Vampire Tales

Edited with an Introduction and Notes by

NICK GROOM

OXFORD
UNIVERSITY PRESS

OXFORD
UNIVERSITY PRESS

Great Clarendon Street, Oxford, OX2 6DP,
United Kingdom

Oxford University Press is a department of the University of Oxford.
It furthers the University's objective of excellence in research, scholarship,
and education by publishing worldwide. Oxford is a registered trade mark of
Oxford University Press in the UK and in certain other countries.

Published in the United States of America by Oxford University Press
198 Madison Avenue, New York, NY 10016, United States of America

British Library Cataloguing in Publication Data
Data available

Library of Congress Control Number: 2026930384

ISBN 9780198814658

Printed and bound by
CPI Group (UK) Ltd., Croydon, CR0 4YY

The manufacturer's authorized representative in the EU for product safety is
Oxford University Press España S.A. of Parque Empresarial San Fernando de Henares,
Avenida de Castilla, 2 – 28830 Madrid (www.oup.es/en or product.safety@oup.com).
OUP España S.A. also acts as importer into Spain of products made by the manufacturer.

FSC
www.fsc.org
MIX
Paper | Supporting responsible forestry
FSC® C013604

ACKNOWLEDGEMENTS

My thanks as ever go to my editors at OUP for their enthusiasm, encouragement, and their patience: Luciana O'Flaherty and her assistants Kizzy Taylor-Richelieu, Emma Varley, Nadine Kolz, and Tara Werger, and my copy editor Dorothy McCarthy, proofreader Hayley Buckley, and project manager Lisa Eaton. I am especially grateful to my colleagues at the University of Macau for their expertise and generosity, in particular Jeremy de Chavez, Man Yin Chiu, Josh Ehrlich, Matthew Gibson, Victoria Harrison, Andrew Moody, Yifeng Sun, Glenn Timmermans, Jo Chengcheng You, and the community of UMGothic. For the first time I have had the benefit of research assistants, Stella Huang Huanrong and Windy Xiao Xue, and it has been a pleasure working with them—if often at a distance: both have been highly efficient, and impressively dedicated to this project in their commitment and attention to detail in preparing the texts. For help with particular points and issues I would like to express my gratitude to Nicholas Allen, Stephen Arata, Fabio Camilletti, Amelia Coughlan, Jo Esra, Christine Faunch, Anna Harding, Rachel Hynes, Sarah Jones, Emma Kelly, Eliza McKee, Kirsty McHugh, Elias Mazzucco, Rachel Sayers, Kathleen Scherf, Emily Selove, Lubna Speitan, Corinna Wagner, Alex Ward, and Jillian Wingfield. A special note of thanks goes to the Ball State University Library, the British Library (especially the Rare Books & Music Reference Team), the James Hardiman Library (National University of Ireland, Galway), the National Library of Scotland, the University of Exeter Library (especially the Document Delivery Team), and the University of Macau Library for allowing me access to MSS, rare books, and electronic resources, as well as to the Hathi Trust and Internet Archive, which deserve acknowledgement for enabling remote research. In the closing stages of this work I was also very fortunate to receive the support of the Moore Institute at NUIG, and I am extremely grateful to the generosity of Director Professor Dan Carey, and the staff, Martha Shaughnessy and Iwona O'Donoghue, for making me so welcome. For personal reasons, my biggest debts are to the Consulate General of Hong Kong, especially Lawrence Chiu and Nick Heath; to the Honorary Consul of Macao, Glenn McCartney; to Dr Tim Watson; and—certainly not least—to

William Hughes. I am also pleased to be able to acknowledge the gracious staff of the Café de Paris Monte-Carlo, Raffles, and in particular Laax and his team at the Ritz-Carlton Bar and Lounge, where many of the ideas developed here were first formed. My sincerest thanks are due, as ever, to my family: Joanne, Matilda, and Dorothy (and especially to Rowley and Pesky), and to my mother and late father for reporting vampire news items to me. I am particularly grateful to Jonathon Green and Susie Ford, who offered shelter from the storm, as did Siobhán McElduff, Adrian Paterson, and, again, Dan Carey.

This collection is respectfully dedicated to my colleagues Jeremy de Chavez, Victoria Harrison, William Hughes, Andrew Moody, Yifeng Sun, and Jo Chengcheng You for their steadfast support during the worst of times.

CONTENTS

INTRODUCTION

VAMPIRES are a staple of twenty-first-century Gothic literature, horror films, and popular culture. They feature in prize-winning fiction (Elizabeth Kostova's *The Historian*, 2005), long-running movie franchises (*The Twilight Saga*, 2008–12), educational children's TV shows (Count von Count of *Sesame Street*, from 1972), and even at the breakfast table (the cereal Count Chocula, from 1971). Although the vampire has been reworked in multiple ways it is instantly recognizable—an undead corpse that at night rises from the grave to suck blood from its human victims, and in doing so vampirizes them; it can be slain only by having a stake driven through its heart.

This stereotypical vampire derives from Bram Stoker's *Dracula* (1897) and the novel's rich legacy in the cinema, on television, on the stage, in comics, in video games, in music, and in fashion; it also persists in literature, and countless stories derived from the Transylvanian Count continue to be published. But it may come as a surprise to learn that not only is there an abundant tradition of vampire literature before *Dracula*, but that vampires of the eighteenth and nineteenth centuries are often very different to those portrayed by Stoker. Count Dracula and his she-vampires represent in effect the culmination of many different depictions of vampires in the years that preceded Stoker's iconic work, and it is the aim of this collection to reveal the extraordinary diversity of vampire tales written in the nineteenth century. If it was once believed that 'every age embraces the vampire it needs', it now appears that every age creates an *array* of vampires.[1] So, in the century before *Dracula* there are classical vampires and medieval vampires, Islamic vampires and Caribbean vampires, aristocratic vampires and penurious vampires, abject vampires and dandified vampires, erudite vampires and bestial vampires, invisible vampires and psychic vampires, and, perhaps most importantly, many more female vampires than male vampires.[2] Vampires were atypical beings—at least until the advent of the Count.

[1] Nina Auerbach, *Our Vampires, Ourselves* (Chicago and London: University of Chicago Press, 1995), 145; see also p. vii.

[2] I have tried to avoid revealing plot twists in the following Introduction.

Moreover, while some of these vampires certainly helped to shape *Dracula*—if sometimes in subtle or implicit ways—many did not; nevertheless, they were recognizable to readers at the time as vampiric creatures. What we have in the nineteenth century, in other words, is not the vampire as a standard bloodsucker, but a variety of traits, themes, and images that constituted a *culture* of vampirism. Such activities often include bloodsucking, but also a morbid preoccupation with blood and vitality, and, more generally, predation; the exercise of power through possessing and dominating others; the prevalence of dreams and deliria that cast doubt over lived reality; the blurring of boundaries between life and death; and the enthralling intensity of beauty—particularly in bewitching eyes. While *Dracula* shares these features, the following stories reveal that these aspects of vampirism were not necessarily confined to the supernatural realm of the undead but could, for example, be understood as medical or psychological conditions.

Reports of vampire outbreaks had been proliferating since the 1720s in official reports and medical accounts, and were keenly debated by natural historians, theologians, and philosophers—all of which led to vampire imagery being popularized in different milieux as a way of exposing and condemning corruption, exploitation, and the abuse of power. These various tropes inevitably spread into literature and generated a diverse spectrum of vampirism. The origins of Romantic and Victorian vampire tales thus lie in these tangled associations, which account for the sheer range of material before it coalesced into the singular figure of Count Dracula.

Background

The history of the vampire begins at a specific time and in a specific place: in 1725 at Kisolova (then in Hungary, now Kisiljevo in Serbia). Ernst Frombald, Imperial Provisor of the Gradiška District (supervisor of the Northern Bosnian region of the Habsburg Military Frontier), filed a report describing how Serbian guerrilla soldiers had disinterred, staked, and cremated the corpse of a local peasant named Peter Plogojowitz (Petar Blagojević).[3] Plogojowitz had been terrorizing the region by rising from the grave and embarking on a murder-

[3] See Thomas M. Bohn, *The Vampire: Origins of a European Myth*, trans. Francis Ipgrave (New York and Oxford: Berghahn Books, 2019), 78–124; and Álvaro García

ous spree of strangulation and infection, spreading a disease that killed within a day; he also sucked the blood of his victims. Frombald had been present at the exhumation and had seen that Plogojowitz's ten-week-old corpse had not decayed and that there was fresh blood in its mouth; more blood gushed from his body when it was impaled with a wooden stake. In diagnosing Plogojowitz's condition Frombald coined the Latinate plural *vampyri*, based on the regional word for predatory undead; he sent his report to Vienna, where it was duly published.

Many more cases followed, likewise investigated by the Habsburg authorities. Every human culture has superstitions, legends, myths, or religious beliefs concerning the return of the dead, and this fear has meant that for centuries corpses have been staked to the ground or otherwise violated to prevent them rising and wreaking havoc, often as supposed vectors of infectious disease. Such malicious revenants or spirits, like the ancient Roman *striges*—malevolent birds or witches described in Ovid's *Fasti*—also sucked human blood. Serbian folklore—derived in part from Eastern Orthodox, Roman Catholic, and Islamic beliefs combined with remnants of Slavic paganism—was no different. But what brought these characteristics together in the figure of the vampire was Frombald's ostensibly objective and verifiable investigation. This was the moment that Enlightenment thinking was confronted with an outlandish regional superstition, and it responded by carefully documenting the phenomenon. Frombald's report and subsequent accounts accordingly detailed medical exhumations and autopsies as well as witness statements authenticated by military officers, magistrates, and notaries. This level of forensic and factual detail would become typical of nineteenth-century vampire literature, with tales frequently incorporating medical findings, officially recorded evidence, and references as corroborating material.

These early testimonies describe vampires as being active between the hours of noon and midnight, slaughtering and then sucking the blood of both humans and animals, and infecting them with vampirism so they would rise again; their first victims were usually close family members. These *vampyri* would return to their graves with blood flowing from their orifices, saturating their coffins in gore. This

Marín, 'Imperial Provisor Frombald's First Name—Discovered', *Journal of Vampire Studies*, 1.1 (2020), 118–21.

appeared to be actual proof of vampirism, and implied that they were corporeal creatures that could accordingly be combated in physical ways: by staking or chaining them to coffins and to the ground or breaking their legs or teeth, as well as by decapitation, decoronation (cardioectomy—removal of the heart), and cremation. As a result, Habsburg officers were proactive in dealing with vampires: the Count de Cabreras, an early vampire slayer, exhumed one suspected vampire in the presence of 'several officers, a chirurgeon, and a notary' before beheading it, he drove a nail into the head of a second, and cremated a third.[4] Meanwhile, protecting oneself from vampire attacks included eating contaminated earth from the grave of the vampire that had caused the infection.

The regions that initially seemed susceptible to vampirism from 1725 onwards—and which were therefore most often scrutinized by the Habsburg government—tended to be peripheral territories recently seized from the Ottoman Empire. In other words, these cases of vampirism were in part a consequence of the transfer of political power and ensuing military occupation. Vampires arose in communities traumatized by being pawns in imperial power-brokering, territorially redefined, and subject to enforced rule by a remote regime. The outbreaks can therefore be understood as mourning the loss of local and national identities, and challenging the imposition of martial law in the most uncanny way.[5] But the plague soon spread much further, raging across Eastern Europe, the Eastern Mediterranean, and Western Asia, extending from Prussia and Poland to Greece and Turkey.

News of these outbreaks also spread rapidly, and from the 1730s vampires featured regularly in European newspapers and journals, and were the subject of several lengthy treatises. The reasons for this 'vampiromania' lay in the very modernity of the creature. Vampirism appeared to be validated by numerous medical reports, the most detailed of which described blue bruises around the neck; shivering, nausea, and bodily aches; an erratic pulse rate and red marks on the

[4] Dom Augustin Calmet, *Dissertations upon the Apparitions of Angels, Dæmons, and Ghosts, and Concerning the Vampires of Hungary, Bohemia, Moravia, and Silesia* (London, 1759), 198–9.

[5] See Peter J. Bräunlein, 'The Frightening Borderlands of Enlightenment: The Vampire Problem', *Studies in History and Philosophy of Biological and Biomedical Sciences*, 43.3 (2012), 710–19.

skin (sometimes appearing only after death); difficulties in seeing, hearing, and speaking; and nocturnal panic attacks and severe nightmares. These nightmares were caused by the 'incubus', often imagined as a demon bearing down on the chest and asphyxiating the victim. Researchers attempted rational explanations for episodes of vampirism ranging from an 'Epidemical Disease of the Brain' and the mass delusion of crowds to poor diet and the accidental ingestion of hallucinatory or deliriant drugs, as well as typhus or disorders of the blood, cross-species infections, and even the chemistry of local soil affecting the rate of decomposition of a corpse; in contrast, ontological explanations attributed outbreaks to demonic assaults on the human condition.[6]

These theories set the agenda of vampire debate for generations. The fundamental distinctions between life and death, so uncomfortably challenged by the vampire, are not only at the heart of medical science, but they are also the foundation of religious faith. Vampires, like ghosts, seemed to confirm that there were indeed other forces in the world, but vampires were, crucially, tangible: they were physically violent, appeared to need nutrition in the form of blood, and could be slain in corporeal ways—they were less supernatural than simply *un*natural. Vampires consequently became intellectually intriguing and their ambiguous nature could help define what was and what was not human: humans were either alive or dead, but vampires—whose corpses did not decompose and who rose from the grave—were clearly of a different order and comprised a third state of being: the undead. Being beyond human comprehension, they predictably attracted the attention of the Roman Catholic Church, and it was a leading rationalist Catholic theologian—the French Benedictine abbot Dom Augustin Calmet—who wrote the most significant account of vampirism in the eighteenth century: *Dissertations upon the Apparitions of Angels, Dæmons, and Ghosts, and Concerning the Vampires of Hungary, Bohemia, Moravia, and Silesia*, published in France in 1746 and in an English translation in 1759. Calmet's *Dissertations* is an eminently readable sourcebook of vampire lore, covering the history of various supernatural phenomena alongside accounts of specific cases of vampirism. He also considered more

[6] Joseph Pitton de Tournefort, *A Voyage into the Levant: perform'd by Command of the late French King*, 2 vols (London, 1718), i. 144.

practical questions, such as how vampires could leave and return to their graves without disturbing the soil, and how they could pass through locked doors and windows.

These claims for the existence of vampires, preposterous as they might seem, were reluctantly acknowledged because they were strongly supported by witnesses. Intellectual attention duly shifted to questioning the reliability of testimony—a point that particularly engaged the French *philosophes*. This issue of evidence and testimony was of serious concern to both Denis Diderot and Jean-Jacques Rousseau—Rousseau noting that,

> There is not an historical fact in the world more fully attested, than that of the Vampires. It is confirmed by regular information, certificates of Notaries, Surgeons, Vicars, and Magistrates. And yet, with all this, who believes in Vampires? And shall we be all damned for not believing? ... My constant experience, as well as that of mankind in general, is much more convincing in this respect than the testimony of individuals.[7]

This led him to treating vampire reports as equivalent to fables or accounts of miracles—the point was not what could be 'proved', but what individuals experienced to be true.

For some years, then, vampires remained an unlikely snare of the modern Enlightenment world of science, reason, and epistemology, and challenged eighteenth-century thinking across medicine, epidemiology, theology, philosophy, and the social and political sciences. The vampire had a characteristic physiology and, in modern ecological terms, was effectively an apex predator. Could they really exist? Despite everything, not only did it appear possible, but it was, to a degree, a proven fact. By the mid-century bloodsucking chiroptera had been classified by the taxonomist Carl Linnaeus, and the term *vampire bat* was being used by explorers to describe a variety of creatures from flying foxes to carnivorous Ecuadorian bats. Indeed, in 1839 one of the creatures actually made it to London's St Katharine Docks in the hold of a ship—much to the excitement of locals.[8]

The first details of Eastern European vampires had, in the meantime, been published in Britain in March 1732, swiftly followed by an

[7] Jean-Jacques Rousseau, *An Expostulatory Letter from J. J. Rousseau, Citizen of Geneva, to Christopher de Beaumont, Archbishop of Paris* (London, 1763), 56.

[8] [Anon.,] 'Jottings down in London: The Vampire', *The Corsair* (23 August 1839), 383.

article arguing that vampires were allegorical figures of political power in the Habsburg Empire. The commentator extended the analogy of bloodsucking vampires to '*ravenous*' government ministers in Britain and the history of parasitical royal favourites and corrupt noblemen, along with moneylenders and stockbrokers, and crooked officials and swindlers.[9] Vampires were, then, straightaway reinvented as belonging to the upper and middle classes, from traditional landed gentry to new capitalists and traders—wealthy, influential, and lawless. The image of the vampire thus replaced the comparable metaphor of the leech because vampires could plausibly pass as human. Foreign investors in Britain, the British in Ireland (absentee landlords), the British in America (collecting taxes), and slave traders, together with monarchs, sultans, and emperors—all were vampires. The professional classes were infested with the things—charity commissioners, workhouse managers, overseers of estates, creditors, debt collectors, lawyers, and army officers. Vampire imagery increasingly appeared in poems and novels, as well as being identified in earlier works such as hagiographies and Norse sagas, while in the world of letters itself plagiarists, booksellers, and even theatre critics were all labelled vampires.

Across the Channel in France it was the Roman Catholic Church that was considered to be overrun. Voltaire sardonically compared vampiromania to religious extremism, observing that, 'the true vampires' are 'the monks, who eat at the expense of both kings and people' and, as commentators in Britain had noted, 'stock-jobbers, brokers, and men of business, who [suck] the blood of the people in broad daylight'.[10] Notwithstanding this, in addition to the court and the Church the later French revolutionary élite and new bureaucrats of the 1790s were also soon satirized as vampires. So despite their emergence in rural Serbia nearly a thousand miles away, vampires at once captured the imagination of Western Europe. Cases were disseminated through popular accounts such as the Marquis d'Argens's pseudo-epistolary work *Lettres juives* (1736, translated as *The Jewish Spy*, 1739–44) and by writers and artists travelling in Eastern Europe

[9] 'Caleb D'Anvers' [Nicholas Amhurst], *The Craftsman*, 14 vols, no. 307 (Saturday, 20 May 1732), ix. 120–9, at 124.

[10] Voltaire, *Questions sur l'Encyclopedie, distribuées en forme de dictionnaire*, 2nd edn, 9 vols (Londres, 1772), ix. 131.

such as Inigo Born and Louis-François Cassas. The vampire had clearly arrived, and its roots in Eastern European peasant superstition, if not wholly forgotten, were quickly disregarded as it developed into a powerful new symbol of venality and vice.

The vampire inheritance the eighteenth century bequeathed to the nineteenth century is, then, a complex matter. The vampire commanded the attention of officialdom and the military, medical officers and epidemiologists, magistrates and the law, political economists and natural historians, and theologians and philosophers. But despite frequent mentions and allusions, in the literature of the period just one short poem was wholly devoted to vampirism. Heinrich August Ossenfelder's twenty-two-line verse 'Der Vampir' was published in a German scientific journal in 1748 and includes details of the Serbian cases summarized by d'Argens, whose own account had been reprinted in the journal.[11] But 'Der Vampir', for all its sexual menace, had little impact, and it would be another seventy years before the vampire properly arrived in European literature as a character. As such, the case of the vampire is analogous to that of Death: for centuries an abstract personification but in 1958 refashioned as a sophisticated—even vulnerable—character in Ingmar Bergman's acclaimed film *The Seventh Seal*, after which increasingly quirky portrayals have followed, such as those of Terry Pratchett (*Discworld*, 1983–2015) and Neil Gaiman (*The Sandman*, from 1989).

Literature

The transformation of the vampire from an Enlightenment trope into a literary individual occurs at the end of the eighteenth century as part of the European Romantic movement and the burgeoning enthusiasm for Gothic novels. There are a number of strands matted together here, complicated by dates of composition, publication, and translation. First, there are poems haunted by vampiric themes such as Samuel Taylor Coleridge's 'Christabel' (begun in 1797, published in 1816) and Johann Wolfgang von Goethe's 'Die Braut von Korinth' (1798, translated 1819); however, these poems are really reworkings of earlier motifs of the revenant and demon lover. The word *vampire* is

[11] See Heide Crawford, *The Origins of the Literary Vampire* (Lanham, etc.: Rowman & Littlefield, 2016), 23–9.

not used in 'Christabel' or the original 'Die Braut', and it was not until 'The Bride of Corinth' appeared in English in 1819 that she was named a vampire.

In the two decades between the composition of 'Christabel' and the publication of 'The Bride' there were several poems in English featuring vampires. Oneiza, an Arabian maiden and undead bride, figured in Robert Southey's Islamic epic *Thalaba the Destroyer* of 1801. Although Southey glossed this 'vampire corpse' with ten pages of notes on East European vampires drawn from accounts made for the Habsburg authorities, his poem actually introduces an important new source to emergent vampirology: the Islamic ghoul.[12] Ghouls were demons who prowled through graveyards to feast on rotting human corpses. They had first appeared in Anglophone literature in the *Arabian Nights Entertainments* (1721)—where they are described in graphic detail—and later in William Beckford's Orientalist Gothic novel, *Vathek*, published in 1786 as *An Arabian Tale*. Southey's vampire was therefore a hybrid of Orthodox Christian superstition, Slavic paganism, and Islamic demonology—and such Islamic aspects of nineteenth-century vampires are frequently evident, if often overlooked.

In 1807, Lord Byron's friend John Herman Merivale published 'The Dead Men of Pest: A Hungarian Legend'—a poem wholly devoted to vampirism and supplemented by an account of the earlier Slavonic cases and the debates they had inspired in medicine and theology; moreover, Merivale's description of the town of Pest on the River Danube—in which almost the entire population are vampires—includes both Christian churches and Islamic mosques, again highlighting Eastern sources. This conflation of the Eastern-Mediterranean vampire with the Middle-Eastern ghoul is further evident in Byron's own Oriental romance poem *The Giaour* (1813). In this, the Giaour (infidel) is cursed by a Muslim Turk to rise as a vampire, suck the blood from his daughter, sister, and wife, and keep the company of ghouls and afrits—afrits being another order of Islamic demons. Byron too provided notes to his poem, referencing eighteenth-century reports, quoting Southey, and providing his own first-hand

[12] Robert Southey, *Thalaba the Destroyer*, 2nd edn, 2 vols (London: Longman, Hurst, Rees and Orme, 1809), ii. 102–12; these notes were later expanded.

experience of vampire beliefs in Greece.[13] In the same year he also wrote a short poem 'Windsor Poetics', describing Henry VIII and Charles I as 'royal Vampires' who had returned from the dead as the current Prince Regent, later crowned George IV.[14] 'Windsor Poetics', which was published in 1818, thus continued the eighteenth-century practice of denouncing the aristocracy as parasites, demonstrating that Byron's interest in vampires embraced memories of his travels in the Eastern Mediterranean, Eastern European history, Islam, and British and Irish political satire. Other poets such as Erasmus Darwin and Walter Scott made passing references to vampires as vectors of malaria and as bloodsucking sprites, respectively, and John Stagg, the 'Blind Bard' of Cumberland, published a homoerotic poem 'The Vampyre' in 1816, including—like Southey, Merivale, and Byron—explanatory notes outlining eighteenth-century debates on the subject.

In the same year that Stagg's poem appeared, Byron and a small circle of friends spent a rain-sodden summer in the Villa Diodati on the banks of Lake Geneva—one of the most celebrated literary retreats of the Romantic period. Byron had arrived at Diodati with his physician Dr John William Polidori, and they were soon joined by Percy Bysshe Shelley, Shelley's partner Mary Godwin (whom he would marry before the end of the year), and Mary's half-sister Claire Clairmont. Conditions were atrocious: the Indonesian volcano Mount Tambora had erupted the previous year throwing nearly nine cubic miles of dust into the atmosphere and causing a worldwide volcanic winter—1816 being bluntly described as the 'Year Without A Summer'.[15] Unwilling to brave the almost incessant rain and sheltering indoors for much of the time, Byron suggested one evening that he and his guests amuse themselves by writing ghost stories. Mary Shelley (as she was already known) began the novel *Frankenstein*, while Byron started a vampire tale.

Vampires had clearly remained on Byron's mind since *The Giaour*—as is clear from 'Windsor Poetics'; however, his 'ghost story' was aban-

[13] George Gordon, Lord Byron, *The Giaour, A Fragment of a Turkish Tale* (London: John Murray, 1813), 23n.–24n.; again, these notes were later expanded.

[14] George Gordon, Lord Byron, *The Complete Poetical Works*, 7 vols: vol. iii, ed. Jerome McGann (Oxford: Oxford University Press, 1981), 87 (Version C).

[15] See R. Auchmann, S. Brönnimann, L. Breda, M. Bühler, R. Spadin, and A. Stickler, 'Extreme Climate, Not Extreme Weather: The Summer of 1816 in Geneva, Switzerland', *Climate of the Past*, 8.1 (2012), 325–35.

doned after only a few pages and it seems that Byron concluded the tale verbally to his companions at Diodati one evening. In one sense Byron's narrative—unprepossessingly titled 'A Fragment' when it was published in 1819—is the first prose vampire tale in English, but little remains and the text actually breaks off before the themes of vampires and vampirism are introduced. However, Polidori heard Byron recount his story at Diodati and later wrote up his own version, which was published in 1819 as his epoch-making tale 'The Vampyre'.

Things are not, however, quite so straightforward. The development of Byron's fragment into Polidori's 'The Vampyre' is mired in controversy. Although Polidori would make fanciful claims that he had completed Byron's tale at the Villa Diodati in 1816, left it there, and that it had eventually been sent anonymously to England where it was published in 1819 without his consent, this is highly unlikely and almost certainly untrue. The letters of Polidori's editor Alaric Watts reveal that the most probable scenario is that Polidori wrote 'The Vampyre' two and a half years after he left Diodati and in response to the publication of 'The Bride of Corinth'. Goethe's poem was first published in an English translation at the beginning of 1819 as another addition to the growing canon of vampire poetry penned by leading men of letters, which could now number among its advocates not only the British Poet Laureate Robert Southey but the European polymath Goethe. This indicated that there was a buoyant market for such work, and it appears that the English translation of a twenty-year-old poem by a leading German writer started a chain reaction by inspiring the composition and publication of Polidori's 'The Vampyre'.

Eager to steal a march on a rival bookseller, Henry Colburn, publisher and proprietor of *The New Monthly Magazine*, contracted Polidori—who was at the time negotiating a book deal with him—to finish Byron's tale. But when Polidori, with the assistance of the editor Alaric Watts, submitted his completed version of Byron's fragment he was conned by Colburn, who not only appropriated the rights to the story but also duplicitously attributed its authorship to Byron. A furious row resulted that wrecked Polidori's literary career, while Byron and 'The Vampyre' became virtually synonymous for the rest of the century.[16] The initial impact of 'The Vampyre', then, was

[16] For a full account, see Nick Groom, 'Polidori's "The Vampyre": Composition, Publication, Deception', *Romanticism*, 28.1 (2022), 46–59.

not because it was the first vampire tale in English literature, or even that it appeared to showcase a Byronic anti-hero—it was simply because it had supposedly been written by Lord Byron, and at the time there was no literary figure more eminent or more notorious. Even as 'The Vampyre' continued to be keenly discussed in the press and in salons, Byron's own unfinished tale appeared shortly afterwards—and without his permission—focusing yet more attention on 'The Vampyre' and fuelling further debate.

This thorny series of relationships is best unpicked by reading the texts not in chronological order of publication, but as a process of influence, beginning with 'Die Braut von Corinth'. Goethe based his sinister ballad on two myths of ancient Greece, presented as a lament for the pagan gods who wreak their vengeance on the followers of the new Christian religion by raising a woman from the dead. This is a reminder of both the Eastern Mediterranean and non-Christian elements of vampirism, as well as adding a Hellenistic dimension to the creature that located it within high culture. The Bride looks forward to reuniting with the ancient gods, who, by temporarily having given her new life, are shown to wield as much power as the Christian deity. She drinks 'blood-red wine' yet rejects 'wheaten bread'—effectively the sacred host (p. 11)—implying that her wedding night cannot be a complete communion with her husband because she has already crossed the threshold from life to death. The poem is laced with Christian language and superstition, but the violent confrontation between the new religion and the old ways in the final stanza leaves the ending ambiguous. By combining exoticism, Islamic rites, pagan idols, and immolation, Goethe's vampire not only becomes a liminal figure to challenge Eastern Orthodox and Roman Catholic Christianity, but is revealed as a knot of contradictions that casts profound doubt over the quality of Christian mercy.

Although Byron did not speak German, he had encountered Goethe's poem through the work of Madame de Staël, whom he met in 1813—the year in which her essay *De l'Allemagne* had been issued by John Murray, Byron's own publisher. 'Die Braut' may well have piqued Byon's interest in classical equivalents of vampires, following his Islamic and contemporary Greek references in *The Giaour*. Byron's 'Fragment' accordingly concerns a young man travelling into Eastern Europe with a companion named Augustus Darvell. Darvell is 'a man of considerable fortune and ancient family' (p. 3), but at the same time a morbid eccentric driven by a 'shadowy restlessness' (p. 4). These two travellers journey through a broken and antique landscape littered with Hellenistic, Roman, Christian, and Islamic ruins before resting in a Muslim cemetery. Darvell, whose health is failing dramatically, has deliberately gone there to die and insists that the young man swears to perform certain mystifying acts: to conceal Darvell's death, to cast the older man's ring into the sea, and to visit a temple. Darvell then expires, his prematurely blackened corpse is unceremoniously buried in a shallow grave—and there 'A Fragment' ends. Although Byron presumably intended Darvell to rise from the dead, there is no hint at this stage that this is a vampire tale, and the possibility can only be inferred from Polidori's later version; moreover, Byron hints that Darvell is a ghoulish denizen of Turkish cemeteries and, as in *The Giaour*, there are repeated references to Islamic funerary culture. These elements are combined with classical paganism, inspired in part by a renewed British interest in ancient Greek antiquities as well as by Byron's political sympathy for Greek independence.

Polidori's ensuing tale 'The Vampyre' is certainly indebted to Byron's brief 'Fragment' in depicting the travels in Eastern Europe of an inexperienced young man with a mysterious and older companion, and in the mix of Hellenism and Islam, the insistence on concealing the protagonist's death, the swearing of a curious oath, and the unnatural decomposition of the corpse. At the same time, 'The Vampyre'—at four times the length of 'A Fragment'—has a much broader canvas, encompassing both dissolute high society and scenes of picturesque simplicity, and introducing severe psychological disturbances and supernatural terror into a contemporary family drama. The plot of 'The Vampyre' is surprisingly intricate for such a short tale: Aubrey, a young aristocrat, encounters the magnetic and maleficent Lord Ruthven (pronounced *riven*). Ruthven exerts a compelling but lethal charm on society women; despite this, Aubrey travels with him across Europe until he becomes sickened by Ruthven's debauched depravity and parts company with him in Rome. Aubrey then journeys to Greece, meets the charming Ianthe, and falls in love. However, while returning one night after exploring ancient Greek ruins, Aubrey is caught in a thunderstorm and attacked by a mysterious assailant. The plot then takes an alarming turn: Ianthe is murdered—apparently the victim of a vampire—Aubrey becomes delirious, and

Ruthven returns and nurses Aubrey. The two resume their travels, but Ruthven is shot on the road by marauding bandits, dies, and his body rots and disappears. Returning to London, Aubrey seemingly—and inexplicably—encounters Ruthven and again becomes delirious, obsessed by the dread lord who orchestrates Aubrey's final descent into madness and death.

While Byron's Augustus Darvell is merely sketched, Polidori's Lord Ruthven is, then, a complex and ambiguous figure. He is intelligent, independent, calculating, and enigmatic: dangerously fascinating and very much living in the modern world, dividing his time between balls, gambling, and touring. Moreover, it is never clear whether Ruthven really is a vampire or whether vampirism is a figment of Aubrey's deranged imagination. Many commentators, now as then, simply read the tale in the context of its composition and publication, allowing the literary renown of Byron to overshadow any serious critical assessment, and in doing so present Ruthven and Aubrey as crude and uncritical portraits of Byron and Polidori, despite the glaring differences between them. However, reading the tale independently of its surrounding scandals reveals it to be a complex psychological thriller charting Aubrey's mental disintegration. While Polidori and Watts were certainly not the first to raise the vampire to the aristocracy or bring the vampire to Britain or even to eroticize the figure, 'The Vampyre' is nevertheless a watershed in vampire literature because it is the first tale to establish the vampire as a character. Ruthven, unlike his monstrous and metaphorical precursors, has a toxic charisma, a ruinous personality, and a lethal individual agency: he is not a type, he is an original.

The impact of 'The Vampyre' was immense. According to Robert Morrison and Chris Baldick, 'More than any other story, *The Vampyre* heralded a new era of modern British fiction in which the opportunistic sensationalism of the monthly magazines assumed an unprecedented importance'.[17] The ensuing popularity of ghastly accounts of horror, crime, and suspense certainly received tremendous impetus from 'The Vampyre', but its immediate impact was on the international stage.[18] Polidori's tale was published in a French translation

[17] Chris Baldick and Robert Morrison (eds), *The Vampyre and Other Tales of the Macabre* (Oxford: Oxford University Press, 1997), p. xiii; this collection provides salient examples of such ghoulish tales.

[18] See Roxana Stuart, *Stage Blood: Vampires of the 19th-Century Stage* (Bowling Green, OH: Bowling Green State University Popular Press, 1994).

by Henri Faber (1819); meanwhile, Cyprien Bérard wrote a two-volume sequel to Polidori, *Lord Ruthwen ou les Vampires* (1820), and in Germany, E. T. A. Hoffmann's vampire story 'Vampirismus' was published as part of his *Serapionsbrüder* ('the Serapion brethren', 1820). Charles Nodier—who had himself travelled in Illyria on the Balkan peninsula, where, he later told Alexandre Dumas *père*, he had seen real vampires—reworked Faber's translation for the stage with co-writers Pierre-Frédéric-Adolphe Carmouche and Achille de Jouffroy, before writing his own vampire novel (*Smarra, ou les démons de la nuit*, 1821) and introducing vampires into his supernatural miscellany *Infernaliana* (1822).[19] But it was the Nodier–Carmouche–Jouffroy melodrama *Le Vampire* (1820)—improbably set in Ossianic Scotland—that precipitated a vampire craze in the theatres and gave rise to at least five other playhouse versions in Paris alone. It was just as popular in London: less than two months after *Le Vampire* premiered the play was rewritten for English audiences by James Robinson Planché as *The Vampire; or, The Bride of the Isles*, which retained the Scottish setting as well as Polidori's idea that the vampire was revived by the rays of the moon; a further five versions followed in London.

The Nodier–Carmouche–Jouffroy and Planché versions were hugely popular with the public; moreover, Planché's production developed the 'Vampire trap'—a piece of machinery that enabled Ruthven instantly to vanish before the eyes of the audience: the playbill for a benefit at Bridgnorth Theatre promised '*The final Disappearance of the VAMPIRE in a Shower of Fire!!!*' Such productions showed no sign of abating in the following decade: there were vampire operas, ballets, burlesques, pantomimes, and farces played in Britain, France, Germany, and Italy. In Germany, for instance, Heinrich Ludwig Ritter's play *Der Vampyr, oder die Todten Braut* (1821) inspired both Heinrich Marschner's and Peter Joseph von Lindpaintner's operas (both 1828, with librettos by Wilhelm August Wohlbrück and Cäsar Max Hegel, respectively), while Planché himself also adapted Marschner's opera in 1829. The stage hosted vampires in every popular theatrical style of the day, performances that

[19] Daniel Sangsue, 'Nodier et le commerce des vampires', *Revue d'Histoire littéraire de la France*, 98.2 (1998), 231–45, at 242; Dumas went on to write his own play on the subject, *Le Vampire* (1851).

continued throughout the century up to and including the Gilbert and Sullivan operetta *Ruddigore; or, The Witch's Curse* (1887), which featured the undead aristocrat Sir Ruthven Murgatroyd, and the same year saw the opening of *Frankenstein; or, The Vampire's Victim*, a satire on Oscar Wilde. From their first appearance in fiction, then, vampires were a comic staple for theatre audiences.

This popularity on the stage gave birth to a market for sensation fiction in magazines and in cheap mass-produced pamphlets known in Britain as 'bluebooks' or 'shilling shockers'. The bluebooks, so-called because of their cheap blue paper covers, were an early nineteenth-century attempt to capitalize on the popularity of Gothic novels by producing affordable versions for younger readers with little disposable income—as Thomas Medwin, Percy Shelley's cousin and biographer, described them, they were 'stories of haunted castles, bandits, murderers, and other grim personages—a most exciting and interesting sort of food for boys' minds'.[20] By the mid-century these had developed from abridged versions of Gothic novels and true-crime narratives into 'bloods' and weekly serials known as 'penny dreadfuls' that eventually cashed in on every genre of writing that might appeal to the mass-market—from historical fiction to romance to, unsurprisingly, supernatural horror. Typical of the bluebooks is *The Bride of the Isles* (*c*.1820). This short sixpenny narrative was attributed on the title-page to Byron but in fact derived directly from Planché's play, whereas the later appetite for lengthy serials was sated by *Varney, the Vampyre*, as described below.[21]

At the same time that the vampire was, for some, becoming a profitable cultural commodity, the poetic tradition continued. Less than three weeks after the first appearance of 'The Vampyre', John Keats wrote the first version of his medievalist ballad 'La Belle Dame Sans Merci' (1819). This justly celebrated poem is included here to show its place within the heady vampiromania of 1819: 'The Bride of Corinth' was published on 1 March, 'The Vampyre' on 1 April, and Keats wrote the first draft of 'La Belle Dame' on 21 April. His short poem reworks the earlier figure of the perilous woman—Geraldine in 'Christabel'

[20] Thomas Medwin, *The Life of Percy Bysshe Shelley*, ed. H. Buxton Forman, new edn (London, etc.: Oxford University Press, 1913), 24.

[21] See Peter Haining (ed.), *The Shilling Shockers: Stories of Terror from the Gothic Bluebooks* (London: Victor Gollancz Ltd, 1978), 127–51.

and Goethe's Bride—under the lurid shadow of 'The Vampyre', switching the protagonist from an older man to a younger woman. Keats demonstrates how finely he could take a wildly topical subject such as vampirism and, with extraordinary concision, reshape it through English witchery and folklore into something radiantly new. On the face of it 'La Belle Dame' is merely a *femme fatale*—but she is a *femme fatale avant la letter*, a paradigmatic figure. Hence this familiar poem should be read in its direct context to show how Keats took Polidori's insistent images of eyes and surveillance, for instance, and literally magnified them to the extent that the lustrous, unearthly, 'wild wild eyes' of 'La Belle Dame' (p. 41) became central to the Victorian vampire—particularly the she-vampire. Not only did Keats swiftly crystallize a feature of the literary vampire, but the vampire in turn contributed to Keats's subsequent canonization by placing him, uncannily, at the heart of a Victorian culture permeated by posthumous literary celebrities, reaching to fame from beyond the grave, yearning for blood:

> This living hand, now warm and capable
> Of earnest grasping, would, if it were cold
> And in the icy silence of the tomb,
> So haunt thy days and chill thy dreaming nights
> That thou would wish thine own heart dry of blood
> So in my veins red life might stream again,
> And thou be conscience-calm'd—see here it is—
> I hold it towards you.[22]

Yes, Keats was a part of the literature of vampirism, but he also transcended it to create new possibilities—and in a matter of mere days.

While Polidori's 'The Vampyre' generated translations, prose sequels, and especially stage adaptations in Britain and on the Continent, it also instantly had an impact in the United States of America. *The Black Vampyre* by 'Uriah Derick D'Arcy' (pseudonym of Richard Varick Dey, a New Brunswick divinity student and occasional poet) is the first American vampire story; it was published within a few months of 'The Vampyre' in 1819, and focuses on the question of slavery and racial politics in conspicuously odd and

[22] John Keats, 'This living hand, now warm and capable', *Selected Poetry*, ed. Elizabeth Cook (Oxford: Oxford University Press, 1998), 218.

unconventional ways. The subtitle, 'A Legend of St. Domingo', makes direct reference to the Republic of Haiti, formerly the French slave colony of Saint-Domingue. In 1791 the colony had rebelled against French rule and after a dozen years of conflict declared independence on 1 January 1804, a signal event in the anti-slavery movement of the nineteenth century that understandably enthused abolitionists—particularly commentators in New York, which is where the tale was first published.

The 'Black Vampyre' of the narrative is an African prince, who is never named. The Prince is deliberately compared to and contrasted with Polidori's 'White Vampyre' (p. 44), and *The Black Vampyre* is actually presented as a prequel to Polidori's tale. In *The Black Vampyre*, Lord Ruthven is identified as possibly one Spooner Dubois, the child of French plantation owners who was vampirized by the Prince—thus defiantly hijacking Ruthven's aristocratic British lineage and turning him into a hybrid slave-trader-vampire. Furthermore, the Black Prince is not only charismatic, eloquent, physically attractive, and sexually potent, he is also a political revolutionary—a manifestation of the vampire as a masterful, manipulative, and dangerously alluring intellectual that draws on the figure of Toussaint L'Ouverture—former slave, leader of the Haitian people, and saviour of the nation. The Prince is also specifically 'drest in the rich garb of a Moorish Prince' and some of his 'Gouls' too are 'in sumptuous Moorish apparel' (pp. 48, 56)—a reminder of African culture and the Islamic associations of vampires at the time, which are reiterated at several points in the text. Accordingly, the tale includes mixed-race and mixed-species marriage, reflections on the beauties of blackness, mockery of whiteness, a stirring emancipation speech, transhuman (i.e. vampire) perspectives, and carnivalesque scenes.

Yet despite the direct allusions to Polidori—and even the exact same use of a passage from Byron's *The Giaour* as an epigraph—*The Black Vampyre* is entirely different from its source. The convoluted plot begins with the arrival of a slave ship at St Domingo, but the ill-treated slaves soon die save for one young boy who is purchased by Mr Personne, a French plantation owner, who promptly kills him. The boy, however, repeatedly revives under moonlight. Personne then tries to cremate the child, but in an absurd episode of comic Gothickry he immolates himself on his own pyre and, seeing that his own son has been reduced to skin, hair, and nails, dies soon after.

Personne's wife, Euphemia, then marries twice more and is twice more widowed before she meets the Prince and marries him. The Prince vampirizes Euphemia by forcing her to drink a concoction of her dead son's blood, and the Prince then raises her three husbands from the dead and stakes the last two. He does however allow her first husband Mr Personne to live on as a vampire—it transpires that the Prince was the boy that Personne had attempted to kill—and gives him his own slave boy, Zembo. The group then visit a gathering of vampires, ghouls, and slaves preparing for an insurrection, which is attacked by French colonial soldiers, and the story ends with Euphemia pregnant by the vampire Prince.

The return of Personne, the consequences of the slave revolt, and the fate of the Prince seem deliberately confusing, and it is unclear whether *The Black Vampire* is an anti-slavery narrative or not. Such uncertainty is exacerbated by nonsensical scenes, instances of derogatory racial humour, and casual violence—most notably the racially inspired infanticide of the slave boy. The tale also includes a rich vein of ancient Greek myth, a chorus of Muslim ghouls, and grotesque accounts of the human body in various abject states that may be derived from the same African sources that gave rise to zombies—a word that entered the English language from Haiti in 1788.[23] Additionally, in the second edition of the text the vampire imagery is redirected to criticize American society, capitalism, and the modern world through multiple prefaces and supplements. While the prefatory letter, introduction, and a concluding moral are included here, the second edition (also 1819) supplemented this material with a lengthy poem, 'Vampyrism', prefaced by another letter, as well as two further appendices. With this in mind, *The Black Vampyre* has been described as 'hemispheric' Gothic—in contrast to 'trans-Atlantic' Gothic—linking nascent American Gothic, Caribbean slavery, and the New York literary marketplace, suggesting that the tale

> deploys both a self-avowed act of plagiarism [of Polidori] and a series of paratextual diatribes about literary theft [in prefaces and appendices] to gesture at the contemporary hypocrisy of an Anglophone literary market

[23] 'The *Zombies* make a great figure in the superstition of the Negroes. Like the *Larvæ* of the ancients, they are supposed to be the spirits of dead wicked men, that are permitted to wander, and torment the living' ([Anon.,] 'The History of Okano', *Universal Magazine* 83 (September 1788), 115–20, at 117n.).

that was vexed by such issues even as it turned a blind eye toward the much weightier thefts inherent in chattel slavery.[24]

These various paratexts also allude to the rich eighteenth-century legacy and varied sources of vampire lore cited in introductions and notes to earlier poems as well as to 'The Vampyre', and consequently renew eighteenth-century themes of medical, social, and commercial vampirism—as well as slavery—in the contexts of nineteenth-century biology, politics, and economics in North America.

The vampire Prince of *The Black Vampyre* is, then, a striking fusion of ancient Hellenic and western African mythologies mixed with Arabic demonology and Christian superstition—elements that are also touched upon in Charlotte Brontë's *Jane Eyre* (1847), in which the mixed-race Bertha Rochester is herself described as a vampire. However, these African elements went little further in the century's vampire lore, and even the Islamic aspects of vampirism were soon eclipsed by new and often more contemporary articulations of the figure. Similarly, Dey's innovations such as the communal gathering and group identity of vampires and ghouls were superseded in favour of focusing on singular beings—at least until *Dracula*. Unlike Polidori's 'White Vampyre', *The Black Vampyre* was quickly forgotten, and when it was finally republished in 1845 it was in a heavily edited and abridged form. Its extreme and unstable narrative mixing literary lampooning with horrific supernaturalism may shape a compelling plot, but its inconsistent attitude to abolitionism and emancipation, its simplistic anti-capitalist sentiments, and especially its purposefully bombastic style make it a perplexing and challenging read today. That may explain why *The Black Vampyre* was soon forgotten in its own time and has subsequently been neglected by commentators.

In direct contrast to *The Black Vampyre*, Ernst Raupach's 'Wake Not The Dead', published in German in 1823 and anonymously translated into English in the same year, is unequivocally European Gothic: a headlong nightmare of Teutonic medievalism; sensuousness, sensuality, and sorcery; and the destructive powers of the unfettered imagination—a fine example of the German *Schauerroman*, or 'shudder novel'. The tale concerns Walter, a powerful lord of Burgundy, and his two wives: Brunhilda, who died young, and Swanhilda, the

[24] Katie Bray, '"A Climate ... More Prolific ... in Sorcery": *The Black Vampyre* and the Hemispheric Gothic', *American Literature*, 87.1 (2015), 1–22, at 5.

mother of his two children. Swanhilda and Brunhilda are polar opposites, Swanhilda being as pale and meek as Brunhilda was fervently feral—and eventually memories of Brunhilda begin to eclipse the reality of Swanhilda. Walter becomes increasingly fixated by his dead wife, lingering at her grave and ultimately being drawn into making a fateful tryst with a necromancer who has the power to restore her to life. Walter is deeply troubled by this possibility—being as 'inquiet [uneasy] as the murderer who meditates his first deed of blood' (p. 68)—yet finds the prospect irresistible. And when Brunhilda rises, she does so in a startlingly dramatic way, springing from her grave 'borne forward by some invisible power' (p. 69)—a scene that may well have been derived from the stage effects of vampire drama.

Raupach thus develops the classical 'Braut von Korinth' into a revenant of the Dark Ages, reworking conventional vampire lore to develop his own primordial folk-demon. Brunhilda favours a sepulchral look and carries with her not the pungent stench of the grave but the fragrance of violets—symbolic of both fertility and remembrance, sex and death; she is averse to the sun and to gold, but has a love of pale moonlight and is adorned with silver and pearls. Brunhilda also possesses a 'malignant withering glance' (p. 74) and, like Keats's 'Belle Dame', lulls her victims into unconsciousness and leads them through magnificent dreams while she drains their vitality so that they fade and age prematurely. Brunhilda is literally cold-blooded, and without warm blood 'her existence was a mere blank' (p. 75); she particularly relishes fresh meat—the blood of children—to feed her carnal energy. Moreover, the tale also examines the psychology of selfhood and the necessity of disciplining the imagination: Walter cannot control the images that come to him; he is not in control of his own mind—there is another, unruly entity in his head.

Raupach's tale was decidedly influential. Despite—or because of—the multifaceted chaos of *The Black Vampire*, the vampire did not gain much traction in American literature until later in the century, and it was not until fifteen years after 'Wake Not the Dead' that Edgar Allan Poe's 'Ligeia' appeared in 1838. 'Ligeia' indubitably has close affinities with Raupach's tale—not least in having two opposing wives—but Poe develops the vampiric female in different ways: without moral codes or certainties, by mixing familiar northern European conventions with unfamiliar American innovations, and also by avoiding the very word *vampire*. As Poe's editor Thomas Ollive Mabbott points out, 'The heroine is not an orthodox vampire'—and although there is really no such thing as an 'orthodox' nineteenth-century vampire, it is certainly true that Ligeia does not suck blood, and, in common with many vampires of the period, is never explicitly named as such.[25]

Yet 'Ligeia' is nevertheless a vampire tale. The first half of the first-person narrative is a meditation on the eponymous protagonist: her ancient Germanic ancestry, her profound and occult learning, and her anomalous beauty—ashen and emaciated, crowned with raven-black hair. Most ominously, Ligeia's large and fathomless eyes convey a strange gaze: 'Observe the eyes', wrote Poe simply of his tale—she is another woman of deeply aberrant charms.[26] The narrator marries Ligeia, but Ligeia fades and dies and the narrator retires to that most Gothic of retreats, a ruined English abbey—where he tries to piece together his memories through fragments of opium dreams and hallucinatory mirages. There he is married a second time to the fair-haired Lady Rowena—the pair of brides mirroring Swanhilda and Brunhilda of 'Wake Not the Dead', the narrator dwelling like Walter on the memory of his dead bride as the living Rowena in turn fades and dies.

Several vampire themes are entwined in 'Ligeia'—the archaic family line, a crumbling ancient city, the strange seduction of a man (the narrator) by a mysterious woman, the dream-like quality of their encounters, the woman's abnormal physique, her gleaming teeth, her wild ferocity, her colossal learning, her artistry, her power, and her precarious mortality—especially her mortality. Yet at the same time—and for all its Gothic antiquity—the psychological landscape of the narrator and of Ligeia herself is distinctively of the New World, and the mental spells or conjurations that involuntarily reimagine this world are, for Poe, the dark side of American Transcendentalism. There is also a contemporary medical dimension to Ligeia's state: Poe's women—such as Madeline Usher, Ligeia, Berenicë, and Morella—all share a hyper-idealized beauty: translucent skin lit by

[25] Edgar Allan Poe, *The Collected Works*, ed. Thomas Ollive Mabbott, 3 vols (Cambridge, MA: Harvard University Press, 1969–78): ii. *Tales and Sketches, 1831–1842*, ed. T. O. Mabbott, with Eleanor D. Kewer and Maureen C. Mabbott (1978), ii. 305–8 [online edition at www.eapoe.org].

[26] Poe, *Collected Works*, ii. 305.

vivid blushes, deep-set eyes, and dependent frailty. These are the characteristics of pulmonary tuberculosis, or consumption. As John Murray described the disease in 1830, 'consumption, like the vampire, while it drinks up the vital stream, fans with its wing the hopes that flutter in the hectic breast; the transparent colours that flit on the features like those of the rainbow on the cloud, are equally evanescent, and leave its darkness more deeply shaded'.[27]

Ultimately, though, 'Ligeia' is the defining example in Poe's work of extreme, annihilating love: for, as the novelist D. H. Lawrence wrote, 'to try to *know* any living being is to try to suck the life out of that being'—hence love exterminates the object of desire.[28] Ligeia's life is thus qualified by the constraints that death imposes: she has a 'desire for life—*but* for life'—the phrase being repeated almost verbatim (p. 93)—and she can only find the will to live through first dying, after which she determines her return. Poe's repeated and necrophiliac narratives of the death of an ideal woman are furthermore plagued by physical decay—as well as the threat of live burial—which leads to vampiric recurrences in his tales. This is most marked in 'Ligeia', as the narrator cannot relinquish the object of desire and its inevitable putrefaction in the terrifying image of the 'Conquering Worm' that he added to later versions. Once more, then, the vampire imagery dwells upon obsessive and poisonous memories and the treacherous past, as well as paying acute attention to the physical state of bodies and corpses. To be dead, decomposing—or, in the case of Berenicë, in Poe's story of the same name, to be butchered—*yet to stay alive*: that is Poe's horror.

Back across the Atlantic, *Varney, the Vampyre* (1845–7) also describes a vampirized woman, Clara Crofton, but in a very different way to Poe's feverish prose. James Malcolm Rymer's sensational and best-selling 'penny dreadful', or weekly serial, is both much lighter and much more prolonged in its telling. This epic series of episodes (well over half a million words in length) details the exploits of Sir Frances Varney, the vampire of the title—a 'living cadaver' who emerges from a storm-tossed night with eyes 'like polished tin' (p. 138) to persecute

[27] John Murray, *A Treatise on Pulmonary Consumption: Its Prevention and Remedy* (London: Whittaker, Treacher, and Arnot, 1830), 3.

[28] D. H. Lawrence, *Studies in Classic American Literature* (London: Martin Secker, 1933), 71, 74.

his descendants, the Bannerworths. Varney subsequently appears throughout the novel in multiple different guises, such as a middle-ranking army officer and an Italian monk, and, although his background is inconsistent, in the confessions that close the book it is revealed that Varney was a Cromwellian double-agent. This means that the national crises of civil war and dynastic revolution underpin the book, as well as the pragmatic necessities of survival. *Varney* is therefore founded on national history—in the words of one critic it is based on 'a figuration of the self-divided English Commonwealth and its legacy, where the bonds uniting men—brother with brother, father with son—have been destroyed'.[29] The timeline of *Varney* is however sketchy: the plot is evidently set in about 1730—some seventy years after the fall of the Commonwealth—positioning it within the first wave of European vampiromania, and there are also various anachronistic references to contemporary Victorian figures—Rymer even knowingly includes a character with the name 'Count Pollidori'. Nevertheless, in this drama the vampire is, literally, a spook—an insurgent conspiring to manipulate the authorities—and as such *Varney* replays the political power games of *The Black Vampire* while looking forward to Count Dracula's own attempts to infiltrate the British government. *Varney* also typifies the atmosphere of what was to become characteristic of Stoker's *Dracula*: the hallucinatory quality of mistiness and moonlight, of dreams and madness, and of derangement and despair, as well as the horrid laughter suggestive of grisly Jacobean tragedies—all run through the text. It is tempting too to see in the episode of Clara a source for the vampirization of Lucy Westenra, the fiancée of Arthur Holmwood, in *Dracula*: a bride-to-be who is vampirized and who preys on children before being savagely staked. But *Varney, the Vampyre* is perhaps most effective in the sheer narrative drive it brings to the vampire tale, its persistent level of protracted suspense being characteristic of the best 'penny dreadfuls'—and it was so well known that it even provoked later rumours of supposed vampire activity.[30]

'The Mysterious Stranger' (translated into English by an unknown hand, 1854) by Karl von Wachsmann also influenced Stoker's *Dracula*,

[29] Erik Butler, *Metamorphoses of the Vampire in Literature and Film: Cultural Transformations in Europe, 1732–1933* (Rochester, NY: Camden House, 2010), 102.

[30] The fraudulent report of the 'Vampire of Croglin Grange', apparently taken from a diary for 1874, is actually derived from *Varney, the Vampyre* (see Augustus Hare in *The Story of My Life*, 6 vols (London: George Allen, 1900), iv. 98).

as well as Sheridan Le Fanu's 'Carmilla'.[31] The former Prussian soldier Wachsmann was a popular and prolific writer of short stories whose vampire novella *Der Fremde*—from which 'The Mysterious Stranger' is abridged—had appeared in 1844. The tale begins as a seventeenth-century romance set at the frontiers of the Habsburg Empire in the Carpathian Mountains (in the original, the Carniolan Alps), shortly before the first historical cases of vampirism. A small party consisting of the Knight of Fahnenberg, his niece and nephew, his niece's companion, and a guide are travelling to the Knight's newly inherited estates and are engaged in a bitter family row over dynastic marriage plans: the Knight's niece, Franziska, is resisting her arranged betrothal to her cousin and near-namesake Baron Franz von Kronstein. Franziska is a notably strong female, forthrightly dismissing Franz—who is actually present—as 'effeminate' (p. 141), and scorning his 'warm heart' (p. 142). Instead, she masochistically desires a hyper-masculine husband to master her: 'I would rather be tyrannized over, and kept under a little by my future husband, than be loved in such a wearisome manner' (p. 142).

These family storms are mirrored in their physical journey: the party ride through a blizzard and into wild woods, pursued by cannibalistic reed-wolves, before they eventually reach a ruined castle—Castle Klatka—and meet a mysterious stranger who scatters the predators. They later return to the ruins, meet the stranger once again, and invite him to visit them at their new seat. The stranger, Azzo von Klatka, does so—'a man about forty, tall, and extremely thin' with a complexion of 'a sort of gray, or ... dirty white' and 'cold grey eyes, whose glance ... was at times so piercing, that no one could endure it long' (pp. 154–5). He proves to be a grotesque guest—rude, sarcastic, contemptuous, and 'inexpressibly repulsive' (p. 155) to all but Franziska, whom he seems to have bewitched. He repeatedly visits her in dreams, condensing from a mist before dissolving, and leaving a red line on her throat that does not heal. As Franziska's health declines, von Klatka is rejuvenated, strong enough to snap Franz's sword with his bare hand.

31 See Katy Brundan, Melanie Jones, and Benjamin Mier-Cruz, 'Dracula or Draculitz?: Translational Forgery and Bram Stoker's "Lost Version" of *Dracula*', *Victorian Review*, 45.2 (2019), 293–306.

Azzo von Klatka therefore takes shape as a certain sort of male vampire, combining recent fiction with historical cases. He is a loner, of peculiar habits, and with terrifying strength; he appears only in moonlight; he can read minds and mesmerize his prey, who experience his attacks in a state between wakefulness and sleep. As he feeds his cadaverous complexion gradually becomes 'smooth and soft' (p. 160), although he is neither charming nor charismatic and remains repugnant to all but his victim. This sordid aristocracy is derived from Ruthven and Varney, but von Klatka lacks their cruel appeal and is considerably more boorish, and 'The Mysterious Stranger' is, in fact, most strongly embedded in early vampire accounts. Von Klatka's violations of Franziska's dreams, for instance, recall the eighteenth-century incubus of nightmare, he leaves telltale forensic evidence such as the innocuous mark on her throat, and also possesses formidable strength.

For all its deep roots in the expanding spectrum of Enlightenment vampirism, Wachsmann also adds a startlingly modern component. The Knight of Woislaw, governor of Castle Glogau, is an expert in vampire lore comparable to the Habsburg vampire slayer Count de Cabreras, but he is also equipped with a marvellous prosthetic. This device, engineered in gold 'by a celebrated Italian mechanic' (p. 154), replaces Woislaw's right hand, which he lost on the battlefield, and gives him 'superhuman strength' (p. 154). Woislaw is, then, a cyborg—part-human, part-machine—and he is twice mistaken for a vampire *by another vampire* due to his preternatural grip. The idea of using technology to defeat vampires may have been adapted in more sophisticated and cutting-edge ways by Stoker, whose Defenders of Light employ phonographs and cameras against the Count, but Woislaw's automative hand is a reminder that vampire tales of the period—even those set in earlier times—were resolutely contemporary.

Fitz-James O'Brien's weird tale, 'What Was It?' (1859) presents a very different vampire. The plot simply concerns the observation of an invisible creature by the narrator Harry Escott and his companion Dr Hammond following its assault on Escott and subsequent capture. This 'Thing'—the 'Invisible', a 'Something', a 'Mystery', an 'Enigma' (pp. 182–7), as unnameable as Frankenstein's Being—does not have obvious sources in eighteenth-century vampirism, except perhaps as an incarnation of the incubus or nightmare, and neither does O'Brien draw on Polidori's literary legacy. Although he was influenced by authors such as Hoffmann, Dickens, Le Fanu, and Poe—notably by 'Ligeia', which anticipates the tale's very title in the line, 'What *was* it?' (p. 90)—'What Was It?' is really founded on the demonology of jinns, afrits, and ghouls, and so the tale effectively represents the return of the Islamic vampire of *Thalaba the Destroyer* and *The Black Vampyre*. There is a convincing emphasis on the entity's corporeality—its breath, its teeth, its heart. Like the vampire, the entity is a 'horrible semblance of a human being' (p. 187), and the narrator actually describes it as a 'ghoul ... capable of feeding on human flesh' (p. 186). So despite the story being set in an accurately delineated New York City, there are frequent references to Muslim literature and culture which accentuate the vivid shades of Orientalism in the story.

O'Brien, an Irish-American, brings these Eastern influences to bear on the most pressing political and humanitarian issues of the time. The Irish Famine or 'Great Hunger' of 1845–9 was a national catastrophe of horrific magnitude, in which the staple potato harvest was devastated in successive years, depopulating the land: of about 8.4 million inhabitants in 1844, a million Irish people died in the next five years and as many as two million emigrated to the United States—including O'Brien himself. The literary critic Terry Eagleton consequently sees the Famine as a visitation from another, primaeval world:

> Part of the horror of the Famine is its atavistic nature—the mind-shaking fact that an event with all the premodern character of a medieval pestilence happened in Ireland with frightening recentness ... there is something recalcitrant at its core which defeats articulation, some 'real' which stubbornly refuses to be symbolized.[32]

O'Brien had already published a poem with the title 'The Famine' in the Irish nationalist magazine *The Nation* (7 March 1846), and 'What Was It?' has been described as 'perhaps the most apt allegory for the human experience of hunger that exists in the American canon'.[33] The literature of the Famine cannot face the Famine itself, and the

[32] Terry Eagleton, *Heathcliff and the Great Hunger: Studies in Irish Culture* (London and New York: Verso, 1995), 14.

[33] Brian Peter Crowe, 'Irish Hunger/American Eyes: The Great Famine in Antebellum American Literature' (PhD thesis: Lehigh University, 2014), 152–61, at 153.

weird and inexplicable entity of O'Brien's tale thus marks the limit of meaning and understanding, signalling the impossibility of representing the 'Great Hunger'.

But this is also a tale of racism and slavery in America, domestic slavery still being legally practised at the time, especially in the southern states. From 1846, the promoter and showman P. T. Barnum ran an exhibit under the banner 'What Is It?' at the American Museum. This was a 'living curiosity': an African-American man named William Henry Johnson who was presented as a supposed 'missing link', half-human, half-orangutan—it was the most extreme of Barnum's objectifications and dehumanizations of individuals in his museum as 'freaks'.[34] The invisible entity therefore functions as a focal point for both national disasters and xenophobic oppression, from the plight of the Irish to Barnum's despicable pseudo-scientific bigotry. Although Escott and Hammond are unreliable witnesses—not least as they smoke opium—they attempt to assess the entity rationally and as part of their intellectual enquiry the tale includes a discussion on the notion of terror and even has a coda verifying that the entity actually existed. Not only, then, is the entity treated as a certifiable physical and sentient phenomenon demanding explanation—much as the vampire cases of the eighteenth century had been analysed by medical officers, theologians, and philosophers—but, in the end, Harry Escott and Dr Hammond feel compassion for the creature, whatever it is.

Mary Helena Fortune—'Waif Wanderer'—was another Irish author, writing in her case from Australia rather than the United States. 'The White Maniac: A Doctor's Tale' (1867) concerns a French family residing in fashionable London, with Fortune assuming the voice of a successful middle-class male physician, Dr Charles Elveston. The tale recounts Elveston's infatuation with a beautiful aristocratic young lady, Princess Blanche d'Alberville, who lives in an 'enchanted castle' (p. 190)—or rather in upmarket Kensington. Elveston observes that those who enter the house dress in pure white, that Blanche is waited on by 'white mad people' (p. 190), and that everything inside and outside the house is uniformly painted blinding white—which he discovers when he surveys the building from a nearby belfry in an

[34] Joyce L. Huff, 'The Domesticated Monster: Freakishness and Masculinity in Fitz-James O'Brien's "What Was It?"', *Nineteenth-Century Gender Studies*, 4.2 (2008), 7–12.

overgrown graveyard. Elveston thus studies the house and its inmates with the gaze of the patriarchal male, and when he meets Blanche she is objectified as a 'piece of statuary' and 'glassy marble', and is predictably pale—blanched (pp. 196, 198). The doctor is asked to treat her and discovers that her family have incarcerated her as a lunatic, but he comes to believe that it is in fact her guardian who is insane, and indeed a creeping lunacy permeates the tale from its very title—the word 'mad' reverberating through a narrative in which nearly every character is eventually accused of being deranged. Elveston duly proposes to marry Blanche d'Alberville.

Blanche is, then, a character imprisoned in whiteness—in strange counterpoint, for instance, to Poe's women, who are incarcerated in sepulchral gloom. But while this white mania is in eerie contrast to the obscurity, shadows, and darkness of many vampire tales, it offers no clarity; rather, it dazzles and stupefies. Whiteness here is intolerable, a claustrophobic blank, a spectral oppressiveness, 'the colour of death' (p. 197). Even so, this 'leukomania' is not a critique of western society or of white colonialism; rather, it is the medium of the story's suspense, like a blank page or canvas awaiting a mark—a spray of blood. Blood indeed beats through this tale of madness and psychiatry in forensic medical details such as Elveston feeling for Blanche's pulse and, more alarmingly, the gradual disclosure of her condition, disgraceful to her family bloodline. Reports of the disturbing behaviour of young women coming of age had grown throughout the century, often in medical reports on female puberty, menstruation, and hysteria. An anonymous contributor to *The Journal of Psychological Medicine and Mental Pathology* (1851), for example, reported on the inflammatory effect on impressionable girls of the simple appearance of a soldier: 'there is a special susceptibility to the sexual influence of form and colour [that] awake strange mysterious emotions in the young female just bursting into womanhood'.[35] In 'The White Maniac', Blanche's bloodlust is triggered by just such a colour—the colour red: blood begets blood. After coming face to face with the monstrous extent of her condition, Elveston attempts to rationalize it in clinical terms—one of several stories in the period that medicalize vampirism—but the horror of his experience has shattered his

[35] [Anon.,] 'Art. II.—Woman in Her Psychological Relations', *The Journal of Psychological Medicine and Mental Pathology*, 4 (1851), 18–50, at 24.

objectivity, and he cannot bring himself to name what she really is: utterly, ferociously, vampiric. The tale thus dramatizes the collapse of scientific male reason when confronted by furious female passion.

Women are also vampiric in the Decadent poetry of Charles Baudelaire, although his signature contribution, 'Les Métamorphoses du Vampire' (written in 1852)—famously rendering a prostitute as a vampire—was censored and ordered to be removed from the first edition of *Les Fleurs du mal* (1857), and in any case very few of his poems were translated into English in this period. 'Une Charogne' ('A Carcass') was, however, made available by Richard Herne Shepherd and printed in 1869; as a study in decay and putrescence it has an undoubted vampire aesthetic. In this hymn to rottenness, the decomposing remains seem to be animate, stirred not only by the noisome gas that swell the guts—'As if the body, by a wild breath blown, | Lived as it multiplied' (p. 207)—but also enveloped in the teeming proliferation of flies and maggots that swarm about it. Baudelaire is enthralled by putrefaction, but he does not aim vampirically to arrest the rot through incorruptibility, but to embrace it through his carrion muse—what he baptized, in homage to Poe, as 'the phosphorescence of decay'.[36] Baudelaire relishes the impermanence—the 'perishable bliss' (p. 208)—of the hallucinatory horror, haunted by dreams and foetid artistry, that he celebrates and in which he finds a sickening attraction, exhilarating in its intensity. 'A Carcass' is thus shot through with perverse eroticism and sexual lust: the 'legs erected, wanton-like, in air' (p. 207) and 'the insatiate worm, | Who wastes you with his kiss' (p. 208)—akin to the lethal embrace of the vampire, or Poe's 'Conquering Worm'. As the rebel English poet Algernon Charles Swinburne described Baudelaire's reeking majesty in his review of *Les Fleurs du mal*, 'Even of the loathsomest bodily putrescence and decay he can make some noble use; pluck out its meaning and secret, even its beauty, in a certain way, from actual carrion'.[37]

In stark contrast to the repellent decadence of Baudelaire, Sheridan Le Fanu's justly celebrated tale 'Carmilla' (1871–2) presents female beauty in the most extravagant terms of simmering sexuality in the

[36] Théophile Gautier, 'Charles Baudelaire,' in Charles Baudelaire, *Les Fleurs du mal* (Paris: Calmann-Lévy, 1868), 31.

[37] Algernon Charles Swinburne, 'Charles Baudelaire: *Les Fleurs du mal*', *Spectator* (6 September 1862), 999.

first vampire tale to combine fully the vampire cultures of Romanticism with the earlier Enlightenment: blending folklore and superstition, authority and the law, medical science and military service, psychology and seduction, and literature and art, and presenting the imperious and lascivious character of Carmilla—beautiful, bewitching, and fey—in the context of paranormal research, legal evidence, and deductive reasoning. The tale is set in the Austro-Hungarian duchy of Styria—archetypal eighteenth-century vampire country—and follows the growing friendship and incipient love between two young women: Laura, a young English girl, and the puzzling, inscrutable Carmilla—a stranger who arrives unexpectedly and is then taken in by Laura's widowed father while Carmilla's mother is engaged on 'secret' business (p. 221). Laura and Carmilla become smotheringly close to each other, but there is a mysterious sickness in the land and Laura, bedevilled by troubling dreams, seems to be infected with the disease while, for her part, Carmilla starts sleepwalking. There are a number of unsettling occurrences. A hundred-year-old painting of the Countess of Karnstein is restored and returned to Laura's father, and is revealed to be an exact likeness of Carmilla—she is literally a work of art—while a doctor discovers a slight bruise on Laura's throat, which is the sort of clear physical evidence of vampire attacks recorded by Calmet in the eighteenth century. At this point the family are visited by an old friend, General Spielsdorf, who comes with tragic news of the recent death of his daughter: the circumstances are chillingly identical to those of Laura. It is at this point that attention focuses on the nearby ruins of Castle Karnstein, which exerts a malign dominion over the area: 'It was a bad family,' according to the General, 'and here its bloodstained annals were written. ... It is hard that they should, after death, continue to plague the human race with their atrocious lusts' (p. 263). There is a dawning realization, not voiced until the final pages of the narrative, that the Karnsteins were vampires. The General accordingly leads an imperial commission, including two medical men, to investigate, and the tale ends after citing earlier authorities on vampirism and with a summary of the official report.

This contrast between rational Enlightenment thinking, led by a senior military officer, and the ebb and flow of female emotions is highly arresting, and invites the reader to try to make sense of the bond between Laura and Carmilla and their respective characters.

Carmilla is beautiful, passionate, and irresistible, yet indifferent, petulant, and even repulsive—both adored and abhorred. Her relationship with Laura is driven by female power and agency, but is presented in such an insistently sensual way that the tale may well be regarded as a lesbian fantasy. Carmilla's lust for Laura is unequivocal: she gazes at her with 'the ardour of a lover', kisses her with 'hot lips', whispers and sobs, 'You are mine …', and leaves Laura 'trembling' orgasmically (p. 227). Carmilla declares that Laura will be her only love, before succumbing to her own shuddering climax—calling Laura, 'Darling, darling' and murmuring, 'I live in you … I love you so' in post-coital languor (p. 235). This love comes in fierce emotional surges but it is also uncanny—Laura is simultaneously tremulous and aghast, both thrilled and appalled by both Carmilla and herself, something she can only explain as a 'paradox' (p. 227). Her needs and desires battle her moral principles and natural conservatism: 'I experienced a strange tumultuous excitement that was pleasurable, ever and anon, mingled with a vague sense of fear and disgust' (p. 227). These cravings are also incestuous: it transpires that Laura and Carmilla are related through Laura's dead mother—they are flesh and blood—and the tale is troubled by questions of maternity. Carmilla is both a symbolic—or a demonic—mother initiating Laura into womanhood, and at the same time a child suckling at her breast.

Indeed, the tale has many inexplicable and incoherent elements, such as the Black woman who briefly appears, the General's confused letter, the enigmatic 'dirty little book' belonging to the eccentric Baron Vordenburg (p. 270), the repeated appearances of a 'gentleman in black' at society gatherings (p. 257), and the 'Babel' of different languages spoken at Laura's schloss (p. 210). These perplexing elements contribute to the suffocating feverishness of the text, which has been described as 'a narrative of infection' due to the repeated references to contagion and dreams.[38] This plague is supernatural, a disease of the mind—'These poor people infect one another with their superstitions, and so repeat in imagination the images of terror that have infested their neighbours' (pp. 231–2)—and is manifested through physical symptoms of convulsions and feelings of strangulation, and as delirium: a mental disorder. Locked doors and sealed rooms create

[38] Martin Willis, 'Le Fanu's "Carmilla", Ireland, and Diseased Vision', in *Literature and Science*, ed. Sharon Ruston (Woodbridge: Boydell & Brewer, 2008), 111–30, at 111.

a stifling atmosphere of confinement; moreover, dreams and memories are repeated and annexed by different characters, and bloodlines and identities are compounded by the arcane logic of anagrams, further accelerating the psychological disorientation of the characters. This becomes most acute perhaps in an unexpected—and momentary—instance towards the end in which Carmilla appears to teleport (p. 268), as if time and space are collapsing; likewise at its termination the plot itself blurs into new uncertainties. Le Fanu's contribution to vampire literature is in combining physical evidence and testimony with the captivating characterization of Polidori and—daringly—adding the frisson not only of a hyper-sexualized she-vampire, but a she-vampire consumed by same-sex desire.

'Carmilla' has also been seen as a dramatization of Anglo-Irish politics, although such elements are at best ethereal; in 'Ken's Mystery' (1883) by the American writer Julian Hawthorne, however, they are much more emphatic as the tale is explicitly set in Ireland. The tense history of religious sectarianism in Ireland is directly alluded to and forms a troubled backdrop to this strange tale, as does the Great Hunger. The Ireland through which the narrator Keningale travels is eerily deserted, its people either dead as a result of the Famine or cholera, or having migrated to America—but there remains a lingering memory of a lost Gaelic past of nobility and opulence. Ken, who recounts his story to a friend, describes elusive encounters with a beautiful woman (Elsie/Ethelind) that have haunted his dreams since childhood, and which are reminiscent of Laura's visions in 'Carmilla'—except that Ken is male. There are also other hints of 'Carmilla': another 'black woman' (p. 284)—although in this case she is the alluring avatar of the alternative reality into which Ken stumbles on the propitious night of Hallowe'en—an ending as comparably ominous as that of 'Carmilla', and even an ekphrastic passage.

Yet 'Ken's Mystery' has an atmosphere of its own: it is a time-travel story in which an enchantress entices Ken into the past to feed on his energy. Human experience is pitted against the material world of things—a banjo, a ring, a key, tapestries, decorations—and these objects testify. The banjo—described as 'a witness whose silent testimony there was no gainsaying' (p. 281)—attests that Ken has tarried in some sort of faery land, and the tale itself becomes a form of vampiric literature, its telling an act of rejuvenation that gives life to ancient times: 'the mediæval age was alive once more' (p. 292). 'Ken's

Mystery' consequently recalls both 'The Bride of Corinth' and 'La Belle Dame Sans Merci', Ethelind declaring at one point, 'Give me wine as red as your blood and as warm, and I will drain a goblet to the dregs' (p. 294), while Ken himself is left 'pale and haggard' (p. 295). Hawthorne's story thus weaves further material—the imagined Celtic past—into Le Fanu's depiction of the East European she-vampire, which remains a commanding predatory figure, but now becomes a ravishing man-eater.

Margery of Quether is another she-vampire, but different again. Sabine Baring-Gould's West Country tale, first published in 1884, places a regional vampire in a farming community governed by family loyalties, church-going, and tradition, and humming with rural manners, local legends, and a suspicion of metropolitan national politics. Sexual power games are again in the foreground: the half-doppelgängers Margery and Margaret are both strong women, eager to acquire property through marriage by manipulating the weak male protagonist George Rosedhu, but they are also homemakers and farm managers rather than comely temptresses. George is a traditionalist, a supporter of Benjamin Disraeli's Conservative Party and fearing what he calls political 'topsy-turvyism' (p. 296)—the impact on rural communities and farming of the Liberal Party policies of William Gladstone and his government through new tenancy agreements. But George is also a traditionalist in family matters, which are governed by the 'Rosedhu system' (p. 301): 'We Rosedhus always marry late in life, and never have large families' (p. 320). This ensures that their land is left to a single son, enabling the farm to remain viable, and in every generation this sole beneficiary is one 'George Rosedhu', a duplicate of the first George Rosedhu and a declaration of the family's fixed inertia. So George's primary concerns are Rosedhu property rights and inheritance laws—and in this he is not alone.

Unlike previous vampire tales, then, 'Margery of Quether' focuses on the legal status of the vampire—an aspect that Stoker would develop in *Dracula*—although the narrative is also unusual for its strong sense of locale, its attention to everyday farming minutiae, and its conscious use of Devon and Cornish dialect. This rural realism—which is all delivered in the first-person monologue of George and so perhaps invites scepticism—is mixed with a frank acceptance of the supernatural that in turn creates an atmosphere of 'folk horror', which becomes explicit at the end of the tale when the community happily endorses mayhem in the form of a murderous lynch mob cheerily quoting the Bible and calmly discussing live cremation. But the most striking thing about 'Margery of Quether' is that it is a darkly comic tale. There is a mocking humour running through the narrative that escalates as the plot becomes progressively more self-consciously absurd, culminating in one of the most audacious final sentences in fiction and daring the reader to see the whole performance as a shaggy-dog story leading to a dreadful pun. There is really no other vampire tale in the period to compare with it.

In contrast, Robert Louis Stevenson's 'Olalla' (1885) effectively un-parodies 'Margery of Quether'. This eerie tale alludes to vampirism without actually using the word, although, like Baring-Gould, Stevenson plays with language and imagery to insinuate the condition—even to the extent of half-punning on the word *vamped*; yet despite its superficial similarities to 'Margery of Quether' there is nothing comic about 'Olalla'. Stevenson's narrative is set in Spain during the mid-nineteenth century wars over succession, and begins with the unsettling character of Felipe conducting an English patient to his family *residencia* where he is to convalesce; it is an uneasy scene that may have inspired Stoker's account of Jonathan Harker's arrival at Castle Dracula. The 'innocent' (p. 336) Felipe has rancid urges and his appetites are those of a dysfunctional child: he is covetous of the convalescent's bed linen and lubriciously rubs his face across it; he also delights in torturing small animals. Felipe's mother, the Señora, has a peculiar beauty yet is similarly graceless, indolently sprawled across staircases and thresholds, incapable of rational speech. Both are oblivious to human relationships to the point of amorality, sinking the *residencia* into a dreamlike torpor suffused with suppressed violence; even the surrounding landscape lacks reality, the hills appearing 'as if they were of cardboard' (p. 365). The English patient's relationship with the impenetrable and incomprehensible Felipe is tense and occasionally flares into anger and hostility, but he has little interaction with the Señora; to him she simply appears insane.

It is only halfway through the tale that the patient comes face-to-face with the daughter Olalla, who is not only lucid, coherent, and rational, but also dazzlingly attractive: 'Beauty I had seen before, and not been charmed, and I had been often drawn to women, who were not beautiful (except to me); but in Olalla all that I desired and had not dared to imagine was united' (pp. 354–5). So again there is an entrancing siren, this time a poet and a Roman Catholic, who also, like Carmilla, has been prefigured in a portrait of a beguiling young woman hanging in the patient's bedroom: 'red tresses lay like a crown over her brow; her eyes, of a very golden brown, held mine with a look'; however, 'her face, which was perfectly shaped, was yet marred by a cruel, sullen, and sensual expression' (pp. 339–40). The family resemblances evident in the many portraits within the *residencia* emphasize how successive generations carry not only the same physical characteristics but also the same secrets. The bloodline is inescapable, the past determines the present: for Olalla, 'The hands of the dead are in my bosom; they move me, they pluck me, they guide me; I am a puppet at their command' (p. 363). The English patient is in danger of being transfused with this poisoned blood—when he first sees Olalla, 'She passed through my veins; she was one with me' (p. 354). But the shadow that hangs over this enervated dynasty is one of an unspoken ancestral disgrace, and, as the patient unwillingly comes to realize, Olalla carries the same degraded genes as do her mother and brother. Her children will be cursed, and so her duty is to ensure the extinction of her line, concluding the tale in a discomforting imperfect cadence.

Several of these vampire tales are first-person narratives and so the reliability of witnesses is always in question, and this is nowhere more so than in the case of Guy de Maupassant's classic 'The Horla' (first translated by Jonathan Sturges in 1890). Maupassant reworked his tale in different ways, the most effective being as a journal written by the victim, documenting his frenetic sickness and concomitant loss of sanity. The diary records how the narrator is terrorized by the physical incarnation of nightmare, the incubus—an invisible vampire that bears down on him while he sleeps. These fearsome dreams are asphyxiating: 'I feel ... that some one approaches me, looks at me, touches me, mounts upon my bed, kneels upon my breast, seizes my neck in his hands and presses ... presses ... with all his force, to strangle me' (p. 373). The narrator watches its invisible actions in horrified fascination: picking a rose, turning the pages of a book. The trauma affects his nights: 'I was not able to sleep ... [my physician] found my pulse rapid, my eye dilated, my nerves disturbed' (p. 373). Most alarmingly, he becomes somniphobic—panicked by slumber itself: 'I await sleep as one might await an executioner' (p. 373).

The nightmares are interspersed with the chronicle of his everyday life in Rouen and visits to Paris: the narrator witnesses his cousin being hypnotized by a doctor, watches a three-masted ship from Brazil sail up the Seine—which unknown to him is carrying 'tangible beings, resembling vampires' (p. 389)—and disputes metaphysics with a monk. He pieces together his predicament. There appear to be other worlds, worlds invisible to the human eye—as the monk serenely remarks, 'Do we see the hundred-thousandth part of what exists?' (p. 376). The narrator's growing fear is that these invisible powers are independent of the human. He contemplates the profundity of the night sky and his thoughts return to nonhuman beings:

> The stars at the back of the black sky glittered and trembled. Who dwell in those worlds up there? What forms? what living things? what animals? what plants? That which thinks in those distant universes, what knows it more than we? (p. 388)

He investigates the psychic sciences, consults academic papers and reference books, and fears that his identity is split into 'two beings' (p. 377)—self and other. This disturbed sense of doubleness is communicated through the language and vocabulary of the journal, which is neurotically repetitive, fragmented and incoherent, freighted with psychotic non-sequiturs—such as a bizarre anecdote about goats with human faces—and coupled with portentous yet empty prophetic passages.

This jarring mix of styles suggests that the journal is written in torment, that its author is mad or hysteric, even that the tale has multiple authorship. In an insightful reading, the critic Martin Calder considers whether it is 'the diarist who writes the journal, or the journal which writes the diarist, as the anonymous narrator's identity is increasingly alienated from itself and overwhelmed by otherness'.[39] If so, the diary could be seen to be the work of three authors: the sane narrator, the narrator fearful of madness, and the narrator increasingly possessed by the Horla. Indeed, Calder concludes that the Horla, having changed the narrator, is effectively dictating the diary: 'The Other writes the diary which writes the diarist'.[40] Rather than the author creating the text, the written word generates the author as a linguistic dilemma; in doing so, the text becomes the stuff of reality, inverting conventional thinking about literary creativity. This loss of

[39] Martin Calder, 'Something in the Water: Self as Other in Guy de Maupassant's *Le Horla*: A Barthesian Reading', *French Studies*, 52.1 (1998), 42–57, at 42.

[40] Ibid. 50.

his sense of self is most dramatically demonstrated when the diarist-narrator stares into a large mirror, a distorted repetition of an earlier mirror scene with the hypnotist. His reflection is eclipsed by the Horla, 'whose invisible body had absorbed the reflection of mine' (p. 392). Counter-intuitively, then, Maupassant's narrator effectively sees the Horla by not seeing himself, and much as the fractured journal provides a model for the fissiparous structure of *Dracula*, these uncanny effects of mirroring and not-mirroring are the origin of Stoker's notes on Dracula's unreflection: 'no looking glasses in Count's house/never can see him reflected in one—no shadow?'[41]

Vampires are only mentioned towards the end of Maupassant's tale as analogous to the Horla, while the word is not used at all in Ambrose Bierce's 'The Death of Halpin Frayser' (1891); however, Bierce's tale is again steeped in vampirism. The plot of this 'rascally mystery', as it is self-consciously described (p. 409), is by no means clear. The brief précis is that Halpin Frayser visits San Francisco despite his mother having a premonition delivered by her dead grandfather—one Myron Bayne, a poet—that her son will be strangled; in fact, he is shanghaied and compelled to work as a sailor for the next six years. During this time his mother Katy is widowed, remarries, and is murdered. Her assailant is thought to be her second husband—a man named Pardee, now calling himself Branscom—who is being sought by two lawmen who see their job as being to 'arrest one of the corpses in the graveyard' (p. 404). But little of this is explained. While 'The Death of Halpin Frayser' is a detective story of sorts in which there is a murderer to be arrested, the plot unfolds in a non-linear fashion and there are mixed and multiple viewpoints, phantasmic dream sequences, ghostly portents, and the vengeful undead; one character changes his name three times, another twice.

The tale begins with Frayser hunting in the Napa Valley, falling into a reverie in which he has his own premonition of his dead mother, and composing automatic verse. He dreams he is travelling through a sanguinary landscape—'Blood, he then observed, was about him everywhere' (p. 398)—and the landscape is infested with invisible 'malevolent existences' that call to him in broken

[41] Bram Stoker, *Bram Stoker's Notes for Dracula: A Facsimile Edition*, ed. Robert Eighteeen-Bisang and Elizabeth Miller (Jefferson, NC, and London: McFarland & Company, Inc., 2008), 19; Stoker's source in Maupassant has not been acknowledged.

speech—'fragmentary utterances of a monstrous conspiracy against his body and his soul' (p. 397). In this nightmarish world of crypto-botany in which the madroño trees bleed, Frayser is inspired to write a poem in a red notebook, penning the verses in fresh blood, before breaking off when the corpse of his mother suddenly materializes. But Frayser's poem, like the diary of 'The Horla', is an evacuation of selfhood: it is identified by one of the detectives as the work not of Halpin Frayser, but of his maternal great-grandfather Myron Bayne. This in turn exposes the tale's darker subtext of Frayser's repressed Oedipal desire for his mother. Bierce more than hints at this shocking taboo, suggesting that mother and son are united in their shared love of Bayne's poetry: 'The two were nearly inseparable, and by strangers observing their manner, were not infrequently mistaken for lovers' (p. 401). Bierce thus provides an arch critique of the sexual iniquities of those who fall for the charms of poetry, with the associated implication that Katy was abused by her menacingly named poet-grandfather (*bane*). Not only is Branscom's crime purposefully unsolvable, but the appeal of literature is implicated in incest and vampirism: it is incomprehensible, aberrant—which for an author is an impressively self-destructive act.

'A Kiss of Judas' (1893), published under the initials 'X. L.' (Julian Osgood Field), treats vampirism quite differently. The word *vampire* is only used once (p. 439)—and then in jest—and much of the tale gives the impression of being taken up with trivial chit-chat. Yet not only does vampirism pervade the tale—if unrecognized and initially powerless—but the inconsequential high society affairs that occupy most of the narrative drain the characters of identity and purpose: the *beau monde* is not merely vacuous, it is itself vampiric. Moreover, latent motifs such as Eastern European locations and the communicable diseases rabies and cholera run through the text, the events are authenticated by the central character's diary and supported by a military serviceman's testimony, and there is forensic evidence in the distinctive tooth marks on the victim's neck; the tale is also, unusually, cloaked in Judaeo-Christian superstition.

The plot centres on the supposed medical student Isaac Lebedenko, an alarming intruder into the fashionable world of Hippy Rowan. Lebedenko is utterly out of place and poisons the chic vivacity of the idle rich—first by (understandably) taking furious offence at careless insults, and then by his bestial appearance and murderous instincts.

His awful physiognomy and 'animal musk' (p. 416) cause him to be scapegoated as one of the 'Children of Judas' (p. 426), and it is here that the story takes an unexpected turn into Apocryphal legend and occult mysticism, as well as implicit anti-Semitism. Judas's thirty pieces of silver become symbolic of his fateful kiss as the roman numeral *xxx*, while Lebedenko is half-crucified in a parody of the Passion of Christ. The glitterati then decide to test Hippy's courage in an elaborate prank, which is itself superseded by the dreamlike arrival of a party of *laoutari* (gypsy musicians), among which is a beautiful female: a Madonna with 'lustrous violet eyes' (p. 446)—a tantalizing yet vulnerable she-vampire. Although Field places his idiosyncratic vampire lore within an affably sceptical context that almost eclipses the monstrous elements of the story, this is nonetheless a tale of honour and shame, sadism and masochism, the return of the dead and metempsychosis, and same-sex seduction and the lethal consequences of homosexuality. The result is that Hippy Rowan's almost wholly homosocial world is exposed as a venomous environment that masks its vices behind bravado and banality. Field may have lacked the wit of Oscar Wilde, but his ridicule of society, its grotesque posturings, and its rank hypocrisy was no less scathing.

The Decadent movement of late nineteenth-century Britain was pervaded with Greek paganism and Gothic horror, idealized beauty and macabre cruelty, visionary excess and transgressive artistry, and so it was inevitable that the vampire would find a home there. Novels such as Wilde's *The Picture of Dorian Gray* (1891), in which the picture exhibits—or vampirically feeds upon—Dorian's vices were among the most pungent blossoms of the Decadence; so too Stanislaus Eric, Count Stenbock's deceptively slight 'The True Story of a Vampire' (1894). 'The True Story' begins with a knowing wink, suggesting that vampires are becoming a cliché—and the narrator Carmela's name is of course derived from Le Fanu's eighteenth-century vampire—but this story is thoroughly up-to-date, involving modern transport and communication: this vampire travels by train. What is more, Stenbock, who was born in Britain of mixed German and Estonian parentage, writes as a woman—an elderly Baroness remembering her youth as 'a little girl' (p. 451, the phrase occurs twice). In contrast, the central relationship is between an older man, the cosmopolitan Hungarian connoisseur and antiquarian scholar Count Vardalek, and the young boy Gabriel—in other words, homoerotic pederasty—and the plot relates Vardalek's seduction of Gabriel through passing moments and fleeting sensitivities. Their relationship dwells in physical intimacy—holding hands and kissing on the lips, and there is again an emphasis on eyes: Vardalek, for example, has an 'intense sadness of the expression of the eyes' (p. 454) before they dilate 'with a particularly disagreeable expression, dull and dead, yet ... animated by some horrible excitement' (p. 455). Gabriel, also known as Gabryel and Gavril, is an unusual victim—not only a musical prodigy, but 'præter-human, something between the animal and the divine' (p. 452) with his own 'large, wild, gazelle-like eyes' (p. 452), as well as perpetually knotted hair and bare feet. The blonde, effeminate Vardalek seduces Gabriel through performing rhapsodic music on the piano—a pursuit that was briefly associated with homosexuality in the 1890s—feeding most hungrily when Gabriel is intoxicated by his virtuosity.[42] 'The True Story of a Vampire' thus presents music as the medium of vampirism, and aesthetic passions as being profoundly vulnerable to predation.

Another Decadent piece is the short but voluptuous medievalist romance 'The Crimson Weaver' (1895) by R. Murray Gilchrist, a tale that describes an ageing master and his servant travelling through a hyper-real landscape to encounter a vampire witch who has the power to restore youth. At the palace of the Crimson Weaver there are troubling portents of 'strange beasts—dogs and pigs with human limbs,—[that] tore ravenously at something' (p. 462), which foreshadow the terrible fantasy of disembowelment—or 'delirious gynophobia', as one critic puts it—with which the tale climaxes.[43] Although vampirism is once more only latent in this tale, it is at the heart of the topography of this sanguinary world, ruled over by the Crimson Weaver: a merciless and only half-human woman capable both of casting spells of rejuvenation and ripping out the hearts of her victims.

Contemporaneous with these Decadent fantasies, Mary Elizabeth Braddon explores the motif in a very different way in 'Good Lady

[42] See Joe Law, 'The "Perniciously Homosexual Art": Music and Homoerotic Desire in *The Picture of Dorian Gray* and other *Fin-de-Siècle* Fiction', in Sophie Fuller and Nicky Losseff (eds), *The Idea of Music in Victorian Fiction* (Aldershot and Burlington, VT: Ashgate, 2004), 173–96, at 189.

[43] Nicholas Freeman, *1895: Drama, Disaster and Disgrace in Late Victorian Britain* (Edinburgh: Edinburgh University Press, 2011), 160.

Ducayne' (1896), a determinedly non-supernatural tale. There is no Gothic terror or horror here, no inexplicable supernatural events, and in fact there are no vampires—the only mention of the word being in a glib rebuke against a mosquito (p. 478). Even so—and despite her 'shining black eyes' (p. 470)—Lady Ducayne herself is so like one of the undead that, notwithstanding his medical training, the physician Herbert Stafford is staggered by her appearance:

> He had seen terrible faces in the hospital—faces on which disease had set dreadful marks—but he had never seen a face that impressed him so painfully as this withered countenance, with its indescribable horror of death outlived, a face that should have been hidden under a coffin-lid years and years ago. (p. 485)

The old woman is obsessed with her age. She believes that money can purchase years of life, and so her fabulous wealth pays her Italian doctor to keep her alive. For Lady Ducayne, longevity—even immortality—is a financial transaction, and one with a long history. She considers pioneering modern medicine to be continuous with alchemy and the occult sciences of the Middle Ages, enquiring of Stafford whether he knows 'all the new-fangled theories, the modern discoveries—that remind one of the mediæval witchcraft, of Albertus Magnus, and George Ripley; you have studied hypnotism—electricity?' (p. 486). But if Lady Ducayne is thriving, the health of her servant girl, the young Bella Rolleston, steadily and dangerously declines. Stafford analyses Bella's sleep patterns in his professional capacity as a doctor and comes to an alarming diagnosis: Bella is the unconsenting subject of regular and invasive nocturnal surgery. Haematology (the science of blood) was burgeoning in the nineteenth century through treatments for anaemia and a growing number of blood transfusions, as well as in related areas such as vaccination—all of which placed medical ethics and the role of doctors in the public eye. 'Good Lady Ducayne' consequently recasts medical factors seen in the earliest reports of vampire outbreaks by making a physician culpable.

But there is also a much darker shadow hanging over 'Good Lady Ducayne'. In 1885 the journalist W. T. Stead had published 'The Maiden Tribute of Modern Babylon' in the *Pall Mall Gazette*: a shocking article exposing the London underworld. Stead unflinchingly reported on the kidnapping and sale of young girls into prostitution, and in the ensuing scandal the medical profession in particular came under intense scrutiny as girls were often rendered unconscious with chloroform and subjected to internal examination. In other words, Braddon's tale is an extended metaphor for prostitution and human trafficking: a young girl is paid for her body—indeed, Lady Ducayne's appellation 'Good' evokes the conventional madam or brothel-keeper. Neither is the distrust of physicians completely dispelled at the end. Herbert Stafford decides not to take any action against either Dr Parravicini or Lady Ducayne, despite their crimes—which include double manslaughter—and is instead essentially bought off by the 'Good Lady'. The conclusion of the narrative is troubling and the tale ends on a provocatively flippant note, as if Braddon is challenging the reader to reconsider the events of the plot—even that they have been in the hands of a disreputable elderly lady for the past ten thousand words: Good Mary Braddon.

Lady Ducayne represents perhaps the most unlikely *femme fatale* of the period—a deadly superannuated dowager whose powers of seduction lie in her riches. The last piece in this collection consolidates several facets of the she-vampire in forming the archetype of the twentieth-century *femme fatale*. This is Rudyard Kipling's poem and *succès de scandale* 'The Vampire' (1897), written to accompany Philip Burne-Jones's painting of a rapacious she-vampire. While Burne-Jones's painting is effectively an inversion of Henry Fuseli's celebrated composition *The Nightmare* (1781), in which an incubus sits upon the chest of an insensible woman, Kipling's poem lays bare the rotten Baudelairean horrors of the creature—'a rag and a bone and a hank of hair' (p. 491)—while reluctantly admitting to her immodest glamour. The lilting rhythm and rhyme-scheme evoke children's songs and even the nonsense verse of Edward Lear in 'The Jumblies' (1871); at the same time the parenthetical remarks add extra voices—two, even three?—creating an intensely disturbing effect of babbling innocence and Babel-like meaninglessness, as if the reader is surrounded by interrogative pronouncements.

In the poem a young man is destroyed by a vampire who squanders his wealth, dissipates his spirit, and leaves him a wraith. His 'goods ... Honour and faith' are exhausted until 'The fool was stripped to his foolish hide', and 'So some of him lived but the most of him died' (p. 491). His identity drains away; he is spent—financially, sexually, and emotionally. Published in the same year as *Dracula*, Kipling's fetishized portrayal of yet another predatory female led directly to the 'vamp' of the early cinema, and it thus acts as a coda to this collection, a decisive step towards future representations, and a striking—and equally iconic—demon sister to Stoker's Count. While the Count himself would be reinvented through Max Schreck's Orlok, Béla Lugosi's Dracula, and the Hammer Film Productions roles of Peter Cushing, Christopher Lee, and Vincent Price, there is a parallel tradition originating at the very beginning of the nineteenth century—that of the *vamp*: Theda Bara, Ingrid Pitt, Siouxsie Sioux, Catherine Deneuve, and the Queen of the Damned, Aaliyah. They are the true legacy of Romantic and Victorian vampire tales.

NOTE ON THE TEXTS

THE variety of texts included in this collection means that transcription conventions and choice of copy-text is not always consistent. In the main, I have preferred to take the first printed text in the English language as copy-text as these are the versions that had initial impact; when on the rare occasions other texts are selected, reasons are given in the appropriate headnote; where the original text is unclear, other contemporary printings have been consulted. Editing is minimal: obvious typographic errors such as 'foul case' typesetting (e.g. 'u' for 'n'), erroneous or superfluous punctuation (e.g. doubled commas or backwards quotation marks—for example, a double full stop at the end of Watts's 'Letter from Geneva' and various redundant full stops elsewhere), and 'knocked out' type have been silently revised, and obvious misspellings and displaced letters are (sparingly) corrected; however, particular spellings of, for example, names have been retained where these are coherent in the text. Consistency has been introduced only in standardizing the use of small capitals and quotation marks (single inverted commas), and ellipses and spacing, replacing -ise with -ize endings (not least because these themselves are sometimes inconsistent within an individual text), Anglicizing certain American spellings, and removing line numbers and unnecessary ornaments; the texts have not been modernized or edited beyond this, so features such as the idiosyncratic uses of commas, combination marks (in, for example, 'The Black Vampyre'), apostrophes, and the use or indeed abuse of the 'Oxford' comma are preserved—to interfere with these elements would be to meddle in the more subtle (if not always intentional) ambitions of these writers and the impact on their readers. It is hoped that this light touch will impart some of the flavour of these early and diverse publications.

All editors owe a debt to those who have gone before, and I have made grateful use of earlier scholarship and critical insights, as acknowledged in the Explanatory Notes.

BIBLIOGRAPHY

The bibliography of vampirism is huge, but many books, chapters, and articles are unreliable, inaccurate, or simply dated. The following suggested reading is divided into general books that cover points made in the Introduction and which may help readers to think about nineteenth-century vampirism in more informed ways, before short bibliographies on each of the texts included in this collection that provide references for the Explanatory Notes.

General Studies of the Vampire

Artenie, Cristina, *Dracula Invades England: The Text, the Context, and the Readers* (Montreal: Universitas Press, 2015).

Artenie, Cristina, *Dracula: A Study of Editorial Practices* (Montreal: Universitas Press, 2016).

Auerbach, Nina, *Our Vampires, Ourselves* (Chicago and London: University of Chicago Press, 1995).

Baldick, Chris and Robert Mighall, 'Gothic Criticism', in David Punter (ed.), *A New Companion to the Gothic* (Malden, MA, Oxford, and Chichester: Wiley Blackwell, 2015), 267–87.

Barber, Paul, *Vampires, Burial, and Death: Folklore and Reality*, 2nd edn (New Haven and London: Yale University Press, 2010).

Biale, David, *Blood and Belief: The Circulation of a Symbol between Jews and Christians* (Berkeley, Los Angeles, and London: University of California Press, 2007).

Braudy, Leo, *Haunted: On Ghosts, Witches, Vampires, Zombies, and Other Monsters of the Natural and Supernatural Worlds* (New Haven and London: Yale University Press, 2016).

Bräunlein, Peter J., 'The Frightening Borderlands of Enlightenment: The Vampire Problem', *Studies in History and Philosophy of Biological and Biomedical Sciences*, 43.3 (2012), 710–19.

Bronfen, Elisabeth, *Over Her Dead Body: Death, Femininity and the Aesthetic* (Manchester: Manchester University Press, 1992).

Brooks, Chris, *Mortal Remains: The History and Present State of the Victorian and Edwardian Cemetery* (Exeter: Wheaton Publishers in association with the Victorian Society, 1989).

Bynum, W. F., *Science and the Practice of Medicine in the Nineteenth Century* (Cambridge: Cambridge University Press, 1994).

Bulfin, Ailise, *Gothic Invasions: Imperialism, War and Fin-de-Siècle Popular Fiction* (Cardiff: University of Wales Press, 2018).

Butler, Erik, *Metamorphoses of the Vampire in Literature and Film: Cultural Transformations in Europe, 1732–1933* (Rochester, NY: Camden House, 2010).

Calmet, Dom Augustin, *Dissertations upon the Apparitions of Angels, Dæmons, and Ghosts, and Concerning the Vampires of Hungary, Bohemia, Moravia, and Silesia* (London, 1759) [modern edition: *Dissertation sur les revenants en corps, les excommuniés, les oupires ou vampires, brucolaques etc.*, ed. Roland Villeneuve, 2nd edn (Grenoble: Editions Jérôme Millon, 1998)].

Calzone, Raul, 'Liminal Figurations of the Vampire in the German Enlightenment, *Sturm und Drang* and Romanticism', in Raul Calzoni and Greta Perletti (eds), *Monstrous Anatomies: Literary and Scientific Imagination in Britain and Germany during the Long Nineteenth Century* (Gottingen: V&R Unipress, 2015), 41–60.

Cameron, Brooke and Lara Karpenko (eds), *The Vampire in Nineteenth-Century Literature: A Feast of Blood* (Abingdon and New York: Routledge, 2022).

Camporesi, Piero, *Juice of Life: The Symbolic and Magic Significance of Blood*, trans. Robert R. Barr (New York: Continuum, 1995).

Ceglia, Francesco Paolo de, 'The Archbishop's Vampires: Giuseppe Davanzati's *Dissertation* and the Reaction of "Scientific" Italian Catholicism to the "Moravian Events"', *Archives Internationales d'Histoire des Sciences*, 61 (2011), 487–510.

Cohen, Jeffrey Jerome (ed.), *Monster Theory: Reading Culture* (Minneapolis and London: University of Minnesota Press, 1996).

Cooper, Chris, *Blood: A Very Short Introduction* (Oxford: Oxford University Press, 2016).

Crawford, Heide, *The Origins of the Literary Vampire* (Lanham, etc.: Rowman & Littlefield, 2016).

Cruz, Joan Carroll, *The Incorruptibles: A Study of the Incorruption of the Bodies of Various Catholic Saints and Beati* (Charlotte, NC: TAN Books, 2012).

Davenport-Hines, Richard, *Gothic: 400 Years of Excess, Horror, Evil and Ruin* (London: Fourth Estate: 1998).

Davies, Owen, *Witchcraft, Magic and Culture, 1736–1951* (Manchester: Manchester University Press, 1999).

Day, Peter (ed.), *Vampires: Myths and Metaphors of Enduring Evil* (Amsterdam and New York: Rodopi, 2006).

Dijkstra, Bram, *Idols of Perversity: Fantasies of Feminine Evil in Fin-de-Siècle Culture* (New York and Oxford: Oxford University Press, 1986).

Dundes, Alan (ed.), *The Vampire: A Casebook* (Madison: University of Wisconsin Press, 1998).

Faivre, Antoine, 'Du vampire villageois aux discours des clercs', in [collective work] *Les Vampires* (Paris: Albin Michel, 1993), 45–74.

Floresçu, Radu and Raymond T. McNally, *In Search of Dracula: A True History of Dracula and Vampire Legends* (Greenwich, CT: New York Graphic Society, 1972).

Foucault, Michel, *Abnormal: Lectures at the Collège de France, 1974–1975*, ed. Valerio Marchetti and Antonella Salomoni, trans. Graham Burchell (London and New York: Verso, 2003).

Freedman, Jeffrey (ed.), *A Cultural History of Death*, vol. 4: *A Cultural History of Death in the Age of Enlightenment* (London, New York, Oxford, New Delhi, and Sydney: Bloomsbury, 2024).

Gelder, Ken, *Reading the Vampire* (London and New York: Routledge, 1994).

Gibson, Matthew, *Dracula and the Eastern Question: British and French Vampire Narratives of the Nineteenth-Century Near East* (Basingstoke and New York: Palgrave Macmillan, 2006).

Groom, Nick, *The Gothic: A Very Short Introduction* (Oxford: Oxford University Press, 2012).

Groom, Nick, 'Literary Vampires in the Long Eighteenth Century', in Nick Groom and William Hughes (eds), *The Vampire: An Edinburgh Companion* (Edinburgh: Edinburgh University Press, 2025), 54–75.

Groom, Nick, 'The Rise of the Aristocratic Vampire', in *The Palgrave Handbook of the Vampire*, ed. Simon Bacon (London: Palgrave Macmillan [Springer Nature, Switzerland], 2024), 229–46.

Groom, Nick, *The Vampire: A New History*, 2nd edn (New Haven and London: Yale University Press, 2020).

Hamberger, Klaus, *Mortuus Non Mordet: Dokumente zum Vampirismus 1689–1791* (Vienna: Turia & Kant, 1992).

Hoeveler, Diane Long, *Gothic Riffs: Secularizing the Uncanny in the European Imaginary, 1780–1820* (Columbus: Ohio State University Press, 2010).

Houston, Gail Turley, *From Dickens to Dracula: Gothic, Economics, and Victorian Fiction* (Cambridge: Cambridge University Press, 2005).

Huet, Marie-Hélène, 'Deadly Fears: Dom Augustin Calmet's Vampires and the Rule over Death', *Eighteenth-Century Life*, 21.2 (1997), 222–32.

Hughes, William, 'Pathology, Physiology, and the Undead: Medicine, Misdiagnosis, and Vampire Fiction', in Nick Groom and William Hughes (eds), *The Vampire: An Edinburgh Companion* (Edinburgh: Edinburgh University Press, 2025), 33–53.

Jones, Kelly, 'The Theatrical Gothic in the Nineteenth-Century', in Dale Townshend and Angela Wright (eds), *The Cambridge History of the Gothic*, vol. 2: *Gothic in the Nineteenth Century* (Cambridge: Cambridge University Press, 2020), 162–81.

Klaniczay, Gábor, *The Uses of Supernatural Power: The Transformation of Popular Religion in Medieval and Early-Modern Europe* (Cambridge and Oxford: Polity Press, 1990).

Malchow, H. L., *Gothic Images of Race in Nineteenth-Century Britain* (Stanford, CA: Stanford University Press, 1996).

Mulvey-Roberts, Marie, *Dangerous Bodies: Historicising the Gothic Corporeal* (Manchester: Manchester University Press, 2016).

Neocleous, Mark, *The Monstrous and the Dead: Burke, Marx, Fascism* (Cardiff: University of Wales Press, 2005).

Nowosadtko, Jutta, 'Der "Vampyrus Serviensis" und sein Habitat: Impressionen von der österreichischen Militärgrenze', *Arbeitskreis Militär und Gesellschaft in der frühen Neuzeit e.V.*, 8 (2004), 151–67.

Paget, John, *Hungary and Transylvania; with Remarks on their Condition, Social, Political, and Economical*, 2 vols (London: John Murray, 1839).

Perkowski, Jan Louis, *The Darkling: A Treatise on Slavic Vampirism* (1989), in *Vampire Lore: From the Writings of Jan Louis Perkowski* (Bloomington: Slavica Publishers, 2006), 317–488.

'Putoneo' [J. C. Meinig], *Besondere Nachricht von denen Vampyren oder so genannten Blut-Saugern* (Leipzig, 1732).

Stoker, Bram, *Bram Stoker's Notes for Dracula: A Facsimile Edition*, ed. Robert Eighteeen-Bisang and Elizabeth Miller (Jefferson, NC, and London: McFarland & Company, Inc., 2008).

Stuart, Roxana, *Stage Blood: Vampires of the 19th-Century Stage* (Bowling Green, OH: Bowling Green State University Popular Press, 1994).

Tille, Rebecca, *Der Vampir als Element der Literaturgeschichte: Literaturwissenschaftliche Untersuchung zur schwarzromantischen Vampirmotivik* (Hamburg: Diplomica Verlag, 2013).

Vukanović, T. P., 'The Vampire', in Jan Louis Perkowski, *Vampire Lore: From the Writings of Jan Louis Perkowski* (Bloomington: Slavica Publishers, 2006), 230–59.

Lord Byron, 'A Fragment'

Franklin, Caroline, 'The Influence of Madame de Staël's Account of Goethe's *Die Braut von Korinth* in *De l'Allemagne* on the Heroine of Byron's *Siege of Corinth*', *Notes & Queries*, 35.3 (1988), 307–10.

Gordon, George, Lord Byron, *Lord Byron: The Complete Miscellaneous Prose*, ed. Andrew Nicholson (Oxford: Oxford University Press, 1991).

Gordon, George, Lord Byron, *The Giaour, A Fragment of a Turkish Tale* (London: John Murray, 1813).

Gordon, George, Lord Byron, *Mazeppa, A Poem* (London: John Murray, 1819).

Hobhouse, John Cam, *A Journey through Albania, and Other Provinces of Turkey in Europe and Asia, to Constantinople, during the years 1809 and 1810* (London: James Cawthorn, 1813).

MacCarthy, Fiona, *Byron: Life and Legend* (London: John Murray, 2002).

Marín, Álvaro García, 'The Significance of "The Vampire of Vourla" to Nineteenth-Century Vampire Fiction', *Journal of Vampire Studies*, 3 (2023), 46–83.

Marín, Álvaro García (ed.), *The Vampire of Vourla and Other Greek Vampire Tales, 1819–1846* (Richmond, VA: Valancourt Books, 2024).

Miles, Margaret M., 'The Roman Propylon in the City Eleusinion', in Bonna D. Wescoat and Robert G. Ousterhout (eds), *Architecture of the Sacred: Space, Ritual, and Experience from Classical Greece to Byzantium* (Cambridge: Cambridge University Press, 2012).

Nietzsche, Friedrich, *Daybreak: Thoughts on the Prejudices of Morality*, ed. Maudemarie Clark and Brian Leiter, trans. R. J. Hollingdale (Cambridge: Cambridge University Press, 1997).

Southey, Robert, *Thalaba the Destroyer*, 2nd edn, 2 vols (London: Longman, Hurst, Rees and Orme, 1809).

Stauffer, Andrew M., 'Sorting Byron's "Windsor Poetics"', *Keats-Shelley Journal*, 51 (2002), 30–4.

Tales of the Dead (London: White, Cochrane, and Co., 1813).

Johann Wolfgang von Goethe, 'The Bride of Corinth'

Brand, John, *Observations on Popular Antiquities: including the Whole of Mr. Bourne's Antiquitates Vulgares, with Addenda to Every Chapter of that Work* (Newcastle-upon-Tyne, 1777).

The Common-Place Book of Ancient and Modern Ballad [sic] *and Metrical Legendary Tales: An Original Selection, including Many Never Before Published* (Edinburgh: John Anderson et al., 1824).

Endres, Johannes, 'Vampires and the Orient in Goethe's "Die Braut von Corinth"', *The German Quarterly*, 93.2: *The Eighteenth Century* (Spring 2020), 204–20.

Goethe, Johann Wolfgang von, *Faustus, A Dramatic Mystery; The Bride of Corinth; The First Walpurgis Night*, trans. John Anster (London: Longman, Rees, Orme, Brown, Green, & Longman, 1835).

John William Polidori and Alaric Watts, 'Extract of a Letter from Geneva', 'Introduction', and 'The Vampyre'

Apollo's Lyre; Being a Selection of Choice Songs, Sung at Vauxhall, Theatres Royal, Convivial Meetings, &c. (Huddersfield: Silvester Sikes and Co., 1800?).

Aquilina, Conrad, 'The Deformed Transformed; or, From Bloodsucker to Byronic Hero—Polidori and the Literary Vampire', in Sam George and Bill Hughes (eds), *Open Graves, Open Minds: Representations of Vampires and the Undead from the Enlightenment to the Present Day* (Manchester: Manchester University Press, 2013), 24–38.

Ariès, Philippe, *The Hour of Our Death*, trans. Helen Weaver (New York: Vintage Books, 1982).

Ashton, John, *The History of Gambling in England* (London: Duckworth, 1898).

Barbauld, Anna Laetitia, *Hymns for Public Worship: selected from Various Authors, and intended as a Supplement to Dr. Watts's Psalms* (Warrington, 1772).

Camilletti, Fabio, 'A Note on the Publication History of John Polidori's *The Vampyre*', *Gothic Studies*, 22.3 (2020), 330–43.

Fedosov, Dmitry G., 'The First Russian Bruces', in Grant G. Simpson (ed.), *The Scottish Soldier Abroad: 1247–1967* (Edinburgh: John Donald, 1992), 55–66.

Giddey, Ernest, 'Byron and Switzerland', in Paul Graham Trueblood (ed.), *Byron's Political and Cultural Influence in Nineteenth-Century Europe* (London: Palgrave Macmillan, 1981), 179–90.

Goethe, Johann Wolfgang von, *Gespräche mit Goethe*, ed. Ernst Rudolf Beutler (Zurich: Artemis-Verlag, 1948).

Gordon, George, Lord Byron, *Byron's Letters and Journals*, ed. Leslie A. Marchand, 12 vols, iii: *'Alas! The Love of Women'* (London: John Murray, 1972).

Gordon, George, Lord Byron, *Byron's Letters and Journals*, ed. Leslie A. Marchand, 12 vols, v: *'So Late into the Night'* (London: John Murray, 1976).

Gordon, George, Lord Byron, *Byron's Letters and Journals*, ed. Leslie A. Marchand, 12 vols, vi: *'The Flesh is Frail'* (London: John Murray, 1976).

Gordon, George, Lord Byron, *Byron's Letters and Journals*, ed. Leslie A. Marchand, 12 vols, ix: *'In the Wind's Eye'* (London: John Murray, 1979).

Gordon, George, Lord Byron, *Childe Harold's Pilgrimage, A Romaunt: and Other Poems*, 7th edn (London: John Murray, 1814).

Groom, Nick, 'Polidori's "The Vampyre": Composition, Publication, Deception', *Romanticism*, 28.1 (April 2022), 46–59.

Groom, Nick, 'Thomas Chatterton and the Death of John William Polidori: Copycat or Coincidence?', *Notes & Queries*, 265.4 (2020), 534–6.

Groom, Nick, '*The Vampyre*, Aubrey, and *Frankenstein*', in Sam George and Bill Hughes (eds), *The Legacy of John Polidori: The Romantic Vampire and its Progeny* (Manchester: Manchester University Press, 2024), 123–40.

Macdonald, D. L., *Poor Polidori: A Critical Biography of the Author of The Vampyre* (Toronto, Buffalo, and London: University of Toronto Press, 1991).

Phillips, Ivan, '"But if thine eye be evil": Tropes of Vision in the Rise of the Modern Vampire', in Sam George and Bill Hughes (eds), *The Legacy of*

John Polidori: The Romantic Vampire and its Progeny (Manchester: Manchester University Press, 2024), 167–85.

Polidori, John William, *The Diary of Dr. John William Polidori, 1816: Relating to Byron, Shelley, etc.*, ed. William Michael Rossetti (London: Elkin Mathews, 1911).

Polidori, John William, *The Vampyre and Ernestus Berchtold; or, The Modern Oedipus: Collected Fiction of John William Polidori*, ed. D. L. MacDonald and Kathleen Scherf (Toronto, Buffalo, and London: University of Toronto Press, 1994).

Polidori, John William, *The Vampyre and Ernestus Berchtold; or, The Modern Œdipus*, ed. D. L. MacDonald and Kathleen Scherf (Peterborough, ON: Broadview Press, 2008).

Polidori, John William, *The Vampyre and Other Tales of the Macabre*, ed. Robert Morrison and Chris Baldick (Oxford and New York: Oxford University Press, 1998; 2nd edn, 2008).

Polidori, John William, *'The Vampyre' and Other Writings*, ed. Franklin Charles Bishop (Manchester: Carcanet Press, 2005).

Polidori, John William, *'The Vampyre' and Other Works: Selected Writings of Dr John Polidori*, ed. Franklin Charles Bishop (Chislehurst: Gargoyle's Head Press, 1991).

Polidori, John William, *Ximenes, The Wreath, and Other Poems* (London: Longman, Hurst, Rees, Orme, and Brown, 1820).

Russell, Gillian, 'Faro's Daughters: Female Gamesters, Politics, and the Discourse of Finance in 1790s Britain', *Eighteenth Century Studies*, 33 (2000), 481–504.

Shelley, Mary, *Frankenstein or The Modern Prometheus. The 1818 Text*, ed. Nick Groom (Oxford: Oxford University Press, 2019).

Skarda, Patricia L., 'Vampirism and Plagiarism: Byron's Influence and Polidori's Practice', *Studies in Romanticism*, 28.2 (1989), 249–69.

Twitchell, James, *The Living Dead: A Study of the Vampire in Romantic Literature* (Durham, NC: Duke University Press, 1981).

Viets, Henry R., 'The London Editions of Polidori's "The Vampyre"', *Papers of the Bibliographical Society of America*, 63.2 (1969), 83–103.

John Keats, 'La Belle Dame Sans Merci'

Jones, Chris, 'Knight or Wight in Keats's "La Belle Dame"? An Ancient Ditty Reconsidered', *Keats-Shelley Review*, 19 (2005), 39–49.

Keats, John, *The Letters of John Keats*, ed. Maurice Buxton Forman, 2 vols, 4th edn (London, New York, and Toronto: Oxford University Press, 1952).

Murfin, Ross and Christopher Stampone, 'Romantic Quotation in "La Belle Dame sans Merci" and *The Fall of Hyperion: A Dream*', *Keats-Shelley Review*, 31.1 (2017), 25–38.

Percy, Thomas, *Northern Antiquities: or, A Description of the ... Ancient Danes ...*, 2 vols (London, 1770).

Spenser, Edmund, *The Faerie Qveene*, ed. A. C. Hamilton, 2nd edn (Harlow: Pearson Longman, 2007).

'Uriah Derick D'Arcy' [Richard Varick Dey], The Black Vampyre

Aeschylus, *The Tragedies of Æschylus*, trans. Robert Potter (Norwich, 1777).

Barger, Andrew (ed.), *The Best Vampire Stories 1800–1849: A Classic Vampire Anthology*, 3rd edn (n.p.: Bottletree, n.d.).

Boswell, James, *Boswell's Life of Johnson together with Boswell's Journal of a Tour to the Hebrides and Johnson's Diary of a Journey into North Wales*, ed. George Birkbeck Hill, rev. L. F. Powell, 6 vols (Oxford: Clarendon Press, 1979).

Bray, Katie, '"A Climate ... More Prolific ... in Sorcery": *The Black Vampyre* and the Hemispheric Gothic', *American Literature*, 87.1 (2015), 1–22.

The British Board of Trade, *Report of The Lords of the Committee of Council appointed for the Consideration of all Matters relating to Trade and Foreign Plantations* (n.p.: n.p., 1789).

Burdett, William, *Life and Exploits of Mansong, commonly called Three-Finger'd Jack, the Terror of Jamaica* ('Sommers Town' [i.e. London]: A. Neil, 1800).

Cervantes Saavedra, Miguel de, *Don Quixote de la Mancha*, trans. Charles Jarvis, ed. E. C. Riley (Oxford: Oxford University Press, 2008).

Chambers, Ephraim and Abraham Rees, *Cyclopædia: or, An Universal Dictionary of Arts and Sciences*, 4 vols (London, 1778–88).

Defoe, Daniel, *The Life and Strange Surprizing Adventures of Robinson Crusoe, of York, Mariner*, ed. Thomas Keymer and James Kelly (Oxford: Oxford University Press, 2009 [1719]).

Dubay, Noelle Victoria, 'Works like a Charm: The Occult Resistance of Nineteenth-Century American Literature' (PhD thesis: Johns Hopkins University, 2020).

Dupriez, Bernard, *A Dictionary of Literary Devices*, trans. Albert W. Halsall (New York, etc.: Harvester Wheatsheaf, 1991).

Earle, William, *Obi; or, The History of Three-Fingered Jack* (London: Earle and Hemet, 1800).

Edwards, Bryan, *The History, Civil and Commercial, of the British Colonies in the West Indies*, 2 vols (London, 1793).

Edwards, Bryan, *The History, Civil and Commercial, of the British Colonies in the West Indies*, 3 vols (London: John Stockdale, 1801).

Edwards, Bryan, *The History, Civil and Commercial, of the British Colonies in the West Indies*, 4 vols (Philadelphia: James Humphreys, 1806–7).

Edwards, Bryan, *Poems, Written Chiefly in the West-Indies* (Kingston, Jamaica, 1792).

Encyclopædia Perthensis; or Universal Dictionary of Knowledge, collected from Every Source; and intended to Supersede the use of All Other English Books of Reference, 23 vols (Perth: C. Mitchel and Co., 1796–1806).

Farmer, Henry Tudor, MD, *Imagination; The Maniac's Dream, and Other Poems* (New York: Kirk & Mercein, and London: John Miller, 1819).

Garrigus, John D., 'Vincent Ogé *jeune* (1757–91): Social Class and Free Colored Mobilization on the Eve of the Haitian Revolution', *The Americas*, 68.1 (2011), 33–62.

Gordon, George, Lord Byron, *The Giaour, A Fragment of a Turkish Tale* (London: John Murray, 1813).

Halleck, Fitz-Greene, *Fanny* (New York: n.p., 1833).

Homer, *The Iliad of Homer*, trans. Alexander Pope, ed. Steven Shankman (London, etc.: Penguin, 1996).

Huhtamo, Erkki, 'Mechanisms in the Mist: A Media Archaeological Excavation of the Mechanical Theatre', in Nele Wynants (ed.), *Media Archaeology and Intermedial Performance: Deep Time of the Theatre* (London: Palgrave Macmillan, 2019), 23–82.

Lucan, *The Civil War (Pharsalia)*, ed. and trans. Robert A. Kaster, Loeb Classical Library (Cambridge, MA, and London: Harvard University Press, 2011).

McLaren, Archibald, *The Battle of the Dandies; or, The Half-Way House* (London: A. Macpherson, 1818).

Medical Transactions, Published by the College of Physicians in London, 6 vols (London, 1768–1820).

Milton, John, *Paradise Lost*, ed. Alastair Fowler (London and New York: Longman, 1971).

Molina, J. Ignatius, Abbé Don, *The Geographical, Natural, and Civil History of Chili*, 2 vols (London: Longman, Hurst, Rees, and Orme, 1809).

Moore, Thomas, *Tom Crib's Memorial to Congress* (London: Longman, Hurst, Rees, Orme, and Brown, 1819).

Moseley, Benjamin, *A Treatise on Sugar* (London, 1799).

O'Regan, William, *Memoirs of the Legal, Literary, and Political Life of the Late the Right Honourable John Philpot Curran, once Master of the Rolls in Ireland ...* (London: James Harper, and Dublin: Richard Milliken, 1817).

Paton, Diana, *The Cultural Politics of Obeah Religion, Colonialism and Modernity in the Caribbean World* (Cambridge: Cambridge University Press, 2015).

Phillips, Charles, *The Speeches of Charles Phillips, Esq. delivered at the Bar, and on Various Public Occasions, in Ireland and England* (London: Longman, Hurst, Rees, Orme, and Brown, 1817).

Quran: *The Koran, commonly called The Alcoran of Mohammed, translated from the original Arabic ...*, trans. George Sale, new edn, 2 vols (Bath, 1795 [1734]).

Raynal, Guillaume-Thomas-François, 'Abbé', *A Philosophical and Political History of the Settlements and Trade of the Europeans in the East and West Indies*, rev. edn, trans. J. O. Justamond, 6 vols (London, 1798).

Raynal, Guillaume-Thomas-François, 'Abbé', *A Philosophical and Political History of the Settlements and Trade of the Europeans in the East and West Indies*, rev. edn, 6 vols (Edinburgh: Mundell and Son, J. Fairbairn, and J. and A. Duncan, 1804).

Rhodes, William Barnes, *Bombastes Furioso* (Dublin: W. Tyrrell, 1813).

Scott, Walter, *The Lady of the Lake. A Poem*, 4th edn (Edinburgh: John Ballantyne and Co., and London: Longman, Hurst, Rees, Orme, and Brown, and W. Miller, 1810).

Shelley, Mary, *Frankenstein or The Modern Prometheus. The 1818 Text*, ed. Nick Groom (Oxford: Oxford University Press, 2019).

Sterne, Laurence, *The Life and Opinions of Tristram Shandy, Gent.*, 9 vols (London, 1759–67).

Sydney, Lady Morgan, *Florence Macarthy; An Irish Tale*, 2nd American edn, 2 vols (Philadelphia: M. Carey & Son, 1819).

Vieth, Gerhard Ulrich Anton, *The Pleasing Preceptor; or Familiar Instructions in Natural History and Physics ...*, 2 vols (London: G. G. and J. Robinson, 1800–1).

Walpole, Horace, *The Yale Edition of Horace Walpole's Correspondence*, ed. W. S. Lewis et al., 48 vols, vol. xxxii: *Horace Walpole's Correspondence with the Countess of Upper Ossory* (New Haven: Yale University Press, and London: Oxford University Press, 1965).

Weaver, Karol K., *Medical Revolutionaries: The Enslaved Healers of Eighteenth-Century Saint Domingue* (Urbana and Chicago: University of Illinois Press, 2006).

Wegelin, Oscar, *Early American Plays: 1714–1830*, 2nd edn (New York: Literary Collector Press, 1905).

Ernst Benjamin Salomo Raupach, 'Wake Not The Dead'

Crawford, Heide, 'Ernst Benjamin Salomo Raupach's Vampire Story "Wake Not The Dead!"', *Journal of Popular Culture*, 45.6 (2012), 1189–205.

De Quincey, Thomas, *Confessions of an English Opium Eater and Other Writings*, ed. Robert Morrison (Oxford: Oxford University Press, 2013).

Frayling, Christopher, *Vampyres: Lord Byron to Count Dracula* (London: Faber and Faber, 1991).

Groom, Nick, 'Viral Vampires', *Critical Quarterly*, 62.4 (2020), special issue 'CoronaGothic: Cultures of the Pandemic', 9–16.

Lewis, Paul, 'The Intellectual Functions of Gothic Fiction: Poe's "Ligeia" and Tieck's "Wake Not The Dead"', *Comparative Literature Studies*, 16 (1979), 201–21.

Mayo, Herbert, 'Vampyrism', *On the Truths Contained in Popular Superstitions with an Account of Mesmerism*, 2nd edn (Edinburgh and London: William Blackwood and Sons, 1851), 20–40.

Popular Tales and Romances of the Northern Nations, 3 vols (London: W. Simpkin and R. Marshall; and J. H. Bohte, 1823).

Edgar Allan Poe, 'Ligeia'

Bacon, Francis, *The Oxford Francis Bacon*, 16 vols, xv: *The Essayes or Counsels, Civill and Morall*, ed. Michael Kiernan (Oxford: Clarendon Press, 2000).

Dayan, Joan, *Fables of Mind: An Inquiry into Poe's Mind* (Oxford: Oxford University Press, 1987).

Dickens, Charles, *The Pickwick Papers*, ed. James Kinsley (Oxford: Oxford University Press, 2008).

Homer, *The Odyssey*, trans. Walter Shewring, ed. G. S. Kirk (Oxford: Oxford University Press, 1980).

Kennedy, J. Gerald, *Poe, Death, and the Life of Writing* (New Haven: Yale University Press, 1987).

Lopes, Elisabete, 'Unburying the Wife: A Reflection Upon the Female Uncanny in Poe's "Ligeia"', *The Edgar Allan Poe Review*, 11.1 (2010), 40–50.

Milton, John, *Paradise Lost*, ed. Alastair Fowler (London and New York: Longman, 1971).

Poe, Edgar Allan, *The Collected Works of Edgar Allan Poe*, ed. Thomas Ollive Mabbott, 3 vols (Cambridge, MA: Harvard University Press, 1969–78), ii: *Tales and Sketches, 1831–1842*, ed. T. O. Mabbott, with Eleanor D. Kewer and Maureen C. Mabbott (1978) [online edition at www.eapoe.org].

Poe, Edgar Allan, 'The Philosophy of Composition' [1846], *The Fall of the House of Usher and Other Writings*, ed. David Galloway (London: Penguin, 1986), 480–92.

Poe, Edgar Allan, *Tales of the Grotesque and Arabesque*, 2 vols (Philadelphia: Lea and Blanchard, 1840 [published in December 1839, dated 1840]).

Pope, Alexander, *The Dunciad in Four Books*, ed. Valerie Rumbold (Harlow: Longman, 1999).

Shaw, G. F., *The Panorama of Nature, or A Comprehensive View of Natural History and Botany. Comprising the Whole of Goldsmith's History of the Earth & Animated Nature* (London: R. Edwards, 1817).

Sheridan, Frances Chamberlaine, *The History of Nourjahad* (London, 1767).

Stephanou, Aspasia, 'Lovely Apparitions and Spiritualized Corpses: Consumption, Medical Discourse, and Edgar Allan Poe's Female Vampire', *The Edgar Allan Poe Review*, 14.1 (2013), 36–54.

Warton, Thomas, *Observations on The Fairy Queen of Spenser*, 2 vols (London, 1762).

James Malcolm Rymer, Varney, the Vampyre

Dickens, Charles, *The Old Curiosity Shop*, ed. Elizabeth M. Brennan (Oxford: Clarendon Press, 1997).

Killeen, Jarlath, 'Dealing with the Dead: Vampires, Corpses, and Serialisation', in Nick Groom and William Hughes (eds), *The Vampire: An Edinburgh Companion* (Edinburgh: Edinburgh University Press, 2025), 216–33.

Mandal, Anthony, 'Gothic Fiction from Shilling Shockers to Penny Bloods', in Dale Townshend and Angela Wright (eds), *The Cambridge History of the Gothic*, vol. 2: *Gothic in the Nineteenth Century* (Cambridge: Cambridge University Press, 2020), 139–61.

Scott, Walter, *Kenilworth: A Romance*, ed. J. H. Alexander (Edinburgh: Edinburgh University Press, 1993).

Scott, Walter, *Marmion; A Tale of Flodden Field* (Edinburgh: Archibald Constable and Company, 1808).

Scott, Walter, *Minstrelsy of the Scottish Border: Consisting of Historical and Romantic Ballads, Collected in the Southern Counties of Scotland; with a Few of Modern Date, Founded upon Local Tradition*, 2 vols (Kelso: James Ballantyne, 1802).

Stoker, Bram, *Dracula*, ed. Roger Luckhurst (Oxford: Oxford University Press, 2011).

Karl Adolf von Wachsmann, 'The Mysterious Stranger'

Chambers's Repository of Instructive and Amusing Tracts, vol. viii, no. 62 (London and Edinburgh: William and Robert Chambers, 1854).

Erzählungen und Novellen, 3rd series, vol. vii (Leipzig: Carl Focke, 1844).

Fitz-James O'Brien, 'What Was It?'

Arabian Nights' Entertainments, ed. Robert L. Mack (Oxford: Oxford University Press, 2009).

Bleiler, Richard, 'Fitz-James O'Brien (1828–1862)', *The Green Book: Writings on Irish Gothic, Supernatural and Fantastic Literature*, 18 (Samhain 2021), 37–51.

Brown, Charles Brockden, *Wieland; or The Transformation, and Memoirs of Carwin, The Biloquist*, ed. Emory Elliott (Oxford: Oxford University Press, 2009).

Bulla, Irene, '"Impossible Tales": Language and Monstrosity in the Literary Fantastic' (PhD thesis: Columbia University, 2018).
Bulwer-Lytton, Edward, *Zanoni*, 3 vols (London: Saunders & Otley, 1842).
Corstorphine, Kevin, 'Fitz-James O'Brien', *The Green Book: Writings on Irish Gothic, Supernatural and Fantastic Literature*, 5 (Bealtaine 2015), 5–25.
Crowe, Brian Peter, 'Irish Hunger/American Eyes: The Great Famine in Antebellum American Literature' (PhD thesis: Lehigh University, 2014).
De Quincey, Thomas, *Confessions of an English Opium Eater and Other Writings*, ed. Robert Morrison (Oxford: Oxford University Press, 2013).
Eagleton, Terry, *Heathcliff and the Great Hunger: Studies in Irish Culture* (London and New York: Verso, 1995).
Fanning, Charles, *The Irish Voice in America: 250 Years of Irish-American Fiction* (Lexington: University Press of Kentucky, 2000).
Freud, Sigmund, 'The "Uncanny"', *The Complete Standard Edition of the Complete Psychological Works*, ed. and trans. James Strachey et al., 24 vols, xvii: *(1917–1919) An Infantile Neurosis and Other Works* (London: The Hogarth Press, 1971), 218–56.
Grimm, Jacob and Wilhelm Grimm, *Selected Tales*, trans. and ed. Joyce Crick (Oxford: Oxford University Press, 2009).
Huff, Joyce L., 'The Domesticated Monster: Freakishness and Masculinity in Fitz-James O'Brien's "What Was It?"', *Nineteenth-Century Gender Studies*, 4.2 (2008), 7–12.
Jones, Darryl (ed.), *Horror Stories: Classic Tales from Hoffmann to Hodgson* (Oxford: Oxford University Press, 2014).
Morash, Christopher, *Writing the Irish Famine* (Oxford: Clarendon Press, 1995).
O'Brien, Fitz-James, *The Poems and Stories of Fitz-James O'Brien*, ed. William Winter (Boston: James R. Osgood and Company, 1881).
Schmitt, Jean-Claude, *Ghosts in the Middle Ages: The Living and the Dead in Medieval Society*, trans. Teresa Lavender Fagan (Chicago and London: University of Chicago Press, 1998).

'Waif Wanderer' [Mary Helena Fortune], 'The White Maniac'

Baring-Gould, Sabine, *The Book of Were-Wolves: Being an account of a Terrible Superstition* (London: Smith, Elder and Co., 1865).
Corbin, Alain, *Village of Cannibals: Rage and Murder in France, 1870* (Cambridge: Polity Press, 1992).
Fortune, Mary, *The Fortunes of Mary Fortune*, ed. Lucy Sussex (Ringwood, Victoria: Penguin, 1989).
A Greek–English Lexicon, compiled by Henry George Liddell and Robert Scott (Oxford: Clarendon Press, 1940).

Klepač, Tihana, 'Mary Helena Fortune: Waif Wanderer or a Cross-Dresser with a Mission?', *Studia Romanica et Anglica Zagrabiensia*, 62 (2017), 39–54.

Mangham, Andrew, *Violent Women and Sensation Fiction: Crime, Medicine and Victorian Popular Culture* (Basingstoke: Palgrave Macmillan, 2007).

Sussex, Lucy, 'The Fortunes of Mary: Authenticity, Notoriety and the Crime-Writing Life', *Women's Writing*, 14.3 (2007), 449–59.

Charles Baudelaire, 'A Carcass'

Baudelaire, Charles, *Translations from Charles Baudelaire. With a Few Original Poems*, ed. Richard Herne Shepherd (London: John Camden Hotten, 1869).

Garland, Tony W., 'Brothers in Paradox: Swinburne, Baudelaire, and the Paradox of Sin', *Victorian Poetry*, 47.4, *'A Hundred Sleeping Years Ago': In Commemoration of Algernon Charles Swinburne* (2009), 633–45.

Joseph Sheridan Le Fanu, 'Carmilla'

Arabian Nights' Entertainments, ed. Robert L. Mack (Oxford: Oxford University Press, 2009).

Calmet, Dom Augustin, *The Phantom World: or, The Philosophy of Spirits, Apparitions, etc.*, trans. Henry Christmas (London: Richard Bentley, 1850).

Cooke, Nicholas Francis, *Satan in Society* (Cincinnati, OH, and New York: C.F. Vent, 1871).

Gibson, Matthew, 'Jane Anne Cranstoun, Countess Purgstall', *Le Fanu Studies*, 2.2 (2007), online.

Gibson, Matthew, *Dracula and the Eastern Question: British and French Vampire Narratives of the Nineteenth-Century Near East* (Basingstoke: Palgrave Macmillan, 2006).

Hall, Basil, *Schloss Hainfeld; or, a Winter in Lower Styria* (Edinburgh: Robert Cadell, and London: Whittaker and Co., 1836).

Ikin, J. I., 'Medical Notes on the Militia', *British Medical Journal*, s-4-1 (10 January 1857), 24–6.

Killeen, Jarlath, 'In the Name of the Mother: Perverse Maternity in "Carmilla"', in Gary William Crawford, Jim Rockhill, and Brian J. Showers (eds), *Reflections in a Glass Darkly: Essays on J. Sheridan Le Fanu* (New York: Hippocampus Press, 2011), 363–84.

Le Fanu, Sheridan, *Carmilla: A Critical Edition*, ed. Kathleen Costello-Sullivan (New York: Syracuse University Press, 2013).

Le Fanu, Sheridan, *In a Glass Darkly*, 3 vols (London: R. Bentley and Son, 1872).

Le Fanu, Sheridan, *In a Glass Darkly*, ed. Robert Tracy (Oxford: Oxford University Press, 2008).

McCormack, W. J., *Sheridan Le Fanu and Victorian Ireland* (Oxford: Clarendon Press, 1980).

O'Malley, Patrick R., *Catholicism, Sexual Deviance, and Victorian Gothic Culture* (Cambridge: Cambridge University Press, 2006).

Sage, Victor, *Le Fanu's Gothic: The Rhetoric of Darkness* (London: Palgrave, 2004).

Stephanou, Aspasia, *Reading Vampire Gothic Through Blood: Bloodlines* (Basingstoke: Palgrave Macmillan, 2014).

Stoker, Bram, *Dracula*, ed. Roger Luckhurst (Oxford: Oxford University Press, 2011).

Swinburne, Algernon Charles, *Atalanta in Calydon* (London: Edward Moxon & Co., 1865).

Tronson, Adrian, 'Vergil, the Augustans, and the Invention of Cleopatra's Suicide—One Asp or Two?', *Vergilius*, 44 (1998), 31–50.

Ulin, Julieann, 'Sheridan Le Fanu's Vampires and Ireland's Invited Invasion', in Sam George and Bill Hughes (eds), *Open Graves, Open Minds: Representations of Vampires and the Undead from the Enlightenment to the Present Day* (Manchester: Manchester University Press, 2013), 39–55.

Vámbéry, Ármin, 'Vampire', *Encyclopædia Britannica*, 11th edn (1910–11), quoted in Nick Groom, *The Vampire: A New History*, 2nd edn (New Haven and London: Yale University Press, 2020), 15.

Veeder, William, '"Carmilla": The Arts of Repression', in Fred Botting and Dale Townshend (eds), *Gothic: Critical Concepts in Literary and Cultural Studies*, vol. iii: *Nineteenth-Century Gothic: At Home with the Vampire* (London and New York: Routledge, 2004), 117–41.

Willis, Martin, 'Le Fanu's "Carmilla", Ireland, and Diseased Vision', in Sharon Ruston (ed.), *Literature and Science* (Woodbridge: Boydell & Brewer, 2008), 111–30.

Julian Hawthorne, 'Ken's Mystery'

Hamilton, Eoghain, '"Ken's Mystery": Blending Gothic Foundations with Gaelic Folklore', in Eoghain Hamilton (ed.), *The Gothic: Probing the Boundaries* (Oxford: Interdisciplinary Press, 2012), 21–8.

Hawthorne, Julian, *David Poindexter's Disappearance and Other Tales* (New York: D. Appleton and Company, 1888).

Mackintosh, Robert James (ed.), *Memoirs of the Life of the Right Honourable Sir James Mackintosh*, 2 vols (London: Edward Moxon, 1835).

Ó Dónaill, Niall, *Foclóir Gaeilge-Béarla* (Dublin: Richview Browne & Nolan, 1977).

'Speranza' (Lady Wilde), *Ancient Legends, Mystic Charms, and Superstitions of Ireland*, 2 vols (London: Ward and Downey).

Turgenev, Ivan, *Fathers and Sons*, ed. and trans. Richard Freeborn (Oxford: Oxford University Press, 2008).

Sabine Baring-Gould, 'Margery of Quether'

Baring-Gould, Sabine, *A Book of Dartmoor* (London: Methuen & Co., 1900).

Baring-Gould, Sabine, *A Book of the West: Being an Introduction to Devon and Cornwall*, 2 vols (London: Methuen & Co., 1900).

Baring-Gould, Sabine, *Cheap Jack Zita*, 3 vols (London: Methuen & Co., 1893).

Baring-Gould, Sabine, *The Gaverocks: A Tale of the Cornish Coast*, 3 vols (London: Smith, Elder, & Co., 1887).

Baring-Gould, Sabine, *In the Roar of the Sea: A Tale of the Cornish Coast*, 5th edn (London: Methuen & Co., 1895).

Baring-Gould, Sabine, *Margery of Quether: And Other Stories* (London: Methuen & Co., 1891).

Collinson, Patrick, 'What's in a Name? Dudley Fenner and the Peculiarities of Puritan Nomenclature', in Kenneth Fincham and Peter Lake (eds), *Religious Politics in Post-Reformation England* (Cambridge: Boydell and Brewer, 2006), 113–27.

Conan Doyle, Arthur, *The Hound of the Baskervilles*, ed. W. W. Robson (Oxford: Oxford University Press, 2008).

Dickens, Charles, *Bleak House*, ed. Stephen Gill (Oxford: Oxford University Press, 2008).

Dickens, Charles, *Martin Chuzzlewit*, ed. Margaret Cardwell (Oxford: Oxford University Press, 2009).

Ditmars, Raymond and Arthur Greenhall, 'The Vampire Bat: A Presentation of Undescribed Habits and Review of its History' (1933–4), in Jan Louis Perkowski, *Vampire Lore: From the Writings of Jan Louis Perkowski* (Bloomington, IN: Slavica Publishers, 2006), 294–310.

Elworthy, Frederick Thomas, *The Somerset Word Book* (London: English Dialect Society, 1886).

Graebe, Martin, *As I Walked Out: Sabine Baring-Gould and the Search for the Folk Songs of Devon and Cornwall* (Oxford: Signal Books, 2017).

Grose, Francis, *Antiquities of Scotland*, 2 vols (London, 1789–91).

Jago, F. W. P., *The Ancient Language and the Dialect of Cornwall ...* (Truro: Netherton & Worth, 1882).

Johnston, James, *The Place-Names of England and Wales* (London: John Murray, 1915).

Johnston, James B., *Place-Names of Scotland* (Edinburgh: David Douglas, 1892).

Kingsley, Charles, *Westward Ho!*, 3 vols (Cambridge: Macmillan & Co., 1855).

Marx, Karl and Friedrich Engels, *The Communist Manifesto*, ed. David McLellan (Oxford: Oxford University Press, 2008).

Payton, Philip, *Cornwall* (Fowey: Alexander Associates, 1996).

Risdon, Tristan, *The Chorographical Description or Survey of the County of Devon* (London: Rees and Curtis, 1811).

Songs and Ballads of the West, ed. S. Baring-Gould and H. Fleetwood Sheppard (London: Methuen & Co., 1895).

Thackeray, William Makepeace, *Vanity Fair*, ed. Helen Small (Oxford: Oxford University Press, 2015).

Tope, Rebecca, *Sabine Baring-Gould: The Man Who Told a Thousand Stories* (Walterstone: Praxis Books, 2017).

Transactions of the Sabine Baring-Gould Appreciation Society 10 (2010).

White, Troy Nelson, 'The Gothic Threshold of Sabine Baring-Gould: A Study of the Gothic Fiction of a Victorian Squarson' (PhD thesis: University of Warwick, 2010).

Robert Louis Stevenson, 'Olalla'

Beattie, Hilary J., 'Dreaming, Doubling and Gender in the Work of Robert Louis Stevenson: The Strange Case of "Olalla"', *Journal of Stevenson Studies*, 2 (2005), 10–32.

Brake, Laurel and Marysa Demoor (eds), *Dictionary of Nineteenth-Century Journalism* (Ghent: Academia Press, 2009).

Calvin, John, *Institutes of the Christian Religion*, trans. Henry Beveridge, 2 vols (Edinburgh: Calvin Translation Society, 1846).

Catechism of the Catholic Church, <https://www.vatican.va/archive/ccc/index.htm>

Gibson, Matthew, *The Fantastic and European Gothic: History, Literature and the French Revolution* (Cardiff: University of Wales Press, 2013).

Grimm, Jacob and Wilhelm Grimm, *Selected Tales*, trans. and ed. Joyce Crick (Oxford: Oxford University Press, 2009).

Hawthorne, Nathaniel, *The Marble Faun*, ed. Susan Manning (Oxford: Oxford University Press, 2002).

Lombroso, Cesare, *Criminal Man*, ed. Gina Lombroso-Ferrero (New York and London: G. P. Putnam's Sons, 1911).

Macrobius, *Saturnalia*, ed. and trans. J. D. Duff, Loeb Classical Library (Cambridge, MA, and London: Harvard University Press, 1928).

Oliver, John E. (ed.), *Encyclopedia of World Climatology* (Dordrecht: Springer, 2005).

Perrault, Charles, *Histories, or Tales of Past Times* (London, 1729).

Stevenson, Robert Louis, *The Black Arrow: A Tale of Two Roses* (London, etc.: Cassell and Company, 1888).

Stevenson, Robert Louis, 'A Chapter on Dreams', in *Strange Case of Dr Jekyll and Mr Hyde and Other Tales*, ed. Roger Luckhurst (Oxford: Oxford University Press, 2008), 151–61.

Stevenson, Robert Louis, *The Merry Men and Other Tales and Fables* (New York: Charles Scribner, 1887).

Stevenson, Robert Louis, *New Arabian Nights* (New York: Henry Holt and Company, 1882).

Stevenson, Robert Louis, *Strange Case of Dr Jekyll and Mr Hyde and Other Tales*, ed. Roger Luckhurst (Oxford: Oxford University Press, 2008).

Stevenson, Robert Louis, *Treasure Island*, ed. Peter Hunt (Oxford: Oxford University Press, 2011).

Stevenson, Robert Louis, *Virginibus Puerisque and Other Papers* (London: C. Kegan Paul & Co., 1881).

Guy de Maupassant, 'The Horla'

Calder, Martin, 'Something in the Water: Self as Other in Guy de Maupassant's *Le Horla*: A Barthesian Reading', *French Studies*, 52.1 (1998), 42–57.

Claretie, Jules, 'The Shudder in Literature', *The North American Review*, 155.429 (August 1892), 136–48.

Curtis, George William (ed.), *Modern Ghosts Selected and Translated from the Works of Guy de Maupassant, Pedro Antonio de Alarcón, Alexander L. Kielland, Leopold Kompert, Gustavo Adolfo Becquer, and Giovanni Magherini Graziani* (New York and London: Harper & Brothers, 1890).

Maupassant, Guy de, *A Day in the Country and Other Stories*, ed. and trans. David Coward (Oxford: Oxford University Press, 2009).

Maupassant, Guy de, *The Horla*, ed. and trans. Charlotte Mandell (Hoboken, NJ: Melville House, 2005).

Maupassant, Guy de, *A Parisian Affair and Other Stories*, ed. and trans. Siân Miles (London: Penguin, 2004).

Maupassant, Guy de, *Notre Cœur or A Woman's Pastime*, trans. M. Walter Dunne (St Dunstan Society: Akron, OH, 1903).

'Voltaire', *Œuvres complètes*, 50 vols (Paris: Librairie Garnier Frères, 1877–83).

Ambrose Bierce, 'The Death of Halpin Frayser'

Bierce, Ambrose, *Can Such Things Be?* (New York: The Cassell Publishing Co., 1893).

Bierce, Ambrose, *The Devil's Dictionary*, ed. Roy Morris, Jr (New York and Oxford: Oxford University Press, 1999).

Crow, Charles L., *California Gothic: The Dark Side of the Dream* (New York: Anthem Press, 2024).

Shelley, Percy B., *Adonais: An Elegy on the Death of John Keats, Author of Endymion, Hyperion etc.* (Pisa: Types of Didot, 1821).

Stevenson, Robert Louis, *The Silverado Squatters* (Chatto and Windus: London, 1883).

Watts, Isaac, *Hymns and Spiritual Songs*, 2nd edn (London, 1709).

Weinstock, Jeffrey Andrew, 'American Vampires', in Joel Faflak and Jason Haslam (eds), *American Gothic Culture: An Edinburgh Companion* (Edinburgh: Edinburgh University Press, 2016), 203–21.

'X. L.', 'A Kiss of Judas'

Bane, Theresa, *Encyclopedia of Demons in World Religions and Cultures* (Jefferson, NC, and London: McFarland & Company, 2012).

Benzon, Ernest, *How I Lost £250,000 in Two Years* (London: Trischler and Company, n.d. [1889]).

Crisci-Richardson, Roberta, *Mapping Degas: Real Spaces, Symbolic Spaces and Invented Spaces in the Life and Work of Edgar Degas (1834–1917)* (Newcastle upon Tyne: Cambridge Scholars, 2015).

Dumas, Alexandre (*père*), *The Count of Monte Cristo*, ed. and trans. David Coward (Oxford: Oxford University Press, 2004).

Givray, Grillot de, *Witchcraft Magic & Alchemy*, trans. J. Courtenay Locke (London, Bombay, and Sydney: George G. Harrap & Company Limited, n.d. [1931]).

Granville-Barker, Harley (ed.), 'Lord Houghton and his Circle', in *The Eighteen-Seventies: Essays by Fellows of the Royal Society of Literature* (Cambridge: Cambridge University Press, 1929), 1–21.

Kaye, J. W., *Lives of Indian Officers*, 2 vols (London: J. J. Keliher & Co., 1904).

Landor, Walter Savage, *Gebir; A Poem, in Seven Books* (London: Rivingtons, 1798).

Maupassant, Guy de, *A Day in the Country and Other Stories*, ed. and trans. David Coward (Oxford: Oxford University Press, 2009).

Michael, Robert, *A History of Catholic Antisemitism: The Dark Side of the Church* (New York and Basingstoke: Palgrave Macmillan, 2008).

Musset, Alfred de, *Le Chandelier* (Paris: Charpentier, 1850).

Pudles, Lynne, 'Fernand Khnopff, Georges Rodenbach, and Bruges, the Dead City', *The Art Bulletin*, 74.4 (December 1992), 637–54.

Rodenbach, Georges-Raymond-Constantin, *Le Règne du silence: Poème* (Paris: Charpentier, 1891).

Seignolle, Claude, *Les Évangiles du diable selon le croyance populaire le grand et le petit Albert* (Paris: Robert Laffont, 1998).

'Stendhal', *The Red and The Black*, ed. Roger Gard (London: Penguin, 2002).

Summers, Montague, *The Vampire: His Kith and Kin. A Critical Edition*, ed. John Edgar Broughton ([1928] New York: Dover Publications, 2005).

Swinburne, Algernon Charles, *Atalanta in Calydon* (London: Edward Moxon & Co., 1865).

Whitehurst, Felix, *My Private Diary during the Siege of Paris*, 2 vols (London: Tinsley Brothers, 1875).

Wolff, Albert, *La Haute-Noce* (Paris: Victor-Havard, 1885).

Zola, Émile, *The Kill*, ed. and trans. Brian Nelson (Oxford: Oxford University Press, 2004).

Eric, Count Stenbock, 'The True Story of a Vampire'

Borel, Pétrus, *Madame Putiphar*, 2nd edn, 2 vols (Paris: Léon Willem, 1877–8).

Huysmans, Joris-Karl, *Against Nature*, trans. Margaret Mauldon, ed. Nicholas White (Oxford: Oxford University Press, 2009).

Law, Joe, 'The "Perniciously Homosexual Art": Music and Homoerotic Desire in *The Picture of Dorian Gray* and other *Fin-de-Siècle* Fiction', in Sophie Fuller and Nicky Losseff (eds), *The Idea of Music in Victorian Fiction* (Aldershot and Burlington, VT: Ashgate, 2004), 173–96.

Mason, Diane, '"The Mighty Light which Maddens One to Crime": Medicine, Masculinity, Same-Sex Desire and the Gothic in *Teleny*', in William Hughes and Andrew Smith (eds), *Queering the Gothic* (Manchester: Manchester University Press, 2009), 73–88.

Perkowski, Jan Louis, *The Darkling: A Treatise on Slavic Vampirism* (1989), reprinted in Jan Louis Perkowski, *Vampire Lore: From the Writings of Jan Louis Perkowski* (Bloomington, IN: Slavica Publishers, 2006), 317–488.

Stenbock, Stanislaus Eric, Count, *Studies of Death: Romantic Tales* (London: David Nutt, 1894).

Yeats, W. B. (ed.), *The Oxford Book of Modern Verse, 1892–1935* (Oxford: Oxford University Press, 1936).

R. Murray Gilchrist, 'The Crimson Weaver'

Boucard, Adolphous, *Travels of a Naturalist* (London: [Pardy & Son,] 1894).

Freeman, Nicholas, *1895: Drama, Disaster and Disgrace in Late Victorian Britain* (Edinburgh: Edinburgh University Press, 2011).

Gilchrist, Robert Murray, *The Stone Dragon and Other Tragic Romances* (London: Methuen and Co., 1894).

The Poems of Thomas Gray, William Collins, and Oliver Goldsmith, ed. Roger Lonsdale (London: Longman, 1969).

Homer, *The Odyssey*, trans. Walter Shewring, ed. G. S. Kirk (Oxford: Oxford University Press, 1980).

Mary Elizabeth Braddon, 'Good Lady Ducayne'

Aristotle, *Poetics*, ed. and trans. Stephen Halliwell; Longinus, *On the Sublime*, ed. and trans. W. H. Fyfe, rev. Donald Russell; Demetrius, *On Style*, ed. and trans. Doreen C. Innes and W. Rhys Roberts, Loeb Classical Library (Cambridge, MA, and London: Harvard University Press, 1995).

Baring-Gould, Sabine, *The Book of Were-Wolves: Being an account of a Terrible Superstition* (London: Smith, Elder and Co., 1865).
Braddon, Mary Elizabeth, *Lady Audley's Secret*, ed. Lyn Pykett (Oxford: Oxford University Press, 2012).
Braddon, Mary Elizabeth, *Aurora Floyd*, ed. P. D. Edwards (Oxford: Oxford University Press, 2008).
Braddon, Mary Elizabeth, *Mount Royal: A Novel* (London: John and Robert Maxwell, 1883).
Bristowe, John Syer, *A Treatise on the Theory and Practice of Medicine*, 2nd edn (London: Smith, Elder, & Co., 1878).
Dickens, Charles, *Great Expectations*, ed. Margaret Cardwell and Robert Douglas-Fairhurst (Oxford: Oxford University Press, 2008).
Foxton, E. [Sarah Hammond Palfrey], *Prémices* (Boston: Ticknor and Fields, 1855).
Kibbie, Anne Louise, *Transfusion: Blood and Sympathy in the Nineteenth-Century Literary Imagination* (Charlottesville, VA, and London: University of Virginia Press, 2019).
Mills, A. R., 'The Last Illness of Lord Byron', *Proceedings of the Royal College of Physicians of Edinburgh*, 28 (1998), 73–80.
Pamboukian, Sylvia A., 'The "Wretched Italian Quack": Braddon's Critique of Medicine in "Good Lady Ducayne"', *Victorian Literature and Culture*, 43 (2015), 559–75.
Shelley, Mary, *Frankenstein or The Modern Prometheus. The 1818 Text*, ed. Nick Groom (Oxford: Oxford University Press, 2019).
Stephanou, Aspasia, *Reading Vampire Gothic Through Blood: Bloodlines* (Basingstoke: Palgrave Macmillan, 2014).
Stoker, Bram, *Dracula*, ed. Roger Luckhurst (Oxford: Oxford University Press, 2011).
Tomaiuolo, Saverio, *In Lady Audley's Shadow: Mary Elizabeth Braddon and Victorian Literary Genres* (Edinburgh: Edinburgh University Press, 2010).

Rudyard Kipling, 'The Vampire'

Browne, Emerson Porter, *A Fool There Was* (New York: The H. K. Fly Company, 1909).
Dijkstra, Bram, *Idols of Perversity: Fantasies of Feminine Evil in Fin-de-Siècle Culture* (New York and Oxford: Oxford University Press, 1986).
Kipling, Rudyard, *Rudyard Kipling's Verse: Inclusive Edition, 1885–1918* (Garden City, NY: Doubleday, Page and Company, 1919).
Livingston, Flora, *Bibliography of the Works of Rudyard Kipling* (New York: Edgar H. Wells and Company, 1927).
Matthews, Brander, *Essays in English* (New York: Charles Scribner's Sons, 1921).

Mitchell, J. Lawrence, 'Rudyard Kipling, *The Vampire*, and the Actress', *English Literature in Transition, 1880–1920*, 55.3 (2012), 303–14.

Morey, Anne and Claudia Nelson, 'Phallus and Void in Kipling's "The Vampire" and Its Progeny', *Frame*, 24 (2011), 39–55.

The New Gallery, Regent Street: Tenth Summer Exhibition, MDCCCXCVII (London: New Gallery, 1897).

Trotter, David, *Brute Meaning: Essays in Materialist Criticism from Dickens to Hitchcock* (Cambridge: Legenda (Modern Humanities Research Association), 2020).

Further Reading in Oxford World's Classics

Burke, Edmund, *Reflections on the Revolution in France*, ed. L. G. Mitchell (Oxford and New York: Oxford University Press, 1993).

Horror Stories: Classic Tales from Hoffmann to Hodgson, ed. Darryl Jones (Oxford: Oxford University Press, 2014).

Le Fanu, Sheridan, *In a Glass Darkly*, ed. Robert Tracy (Oxford: Oxford University Press, 2008).

Maupassant, Guy de, *A Day in the Country and Other Stories*, ed. and trans. David Coward.

Poe, Edgar Allan, *Selected Tales*, ed. David van Leer (Oxford: Oxford University Press, 2008).

Polidori, John, *The Vampyre and Other Tales of the Macabre*, ed. Robert Morrison and Chris Baldick (Oxford and New York: Oxford University Press, 1998; 2nd edn, 2008).

Shelley, Mary, *Frankenstein or The Modern Prometheus. The 1818 Text*, ed. Nick Groom (Oxford: Oxford University Press, 2019).

Stevenson, Robert Louis, *Strange Case of Dr Jekyll and Mr Hyde and Other Tales*, ed. Roger Luckhurst (Oxford: Oxford University Press, 2008).

Walpole, Horace, *The Castle of Otranto*, ed. Nick Groom (Oxford University Press, 2014).

A CHRONOLOGY OF SIGNIFICANT VAMPIRE CASES AND PUBLICATIONS PRIOR TO *DRACULA* (1897)

Publications are listed by year and alphabetically by author; British translations noted. Only selected texts that make notable references to vampires are listed.

1704 Karl Ferdinand Schertz, *Magia Posthuma* (Moravia)

1718 Joseph Pitton de Tournefort, *A Voyage into the Levant* (Britain; French report dated 1701)

1721 *The Arabian Nights Entertainments* (Britain)

Fr Gabriel Rzączyński, SJ, *Historia Naturalis Curiosa Regni Poloniæ* (Poland)

1725 First use of word *vampyri* to describe attacks of Peter Plogojowitz (Habsburg Empire)

1727 Attacks of Arnond Paole (Habsburg Empire)

1731 Revival of Arnond Paole case; more attacks (Habsburg Empire)

1732 First publications in *Commercium Literarium* (Habsburg Empire)

Anon., 'Political Vampyres', *The London Magazine* (Britain)

'Caleb D'Anvers' [Nicholas Amhurst], *The Craftsman* (Britain)

'Putoneo' [J. C. Meinig], *Besondere Nachricht von denen Vampyren oder so genannten Blut-Saugern* (Germany)

1733 Charles Forman, *A Second Letter to the Right Honourable Sir Robert Walpole* (Britain)

Johann Christoph Harenberg, *Vernünftige und Christliche Gedancken über die Vampirs Oder Blutsaugende Todten* (Germany)

Johann Heinrich Zopf, *Dissertation de Vampiris Serviensibus* (Germany)

1737 Anon., 'A Confutation of the Stories about Vampires, or Dead Bodies sucking the Living, in Hungary, &c.', *The London Magazine* (Britain)

1739–44 Jean Baptiste de Boyer, Marquis d'Argens, *The Jewish Spy* (Britain)

1741 Charles Forman, *Some Queries and Observations upon the Revolution in 1688, and its Consequences* (Britain)

1744–6 Anon., 'The Travels of Three English Gentlemen, from Venice to Hamburgh, being the Grand Tour of Germany, in the Year 1734' (Britain)

1746 Dom Augustin Calmet, *Dissertation sur les revenants en corps, les excommuniés, les oupires ou vampires, brucolaques etc.* (France)

1748 Heinrich August Ossenfelder, 'Der Vampir' (Germany)

1751 John Cleland, *Memoirs of a Coxcomb* (Britain)

1753 John Bond, *Essay on the Incubus, or Night-Mare* (Britain)

1759 Dom Augustin Calmet, *Dissertations upon the Apparitions of Angels, Dæmons, and Ghosts, and Concerning the Vampires of Hungary, Bohemia, Moravia, and Silesia* (Britain)

1763 Jean-Jacques Rousseau, *An Expostulatory Letter* (Britain)

1768 Gerhard van Swieten, *Vampyrismus* (Habsburg Empire)

1772 Voltaire, *Questions sur l'Encyclopedie*, 2nd edn (France)

1774 Gottfried August Bürger, 'Lenore' (Germany)

Guiseppe Davanzati, *Dissertazione sopra I Vampiri* (Italy)

Alberto Fortis, *Travels into Dalmatia* (Britain)

1777 Inigo Born, *Travels through the Bannat of Temeswar, Transylvania, and Hungary, in the Year 1770* (Britain)

1781 Henry Fuseli, *The Nightmare* (Britain, painting)

1785 Georg Tallar, *Visum repertum anatomico-chirurgicum von den sogenannten Vampier* (Germany)

1785 Louis Sébastien Mercier, *The Nightcap* (Britain)

1786 John Ferriar, 'Of Popular Illusions, and Particularly of Medical Demonology' (Britain)

William Beckford, *Vathek* (*An Arabian Tale*) (Britain)

1790 *Edmund Burke, Reflections on the Revolution in France* (Britain)

Henry Fuseli, *The Nightmare* (Britain, painting: later version)

1791 Erasmus Darwin, 'Loves of the Plants' (Britain)

1796 Gottfried August Bürger, 'Lenore' (Britain)

1797 Johann Wolfgang von Goethe, 'Die Braut von Korinth' (Germany)

1799 Robert Southey, 'The Old Woman of Berkeley' (Britain)

1801 Ignaz Ferdinand Arnold, *Der Vampir* (Germany; not extant)

James Bland Burges, *Richard the First* (Britain)

Robert Southey, *Thalaba the Destroyer* (Britain)

1807 'Arminius' [John Herman Merivale], 'The Dead Men of Pest: A Hungarian Legend' (Britain)

1809 Lady Morgan, Sydney Owenson, *Patriotic Sketches of Ireland, written in Connaught* (Ireland)

1812 Anon., *Der Vampyr oder die blutige Hochzeit mit der schönen Kroatin* (Germany; not extant)

Anon., *Fantasmagoriana, ou recueil d'histoires d'apparitions de spectres, revenans, fantômes, etc.* (France)

Giuseppe Palomba and Silvestro di Palma, *I Vampiri* (Italy)

Ludwig Tieck, 'Liebeszauber' (Germany)

1813 Lord Byron, *The Giaour* (Britain)

Walter Scott, *Rokeby* (Britain)

1815 Richard Polwhele, *The Fair Isabel of Cotehele* (Britain)

1816 Samuel Taylor Coleridge, 'Christabel' (Britain; begun in 1797)

Joseph Freiherr von Eichendorff, 'Das Kalte Liebchen' (Germany)

Lady Caroline Lamb, *Glenarvon* (Britain)

John Stagg, 'The Vampyre' (Britain)

1818 Mary Shelley, *Frankenstein; or, The Modern Prometheus* (Britain)

1819 Lord Byron, 'A Fragment' (written 1816); 'Windsor Poetics' (written 1813) (Britain)

'Uriah Derick D'Arcy' [Richard Varick Dey], *The Black Vampire* (United States)

Henri Faber, *Le Vampire, nouvelle traduite de l'Anglais de Lord Byron* (France)

Johann Wolfgang von Goethe, 'The Bride of Corinth' (Britain)

John William Polidori, 'The Vampyre' and *Ernestus Berchtold; or, The Modern Œdipus* (Britain)

Alaric Watts, 'Introduction' to 'The Vampyre' (Britain)

1820 Cyprien Bérard, *Lord Ruthwen ou les vampires* (France)

John Keats, 'La Belle Dame Sans Merci' (Britain, written 1819)

E. T. A. Hoffmann, 'Vampirismus' (Germany)

Charles Nodier, Pierre-Frédéric-Adolphe Carmouche, and Achille de Jouffroy, *Le Vampire* (France, and several other stage productions in the decade)

James Robinson Planché, *The Vampire; or, The Bride of the Isles* (Britain, and, likewise, several other stage productions in the decade)

John William Polidori, *Ximenes, The Wreath, and Other Poems* (Britain)

1821 Charles Nodier, *Smarra, ou les démons de la nuit* (France)

Heinrich Ludwig Ritter, *Der Vampyr, oder die Todten Braut* (Germany)

1822 Anon., 'The Vampires of London: A Tale of the Last Pestilence' (Britain)

Charles Nodier, *Infernaliana* (France)

Percy Bysshe Shelley, 'The Triumph of Life' (Britain)

1823 Ernst Benjamin Salomo Raupach, 'Wake Not The Dead' (Germany and Britain)

1825 Etienne-Léon Lamothe-Langon, *La Vampire, ou La Vierge de Hongrie* (France)

Charles Waterton, *Wanderings in South America, the North-West of the United States, and the Antilles* (Britain)

1826 Martin Joseph Mengal, *Le Vampire* (France)

Wilhelm August Wohlbrück and Heinrich August Marschner, *Der Vampyr* (Germany)

1827 Prosper Mérimée, *La Guzla* (France)

1828 Joseph Freiherr von Eichendorff, 'Die Späte Hochzeit' (Germany)

Theodor Hildebrand, *Der Vampyr oder die Todtenbraut* (Germany)

Peter Joseph von Lindpaintner, *Der Vampyr* (Germany)

Heinrich Marschner, *Der Vampyr* (Germany)

1830 George Blink, *The Vampire Bride: or, The Tenant of the Tomb* (Britain)

1833 Henry Thomas Liddell, 'The Vampire Bride' (Britain)

1835 Edgar Allan Poe, 'Berenicë', 'Morella' (United States)

1836 Théophile Gautier, 'Clairmonde' (France)

Alexander Pushkin, *Wurdulac* (Russia)

1836–7 Charles Dickens, *The Pickwick Papers* (Britain)

1838 Edgar Allan Poe, 'Ligeia' (United States)

1839 Appearance of a vampire bat at St Katharine Docks, London (Britain)

Edgar Allan Poe, 'The Fall of the House of Usher' (United States)

1840–1 Charles Dickens, *The Old Curiosity Shop* (Britain)

1844 Karl Adolf von Wachsmann, 'Der Fremde' (Germany)

1845 [Anon.,] 'The Vampire of Vourla; Leaves from a Mediterranean Log' (Britain)

James Clerk Maxwell, 'The Vampyre' (Britain)

1845–7 James Malcolm Rymer, *Varney, the Vampire or, The Feast of Blood* (Britain)

1845–9 Irish Famine or 'Great Hunger'

1847 Charlotte Brontë, *Jane Eyre* (Britain)

1848 Alexandre Dumas (*père*), 'La Dame pâle' (France)

Karl Marx and Friedrich Engels, *The Communist Manifesto* (Britain)

1850 Thomas Lovell Beddoes, *Death's Jest-Book* (Britain, written 1825–48)

Dom Augustin Calmet, *The Phantom World: The History and Philosophy of Spirits, Apparitions, &c. &c.* (new edition of 1746 *Dissertations*, trans. Henry Christmas, Britain)

Edgar Allan Poe, 'The Oval Portrait' (United States)

1851 Alexandre Dumas (*père*), *Le Vampire* (France)

Herbert Mayo, *On the Truths Contained in Popular Superstitions with An Account of Mesmerism*, 2nd edn (Britain)

1852 Dion Boucicault, *The Vampire*

1852–3 Charles Dickens, *Bleak House* (Britain)

1853 Pierre-Alexis Ponson du Terrail, *La Baronne trépassée (France)*

1854 Karl Adolf von Wachsmann, 'The Mysterious Stranger' (Britain)

1855 E. Foxton [Sarah Hammond Palfrey], 'The Princess' Bath: or The Three Maids' (United States)

1856 Henry Wallis, *The Death of Chatterton* (Britain, painting)

1857 Charles Baudelaire, *Les Fleurs du mal* (France)

1859 Fitz-James O'Brien, 'What Was It?: A Mystery' (United States)

1860 Paul Féval, *Le Chevalier ténèbre* (France)

1862 Christina Rossetti, 'Goblin Market' (Britain)

1863 William Henry Giles Kingston, 'The Vampire; or, Pedro Pacheco and the Bruxa' (Britain)

1865 Sabine Baring-Gould, *The Book of Were-Wolves: Being an account of a Terrible Superstition* (Britain)

Jules Dornay, *Douglas le vampire* (France)

Paul Féval, *La Vampire* (France)

1867 Paul Féval, *La Ville-Vampire* (France)

William Gilbert, 'The Last Lords of Gardonal' (Britain)

Karl Marx, *Capital* (Britain)

'Waif Wanderer' [Mary Helena Fortune], 'The White Maniac: A Doctor's Tale' (Australia)

1869 Charles Baudelaire, 'A Carcass' (Britain)

G. J. Whyte-Melville, *Bones and I* (Britain)

1870 Sir Richard Burton, *Vikram and the Vampire* (Britain)

1871 Edward Tylor, *Primitive Culture: Researches into the Development of Mythology, Philosophy, Religion, Art, and Custom* (Britain)

1871–2 George Eliot, *Middlemarch* (Britain)

Joseph Sheridan Le Fanu, 'Carmilla' (Britain)

1873 Walter Pater, *The Renaissance: Studies in Art and Poetry* (Britain)

1880 Milovan Glisic, *After Ninety Years: The Story of Serbian Vampire Sava Savanovic* (Serbia)

Eliza Lynn Linton, 'The Fate of Madame Cabanel' (Britain)

1882 Théophile Gautier, 'Les Taches Jaunes' (Britain)

1883 Julian Hawthorne, 'Ken's Mystery' (United States)

1884 Sabine Baring-Gould, 'Margery of Quether' (Britain)

Count Aleksey Konstantinovich Tolstoy, 'The Family of the Vourdalak' (Britain, written 1839)

1885 Emily Gerard, 'Transylvanian Superstitions' (Britain)

Guy de Maupassant, 'Lettre d'un fou' (France)

Robert Louis Stevenson, 'Olalla' (Britain)

1886 Robert Louis Stevenson, *Strange Case of Dr Jekyll and Mr Hyde* (Britain)

1887 Anne Crawford, 'A Mystery of the Campagna' (Britain)

Gilbert and Sullivan, *Ruddigore; or, The Witch's Curse* (Britain)

1889 Phil Robinson, 'Medusa' (Britain)

1890 Mary Cholmondeley, *Let Loose* (Britain)

Hume Nisbet, 'The Vampire Maid' (Britain)

Guy de Maupassant, 'The Horla' (Britain)

Owen Meredith, Lord Lytton, 'The Vampire' (Britain)

Oscar Wilde, *The Picture of Dorian Gray*

1891 Ambrose Bierce, 'The Death of Halpin Frayser' (America)

1892 Max Nordau, *Degeneration* (Britain)

Jules Verne, *The Carpathian Castle* [*Le Château des Carpathes*] (Britain)

1893 Oscar Wilde, *Salomè* (Britain)

'X. L.' [Julian Osgood Field], 'A Kiss of Judas' (Britain)

1894 Arthur Conan Doyle, *The Parasite* (Britain)

Edvard Munch, *Vampyr* (painting, Norway)

Eric, Count Stenbock, 'The True Story of a Vampire' (Britain)

1895 R. Murray Gilchrist, 'The Crimson Weaver' (Britain)

1896 Mary Elizabeth Braddon, 'Good Lady Ducayne' (Britain)

Georges Méliès, *Le Manoir du diable* (film, France)

George Stetson, 'The Animistic Vampire in New England' (United States)

1897 Philip Burne-Jones, *The Vampire* (Britain, painting)

Rudyard Kipling, 'The Vampire' (Britain)

Florence Marryat, *Blood of the Vampire* (Britain)

Bram Stoker, *Dracula* (Britain)

VAMPIRE TALES

GEORGE GORDON, LORD BYRON

A FRAGMENT

June 17, 1816

In the year 17—, having for some time determined on a journey through countries not hitherto much frequented by travellers, I set out, accompanied by a friend, whom I shall designate by the name of Augustus Darvell.* He was a few years my elder, and a man of considerable fortune and ancient family—advantages which an extensive capacity prevented him alike from undervaluing or overrating. Some peculiar circumstances in his private history had rendered him to me an object of attention, of interest, and even of regard, which neither the reserve of his manners, nor occasional indications of an inquietude* at times nearly approaching to alienation of mind, could extinguish.

I was yet young in life, which I had begun early; but my intimacy with him was of a recent date: we had been educated at the same schools and university; but his progress through these had preceded mine, and he had been deeply initiated into what is called the world, while I was yet in my noviciate. While thus engaged, I had heard much both of his past and present life; and although in these accounts there were many and irreconcileable contradictions, I could still gather from the whole that he was a being of no common order, and one who, whatever pains he might take to avoid remark, would still be remarkable. I had cultivated his acquaintance subsequently, and endeavoured to obtain his friendship, but this last appeared to be unattainable; whatever affections he might have possessed seemed now, some to have been extinguished, and others to be concentred:* that his feelings were acute, I had sufficient opportunities of observing; for, although he could control, he could not altogether disguise them: still he had a power of giving to one passion the appearance of another in such a manner that it was difficult to define the nature of what was working within him; and the expressions of his features would vary so rapidly, though slightly, that it was useless to trace them to their sources. It was evident that he was a prey to some cureless disquiet; but whether it arose from ambition, love, remorse, grief, from one or all of these, or merely from a morbid temperament akin to disease, I could not discover: there were circumstances alleged, which might have justified the application to each of these causes; but, as I have before said, these were so contradictory and contradicted, that none could be fixed upon with accuracy. Where there is mystery, it is generally supposed that there must also be evil: I know not how this may be, but in him there certainly was the one, though I could not ascertain the extent of the other—and felt loth, as far as regarded himself, to believe in its existence. My advances were received with sufficient coldness; but I was young, and not easily discouraged, and at length succeeded in obtaining, to a certain degree, that common-place intercourse and moderate confidence of common and every day concerns, created and cemented by similarity of pursuit and frequency of meeting, which is called intimacy, or friendship, according to the ideas of him who uses those words to express them.

Darvell had already travelled extensively; and to him I had applied for information with regard to the conduct of my intended journey. It was my secret wish that he might be prevailed on to accompany me: it was also a probable hope, founded upon the shadowy restlessness which I had observed in him, and to which the animation which he appeared to feel on such subjects, and his apparent indifference to all by which he was more immediately surrounded, gave fresh strength. This wish I first hinted, and then expressed: his answer, though I had partly expected it, gave me all the pleasure of surprise—he consented; and, after the requisite arrangements, we commenced our voyages. After journeying through various countries of the south of Europe, our attention was turned towards the East, according to our original destination; and it was in my progress through those regions that the incident occurred upon which will turn what I may have to relate.

The constitution of Darvell, which must from his appearance have been in early life more than usually robust, had been for some time gradually giving way, without the intervention of any apparent disease: he had neither cough nor hectic,* yet he became daily more enfeebled: his habits were temperate, and he neither declined nor complained of fatigue, yet he was evidently wasting away: he became more and more silent and sleepless, and at length so seriously altered, that my alarm grew proportionate to what I conceived to be his danger.

We had determined, on our arrival at Smyrna,* on an excursion to the ruins of Ephesus and Sardis,* from which I endeavoured to dissuade him in his present state of indisposition—but in vain: there appeared to be an oppression on his mind, and a solemnity in his manner, which ill corresponded with his eagerness to proceed on what I regarded as a mere party of pleasure, little suited to a valetudinarian; but I opposed him no longer—and in a few days we set off together, accompanied only by a serrugee and a single janizary.*

We had passed halfway towards the remains of Ephesus, leaving behind us the more fertile environs of Smyrna, and were entering upon that wild and tenantless track through the marshes and defiles which lead to the few huts yet lingering over the broken columns of Diana*—the roofless walls of expelled Christianity, and the still more recent but complete desolation of abandoned mosques—when the sudden and rapid illness of my companion obliged us to halt at a Turkish cemetery, the turbaned tombstones* of which were the sole indication that human life had ever been a sojourner in this wilderness. The only caravansera* we had seen was left some hours behind us, not a vestige of a town or even cottage was within sight or hope, and this 'city of the dead'* appeared to be the sole refuge for my unfortunate friend, who seemed on the verge of becoming the last of its inhabitants.

In this situation, I looked round for a place where he might most conveniently repose:—contrary to the usual aspect of Mahometan burial-grounds, the cypresses were in this few in number, and these thinly scattered over its extent: the tombstones were mostly fallen, and worn with age:—upon one of the most considerable of these, and beneath one of the most spreading trees, Darvell supported himself, in a half-reclining posture, with great difficulty. He asked for water. I had some doubts of our being able to find any, and prepared to go in search of it with hesitating despondency—but he desired me to remain; and turning to Suleiman, our janizary, who stood by us smoking with great tranquillity, he said, 'Suleiman, verbana su,' (i.e. bring some water,*) and went on describing the spot where it was to be found with great minuteness, at a small well for camels, a few hundred yards to the right: the janizary obeyed. I said to Darvell, 'How did you know this?'—He replied, 'From our situation; you must perceive that this place was once inhabited, and could not have been so without springs: I have also been here before.'*

'You have been here before!—How came you never to mention this to me? and what could you be doing in a place where no one would remain a moment longer than they could help it?'

To this question I received* no answer. In the mean time Suleiman returned with the water, leaving the serrugee and the horses at the fountain. The quenching of his thirst had the appearance of reviving him for a moment; and I conceived hopes of his being able to proceed, or at least to return, and I urged the attempt. He was silent—and appeared to be collecting his spirits for an effort to speak. He began.

'This is the end of my journey, and of my life—I came here to die: but I have a request to make,* a command—for such my last words must be—You will observe it?'

'Most certainly; but have better hopes.'

'I have no hopes, nor wishes, but this—conceal my death from every human being.'

'I hope there will be no occasion; that you will recover, and—'

'Peace!—it must be so: promise this.'

'I do.'

'Swear it, by all that.'—He here dictated an oath of great solemnity.

'There is no occasion for this—I will observe your request; and to doubt me is—'

'It cannot be helped,—you must swear.'

I took the oath: it appeared to relieve him. He removed a seal ring from his finger, on which were some Arabic characters, and presented it to me. He proceeded—

'On the ninth day of the month, at noon precisely (what month you please, but this must be the day), you must fling this ring into the salt springs which run into the Bay of Eleusis:* the day after, at the same hour, you must repair to the ruins of the temple of Ceres,* and wait one hour.'

'Why?'

'You will see.'

'The ninth day of the month,* you say?'

'The ninth.'

As I observed that the present was the ninth day of the month, his countenance changed, and he paused. As he sate, evidently becoming more feeble, a stork, with a snake in her beak,* perched upon a tombstone near us; and, without devouring her prey, appeared to be stedfastly regarding us. I know not what impelled me to drive it away, but the attempt was useless; she made a few circles in the air, and returned exactly to the same spot. Darvell pointed to it, and smiled: he spoke—I know not whether to himself or to me—but the words were only, ''Tis well!'

'What is well? what do you mean?'

'No matter: you must bury me here this evening, and exactly where that bird is now perched. You know the rest of my injunctions.'

He then proceeded to give me several directions as to the manner in which his death might be best concealed. After these were finished, he exclaimed, 'You perceive that bird?'

'Certainly.'

'And the serpent writhing in her beak?'

'Doubtless: there is nothing uncommon in it; it is her natural prey. But it is odd that she does not devour it.'

He smiled in a ghastly manner, and said, faintly, 'It is not yet time!' As he spoke, the stork flew away. My eyes followed it for a moment, it could hardly be longer than ten might be counted.* I felt Darvell's weight, as it were, increase upon my shoulder, and, turning to look upon his face, perceived that he was dead!

I was shocked with the sudden certainty which could not be mistaken—his countenance in a few minutes became nearly black. I should have attributed so rapid a change to poison, had I not been aware that he had no opportunity of receiving it unperceived. The day was declining, the body was rapidly altering, and nothing remained but to fulfil his request. With the aid of Suleiman's ataghan* and my own sabre, we scooped a shallow grave upon the spot which Darvell had indicated: the earth easily gave way, having already received some Mahometan tenant.* We dug as deeply as the time permitted us, and throwing the dry earth upon all that remained of the singular being so lately departed, we cut a few sods of greener turf from the less withered soil around us, and laid them upon his sepulchre.

Between astonishment and grief, I was tearless.

THE END

JOHANN WOLFGANG VON GOETHE

THE BRIDE OF CORINTH

I

A STRANGER youth from Athens came
To Corinth*—tho' himself unknown,
Relying on his father's name;—
Nor hospitable ties alone
Secured him a Corinthian friend,
For, plighted* by his father's vows,
He longed to see his plighted spouse,
And hence his journey's aim and end.

II

But shall the stranger welcome be?
Or must her love be dearly bought?
Alas! a heathen still is he,
And they the Christian faith are taught!
And when new forms of faith arise,
How soon love's tender blossom dies,
Without a sigh, without a thought!

III

The house in midnight silence lies,
Father and daughters, all at rest!
Sleep only shuns the mother's eyes—
She rises to receive the guest—
She leads him to a chamber bright,
And wine and bread before him laid;
She bows, and wishes him 'Good night!'

IV

He thought not of the wine and bread,
He only felt a wish for rest—
At once he flung him on the bed—
His weary limb's scarce feel repose,
When, hush! the chamber doors unclose,
And in there steals a timid guest.

V

He wakes—and by the lamp's faint light,
    Behold a maiden tall and fair!
Her veil is white—her robes are white—
    Black is the band that twines her hair;
'Tis black, but streaked with lines of gold—
She screams, and shudders to behold
The stranger youth reclining there,
And, lifting her white arm in air,

VI

Exclaims, 'then am I nothing here!
    Guests come and go, and none tells me!
Dark is my chamber, lone and drear,
    And here to come is infamy.
To wander here is scathe* and shame,
Sleep on, young stranger, quietly,
    And I will vanish as I came!'

VII

'Stay,' cries the youth, 'stay maiden dear,'
    As lightly from the couch springs he,
'CERES and BACCHUS, lo! are here,
    And LOVE, sweet maid, hath come with thee,
Ah! thou art pale with idle fear,
    The Gods are good, and blest are we!'—

VIII

'Away—young man—stand far away,
    What pleasure is, I feel not now—
Joy hath forever fled from me,
    Scared by a mother's gloomy vow;—
    She feared to die,—my youthful bloom—
My hopes of love—her stern decree
    Hath destined to a living tomb!

IX

'Our ancient Gods no longer deign,
    In this dull mansion to reside—
But one, who dwells in heaven unseen,
    And one, upon the cross who died,

Are worshipped with sad rite severe;
No offering falls* of lamb or steer,
But human victims suffer here!'

X

He ponders with a trembling heart,
Each word that falls upon his ear,
'And art thou then—ah! sure thou art
My plighted spouse, that meets me here?
Be mine, my love, our father's vow
Hath blessed our loves—be mine even now!'

XI

'Have they not told thee then,' she cried,
'That I thy consort may not be—
My sister is thy destined bride;
But in her arms, ah! think of me,
Who in my cell will think of thee,
Who pine and die with love of thee,
The cold earth soon my woes will hide.'

XII

'No!—never!—by this lamp I swear,
That glowing emblems Hymen's torch,
Thou shalt not perish thus from me.
Oh! we will seek my father's porch,
And from this home of sorrow flee;
Be mine, my love, be mine to-night,
To-morrow's sun will guide our flight.'

XIII

She reached to him a chain of gold,
Of deathless love a token fair;
He reached to her a silver cup,
Adorned with gravings* rich and rare;
'The cup, my love, I may not take,
But give me, for thine own dear sake,
One only ringlet* of thy hair!'

XIV

Damp strikes the hour that spirits know—
Her eyes with eager pleasure shine,

Her cheek assumes a sparkling glow,
    Her pale lips quaff the blood-red wine;
But vainly may the youth entreat,
The wheaten bread she will not eat!

XV

She reached the wine-cup to his hand,
    Like her, with eager joy, he drinks,
He speaks to her with words of love;
    On love, on love alone he thinks;
In vain his warm intreaties prove
No words have charms her breast to move—
    In tears, upon the bed he sinks!

XVI

She leans above him o'er the couch,
    'Thy pangs I mourn but cannot heal—
What!—ha!—my limbs have met thy touch,
    And tell thee what I would conceal;
White, white as snow! cold, cold as sleet,
Is she whose love thou dost entreat!'

XVII

He strains* her in his closing arm
    With strength that youth and passion gave;
'Cold as thou art, thy blood shall warm,
    Even if thy dwelling were the grave.'
With frenzied clasp of wild desire,
He strains her to his breast of fire.

XVIII

Strange was, I ween,* that bridal scene,
    For with their kisses mingle tears;
    But what is coldness, what are fears,
While in her lover's bosom prest,
    The blood that stirs
    In his veins warms hers,
But, oh! no heart throbs in her breast!

XIX

Without the door the mother stood,
    That under-voice what may it be,

She knows not—and she lingers there,
She listens long and anxiously;
Oh, is it, that she hears aright,
Voices like lovers', low and light?

XX

Breathless she stands, and motionless,
Till of these low words satisfied—
The vows of lisping tenderness,
The words of lover and of bride—
'Hark! the cock crows*—day soon will shine,
To-morrow night, again, my love,
To-morrow night thou wilt be mine.'

XXI

The mother hears no more—in wrath
She bursts into the stranger's room;—
'And is there in my house a maid
Thus shameless,* who can thus presume
To wanton—with a stranger too?'—
Thus thinks she angrily—when, lo!
By the lamp's decaying glow,
Her own—her daughter meets her view!

XXII

In the first impulse of his fear
He strove to hide the maiden's face—
In vain he drew the curtain's fold,
In vain he strove her veil to place,
Still from his reaching hand she rose,
Tall and more tall her stature grows.

XXIII

'Oh, mother! mother!' hollow sounds,
Unearthly, formed each fearful word;
'Thou enviest me this bridal night,
These few short moments of delight,
To pain am I again restored!
And is it not enough that I
For thee in funeral pall should lie?
For thee in youth should fade and die?

XXIV

'Me, from my narrow silent bed,
    Hither a wondrous doom hath driven:
Your priests, their mummery song* have said,
    But, oh! it hath no weight in heaven!
In vain your mystic spells ye prove!
The grave is cold—but chills not love!

XXV

'I was his doomed and destined bride
    In days, while Venus' fane* still stood,
But ye your former vows belied,
    And sealed your late-learned creed* in blood;
Alas! no heavenly power stood by,
When thou didst doom thy child to die!

XXVI

'And hither from the grave I roam
    To seek the joys denied in life;
Hither, to seek my spouse I come
    To drain his veins, a vampire wife!
His doom is past—his fate severe—
For Madness hath been Bride-maid here!

XXVII

'Young man, thy life is o'er—the pain
    Is on thee that must end in death;
Round thee still hangs my fatal chain—
    Thy ringlet I must bear beneath.
Farewell! farewell! away! away!
Yonder the morning rises gray!

XXVIII

'Hear, mother, hear a last request,
    Build high for us a funeral pile;*
Oh, from that narrow cell released,
    My spirit shall rejoicing smile;
And when the embers fall away,
    And when the funeral flames arise,
We'll journey to a home of rest,—
    Our ancient gods!—our ancient skies!'

JOHN WILLIAM POLIDORI, ED. ALARIC WATTS

EXTRACT OF A LETTER FROM GENEVA, WITH ANECDOTES OF LORD BYRON, &C.

[We received several private letters in the course of last autumn from a friend travelling on the Continent, and among others the following, which we give to the public on account of its containing anecdotes of an Individual, concerning whom the most trifling circumstances, if they tend to mark even the minor features of his mind, cannot fail of being considered important and valuable by those who know how to appreciate his erratic but transcendent genius. The tale which accompanied the letter we have much pleasure in presenting to our readers.—*Ed.**]

'I Breathe freely in the neighbourhood of this lake; the ground upon which I tread has been subdued from the earliest ages; the principal objects which immediately strike my eye, bring to my recollection, scenes, in which man acted the hero and was the chief object of interest. Not to look back to earlier times of battles and sieges, here is the bust of Rousseau—here is the house with an inscription denoting that the Genevan philosopher first drew breath under its roof.* A little out of the town is Ferney the residence of Voltaire;* where that wonderful, though certainly in many respects contemptible, character, received, like the hermits of old, the visits of pilgrims, not only from his own nation, but from the farthest boundaries of Europe. Here too is Bonnet's abode,* and, a few steps beyond, the house of that astonishing woman Madame de Stael,* perhaps the first of her sex, who has really proved its often claimed equality with the nobler man. We have had before, women who have written interesting novels and poems, in which their tact at observing drawing-room characters has availed them; but never since the days of Heloise have those faculties which are peculiar to man, been developed as the possible inheritance of woman. Though even here, as in the case of Heloise, our sex have not been backward in alleging the existence of an Abeilard* in the person of M. Schlegel* as the inspirer of her works. But to proceed: upon the same side of the lake, Gibbon, Bonnivard, Bradshaw* and others, mark, as it were, the stages for our progress; whilst upon the other side there is one house built by Diodati,* the friend of Milton, which has contained within its walls, for several months, that poet whom we have so often read together, and who—if human passions remain the same, and human feelings, like chords, on being swept by nature's impulses shall vibrate as before—will be placed by posterity in the first rank of our English Poets. You must have heard, or the Third Canto of Childe Harold* will have informed you, that Lord Byron resided many months in this neighbourhood.* I went with some friends a few days ago, after having seen Ferney, to view this mansion. I trod the floors with the same feelings of awe and respect as we did, together, those of Shakspeare's dwelling at Stratford. I sat down in a chair of the saloon, and satisfied myself that I was resting on what he had made his constant seat. I found a servant there who had lived with him; she, however, gave me but little information. She pointed out his bed-chamber upon the same level as the saloon and dining-room, and informed me that he retired to rest at three, got up at two, and employed himself a long time over his toilette; that he never went to sleep without a pair of pistols and a dagger by his side, and that he never eat animal food.* He apparently spent some part of every day upon the lake in an English boat.* There is a balcony from the saloon which looks upon the lake and the mountain Jura; and, I imagine, that it must have been hence, he contemplated the storm so magnificently described in the Third Canto; for you have from here a most extensive view of all the points he has therein depicted. I can fancy him like the scathed* pine, whilst all around was sunk to repose, still waking to observe, what gave but a weak image of the storms which had desolated his own breast.

The sky is changed!—and such a change; Oh, night!
And storm and darkness, ye are wond'rous strong,
Yet lovely in your strength, as is the light
Of a dark eye in woman! Far along
From peak to peak, the rattling crags among,
Leaps the live thunder! Not from one lone cloud,
But every mountain now hath found a tongue,
And Jura answers thro' her misty shroud,
Back to the joyous Alps who call to her aloud!

And this is in the night:—Most glorious night!
Thou wer't not sent for slumber! let me be
A sharer in thy far and fierce delight,—
A portion of the tempest and of me!

How the lit lake shines a phosphoric sea,
And the big rain comes dancing to the earth!
And now again 'tis black,—and now the glee
Of the loud hill shakes with its mountain mirth,
As if they did rejoice o'er a young earthquake's birth.

Now where the swift Rhine cleaves his way between
Heights which appear, as lovers who have parted
In haste, whose mining depths so intervene,
That they can meet no more, tho' broken hearted;
Tho' in their souls which thus each other thwarted,
Love was the very root of the fond rage
Which blighted their life's bloom, and then departed—
Itself expired, but leaving them an age
Of years all winter—war within themselves to wage.*

I went down to the little port, if I may use the expression, wherein his vessel used to lay, and conversed with the cottager, who had the care of it. You may smile, but I have my pleasure in thus helping my personification of the individual I admire, by attaining to the knowledge of those circumstances which were daily around him. I have made numerous enquiries in the town concerning him, but can learn nothing. He only went into society there once, when M. Pictet* took him to the house of a lady to spend the evening. They say he is a very singular man, and seem to think him very uncivil. Amongst other things they relate, that having invited M. Pictet and Bonstetten* to dinner, he went on the lake to Chillon, leaving a gentleman who travelled with him* to receive them and make his apologies. Another evening, being invited to the house of Lady D——H——,* he promised to attend, but upon approaching the windows of her ladyship's villa, and perceiving the room to be full of company, he put down his friend, desiring him to plead his excuse, and immediately returned home. This will serve as a contradiction to the report which you tell me is current in England, of his having been avoided by his countrymen on the continent. The case happens to be directly the reverse, as he has been generally sought after by them, though on most occasions, apparently without success. It is said, indeed, that upon paying his first visit at Coppet, following the servant who had announced his name, he was surprised to meet a lady carried out fainting;* but before he had been seated many minutes, the same lady, who had been so affected at the sound of his name, returned and conversed with him a considerable time—such is female curiosity and affectation! He visited Coppet frequently, and of course associated there with several of his countrymen, who evinced no reluctance to meet him whom his enemies alone would represent as an outcast.*

Though I have been so unsuccessful in this town, I have been more fortunate in my enquiries elsewhere. There is a society three or four miles from Geneva, the centre of which is the Countess of Breuss,* a Russian lady, well acquainted with the *agrémens de la Société*,* and who has collected them round herself at her mansion. It was chiefly here, I find, that the gentleman who travelled with Lord Byron, as physician, sought for society. He used almost every day to cross the lake by himself, in one of their flat-bottomed boats, and return after passing the evening with his friends about eleven or twelve at night, often whilst the storms were raging in the circling summits of the mountains around. As he became intimate, from long acquaintance, with several of the families in this neighbourhood, I have gathered from their accounts some excellent traits of his lordship's character, which I will relate to you at some future opportunity. I must, however, free him from one imputation attached to him—of having in his house two sisters as the partakers of his revels. This is, like many other charges which have been brought against his lordship, entirely destitute of truth. His only companion was the physician I have already mentioned. The report originated from the following circumstance: Mr. Percy Bysshe Shelly, a gentleman well known for extravagance of doctrine, and for his daring in their profession, even to sign himself with the title of Αθεος in the Album at Chamouny,* having taken a house below, in which he resided with Miss M. W. Godwin and Miss Clermont, (the daughters of the celebrated Mr. Godwin)* they were frequently visitors at Diodati, and were often seen upon the lake with his Lordship, which gave rise to the report, the truth of which is here positively denied.

Among other things which the lady, from whom I procured these anecdotes, related to me, she mentioned the outline of a ghost story by Lord Byron. It appears that one evening Lord B., Mr. P. B. Shelly, the two ladies and the gentleman before alluded to, after having perused a German work, which was entitled Phantasmagoriana,* began relating ghost stories; when his lordship having recited the beginning of Christabel, then unpublished, the whole took so strong a hold of Mr. Shelly's mind, that he suddenly started up and ran out of the room.* The physician and Lord Byron followed, and discovered him leaning against a mantle-piece, with cold drops of perspiration trickling down his face. After having given him something to refresh him, upon enquiring into the cause of his alarm, they found that his wild imagination having pictured to him the bosom of one of the ladies with eyes* (which was reported of a lady in the neighbourhood where he lived) he was obliged to leave the room in order to destroy the impression. It was afterwards proposed, in the course of conversation, that each of the company present should write a tale depending upon some supernatural agency, which was undertaken by Lord B., the physician, and Miss M. W. Godwin. My friend, the lady above referred to, had in her possession the outline of each of these stories, I obtained them as a great favour, and herewith forward them to you, as I was assured you would feel as much curiosity as myself, to peruse the *ebauches** of so great a genius, and those immediately under his influence.'[1]

[1] We have in our possession the Tale of Dr.——, as well as the outline of that of Miss Godwin. The latter has already appeared under the title of 'Frankenstein, or the modern Prometheus;' the former, however, upon consulting with its author, we may, probably, hereafter give to our readers.—ED.

ALARIC WATTS

INTRODUCTION TO THE VAMPYRE

THE superstition upon which this tale is founded is very general in the East. Among the Arabians it appears to be common: it did not, however, extend itself to the Greeks until after the establishment of Christianity; and it has only assumed its present form since the division of the Latin and Greek churches;* at which time, the idea becoming prevalent, that a Latin body could not corrupt if buried in their territory, it gradually increased, and formed the subject of many wonderful stories, still extant, of the dead rising from their graves, and feeding upon the blood of the young and beautiful. In the West it spread, with some slight variation, all over Hungary, Poland, Austria, and Lorraine,* where the belief existed, that vampyres nightly imbibed a certain portion of the blood of their victims, who became emaciated, lost their strength, and speedily died of consumptions; whilst these human blood-suckers fattened—and their veins became distended to such a state of repletion as to cause the blood to flow from all the passages of their bodies, and even from the very pores of their skins.

In the London Journal of March, 1732, is a curious, and of course *credible* account of a particular case of vampyrism, which is stated to have occurred at Madreyga, in Hungary. It appears, that upon an examination of the commander in chief and magistrates of the place, they positively and unanimously affirmed that, about five years before, a certain Heyduke, named Arnold Paul,* had been heard to say, that, at Cassovia, on the frontiers of the Turkish Servia, he had been tormented by a vampyre, but had found a way to rid himself of the evil, by eating some of the earth out of the vampyre's grave, and rubbing himself with his blood. This precaution, however, did not prevent him from becoming a vampyre[1] himself; for, about twenty or thirty days after his death and burial, many persons complained of having been tormented by him, and a deposition was made, that four persons had been deprived of life by his attacks. To prevent further

[1] The universal belief is, that a person sucked by a vampyre becomes a vampyre himself, and sucks in his turn.

mischief, the inhabitants having consulted their Hadagni,[1] took up the body, and found it (as is supposed to be usual in cases of vampyrism) fresh, and entirely free from corruption, and emitting at the mouth, nose, and ears, pure and florid blood. Proof having been thus obtained, they resorted to the accustomed remedy. A stake was driven entirely through the heart and body of Arnold Paul, at which he is reported to have cried out as dreadfully as if he had been alive. This done, they cut off his head, burned his body, and threw the ashes into his grave. The same measures were adopted with the corses* of those persons who had previously died from vampyrism, lest they should, in their turn, become agents upon others who survived them.

We have related this monstrous rodomontade, because it seems better adapted to illustrate the subject of the present observations than any other instance we could adduce. In many parts of Greece it is considered as a sort of punishment after death, for some heinous crime committed whilst in existence, that the deceased is doomed to vampyrize, but be compelled to confine his infernal visitations solely to those beings he loved most while upon earth—those to whom he was bound by ties of kindred and affection. This supposition is, we imagine, alluded to in the following fearfully sublime and prophetic curse from the 'Giaour.'

But first on earth, as Vampyre sent,
Thy corse shall from its tomb be rent;
Then ghastly haunt the native place,
And suck the blood of all thy race;
There from thy *daughter*, *sister*, *wife*,
At midnight drain the stream of life;
Yet loathe the banquet, which perforce
Must feed thy livid living corse,
Thy victims, ere they yet expire,
Shall know the demon for their sire;
As cursing thee, thou cursing them,
Thy flowers are withered on the stem.
But one that for *thy crime* must fall,
The youngest, best beloved of all,
Shall bless thee with a *father's* name—
That word shall wrap thy heart in flame!
Yet thou must end thy task and mark

[1] Chief bailiff.

Her cheek's last tinge—her eye's last spark,
And the last glassy glance must view
Which freezes o'er its lifeless blue;
Then with unhallowed hand shall tear
The tresses of her yellow hair,
Of which, in life a lock when shorn
Affection's fondest pledge was worn—
But now is borne away by thee
Memorial of thine agony!
Yet with thine own best blood shall drip
Thy gnashing tooth, and haggard lip;
Then stalking to thy sullen grave,
Go—and with Gouls and Afrits rave,
Till these in horror shrink away
From spectre more accursed than they.*

Mr. Southey has also introduced in his wild but beautiful poem of 'Thalaba,'* the vampyre corse of the Arabian maid Oneiza, who is represented as having returned from the grave for the purpose of tormenting him she best loved whilst in existence. But this cannot be supposed to have resulted from the sinfulness of her life, she being pourtrayed throughout the whole of the tale as a complete type of purity and innocence. The veracious Tournefort gives a long account in his travels of several astonishing cases of vampyrism, to which he pretends* to have been an eye-witness; and Calmet,* in his great work upon this subject, besides a variety of anecdotes, and traditionary narratives illustrative of its effects, has put forth some learned dissertations, tending to prove it to be a classical, as well as barbarian error.

We could add many curious and interesting notices on this singularly horrible superstition, and we may, perhaps, resume our observations upon it at some future opportunity; for the present, we feel that we have very far exceeded the limits of a note, necessarily devoted to the explanation of the strange production to which we now invite the attention of our readers; and we shall therefore conclude by merely remarking, that though the term Vampyre is the one in most general acceptation, there are several others synonimous with it, which are made use of in various parts of the world, namely, Vroucolocha, Vardoulacha, Goul, Broucoloka,* &c.—Ed.

JOHN WILLIAM POLIDORI, ED. ALARIC WATTS

THE VAMPYRE

It happened that in the midst of the dissipations attendant upon a London winter, there appeared at the various parties of the leaders of the *ton** a nobleman, more remarkable for his singularities, than his rank. He gazed upon the mirth around him, as if he could not participate therein. Apparently, the light laughter of the fair only attracted his attention, that he might by a look quell it, and throw fear into those breasts where thoughtlessness reigned. Those who felt this sensation of awe, could not explain whence it arose: some attributed it to the dead grey eye,* which, fixing upon the object's face, did not seem to penetrate, and at one glance to pierce through to the inward workings of the heart; but fell upon the cheek with a leaden ray that weighed upon the skin it could not pass. His peculiarities caused him to be invited to every house; all wished to see him, and those who had been accustomed to violent excitement, and now felt the weight of *ennui*,* were pleased at having something in their presence capable of engaging their attention. In spite of the deadly hue of his face,* which never gained a warmer tint, either from the blush of modesty, or from the strong emotion of passion, though its form and outline were beautiful, many of the female hunters after notoriety attempted to win his attentions, and gain, at least, some marks of what they might term affection. Lady Mercer,* who had been the mockery of every monster shewn in drawing rooms since her marriage, threw herself in his way, and did all but put on the dress of a mountebank,* to attract his notice;—though in vain:—when she stood before him, though his eyes were apparently fixed upon her's, still it seemed as if they were unperceived—even her unappalled impudence was baffled, and she left the field. But though the common adultress could not influence even the guidance of his eyes, it was not that the female sex was indifferent to him: yet such was the apparent caution with which he spoke to the virtuous wife and innocent daughter, that few knew he ever addressed himself to females. He had, however, the reputation of a winning tongue; and whether it was that it even overcame the dread of his singular character, or that they were moved by his apparent hatred of vice, he was as often among those females who form the boast of their sex from their domestic virtues, as among those who sully it by their vices.

About the same time, there came to London a young gentleman of the name of Aubrey:* he was an orphan left with an only sister in the possession of great wealth, by parents who died while he was yet in childhood. Left also to himself by guardians, who thought it their duty merely to take care of his fortune, while they relinquished the more important charge of his mind to the care of mercenary subalterns, he cultivated more his imagination than his judgment. He had, hence, that high romantic feeling of honour and candour, which daily ruins so many milliners' apprentices. He believed all to sympathize with virtue, and thought that vice was thrown in by Providence merely for the picturesque effect of the scene, as we see in romances; he thought that the misery of a cottage merely consisted in the vesting of clothes, which were as warm, but which were better adapted to the painter's eye* by their irregular folds and various coloured patches. He thought, in fine,* that the dreams of poets were the realities of life.* He was handsome, frank, and rich: for these reasons, upon his entering into the gay* circles, many mothers surrounded him, striving which should describe with least truth their languishing or romping favourites: the daughters at the same time, by their brightening countenances when he approached, and by their sparkling eyes, when he opened his lips, soon led him into false notions of his talents and his merit. Attached as he was to the romance of his solitary hours, he was startled at finding that except in the tallow and wax candles, that flickered not from the presence of a ghost, but from want of snuffing, there was no foundation in real life for any of that congeries* of pleasing pictures and descriptions contained in those volumes, from which he had formed his study. Finding, however, some compensation in his gratified vanity, he was about to relinquish his dreams, when the extraordinary being we have above described, crossed him in his career.

He watched him; and the very impossibility of forming an idea of the character of a man entirely absorbed in himself, who gave few other signs of his observation of external objects, than the tacit assent to their existence, implied by the avoidance of their contact; allowing his imagination to picture every thing that flattered its propensity to extravagant ideas, he soon formed this object into the hero of a romance, and determined to observe the offspring of his fancy, rather than the person before him. He became acquainted with him, paid him attentions, and had so far advanced upon his notice, that his presence was always recognized. He gradually learnt that Lord Ruthven's* affairs were embarrassed, and soon found, from the notes of preparation in——Street, that he was about to travel.* Desirous of gaining some information respecting this singular character, who, till now, had only whetted his curiosity, he hinted to his guardians, that it was time for him to perform the tour, which for many generations has been thought necessary to enable the young to take some rapid steps in the career of vice, towards putting themselves upon an equality with the aged, and not allowing them to appear as if fallen from the skies, whenever scandalous intrigues are mentioned as the subjects of pleasantry or of praise, according to the degree of skill shewn in carrying them on. They consented: and Aubrey immediately mentioning his intentions to Lord Ruthven, was surprised to receive from him a proposal to join him. Flattered, by such a mark of esteem from him, who, apparently, had nothing in common with other men, he gladly accepted it, and in a few days they had passed the circling waters.*

Hitherto, Aubrey had had no opportunity of studying Lord Ruthven's character, and now he found, that, though many more of his actions were exposed to his view, the results offered different conclusions from the apparent motives to his conduct. His companion was profuse in his liberality;—the idle, the vagabond, and the beggar, received from his hand more than enough to relieve their immediate wants. But Aubrey could not avoid remarking, that it was not upon the virtuous, reduced to indigence by the misfortunes attendant even upon virtue, that he bestowed his alms;—these were sent from the door with hardly suppressed sneers; but when the profligate came to ask something, not to relieve his wants, but to allow him to wallow in his lust, or to sink him still deeper in his iniquity, he was sent away with rich charity. This was, however, attributed by him to the greater importunity of the vicious, which generally prevails over the retiring bashfulness of the virtuous indigent. There was one circumstance about the charity of his Lordship, which was still more impressed upon his mind: all those upon whom it was bestowed, inevitably found that there was a curse upon it, for they were all either led to the scaffold, or sunk to the lowest and the most abject misery. At Brussels and other towns through which they passed, Aubrey was surprized at the apparent eagerness with which his companion sought for the centres of all fashionable vice; there he entered into all the spirit of the faro table:* he betted, and always gambled with success, except where the known sharper was his antagonist, and then he lost even more than he gained; but it was always with the same unchanging face, with which he generally watched the society around: it was not, however, so when he encountered the rash youthful novice, or the luckless father of a numerous family: then his very wish seemed fortune's law—this apparent abstractedness of mind was laid aside, and his eyes sparkled with more fire than that of the cat whilst dallying with the half dead mouse. In every town, he left the formerly affluent youth, torn from the circle he adorned, cursing, in the solitude of a dungeon, the fate that had drawn him within the reach of this fiend: whilst many a father sat frantic, amidst the speaking looks of mute hungry children, without a single farthing of his late immense wealth, wherewith to buy even sufficient to satisfy their present craving. Yet he took no money from the gambling table; but immediately lost, to the ruiner of many, the last gilder* he had just snatched from the convulsive grasp of the innocent: this might but be the result of a certain degree of knowledge, which was not, however, capable of combating the cunning of the more experienced. Aubrey often wished to represent this to his friend, and beg him to resign that charity and pleasure which proved the ruin of all, and did not tend to his own profit;—but he delayed it—for each day he hoped his friend would give him some opportunity of speaking frankly and openly to him; however, this never occurred. Lord Ruthven in his carriage,* and amidst the various wild and rich scenes of nature, was always the same: his eye spoke less than his lip; and though Aubrey was near the object of his curiosity, he obtained no greater gratification from it than the constant excitement of vainly wishing to break that mystery, which to his exalted imagination began to assume the appearance of something supernatural.

They soon arrived at Rome, and Aubrey for a time lost sight of his companion; he left him in daily attendance upon the morning circle of an Italian countess, whilst he went in search of the memorials of another almost deserted city. Whilst he was thus engaged, letters arrived from England, which he opened with eager impatience; the first was from his sister, breathing nothing but affection; the others were from his guardians, the latter astonished him; if it had before entered into his imagination that there was an evil power resident in his companion, these seemed to give him almost sufficient reason for the belief. His guardians insisted upon his immediately leaving his friend, and urged, that his character was dreadfully vicious, for that the possession of irresistible powers of seduction, rendered his licentious habits more dangerous to society. It had been discovered, that his contempt for the adultress had not originated in hatred of her character; but that he had required, to enhance his gratification, that his victim, the partner of his guilt, should be hurled from the pinnacle of unsullied virtue, down to the lowest abyss of infamy and degradation: in fine, that all those females whom he had sought, apparently on account of their virtue, had, since his departure, thrown even the mask aside, and had not scrupled to expose the whole deformity of their vices to the public gaze.

Aubrey determined upon leaving one, whose character had not yet shown a single bright point on which to rest the eye. He resolved to invent some plausible pretext for abandoning him altogether, purposing, in the mean while, to watch him more closely, and to let no slight circumstances pass by unnoticed. He entered into the same circle, and soon perceived, that his Lordship was endeavouring to work upon the inexperience of the daughter of the lady whose house he chiefly frequented. In Italy, it is seldom that an unmarried female is met with in society; he was therefore obliged to carry on his plans in secret; but Aubrey's eye followed him in all his windings, and soon discovered that an assignation had been appointed, which would most likely end in the ruin of an innocent, though thoughtless girl. Losing no time, he entered the apartment of Lord Ruthven, and abruptly asked him his intentions with respect to the lady, informing him at the same time that he was aware of his being about to meet her that very night. Lord Ruthven answered, that his intentions were such as he supposed all would have upon such an occasion; and upon being pressed whether he intended to marry her, merely laughed. Aubrey retired; and, immediately writing a note, to say, that from that moment he must decline accompanying his Lordship in the remainder of their proposed tour, he ordered his servant to seek other apartments, and calling upon the mother of the lady, informed her of all he knew, not only with regard to her daughter, but also concerning the character of his Lordship. The assignation was prevented. Lord Ruthven next day merely sent his servant to notify his complete assent to a separation; but did not hint any suspicion of his plans having been foiled by Aubrey's interposition.

Having left Rome, Aubrey directed his steps towards Greece, and, crossing the Peninsula, soon found himself at Athens. He then fixed his residence in the house of a Greek; and soon occupied himself in tracing the faded records of ancient glory upon monuments that apparently, ashamed of chronicling the deeds of freemen only before slaves, had hidden themselves beneath the sheltering soil or many coloured lichen. Under the same roof as himself, existed a being, so beautiful and delicate, that she might have formed the model for a painter wishing to pourtray on canvass the promised hope of the faithful in Mahomet's paradise, save that her eyes spoke too much mind for any one to think she could belong to those who had no souls. As she danced upon the plain, or tripped along the mountain's side, one would have thought the gazelle* a poor type of her beauties, for who would have exchanged her eye, apparently the eye of animated nature, for that sleepy luxurious look of the animal suited but to the taste of an epicure. The light step of Ianthe* often accompanied Aubrey in his search after antiquities, and often would the unconscious girl, engaged in the pursuit of a Kashmere butterfly,* show the whole beauty of her form, floating as it were upon the wind, to the eager gaze of him, who forgot the letters he had just decyphered upon an almost effaced tablet, in the contemplation of her sylph-like figure. Often would her tresses falling, as she flitted around, show in the sun's ray such delicately brilliant and swiftly fading hues, as might well excuse the forgetfulness of the antiquary, who let escape from his mind the very object he had before thought of vital importance to the proper interpretation of a passage in Pausanias.* But why attempt to describe charms which all feel, but none can appreciate?—It was innocence, youth, and beauty, unaffected by crowded drawing rooms, and stifling balls. Whilst he drew those remains of which he wished to preserve a memorial for his future hours, she would stand by, and watch the magic effects of his pencil, in tracing the scenes of her native place; she would then describe to him the circling dance upon the open plain, would paint to him in all the glowing colours of youthful memory, the marriage pomp she remembered viewing in her infancy; and then, turning to subjects that had evidently made a greater impression upon her mind, would tell him all the supernatural tales of her nurse. Her earnestness and apparent belief of what she narrated, excited the interest even of Aubrey; and often as she told him the tale of the living vampyre,* who had passed years amidst his friends, and dearest ties, forced every year, by feeding upon the life of a lovely female to prolong his existence for the ensuing months, his blood would run cold, whilst he attempted to laugh her out of such idle and horrible fantasies; but Ianthe cited to him the names of old men, who had at last detected one living among themselves, after several of their near relatives and children had been found marked with the stamp of the fiend's appetite: and when she found him so incredulous, she begged of him to believe her, for it had been remarked, that those who had dared to question their existence, always had some proof given, which obliged them, with grief and heartbreaking, to confess it was true. She detailed to him the traditional appearance of these monsters, and his horror was increased, by hearing a pretty accurate description of Lord Ruthven; he, however, still persisted in persuading her, that there could be no truth in her fears, though at the same time he wondered at the many coincidences which had all tended to excite a belief in the supernatural power of Lord Ruthven.

Aubrey began to attach himself more and more to Ianthe, her innocence, so contrasted with all the affected virtues of the women among whom he had sought for his vision of romance, won his heart; and while he ridiculed the idea of a young man of English habits, marrying an uneducated Greek girl, still he found himself more and more attached to the almost fairy form before him. He would tear himself at times from her, and, forming a plan for some antiquarian research, he would depart, determined not to return until his object was attained; but he always found it impossible to fix his attention upon the ruins around him, whilst in his mind he retained an image that seemed alone the rightful possessor of his thoughts. Ianthe was unconscious of his love, and was ever the same frank infantile being he had first known. She always seemed to part from him with reluctance; but it was because she had no longer any one with whom she could visit her favourite haunts, whilst her guardian was occupied in sketching or uncovering some fragment which had yet escaped the destructive hand of time. She had appealed to her parents on the subject of Vampyres, and they both, with several present, affirmed their existence, pale with horror at the very name. Soon after, Aubrey determined to proceed upon one of his excursions, which was to detain him for a few hours; when they heard the name of the place, they all at once begged of him not to return at night, as he must necessarily pass through a wood, where no Greek would ever remain after the day had closed, upon any consideration. They described it as the resort of the vampyres in their nocturnal orgies,* and denounced the most heavy evils as impending upon him who dared to cross their path. Aubrey made light of their representations, and tried to laugh them out of the idea; but when he saw them shudder at his daring thus to mock a superior, infernal power, the very name of which apparently made their blood freeze, he was silent.

Next morning Aubrey set off upon his excursion unattended; he was surprised to observe the melancholy face of his host, and was concerned to find that his words, mocking the belief of those horrible fiends, had inspired them with such terror.—When he was about to depart, Ianthe came to the side of his horse, and earnestly begged of him to return, ere night allowed the power of these beings to be put in action—he promised. He was, however, so occupied in his research, that he did not perceive that daylight would soon end, and that in the horizon there was one of those specks which in the warmer climates so rapidly gather into a tremendous mass and pour all their rage upon the devoted country.—He at last, however, mounted his horse, determined to make up by speed for his delay: but it was too late. Twilight in these southern climates is almost unknown; immediately the sun sets, night begins; and ere he had advanced far, the power of the storm was above—its echoing thunders had scarcely an interval of rest—its thick heavy rain forced its way through the canopying foliage, whilst the blue forked lightning* seemed to fall and radiate at his very feet. Suddenly his horse took fright, and he was carried with dreadful rapidity through the entangled forest. The animal at last, through fatigue, stopped, and he found, by the glare of lightning, that he was in the neighbourhood of a hovel that hardly lifted itself up from the masses of dead leaves and brushwood which surrounded it. Dismounting, he approached, hoping to find some one to guide him to the town, or at least trusting to obtain shelter from the pelting of the storm. As he approached, the thunders, for a moment silent, allowed him to hear the dreadful shrieks of a woman mingling with the stifled exultant mockery of a laugh, continued in one almost unbroken sound; he was startled: but, roused by the thunder which again rolled over his head, he with a sudden effort forced open the door of the hut. He found himself in utter darkness; the sound, however, guided him. He was apparently unperceived; for though he called, still the sounds continued, and no notice was taken of him. He found himself in contact with some one, whom he immediately seized, when a voice cried 'again baffled,'* to which a loud laugh succeeded, and he felt himself grappled by one whose strength seemed superhuman: determined to sell his life as dearly as he could, he struggled; but it was in vain: he was lifted from his feet and hurled with enormous force* against the ground:—his enemy threw himself upon him, and kneeling upon his breast, had placed his hands upon his throat, when the glare of many torches penetrating through the hole that gave light in the day, disturbed him—he instantly rose and, leaving his prey, rushed through the door, and in a moment the crashing of the branches, as he broke through the wood, was no longer heard.—The storm was now still; and Aubrey, incapable of moving, was soon heard by those without.—They entered; the light of their torches fell upon the mud walls, and the thatch loaded on every individual straw with heavy flakes of soot. At the desire of Aubrey they searched for her who had attracted him by her cries; he was again left in darkness; but what was his horror, when the light of the torches once more burst upon him, to perceive the airy form of his fair conductress brought in a lifeless corse. He shut his eyes, hoping that it was but a vision arising from his disturbed imagination; but he again saw the same form, when he unclosed them, stretched by his side. There was no colour upon her cheek, not even upon her lip; yet there was a stillness about her face that seemed almost as attaching as the life that once dwelt there:—upon her neck and breast was blood, and upon her throat were the marks of teeth having opened the vein:*—to this the men pointed, crying, simultaneously struck with horror, 'a Vampyre! a Vampyre!' A litter was quickly formed, and Aubrey was laid by the side of her who had lately been to him the object of so many bright and fairy visions, now fallen with the flower of life that had died within her. He knew not what his thoughts were—his mind was benumbed and seemed to shun reflection and take refuge in vacancy—he held almost unconsciously in his hand a naked dagger of a particular construction, which had been found in the hut.—They were soon met by different parties who had been engaged in the search of her whom a mother had soon missed.—Their lamentable cries, as they approached the city, forewarned the parents of some dreadful catastrophe.—To describe their grief would be impossible; but when they ascertained the cause of their child's death, they looked at Aubrey and pointed to the corpse.—They were inconsolable; both died broken hearted.

Aubrey being put to bed was seized with a most violent fever, and was often delirious; in these intervals he would call upon Lord Ruthven and upon Ianthe—by some unaccountable combination he seemed to beg of his former companion to spare the being he loved.—At other times he would imprecate maledictions upon his head, and curse him as her destroyer. Lord Ruthven chanced at this time to arrive at Athens, and, from whatever motive, upon hearing of the state of Aubrey, immediately placed himself in the same house and became his constant attendant. When the latter recovered from his delirium he was horrified and startled at the sight of him whose image he had now combined with that of a Vampyre; but Lord Ruthven by his kind words, implying almost repentance for the fault that had caused their separation, and still more by the attention, anxiety, and care which he showed, soon reconciled him to his presence. His Lordship seemed quite changed; he no longer appeared that apathetic being who had so astonished Aubrey; but as soon as his convalescence began to be rapid, he again gradually retired into the same state, of mind, and Aubrey perceived no difference from the former man, except, that at times he was surprised to meet his gaze fixed intently upon him with a smile of malicious exultation playing upon his lips; he knew not why, but this smile haunted him. During the last stage of the invalid's recovery, Lord Ruthven was apparently engaged in watching the tideless waves* raised by the cooling breeze, or in marking the progress of those orbs, circling, like our world, the moveless sun;—indeed he appeared to wish to avoid the eyes of all.

Aubrey's mind, by this shock, was much weakened, and that elasticity of spirit which had once so distinguished him now seemed to have fled for ever.—He was now as much a lover of solitude and silence as Lord Ruthven; but much as he wished for solitude, his mind could not find it in the neighbourhood of Athens; if he sought it amidst the ruins he had formerly frequented, Ianthe's form stood by his side—if he sought it in the woods, her light step would appear wandering amidst the underwood, in quest of the modest violet;* then suddenly turning round would show, to his wild imagination, her pale face and wounded throat with a meek smile upon her lips.

He determined to fly scenes, every feature of which created such bitter associations in his mind. He proposed to Lord Ruthven, to whom he held himself bound by the tender care he had taken of him during his illness, that they should visit those parts of Greece neither had yet seen. They travelled in every direction, and sought every spot to which a recollection could be attached; but though they thus hastened from place to place yet they seemed not to heed what they gazed upon.—They heard much of robbers, but they gradually began to slight these reports, which they imagined were only the invention of individuals, whose interest it was to excite the generosity of those whom they defended from pretended dangers. In consequence of thus neglecting the advice of the inhabitants, on one occasion they travelled with only a few guards, more to serve as guides than as a defence.—Upon entering, however, a narrow defile,* at the bottom of which was the bed of a torrent, with large masses of rock brought down from the neighbouring precipices, they had reason to repent their negligence—for, scarcely were the whole of the party engaged in the narrow pass, when they were startled by the whistling of bullets close to their heads, and by the echoed report of several guns. In an instant their guards had left them, and placing themselves behind rocks had began to fire in the direction whence the report came. Lord Ruthven and Aubrey, imitating their example, retired for a moment behind a sheltering turn of the defile; but ashamed of being thus detained by a foe, who with insulting shouts bade them advance, and being exposed to unresisting slaughter, if any of the robbers should climb above and take them in the rear, they determined at once to rush forward in search of the enemy.—Hardly had they lost the shelter of the rock, when Lord Ruthven received a shot in the shoulder that brought him to the ground.—Aubrey hastened to his assistance, and no longer heeding the contest or his own peril, was soon surprised by seeing the robbers' faces around him; his guards having, upon Lord Ruthven's being wounded, immediately thrown up their arms and surrendered.

By promises of great reward, Aubrey soon induced them to convey his wounded friend to a neighbouring cabin, and having agreed upon a ransom he was no more disturbed by their presence, they being content to merely guard the entrance till their comrade should return with the promised sum for which he had an order.*—Lord Ruthven's strength rapidly decreased, in two days mortification ensued,* and death seemed advancing with hasty steps.—His conduct and appearance had not changed; he seemed as unconscious of pain as he had been of the objects about him; but towards the close of the last evening his mind became apparently uneasy, and his eye often fixed upon Aubrey, who was induced to offer his assistance with more than usual earnestness—'Assist me! you may save me—you may do more than that—I mean not my life, I heed the death of my existence as little as that of the passing day; but you may save my honour, your friend's honour.'—'How? tell me how; I would do any thing,' replied Aubrey, 'I need but little—my life ebbs apace—I cannot explain the whole—but if you would conceal all you know of me, my honour were free from stain in the world's mouth—and if my death were unknown for some time in England—I—I—but life.'—'It shall not be known,'—'Swear!' cried the dying man,* raising himself with exultant violence, 'Swear by all your soul reveres, by all your nature fears, swear that for a year and a day you will not impart your knowledge of my crimes or death to any living being in any way, whatever may happen, or whatever you may see.'—His eyes seemed bursting from their sockets: 'I swear!' said Aubrey; he sunk laughing upon his pillow and breathed no more.

Aubrey retired to rest, but did not sleep, the many circumstances attending his acquaintance with this man rose upon his mind, and he knew not why; when he remembered his oath a cold shivering came over him, as if from the presentiment of something horrible awaiting him. Rising early in the morning he was about to enter the hovel in which he had left the corpse, when a robber met him, and informed him that it was no longer there, having been conveyed by himself and comrades, upon his retiring, to the pinnacle of a neighbouring mount, according to a promise they had given his lordship, that it should be exposed to the first cold ray of the moon* that rose after his death. Aubrey astonished,* and taking several of the men, determined to go and bury it upon the spot where it lay. But, when he had mounted to the summit he found no trace of either the corpse or the clothes, though the robbers swore they pointed out the identical rock on which they had laid the body. For a time his mind was bewildered in conjectures, but he at last returned, convinced that they had buried the corpse for the sake of the clothes.

Weary of a country in which he had met with such terrible misfortunes, and in which all apparently conspired to heighten that superstitious melancholy that had seized upon his mind, he resolved to leave it, and soon arrived at Smyrna.* While waiting for a vessel to convey him to Otranto,* or to Naples, he occupied himself in arranging those effects he had with him belonging to Lord Ruthven. Amongst other things there was a case containing several weapons of offence, more or less adapted to ensure the death of the victim. There were several daggers and ataghans.* Whilst turning them over, and examining their curious forms, what was his surprise at finding a sheath apparently ornamented in the same style as the dagger discovered in the fatal hut; he shuddered; hastening to gain further proof, he found the weapon, and his horror may be imagined when he discovered that it fitted, though peculiarly shaped, the sheath he held in his hand. His eyes seemed to need no further certainty—they seemed gazing to be bound to the dagger; yet still he wished to disbelieve; but the particular form, the same varying tints upon the haft and sheath were alike in splendour on both, and left no room for doubt; there were also drops of blood on each.

He left Smyrna, and on his way home, at Rome, his first inquiries were concerning the lady he had attempted to snatch from Lord Ruthven's seductive arts. Her parents were in distress, their fortune ruined, and she had not been heard of since the departure of his lordship. Aubrey's mind became almost broken under so many repeated horrors; he was afraid that this lady had fallen a victim to the destroyer of Ianthe. He became morose and silent, and his only occupation consisted in urging the speed of the postilions, as if he were going to save the life of some one he held dear. He arrived at Calais; a breeze, which seemed obedient to his will, soon wafted him to the English shores; and he hastened to the mansion of his fathers, and there, for a moment, appeared to lose, in the embraces and caresses of his sister, all memory of the past. If she before, by her infantine* caresses, had gained his affection, now that the woman began to appear, she was still more attaching as a companion.

Miss Aubrey had not that winning grace which gains the gaze and applause of the drawing-room assemblies. There was none of that light brilliancy which only exists in the heated atmosphere of a crowded apartment. Her blue eye was never lit up by the levity of the mind beneath. There was a melancholy charm about it which did not seem to arise from misfortune, but from some feeling within, that appeared to indicate a soul conscious of a brighter realm. Her step was not that light footing, which strays where'er a butterfly or a colour may attract—it was sedate and pensive. When alone, her face was never brightened by the smile of joy; but when her brother breathed to her his affection, and would in her presence forget those griefs she knew destroyed his rest, who would have exchanged her smile for that of the voluptuary?* It seemed as if those eyes,—that face were then playing in the light of their own native sphere. She was yet only eighteen, and had not been presented to the world; it having been thought by her guardians more fit that her presentation should be delayed until her brother's return from the continent, when he might be her protector. It was now, therefore, resolved that the next drawing room,* which was fast approaching, should be the epoch of her entry into the 'busy scene.'* Aubrey would rather have remained in the mansion of his fathers, and fed upon the melancholy which overpowered him. He could not feel interest about the frivolities of fashionable strangers, when his mind had been so torn by the events he had witnessed; but he determined to sacrifice his own comfort to the protection of his sister. They soon arrived in town, and prepared for the next day, which had been announced as a drawing-room.

The crowd was excessive—a drawing room had not been held for a long time, and all who were anxious to bask in the smile of royalty, hastened thither. Aubrey was there with his sister. While he was standing in a corner by himself, heedless of all around him, engaged in the remembrance that the first time he had seen Lord Ruthven was in that very place—he felt himself suddenly seized by the arm, and a voice he recognized too well, sounded in his ear—'Remember your oath.' He had hardly courage to turn, fearful of seeing a spectre that would blast him, when he perceived, at a little distance, the same figure which had attracted his notice on this spot upon his first entry into society. He gazed till his limbs almost refusing to bear their weight, he was obliged to take the arm of a friend, and forcing a passage through the crowd, he threw himself into his carriage, and was driven home. He paced the room with hurried steps, and fixed his hands upon his head, as if he were afraid his thoughts were bursting from his brain. Lord Ruthven again before him—circumstances started up in dreadful array—the dagger—his oath.—He roused himself, he could not believe it possible—the dead rise again!—He thought his imagination had conjured up the image his mind was resting upon. It was impossible that it could be real—he determined, therefore, to go again into society; for though he attempted to ask concerning Lord Ruthven, the name hung upon his lips, and he could not succeed in gaining information. He went a few nights after with his sister to the assembly of a near relation. Leaving her under the protection of a matron, he retired into a recess, and there gave himself up to his own devouring thoughts. Perceiving, at last, that many were leaving, he roused himself, and entering another room, found his sister surrounded by several, apparently in earnest conversation; he attempted to pass and get near her, when one, whom he requested to move, turned round, and revealed to him those features he most abhorred. He sprung forward, seized his sister's arm, and, with hurried step, forced her towards the street: at the door he found himself impeded by the crowds of servants who were waiting for their lords; and while he was engaged in passing them, he again heard that voice whisper close to him—'Remember your oath!'—He did not dare to turn, but, hurrying his sister, soon reached home.

Aubrey became almost distracted. If before his mind had been absorbed by one subject, how much more completely was it engrossed, now that the certainty of the monster's living again pressed upon his thoughts. His sister's attentions were now unheeded, and it was in vain that she intreated him to explain to her what had caused his abrupt conduct. He only uttered a few words, and those terrified her. The more he thought, the more he was bewildered. His oath startled him;—was he then to allow this monster to roam, bearing ruin upon his breath, amidst all he held dear, and not avert its progress? His very sister might have been touched by him. But even if he were to break his oath, and disclose his suspicions, who would believe him? He thought of employing his own hand to free the world from such a wretch; but death, he remembered, had been already mocked. For days he remained in this state, shut up in his room, he saw no one, and eat only when his sister came, who, with eyes streaming with tears, besought him, for her sake, to support nature.* At last, no longer capable of bearing stillness and solitude, he left his house, roamed from street to street, anxious to fly that image which haunted him. His dress became neglected, and he wandered, as often exposed to the noon-day sun as to the midnight damps. He was no longer to be recognized; at first he returned with the evening to the house; but at last he laid him down to rest wherever fatigue overtook him. His sister, anxious for his safety, employed people to follow him; but they were soon distanced by him who fled from a pursuer swifter than any—from thought. His conduct, however, suddenly changed. Struck with the idea that he left by his absence the whole of his friends, with a fiend amongst them, of whose presence they were unconscious, he determined to enter again into society, and watch him closely, anxious to forewarn, in spite of his oath, all whom Lord Ruthven approached with intimacy. But when he entered into a room, his haggard and suspicious looks were so striking, his inward shudderings so visible, that his sister was at last obliged to beg of him to abstain from seeking, for her sake, a society which affected him so strongly. When, however, remonstrance proved unavailing, the guardians thought proper to interpose, and, fearing that his mind was becoming alienated, they thought it high time to resume again that trust which had been before imposed upon them by Aubrey's parents.

Desirous of saving him from the injuries and sufferings he had daily encountered in his wanderings, and of preventing him from exposing to the general eye those marks of what they considered folly, they engaged a physician to reside in the house, and take constant care of him. He hardly appeared to notice it, so completely was his mind absorbed by one terrible subject. His incoherence became at last so great, that he was confined to his chamber. There he would often lie for days, incapable of being roused. He had become emaciated, his eyes had attained a glassy lustre;—the only sign of affection and recollection remaining displayed itself upon the entry of his sister: then he would sometimes start, and, seizing her hands, with looks that severely afflicted her, he would desire her not to touch him. 'Oh, do not touch him—if your love for me is aught, do not go near him!' When, however, she inquired to whom he referred, his only answer was—'True! true!' and again he sank into a state, whence not even she could rouse him. This lasted many months: gradually, however, as the year was passing, his incoherences became less frequent, and his mind threw off a portion of its gloom, whilst his guardians observed, that several times in the day he would count upon his fingers a definite number, and then smile.

The time had nearly elapsed, when, upon the last day of the year, one of his guardians entering his room, began to converse with his physician upon the melancholy circumstance of Aubrey's being in so awful a situation when his sister was going next day to be married. Instantly Aubrey's attention was attracted; he asked anxiously to whom. Glad of this mark of returning intellect, of which they feared he had been deprived, they mentioned the name of the Earl of Marsden.* Thinking this was a young Earl whom he had met with in society, Aubrey seemed pleased, and astonished them still more by his expressing his intention to be present at the nuptials, and desiring to see his sister. They answered not, but in a few minutes his sister was with him. He was apparently again capable of being affected by the influence of her lovely smile; for he pressed her to his breast, and kissed her cheek, wet with tears, flowing at the thought of her brother's being once more alive to the feelings of affection. He began to speak with all his wonted warmth, and to congratulate her upon her marriage with a person so distinguished for rank and every accomplishment; when he suddenly perceived a locket upon her breast; opening it, what was his surprise at beholding the features of the monster who had so long influenced his life. He seized the portrait in a paroxysm of rage, and trampled it under foot. Upon her asking him why he thus destroyed the resemblance of her future husband, he looked as if he did not understand her—then seizing her hands, and gazing on her with a frantic expression of countenance, he bade her swear that she would never wed this monster, for he——But he could not advance—it seemed as if that voice again bade him remember his oath—he turned suddenly round, thinking Lord Ruthven was near him, but saw no one. In the meantime the guardians and physician, who had heard the whole, and thought this was but a return of his disorder, entered, and forcing him from Miss Aubrey, desired her to leave him. He fell upon his knees to them, he implored, he begged of them to delay but for one day. They, attributing this to the insanity they imagined had taken possession of his mind, endeavoured to pacify him, and retired.

Lord Ruthven had called the morning after the drawing room, and had been refused with every one else. When he heard of Aubrey's ill health, he readily understood himself to be the cause of it: but when he learned that he was deemed insane, his exultation and pleasure could hardly be concealed from those among whom he had gained this information. He hastened to the house of his former companion, and, by constant attendance, and the pretence of great affection for the brother and interest in his fate, he gradually won the ear of Miss Aubrey. Who could resist his power? His tongue had dangers and toils to recount—could speak of himself as of an individual having no sympathy with any being on the crowded earth, save with her to whom he addressed himself;—could tell how, since he knew her, his existence, had begun to seem worthy of preservation, if it were merely that he might listen to her soothing accents;—in fine, he knew so well how to use the serpent's art,* or such was the will of fate, that he gained her affections. The title of the elder branch falling at length to him, he obtained an important embassy, which served as an excuse for hastening the marriage, (in spite of her brother's deranged state,) which was to take place the very day before his departure for the continent.

Aubrey, when he was left by the physician and his guardian, attempted to bribe the servants, but in vain. He asked for pen and paper; it was given him; he wrote a letter to his sister, conjuring* her, as she valued her own happiness, her own honour, and the honour of those now in the grave, who once held her in their arms as their hope and the hope of their house, to delay but for a few hours, that marriage, on which he denounced the most heavy curses. The servants promised they would deliver it; but giving it to the physician, he thought it better not to harass any more the mind of Miss Aubrey by, what he considered, the ravings of a maniac. Night passed on without rest to the busy inmates of the house; and Aubrey heard, with a horror that may more easily be conceived than described, the notes of busy preparation. Morning came, and the sound of carriages broke upon his ear. Aubrey grew almost frantic. The curiosity of the servants at last overcame their vigilance, they gradually stole away, leaving him in the custody of an helpless old woman. He seized the opportunity, with one bound was out of the room, and in a moment found himself in the apartment where all were nearly assembled. Lord Ruthven was the first to perceive him: he immediately approached, and, taking his arm by force, hurried him from the room, speechless with rage. When on the staircase, Lord Ruthven whispered in his ear—'Remember your oath, and know, if not my bride to day, your sister is dishonoured. Women are frail!' So saying, he pushed him towards his attendants, who, roused by the old woman, had come in search of him. Aubrey could no longer support himself; his rage, not finding vent, had broken a blood-vessel, and he was conveyed to bed. This was not mentioned to his sister, who was not present when he entered, as the physician was afraid of agitating her. The marriage was solemnized, and the bride and bridegroom left London.

Aubrey's weakness increased; the effusion of blood produced symptoms of the near approach of death. He desired his sister's guardians might be called, and when the midnight hour had struck, he related composedly what the reader has perused—he died immediately after.

The guardians hastened to protect Miss Aubrey; but when they arrived, it was too late. Lord Ruthven had disappeared,* and Aubrey's sister had glutted the thirst of a VAMPYRE!

JOHN KEATS

LA BELLE DAME SANS MERCI

O what can ail thee Knight at arms
  Alone and palely loitering?
The sedge* has withered from the Lake
  And no birds sing!

O what can ail thee Knight at arms
  So haggard, and so woe begone?
The Squirrel's granary is full
  And the harvest's done.

I see a lilly on thy brow
  With anguish moist and fever dew,
And on thy cheeks a fading rose
  Fast Withereth too—

I met a Lady in the Meads*
  Full beautiful, a faery's child*
Her hair was long, her foot was light
  And her eyes were wild—

I made a Garland for her head,
  And bracelets too, and fragrant Zone*
She look'd at me as she did love
  And made sweet moan—

I set her on my pacing steed
  And nothing else saw all day long
For sidelong would she bend and sing
  A faery's song—

She found me roots of relish sweet
  And honey wild and manna dew*
And sure in language strange she said
  I love thee true—

She took me to her elfin grot*
  And there she wept and sigh'd full sore,
And there I shut her wild wild eyes
  With Kisses four—

And there she lulled* me asleep
  And there I dream'd Ah Woe betide!
The latest dream I ever dreamt
  On the cold hill side.

I saw pale Kings and Princes too
  Pale warriors death pale were they all
Who cried La belle dame sans merci
  Thee hath in thrall.*

I saw their starv'd lips in the gloam*
  With horrid warning gaped* wide,
And I awoke, and found me here
  On the cold hill's side.

And this is why I sojourn* here
  Alone and palely loitering;
Though the sedge is withered from the Lake
  And no birds sing—

'URIAH DERICK D'ARCY' [RICHARD VARICK DEY]

THE BLACK VAMPYRE; A LEGEND OF ST. DOMINGO

So have I seen, upon another shore,
Another Lion give a grievous roar;
And the last Lion thought the first—A BOAR!
*Bombast. Furios.**

TO THE AUTHOR OF 'WALL-STREET.'*
MY DEAR SIR,

CHARMED with the success of your anomalous drama, which, without aspiring even to the character of nonsense, has already seen three editions, I have been myself induced to venture on publishing; with the sanguine hope of also scraping together a few shillings, in these hard times. Permit me to inscribe this tale to you, with a fellow-feeling for your lack of genius; and a fervent hope, that our names may be encircled by the same evergreen in the temple of the Muses;* and that we may long flourish together, on the same pedestal, embellishing and elevating the literature of the Auction Room.*

I remain,
My dear Sir,
Your affectionate Friend,
And obedient Servant,
THE AUTHOR.

Introduction

IF any person should have patience to read the following narrative, and can discover the Author's drift, it is more than he can do himself. If it be thought exquisite nonsense, it is more than the writer dares hope: and if it be pronounced simple, stupid, and unadulterated absurdity, his own private opinion will perfectly coincide with that of the public. He began to write without any fable, and before he had found any had spun out the thread of his ideas.

This tangled skein* of absurdities is now exposed to criticism, from the laudable motive of showing, of how much nonsense an individual may be delivered, in the short space of two afternoons;* without any excuse but idleness, or any object but amusement.

The prominent descriptions, which it is here attempted to ridicule, are fresh in the memory of all who have read the 'White Vampyre;'* and to those who have not, the Superstition must be so familiar, that it is unnecessary to make useless extracts.

That the Author may not, however, be misunderstood, it may be necessary to state, that in the speech of the Vampyre, he had no design of descending to that meanest of all intellectual exercises, a travestie on authors who are justly admired: but meant, if any thing, simply to show how passages, which were fine in their original use, when garbelled* by the ignorant and tasteless, become a melancholy rhapsody of nonsense.

'But first on earth, as Vampyre sent,
Thy corse shall from its tomb be rent;
Then ghastly haunt thy native place,
And suck the blood of all thy race;
There from thy *daughter*, *sister*, *wife*,
At midnight drain the stream of life;
Yet loathe the banquet, which perforce
Must feed thy livid living corse.
Thy victims, ere they yet expire,
Shall know the demon for their sire;
As cursing thee, thou cursing them,
Thy flowers are withered on the stem.
But one that for *thy crime* must fall,
The youngest, best beloved of all,
Shall bless thee with a *father's* name—
That word shall wrap thy heart in flame!
Yet thou must end thy task and mark
Her cheek's last tinge—her eye's last spark,
And the last glassy glance must view
Which freezes o'er its lifeless blue;
Then with unhallowed hand shall tear
The tresses of her yellow hair,
Of which, in life a lock when shorn
Affection's fondest pledge was worn—
But now is borne away by thee
Memorial of thine agony!
Yet with thine own best blood shall drip
Thy gnashing tooth, and haggard lip;

Then stalking to thy sullen grave,
Go—and with Gouls and Afrits rave,
Till these in horror shrink away
From spectre more accursed than they.'
BYRON.*

The Black Vampyre

MR. ANTHONY GIBBONS was a gentleman of African extraction. His ancestors* emigrated from the eastern coast of GUINEA, in a French ship, and were sold in ST. DOMINGO* remarkably cheap; as they were reduced to mere skeletons by the yaws* on the passage; and all died shortly after their arrival, except one small negro, of a very slender constitution, and fit for no work whatever. The gentleman who purchased *him,* charitably knocked out his brains; and the body was thrown into the ocean. The tide returning in the night, it was washed upon the sands; and the moon then shining bright,* the gentleman was taking a walk to enjoy the coolness of the evening; judge of his surprise, when the little corpse got up, and complaining of a pain in its bowels, begged for some bread and butter!

The PLANTER supposing his business to have been but half done, kicked him back in the water. The element seemed very familiar to him; and he swam back with much grace and agility; parting the sparkling waves with his jet black members, polished like ebony, but reflecting no single beam of light. His complexion was a dead black;—his eyes a pure white;—the iris was flame colour;—and the pupils of a clear, moonshiny lustre;—but so peculiarly constructed, that, though prominent, they seemed to look into his own head. His hair was neither curled nor straight; but feathery, like the plumage of a crow. Having paddled again on shore, he came crawling crab fashion, to the feet of Mr. PERSONNE.* The latter gentleman, in considerable alarm, (not knowing whether it was Satan, Obi,* or some other worthy, with whom he had to deal,) mustered up sufficient resolution, to tie a large stone round the boy's middle: then, with a main exertion of strength, he hurled him into the sparkling ocean. He fell where the reflection of the moon was brightest, and sunk like lead; but immediately rose again like cork, perpendicularly, with the stone under his arm; while the radiant lustre of the planet retreated from his dark figure, exhibiting in its most striking contrast its utter blackness!

In this predicament, he came buoyant to land; surrounded, as he seemed, by a sphere of magic lustre. He now walked up to the Frenchman, with his arms a-kimbo, and looking remarkably fierce. Mr. PERSONNE's particular hairs stood up on end,

> ——————Tunc perculit horror
> Membra ducis, riguere comæ, gressumque coercens
> Languor in extrema tenuit vestigia ripa. LVC.*

but being ashamed that a little negro of ten years old, should put him in bodily fear, he knocked him down. The Guineaman rose again, without bending a joint; as fast as Mr. PERSONNE could upset him, he recovered his altitude;* just like one of those small toys, fabricated from pith, tipt with lead, called witches and hobgoblins* by the rising generation!

The PLANTER, in utter amazement and despair, took hold of the child by both his extremities; and pressing him to the earth, set down upon him! Then, halloing* for his attendants, he ordered a tremendous fire to be kindled on the sand!! This was accordingly done. The GAUL congratulated himself on his perseverance and sagacity; and as he had never heard of ignaqueous* animals, was confident that though the water fiend was so expert in his own element, he could not stand the fiery ordeal. The boy, meanwhile, lay perfectly passive, as if he had been a mere log; but presently, when the pile was all in a light blaze, with a sudden expansion, like that of a compressed Indian Rubber,* he popped Mr. PERSONNE up into the air many yards, and he alighted head-foremost into the fire, where he had intended to have dedicated the sable brat, with his nine lives, to Moloch!!!*

Whatever the negro was, it is notorious that Mr. PERSONNE was no salamander.* He was rescued from the pyre, which, like Hercules,* he had, (though unwittingly,) erected for himself; looking like a squizzed* cat, and having apparently no life left in his body. The attention of the domestics was drawn entirely to their master; who soon betrayed signs of animation, though he exhibited a most awful spectacle: being one continual sore and blister. 'His whole body was one wound,' as Virgil or some other poet* has hyperbolically expressed himself.

Mr. PERSONNE, when he perfectly recovered his senses, found himself in his own bed, wrapt in greasy sheets, and smarting as if in a Cayenne bath.* He called for a glass of brandy,—his dear wife EUPHEMIA,*—and his infant son, who had not yet been christened. His lady, with streaming eyes, presented herself before him; and, after tenderly inquiring into the state of his health, told him, (with a voice interrupted with sobs and hiccups,) that when she went in the morning to see her baby, whom she had left in the cradle, there was nothing to *be* seen, but the *skin*, *hair*, and *nails!!!** She declared that there never was such another object; except, indeed, the exsiccation* in Scudder's Museum!*

On the receipt of this horrid intelligence, Mr. PERSONNE was seized with a violent spasmodic affection;* and shortly after expired, muttering something about *sacre*,* and the Guinea-negro!

The amiable, but unfortunate Euphemia, was thrown into several hysterical convulsions; as well she might be, poor woman! when her husband had been made a holocaust,* and served up like a broiled and peppered chicken, to feed the grim maw of death; and her interesting infant,* the first pledge of her pure and perfect love, had been precociously sucked, like an unripe orange,* and nothing left but its beautiful and tender skin. The disconsolate widow caused her husband to be embalmed; and he was buried amid the lamentations and tears of all the funeral; much regretted by all who had the honour of his acquaintance, particularly by his negroes; who could not soon forget him; as he had left too many sincere marks of his regard upon their backs,* to be ever obliterated from their recollections.

Time, as all the Greek tragedians, Solomon,* and others have remarked, is a benevolent deity. Mrs. PERSONNE's grief yielded to the soothing hand of the consoling power; and her bloom and spirits returned with more lustre and elasticity* than they had before exhibited: as the rose, that had drooped in the fury of the passing storm, erects its blushing honours, and shows more beautiful and vivid tints, when the squall is over!

Many years after these occurrences took place, while EUPHEMIA was in second mourning* for her third husband, she was indulging in the luxury of solitary grief; and reading Burton's Anatomy of Melancholy, and The Melancholy Poems of Dr. Farmer,* in an orangerie.* The refreshing breezes from the ocean, which now tempered the sultry heats of the declining day,—the soft perfume of the opening blossoms;—and the mellow tints of the evening sky, shedding that holy light, so dear to sensitive hearts, diffused a calm over her soul, wrapt in the contemplation of departed days. While lost in this pensive reverie, she perceived two strangers approaching her, in the extremity of the long vista of the grove. One of them was a coloured gentleman, of remarkable height, and deep jetty blackness; a perfect model of the CONGO Apollo.* He was drest in the rich garb of a Moorish Prince;* and led by the hand a pale European boy, in an Asiatic dress; whose languid countenance, slender form and tristful* gait, were strongly contrasted with the portly appearance and majestic step of his conductor!

They both saluted the lovely widow, and after an interchange of compliments, accepted her polite invitation to set down,* and take tea with her in the bower. She learned from the elder stranger, that he had brought out* a cargo of slaves, whom his subjects had lately taken prisoners in war; and whom he had resolved to dispose of himself; as he was desirous of seeing the world. His Page, he said, was an orphan, left by a slave merchant in Africa.

The manners and conversation of the PRINCE had an irresistible charm. The regal port* was manifest in his gigantic and well proportioned frame; and majesty was conspicuous on his brow, without its diadem. The turban and crescent* had never graced a nobler front; but the winning condescension of his tones and language, while they could not banish the feeling of the presence of royalty, removed every restraint incident to that consciousness. He criticized* the works, which EUPHEMIA had been perusing, with masterly precision; and displayed more knowledge than even the accomplished ideologist of Lady Morgan;* with infinitely more discretion and good sense.

It is remarked by the Abbe Reynal,* that there is a peculiar elegance and beauty in the complexion of the Africans, (when the eyes and nose are accustomed to their hue and odour.) This truth was realized by EUPHEMIA, as she gazed on the open visage of her illustrious guest. She thought surely that in him Nature might stand up and say 'This was a man!'* And certainly it is only the weakness and imperfection of our human senses, which, penetrating no further than the surface, is for ever deceived by superficial shadows. The empyrean* is always blue, whatever vapours may float in our contracted atmosphere. And if we gaze on the rows of skulls, which festoon and garnish Surgeon's Hall,* we can apply no standard, to determine their relative beauty. They are all equally ugly; and the block of Helen* might be mistaken for that of Medusa.* Shakspeare, true to nature, has also remarked, 'Black men are pearls in beauteous ladies' eyes.'*

The beauty then, the royalty, gentility, and various accomplishments of the BAMBUCK* monarch, made captive the too sensible heart of the French widow. She forgot her ogles, graces, and even her loquacity; rooted to her seat, and fixed in immoveable contemplation of the AFRICAN's face. What peculiar feature or lineament attracted her attention, she knew not: his eyes, though bright, did not sparkle; and the iris, though of a more vivid red than the roseate line in the rainbow, emitted no scintillations. In fact, *his whole countenance seemed to look, and to perambulate* her own.*

The conversation gradually assumed a more empassioned and amorous complexion; and the little page, (who, though meagre and emaciated, evidently showed that he was no gump* for his years,) taking certain broad hints, cast a mournful and intelligent look on the widow, said he would fetch a short walk in the plantation, and left the orangerie.

The PRINCE then spreading his glittering sash upon the grass, went down on his knees upon it; and broke out into the most ardent exclamations, of love and admiration; and professions of constant attachment. He said that the flat-nosed beauties of Zara;* the scarred, squab figures of the golden coast;* the well proportioned Zilias, Calypsos, and Zamas on the banks of the Niger;[1] and even the great Hottentot Venus* herself, had never for a moment made the least impression on his heart! His passion was a mystery to himself; its origin secret as the sources of the Nile; but full and impetuous as its ample channel, when replenished from the celestial fountains of ABYSSINIA;* while if Mrs. DUBOIS* would shine upon its waves, its enlivened currents would fertilize his vast dominions, in the luxuriant realms of central Africa; making them to fructify* yet more abundantly, with burning gold, and radiant diamonds!!!

What female heart could resist such pleadings, and the compliment implied in such a preference? When ZEMBO* (the page) returned, the parties had agreed to be privately united on the same evening. The ceremony was accordingly performed, on the spot, by the family chaplain of Mrs. DUBOIS: not without many remonstrances on his part, as to the impropriety of marrying a negro. The PRINCE did not see to resent the affront; which, by the by, he had no right to do; as the priest got nothing for the job. ZEMBO, too, was

[1] See Reynal, Vol. III. pp. 385 and 387.*

extremely restless; till Mrs. DUBOIS gave him some sweetmeats,* which seemed to quiet his conscience; after which he took some stiff punch, and fell asleep!

About midnight, the PRINCE came to him; and, shaking him by the ears, bade him rise and follow him. His bride was hanging on his arm, in an enchanting dishabille;* and did not seem to be in perfect possession of her right senses. ZEMBO mournfully followed the new married pair.

They went silently out of the back door, with cautious steps, and proceeded through the orangerie. No breath of wind was stirring. The moon was on the zenith, surrounded by a pale halo of ghostly lustre. When they had crossed the plantation, they came to a place of sepulture;* where the dark cypresses, and lugubrious mahogany, admitted but sparse and glimmering streaks of funereal light; which, falling on the rank foliage, the white monuments and broken ground beneath, presented a thousand dusky shapes, flitting in the dim uncertainty dear to superstition.

Vague terrors seized on the mind of the bride; and she began very naturally to inquire, what was the use of getting out of a comfortable bed, and trailing through the heavy dew, in her undress, to such an unusual spot for midnight recreation.

They now stood near the spot, where her three husbands, several children, and the *skin*, *hair* and *nails* of her first baby, were deposited in a row. At the foot of a tamarind,* lay her third son; whose christian name was SPOONER, and who died, according to the tombstone, in a fit of intoxication, aged seven years and six months. On him she had bestowed a greater share of tenderness, than any of her other offspring; and his loss had caused her most affliction.[1] The African, making observations on the grave, began to strip himself very expeditiously, assisted by ZEMBO; who seemed to recover from his blues;* and by his activity and eagerness, manifested his expectation of soon seeing some fine sport.

Presently the two genii,* or gentlemen, or whatever they were, turned towards the East, and performed certain antic prostrations; throwing handfuls of earth three times over their heads.* Then

[1] This Spooner Dubois having never been heard of since, it is probable that he has been roaming about the world; and it is possible, that he may be the same Lord Ruthven, whose adventures have been recently related.

returning to the tomb, they tore up the sods with ravenous fury; and soon drew out the last-mentioned son of the Lady, and threw him on the grass, beside the grave. ZEMBO fell as fiercely upon the corpse, as a hungry dog upon his dinner; but was arrested by the AFRICAN, who lent him a severe box on the ear, which sent him blubbering to a corner of the cemetery.

What added both to the mother's horrors and admiration, was, that the body of her child was perfectly fresh, and the olfactory nerves experienced no unsavoury sensation from its proximity; while its cheeks were diffused with so deep a tinge of scarlet, that they shone like ruddy fireballs in the darkness of the spot.[1] Her husband drew a golden goblet from beneath a large stone; then, bending over the corse, he scooped out the heart, with his long and polished nails; and, having pressed the blood into the chalice, mingled with it some dark particles, gathered from the newly turned up earth.* From the pure and scanty lymph,* which gushed near by and flickered like a streak of quicksilvery-light in the moonbeam, he added a third ingredient of the potion. Then seizing his passive and trembling spouse by the throat, and presenting the unnatural mixture to her lips; he cried in a hollow voice, whose very inflection thrilled through each fibre of its victim,—'Swear, or if that is against your principles, affirm, by this dirty blood,—and bloody dirt;—by this watery blood,—and bloody water;—by this watery dirt, and dirty water;—that you will never disclose in any manner, aught of what you have seen and shall see this night. Call them all to witness your wish, that in the moment when you even conceive the thought of perjury, your bowels may burst out, and your bones rot! Swear and drink!'[2]

The affrighted woman murmured, (as articulately as the iron gripe* of the monster would suffer her,) that she was not thirsty; and had not breath enough to aspirate such a terrible conjuration. 'No trifling;' roared the fiend, 'you have not a moment to deliberate.' But his bellowing and threats were vain; and he found to his mortifica-

[1] 'The universal belief is, that a person sucked by a Vampyre becomes a Vampyre himself, and sucks in his turn'—*Ed. New Mon. Mag.**

[2] See Edwards, vol. II. p. 86. 'Among their other superstitions also, must not be omitted their mode of administering an oath of secrecy or purgation. Human blood, and earth taken from the grave of some near relation, are mixed with water, and given to the party to be sworn, who is compelled to drink the mixture, with an imprecation, that it may cause the belly to burst, and the bones to rot, if the truth be not spoken.'*

tion that he had gotten the wrong sow by the ear,* or rather by the throat. She stuttered out, in the most pitiful accents, which would have softened any heart, (but a Vampyre has none,) that though she was by no means partial to the delectable confectionary of the pharmacopeia,* calomel and jalap, ipecacuanha, rhubarb, and tartar-emetic,* she would rather take them all, collectively and individually, than the unchristian decoction he held against her teeth.

Foaming with madness, till the white slaver* flowed down his sable limbs, the African hurled MRS. PERSONNE, DUBOIS, &c. &c. on the grave of her first husband, and stamping violently on the earth, it seemed to heave as with the throes of an earthquake. Immediately the tumuli* yawned! The ponderous stones and slabs were shaken from their ancient sockets; and the ghastly dead, in uncouth attitudes, crawled from their nooks; with their hair curling in tortuous and serpent twinings; and their eyeballs of fire bursting from their heads; while, as they extended their withered arms, and tapering fingers, furnished with blood-hound claws, their gory shrouds fell in wild drapery around them, transiently revealing their forms, bloated as if to bursting, and often incarnadined with clotted blood, yet warm and dripping!!!

The Lady, (as those who have been in similar predicaments may suppose,) soon lost her recollection; not, however, before she had seen ZEMBO busily employed in tearing up the grave of her first husband; she saw herself surrounded by the spectres, and lost all consciousness.

When reason and sense returned, she found herself in the same place; and it was also the midnight hour. She was laying by the grave of Mr. PERSONNE, and her breast was stained with blood. A wide wound appeared to have been inflicted there, but was now cicatrized.* Imagine if you can, her surprise; when, by a certain carniverous craving in her maw, and by putting this and that together, she found she was a——VAMPYRE!!! and gathered from her indistinct reminiscences, of the preceding night, that she had been then sucked; and that it was now her turn to eject the peaceful tenants of the grave!

With this delightful prospect of immortality before her,* she began to examine the graves, for a subject to satisfy* her furious appetite. When she had selected one to her mind, a new marvel arrested her attention. Her first husband got up out of his coffin,* and with all the grace so natural to his countrymen, made her a low bow in the last fashion, and opened his arms to receive her!

What were the emotions of this fond couple, when, after a lingering separation for sixteen years, they again embraced each other, with the ardour of an affection equal to their earliest transports, and which their long divorce* served only to increase; tenderly inquiring into the state of each other's health; and the accidents which had befallen them during their disjunction. They forgot even their hunger and thirst; and sitting down on a tombstone, made a thousand inquiries; which, however, as they related to family concerns, might not be as interesting to the reader as they were to the parties concerned.

Mr. PERSONNE, however, looked rather glum, when he learned that his Lady had been thrice married, since his decease. But she assured him, that she would never more tolerate the addresses of another suitor: and as for the two husbands, they were rotten enough by this time; as she was confident they had not attended the Vampyre Ball, on the preceding night. As for her sable spouse, she trusted that he would never again appear to interrupt their happiness. But while she was expressing this hope, the gentleman in question, (like his relation below, according to the old proverb,*) came upon the ground, with ZEMBO. Mr. PERSONNE, having neither sword nor pistols at hand, armed himself with a gigantic thigh-bone; and warned the BLACK PRINCE to stand upon his guard as he meant to punish him severely.

But ZEMBO, rushing between the parties, raised his hands in a supplicating posture; while the generous monarch, making a Salam* to his antagonist, begged him to keep himself quiet, and look behind him. They both turned round on this intimation when, to the utter confusion of the Lady, her second and third husbands, Messieurs MARQUAND and DUBOIS, arose from the graves, where they had been lovingly deposited by the side of each other. They both advanced to salute their wife; but Mr. PERSONNE, brandishing his thigh-bone, warned them to stand off, as he had the first title to the Lady. Much confusion would have ensued, had not the African Prince interfered. He told the gentlemen that so delicate a point could only be settled in an *honourable* way; and proposed that Mr. MARQUAND and Mr. DUBOIS should first settle their difference in a personal encounter; after which Mr. PERSONNE might give the survivor *gentlemanly satisfaction*.* To this all parties assented.

As they were already stripped, the combatants shook hands, to show their mutual good-will; and proceeded to action, without further ceremony. Mr. DUBOIS soon brought claret* from Mr. MARQUAND; who, in returning the compliment, fibbed* Mr. DUBOIS so severely in the bowels, that he lost his wind; and gasping for breath, smote the air on all sides, without any of his blows telling. He came to the ground, and his bones rattled as he fell. But soon recovering his breath, he made a desperate attack on Mr. MARQUAND's sconce;* and favoured him with so terrible a facer under the gills,* that he fell incontinently like a bull smitten in his front; but entangling his own heels with those of Mr. DUBOIS, they both came simultaneously to the ground; striking their heads against different tombstones; and knocking out their own brains.

They rose again, refreshed like the giant of old,* by their grappling with the earth, and all the better for the loss of their wits, which, indeed, was a mere trifle. But the AFRICAN, who had no time to see more sport, fixed them to the sod by his superior strength; and ZEMBO dexterously pinned them fast, by driving stakes through their hearts, with a large sledge hammer,* (which he carried about his person for such emergencies.) During the operation, their roaring surpassed that which is performed by the Lioness, when bereft of her whelps; but as soon as they were fairly nailed to the counter,* they lay motionless and breathless—a horrible pair of spectacles of sin and misery!

The AFRICAN assured the Lady, that she need never fear their second resurrection; and Mr. PERSONNE politely offered to settle their controversy, in any mode most agreeable to the PRINCE:—either to box with him on the spot, or appoint a meeting in future, with pistols, rifles, small or broad sword;* or else they might toss up, who should set fire to a barrel of gunpowder. The PRINCE said that quarrelling was all nonsense, and offered his hand; but Mr. PERSONNE refused, saying, 'Don't be too familiar, Blackey;' and renewing his threats of cracking him over the noddle* with the thigh-bone.

The generous monarch pocketed the affront.* 'You have been,' he said, 'sufficiently rewarded, for the cruelties you practised upon my person, several years ago. I forgive you, my dear sir, what you performed, and intended to perform on me. Here is your son, who has grown considerably, as you may observe; and I assure you that his education has not been neglected. To his exertions last night you are indebted for your revivification. And as, you may remember, you were embalmed, you have kept quite sweet and fresh ever since your interment. Amiable and virtuous VAMPYRES! may you long enjoy that tranquillity and contentment, which your merit and accomplishments so eminently deserve! A vessel lies in the port, ready to sail for

Europe in an hour. The Island is no longer a place for you. Here is money to pay your passages, and all I have to say, is, that the sooner you're off the better.—Farewell!' So saying he departed, without waiting for the acknowledgments of the party.

Mr. PERSONNE and his Lady, whom we shall again call by her first marriage name, did not exactly comprehend what their dingy* benefactor meant, by bidding them take French leave* of the Island, like pickpockets and outlaws; but, as they were yet wondering at their own existence, like Adam and Eve, the first day of their creation, and as they had reason to believe the PRINCE a potent magician, who could rouse the dead from their searments,* and turn the planets from their courses;—for these reasons, they concluded to follow his bidding, without any impertinent scruples. But as the keen edge of their hunger had been whetted by delay, they would fain have taken supper, and digested a little something wherewithal to strengthen them, before they set out.

ZEMBO, who had filled his own bread-basket* very lately, and was in no such urgent necessity, protested with all the vehemence which filial reverence would permit, against the unseasonable gratification of their unnatural craving; and recited, with just emphasis and good discretion, an extract from Counsellor Phillips's harangue, about 'the cannibal appetite of his rejected altar;'* which his parents did not understand, and of course thought very sublime! But even this master-piece of mystical eloquence would have been delivered in vain; had not the boy given other reasons, of such cogency, that they licked their lips—cast a longing, lingering look at the graveyard,—and followed him without more opposition.

They prosecuted their nocturnal march, through closely woven and solemn groves; until they descended into a profound valley, where the light of the pale planet of magic adoration,* streamed and quivered on serried files* of bright armoury.* The leader of the band seemed to have expected their arrival; and mutual tokens of recognition passed between him and ZEMBO. The whole company then set forward their array in silence;—

No cymbal clash'd, no clarion rang,
  Still were the pipe and drum;
Save heavy tread, and armour's clang,
  The sullen march was dumb.*

By continual descent, they seemed to have penetrated the bowels of a cavern,[1] whose ramifications* ran under the sea; as they heard a murmuring roar, as of the ocean, above their heads. The party, by the instructions of ZEMBO, dispersed themselves in different directions; until they had enclosed the interior of the rock, where its largest chamber was, to speak catachrestically,* so artfully concealed by nature, that no one, not instructed by an adept in its subterranean topography, could ever have detected the secret of its existence. It had been, in former days, a place of deposit and asylum for the Buccaniers;* and its situation had been since known only to the Professors of the OBEAH art,* who held here their midnight orgies.*

Mr. and Mrs. PERSONNE, guided by their son, were placed in a situation, where, through the crevices of the inner partition of the rock, they could observe what was passing in the interior.

It seemed, at first view, a vast hall of Arabian romance; supported by immense shafts, and studded with precious stones; so various and beautiful were the hues, which the different spars* assumed, in the light of an hundred torches, blazing in every quarter, and illuminating the farthest recesses of the cave. The walls were decorated with other appendages, which added to the mystery, if not to the embellishment of the scene: being irregularly stained with blood; decorated with rude tapestry of many coloured plumage;—and stuccoed with the beaks of parrots;—the teeth of dogs, and alligators;—bones of cats;—broken glass and eggshells; plastered with a composition of rum and grave-dirt, the implements of NEGRO witchcraft![2]

At one extremity of the extensive apartment, on a kind of natural throne, sat several blackamoors* in sumptuous Moorish apparel; whom, by their swollen forms, and remarkable eyes, Mrs. PERSONNE knew to be GOULS;* and among whom she recognized her late husband.* The whole range of this vast amphitheatre, sweeping from before the throne, was occupied by slaves, rudely attired, and imperfectly armed with clubs and missiles; a decent platoon of black-guards were posted before the Vampyre monarchs; and, in the centre, a band of musicians performed an exquisite symphony. The soft strains of the MERRIWANG;—the lively notes of the DUNDO;—and the martial

[1] 'The ring-leaders held their meetings in certain subterranean passages or caves, in the parish of the La Grande Riviere,' &c.—Edwards, Vol. III. p. 52.*

[2] See Edwards, Vol. II. p. 111.*

accompaniment of the GOOMBAY,* made, with their united noises, a discordant harmony, whose powers the lyre of Orpheus* could not equal; and which would certainly be enough to frighten all the hosts of Pandemonium.*

The oratorio being finished, the AFRICAN PRINCE arose, and making an obeisance to the company,—cleared his throat, and began to address them as follows:—'Gentlemen and Vampyres!'—but the VAMPYRES expressing their resentment against this breach of etiquette, he corrected himself:—'Vampyres and Gentlemen!'—but the NEGROES were no more willing to come last, than the Vampyres, and a loud growl, accompanied by a slight hiss, again interrupted the orator. He was not, however, disconcerted, but like Mr. Burke,* thundered out an iteration of the offensive sentence.

'Yes,' said he, 'I repeat it, Vampyres and Gentlemen? Shall not the immortal precede the mortal?—Shall not those whose diet surpasses the nectar and ambrosia of celestials, precede the ephemeral race, who fatten on the unclean juice of brutes,—the rank essence of esculent* productions,—or the nauseous liquor of the distillery? (*applause—hear! hear! and see-boy! from the Vampyres—groans from the negroes!*) Gentlemen of colour!* I appeal to yourselves; shall not the descendants of the Gods be named before the offspring of the earth-born image, whom Titan impregnated with celestial fire?—For Prometheus was the first Vampyre. You must all know, as you have undoubtedly read Æschylus, that the vulture, who preyed on his liver, was neither fish, flesh, nor fowl.[1] He is called a dog, which makes him a quadruped;—he is represented as ερπωυ, creeping, which proves him an insect; and is said to have wings, which shows that he was a bird.* Now, from this amphibious monster have descended the Crows,—the Jackalls,—and the Bloodhounds;—the pirate Bat of Madagascar,—and the man-killing Ivunches of Chili;—the Sharks;—the Crocodiles;—the Krakens;—the Horse-leeches;—the Cape-cod Sea Serpents;—the Mermaids;—the Incubi;—and the Succubi!!!* (*loud cheering from the Vampyres.*) From Titan himself, descended the Cyclopes, and all other ancient and modern Anthropophagi;* and, in lineal descent, the Moco tribe of our own EBOES,[2] to whom I have the honour of being related. Those of you,

[1] See Prometheus Vinctus.*

[2] See Edwards, Vol. II. p. 90, and Reynal, Vol. III. p. 388.*

too, are his posterity, who, after your deaths, return to your native land—the true Elysium; where the balmy bowl of the Coco, the soft bloom of the ANANA,* and the coal-black beauties of the clime of love, shall for ever reward your fortitude, and steep in forgetfulness the memory of your wrongs. (*hear! hear! from the negroes.*) But none of these genera or species of our order, must longer engage your dignified and charitable attention. I come to ourselves, full-blooded—unadulterated—immortal bloodsuckers!—To ourselves—whether Gouls,—or Afrits,—or Vampyres;—Vroucolochas,—Vardoulachos,—or Broucolokas;*—To ourselves—the terror of the living and of the dead, and the participants of the nature of both;—To ourselves—the emblems at once of corruption and of vitality;—blotted from the records of existence, and replenished to repletion with circulating life;—abandoned by the quick, and unrecognized by the dead:—at once relics and relicts;*—rocked on the bases of our own eternities;—the chronicles of what was—the solemn and sublime mementoes of what must be!'* (*unqualified approbation from both sides of the house.*)

'The estate of Vampyrism is a fee-tail,* and may be docked* in two different ways. The first mode is the sanguinary practice of perforating the subject with a stake; and this is final. The other is produced by the gentler operation of the narcotic potion you behold in this phial; by whose lenient and opiate influence, the individual is restored to the plight, in which he was previous to his death, or his becoming a Vampyre, and belongs to the OBEAH mysteries.

'But to come to the object of our present meeting. Sublime and soul-elevating theme!—The emancipation of the Negroes!—The consecration of the soil of ST. DOMINGO to the manes* of murdered patriots in all ages!—No matter whether the bill of sale was scrawled in French or in English;—No matter whether we were taken prisoners, in a battle between the LEOPHARES and the JAKOFFS,* or in a skirmish between the SAMBOES and the SAWPITS;*—No matter whether we were bought for calico and cotton, or for gunpowder or for shot;—No matter whether we were transported in chains or in ropes—in a brig, or a schooner, or a seventy-four*—the first moment we come ashore on ST. DOMINGO, our souls shall swell like a sponge in the liquid element;—our bodies shall burst from their fetters, glorious as a curculio* from its shell;—our minds shall soar like the car of the æronaut, when its ligaments are cut;* in a word,

O my brethren, we shall be free!—Our fetters discandied,* and our chains dissolved, we shall stand liberated,—redeemed,—emancipated,—and disenthralled by the irresistible genius of UNIVERSAL EMANCIPATION!!!' (*Unparalleled bursts of unprecedented applause!!!*)

Such was the report of this oration, taken down in short hand by ZEMBO; of whose extraordinary sagacity so many proofs have been exhibited; and who was never unprovided with materials for any emergency. The fiery oratory of the Prince communicated such inspiration to the auditors, that the whole mass of their thick blood leaped up with the quickening pulse of anticipated freedom; they danced and sung, with violent gesticulations, like perfect Corybantes;* but unfortunately, their Phyrricks* were interrupted by the glittering bayonets of the soldiery; who poured in upon them from every quarter, and hemmed them in, with a bristling chevaux-de-frise* of steel. The Vampyres, surprised but undaunted, unsheathed their sabres, and drew up in a gallant style, as if determined to die game;* being, indeed, assured, that like so many Phœnixes, they would rise from their own ashes, as often as they might be cut down.

A desperate conflict ensued, during which Mrs. PERSONNE observed the phial, mentioned by the Prince, lying on the ground; and very thoughtfully put it in her ridicule.* The slaves, seeing how the business was likely to terminate, prudently sneaked off, while the attention of the military was occupied by the Vampyres. The former were violently exasperated to find all their labour so unprofitable; since while they themselves were wounded by every blow of their opponents, the latter, like so many ninepins, were set up, as fast as they were bowled down; bending to the storm, like masts on a tempestuous ocean, and rising again upon the billow in perpendicular triumph.

But, being instructed by ZEMBO, the soldiers pinioned them as fast as they fell; and prevented their rising, by sitting in great numbers on their bodies; though the task was somewhat like that of detaining quicksilver* beneath the fingers. The PRINCE, however, still fought desperately. Brandishing a huge scimitar in either hand, he swayed his arms like the sails of a windmill; while limbs, heads, and bodies flew about him, curvetting* and dancing in the air; as when the ingenious Mr. MAFFEY* pulls to pieces a coach, or an old woman, children, chickens, friars, and petticoats dance about in wild confusion, till the artist's hand again brings order out of chaos:—Or, as when the renowned knight of the BED-CHAMBER,* whose name eternal vases shall record, saw the ungenerous caricature on the wall, wielding a ponderous jug, he smote the innocent tables, chairs, and bed-posts, and strode victorious over the gory field: So fought the PRINCE; till being neatly pricked in the spine, unexpectedly, he soused* (as Johannes Porco Latinus* remarks) 'in principia fundimentalia,'* and was immediately set upon by a host. So when a Gœtulian lion* is pierced by the light bamboo, overpowered by the hunters, he struggles in his thrall like an Enceladus under Ætna,* and dies at last with heart-wrung tears of anguish, and reverberating roars of hatred!!!

Stakes were immediately procured, and the whole infernal fraternity securely disposed of: as their compeers,* described by Homer,

> With burning chains fixed to the brazen floors
> And lock'd by hell's inexorable doors.*

With their bellowings, the vast chambers of the subterranean rung like the caverns of Delphos,* when the inflammable air was fired by the crafty priests. The Inhabitants of the Island started up from their slumbers in shuddering terror, and believed that an earthquake was rumbling beneath their feet.

Mr. and Mrs. PERSONNE and ZEMBO lost no time in trying the effects of the African's stolen prescription. Being thrown into a tranquil slumber they were conveyed to their plantation; and awoke the next morning, perfectly well, excepting slight colds in the head. Mr. PERSONNE, having been in statu quo,* for sixteen years, was now much younger than his lady; a circumstance, for which she was not at all sorry; and which he himself declared by no means displeased him. The remainder of their life was serene as a tropic night:—illumined by the mild effulgence of domestic love;—fanned by the soft aspirations of peaceful bosoms;—and enlivened by the fire-fly scintillations of rapture!!!

ZEMBO, to whose taste and ingenuity they were indebted for their happiness, and who was baptized with the Christian name of BARABBAS,* after an uncle of his mother's, recorded what the reader has perused. One only circumstance, like one of those claps of thunder, frequently heard in the unclouded sky, passed over the tranquillity of their bosoms. Mrs. PERSONNE's fourth husband's child was a mulatto,* and of Vampyrish propensities; of which his mother and

Mr. PERSONNE were never able entirely to cure him, having used up all the African's preparation.

The intelligent reader, (if any such there be,) will remember that this narrative commenced with the name of Mr. ANTHONY GIBBONS, of whom nothing has since been said; and whose adventures (to use a FORUM trope*) 'must remain buried in the bowels of futurity,'* until a more convenient opportunity. He is a lineal descendant from the last-mentioned mulatto; and the manuscript, which is now given to the public, was transmitted to him from his ancestors. He is a resident in Essex county, New-Jersey; and candour requires us to state, that he is no relation to his celebrated namesake at ELIZABETH-TOWN;* as it is notorious to all who have had the pleasure of witnessing the size of the latter gentleman's waist, that he has too much bowels for so diabolical a profession;* and it is to be hoped in charity, that though he is such a delicate morsel, when he is laid in the sepulchre of his fathers, he may not prove a titbit, to GLUT THE THIRST OF A VAMPYRE!!!*

Moral

IN this happy land of liberty and equality, we are free from all traditional superstitions, whether political, religious, or otherwise. Fiction has no materials for machinery;*—Romance no horrors for a tale of mystery. Yet in a figurative sense, and in the moral world, our climate is perhaps more prolific than any other, in enchanters,*—Vampyres,—and the whole infernal brood of sorcery and witchcraft.

The accomplished dandy, who in maintaining his horses,—his taylor, &c.—absorbs in the forced and unnatural excitement of his senseless orgies, the life-blood of that wealth which his prudent Sire had accumulated by a long devotion to the counter,*—What is he but a Vampyre?

The fraudulent trafficker in stock and merchandize, who, having sucked the whole substance of an hundred honest men, is consigned for a few weeks to the sepulchre of the jail; and then, by the potent magic of an insolvent law, stalks forth, triumphant with bloated villany, more elated in his shameless resurrection to renew his career of iniquity and of disgrace,—what is he but a Vampyre?

The corrupted and senseless Clerk, who being placed near the vitals of a moneyed institution, himself exhausted to feed the appetite of sharpers, drains, in his turn, the coffers he was appointed to guard,—is *he* not, I appeal to the Stockholders,—is *he* not a Vampyre?

Brokers, Country Bank Directors, and their disciples—all whose hunger and thirst for money, unsatisfied with the tardy progression of honest industry, by creating fictitious and delusive credit, has preyed on the heart and liver of public confidence, and poisoned the currents of public morals,—are they not all Vampyres?

The whole tribe of Plagiarists, under every denomination;—The Critic, who, by eviscerating authors, and stuffing his own meagre show of learning with the pilfered entrails, ekes out his periodical fulmination against public taste;—the Forum Orator, who, without compunction, barbarously exenterates* Burke, and Curran, and Phillips,*—the Second-handed* Lawyer,—Scholar,—Theologue,*—who quote from quotations, and steal stolen property:—the Divine, who preaches Tillotson and Toplady;*—what are they all but Vampyres?

The Empiric,* who fills his own stomach, while he empties his shop into the bowels of the hypochondriac;—the Bibliopolist,* 'who guts the fobs'* of the whole reading community, by ascribing to Lord Byron works which that author never saw;* the philanthropic Contractor for the Army, who charges more for lime and horse-beef,* than his quantum-meruit* for the best provisions; who sets up his carriage and his palace, by blistering the mouths and destroying the intestines of thousands,—what are these but Vampyres?

The Professors and Disciples of Surgeon's Hall, who, when a fine fat corse is rolled out of the resurrectionist's* budget, set up a howl of horrible transport, like the anthropophagous Caribs in Robinson Crusoe;*—glut their gloating eyes with the pinguidity and unctuousness* of the subject; and whet their blades like Shylock, impatient to attack the ilia,*—what are they but Vampyres?

And I, who, as Johnson said of an hypochondriac Lady, 'have spun this discourse out of my own bowels,'* and made as free with those of others—I am a VAMPYRE!

ERNST BENJAMIN SALOMO RAUPACH

WAKE NOT THE DEAD

Wake not the Dead:—they bring but gloomy night
And cheerless desolation into day;
For in the grave who mouldering lay,
No more can feel the influence of light,
Or yield them to the sun's prolific might;
Let them repose within their house of clay—
Corruption, vainly wilt thou e'er essay
To quicken:—it sends forth a pest'lent blight;
And neither fiery sun, nor bathing dew,
Nor breath of spring the dead can e'er renew.
That which from life is pluck'd, becomes the foe
Of life, and whoso wakes it waketh woe.
Seek not the dead to waken from that sleep
In which from mortal eye they lie enshrouded deep.*

'Wilt thou for ever sleep? Wilt thou never more awake, my beloved? but henceforth repose for ever from thy short pilgrimage on earth? O yet once again return! and bring back with thee the vivifying dawn of hope to one whose existence hath, since thy departure, been obscured by the dunnest shades. What! dumb? for ever dumb? Thy friend lamenteth, and thou heedest him not? He sheds bitter, scalding tears, and thou reposest unregarding his affliction? He is in despair, and thou no longer openest thy arms to him as an asylum from his grief? Say then, doth the paly shroud become thee better than the bridal veil? Is the chamber of the grave a warmer bed than the couch of love? Is the spectre death more welcome to thy arms than thy enamoured consort? O return, my beloved, return once again to this anxious, disconsolate bosom.' Such were the lamentations which Walter poured forth for his Brunhilda,* the partner of his youthful, passionate love: thus did he bewail over her grave at the midnight hour, what time the spirit that presides in the troublous atmosphere, sends his legions of monsters through mid-air; so that their shadows, as they flit beneath the moon and across the earth, dart as wild, agitating thoughts that chase each other o'er the sinner's bosom:—thus did he lament under the tall linden trees by her grave, while his head reclined on the cold stone.

Walter was a powerful lord in Burgundy, who, in his earliest youth, had been smitten with the charms of the fair Brunhilda, a beauty far surpassing in loveliness all her rivals; for her tresses, dark as the raven face of night, streaming over her shoulders, set off to the utmost advantage the beaming lustre of her slender form, and the rich dye of a cheek whose tint was deep and brilliant as that of the western heaven: her eyes did not resemble those burning orbs whose pale glow gem* the vault of night, and whose immeasurable distance fills the soul with deep thoughts of eternity, but rather as the sober beams which cheer this nether world, and which, while they enlighten, kindle the sons of earth to joy and love. Brunhilda became the wife of Walter, and both being equally enamoured and devoted, they abandoned themselves to the enjoyment of a passion that rendered them reckless of aught besides, while it lulled them in a fascinating dream. Their sole apprehension was lest aught should awaken them from a delirium which they prayed might continue for ever. Yet how vain is the wish that would arrest the decrees of destiny! as well might it seek to divert the circling planets from their eternal course. Short was the duration of this phrenzied passion; not that it gradually decayed and subsided into apathy, but death snatched away his blooming victim, and left Walter to a widowed couch. Impetuous, however, as was his first burst of grief, he was not inconsolable, for ere long another bride became the partner of the youth.

Swanhilda* also was beautiful; although nature had formed her charms on a very different model from those of Brunhilda. Her golden locks waved bright as the beams of morn: only when excited by some emotion of her soul did a rosy hue tinge the lily paleness of her cheek: her limbs were proportioned in the nicest symmetry, yet did they not possess that luxuriant fullness of animal life:* her eye beamed eloquently, but it was with the milder radiance of a star tranquillizing to tenderness rather than exciting to warmth. Thus formed, it was not possible that she should steep him in his former delirium, although she rendered happy his waking hours: tranquil and serious, yet cheerful, studying in all things her husband's pleasure, she restored order and comfort in his family, where her presence shed a general influence all around. Her mild benevolence tended to restrain the fiery, impetuous disposition of Walter: while at the same time her prudence recalled him in some degree from his vain, turbulent wishes, and his aspirings after unattainable enjoyments, to the duties and pleasures of actual life. Swanhilda bore her husband two children, a son and a daughter; the latter was mild and patient as her mother, well contented with her solitary sports, and even in these recreations displayed the serious turn of her character. The boy possessed his father's fiery, restless disposition, tempered, however, with the solidity of his mother. Attached by his offspring more tenderly towards their mother, Walter now lived for several years very happily: his thoughts would frequently, indeed, recur to Brunhilda, but without their former violence, merely as we dwell upon the memory of a friend of our earlier days, borne from us on the rapid current of time to a region where we know that he is happy.

But clouds dissolve into air, flowers fade, the sand of the hour-glass runs imperceptibly away, and even so, do human feelings dissolve, fade, and pass away, and with them too, human happiness. Walter's inconstant breast again sighed for the exstatic dreams of those days which he had spent with his equally romantic, enamoured Brunhilda: again did she present herself to his ardent fancy in all the glow of her bridal charms, and he began to draw a parallel between the past and the present; nor did imagination, as it is wont, fail to array the former in her brightest hues, while it proportionably obscured the latter; so that he pictured to himself, the one much more rich in enjoyment, and the other, much less so than they really were. This change in her husband did not escape Swanhilda; whereupon, redoubling her attentions towards him, and her cares towards their children, she expected, by this means, to reunite the knot that was slackened; yet the more she endeavoured to regain his affections, the colder did he grow,—the more intolerable did her caresses seem, and the more continually did the image of Brunhilda haunt his thoughts. The children, whose endearments were now become indispensable to him, alone stood between the parents as genii eager to affect a reconciliation; and, beloved by them both, formed a uniting link between them. Yet, as evil can be plucked from the heart of man, only ere its root has yet struck deep, its fangs being afterwards too firm to be eradicated; so was Walter's diseased fancy too far affected to have its disorder stopped, for, in a short time it completely tyrannized over him. Frequently of a night, instead of retiring to his consort's chamber, he repaired to Brunhilda's grave, where he murmured forth his discontent, saying: 'Wilt thou sleep for ever?'

One night as he was thus reclining on the turf, indulging in his wonted sorrow, a sorcerer from the neighbouring mountains, entered into this field of death for the purpose of gathering, for his mystic spells, such herbs as grow only from the earth wherein the dead repose, and which, as if the last production of mortality, are gifted with a powerful and supernatural influence. The sorcerer perceived the mourner, and approached the spot where he was lying.

'Wherefore, fond wretch, dost thou grieve thus, for what is now a hideous mass of mortality—mere bones, and nerves, and veins? Nations have fallen unlamented; even worlds themselves, long ere this globe of ours was created, have mouldered into nothing; nor hath any one wept over them; why then should thou indulge this vain affliction for a child of the dust—a being as frail as thyself, and like thee the creature but of a moment?'

Walter raised himself up:—'Let yon worlds that shine in the firmament,' replied he, 'lament for each other as they perish. It is true, that I who am myself clay, lament for my fellow-clay: yet is this clay impregnated with a fire,—with an essence, that none of the elements of creation possess—with love: and this divine passion, I felt for her who now sleepeth beneath this sod.'

'Will thy complaints awaken her: or could they do so, would she not soon upbraid thee for having disturbed that repose in which she is now hushed?'

'Avaunt, cold-hearted being: thou knowest not what is love. Oh! that my tears could wash away the earthy covering that conceals her from these eyes;—that my groan of anguish could rouse her from her slumber of death!—No, she would not again seek her earthy couch.'

'Insensate that thou art, and couldst thou endure to gaze without shuddering on one disgorged from the jaws of the grave? Art thou too thyself the same from whom she parted; or hath time passed o'er thy brow and left no traces there? Would not thy love rather be converted into hate and disgust?'

'Say rather that the stars would leave yon firmament, that the sun will henceforth refuse to shed his beams through the heavens. O that she stood once more before me;—that once again she reposed on this bosom!—how quickly should we then forget that death or time had ever stepped between us.'

'Delusion! mere delusion of the brain, from heated blood, like to that which arises from the fumes of wine. It is not my wish to tempt thee;—to restore to thee thy dead; else wouldst thou soon feel that I have spoken sooth.'*

'How! restore her to me,' exclaimed Walter casting himself at the sorcerer's feet. 'Oh! if thou art indeed able to effect that, grant it to my earnest supplication; if one throb of human feeling vibrates in thy bosom, let my tears prevail with thee: restore me my beloved; so shalt thou hereafter bless the deed, and see that it was a good work.'

'A good work! a blessed deed!'—returned the sorcerer with a smile of scorn; 'for me there exists nor good, nor evil; since my will is always the same. Ye alone know evil, who will that which ye would not. It is indeed in my power to restore her to thee: yet, bethink thee well, whether it will prove thy weal.* Consider too, how deep the abyss between life and death; across this, my power can build a bridge, but it can never fill up the frightful chasm.'

Walter would have spoken, and have sought to prevail on this powerful being by fresh entreaties, but the latter prevented him, saying: 'Peace! bethink thee well! and return hither to me to-morrow at midnight. Yet once more do I warn thee, "wake not the dead."'

Having uttered these words, the mysterious being disappeared. Intoxicated with fresh hope, Walter found no sleep on his couch; for fancy, prodigal of her richest stores, expanded before him the glittering web of futurity; and his eye, moistened with the dew of rapture, glanced from one vision of happiness to another. During the next day he wandered through the woods, lest wonted objects by recalling the memory of later and less happier times, might disturb the blissful idea, that he should again behold her—again fold her in his arms, gaze on her beaming brow by day, repose on her bosom at night: and, as this sole idea filled his imagination, how was it possible that the least doubt should arise; or that the warning of the mysterious old man should recur to his thoughts?

No sooner did the midnight hour approach, than he hastened before the grave-field where the sorcerer was already standing by that of Brunhilda. 'Hast thou maturely considered?' enquired he.

'Oh! restore to me the object of my ardent passion,' exclaimed Walter with impetuous eagerness. 'Delay not thy generous action, lest I die even this night, consumed with disappointed desire; and behold her face no more.'

'Well then,' answered the old man, 'return hither again to-morrow at the same hour. But once more do I give thee this friendly warning, "wake not the dead."'

In all the despair of impatience, Walter would have prostrated himself at his feet, and supplicated him to fulfill at once a desire now increased to agony; but the sorcerer had already disappeared. Pouring forth his lamentations more wildly and impetuously than ever, he lay upon the grave of his adored one, until the grey dawn streaked the east. During the day, which seemed to him longer than any he had ever experienced, he wandered to and fro, restless and impatient, seemingly without any object, and deeply buried in his own reflections, inquiet* as the murderer who meditates his first deed of blood: and the stars of evening found him once more at the appointed spot. At midnight the sorcerer was there also.

'Hast thou yet maturely deliberated?' enquired he, 'as on the preceding night?'

'On what should I deliberate?' returned Walter impatiently. 'I need not to deliberate: what I demand of thee, is that which thou hast promised me—that which will prove my bliss. Or dost thou but mock me? if so, hence from my sight, lest I be tempted to lay my hand on thee.'

'Once more do I warn thee,' answered the old man with undisturbed composure, "wake not the dead"—let her rest.'

'Aye, but not in the cold grave: she shall rather rest on this bosom which burns with eagerness to clasp her.'

'Reflect, thou may'st not quit her until death, even though aversion and horror should seize thy heart. There would then remain only one horrible means.'

'Dotard!' cried Walter, interrupting him, 'how may I hate that which I love with such intensity of passion? how should I abhor that for which my every drop of blood is boiling?'

'Then be it even as thou wishest,' answered the sorcerer; 'step back.'

The old man now drew a circle round the grave, all the while muttering words of enchantment. Immediately the storm began to howl among the tops of the trees; owls flapped their wings, and uttered their low voice of omen; the stars hid their mild, beaming aspect, that they might not behold so unholy and impious a spectacle; the stone then rolled from the grave with a hollow sound, leaving a free passage for the inhabitant of that dreadful tenement. The sorcerer scattered into the yawning earth, roots and herbs of most magic power, and of most penetrating odour, so that the worms crawling forth from the earth congregated together, and raised themselves in a fiery column over the grave: while rushing wind burst from the earth, scattering the mould before it, until at length the coffin lay uncovered. The moonbeams fell on it, and the lid burst open with a tremendous sound. Upon this the sorcerer poured upon it some blood from out of a human skull, exclaiming at the same time:—'Drink, sleeper, of this warm stream,* that thy heart may again beat within thy bosom.' And, after a short pause, shedding on her some other mystic liquid, he cried aloud with the voice of one inspired: 'Yes, thy heart beats once more with the flood of life: thine eye is again opened to sight. Arise, therefore, from thy tomb.'

As an island suddenly springs forth from the dark waves of the ocean, raised upwards from the deep by the force of subterraneous fires, so did Brunhilda start from her earthy couch, borne forward by some invisible power. Taking her by the hand, the sorcerer led her towards Walter, who stood at some little distance, rooted to the ground with amazement.

'Receive again,' said he, 'the object of thy passionate sighs: mayest thou never more require my aid; should that however happen, so wilt thou find me, during the full of the moon, upon the mountains in that spot and where the three roads meet.'

Instantly did Walter recognize in the form that stood before him, her whom he so ardently loved; and a sudden glow shot through his frame at finding her thus restored to him: yet the night-frost had chilled his limbs and palsied his tongue. For a while he gazed upon her without either motion or speech, and during this pause, all was again become hushed and serene; and the stars shone brightly in the clear heavens.

'Walter!' exclaimed the figure; and at once the well-known sound, thrilling to his heart, broke the spell by which he was bound.

'Is it reality? is it truth?' cried he, 'or a cheating delusion?'

'No, it is no imposture; I am really living:—conduct me quickly to thy castle in the mountains.'

Walter looked around: the old man had disappeared, but he perceived close by his side, a coal-black steed of fiery eye, ready equipped to conduct him thence; and on his back lay all proper attire for Brunhilda, who lost no time in arraying herself. This being done, she cried: 'Haste, let us away ere the dawn breaks, for my eye is yet too weak to endure the light of day.'* Fully recovered from his stupor, Walter leaped into his saddle, and catching up, with a mingled feeling of delight and awe, the beloved being thus mysteriously restored from the power of the grave, he spurred on across the wild, towards the mountains, as furiously as if pursued by the shadows of the dead, hastening to recover from him their sister.

The castle to which Walter conducted his Brunhilda, was situated on a rock between other rocks rising up above it. Here they arrived, unseen by any, save one aged domestic, on whom Walter imposed secrecy by the severest threats.

'Here will we tarry,' said Brunhilda, 'until I can endure the light, and until thou canst look upon me without trembling: as if struck with a cold chill.' They accordingly continued to make that place their abode: yet no one knew that Brunhilda existed, save only that aged attendant, who provided their meals. During seven entire days, they had no light except that of tapers; during the next seven, the light was admitted through the lofty casements only while the rising or setting-sun faintly illumined the mountain-tops, the valleys being still enveloped in shade.

Seldom did Walter quit Brunhilda's side: a nameless spell seemed to attach him to her; even the shudder which he felt in her presence, and which would not permit him to touch her, was not unmixed with pleasure, like that thrilling aweful* emotion felt when strains of sacred music float under the vault of some temple;* he rather sought, therefore, than avoided this feeling. Often too as he had indulged in calling to mind the beauties of Brunhilda, she had never appeared so fair, so fascinating, so admirable when depicted by his imagination, as when now beheld in reality. Never till now had her voice sounded with such tones of sweetness; never before did her language possess such eloquence as it now did, when she conversed with him on the subject of the past. And this was the magic fairy-land towards which her words constantly conducted him. Ever did she dwell upon the days of their first love, those hours of delight which they had participated together when the one derived all enjoyment from the other: and so rapturous, so enchanting, so full of life did she recall to his imagination that blissful season, that he even doubted whether he had ever experienced with her so much felicity, or had been so truly happy. And, while she thus vividly pourtrayed their hours of past delight, she delineated in still more glowing, more enchanting colours, those hours of approaching bliss which now awaited them, richer in enjoyment than any preceding ones. In this manner did she charm her attentive auditor with enrapturing hopes for the future, and lull him in dreams of more than mortal exstasy; so that while he listened to her syren strain, he entirely forgot how little blissful was the latter period of their union, when he had often sighed at her imperiousness, and at her harshness both to himself and all his household. Yet even had he recalled this to mind would it have disturbed him in his present delirious trance? Had she not now left behind in the grave all the frailty of mortality? Was she not cheerful as the morning hour in spring—affectionate and mild as the last beams of an autumnal sun? Was not her whole being refined and purified by that long sleep in which neither passion nor sin had approached her even in dreams? How different now was the subject of her discourse! Only when speaking of her affection for him, did she betray anything of earthly feeling: at other times, she uniformly dwelt upon themes relating to the invisible and future world; when in descanting and declaring the mysteries of eternity, a stream of prophetic eloquence would burst from her lips.

In this manner had twice seven days elapsed, and, for the first time, Walter beheld the being now dearer to him than ever, in the full light of day. Every trace of the grave had disappeared from her countenance: a roseate tinge like the ruddy streaks of dawn again beamed on her pallid cheek; the faint, mouldering taint of the grave was changed into a delightful violet scent; the only sign of earth that never disappeared.* He no longer felt either apprehension or awe, as he gazed upon her in the sunny light of day: it was not until now, that he seemed to have recovered her completely; and, glowing with all his former passion towards her, he would have pressed her to his bosom, but she gently repulsed him, saying: 'Not yet: spare your caresses until the moon has again filled her horn.'*

Spite of his impatience, Walter was obliged to await the lapse of another period of seven days; but, on the night when the moon was arrived at the full, he hastened to Brunhilda, whom he found more lovely than she had ever appeared before. Fearing no obstacles to his transports, he embraced her with all the fervour of a deeply-enamoured and successful lover. Brunhilda, however, still refused to yield to his passion. 'What!' exclaimed she, 'is it fitting that I who have been purified by death from the frailty of mortality, should become thy concubine, while a mere daughter of the earth bears the title of thy wife: never shall it be. No, it must be within the walls of thy palace, within that chamber where I once reigned as queen, that thou obtainest the end of thy wishes,—and of mine also,' added she, imprinting a glowing kiss on his lips, and immediately disappeared.

Heated with passion, and determined to sacrifice every thing to the accomplishment of his desires, Walter hastily quitted the apartment, and shortly after the castle itself. He travelled over mountain and cross heath,* with the rapidity of a storm, so that the turf was flung up by his horse's hoofs; nor once stopped until he arrived home.

Here, however, neither the affectionate caresses of Swanhilda, or those of his children could touch his heart, or induce him to restrain his furious desires. Alas! is the impetuous torrent to be checked in its devastating course by the beauteous flowers over which it rushes, when they exclaim: 'Destroyer, commiserate our helpless innocence and beauty, nor lay us waste?'—the stream sweeps over them unregarding, and a single moment annihilates the pride of a whole summer.

Shortly afterwards, did Walter begin to hint to Swanhilda, that they were ill-suited to each other;—that he was anxious to taste that wild, tumultuous life, so well according with the spirit of his sex, while she, on the contrary, was satisfied with the monotonous circle of household enjoyments:—that he was eager for whatever promised novelty, while she felt most attached to what was familiarized to her by habit; and lastly, that her cold disposition, bordering upon indifference, but ill assorted with* his ardent temperament: it was therefore more prudent that they should seek apart from each other, that happiness which they could not find together. A sigh, and a brief acquiescence in his wishes was all the reply that Swanhilda made: and, on the following morning upon his presenting her with a paper of separation, informing her that she was at liberty to return home to her father, she received it most submissively: yet, ere she departed, she gave him the following warning: 'Too well do I conjecture to whom I am indebted for this our separation. Often have I seen thee at Brunhilda's grave, and beheld thee there even on that night when the face of the heavens was suddenly enveloped in a veil of clouds. Hast thou rashly dared to tear aside the awful veil that separates the mortality that dreams, from that which dreameth not? O! then woe to thee, thou wretched man, for thou hast attached to thyself that which will prove thy destruction.' She ceased: nor did Walter attempt any reply, for the similar admonition uttered by the sorcerer flashed upon his mind, all obscured as it was by passion, just as the lightning glares momentarily through the gloom of night without dispersing the obscurity.

Swanhilda then departed, in order to pronounce to her children, a bitter farewell, for they, according to the custom of his nation, belonged to the father; and, having bathed them in her tears, and consecrated them with the holy water of maternal love, she quitted her husband's residence, and departed to the home of her fathers.

Thus was the kind and benevolent Swanhilda, driven an exile from those halls, where she had presided with such grace;—from halls which were now newly decorated to receive another mistress. The day at length arrived, on which Walter, for the second time, conducted Brunhilda home, as a newly-made bride. And he caused it to be reported among his domestics, that his new consort had gained his affections by her extraordinary likeness to Brunhilda, their former mistress. How ineffably happy did he deem himself, as he conducted his beloved once more into the chamber which had often witnessed their former joys, and which was now newly gilded and adorned in a most costly style: among the other decorations were figures of angels scattering roses, which served to support the purple draperies, whose ample folds o'ershadowed the nuptial couch. With what impatience did he await the hour that was to put him in possession of those beauties, for which he had already paid so high a price, but, whose enjoyment was to cost him most dearly yet! Unfortunate Walter! revelling in bliss, thou beholdest not the abyss that yawns beneath thy feet, intoxicated with the luscious perfume of the flower thou hast plucked, thou little deemest how deadly is the venom with which it is fraught, although, for a short season, its potent fragrance bestows new energy on all thy feelings.

Happy however, as Walter was now, his household were far from being equally so. The strange resemblance between their new lady and the deceased Brunhilda, filled them with a secret dismay,—an undefinable horror; for there was not a single difference of feature, of tone of voice, or of gesture. To add too to these mysterious circumstances, her female attendants discovered a particular mark on her back, exactly like one which Brunhilda had. A report was now soon circulated, that their lady was no other than Brunhilda herself, who had been recalled to life by the power of necromancy. How truly horrible was the idea of living under the same roof with one who had been an inhabitant of the tomb, and of being obliged to attend upon her, and acknowledge her as mistress! There was also in Brunhilda, much to increase this aversion, and favour their superstition: no ornaments of gold ever decked her person; all that others were wont to wear of this metal, she had formed of silver:* no richly coloured, and sparkling jewels glittered upon her; pearls* alone, lent their pale lustre to adorn her bosom. Most carefully did she always avoid the cheerful light of the sun, and was wont to spend the brightest days in the most retired and gloomy apartments: only during the twilight of the commencing, or declining day did she ever walk abroad, but her favourite hour was, when the phantom light of the moon bestowed on all objects a shadowy appearance, and a sombre hue; always too at the crowing of the cock,* an involuntary shudder was observed to seize her limbs. Imperious as before her death, she quickly imposed her iron yoke on every one around her, while she seemed even far more terrible than ever, since a dread of some supernatural power attached to her, appalled all who approached her. A malignant withering glance seemed to shoot from her eye* on the unhappy object of her wrath, as if it would annihilate its victim. In short, those halls which, in the time of Swanhilda were the residence of cheerfulness and mirth, now resembled an extensive desert tomb. With fear imprinted on their pale countenances, the domestics glided through the apartments of the castle; and, in this abode of terror, the crowing of the cock caused the living to tremble, as if they were the spirits of the departed; for the sound always reminded them of their mysterious mistress. There was no one but who shuddered at meeting her in a lonely place, in the dusk of evening, or by the light of the moon, a circumstance that was deemed to be ominous of some evil: so great was the apprehension of her female attendants, that they pined in continual disquietude, and, by degrees, all quitted her. In the course of time even others of the domestics fled, for an insupportable horror had seized them.

The art of the sorcerer had indeed bestowed upon Brunhilda an artificial life, and due nourishment had continued to support the restored body: yet, this body was not able of itself to keep up the genial glow of vitality, and to nourish the flame whence springs all the affections and passions, whether of love or hate; for death had for ever destroyed and withered it: all that Brunhilda now possessed was a chilled existence, colder than that of the snake. It was nevertheless necessary that she should love, and return with equal ardour the warm caresses of her spell-enthralled husband, to whose passion alone she was indebted for her renewed existence. It was necessary that a magic draught should animate the dull current in her veins, and awaken her to the glow of life and the flame of love—a potion of abomination—one not even to be named without a curse—human blood, imbibed whilst yet warm, from the veins of youth. This was the hellish drink for which she thirsted: possessing no sympathy with the purer feelings of humanity; deriving no enjoyment from aught that interests in life, and occupies its varied hours; her existence was a mere blank, unless when in the arms of her paramour husband, and therefore was it that she craved incessantly after the horrible draught. It was even with the utmost effort that she could forbear sucking even the blood of Walter himself, as he reclined beside her. Whenever she beheld some innocent child, whose lovely face denoted the exuberance of infantine* health and vigour, she would entice it by soothing words and fond caresses into her most secret apartment, where, lulling it to sleep in her arms, she would suck from its bosom the warm, purple tide of life. Nor were youths of either sex safe from her horrid attack: having first breathed upon her unhappy victim, who never failed immediately to sink into a lengthened sleep, she would then in a similar manner drain his veins of the vital juice. Thus children, youths, and maidens quickly faded away, as flowers gnawn by the cankering worm: the fullness of their limbs disappeared; a sallow hue succeeded to the rosy freshness of their cheeks, the liquid lustre of the eye was deadened, even as the sparkling stream when arrested by the touch of frost; and their locks became thin and grey, as if already ravaged by the storm of life. Parents beheld with horror this desolating pestilence* devouring their offspring; nor could simple* or charm, potion or amulet avail aught against it. The grave swallowed up one after the other; or did the miserable victim survive, he became cadaverous and wrinkled even in the very morn of existence. Parents observed with horror, this devastating pestilence snatch away their offspring—a pestilence which, nor herb however potent, nor charm, nor holy taper, nor exorcism could avert. They either beheld their children sink one after the other into the grave, or their youthful forms withered by the unholy, vampire embrace of Brunhilda, assume the decrepitude of sudden age.

At length strange surmises and reports began to prevail; it was whispered that Brunhilda herself was the cause of all these horrors; although no one could pretend to tell in what manner she destroyed her victims, since no marks of violence were discernible. Yet when young children confessed that she had frequently lulled them asleep in her arms, and elder ones said that a sudden slumber had come upon them whenever she began to converse with them, suspicion became converted into certainty, and those whose offspring had hitherto escaped unharmed, quitted their hearths and home—all their little possessions—the dwellings of their fathers and the inheritance of their children, in order to rescue from so horrible a fate those who were dearer to their simple affections than aught else the world could give.

Thus did the castle daily assume a more desolate appearance; daily did its environs become more deserted: none but a few aged decrepit old women and grey-headed menials were to be seen remaining of the once numerous retinue. Such will, in the latter days of the earth, be the last generation of mortals, when child-bearing shall have ceased, when youth shall no more be seen, nor any arise to replace those who shall await their fate in silence.

Walter alone noticed not, or heeded not, the desolation around him; he apprehended not death, lapped as he was in a glowing elysium of love. Far more happy than formerly did he now seem in the possession of Brunhilda. All those caprices and frowns which had been wont to overcloud their former union had now entirely disappeared. She even seemed to dote on him with a warmth of passion that she had never exhibited even during the happy season of bridal love; for the flame of that youthful blood, of which she drained the veins of others, rioted in her own. At night, as soon as he closed his eyes, she would breathe on him till he sank into delicious dreams, from which he awoke only to experience more rapturous enjoyments. By day she would continually discourse with him on the bliss experienced by happy spirits beyond the grave, assuring them* that, as his affection had recalled her from the tomb, they were now irrevocably united. Thus fascinated by a continual spell, it was not possible that he should perceive what was taking place around him. Brunhilda, however, foresaw with savage grief that the source of her youthful ardour was daily decreasing, for, in a short time, there remained nothing gifted with youth, save Walter and his children, and these latter she resolved should be her next victims.*

On her first return to the castle, she had felt an aversion towards the offspring of another, and therefore abandoned them entirely to the attendants appointed by Swanhilda. Now, however, she began to pay considerable attention to them, and caused them to be frequently admitted into her presence. The aged nurses were filled with dread at perceiving these marks of regard from her towards their young charges, yet dared they not to oppose the will of their terrible and imperious mistress. Soon did Brunhilda gain the affection of the children, who were too unsuspecting of all guile to apprehend any danger from her; on the contrary, her caresses won them completely to her. Instead of ever checking their mirthful gambols, she would rather instruct them in new sports; often too did she recite to them tales of such strange and wild interest as to exceed all the stories of their nurses. Were they wearied either with play or with listening to her narratives, she would take them on her knees and lull them to slumber. Then did visions of the most surpassing magnificence attend their dreams:* they would fancy themselves in some garden, where flowers of every hue rose in rows one above the other, from the humble violet to the tall sun-flower, forming a party-coloured broidery* of every hue, sloping upwards towards the golden clouds, where little angels, whose wings sparkled with azure and gold, descended to bring them delicious cates* or splendid jewels; or sung to them soothing melodious hymns. So delightful did these dreams in short time become to the children, that they longed for nothing so eagerly as to slumber on Brunhilda's lap, for never did they else enjoy such visions of heavenly forms. Thus were they most anxious for that which was to prove their destruction:—yet do we not all aspire after that which conducts us to the grave—after the enjoyment of life? These innocents stretched out their arms to approaching death, because it assumed the mask of pleasure; for, while they were lapped in these exstatic slumbers, Brunhilda sucked the life-stream from their bosoms. On waking, indeed, they felt themselves faint and exhausted, yet did no pain, nor any mark betray the cause. Shortly, however, did their strength entirely fail, even as the summer brook is gradually dried up: their sports became less and less noisy; their loud, frolicsome laughter was converted into a faint smile; the full tones of their voices died away into a mere whisper. Their attendants were filled with horror and despair; too well did they conjecture the dreadful truth, yet dared not to impart their suspicions to Walter, who was so devotedly attached to his horrible partner. Death had already smote his prey: the children were but the mere shadows of their former selves, and even this shadow quickly disappeared.

The anguished father deeply bemoaned their loss, for, notwithstanding his apparent neglect, he was strongly attached to them, nor until he had experienced their loss, was he aware that his love was so great. His affliction could not fail to excite the displeasure of Brunhilda: 'Why dost thou lament so fondly,' said she, 'for these little ones? What satisfaction could such unformed beings yield to thee, unless thou wert still attached to their mother? Thy heart then is still hers? Or dost thou now regret her and them, because thou art satiated with my fondness, and weary of my endearments? Had these young ones grown up, would they not have attached thee, thy spirit and thy affections more closely to this earth of clay—to this dust, and have alienated thee from that sphere to which I, who have already passed the grave, endeavour to raise thee? Say is thy spirit so lumpish, or thy love so weak, or thy faith so hollow, that the hope of being mine for ever is unable to touch thee?' Thus did Brunhilda express her indignation at her consort's grief, and forbade him her presence. The fear of offending her beyond forgiveness, and his anxiety to appease her soon dried up his tears; and he again abandoned himself to his fatal passion, until approaching destruction, at length awakened him from his delusion.

Neither maiden, nor youth, was any longer to be seen, either within the dreary walls of the castle, or the adjoining territory:—all had disappeared; for those whom the grave had not swallowed up, had fled from the region of death. Who, therefore, now remained to quench the horrible thirst of the female vampire, save Walter himself? and his death she dared to contemplate unmoved; for that divine sentiment that unites two beings in one joy and one sorrow was unknown to her bosom. Was he in his tomb, so was she free to search out other victims, and glut herself with destruction, until she herself should, at the last day, be consumed with the earth itself: such is the fatal law, to which the dead are subject, when awoke by the arts of necromancy from the sleep of the grave.

She now began to fix her blood-thirsty lips on Walter's breast, when cast into a profound sleep by the odour of her violet breath, he reclined beside her quite unconscious of his impending fate: yet soon did his vital powers begin to decay; and many a grey hair peeped through his raven locks. With his strength, his passion also declined; and he now frequently left her in order to pass the whole day in the sports of the chase,* hoping thereby, to regain his wonted vigour. As he was reposing one day in a wood beneath the shade of an oak, he perceived, on the summit of a tree, a bird of strange appearance, and quite unknown to him; but, before he could take aim at it with his bow, it flew away into the clouds; at the same time, letting fall a rose-coloured root which dropped at Walter's feet, who immediately took it up, and, although he was well acquainted with almost every plant, he could not remember to have seen any at all resembling this. Its delightfully odoriferous scent induced him to try its flavour, but ten times more bitter than wormwood, it was even as gall in his mouth; upon which, impatient of the disappointment, he flung it away with violence. Had he, however, been aware of its miraculous quality, and that it acted as a counter-charm against the opiate perfume of Brunhilda's breath, he would have blessed it in spite of its bitterness: thus do mortals often blindly cast away in displeasure, the unsavoury remedy that would otherwise work their weal.

When Walter returned home in the evening, and laid him down to repose as usual by Brunhilda's side, the magic power of her breath produced no effect upon him; and, for the first time during many months did he close his eyes in a natural slumber. Yet hardly had he fallen asleep, ere a pungent,* smarting pain disturbed him from his dreams; and, opening his eyes, he discerned, by the gloomy rays of a lamp, that glimmered in the apartment, what for some moments transfixed him quite aghast, for it was Brunhilda, drawing with her lips, the warm blood from his bosom. The wild cry of horror which at length escaped him, terrified Brunhilda, whose mouth was besmeared with the warm blood. 'Monster!' exclaimed he, springing from the couch, 'is it thus that you love me?'

'Aye, even as the dead love,' replied she, with a malignant coldness.

'Creature of blood!' continued Walter, 'the delusion which has so long blinded me is at an end: thou art the fiend who hast destroyed my children—who hast murdered the offspring of my vassals.' Raising herself upwards, and, at the same time, casting on him a glance that froze him to the spot with dread, she replied: 'It is not I who have murdered them:—I was obliged to pamper* myself with warm youthful blood, in order that I might satisfy thy furious desires—thou art the murderer!'—These dreadful words summoned, before Walter's terrified conscience, the threatening shades of all those who had thus perished; while despair choked his voice. 'Why,' continued she, in a tone that increased his horror, 'why dost thou make mouths at me like a puppet?* Thou who hadst the courage to love the dead—to take into thy bed, one who had been sleeping in the grave, the bed-fellow of the worm—who hast clasped in thy lustful arms, the corruption of the tomb—dost thou, unhallowed as thou art, now raise this hideous cry for the sacrifice of a few lives?—They are but leaves swept from their branches by a storm.—Come, chase these ideot* fancies, and taste the bliss thou hast so dearly purchased.' So saying, she extended her arms towards him; but this motion served only to increase his terror, and exclaiming: 'Accursed Being,'—he rushed out of the apartment.

All the horrors of a guilty, upbraiding conscience became his companions, now that he was awakened from the delirium of his unholy pleasures. Frequently did he curse his own obstinate blindness, for having given no heed to the hints and admonitions of his children's nurses, but treating them as vile calumnies. But his sorrow was now too late, for, although repentance may gain pardon for the sinner, it cannot alter the immutable decrees of fate—it cannot recall the murdered from the tomb. No sooner did the first break of dawn appear, than he set out for his lonely castle in the mountains, determined no longer to abide under the same roof with so terrific* a being; yet vain was his flight, for, on waking the following morning, he perceived himself in Brunhilda's arms, and quite entangled in her long raven tresses, which seemed to involve him, and bind him in the fetters of his fate; the powerful fascination of her breath held him still more captivated, so that, forgetting all that had passed, he returned her caresses, until awakening as if from a dream he recoiled in unmixed horror from her embrace. During the day he wandered through the solitary wilds of the mountains, as a culprit seeking an asylum from his pursuers; and, at night, retired to the shelter of a cave; fearing less to couch himself within such a dreary place, than to expose himself to the horror of again meeting Brunhilda; but; alas! it was in vain that he endeavoured to flee her. Again, when he awoke, he found her the partner of his miserable bed. Nay, had he sought the centre of the earth as his hiding place; had he even imbedded himself beneath rocks, or formed his chamber in the recesses of the ocean, still had he found her his constant companion; for, by calling her again into existence, he had rendered himself inseparably hers; so fatal were the links that united them.

Struggling with the madness that was beginning to seize him, and brooding incessantly on the ghastly visions that presented themselves to his horror-stricken mind, he lay motionless in the gloomiest recesses of the woods, even from the rise of sun till the shades of eve. But, no sooner was the light of day extinguished in the west, and the woods buried in impenetrable darkness, than the apprehension of resigning himself to sleep drove him forth among the open mountains. The storm played wildly with the fantastic clouds, and with the rattling leaves, as they were caught up into the air, as if some dread spirit was sporting with these images of transitoriness and decay: it roared among the summits of the oaks as if uttering a voice of fury, while its hollow sound rebounding among the distant hills, seemed as the moans of a departing sinner, or as the faint cry of some wretch expiring under the murderer's hand: the owl too, uttered its ghastly cry as if foreboding the wreck of nature. Walter's hair flew disorderly in the wind, like black snakes wreathing around his temples and shoulders; while each sense was awake to catch fresh horror. In the clouds he seemed to behold the forms of the murdered; in the howling wind to hear their laments and groans; in the chilling blast itself he felt the dire kiss of Brunhilda; in the cry of the screeching bird he heard her voice; in the mouldering leaves he scented the charnel-bed out of which he had awakened her. 'Murderer of thy own offspring,' exclaimed he in a voice making night, and the conflict of the element still more hideous, 'paramour of a blood-thirsty vampire, reveller with the corruption of the tomb!' while in his despair he rent the wild locks from his head. Just then the full moon darted from beneath the bursting clouds; and this sight recalled to his remembrance the advice of the sorcerer, when he trembled at the first apparition of Brunhilda rising from her sleep of death;—namely, to seek him, at the season of the full moon, in the mountains, where three roads met. Scarcely had this gleam of hope broke in on his bewildered mind than he flew to the appointed spot.

On his arrival, Walter found the old man seated there upon a stone, as calmly as though it had been a bright sunny day, and completely regardless of the uproar around. 'Art thou come then?' exclaimed he to the breathless wretch, who, flinging himself at his feet, cried in a tone of anguish: 'Oh save me—succour me—rescue me from the monster that scattereth death and desolation around her.'

'I am acquainted with all,' returned the sorcerer; 'thou now perceivest how wholesome was the advice—"WAKE NOT THE DEAD."'

'And wherefore a mere mysterious warning? why didst thou not rather disclose to me, at once, all the horrors that awaited my sacrilegious profanation of the grave?'

'Wert thou able to listen to any other voice than that of thy impetuous passions? Did not thy eager impatience shut my mouth at the very moment I would have cautioned thee?'

'True, true:—thy reproof is just: but what does it avail now;—I need the promptest aid.'

'Well,' replied the old man, 'there remains even yet a means of rescuing thyself, but it is fraught with horror, and demands all thy resolution.'

'Utter it then, utter it; for what can be more appalling, more hideous than the misery I now endure?'

'Know then,' continued the sorcerer, 'that only on the night of the new moon, does she sleep the sleep of mortals; and then all the supernatural power which she inherits from the grave totally fails her. 'Tis then that thou must murder her.'

'How! murder her!' echoed Walter.

'Aye,' returned the old man calmly, 'pierce her bosom with a sharpened dagger,* which I will furnish thee with; at the same time renounce her memory for ever, swearing* never to think of her intentionally, and that, if thou dost involuntarily, thou wilt repeat the curse.'

'Most horrible!* yet what can be more horrible than she herself is?—I'll do it.'*

'Keep then this resolution until the next new moon.'

'What, must I wait until then?' cried Walter, 'alas ere then, either her savage thirst for blood will have forced me into the night of the tomb, or horror will have driven me into the night of madness.'

'Nay,' replied the sorcerer, 'that I can prevent;' and, so saying, he conducted him to a cavern further among the mountains. 'Abide here twice seven days,' said he; 'so long can I protect thee against her deadly caresses. Here wilt thou find all due provision for thy wants; but take heed that nothing tempt thee to quit this place. Farewell, when the moon renews itself, then do I repair hither again.' So saying, the sorcerer drew a magic circle around the cave, and then immediately disappeared.

Twice seven days did Walter continue in this solitude, where his companions were his own terrifying thoughts, and his bitter repentance. The present was all desolation and dread; the future presented the image of a horrible deed, which he must perforce commit; while the past was empoisoned* by the memory of his guilt. Did he think on his former happy union with Brunhilda, her horrible image presented itself to his imagination with her lips defiled with dropping blood: or, did he call to mind the peaceful days he had passed with Swanhilda, he beheld her sorrowful spirit, with the shadows of her murdered children. Such were the horrors that attended him by day: those of night were still more dreadful, for then he beheld Brunhilda herself, who, wandering round the magic circle which she could not pass, called upon his name, till the cavern re-echoed the horrible sound. 'Walter, my beloved,' cried she, 'wherefore dost thou avoid me? art thou not mine? for ever mine—mine here, and mine hereafter? And dost thou seek to murder me?—ah! commit not a deed which hurls us both to perdition—thyself as well as me.' In this manner did the horrible visitant torment him each night, and, even when she departed, robbed him of all repose.

The night of the new moon at length arrived, dark as the deed it was doomed to bring forth. The sorcerer entered the cavern; 'Come,' said he to Walter, 'let us depart hence, the hour is now arrived:' and he forthwith conducted him in silence from the cave* to a coal-black steed, the sight of which recalled to Walter's remembrance the fatal night. He then related to the old man Brunhilda's nocturnal visits, and anxiously inquired whether her apprehensions of eternal perdition would be fulfilled or not. 'Mortal eye,' exclaimed the sorcerer, 'may not pierce the dark secrets of another world, or penetrate the deep abyss that separates earth from heaven.' Walter hesitated to mount the steed. 'Be resolute,' exclaimed his companion, 'but this once is it granted to thee to make the trial, and, should thou fail now, nought can rescue thee from her power.'

'What can be more horrible than she herself?—I am determined:' and he leaped on the horse, the sorcerer mounting also behind him.

Carried with a rapidity equal to that of the storm that sweeps across the plain, they in brief space arrived at Walter's castle. All the doors flew open at the bidding of his companion, and they speedily reached Brunhilda's chamber, and stood beside her couch. Reclining in a tranquil slumber; she reposed in all her native loveliness, every trace of horror had disappeared from her countenance; she looked so pure, meek and innocent that all the sweet hours of their endearments rushed to Walter's memory, like interceding angels pleading in her behalf. His unnerved* hand could not take the dagger which the sorcerer presented to him. 'The blow must be struck even now:' said the latter, 'shouldst thou delay but an hour, she will lie at day-break on thy bosom, sucking the warm life-drops from thy heart.'

'Horrible! most horrible!' faultered the trembling Walter, and turning away his face, he thrust the dagger into her bosom, exclaiming: 'I curse thee for ever!'—and the cold blood gushed upon his hand. Opening her eyes once more, she cast a look of ghastly horror on her husband, and, in a hollow dying accent said:—'Thou too art doomed to perdition.'

'Lay now thy hand upon her corse,'* said the sorcerer, 'and swear the oath.'—Walter did as commanded, saying,—'Never will I think of her with love, never recall her to mind intentionally, and, should her image recur to my mind involuntarily, so will I exclaim to it: be thou accursed.'

'Thou hast now done everything,' returned the sorcerer;—'restore her therefore to the earth, from which thou so foolishly recalled her; and be sure to recollect thy oath: for, shouldst thou forget it but once, she would return, and thou wouldst be inevitably lost. Adieu: we see each other no more.' Having uttered these words he quitted the apartment, and Walter also fled from this abode of horror, having first given direction that the corse should be speedily interred.

Again did the terrific Brunhilda repose within her grave; but her image continually haunted Walter's imagination, so that his existence was one continued martyrdom, in which he continually struggled, to dismiss from his recollection the hideous phantoms of the past; yet, the stronger his effort to banish them, so much the more frequently and the more vividly did they return; as the night-wanderer, who is enticed by a fire-wisp* into quagmire or bog, sinks the deeper into his damp grave the more he struggles to escape. His imagination seemed incapable of admitting any other image than that of Brunhilda: now he fancied he beheld her expiring, the blood streaming from her beautiful bosom: at others he saw the lovely bride of his youth, who reproached him with having disturbed the slumbers of her tomb: and to both he was compelled to utter the dreadful words, 'I curse thee for ever.' The terrible imprecation was constantly passing his lips; yet was he in incessant terror lest he should forget it, or dream of her without being able to repeat it, and then, on awaking, find himself in her arms. Else would he recall her expiring words, and, appalled at their terrific import, imagine that the doom of his perdition was irrecoverably passed. Whence should he fly from himself? or how erase from his brain these images and forms of horror? In the din of combat, in the tumult of war and its incessant pour* of victory to defeat; from the cry of anguish to the exultation of victory—in these he hoped to find at least the relief of distraction: but here too he was disappointed. The giant fang of apprehension now seized him who had never before known fear: each drop of blood that sprayed upon him seemed the cold blood that had gushed from Brunhilda's wound; each dying wretch that fell beside him looked like her, when expiring, she exclaimed,—'Thou too art doomed to perdition,' so that the aspect of death seemed more full of dread to him than aught beside, and this unconquerable terror compelled him to abandon the battle-field. At length, after many a weary and fruitless wandering he returned to his castle. Here all was deserted and silent, as if the sword, or a still more deadly pestilence had laid everything waste: for the few inhabitants that still remained, and even those servants who had once shewn themselves the most attached, now fled from him, as though he had been branded with the mark of Cain.* With horror he perceived that, by uniting himself as he had done with the dead, he had cut himself off from the living, who refused to hold any intercourse with him. Often, when he stood on the battlements of his castle, and looked down upon desolate fields, he compared their present solitude with the lively activity they were wont to exhibit, under the strict but benevolent discipline of Swanhilda. He now felt that she alone could reconcile him to life, but durst he hope that one, whom he so deeply aggrieved, could pardon him, and receive him again? Impatience at length got the better of fear; he sought Swanhilda, and, with the deepest contrition, acknowledged his complicated* guilt; embracing her knees as he beseeched her to pardon him, and to return to his desolate castle, in order that it might again become the abode of contentment and peace. The pale form which she beheld at her feet, the shadow of the lately blooming youth, touched Swanhilda. 'Thy folly,' said she gently, 'though it has caused me much sorrow, has never excited my resentment or my anger. But say, where are my children?' To this dreadful interrogation the agonized father could for a while frame no reply: at length he was obliged to confess the dreadful truth. 'Then we are asundered for ever,' returned Swanhilda; nor could all his tears or supplications prevail upon her to revoke the sentence she had given.

Stripped of his last earthly hope, bereft of his last consolation, and thereby rendered as poor as mortal can possibly be on this side of the grave, Walter returned homewards; when, as he was riding through the forest in the neighbourhood of his castle, absorbed in his gloomy meditations, the sudden sound of a horn roused him from his reverie. Shortly after he saw appear a female figure clad in black, and mounted on a steed of the same colour: her attire was like that of a huntress, but, instead of a falcon she bore a raven* in her hand; and she was attended by a gay troop of cavaliers and dames. The first salutations being passed, he found that she was proceeding the same road as himself; and, when she found that Walter's castle was close at hand, she requested that he would lodge her for that night, the evening being far advanced. Most willingly did he comply with this request, since the appearance of the beautiful stranger had struck him greatly; so wonderfully did she resemble Swanhilda, except that her locks were brown, and her eye dark and full of fire. With a sumptuous banquet did he entertain his guests, whose mirth and songs enlivened the lately silent halls. Three days did this revelry continue, and so exhilarating did it prove to Walter, that he seemed to have forgotten his sorrows and his fears; nor could he prevail upon himself to dismiss his visitors, dreading lest, on their departure, the castle would seem a hundred times more desolate than before, and his grief be proportionably increased. At his earnest request, the stranger consented to stay seven days, and again another seven days. Without being requested, she took upon herself the superintendence of the household, which she regulated as discreetly and cheerfully as Swanhilda had been wont to do, so that the castle, which had so lately been the abode of melancholy and horror, became the residence of pleasure and festivity, and Walter's grief disappeared altogether in the midst of so much gaiety. Daily did his attachment to the fair unknown increase; he even made her his confidant; and, one evening as they were walking together apart from any of her train, he related to her his melancholy and frightful history. 'My dear friend,' returned she, as soon as he had finished his tale, 'it ill beseems a man of thy discretion to afflict thyself, on account of all this. Thou hast awakened the dead from the sleep of the grave, and afterwards found,—what might have been anticipated, that the dead possess no sympathy with life. What then? thou wilt not commit this error a second time. Thou hast however murdered the being whom thou hadst thus recalled again into existence—but it was only in appearance, for thou couldst not deprive that of life, which properly had none. Thou hast too, lost a wife and two children: but, at your years, such a loss is most easily repaired. There are beauties who will gladly share your couch, and make you again a father. But you dread the reckoning of hereafter:—go, open the graves and ask the sleepers there whether that hereafter disturbs them.' In such manner would she frequently exhort and cheer Walter, and, so successful were her efforts, that, in a short time, his melancholy entirely disappeared. He now ventured to declare to the unknown the passion with which she had inspired him, nor did she refuse him her hand. Within seven days afterwards the nuptials were celebrated with the utmost magnificence: with the first dawn of day commenced the labours of those who were busied in preparing the festival; and, if the walls of the castle had often echoed before to the sounds of mirth and revelry, the very foundations now seemed to rock from the wild tumultuous uproar of unrestrained riot.* The wine streamed in abundance; the goblets circled incessantly; intemperance reached its utmost bounds, while shouts of laughter, almost resembling madness, burst from the numerous train belonging to the unknown. At length Walter, heated with wine and love, conducted his bride into the nuptial chamber: but, oh horror! scarcely had he clasped her in his arms, ere she transformed herself into a monstrous serpent, which, entwining him in its horrid folds, crushed him to death. Flames crackled* on every side of the apartment; in a few minutes after, the whole castle was enveloped in a blaze that consumed it entirely: while, as the walls fell in with a horrid crash, a voice exclaimed aloud—WAKE NOT THE DEAD.

EDGAR ALLAN POE

LIGEIA

> And the will therein lieth, which dieth not. Who knoweth the mysteries of the will, with its vigor? For God is but a great will pervading all things by nature of its intentness. Man doth not yield himself to the angels, nor unto death utterly, save only through the weakness of his feeble will.
>
> *Joseph Glanvill**

I CANNOT, for my soul, remember how, when, or even precisely where, I first became acquainted with the Lady Ligeia.* Long years have since elapsed, and my memory is feeble through much suffering. Or, perhaps, I cannot *now* bring these points to mind, because, in truth, the character of my beloved, her rare learning, her singular yet placid cast of beauty, and the thrilling and enthralling eloquence of her low, musical language, made their way into my heart by paces so steadily and stealthily progressive, that they have been unnoticed and unknown. Yet I believe that I met her most frequently in some large, old, decaying city near the Rhine.* Of her family—I have surely heard her speak—that they are of a remotely ancient date cannot be doubted. Ligeia! Buried in studies of a nature more than all else adapted to deaden impressions of the outward world, it is by that sweet word alone—by Ligeia—that I bring before mine eyes in fancy the image of her who is no more. And now, while I write, a recollection flashes upon me that I have *never known* the paternal name of her who was my friend and my betrothed, and who became the partner of my studies, and eventually the wife of my bosom. Was it a playful charge on the part of my Ligeia? or was it a test of my strength of affection that I should institute no inquiries upon this point? or was it rather a caprice of my own—a wildly romantic offering on the shrine of the most passionate devotion? I but indistinctly recall the fact itself—what wonder that I have utterly forgotten the circumstances which originated or attended it? And, indeed, if ever that spirit which is entitled *Romance*—if ever she, the wan, and the misty-winged *Ashtophet** of idolatrous Egypt, presided, as they tell, over marriages ill-omened, then most surely she presided over mine.

There is one dear topic, however, on which my memory faileth me not. It is the person of Ligeia. In stature she was tall, somewhat slender, and in her latter days even emaciated. I would in vain attempt to portray the majesty, the quiet ease, of her demeanor, or the incomprehensible lightness and elasticity of her footfall. She came and departed like a shadow. I was never made aware of her entrance into my closed study save by the dear music of her low sweet voice, as she placed her delicate hand upon my shoulder. In beauty of face no maiden ever equalled her. It was the radiance of an opium dream—an airy and spirit-lifting vision more wildly divine than the phantasies which hovered about the slumbering souls of the daughters of Delos.* Yet her features were not of that regular mould which we have been falsely taught to worship in the classical labors of the heathen. 'There is no exquisite beauty,' says Bacon, Lord Verülam,* speaking truly of all the forms and *genera* of beauty, 'without some *strangeness* in the proportions.'* Yet, although I saw that the features of Ligeia were not of classic regularity, although I perceived that her loveliness was indeed 'exquisite,' and felt that there was much of 'strangeness' pervading it, yet I have tried in vain to detect the irregularity, and to trace home my own perception of 'the strange.' I examined the contour of the lofty and pale forehead—it was faultless—how cold indeed that word when applied to a majesty so divine!—the skin rivalling the purest ivory, the commanding extent and repose, the gentle prominence of the regions above the temples, and then the raven-black, the glossy, the luxuriant and naturally-curling tresses, setting forth the full force of the Homeric epithet, 'hyacinthine!'* I looked at the delicate outlines of the nose—and nowhere but in the graceful medallions of the Hebrews had I beheld a similar perfection. There was the same luxurious smoothness of surface, the same scarcely perceptible tendency to the aquiline, the same harmoniously curved nostril speaking the free spirit. I regarded the sweet mouth. Here was indeed the triumph of all things heavenly—the magnificent turn of the short upper lip—the soft, voluptuous slumber of the under—the dimples which sported, and the color which spoke—the teeth glancing back, with a brilliancy almost startling, every ray of the holy light which fell upon them in her serene, and placid, yet most exultingly radiant of all smiles. I scrutinized the formation of the chin—and here, too, I found the gentleness of breadth, the softness and the majesty, the fulness and the spirituality, of the Greek,—the contour which the god Apollo revealed but in a dream, to Cleomenes, the son of the Athenian.* And then I peered into the large eyes of Ligeia.

For eyes we have no models in the remotely antique. It might have been, too, that in these eyes of my beloved lay the secret to which Lord Verülam alludes. They were, I must believe, far larger than the ordinary eyes of our race.* They were even far fuller than the fullest of the Gazelle* eyes of the tribe of the valley of Nourjahad.* Yet it was only at intervals—in moments of intense excitement—that this peculiarity became more than slightly noticeable in Ligeia. And at such moments was her beauty—in my heated fancy thus it appeared perhaps—the beauty of beings either above or apart from the earth—the beauty of the fabulous Houri* of the Turk. The color of the orbs was the most brilliant of black, and far over them hung jetty lashes* of great length. The brows, slightly irregular in outline, had the same hue. The 'strangeness,' however, which I found in the eyes was of a nature distinct from the formation, or the color, or the brilliancy of the features, and must, after all, be referred to the *expression*. Ah, word of no meaning! behind whose vast latitude of mere sound we intrench our ignorance of so much of the spiritual. The expression of the eyes of Ligeia! How, for long hours have I pondered upon it! How have I, through the whole of a midsummer night, struggled to fathom it! What was it—that something more profound* than the well of Democritus*—which lay far within the pupils of my beloved? What *was* it? I was possessed with a passion to discover. Those eyes! those large, those shining, those divine orbs! they became to me twin stars of Leda,* and I to them devoutest of astrologers. Not for a moment was the unfathomable meaning of their glance, by day or by night, absent from my soul.*

There is no point, among the many incomprehensible anomalies of the science of mind, more thrillingly exciting than the fact—never, I believe, noticed in the schools—that in our endeavors to recall to memory something long forgotten we often find ourselves *upon the very verge* of remembrance without being able, in the end, to remember. And thus, how frequently, in my intense scrutiny of Ligeia's eyes, have I felt approaching the full knowledge of the secret of their expression—felt it approaching—yet not quite be mine—and so at length entirely depart. And (strange, oh strangest mystery of all!) I found, in the commonest objects of the universe, a circle of analogies to that expression. I mean to say that, subsequently to the period when Ligeia's beauty passed into my spirit, there dwelling as in a shrine, I derived, from many existences in the material world, a sentiment such as I felt always aroused within me by her large and luminous orbs. Yet not the more could I define that sentiment, or analyze, or even steadily view it. I recognized it, let me repeat, sometimes in the commonest objects of the universe. It has flashed upon me in the survey of a rapidly-growing vine—in the contemplation of a moth, a butterfly, a chrysalis, a stream of running water. I have felt it in the ocean, in the falling of a meteor. I have felt it in the glances of unusually aged people. And there are one or two stars in heaven—(one especially, a star of the sixth magnitude, double and changeable, to be found near the large star in Lyra*) in a telescopic scrutiny of which I have been made aware of the feeling. I have been filled with it by certain sounds from stringed instruments, and not unfrequently by passages from books. Among innumerable other instances, I well remember something in a volume of Joseph Glanvill, which (perhaps merely from its quaintness—who shall say?) never failed to inspire me with the sentiment,—'And the will therein lieth, which dieth not. Who knoweth the mysteries of the will, with its vigor? For God is but a great will pervading all things by nature of its intentness. Man doth not yield him to the angels, nor unto death utterly, but* only through the weakness of his feeble will.'

Length of years, and subsequent reflection, have enabled me to trace, indeed, some remote connexion between this passage in the old* English moralist and a portion of the character of Ligeia. An *intensity* in thought, action, or speech, was possibly, in her, a result, or at least an index, of that gigantic volition which, during our long intercourse, failed to give other and more immediate evidence of its existence. Of all women whom I have ever known she, the outwardly calm, the ever-placid Ligeia, was the most violently a prey to the tumultuous vultures of stern passion. And of such passion I could form no estimate, save by the miraculous expansion of those eyes which at once so delighted and appalled me, by the almost magical melody, modulation, distinctness and placidity of her very low voice, and by the fierce energy (rendered doubly effective by contrast with her manner of utterance) of the words which she uttered.

I have spoken of the learning of Ligeia: it was immense—such as I have never known in woman. In the classical tongues was she deeply proficient, and as far as my own acquaintance extended in regard to the modern dialects of Europe, I have never known her at fault. Indeed upon any theme of the most admired, because simply the most abstruse, of the boasted erudition of the academy, have I *ever* found Ligeia at fault? How singularly, how thrillingly, this one point in the nature of my wife has forced itself, at this late period only, upon my attention! I said her knowledge was such as I had never known in woman. Where breathes the man who, like her, has traversed, and successfully, *all* the wide areas of moral, natural, and mathematical science? I saw not then what I now clearly perceive, that the acquisitions of Ligeia were gigantic, were astounding—yet I was sufficiently aware of her infinite supremacy to resign myself, with a child-like confidence, to her guidance through the chaotic world of metaphysical investigation at which I was most busily occupied during the earlier years of our marriage. With how vast a triumph—with how vivid a delight—with how much of all that is ethereal in hope—did I *feel*, as she bent over me in studies but little sought for—but less known—that delicious vista by slow but perceptible degrees expanding before me, down whose long, gorgeous, and all untrodden path, I might at length pass onward to the goal of a wisdom too divinely precious not to be forbidden!

How poignant, then, must have been the grief with which, after some years, I beheld my well-grounded expectations take wings to themselves and flee* away! Without Ligeia I was but as a child groping benighted. Her presence, her readings alone, rendered vividly luminous the many mysteries of the transcendentalism* in which we were immersed. Letters, lambent and golden, grew duller than Saturnian lead,* wanting the radiant lustre of her eyes.* And now those eyes shone less and less frequently upon the pages over which I pored. Ligeia grew ill. The wild eye blazed with a too—too glorious effulgence; the pale fingers became of the transparent waxen hue of the grave—and the blue veins upon the lofty forehead swelled and sunk impetuously with the tides of the most gentle emotion. I saw that she must die—and I struggled desperately in spirit with the grim Azrael.* And the struggles of the passionate wife were, to my astonishment, even more energetic than my own. There had been much in her stern nature to impress me with the belief that, to her, death would have come without its terrors—but not so. Words are impotent to convey any just idea of the fierceness of resistance with which she wrestled with the dark shadow. I groaned in anguish at the pitiable spectacle. I would have soothed—I would have reasoned; but in the intensity of her wild desire for life—for life—*but* for life, solace and reason were alike the uttermost of folly. Yet not for an instant, amid the most convulsive writhings of her fierce spirit, was shaken the external placidity of her demeanor. Her voice grew more gentle—grew more low—yet I would not wish to dwell upon the wild meaning of the quietly-uttered words. My brain reeled as I hearkened, entranced, to a melody more than mortal—to assumptions and aspirations which mortality had never before known.

That she loved me, I should not have doubted; and I might have been easily aware that, in a bosom such as hers, love would have reigned no ordinary passion. But in death only, was I fully impressed with the strength of her affection. For long hours, detaining my hand, would she pour out before me the overflowings of a heart whose more than passionate devotion amounted to idolatry. How had I deserved to be so blessed by such confessions?—how had I deserved to be so cursed with the removal of my beloved in the hour of her making them? But upon this subject I cannot bear to dilate. Let me say only, that in Ligeia's more than womanly abandonment to a love, alas! all unmerited, all unworthily bestowed, I at length recognized the principle of her longing with so wildly earnest a desire for the life which was now fleeing so rapidly away. It is this wild longing—it is this eager vehemence of desire for life—*but* for life—that I have no power to portray—no utterance capable of expressing. Methinks I again behold the terrific struggles of her lofty, her nearly idealized nature, with the might and the terror, and the majesty, of the great Shadow. But she perished. The giant *will* succumbed to a power more stern. And I thought, as I gazed upon the corpse, of the wild passage in Joseph Glanvill: 'The will therein lieth, which dieth not. Who knoweth the mysteries of the will, with its vigor? For God is but a great will pervading all things by nature of its intentness. Man doth not yield him to the angels, *nor unto death utterly*, save only through the weakness of his feeble will.'*

She died—and I, crushed into the very dust with sorrow, could no longer endure the lonely desolation of my dwelling in the dim and decaying city by the Rhine. I had no lack of what the world terms wealth—Ligeia had brought me far more, very far more, than falls ordinarily to the lot of mortals. After a few months, therefore, of weary and aimless wandering, I purchased, and put in some repair, an abbey, which I shall not name, in one of the wildest and least frequented portions of fair England. The gloomy and dreary grandeur of the building, the almost savage aspect of the domain, the many melancholy and time-honored memories connected with both, had much in unison with the feelings of utter abandonment which had driven me into that remote and unsocial region of the country. Yet although the external abbey, with its verdant decay hanging about it, suffered but little alteration, I gave way, with a child-like perversity, and perchance with a faint hope of alleviating my sorrows, to a display of more than regal magnificence within. For such follies even in childhood I had imbibed a taste, and now they came back to me as if in the dotage of grief. Alas, I feel how much even of incipient madness might have been discovered in the gorgeous and fantastic draperies, in the solemn carvings of Egypt, in the wild cornices and furniture, in the bedlam* patterns of the carpets of tufted gold! I had become a bounden slave in the trammels of opium, and my labors and my orders had taken a coloring from my dreams. But these absurdities I must not pause to detail. Let me speak only of that one chamber, ever accursed, whither, in a moment of mental alienation, I led from the altar as my bride—as the successor of the unforgotten Ligeia—the fair-haired and blue-eyed Lady Rowena Trevanion, of Tremaine.*

There is not any individual portion of the architecture and decoration of that bridal chamber which is not now visibly before me. Where were the souls of the haughty family of the bride, when, through thirst of gold, they permitted to pass the threshold of an apartment *so* bedecked, a maiden and a daughter so beloved? I have said that I minutely remember the details of the chamber—yet I am sadly forgetful on topics of deep moment—and here there was no system, no keeping, in the fantastic display, to take hold upon the memory. The room lay in a high turret of the castellated abbey, was pentagonal* in shape, and of capacious size. Occupying the whole southern face of the pentagon was the sole window—an immense sheet of unbroken glass from Venice—a single pane, and tinted of a leaden hue, so that the rays of either the sun or moon, passing through it, fell with a ghastly lustre upon the objects within. Over the upper portion of this huge window extended the open trellice-work of an aged vine which clambered up the massy walls of the turret. The ceiling, of gloomy-looking oak, was excessively lofty, vaulted, and elaborately fretted with the wildest and most grotesque specimens of a semi-Gothic, semi-Druidical* device. From out the most central recess of this melancholy vaulting, depended, by a single chain of gold, with long links, a huge censer of the same metal, Saracenic* in pattern, and with many perforations so contrived that there writhed in and out of them, as if endued with a serpent vitality, a continual succession of particolored fires. Some few ottomans and golden candelabra of Eastern figure were in various stations about—and there was the couch, too, the bridal couch, of an Indian model, and low, and sculptured of solid ebony, with a canopy above. In each of the angles of the chamber, stood on end a gigantic sarcophagus of black granite, from the tombs of the kings over against Luxor,* with their aged lids full of immemorial sculpture. But in the draping of the apartment lay, alas! the chief phantasy of all. The lofty walls—gigantic in height—even unproportionably so, were hung from summit to foot, in vast folds, with a heavy and massive looking tapestry—tapestry of a material which was found alike as a carpet on the floor, as a covering for the ottomans and the ebony bed, as a canopy for the bed, and as the gorgeous volutes* of the curtains which partially shaded the window. This material was the richest cloth of gold. It was spotted all over, at irregular intervals, with arabesque figures, of about a foot in diameter, and wrought upon the cloth in patterns of the most jetty black. But these figures partook of the true character of the arabesque only when regarded from a single point of view. By a contrivance now common, and indeed traceable to a very remote period of antiquity, they were made changeable in aspect. To one entering the room they bore the appearance of simple monstrosities; but, upon a farther advance, this appearance suddenly* departed; and, step by step, as the visiter moved his station in the chamber, he saw himself surrounded by an endless succession of the ghastly forms which belong to the superstition of the Northman,* or arise in the guilty slumbers of the monk. The phantasmagoric* effect was vastly heightened by the artificial introduction of a strong continual current of wind behind the draperies—giving a hideous and uneasy animation to the whole.

In halls such as these—in a bridal chamber such as this—I passed, with the Lady of Tremaine, the unhallowed hours of the first month of our marriage—passed them with but little disquietude. That my wife dreaded the fierce moodiness of my temper—that she shunned me, and loved me but little—I could not help perceiving—but it gave me rather pleasure than otherwise. I loathed her with a hatred belonging more to demon than to man. My memory flew back, (oh, with what intensity of regret!) to Ligeia, the beloved, the beautiful, the entombed. I revelled in recollections of her purity, of her wisdom, of her lofty, her ethereal nature, of her passionate, her idolatrous love. Now, then, did my spirit fully and freely burn with more than all the fires of her own. In the excitement of my opium dreams (for I was habitually fettered in the iron shackles of the drug) I would call aloud upon her name, during the silence of the night, or among the sheltered recesses of the glens by day, as if, through the wild eagerness, the solemn passion, the consuming ardor of my longing for the departed Ligeia,* I could restore the departed Ligeia* to the pathway she had abandoned upon earth.

About the commencement of the second month of the marriage, the Lady Rowena was attacked with sudden illness from which her recovery was slow. The fever which consumed her rendered her nights uneasy, and, in her perturbed state of half-slumber, she spoke of sounds, and of motions, in and about the chamber of the turret, which had no origin save in the distemper of her fancy, or, perhaps, in the phantastic influences of the chamber itself. She became at length convalescent—finally well. Yet but a brief period elapsed, ere a second more violent disorder again threw her upon a bed of suffering—and from this attack her frame, at all times feeble, never altogether recovered. Her illnesses were, after this epoch, of alarming character, and of more alarming recurrence, defying alike the knowledge and the great exertions of her medical men. With the increase of the chronic disease which had thus, apparently, taken too sure hold upon her constitution to be eradicated by human means, I could not fail to observe a similar increase in the nervous irritation of her temperament, and in her excitability by trivial causes of fear. Indeed reason seemed fast tottering from her throne. She spoke again, and now more frequently and pertinaciously, of the sounds, of the slight sounds, and of the unusual motions among the tapestries, to which she had formerly alluded.

One night near the closing in of September, she pressed this distressing subject with more than usual emphasis upon my attention. She had just awakened from an unquiet slumber, and I had been watching, with feelings half of anxiety, half of a vague terror, the workings of her emaciated countenance. I sat by the side of her ebony bed, upon one of the ottomans of India. She partly arose, and spoke, in an earnest low whisper, of sounds which she *then* heard, but which I could not hear, of motions which she *then* saw, but which I could not perceive. The wind was rushing hurriedly behind the tapestries, and I wished to show her (what, let me confess it, I could not *all* believe) that those faint, almost inarticulate breathings, and the very gentle variations of the figures upon the wall, were but the natural effects of that customary rushing of the wind. But a deadly pallor, overspreading her face, had proved to me that my exertions to reassure her would be fruitless. She appeared to be fainting, and no attendants were within call. I remembered where was deposited a decanter of some light wine which had been ordered by her physicians, and hastened across the chamber to procure it. But, as I stepped beneath the light of the censer, two circumstances of a startling nature attracted my attention. I had felt that some palpable object had passed lightly by my person; and I saw that there lay a faint indefinite shadow upon the golden carpet, in the very middle of the rich lustre thrown from the censer. But I was wild with the excitement of an immoderate dose of opium, and heeded these things but little, nor spoke of them to Rowena. Finding the wine, I recrossed the chamber, and poured out a gobletful, which I held to the lips of the fainting lady. She had now partially recovered, however, and took, herself, the vessel, while I sank upon the ottoman near me, with my eyes rivetted upon her person. It was then that I became distinctly aware of a gentle foot-fall upon the carpet, and near the couch; and, in a second thereafter, as Rowena was in the act of raising the wine to her lips, I saw, or may have dreamed that I saw, fall within the goblet, as if from some invisible spring in the atmosphere of the room, three or four large drops of a brilliant and ruby-colored fluid. If this I saw—not so Rowena. She swallowed the wine unhesitatingly, and I forbore to speak to her of a circumstance which must, after all, I considered, have been but the suggestion of a vivid imagination, rendered morbidly active by the terror of the lady, by the opium, and by the hour.

Yet—I cannot conceal it from myself—after this period, a rapid change for the worse took place in the disorder of my wife; so that, on the third subsequent night, the hands of her menials prepared her for the tomb, and on the fourth, I sat alone, with her shrouded body, in that fantastic chamber which had received her as my bride. Wild visions, opium engendered, flitted, shadow-like, before me. I gazed with unquiet eye upon the sarcophagi in the angles of the room, upon the varying figures of the drapery, and upon the writhing of the parti-colored fires in the censer overhead. My eyes then fell, as I called to mind the circumstances of a former night, to the spot beneath the glare of the censer where I had beheld the faint traces of the shadow. It was there, however, no longer, and, breathing with greater freedom, I turned my glances to the pallid and rigid figure upon the bed. Then rushed upon me a thousand memories of Ligeia—and then came back upon my heart, with the turbulent violence of a flood, the whole of that unutterable wo* with which I had regarded *her* thus enshrouded. The night waned; and still, with a bosom full of bitter thoughts of the one only and supremely beloved, I remained with mine eyes rivetted upon the body of Rowena.

It might have been midnight, or perhaps earlier, or later, for I had taken no note of time, when a sob, low, gentle, but very distinct, startled me from my revery. I *felt* that it came from the bed of ebony—the bed of death. I listened in an agony of superstitious terror—but there was no repetition of the sound; I strained my vision to detect any motion in the corpse, but there was not the slightest perceptible. Yet I could not have been deceived. I *had* heard the noise, however faint, and my whole soul was awakened within me, as I resolutely and perseveringly kept my attention rivetted upon the body. Many minutes elapsed before any circumstance occurred tending to throw light upon the mystery. At length it became evident that a slight, a very faint, and barely noticeable tinge of color had flushed up within the cheeks, and along the sunken small veins of the eyelids. Through a species of unutterable horror and awe, for which the language of mortality has no sufficiently energetic expression, I felt my brain reel,* my heart cease to beat, my limbs grow rigid where I sat. Yet a sense of duty finally operated to restore my self-possession. I could no longer doubt that we had been precipitate in our preparations for interment—that Rowena still lived. It was necessary that some immediate exertion be made; yet the turret was altogether apart from the portion of the Abbey tenanted by the servants—there were none within call,—I had no means of summoning them to my aid without leaving the room for many minutes—and this I could not venture to do. I therefore struggled alone in my endeavors to call back the spirit still hovering. In a short period it was certain, however, that a relapse had taken place; the color utterly disappeared from both eyelid and cheek, leaving a wanness even more than that of marble; the lips became doubly shrivelled and pinched up in the ghastly expression of death; a repulsive clamminess and coldness overspread rapidly the surface of the body; and all the usual rigorous stiffness immediately supervened. I fell back with a shudder upon the couch from which I had been so startlingly aroused, and again gave myself up to passionate waking visions of Ligeia.

An hour thus elapsed when, (could it be possible?) I was a second time aware of some vague sound issuing from the region of the bed. I listened—in extremity of horror. The sound came again—it was a sigh. Rushing to the corpse, I saw—distinctly saw—a tremor upon the lips. In a minute after, they slightly relaxed, disclosing a bright line of the pearly teeth. Amazement now struggled in my bosom with the profound awe which had hitherto reigned therein alone. I felt that my vision grew dim, that my reason wandered, and it was only by a convulsive effort that I at length succeeded in nerving myself to the task which duty thus, once more, had pointed out. There was now a partial glow upon the forehead and upon the cheek and throat—a perceptible warmth pervaded the whole frame—there was even a slight pulsation at the heart. The lady *lived*; and with redoubled ardor I betook myself to the task of restoration. I chafed and bathed the temples and the hands, and used every exertion which experience, and no little medical reading, could suggest. But in vain. Suddenly, the color fled, the pulsation ceased, the lips resumed the expression of the dead, and, in an instant afterwards, the whole body took upon itself the icy chillness, the livid hue, the intense rigidity, the sunken outline, and each and all of the loathsome peculiarities of that which has been, for many days, a tenant of the tomb.

And again I sunk into visions of Ligeia—and again, (what marvel that I shudder while I write?) *again* there reached my ears a low sob from the region of the ebony bed. But why shall I minutely detail the unspeakable horrors of that night? Why shall I pause to relate how, time after time, until near the period of the gray dawn, this hideous drama of revivification* was repeated, and* how each terrific relapse was only into a sterner and apparently more irredeemable death?* Let me hurry to a conclusion.

The greater part of the fearful night had worn away, and the corpse of Rowena once again stirred—and now more vigorously than hitherto, although arousing from a dissolution more appalling in its utter hopelessness than any. I had long ceased to struggle or to move, and remained sitting rigidly upon the ottoman, a helpless prey to a whirl of violent emotions, of which extreme awe was perhaps the least terrible, the least consuming. The corpse, I repeat, stirred, and* now more vigorously than before. The hues of life flushed up with unwonted energy into the countenance—the limbs relaxed*—and,* save that the eyelids were yet pressed heavily together, and that the bandages and draperies of the grave still imparted their charnel character to the figure, I might have dreamed that Rowena had indeed shaken off, utterly, the fetters of Death. But if this idea was not, even then, altogether adopted, I could, at least, doubt no longer, when, arising from the bed, tottering, with feeble steps, with closed eyes, and with the manner of one bewildered in a dream, the Lady of Tremaine advanced bodily and palpably into the middle of the apartment.

I trembled* not—I stirred not—for a crowd of unutterable fancies connected with the air,* the demeanor of the figure, rushing hurriedly through my brain, had paralyzed, had chilled me into stone. I stirred not—but gazed upon the apparition. There was a mad disorder in my thoughts—a tumult unappeasable. Could it, indeed, be the *living* Rowena who confronted me? Why, *why* should I doubt it? The bandage lay heavily about the mouth—but then it was* the mouth of the breathing Lady of Tremaine.* And the cheeks—there were the roses as in her noon of life—yes, these were indeed the fair cheeks of the living Lady of Tremaine. And the chin, with its dimples, as in health, was it not hers?—but *had she then grown taller since her malady*? What inexpressible madness seized me with that thought? One bound, and I had reached her feet! Shrinking from my touch, she let fall from her head, unloosened, the ghastly cerements which had confined it, and there streamed forth, into the rushing atmosphere of the chamber, huge masses of long and dishevelled hair. *It was blacker than the raven wings of the midnight!* And now *the eyes* opened of the figure which stood before me. 'Here then, at least,' I shrieked aloud, 'can I never—can I never be mistaken—these are the full, and the black, and the wild eyes of the lady—of the Lady Ligeia!'*

JAMES MALCOLM RYMER

EXTRACT FROM *VARNEY, THE VAMPYRE; OR, THE FEAST OF BLOOD*

CHAPTER XCVIII

Will Stephens' Visit to the Family Vault with the Sawdust, and what he saw there

Will Stephens waited at the ale-house much longer than he intended. To be sure the rain cleared off, but what of that? It was not a circumstance that made the ale anything the worse, and so he waited to drink it with a gusto that improved each glass amazingly, and then some of those who were present—jolly topers like himself—began to laugh and to say—

'Ah, Will, you may as well poke that bag of sawdust* into some corner; you won't do anything with it to-night, old fellow, we know.'

Now, some people get good tempered and complying when they have had the drop too much, and others again get particularly obstinate and contradictory. Will of the two certainly had more pretensions to belong to the latter class than the former, so when he heard such a prophecy concerning his movements and knew it was all an assumption based upon the ale he had drank, he felt indignant.

'Not go!' he cried. 'Not go! You may fancy if you please that I will not go, but you will find yourselves mistaken: I will go.'

'What, so late!'

'What's the odds to me. Any of you now would be frightened out of your lives to set foot in the old church at such a time as this, I know; but I'm none of the timid sort; I'm afraid of nobody living, and it ain't likely that I'm now going to be afraid of anybody dead.'

'Then you really will go?'

The only reply that he made to this was to finish off the glass of ale that was before him, shoulder the bag of sawdust, and sally out into the open air. Will Stephens felt highly indignant and touchy about his honour, and as he had said he would go and then somebody chose to imply a doubt still, he was grievously offended.

When he got out, he found that the night was anything but an inviting one. He was still sober enough to see that, and to feel that although the heavy rain had ceased, there was a little disagreeable misty sort of vapour* in the air.

He staggered at the first turning he came to, for rather an uncomfortable gust of wind blew in his face, carrying along with it such a shower of small cold rain that he was, or fancied himself to be, wet through in a moment.

'Pleasant this,' thought Will; 'but I will not go back to be laughed at.'

As for the sawdust he was carrying, its weight was by no means any great consideration, for it was just as light as it could be.

'No, I won't go back—back, indeed, not I; they would make me stand a pot of ale to a certainty if I were to go back; and, besides, it would be all over the parish to-morrow that Will Stephens, after he got half way to the church, was afraid to go any further. Confound the small rain, it pricks like pins and needles.'

Nothing is more sobering than rain, and as he, Will, gradually got saturated with the small aquaeous particles, the effect of the strong ale as gradually wore off, until by the time the dim, dusky outline of the church rose before him he was almost as sober as need be.

'Ah!' he said, 'here I am at last at any rate. I do hate this sort of rain, you can hardly make up your mind that it is raining at all, and yet, somehow you get soaked before you know where you are. It's just like going through a damp cloud, that it is, and yet somehow or another, I don't much mind it; I'm earning a guinea* easy enough. Ha—ha!'

This was by no means an unpleasant reflection.

'Yes,' he added, 'I am earning a guinea easily enough, that's quite clear, but then it's not everybody who would, for a guinea, go into anybody's family vault at such a time. By-the-by, I wonder now what the time is exactly?'

Scarcely had Will spoken those words when the old church-clock struck the hour of twelve.

It was a very serious, deliberate sort of clock that, and it took a long time to strike twelve, and Will listened with the greatest attention with the hope of persuading himself that it was only eleven, but there could be no mistake, twelve it was.

'Really,' he said, 'is it so late? Well, I didn't think—'

Will stood within the porch of the church door, and he gave a sort of shiver, and then, with the bag of sawdust in his hand, he stopped to listen attentively, for he thought he heard a slight sound.

'What was that, eh? what—I thought, nay, I am sure I heard something; it's very odd—very odd, indeed.'

As if then to afford Will an excuse for resolving the sound to be something else, the wind at this moment came in such a sudden gale round the ancient edifice, that he quite congratulated himself he was within the porch and protected from its fury; and, besides, it to his mind was a sufficing explanation of the noise he had heard.

'Some of the old doors,' he muttered, 'rattled by the wind, that's all. Now I suppose we shall have a clear night after all the rain. Such a gale will soon blow off the damp clouds.'

Will was right. The gale, for a gale it was, blew from the north, and away went the rain clouds as if a curtain had been drawn aside by some invisible hand.

After some rummaging Will found in his pocket the key of the church; it was not the key of the principal door, but of a smaller side entrance, at which the officials who required at all times free ingress and egress* made application. The little arched door creaked upon its hinges, and then Will stood in a sort of vestibule, for another door that was never fast had to be opened before he could be fairly said to be within the church.

This second door was covered with green baize,* and could be opened and shut very noiselessly, indeed.

Will Stephens stood in the vestibule until he had got a small lantern out of one pocket, and some matches from another. Then in a few moments he had a light, and once again shouldering the bag of sawdust, he pushed open the inner door, and stood in the church.

It might have been fancy—nay, he felt certain, it could be nothing else—but he thought as he opened the door that a faint sort of sigh came upon his ears.

Fancy or not, though, it was an uncomfortable thing at such an hour, and in such a place, too, and he had never before heard anything of the sort upon his visits to the church, and he had visited it at all hours, many and many a time.

'It's odd,' he said, 'it's uncommonly odd. I never felt so uncomfortable in the church before. I—I never used to mind coming to it in the middle of the night. But now, I—eh?—what was that?'

Again an odd sort of noise came upon his ears, and he dropped the bag of sawdust.

All was still again, save the regular roar of wind, as it swept round the sacred building, and although Will Stephens stood for nearly ten minutes in an attitude of listening, he heard nothing to augment his terrors. But let an impulse once be given to fear, and it will go on accumulating material from every trivial circumstance. The courage of the sexton was broken down, and there was no knowing, now, what tricks his awakened imagination might play him.

He began to wish he had not come, and from that wish, to think that he might as well go back, only shame forbade him, for it would be easily known on the morrow that he had not placed the sawdust in the vault, and, lastly, he began to think that some one might be playing him a trick.

This last supposition, probably, had more effect in raising his courage than any preceding one. Indignation took possession of him, and he no longer thought of retreating. He went forward at once, and fell over the bag of sawdust.

'Murder!' shouted Will.

The moment he did so, he recollected what it was that had occasioned his fall, and being ashamed of himself he called out impulsively, as if somebody was there to hear him—

'No—no, it's only the sawdust. No—no.'

He rose to his feet again, heartily ashamed of his own fears. Luckily his lantern had not been broken nor extinguished, in his fall, and now, without another word, he prepared himself to execute the work he came to do, and leave the church to its repose as quickly as possible.

At one end of the church, the southern end, there was a large window, which might be said to light the whole of the interior, for the little windows at the sides were more ornamental than useful, being nothing but lattices; and across this window was drawn a heavy cloth curtain, so that when the sun shone too brightly upon the congregation on a summer's day, it could be wholly or partially excluded upon a sign from the clergyman.

The curtain was drawn close on the window now, at night, and Will just glanced up to it, as he walked on towards the aisle where the opening to the family vault of the Croftons was situated.

'All's right,' he said, 'what a fool I have been to be sure.' Upon my word, I might have continued frightening myself all night, and some people would too, but that's not my way of doing business. So here we are, all right. The door is on one side, so that I have just room enough to go down in the vault. Oh! when one comes to think of it, it was rather a melancholy thing, the death of such a young girl as she was, going to be married, too. Well, that's the way the world goes.'

The stone steps leading down to the vault were rather steep, and Will threw down the bag of sawdust first, in preference to carrying it, and then, with his lantern in his hand, he commenced his own descent.

'That'll do,' said Will, when he felt his feet upon the soft old sawdust that was on the floor of the vault. 'That'll do—now for it, I shall soon have this job settled, and then I'll get home no faster than I can.'

Somehow or another, he felt very much inclined to talk; the sound of his own voice, conversing, as he might be said to be, with himself, gave him a sort of courage, and made the place not appear to be altogether so desperately lonely as it really was.

That, no doubt, was the feeling that brought forth so many indifferent remarks from Will Stephens. He held up his light to look round him, and turned gradually upon his heels as he did so.

The light shook in his hand. The hair almost stood on end on his head—his teeth chattered, and he tried to speak in vain, as he saw lying at his feet, a coffin lid.

It was new. The nails that held the blue cloth upon it were bright, and fast—the plate shone like silver. Yes, it was the lid of the coffin of Miss Clara Crofton;* but how came it off—unsecured, and lying upon the floor of the vault, while the coffin was in its proper niche?

'Gracious goodness!' gasped Will, at length. 'What does this mean?'

The question was easy to ask, but most difficult to answer, and he stood trembling and turning over in his mind all the most frightful explanations of what he saw that could occur to any one.

'Has she been buried alive? Have the body snatchers* been after her? How is it—what—what has happened?'

Then it occurred to Will, that it would be just as well to look into the coffin, and see if it were tenantless or not. If it were, he thought he should know what to think, and if the dead body was there, then he could only conclude that she had been buried alive, and had had just strength enough to force open the coffin, and cast the lid of it on the floor of the vault, and then to die in that horrible place.

It required almost more courage than Will could muster to go and look into the coffin, for now that his usual indifference was completely broken down, he was as timid as any stranger to graves and vaults would have been. But curiosity is, after all, a most exciting passion, and that lent him power.

'Yes,' he said, 'I—I will look in the coffin, I shall have but a poor tale to tell to Sir George Crofton,* if I do not look in the coffin. I—I—have nothing to be afraid of.'

He advanced with trembling steps, the light shaking in his hands as he did so. He reached the coffin, and with eyes unusually wide, he looked in: it was empty.

CHAPTER XCIX

The Apparition in the Church—Will Stephens' Swoon—the Morning

For some minutes, Will Stephens continued to gaze in the empty coffin, as if there was something peculiarly fascinating in it, and most attractive, and yet nothing was in it, no vestige even of the vestments of the dead. If Clara Crofton had herself risen, and left the vault, it was quite clear she had taken with her the apparel of the grave.

Will had thought that if he found the coffin empty, all his fears would vanish, and that he should be able to come at once to the conclusion, that she had become the prey of resurrectionists.* But new ideas, as he gazed at that abandoned receptacle of the dead, began to creep across him.

'I—I—don't know,' he muttered, 'but she may in a ghost-like kind of way be going about. I don't know whether ghosts is corpses or not. I—I wish I was out of this.'

The idea of spreading the sawdust in the vault now completely left him; all he thought of was to get away, and the dread that Clara Crofton was, perhaps, hiding somewhere, and might come suddenly out upon him with a yell, got so firm a hold of him, that several times he thought he should faint with excess of terror.

'That would be too horrible,' he said, 'I am sure I should go mad—mad—mad.'

He retreated backward to the stairs, for the coffin, empty though it was, held his gaze with a strange kind of fascinating power. He thought that if he turned round something would be sure to lay hold of him. It was a most horrifying and distressing idea that, and yet he could not conquer it.

Of course he must turn round, it would be an awkward thing to attempt ascending the staircase, short as it was, backward, so he felt the necessity of turning his back upon the vault.

'I—I will do so,' he thought, 'and then make such a rush up the steps, that I shall be in the church in a moment, I—I can surely do that, and—and after all it's nothing really to be afraid of—it's only a matter of imagination, after all! oh, yes, that's all, that's all. I—I will do that.'

He put this notable scheme into execution by turning suddenly round and making a dash at the stairs, but as people generally do things badly when they do things in a hurry, he stumbled when about half-way and felt himself at the mercy of the whole of the supernatural world.

'Have mercy on me,' he cried, 'I am going. Have mercy on me.'

He had struck the lantern so hard against the stone stairs that he had broken it into fragments, and now all was intense darkness around him.

He gave himself up for lost.

He lay, expecting each moment to feel some dead bony fingers clutching him, and he only groaned, thinking that surely now his last hour was come; and it is a wonder that his fancy, excited as it was, did not conjure up to him the very effect he dreaded, but it did not do so, strange to say, and he lay for full five minutes without anything occurring to add to his terrors.

Then he began gradually to recover.

'If—if,' he gasped, 'I could but reach the church, I—I think I should be safe. Yes, I should surely be safe in the body of the church. Have mercy on me, good ghosts; I never harmed any of you, I—I respect you very much, indeed I do. Let me go, and—I'll never say a light word of any of you again, no, never, if I were to live for a thousand years.'

As he uttered these words, he crawled up the remaining stairs, and to his great satisfaction, made his way fairly into the church.

But then a new surprise, if it was not exactly a new fright, perhaps it was something of both, awaited him.

The curtain that had been, as he had observed when he was walking down the aisle, closely drawn across the large south window was now drawn on one side, so that a large portion of that window was exposed, and the north wind having chased away by this time entirely the damp clouds, the moon was sailing in a cloudless sky, and sending into the old church a glorious flood of light.

'What a change,' said Will Stephens.

It was indeed a change; the church was as light as day, save in some places where shadows fell, and they, in contrast to the silvery lightness of the moonbeams, were of a jetty* blackness.

But still, let the moon shine ever so brightly, there is not that distinctness and freshness of outline produced as in the direct daylight. A strange kind of hazy vapour seems to float between the eye and all objects—an indistinctness and mysteriousness of aspect, which belongs not to the sun's unreflected rays. Thus it was, that although the church was illuminated by the moon, it had a singular aspect, and would scarcely have been recognized by any one who had only seen it by the mild searching light of day.

But of course Will Stephens the sexton knew it well, and as he wiped the perspiration from his face, he said—

'What a relief to get out of that vault, and find now that the night has turned out so fair and beautiful. I—I begin to think I have frightened myself more than I need have done—but it was that coffin-lid that did the business. I wasn't my own man after that. But now that I have got out of the vault, I feel quite different—oh, quite another thing.'

Suddenly, then, it occurred to him, that the curtain had been close on the window, when he came into the church, and following upon that thought came another, namely, that it could not very well remove itself from before the casement, and that consequently some hands, mortal or ghostly, must have done that part of the business.

Here there was ample food again for all his fears, and Will Stephens almost on the instant relapsed into his former trembling and nerveless state.

'What shall I do?' he said; 'it ain't all over yet. What will become of me? There's something horrid going to happen, I feel certain, and that curtain has only been drawn aside to let the moonlight come in for me to see it.'

With a painful expectation of his eyes being blasted by some horrible sight, he glared round him, but he saw nothing, although the dense little mass of pews before him might have hidden many a horror.

His next movement was to turn his eyes to the gallery, and all round it he carried them until he came to the window again, but he saw nothing.

'Who knows,' he muttered, 'who knows, after all, but that the wind in some odd sort of way may have blown the curtain on one side? I—I wish I had the courage now to go up to the gallery, and see, but I—I don't think I should like to do that.'

He hesitated. He knew that it would sound well on the morrow for him to be able to say that he went up, and yet it was rather a fearful thing.

'A—hem!' he said at length, 'is any one here?'

As he made this inquiry, he took care to keep himself ready to make a dart out at the door into the churchyard, but as there was no response to it, he was a little encouraged. The gallery staircase was close to where he stood, and after the not unnatural hesitation of a few moments more, he approached them, and began slowly to ascend.

Nothing interrupted him, all was profoundly still, and at length he did reach the south window, and he found that the curtain was most deliberately drawn on one side, and that the window was fast, so that no vagary of the wind could have accomplished the purpose.

'Now I'll go—I'll go at once,' he said, 'I can't stand this any longer! I'll go and alarm the village—I'll—I'll make a disturbance of some sort.'

'Awake!' said a deep, hollow voice.

Will sunk upon his knees with a groan, and mechanically his eyes wandered to the direction from whence the sound came, and he saw in a pew just beneath him, and on which the moonlight now fell brightly, a human form.

It was lying in a strange huddled up position in the pew, and a glance showed the experienced eye of the sexton that it was arrayed in the vestments of the dead.

He tried to speak—he tried to scream—he tried to pray, but all was in vain. Intense terror froze up every faculty of his body, and he could only kneel there with his face resting upon the front of the gallery, and glare with aching eyes, that would not close for a moment, upon the scene below.

'Awake!' said the deep strange voice again. 'Awake!'

It was quite clear that that voice did not come from the figure in the pew, but from some one close at hand. The sexton soon saw another form.

In the adjoining pew, standing upright as a statue, with one hand pointing upwards to the window, where came in the moonlight, was a tall figure enveloped in a cloak. It was from the lips of that figure that the sound came, so deeply and so solemnly.

'Sister,' it said, 'be one of us—let the cold, chaste moonbeams endow thee with your new, and strange, and horrible existence. Be one of us—be one of us! Hours must yet elapse, ere the faint flash of morning will kill the moonbeams. There is time, sister. Awake, be one of us.'

There was a passing cloud that swept for an instant over the face of the moon, obscuring its radiance, and the figure let its arm fall to its side. But when the silvery beams streamed into the church, it again pointed to the window.

''Tis done!—she moves,' he said. 'I have fulfilled my mission. Ha! ha! ha!'

The laugh was so terrific* and unmirthful that it froze the very blood in the veins of Will, and he thought he was surely at that moment going mad.

But still he did not close his eyes, still he moved not from the position which he had first assumed when the horrible noise met his ears.

''Tis done,' said the figure, and the arm that had been outstretched was let fall to his side.

Will Stephens looked in the pew, where he had seen what appeared to be a corpse. It had altered its position. He saw it move and wave its arms about strangely, and deep sighs came from its lips. It was a dreadful sight to see, but at length it rose up in the grave clothes, and moved to the door of the pew.

The figure in the adjoining pew opened the door and stood on one side, and the revivified corpse passed out.

Slowly and solemnly it passed down the aisle. It reached the door at which Will Stephens had entered, and then it passed away from his sight. The tall figure followed closely, and Will Stephens was alone in the church.

What could he do? How could he give a sufficient alarm? Would the two horrible personages return or not? Alas! poor Will Stephens, never was an unhappy mortal sexton in such frightful tribulation before. He knelt and shook like an aspen. At length a lucky thought entered his head.

'The bell. The bell,' he cried, all at once finding his voice. 'To the bell.'

He sprung to his feet, for what he was now about to do did not involve the necessity of going down again into the body of the church. There was a narrow staircase at the corner of the gallery, leading to the belfry. It was up that staircase that Will now struggled and tore.

[CHAPTERS C, CI, CII, CIII]*

CHAPTER CIV

The Midnight Hour—The Stone Slab—The Vampyre

YES, it was just twelve o'clock, that hour when all that is human feels a sort of irksome* dread, as if the spirits of those who have gone from the great world were too near, loading the still night air with the murky vapours of the grave—that mysterious hour at which it is believed by many that

> 'Graves give up their dead,
> And many a ghost in church-yard decay,
> Rise from their cold, cold bed
> To make night horrible with wild vagary.'*

A chilliness came over Ringwood,* and he fancied a strange kind of light was in the church, making objects more visible than in their dim and dusky outlines they had been before.

'Why do I tremble?' he said, 'why do I tremble? Clouds pass away from before the moon, that is all. Soon there may be a bright light here, and lo, all is still; I hear nothing but my own breathing; I see nothing but what is common and natural. Thank heaven, all will pass away in quiet. There will be no horror to recount—no terrific sight to chill my blood. Rest, Clara, rest in Heaven.'

Ten minutes passed away, and there was no alarm; how wonderfully relieved was Ringwood. Tears came to his eyes, but there were the natural tears of regret, such as he had shed before for her who had gone from him to the tomb, and left no trace behind, but in the hearts of those who loved her.

'Yes,' he said, mournfully, 'she has gone from me, but I love her still. Still does the fond remembrance of all that she was to me linger at my heart. She is my own, my beautiful Clara, as she ever was, and as, while life remains to me she, ever will be.'

At the moment that he uttered these words a slight noise met his ears.

In an instant he sprang to his feet in the pulpit, and looked anxiously around him.

'What was that?' he said. 'What was that?'

All was still again, and he was upon the point of convincing himself that the noise was either some accidental one, or the creation of his own fancy, when it came again.

He had no doubt this time. It was a perceptible, scraping, strange sort of sound, and he turned his whole attention to the direction from whence it came. With a cold creeping chill through his frame, he saw that that direction was the one where was the family vault of the Croftons, the last home of her whom he held still in remembrance, and whose memory was so dear to him.

He felt the perspiration standing upon his brow, and if the whole world had been the recompense to him for moving away from where he was he could not have done so. All he could do was to gaze with bated breath and distended eyes upon the aisle of the church from whence the sound came.

That something of a terrific nature was now about to exhibit itself, and that the night would not go off without some terrible and significant adventure to make it remembered, he felt convinced. All he dreaded was to think for a moment what it might be.

His thoughts ran on Clara, and he murmured forth in the most agonising accents—

'Anything—any sight but the sight of her. Oh, no, no, no!'*

But it was not altogether the sight of her that he dreaded; oh no, it was the fact that the sight of her on such an occasion would bring the horrible conviction with it that there was some truth in the dreadful apprehension that he had of the new state of things that had ensued regarding the after death condition of that fair girl.

The noise increased each moment, and finally there was a sudden crash.

'She comes—she comes!'* gasped Ringwood.

He grasped the front of the pulpit with a frantic violence, and then slowly and solemnly there crossed his excited vision a figure all clothed in white. Yes, white flowing vestments, and he knew by their fashion that they were not worn by the living, and that it was some inhabitant of the tomb that he now looked upon.

He did not see the face. No, that for a time was hidden from him, but his heart told him who it was. Yes, it was his Clara.

It was no dream. It was no vision of a too excited fancy, for until those palpable sounds, and that most fearfully palpable form crossed his sight, he was rather inclined to go the other way, and to fancy what the sexton had reported was nothing but a delusion of his overwrought brain. Oh, that he could but for one brief moment have found himself deceived.

'Speak!' he gasped; 'speak, speak!'

There was no reply.

'I conjure you, I pray you, though the sound of your voice should hurl me to perdition—I implore you, speak.'

All was silent, and the figure in white moved on slowly but surely towards the door of the church, but ere it passed out, it turned for a moment, as if for the very purpose of removing from the mind of Ringwood any lingering doubt as to its identity.

He then saw the face, oh, so well-known, but so pale. It was Clara Crofton!

''Tis she!—'tis she!' was all he could say.

It seemed, too, as if some crevice in the clouds had opened at the moment, in order that he should with an absolute certainty see the countenance of that solemn figure, and then all was more than usually silent again. The door closed, and the figure was gone.

He rose in the pulpit, and clasped his hands. Irresolution seemed for a few moments to sway him to and fro, and then he rushed down into the body of the church.

'I'll follow it,' he cried, 'though it lead me to perdition. Yes, I'll follow it.'

He made his way to the door, and even as he went he shouted—'Clara—Clara—Clara!'

He reached the threshold of the ancient church; he gazed around him distractedly, for he thought that he had lost all sight of the figure. No—no, even in the darkness and against the night sky, he saw it once again in its sad-looking death raiments. He dashed forward.

The moonbeams at this instant being freed from some dense clouds that had interposed between them and this world, burst forth with resplendent beauty.

There was not a tree, a shrub, nor a flower, but what was made distinct and manifest, and with the church, such was the almost unprecedented lustre of the beautiful planet, that even the inscriptions upon the old tablets and tombs were distinctly visible.

Such a refulgence lasted not many minutes, but while it did, it was most beautiful, and the gloom that followed it seemed doubly black.

'Stay, stay,' he shouted, 'yet a moment, Clara; I swear that what you are, that will I be. Take me over to the tomb with you, say but that it is your dwelling-place, and I will make it mine, and declare it a very palace of the affections.'

The figure glided on.

It was in vain that he tried to keep up with it. It threaded the churchyard among the ancient tombs, with a gliding speed that soon distanced* him, impeded, as he continually was, by some obstacle or another, owing to looking at the apparition he followed, instead of the ground before him.

Still, on he went, heedless whither he was conveyed, for he might be said to be dragged onward, so much were all his faculties both of mind and body intent upon following the apparition of his beloved.

Once, and once only, the figure paused, and seemed to be aware that it was followed, for it flitted round an angle made by one of the walls of the church, and disappeared from his eyes.

In another moment he had turned the same point.

'Clara—Clara!' he shouted. ''Tis I—you know my voice, Clara—Clara!'

She was not to be seen, and then the idea struck him that she must have re-entered the church, and he, too, turned, and crossed the threshold. He lingered there for a moment or two, and the whole building echoed to the name of Clara, as with romantic eagerness he called upon her by name to come forth to him.

Those echoes were the only reply.

Maddened—rendered desperate beyond all endurance, he went some distance into the building in search of her, and again he called.

It was in vain; she had eluded him, and with all the carefulness and all the energy and courage he had brought to bear upon that night's proceedings, he was foiled. Could anything be more agonising than this to such a man as Ringwood—he who loved her so, that he had not shrunk from her, even in death, although she had so shrunk from him?

'I will find her—I will question her,' he cried. 'She shall not escape me; living or dead, she shall be mine. I will wait for her, even in the tomb.'

Before he carried out the intention of going actually into the vault to await her return, he thought he would take one more glance at the churchyard with the hope of seeing her there, as he could observe no indications of her presence in the church.

With this view he proceeded to the door, and emerged into the dim light. He called upon her again by name, and he thought he heard some faint sound in the church behind him. To turn and make a rush into the building was the work of a moment.

He saw something—it was black instead of white—a tall figure—it advanced towards him, and with great force,* before he was aware that an attack was at all intended, it felled him to the ground.

The blow was so sudden, so unexpected, and so severe, that it struck him down in a moment before he could be aware of it. To be sure, he had arms with him, but the anxiety and agony of mind he endured that night, since seeing the apparition come from the tomb, had caused him to forget them.

CHAPTER CV

The Young Girl in the Village, and the Awful Visit

It is now necessary that we draw the reader's attention to an humbler place of residence than the Grange,* with its spacious chambers and lordly halls.

Situated not very far from the church, and almost close to the churchyard, upon which its little garden abutted, was a cottage, the very picture of rural neatness and beauty. In the winter it was beautiful and picturesque, but in the summer time, when its porch was overrun with the woodbine and the sweet clematis, it was one of the sweetest of abodes that content and happiness could ever live in.

This cottage was inhabited by an old woman and her only child, a young girl of sixteen, beautiful as a rose, and as guileless as an angel. They contrived to live upon a small annuity that the mother had from a family in whose service she spent the best years of her life, and who, with a generosity that would be well to be abundantly and extensively imitated, would not see their old dependant want.

These two innocent and blameless persons had retired to rest at nine o'clock, their usual hour, and had slept the calm sleep of contentment until about half-past one, when the mother was awakened by a loud and piercing shriek from her daughter's chamber.

To spring from her humble couch was the work of a moment.

'Anna, Anna! my child, Anna!' she shrieked.

As she did so, she rushed across the small stair landing which separated the two, and the only two upper rooms of the cottage, and was about to enter her daughter's room, when the door of it was opened from within, and the old dame's heart died within her, as she saw a figure upon the threshold, attired in the vestments of the grave, and opposing her entrance.

Was it a dream, or did she really see such a sight?

Aghast and trembling the mother stood, unable for a moment or two to speak, and as she lay fainting upon the landing, she thought that something passed her, but she could not be quite sure, as it was at the instant her faculties were flitting from her.

How long she lay in that seeming death she knew not, and when she recovered, it was some few minutes before recollection came back to her, and she really remembered what had so completely overpowered her.

But when her reason did resume its sway, and she recollected that it was some danger to Anna which had first alarmed her, she called her loudly by name.

'Anna, Anna, speak to me.'

'Mother, mother,' replied the young girl. 'Oh, come to me.'

These words supplied strength to the old woman, and rising, she made her way immediately into the chamber of her daughter, whom she found in an agony of fear; a light was procured, and then Anna flung herself upon her mother's neck, and wept abundantly.

'Oh, mother, tell me, convince me that it was only a dream.'

'What, my child?—oh, what?'

The girl trembled so much that it was only by the utmost persuasion that the following account was got from her of the cause of her fright.

She said that she had gone to sleep as usual within a very few minutes after going to bed, that she enjoyed a calm, and uninterrupted slumber the duration of which she had no means whatever of guessing, but she was partially awakened by a noise at the window of her room.

She instantly rose and stood looking at the window, on which a sort of shadow seemed to pass without, which alarmed her exceedingly.

Still as it did not come again, and as she certainly had not been fully awake when she sprung from her bed, she had thought it quite possible that all might be a dream, and had forborne from making any alarm upon the subject.

After some hesitation, she had persuaded herself to go to bed again, and when there, although she sometimes started awake fancying she heard something, she at length yielded to sleep, and again slept soundly for a time, until a new circumstance awakened her.

She thought she felt something touching her about the neck, and after opening her eyes, the moonlight, which at that moment happened to be very bright, disclosed to her a white figure standing by the side of her bed, the face of which figure was leaning over her, and within a very few inches of her own.

Terror at first deprived her of all power of speech or motion, but as the figure did not move, she at length gave utterance to her fears in that shriek which had come from her lips, and so much alarmed the mother.

This was all the young girl could say, with the exception that the figure when she shrieked appeared to glide away, but where to she had no means of telling, for some clouds at that moment came again over the face of the moon.

The mother was much affected and terrified, and at first she thought of calling up her neighbours, but at length, as the night was considerably advanced, and the intruder gone, they agreed to let the matter rest till morning, and the mother retired to her room again.

How long it was before the shriek from her daughter's room came again she did not know, but come again it did.

Yes, again came the dreadful shriek. It was—it could be no delusion now—and the mother once more sprung from her couch to rush to the rescue of her child.

Confused and bewildered, she darted onward to the chamber, but the door was fast, nor could all her exertions suffice to open it.

'Anna, Anna!' she shouted, 'speak to me. One word only, my child, my child.'

All was still. The trembling mother placed her ear to the door, and she heard a strange sucking sound,* as if an animal was drinking with labour and difficulty. Her head seemed to be on fire, and her senses were upon the point of leaving her, but she did manage to reach her own room. She flew to the little casement—she dashed it open.

'Help! help! help!—for the love of God, help!'

There was no reply.

Again she raised her voice in shrieking wild accents.

'Help!—murder!—help!'

'What is it?' shouted a man's voice. It was one who was going some distance to take in his fishing nets.

'Oh! thank God, some human being hears me! Come in, come in!'

'How am I to get in?'

'Stay a moment, and I will come down and open the cottage door for you. For the love of mercy do not go away.'

Trembling and terrified to a dreadful excess, the old woman went down stairs and let the man into the cottage, when they both proceeded up to the chamber of the daughter.

'What do you suppose is the matter?' asked the fisherman.

'Oh! I know not—I know not; but twice to-night—twice has this dreadful alarm happened. Do not leave us—oh, do not.'

'I don't want; but I should hardly think thieves would find it worth their while to come here at all for what they would get. You must have been dreaming.'

'Oh, that I could think so!'

Anna's chamber was reached; and there, to the horror of the mother, she was found lying perfectly insensible on her bed, with a quantity of blood smeared about her neck.

'Why, it's a murder!' cried the fisherman; and firmly impressed with such a belief, he ran out of the house to spread an alarm.

The window of the chamber was wide open, and from that the mother now cried aloud for help; so that between her and the fisherman, such a disturbance was made all over the neighbourhood, that they were soon likely to have more assistance than could be useful.

The people living the nearest were soon roused, and they roused others, while the distracted woman, who believed Anna was dead, called for justice and for vengeance.

The alarm spread from house to house—from cottage to hall—and, in the course of half-an-hour, most of the inhabitants of the village had risen to hear the old dame's account of the horrible proceeding that had taken place that night in the cottage.

Exaggeration was out of the question. The fact itself was more than sufficient to induce the greatest amount of horror in the minds of all who heard it; and there was one, and only one, whose information enabled him to give a name to the apparition that had assaulted Anna. That one was the schoolmaster of the place, and he, after hearing the story, said—'If one could persuade oneself at all of the existence of such horrors, one would suppose that a vampyre had visited the cottage.'

This was a theme that was likely to be popular. The schoolmaster foolishly gave way to the vanity, and explained what a vampyre was—or was supposed and said to be; and soon the whole place was in a state of the most indescribable alarm upon the subject.

As yet the horrible news had not reached the Grange, but it was destined soon to do so; and better would it have been that any one had at once plunged a dagger in the heart of poor Sir George Crofton than that there should be thought to be such a horrible confirmation of his worst fears.

To be sure, his daughter was not named, but he received the news with a scream of anguish, and fell insensible into the arms of his son.

All was confusion. The servants ran hither and thither, not knowing what to do, and it was not until Mr. Bevan* arrived that something like order was restored. He as a privileged friend assumed for the nonce* a kind of dictatorship at the Grange, and gave orders, which were cheerfully and promptly obeyed. Then he desired a strictly private interview with Sir George.

It was, or course, granted to him; but the old baronet begged that Charles and Edwin* might now know all. It was Emma* alone from whom he wished to keep the awful truth.

CHAPTER CVI

The Awful Supposition—A Resolution

It was with some reluctance that the clergyman spoke.

'Sir,' he said to the old baronet, 'and you, my young gentleman, I am afraid—very much afraid, that I am doing anything but right in countenancing a supposition so utterly at variance with all my own notions and feelings; but my abhorrence of a secret impels me to speak.'

'Say on, sir—say on,' cried Sir George. 'Perhaps we are better prepared to hear what you have to tell us, than you imagine.'

After this Mr. Bevan had less reluctance to speak, and he said,—

'I was aware, although you all were not, that Mr. Ringwood intended to keep watch last night in the church, in order to test the truth of what had been told by Will Stephens, the sexton. I did all I could to persuade him from making the attempt, but when I found that nothing else would satisfy him, I thought it prudent to give him the means of carrying out what had become such a fixed intention with him, that to oppose it was to do far more mischief than to grant it all the aid I had in my power to do.'

Sir George gave a nod of assent.

'He went there,' continued Mr. Bevan, 'with a private key of my own, and took his place in the church.'

'I wish, sir, you had been with him,' said Edwin.

'Yes,' added Charles. 'If you, with your cool, calm, unbiassed judgment had been there, we should have been much better able to come to a correct conclusion about what occurred; for that something did occur, or was supposed by Ringwood to do so, we can well guess.'

'I wish, indeed, I had been there,' said Mr. Bevan, 'but he begged so earnestly to be allowed to go alone, that I had not the heart to refuse him.'

'And what happened, sir?'

'I will tell you. I gave him a key which admitted him to the church, by the small private entrance at which I usually go in myself; in fact, it was my own private key, for I at times visit the church, and wish to do so, when I am not expected by those who have the ordinary charge of it.'

'We have heard as much.'

'No doubt. Well, then, I say I gave that key, but it was my sympathy with his evident distress rather than my judgment which consented to do so, and I had hardly done it, when I began to busy myself with conjectures, and to deeply regret that I had yielded to him so easily. "What if he, in his excited and grief-stricken state of mind, should come to some serious mischief?" I said to myself, "should not I be very much to blame? Would not all prudent persons say that I did very wrong to send a man in such a condition of mind into a church at midnight, alone?"'

'Your motives and your known character, sir, would protect you,' said Charles.

'I hope so,' continued Mr. Bevan. 'I think it would from all other charges, but imprudence; and if any great mischance had befallen Ringwood, I should not so readily have forgiven myself, as others might have been induced to forgive me.'

'I understand that feeling,' said Sir George.

'Well, then, with such sensations tugging at my heart, no wonder I could not rest, and so at a little after twelve I rose, and hastily dressing myself, I left my house as noiselessly as possible, and made my way towards the church. The moon's light was at that time obscured, but every spot was so familiar to me, that I was able to go with speed, and I soon reached the venerable building. I walked round it, until I came to the door, the key of which I had given to Mr. Ringwood; it was open, but the moment I crossed the threshold, I stumbled on his insensible form.'

'Go on! go on! He had seen something terrible,' gasped Sir George; 'I am nerved, I think, for the very worst; I pray you, sir, go on, and tell me all.'

'I will, Sir George, because I feel convinced it is my duty to conceal nothing in this transaction, and because I think you had better more calmly and dispassionately, and without exaggeration, hear from me all that is to be told.'

'That is a good reason, sir,' said Edwin. 'We should, of course, hear all from other sources, and, probably, with all the aids that a feeling for the marvellous could append to it.'

'That is my impression. When, then, I stumbled over a person lying just within the little private door of the church, I had no immediate means of knowing who it was; I tell you it was Ringwood, because I afterwards discovered as much. I had the means of getting a light; when I did so, I found Ringwood lying in a swoon, while, at the same time, I could not but notice a large bruise upon his forehead.

'Of course, my first duty was to look after him, instead of troubling myself about his assailant, and having placed him in as convenient a posture as I could, I hurried home again, and roused up my servants. With their assistance I got him to my house, and placed him in bed.'

'And did you search the church, sir?'

'I did. I went back and searched it thoroughly, but found nothing at all suspicious. Everything was in its right place, and I could not account for the affair at all, because of the wound that Ringwood had. I was most anxious to hear from him that he had had a fall.'

'But—but,' said Sir George, falteringly, 'he told a different story?'

'He did.'

'A story which you will not keep from us.'

'I do not feel myself justified, as I have said, in keeping it from you. This is it.'

The clergyman then related to the family of the Croftons what is already known to the reader concerning the adventures of Ringwood in the old church, and which that morning, upon his recovery, Ringwood had told to him most circumstantially.

We need scarcely say that this recital was listened to with the most agonized feelings. Poor Sir George appeared to be most completely overcome by it. He trembled excessively, and could not command himself sufficiently to speak.

The two brothers looked at each other in dismay.

'Now, I pray you all to consider this matter more calmly,' said Mr. Bevan, 'than you seem inclined to do.'

'Calmly!' gasped Sir George, 'calmly!'

'Yes—what evidence have we after all that the whole affair is anything more than a dream of Mr. Ringwood's?'

'Does he doubt it?'

'No—I am bound to tell you that he does not; but we may well do so for all that. He is the last person who is likely to give in to the opinion that it is a mere vision, so strangely impressed as it is upon his imagination. Recollect always that he went to the church prepared to see something.'

'Oh, if we could but think it unreal,' said Sir George, glancing at his sons, as if to gather their opinions of the matter from their countenances.

'I will cling to such a thought,' said Charles, 'until I am convinced otherwise through the medium of my own senses.'

'And I,' said Edwin.

'You are right,' added Mr. Bevan. 'I never, in the whole course of my experience, heard of anything of which people should be so slow of believing in, as this most uncomfortable affair. You now know all, and it is for yourselves, of course to make whatever determination you think fit. If I might advise, it would be that you all take a short tour, perhaps on the continent, for a time.'

'Mr. Bevan,' said Sir George, in a kindly tone, 'I am greatly obliged to you. The suggestion, I know, springs from the very best and friendly motives; but it carries with it a strong presumption that you really do think there is something in all this affair which it would have been as well to have settled in my absence.'

The clergyman could not deny but that some such feeling was at the bottom of his advice; but still he would not admit that he was at all convinced of the reality of what was presumed to have happened, and a short pause in the conversation ensued, after which Sir George spoke with a solemn air of determination, saying to his sons, as well as to his friend and pastor, Mr. Bevan:

'When I tell you that I have made a determination from which nothing but the hand of Heaven visiting me with death shall move me, I hope no one here will try to dissuade me from carrying it out.'

After such an exordium* it was a difficult thing to say anything to him, so he continued—

'My child was dear—very dear to me in life, and I have no superstitious fears concerning one who held such a place in my affections. I am resolved that to-night I will watch her poor remains, and at once convince myself of a horror that may drive me mad, or take a mountain of grief and apprehension off my heart.'

'Father,' cried Charles, 'you will allow me to accompany you?'

'And me?' added Edwin.

'My sons, you are both deeply interested in* this matter—you would be miserable while I was gone if you were not with me. Moreover, I will not trust my own imagination entirely—we will all three go, and then we cannot be deceived. This is my most solemn resolution.'

'I have only one thing to say regarding it,' said Mr. Bevan; 'that is, to prefer an earnest request that you will allow me to be one of the party—you shall sit in a pew of the church, that shall command a view of the whole building.'

'Accompany us, Mr. Bevan, if you will,' said Sir George, 'but I sit in no pew.'

'No pew?'

'No. By my child's coffin, in the vault where repose the remains of more than one of my race who had been dear to me in life, will I take my place.'

There was an earnest resolved solemnity about Sir George's manner, which showed that he was not to be turned from his purpose, and Mr. Bevan accordingly did not attempt to do so. He had done what he scarcely expected, that is, got a consent to accompany him to the night vigil, and at all events, let what would happen, he, as a more disinterested party than the others, would be able, probably, to interfere and prevent any disastrous circumstances from arising.

Besides, his mind was more clear than Sir George's, he considered, after the severe shock it had sustained in the loss of his dear child, and the other melancholy attendant circumstances with which the reader is well acquainted. Mr. Bevan also argued in his mind, that if anything of an extraordinary character should take place—something out of the common methodical calculation of mankind, he should be enabled to make his deductions from what he saw and heard with far greater clearness and fairness than could be the case in so interested a person as Sir George really was. In the pursuits of life Sir George had been active and energetic, and anything in the ordinary run of matters might be well placed in his hands; but where the imagination was likely to be played on through the feelings, Mr. Bevan thought any but Sir George's judgment would be preferable.

'Say nothing of what has been determined on to any one,' said Sir George, 'keep it a profound secret, sir, and this night will put an end to the agony of doubt.'

'Depend upon me. Will you come to my house at eleven o'clock, or shall I come here?'

'We will come to you; it is in the way.'

Thus then the affair was settled, so far satisfactorily, that there was to be a watch actually now in the vault, so that there could be no delusion, no trick practised. What will be the result will be shown very shortly; in the meantime we cannot but tremble at what that attached and nearly heart-broken father may have still to go through.

The excitement, too, in the village was immense; for the story of the vampyre's attack upon the young girl was fresh in everybody's mouth, and it lost nothing of its real horrors by the frequency with which it was repeated, and the terror-stricken manner in which it was dilated upon.

[CHAPTERS CVII, CVIII]*

CHAPTER CIX

The Madman—The Vampyre

'WHAT does this mean?' cried Sir George Crofton, excitedly.

'Hush!' said Mr. Bevan, 'I pray you be calm, sir. If you are to make any discovery that will give you peace of mind, rest assured it will not be made by violence.'

'You do not answer my question.'

'I cannot answer it. Remember that I know no more than you do, and that, like yourselves, I am an adventurer here in search of the truth.'

Sir George said no more upon that head, but with clasped hands and downcast eyes he stood in silence, while his two sons, armed with the crowbars that Mr. Bevan had provided for the occasion, proceeded to lift up the marble slab that covered the vault where lay their sister's remains.

The work was not one of great difficulty, for the slab was not very large, and as it was not cemented down, it yield at once to the powerful leverage that was brought to play against it, and in a few minutes it was placed aside, and the yawning abyss appeared before them.

'Oh, sir,' said Mr. Bevan, 'even now at this late hour, when the proceedings have commenced, I pray you to pause.'

'Pause!' cried Sir George, passionately, 'pause for what?'

'Disturb not the dead, and let them rest in peace. Absolve your mind from the dangerous and perhaps fatal fancies that possess it, and let us say a prayer, and close again this entrance to the tomb.'

The sons hesitated, and they probably would have taken the clergyman's advice, but Sir George was firm.

'No, sir,' he said, 'already have I suffered much in coming thus far; I will not retreat until I have effected all my purpose. I swear it, by Heaven, whose temple we now are in. You would not, Mr. Bevan, have me break such an oath.'

'I would not; but I regret you made it. Since, however, it must be so, and this rash adventure is determined upon, follow me; I will lead you the way into these calm regions, where you can sleep, I trust, in peace.'

Sir George Crofton made a step forward, as if he would have arrested Mr. Bevan's progress and led the way himself, but already the clergyman had descended several steps, so he had nothing to do but to follow him.

This they all did, Sir George going immediately after him, and his two sons, with pale anxious-looking faces, as if they had a suspicion that the adventure would end in something terrific, came after him, and glanced nervously and suspiciously about them; but they said not a word, for if they had spoken, it would have been to express great apprehension, and that was what they were ashamed to do.

Mr. Bevan carried the light, and when he felt that he was at the bottom of the stone steps, by finding that he was treading upon the sawdust that was strewn on the floor of the vault, he turned and held the lamp up at arm's length, so that his companions might see their way down the steps.

In another minute they all stood on the floor of the vault.

The light burnt with rather a faint and sickly glare, for so rapidly were noxious gases evolved* in that receptacle for the dead, that notwithstanding it had been so frequently opened as it had been lately, they had again accumulated.

In a few moments, however, this was partially remedied by the air from the church above, and the light burnt more brilliantly—indeed, quite sufficiently so to enable them to look around them in the vault.

Sir George Crofton's feelings at that moment must have been of the most painful and harrowing description. He had lived long enough to be a witness of the death and the obsequies of many members of his family, whom he had loved fondly, and there he stood in that chamber of death, surrounded by all the remains of those beings, the memory of whose appearance and voices came at once freshly upon his mind.

Mr. Bevan could well guess the nature of the sad thoughts that transpired in the breast of the baronet, and the sons having by accident cast their eyes upon the coffin that contained the remains of their mother, regarded it in silence, while memory was busy, too, within them in conjuring up her image.

'And it has come to this,' said Sir George, solemnly.

'We must all come to this,' interposed Mr. Bevan; 'this is indeed a place for solemn and holy thoughts—for self-examination, for self-condemnation.'

'But there is peace here.'

'There is—the peace that shall be eternal.'

'Hark! hark!' said Charles; 'what is that?'

'The wind,' said Mr. Bevan; 'nothing but the wind howling round and through the old belfry—you will remember that it is a boisterous night.'

'Turn, turn, father.'

Sir George turned and looked at Charles, who pointed in silence to the coffin which contained the corpse of his mother. The light gleamed upon the plate on which was engraved her name. Sir George's features moved convulsively as he read it, and he turned aside to hide a sudden gush of emotion that came over him.

After a few minutes, he touched Mr. Bevan on the arm, and said in a whisper—

'Where did they place my child?'

The clergyman pointed to the narrow shelf on which was the coffin of Clara Crofton, and then Sir George, making a great effort to overcome his feelings, said—

'Mr. Bevan, our worthy minister and friend, and you, likewise, my boys, hear me. You can guess to some extent, but not wholly—that can only be known by God—the agony that a sight of the poor remains of her who has gone from me in all the pride of her youth and beauty must be to me; yet now that I am here I consider it to be my duty to look once again upon the face of my child—my—my lost Clara.'

'Oh! father, father,' said Edwin, 'forego this purpose.'

'You will spare us this,' cried Charles.

'Repent you, sir,' said Mr. Bevan, 'of the wish. Let her rest in peace. The dead are sanctified.'

'The dead are sanctified—but I am her father.'

'Nay, Sir George, let me implore you.'

'Implore me to what, sir? Not to look upon the face of my own child? Peace—peace. It is no profanation for one who loved her as I loved her, to look upon her once again. Urge me no more.'

'This is in vain,' said Charles.

'You are right—it is in vain.'

A shriek burst from the lips of Edwin at this moment, and flinging his arms around his father, he held him back. Mr. Bevan, too, gave a cry of terror, and Charles stood with his hands clasped, as if turned to stone.

Their eyes were all bent upon Clara's coffin.

The lid moved, and a strange sound was heard from within that receptacle for the dead—the clock of the old church struck twelve—the coffin lid moved again, and then sliding on one side, it eventually fell upon the floor of the vault.

The four spectators of this scene were struck speechless for the time with terror. Then they stood gazing at the coffin as if they were so many statues.

And now the light which Mr. Bevan still, for a miracle, held in his trembling grasp, shone on a mass of white clothing within the coffin, and in another moment that white clothing was observed to be in motion. Slowly the dead form that was there rose up, and they all saw the pale and ghastly face. A streak of blood was issuing from the mouth, and the eyes were open.

Sir George Crofton lifted up both his hands, and struck his head, and then he burst into a wild frightful laugh. It was the laugh of insanity.

Mr. Bevan dropped the light, and all was darkness.

'Ha, ha, ha, ha, ha!' laughed Sir George Crofton. 'Ha, ha, ha, ha, ha!' and the horrible laugh was taken up by many an echo in the old church, and responded to with strange and most unearthly reverberations. 'Ha, ha, ha, ha!' Oh, what a dreadful sound that was, coming at such a time from the lips of the father.

'Fly Edwin—oh, fly,' cried Charles.

Edwin screamed twice, for he was full of horror, and then he fell on the floor of the vault in a state of insensibility.

Charles had just sense left him to spring towards the steps, and make a frantic effort to reach the church; in his hurry he fell twice, but each time rising again with a shout of despair he resumed his efforts, and all the while the horrible laugh of his maniac father sounded in his ears, a sound which he felt that he should never forget.

By a great effort he did reach the aisle of the church, and when there, he called aloud—

'Mr. Bevan, Mr. Bevan, help—oh help! For the love of God speak! Help, help, Mr. Bevan! where are you? Speak, I implore you! Am I, too, going mad? Oh yes, I shall—I must! What mortal intellect can stand such a scene as this. Help, help—oh, help!'

The church was suddenly lit up by a flash of light, and turning in the direction from whence it proceeded, Charles saw Mr. Bevan approaching with a light which he had procured from the chancel,* and it would appear that immediately upon dropping in his horror the light in the vault, he had run up the stairs with the intent of getting another.

'Who calls me? Who calls me?' he cried.

'I—I,' said Charles. 'Oh, God, what a dreadful night is this.'

The clergyman was trembling violently, and was very pale, but he made his way up to Charles, from whose brow the perspiration was falling in heavy drops, and then again they heard the mad Sir George laughing in the vault.

'Ha, ha, ha! ha, ha, ha! ha, ha, ha!'

'Oh, God, is not that horrible?' said Charles.

'Most horrible,' responded Mr. Bevan.

Bang—bang—bang! at this moment came a violent knocking at the church door, and then several voices were heard without shouting—

'The vampyre—the vampyre—the vampyre.'

'What is that? What is that?' said Charles.

'Nay, I know not,' replied Mr. Bevan, 'I am nearly distracted already. Where is your brother? Did he not escape from the vault? Where is he? Oh, that horrible laugh! Good God! that knocking, too, at the church door. What can be the meaning of it? Heaven in its mercy guide us now what to do.'

The reader will understand the meaning of the knocking, although those bewildered persons who heard it in the church did not. The fact is, that the party from the alehouse, headed by the valiant blacksmith, and heated by their too liberal potations, had just arrived at the church, and were clamouring for admission.

They had seen through one of the old painted windows the reflection of the light which Mr. Bevan carried, and that it was that convinced them some one was there who might, if he would, pay attention to the uproarious summons.

The knocking lasted with terrible effect, for the old door of the sacred edifice shook again, it seemed as if certainly it could not resist the making of such an attack.

Mr. Bevan was confounded. A horrible suspicion came across him of what was meant by those violent demands for admission, and he shook with great trepidation as he conjectured what might be the effect of the proceedings of a lawless mob.

'Now Heaven help us,' he said, 'for we shall soon, I fear, be powerless.'

'Good God! what mean you?' said Charles.

'I scarcely know how to explain to you all my fears. They are too dreadful to think of, but while that knocking continues, what can I think?'

'I understand! they call for my sister.'

'Oh, call her not now by that name. Remember, and remember with a shudder, what she now is.'

CHAPTER CX

The Hunt of the Vampyre

ALL these occurrences which have taken a considerable time in telling, occurred so simultaneously, that although it would appear Mr. Bevan and Charles Crofton rather neglected Sir George and Edwin, who were still in the vault, they had really not had time to think of them, to say nothing of making an effort to extricate them from the frightful situation in which they were placed.

Probably, after procuring a light, Mr. Bevan would have rushed to their rescue had not that incessant knocking at the church-door suggested a new and more horrible danger still, from the evil passions of an infuriated multitude.

'Oh, Mr. Charles,' he said, 'if we could but get your father away from the church, there is no knowing what an amount of misery he might be spared.'

'Misery, sir? Surely there is no more misery in store for us—have we not suffered enough—more than enough? Oh, Mr. Bevan, we have fallen upon evil times, and I dread to think what will yet be the end of these most frightful transactions.'

The mass of persons who at that unseemly hour of the night had made their way to the church door, again made an unmistakable summons for admission by striking with force the oak panels of the door; but fortunately for those within they resisted their united efforts. Such a state of affairs could not last long; no bolts, locks or wood would be long in giving way to the dogged perseverance of the mob, which was composed of men, women, and children of all ages, amounting to some hundreds.

'A crowbar! go and fetch a crowbar!' shouted a stentorian voice. 'Without a crowbar, it is impossible to force an entrance.'

Following this demand there was a tumultuous noise, for every one was giving his advice or instructions as to where such an implement was to be obtained. In a few minutes, however, a rough voice exclaimed—

'Clear the way there, I'll soon make an entrance;' as he spoke he held aloft a huge bar of iron bevelled at one end. Charles, hearing the continued noise, but not catching the purport of the words uttered, indicated a wish to proceed there to ascertain what it was, but Mr. Bevan stopped him, saying—

'No, Charles, no—let them be, I hardly think they will venture to break into the sacred edifice, but whether they do or not, remember that your duty and mine, yours being the duty of a son, and mine that of a friend, should take us now to your father's vault.'

'That is true, sir,' said Charles, 'lead on, I will follow you.'

Mr. Bevan, who had all the intellectual courage of a man of education, and of regular habits, led the way again to the vault with the light in his hand. It was a great relief that the insane and horrible laugh of Sir George Crofton had ceased; the best friend of any man could almost have wished him dead, ere their ears had drunk in such horrible sounds.

The shouts and cries from without now became incessant, and it seemed as if some weapon had been procured, wherewith to hammer violently upon the church-door, for the strokes were regular and incessant, and it was evident that if they continued long that frail defence against the incursions of the rabble rout without must soon give way.

The only effect, however, which these sounds had upon Mr. Bevan was to make him hasten his progress towards the vault, for anything in the shape of a collision between those who wanted to take the church by storm, and Sir George Crofton, was, indeed, most highly to be deprecated.*

The steps were not many in number, and once again the clergyman and Charles Crofton stood upon the sawdust that covered the flooring of the vault.

At first, in consequence of the flaring of the light, the state of affairs in that dismal region could not be ascertained; but as soon as they could get a view, they found Sir George lying apparently in a state of insensibility across the coffin of his daughter Clara, while Edwin was in a swoon close to his feet.

'Sir George—Sir George,' cried Mr. Bevan; 'arouse yourself; it is necessary that you leave this place at once.'

The baronet got up and glanced at the intruders. Charles uttered a deep groan, for the most superficial observation of his father's face was sufficient to convince him that reason had fled, and that wildness had set up his wild dominion* in his brain.

'Father—father!' he cried, 'speak to me, and dissipate a frightful thought.'

'What would you have of me?' said Sir George; 'I am a vampyre, and this is my tomb—you should see me in the rays of the cold moon gliding 'twixt earth and heaven, and panting for a victim. I am a vampyre.'

At this moment Edwin seemed to be partially recovering, for his eyes opened as he lay upon the floor, and he looked around him with a bewildered gaze, which soon settled into one of more intelligence as memory resumed her sway, and he recollected the various circumstances that had brought him into his present position.

'Rouse yourself, Edwin, rouse yourself,' cried Mr. Bevan, 'you must aid us to remove your father.'

'Do you talk of me?' said Sir George, 'know you not that I am one of those supernatural existences known as the death and despair-dealing vampyres—it's time I took my nightly prowl to look for victims. I must have blood—I must have blood!'

'Gracious Heaven! he raves,' said Charles.

'Heed him not,' said Mr. Bevan—'heed him not, and touch him not, so that he leave the place—when we have him once clear of the church we can procure assistance, and take him to his own home.'

'Edwin,' whispered Charles, 'what of our sister?'

Edwin shook his head and shuddered. 'I know nothing but that I saw her—oh, horrible sight, rising from her coffin, and then in a convulsion of terror my senses fled—a frightful ringing laugh came on my ears, and from that time till now, be the period long or short, I have been blessed by a death-like trance.'

'Blessed, indeed,' said Mr. Bevan; 'tarry* one moment.'

Sir George Crofton was ascending the steps of the vault, but his two sons paused for an instant at the request of Mr. Bevan, and then the latter approaching Clara's coffin slightly removed the lid, and was gratified, as far as any feeling could be considered gratification under such circumstances, to find that the corpse occupied an ordinary position in its narrow resting place.

'All's right,' he said, 'let us persuade ourselves that this, too, has been but a dream, that we have been deceived, and that imagination has played us tricks it is accustomed to play to those who give it the rein at such hours as these—let us think and believe anything rather than that what we have seen to-night is a reality.'

As he spoke these words, he ascended hastily the steps in pursuit of Sir George, who, by this time, had alone reached the door.

The heavy strokes against the door of the church had ceased, but an odd sort of scraping, rattling sound at the lock, convinced the clergyman that a workman of more skill than he who had wielded the hammer was now at work, endeavouring to force an entrance.

'Oh, if we could but get out,' he said, 'by the small private entrance, all might be well; Charles, urge your father, I pray you.'

Charles did so to the best of his ability; but the blacksmith who had originally incited the crowd to attack the church, in order to get possession of the body of the vampyre, had sent to his workshop for the tools of his craft, and soon quietly accomplished by skill, what brute force would have been a long time about, namely, the opening of the church-door.

It was flung wide open, before Sir George Crofton and his sons could reach the small private entrance, of which Mr. Bevan had the key.

The sight of the multitude of persons, for they looked such crowds in the church-porch, materially increased the incipient madness of the bereaved father.

CHAPTER CXI

The Fate of Sir George—The Cross Road

Sir George, when he saw the crowd of persons, seemed to have some undefined idea that they were enemies, but this would not have been productive of any serious consequences, if it had not most unfortunately happened that a most formidable weapon was within his grasp.

That weapon consisted of one of the long iron crowbars which had been successfully used by his own sons in order to force a passage to the family vault, where such horrors had been witnessed.

Suddenly, then, seizing this weapon, which, in the hands of a ferocious man, was a most awful one, he swung it once round his head, and then rushed upon those he considered his foes.

He dealt but three blows, and at each of those one of the assailants fell lifeless in the church-porch.

To resist, or, to attempt to contend with a man so armed, and apparently possessed of such preternatural strength, was what none of the party wished, and accordingly a free passage was left for him, and he rushed out of the church into the night air shouting for vengeance, and still at intervals accusing himself of being a vampyre, a most dangerous theme to touch upon, considering the then state of feeling in that little district.

Anxiety for the safety of Sir George induced his sons and Mr. Bevan to rush after him, regardless of all other consequences, so that the church, the vaults, and everything they contained, were left to the mercy of a mob infuriated by superstition, rendered still more desperate by the loss of three of their number in so sudden and unexampled a manner.

They opposed no obstacle to the leaving of those persons, who thus for dearer considerations abandoned the old church, but they rushed with wild shouts and gesticulations into the building.

'The vampyre, the vampyre,' cried the blacksmith, 'death to the vampyre—death and destruction to the vampyre!'

'Hurrah!' cried another, 'to the vaults—this way to Sir George Crofton's vault.'

There seemed to be little doubt now but that this disorderly rabble would execute summary vengeance upon the supposed nocturnal disturber of the peace of the district.

Ever and anon, too, as these shouts of discord and of threatening vengeance rose upon the night air, there would come the distant muttering of thunder, for the storm had not yet ceased, although its worst fury had certainly passed away.

Dark and heavy clouds were sweeping up from the horizon, and it seemed to be tolerably evident that some heavy deluge of rain would eventually settle the fury of the elements, and reconcile the discord of wind and electricity.

Several of the rioters were provided with links and matches,* so that in a few moments the whole interior of the church was brilliantly illuminated, while at the same time it presented a grotesque appearance, in consequence of the unsteady and wavering flame from the links, throw myriads of dancing shadows upon the walls.

There would have been no difficulty, under any ordinary circumstances, in finding the entrance to the vault, where the dead of the Crofton family should have lain in peace, but now since the large flagstone that covered the entrance to that receptacle of the grave was removed, it met their observation at once.

It was strange now to perceive how, for a moment, superstition having led them on so far, the same feeling should induce them to pause, ere they ventured to make their way down these gloomy steps.

It was a critical moment, and probably if any one or two had taken a sudden panic, the whole party might have left the church with precipitation, having done a considerable amount of mischief, and yet, as it is so usual with rioters, having left their principal object unaccomplished.

The blacksmith put an end to this state of indecision, for, seizing a link from the man who was nearest to him, he darted hastily down the steps, exclaiming as he did so—

'Whoever's afraid, need not follow me.'

This was a taunt they were not exactly prepared to submit to, and the consequence was, that in a very few moments the ancient and time-honoured vault of the Croftons was more full of the living than of the dead.

The blacksmith laid his hand upon Clara's coffin.

'Here it is,' he said; 'I know the very pattern of the cloth, and the fashion of the nails. I saw it at Grigson's the undertaker's before it was taken to the Grange.'

'Is she there—is she there?' cried half-a-dozen voices at once.

Even the blacksmith hesitated a moment ere he removed the lid from the receptacle of death, but when he did so, and his eyes fell upon the face of the presumed vampyre, he seemed rejoiced to find in the appearances then exhibited some sort of justification for the act of violence of which already he had been the instigator.

'Here you are,' he said, 'look at the bloom upon her lips; why her cheeks are fresher and rosier than ever they were while she was alive; a vampyre, my mates, this is a vampyre, or may I never break bread again; and now what's to be done?'

'Burn her—burn her!' cried several.

'Well,' said the blacksmith, 'mind it's as you like. I've brought you here, and shown you what it is, and now you can do what you like, and of course I'll lend you a hand to do it.'

Any one who had been very speculative in this affair might have detected in these last words of the blacksmith something like an inclination to creep out of the future consequences of what might next be done, while at the same time shame deterred him from exactly leaving his companions in the lurch.

After some suggestions then, and some argumentation as to the probability or possibility of interruption—the coffin itself was, with its sad and wretched occupant, lifted from the niche where it should have remained until that awful day when the dead shall rise for judgment, and carried up the steps into the church; from thence they passed into the graveyard, but scarcely had they done so, when the surcharged clouds burst over their heads, and the rain came down in perfect torrents.

The deluge was of so frightful and continuous a character, that they shrank back again beneath the shelter of the church porch, and there waited until its first fury had passed away.

Such an even down storm seldom lasts long in our climate, and the consequence was that in about ten minutes the shower had so far subsided that, although a continuous rain was falling, it bore but a very distant comparison to what had taken place.

'How are we to burn the body on such a night as this?'

'Aye, how indeed,' said another; 'you could not so much as kindle a fire, and if you did, it would not live many minutes.'

'I'll tell you what to do at once,' said one who had as yet borne but a quiet part in the proceedings; 'I'll tell you what to do at once, for I saw it done myself; a vampyre is quite as secure buried in a cross-road with a stake through its body,* as if you burned it in all the fires in the world; come on, the rain won't hinder you doing that.'

This was a suggestion highly approved of, and the more so as there was a cross-road close at hand, so that the deed would be done quick, and the parties dispersed to their respective homes, for already the exertion they had taken, and the rain that had fallen, had had a great effect in sobering them.

And even now the perilous and disgusting operation of destroying the body, by fire or any other way, might have been abandoned, had any one of the party suggested such a course—but the dread of a future imputation of cowardice kept all silent.

Once more the coffin was raised by four of the throng, and carried through the church-yard, which was now running in many little rivulets, in consequence of the rain. The cross-road was not above a quarter of a mile from the spot, and while those who were disengaged from carrying the body were hurrying away to get spades and mattocks, the others walked through the rain, and finally paused at the place they thought suitable for that ancient superstitious rite, which it was thought would make the vampyre rest in peace.

It is hard to suppose that Sir George Crofton, his sons, and Mr. Bevan were all deceived concerning these symptoms of vitality which they had observed in the corpse of Clara; but certainly now, there was no appearance of anything of the kind, and the only suspicious circumstances appeared to be the blood upon the lips, and the very fresh-like appearance of the face.

If it were really a fact that the attack of Varney the Vampyre upon this fair young girl had converted her into one of those frightful existences, and that she had been about to leave her tomb for the purpose of seeking a repast of blood, it would appear that the intention had been checked and frustrated by the presence of Sir George and his party in the vault.

At last a dozen men now arrived well armed with spades and picks, and they commenced the work of digging a deep, rather than a capacious grave in silence.

A gloomy and apprehensive spirit seemed to come over the whole assemblage, and the probability is that this was chiefly owing to the fact that they now encountered no opposition, and that they were permitted unimpeded to accomplish a purpose which had never yet been attempted within the memory of any of the inhabitants of the place.

The grave was dug, and about two feet depth of soil was thrown in a huge mound upon the surface; the coffin was lowered, and there lay the corpse within that receptacle of poor humanity, unimprisoned by any lid, for that had been left in the vault, and awaiting the doom which they had decreed upon it, but which they now with a shuddering horror shrunk from performing.

A hedge-stake with a sharp point had been procured, and those who held it looked around them with terrified countenances, while the few links that had not been extinguished by the rain shed a strange and lurid glare upon all objects.

'It must be done,' said the blacksmith, 'don't let it be said that we got thus far and then were afraid.'

'Do it then yourself,' said the man that held the stake, 'I dare not.'

'Aye, do,' cried several voices; 'you brought us here, why don't you do it—are you afraid after all your boasting?'

'Afraid—afraid of the dead? I'm not afraid of any of you that are alive, and it's not likely I'm going to be afraid of a dead body; you're a pretty set of cowards. I've no animosity against the girl, but I want that we shall all sleep in peace, and that our wives and children should not be disturbed nocturnally in their blessed repose. I'll do it if none of you'll do it, and then you may thank me afterwards for the act, although I suppose if I get into trouble I shall have you all turn tail upon me.'

'No, we won't—no, we won't.'

'Well, well, here goes, whether you do or not. I—I'll do it directly.'

'He shrinks,' cried one.

'No,' said another; 'he'll do it—now for it, stand aside.'

'Stand aside yourself—do you want to fall into the grave?'

The blacksmith shuddered as he held the stake in an attitude to pierce the body, and even up to that moment it seemed to be a doubtful case whether he would be able to accomplish his purpose or not; at length, when they all thought he was upon the point of abandoning his design, and casting the stake away, he thrust it with tremendous force through the body and the back of the coffin.

The eyes of the corpse opened wide—the hands were clenched, and a shrill, piercing shriek came from the lips—a shriek that was answered by as many as there were persons present, and then with pallid fear upon their countenances they rushed headlong from the spot.

CHAPTER CXII

The Solitary Man—Varney's Despair

THERE lay the dead, alone, in that awful grave, dabbled in blood, and the victim of the horrible experiment that had been instituted to lay a vampyre.

The rain still fell heavily.

Oh, surely, pitying Heaven sent those drops to wash out the remembrance of such a deed. The grave slowly began to be a pool of water; it rose up the sides of the coffin, and in a few minutes more nothing of the ghastly and the terrible contents of that grave could have been seen.

Before that took place, a man of tall stature and solemn gait stepped up and stood upon the brink of the little excavation.

For a time he was as still as that sad occupant of the little space of earth that served her for a resting place; but at length in a tone of deep anguish, he spoke—'And has it come to this?' he said, 'is this my work? Oh, horror! horror, unspeakable. Is this some hideous dream, or a reality of tragedy, so far transcending all I looked for, that if I had tears I should shed them now? But I have none. A hundred years ago that fount was dry. I thought that I had steeled my heart against all gentle impulses; that I had crushed—ay, completely crushed dove-eyed pity in my heart; but it is not so, and still sufficient of my once human feelings clings to me to make me grieve for thee, Clara Crofton, thou victim!'

We need not tell our readers now, that it was no other than Varney the vampyre* himself from whom these words came. ...

KARL ADOLF VON WACHSMANN

THE MYSTERIOUS STRANGER

'To die?—to sleep!
Perchance to dream? Ay, there's the rub.'—*Hamlet*.*

Boreas,* that fearful north-west wind, which in the spring and autumn stirs up the lowest depths of the wild Adriatic,* and is then so dangerous to vessels, was howling through the woods, and tossing the branches of the old knotty oaks in the Carpathian Mountains,* when a party of five riders, who surrounded a litter drawn by a pair of mules, turned into a forest-path, which offered some protection from the April weather, and allowed the travellers in some degree to recover their breath. It was already evening, and bitterly cold; the snow fell every now and then in large flakes. A tall old gentleman, of aristocratic appearance, rode at the head of the troop. This was the Knight of Fahnenberg,* in Austria. He had inherited from a childless brother a considerable property, situated in the Carpathian Mountains; and he had set out to take possession of it, accompanied by his daughter Franziska, and a niece about twenty years of age, who had been brought up with her. Next to the knight rode a fine young man some twenty and odd years—the Baron Franz von Kronstein; he wore, like the former, the broad-brimmed hat with hanging feathers, the leather collar, the wide riding-boots—in short, the travelling-dress which was in fashion at the commencement of the seventeenth century. The features of the young man had much about them that was open and friendly, as well as some mind; but the expression was more that of dreamy and sensitive softness than of youthful daring, although no one could deny that he possessed much of youthful beauty. As the cavalcade turned into the oak wood, the young man rode up to the litter, and chatted with the ladies who were seated therein. One of these—and to her his conversation was principally addressed—was of dazzling beauty. Her hair flowed in natural curls round the fine oval of her face, out of which beamed a pair of star-like eyes, full of genius, lively fancy, and a certain degree of archness. Franziska von Fahnenberg seemed to attend but carelessly to the speeches of her admirer, who made many kind inquiries as to how she felt herself during the journey, which had been attended with many difficulties: she always answered him very shortly, almost contemptuously; and at length remarked, that if it had not been for her father's objections, she would long ago have requested the baron to take her place in their horrid cage of a litter, for, to judge by his remarks, he seemed incommoded by the weather; and she would so much rather be mounted on the spirited horse, and face wind and storm, than be mewed up* there, dragged up the hills by those long-eared animals, and mope herself to death with ennui. The young lady's words, and, still more, the half-contemptuous tone in which they were uttered, appeared to make the most painful impression on the young man: he made her no reply at the moment, but the absent air with which he attended to the kindly-intended remarks of the other young lady, shewed how much he was disconcerted.

'It appears, dear Franziska,' said he at length in a kindly tone, 'that the hardships of the road have affected you more than you will acknowledge. Generally so kind to others, you have been very often out of humour during the journey, and particularly with regard to your humble servant and cousin, who would gladly bear a double or treble share of the discomforts, if he could thereby save you from the smallest of them.'

Franziska shewed by her look that she was about to reply with some bitter jibe, when the voice of the knight was heard calling for his nephew, who galloped off at the sound.

'I should like to scold you well, Franziska,' said her companion somewhat sharply, 'for always plaguing your poor Cousin Franz in this shameful way; he who loves you so truly, and who, whatever you may say, will one day be your husband.'

'My husband!' replied the other angrily. 'I must either completely alter my ideas, or he his whole self, before that takes place. No, Bertha! I know that this is my father's darling wish, and I do not deny the good qualities Cousin Franz may have, or really has, since I see you are making a face; but to marry an effeminate* man—never!'

'Effeminate! you do him great injustice,' replied her friend quickly. 'Just because instead of going off to the Turkish war, where little honour was to be gained, he attended to your father's advice, and stayed at home, to bring his neglected estate into order, which he accomplished with care and prudence; and because he does not represent this howling wind as a mild zephyr—for reasons such as these you are pleased to call him effeminate.'

'Say what you will, it is so,' cried Franziska obstinately. 'Bold, aspiring, even despotic, must be the man who is to gain my heart; these soft, patient, and thoughtful natures are utterly distasteful to me. Is Franz capable of deep sympathy, either in joy or sorrow? He is always the same—always quiet, soft, and tiresome.'

'He has a warm heart, and is not without genius,' said Bertha.

'A warm heart! that may be,' replied the other; 'but I would rather be tyrannized over, and kept under a little by my future husband, than be loved in such a wearisome manner. You say he has genius, too. I will not exactly contradict you, since that would be unpolite, but it is not easily discovered. But even allowing you are right in both statements, still the man who does not bring these qualities into action is a despicable creature. A man may do many foolish things, he may even be a little wicked now and then, provided it is in nothing dishonourable; and one can forgive him, if he is only acting on some fixed theory for some special object. There is, for instance, your own faithful admirer, the Castellan of Glogau, Knight of Woislaw;* he loves you most truly, and is now quite in a position to enable you to marry comfortably. The brave man has lost his right hand—reason enough for remaining seated behind the stove, or near the spinning-wheel of his Bertha; but what does he do?—He goes off to the war in Turkey; he fights for a noble thought'—

'And runs the chance of getting his other hand chopped off, and another great scar across his face,' put in her friend.

'Leaves his lady-love to weep and pine a little,' pursued Franziska, 'but returns with fame, marries, and is all the more honoured and admired! This is done by a man of forty, a rough warrior, not bred at court, a soldier who has nothing but his cloak and sword. And Franz—rich, noble—but I will not go on. Not a word more on this detested point, if you love me, Bertha.'

Franziska leaned back in the corner of the litter with a dissatisfied air, and shut her eyes, as though, overcome by fatigue, she wished to sleep.

'This awful wind is so powerful, you say, that we must make a detour to avoid its full force,' said the knight to an old man, dressed in a fur-cap and a cloak of rough skin, who seemed to be the guide of the party.

'Those who have never personally felt the Boreas storming over the country between Sessano and Trieste,* can have no conception of the reality,' replied the other. 'As soon as it commences, the snow is blown in thick long columns along the ground. That is nothing to what follows. These columns become higher and higher, as the wind rises, and continue to do so until you see nothing but snow above, below, and on every side—unless, indeed, sometimes, when sand and gravel are mixed with the snow, and at length it is impossible to open your eyes at all. Your only plan for safety is to wrap your cloak around you, and lie down flat on the ground. If your home were but a few hundred yards off, you might lose your life in the attempt to reach it.'

'Well, then, we owe you thanks, old Kumpan,' said the knight, though it was with difficulty he made his words heard above the roaring of the storm; 'we owe you thanks for taking us this round, as we shall thus be enabled to reach our destination without danger.'

'You may feel sure of that, noble sir,' said the old man. 'By midnight we shall have arrived, and that without any danger by the way, if'—Suddenly the old man stopped, he drew his horse sharply up, and remained in an attitude of attentive listening.

'It appears to me we must be in the neighbourhood of some village,' said Franz von Kronstein; 'for between the gusts of the storm, I hear a dog howling.'

'It is no dog, it is no dog!' said the old man uneasily, and urging his horse to a rapid pace. 'For miles around there is no human dwelling; and except in the castle of Klatka,* which indeed lies in the neighbourhood, but has been deserted for more than a century, probably no one has lived here since the creation.—But there again,' he continued; 'well, if I wasn't sure of it from the first.'

'That howling seems to fidget* you, old Kumpan,' said the knight, listening to a long-drawn fierce sound, which appeared nearer than before, and seemed to be answered from a distance.

'That howling comes from no dogs,' replied the old guide uneasily. 'Those are reed-wolves;* they may be on our track; and it would be as well if the gentlemen looked to their firearms.'

'Reed-wolves? What do you mean?' inquired Franz in surprise.

'At the edge of this wood,' said Kumpan, 'there lies a lake about a mile long, whose banks are covered with reeds. In these a number of wolves have taken up their quarters, and feed on wild birds, fish, and such like. They are shy in the summer-time, and a boy of twelve might scare them; but when the birds migrate, and the fish are frozen up, they prowl about at night, and then they are dangerous. They are worst, however, when Boreas rages, for then it is just as if the fiend himself possessed them: they are so mad and fierce, that man and beast become alike their victims; and a party of them have been known even to attack the ferocious bears of these mountains, and, what is more, to come off victorious.' The howl was now again repeated more distinctly, and from two opposite directions. The riders in alarm felt for their pistols, and the old man grasped the spear which hung at his saddle.

'We must keep close to the litter; the wolves are very near us,' whispered the guide. The riders turned their horses, surrounded the litter, and the knight informed the ladies, in a few quieting words, of the cause of this movement.

'Then we *shall* have an adventure—some little variety!' cried Franziska with sparkling eyes.

'How can you talk so foolishly?' said Bertha in alarm.

'Are we not under manly protection? Is not Cousin Franz on our side?' said the other mockingly.

'See, there is a light gleaming among the twigs; and there is another,' cried Bertha. 'There must be people close to us.'

'No, no,' cried the guide quickly. 'Shut up the door, ladies. Keep close together, gentlemen. It is the eyes of wolves you see sparkling there.' The gentlemen looked towards the thick underwood, in which every now and then little bright spots appeared, such as in summer would have been taken for glow-worms; it was just the same greenish-yellow light, but less unsteady, and there were always two flames together. The horses began to be restive, they kicked and dragged at the rein; but the mules behaved tolerably well.

'I will fire on the beasts, and teach them to keep their distance,' said Franz, pointing to the spot where the lights were thickest.

'Hold, hold, Sir Baron!' cried Kumpan quickly, and seizing the young man's arm. 'You would bring such a host together by the report, that, encouraged by numbers, they would be sure to make the first assault. However, keep your arms in readiness, and if an old she-wolf springs out—for these always lead the attack—take good aim and kill her, for then there must be no further hesitation.' By this time, the horses were almost unmanageable, and terror had also infected the mules. Just as Franz was turning towards the litter to say a word to his cousin, an animal, about the size of a large hound, sprang from the thicket and seized the foremost mule.

'Fire, baron! A wolf!' shouted the guide.

The young man fired, and the wolf fell to the ground. A fearful howl rang through the wood.

'Now, forward! Forward without a moment's delay!' cried Kumpan. 'We have not above five minutes' time. The beasts will tear their wounded comrade to pieces, and, if they are very hungry, partially devour her. We shall, in the meantime, gain a little start, and it is not more than an hour's ride to the end of the forest. There—do you see—these are the towers of Klatka between the trees—out there where the moon is rising, and from that point the wood becomes less dense.'

The travellers endeavoured to increase their pace to the utmost, but the litter retarded their progress. Bertha was weeping with fear, and even Franziska's courage had diminished, for she sat very still. Franz endeavoured to reassure them. They had not proceeded many moments when the howling recommenced, and approached nearer and nearer.

'There they are again, and fiercer and more numerous than before,' cried the guide in alarm.

The lights were soon visible again, and certainly in greater numbers. The wood had already become less thick, and the snowstorm having ceased, the moonbeams discovered many a dusky form amongst the trees, keeping together like a pack of hounds, and advancing nearer and nearer till they were within twenty paces, and on the very path of the travellers. From time to time a fierce howl arose from their centre, which was answered by the whole pack, and was at length taken up by single voices in the distance.

The party now found themselves some few hundred yards from the ruined castle of which Kumpan had spoken. It was, or seemed by moonlight to be, of some magnitude. Near the tolerably preserved principal building lay the ruins of a church, which must have once been beautiful, placed on a little hillock, dotted with single oak-trees and bramble-bushes. Both castle and church were still partially roofed in; and a path led from the castle gate to an old oak-tree, where it joined at right angles the one along which the travellers were advancing.

The old guide seemed in much perplexity.

'We are in great danger, noble sir,' said he. 'The wolves will very soon make a general attack. There will then be only one way of escape: leaving the mules to their fate, and taking the young ladies on your horses.'

'That would be all very well, if I had not thought of a better plan,' replied the knight. 'Here is the ruined castle; we can surely reach that, and then, blocking up the gates, we must just await the morning.'

'Here? In the ruins of Klatka?—Not for all the wolves in the world!' cried the old man. 'Even by daylight no one likes to approach the place, and, now by night!—The castle, Sir Knight, has a bad name.'

'On account of robbers?' asked Franz.

'No; it is haunted,' replied the other.

'Stuff and nonsense!' said the baron. 'Forward to the ruins; there is not a moment to be lost.'

And this was indeed the case. The ferocious beasts were but a few steps behind the travellers. Every now and then they retired, and set up a ferocious howl. The party had just arrived at the old oak before mentioned, and were about to turn into the path to the ruins, when the animals, as though perceiving the risk they ran of losing their prey, came so near that a lance could easily have struck them. The knight and Franz faced sharply about, spurring their horses amidst the advancing crowds, when suddenly, from the shadow of the oak stepped forth a man, who in a few strides placed himself between the travellers and their pursuers. As far as one could see in the dusky light, the stranger was a man of a tall and well-built frame; he wore a sword by his side, and a broad-brimmed hat was on his head. If the party were astonished at his sudden appearance, they were still more so at what followed. As soon as the stranger appeared, the wolves gave over their pursuit, tumbled over each other, and set up a fearful howl. The stranger now raised his hand, appeared to wave it, and the wild animals crawled back into the thickets like a pack of beaten hounds.

Without casting a glance at the travellers, who were too much overcome by astonishment to speak, the stranger went up the path which led to the castle, and soon disappeared beneath the gateway.

'Heaven have mercy on us!' murmured old Kumpan in his beard, as he made the sign of the cross.

'Who was that strange man?' asked the knight with surprise, when he had watched the stranger as long as he was visible, and the party had resumed their way.

The old guide pretended not to understand, and riding up to the mules, busied himself with arranging the harness, which had become disordered in their haste: more than a quarter of an hour elapsed before he rejoined them.

'Did you know the man who met us near the ruins, and who freed us from our four-footed pursuers in such a miraculous way?' asked Franz of the guide.

'Do I know him? No, noble sir; I never saw him before,' replied the guide hesitatingly.

'He looked like a soldier, and was armed,' said the baron. 'Is the castle, then, inhabited?'

'Not for the last hundred years,' replied the other. 'It was dismantled because the possessor in those days had iniquitous dealings with some Turkish-Sclavonian* hordes, who had advanced as far as this; or rather'—he corrected himself hastily—'he is *said* to have had such, for he might have been as upright and good a man as ever ate cheese fried in butter.'[1] *

'And who is now the possessor of the ruins and of these woods?' inquired the knight.

'Who but yourself, noble sir?' replied Kumpan. 'For more than two hours we have been on your estate, and we shall soon reach the end of the wood.'

'We hear and see nothing more of the wolves,' said the baron after a long pause. 'Even their howling has ceased. The adventure with the stranger still remains to me inexplicable, even if one were to suppose him a huntsman'—

'Yes, yes; that is most likely what he is,' interrupted the guide hastily, whilst he looked uneasily round him. 'The brave good man, who came so opportunely to our assistance, must have been a huntsman. Oh, there are many powerful woodsmen in this neighbourhood! Heaven be praised!' he continued, taking a deep breath, 'there is the end of the wood, and in a short hour we shall be safely housed.'

And so it happened. Before an hour had elapsed, the party passed through a well-built village, the principal spot on the estate, towards the venerable castle, the windows of which were brightly illuminated, and at the door stood the steward and other dependents, who, having

[1] A favourite dish in those parts.

received their new lord with every expression of respect, conducted the party to the splendidly furnished apartments.

Nearly four weeks passed before the travelling adventures again came on the tapis.* The knight and Franz found such constant employment in looking over all the particulars of the large estate, and endeavouring to introduce various German improvements, that they were very little at home. At first, Franziska was charmed with everything in a neighbourhood so entirely new and unknown. It appeared to her so romantic, so very different from her German Fatherland, that she took the greatest interest in everything, and often drew comparisons between the countries, which generally ended unfavourably for Germany. Bertha was of exactly the contrary opinion: she laughed at her cousin, and said that her liking for novelty and strange sights must indeed have come to a pass, when she preferred hovels in which the smoke went out of the doors and windows instead of the chimney, walls covered with soot, and inhabitants not much cleaner, and of unmannerly habits, to the comfortable dwellings and polite people of Germany. However, Franziska persisted in her notions, and replied that everything in Austria was flat, *ennuyant*,* and common; and that a wild peasant here, with his rough coat of skin, had ten times more interest for her than a quiet Austrian in his holiday suit, the mere sight of whom was enough to make one yawn.

As soon as the knight had got the first arrangements into some degree of order, the party found themselves more together again. Franz continued to shew great attention to his cousin, which, however, she received with little gratitude, for she made him the butt of all her fanciful humours, that soon returned when after a longer sojourn she had become more accustomed to her new life. Many excursions into the neighbourhood were undertaken, but there was little variety in the scenery, and these soon ceased to amuse.

The party were one day assembled in the old-fashioned hall, dinner had just been removed, and they were arranging in which direction they should ride. 'I have it,' cried Franziska suddenly. 'I wonder we never thought before of going to view by day the spot where we fell in with our night-adventure with wolves and the Mysterious Stranger.'

'You mean a visit to the ruins—what were they called?' said the knight.

'Castle Klatka,' cried Franziska gaily. 'Oh, we really must ride there! It will be so charming to go over again by daylight, and in safety, the ground where we had such a dreadful fright.'

'Bring round the horses,' said the knight to a servant; 'and tell the steward to come to me immediately.' The latter, an old man, soon after entered the room.

'We intend taking a ride to Klatka,' said the knight: 'we had an adventure there on our road'—'So old Kumpan told me,' interrupted the steward.

'And what do you say about it?' asked the knight.

'I really don't know what to say,' replied the old man, shaking his head. 'I was a youth of twenty when I first came to this castle, and now my hair is grey; half a century has elapsed during that time. Hundreds of times my duty has called me into the neighbourhood of those ruins, but never have I seen the Fiend of Klatka.'

'What do you say? Whom do you call by that name?' inquired Franziska, whose love of adventure and romance was strongly awakened.

'Why, people call by that name the ghost or spirit who is supposed to haunt the ruins,' replied the steward. 'They say he only shews himself on moonlight nights'—

'That is quite natural,' interrupted Franz smiling. 'Ghosts can never bear the light of day; and if the moon did not shine, how could the ghost be seen? for it is not to be supposed that any one for a mere freak* would visit the ruins by torch-light.'

'There are some credulous people, who pretend to have seen this ghost,' continued the steward. 'Huntsmen and wood-cutters say they have met him by the large oak on the cross-path. That, noble sir, is supposed to be the spot he inclines most to haunt, for the tree was planted in remembrance of the man who fell there.'

'And who was he?' asked Franziska with increasing curiosity.

'The last owner of the castle, which at that time was a sort of robber's den, and the headquarters of all depredators in the neighbourhood,' answered the old man. 'They say this man was of superhuman strength, and was feared not only on account of his passionate temper, but of his treaties with the Turkish hordes. Any young woman, too, in the neighbourhood to whom he took a fancy, was carried off to his tower, and never heard of more. When the measure of his iniquity was full, the whole neighbourhood rose in a mass, besieged his stronghold, and at length he was slain on the spot where the huge oak-tree now stands.'

'I wonder they did not burn the whole castle, so as to erase the very memory of it,' said the knight.

'It was a dependency of the church, and that saved it,' replied the other. 'Your great-grandfather afterwards took possession of it, for it had fine lands attached. As the Knight of Klatka was of good family, a monument was erected to him in the church, which now lies as much in ruin as the castle itself.'

'Oh, let us set off at once! Nothing shall prevent my visiting so interesting a spot,' said Franziska eagerly. 'The imprisoned damsels who never reappeared, the storming of the tower, the death of the knight, the nightly wanderings of his spirit round the old oak, and, lastly, our own adventure, all draw me thither with an indescribable curiosity.'

When a servant announced that the horses were at the door, the young girls tripped laughingly down the steps which led to the coach-yard. Franz, the knight, and a servant well acquainted with the country, followed; and in a few minutes the party were on their road to the forest.

The sun was still high in the heavens when they saw the towers of Klatka rising above the trees. Everything in the wood was still, except the cheerful twitterings of the birds as they hopped about amongst the bursting buds and leaves, and announced that spring had arrived.

The party soon found themselves near the old oak at the bottom of the hill on which stood the towers, still imposing in their ruin. Ivy and bramble bushes had wound themselves over the walls, and forced their deep roots so firmly between the stones, that they in a great measure held these together. On the top of the highest point, a small bush in its young fresh verdure swayed lightly in the breeze.

The gentlemen assisted their companions to alight, and leaving the horses to the care of the servant, ascended the hill to the castle. After having explored this in every nook and cranny, and spent much time in a vain search for some trace of the extraordinary stranger, whom Franziska declared she was determined to discover, they proceeded to an inspection of the adjoining church. This they found to have better withstood the ravages of time and weather; the nave, indeed, was in complete dilapidation, but the chancel and altar were still under roof, as well as a sort of chapel which appeared to have been a place of honour for the families of the old knights of the castle. Few traces remained, however, of the magnificent painted glass which must once have adorned the windows, and the wind entered at pleasure through the open spaces.

The party were occupied for some time in deciphering the inscriptions on a number of tombstones, and on the walls, principally within the chancel. They were generally memorials of the ancient lords, with figures of men in armour, and women and children of all ages. A flying raven and various other devices were placed at the corners. One gravestone, which stood close to the entrance of the chancel, differed widely from the others: there was no figure sculptured on it, and the inscription, which, on all besides, was a mere* mass of flattering eulogies, was here simple and unadorned; it contained only these words: 'Ezzelin von Klatka* fell like a knight at the storming of the castle'—on such a day and year.

'That must be the monument of the knight whose ghost is said to haunt these ruins,' cried Franziska eagerly. 'What a pity he is not represented in the same way as the others—I should so like to have known what he was like!'

'Oh, there is the family vault, with steps leading down to it, and the sun is lighting it up through a crevice', said Franz, stepping from the adjoining vestry.

The whole party followed him down the eight or nine steps which led to a tolerably airy chamber, where were placed a number of coffins of all sizes, some of them crumbling into dust. Here, again, one close to the door was distinguished from the others by the simplicity of its design, the freshness of its appearance, and the brief inscription: 'Ezzelinus de Klatka, Eques.'*

As not the slightest effluvium was perceptible, they lingered some time in the vault; and when they reascended to the church, they had a long talk over the old possessors, of whom the knight now remembered he had heard his parents speak. The sun had disappeared, and the moon was just rising as the explorers turned to leave the ruins. Bertha had made a step into the nave, when she uttered a slight exclamation of fear and surprise. Her eyes fell on a man who wore a hat with drooping feathers, a sword at his side, and a short cloak of somewhat old-fashioned cut over his shoulders. The stranger leaned carelessly on a broken column at the entrance; he did not appear to take any notice of the party; and the moon shone full on his pale face.

The party advanced towards the stranger.

'If I am not mistaken,' commenced the knight; 'we have met before.'

Not a word from the unknown.

'You released us in an almost miraculous manner,' said Franziska, 'from the power of those dreadful wolves. Am I wrong in supposing it is to you we are indebted for that great service?'

'The beasts are afraid of me,' replied the stranger in a deep fierce tone, while he fastened his sunken eyes on the girl, without taking any notice of the others.

'Then you are probably a huntsman,' said Franz, 'and wage war against the fierce brutes.'

'Who is not either the pursuer or the pursued? All persecute or are persecuted, and Fate persecutes all,' replied the stranger without looking at him.

'Do you live in these ruins?' asked the knight hesitatingly.

'Yes; but not to the destruction of your game, as you may fear, Knight of Fahnenberg,' said the unknown contemptuously. 'Be quite assured of this; your property shall remain untouched'—

'Oh! my father did not mean that,' interrupted Franziska, who appeared to take the liveliest interest in the stranger. 'Unfortunate events and sad experiences have, no doubt, induced you to take up your abode in these ruins, of which my father would by no means dispossess you.'

'Your father is very good, if that is what he meant,' said the stranger in his former tone; and it seemed as though his dark features were drawn into a slight smile; 'but people of my sort are rather difficult to turn out.'

'You must live very uncomfortably here,' said Franziska, half vexed, for she thought her polite speech had deserved a better reply.

'My dwelling is not exactly uncomfortable, only somewhat small, still quite suitable for quiet people,' said the unknown with a kind of sneer. 'I am not, however, always quiet; I sometimes pine to quit the narrow space, and then I dash away through forest and field, over hill and dale; and the time when I must return to my little dwelling always comes too soon for me.'

'As you now and then leave your dwelling,' said the knight, 'I would invite you to visit us, if I knew'—

'That I was in a station to admit of your doing so,' interrupted the other; and the knight started slightly, for the stranger had exactly expressed the half-formed thought. 'I lament,' he continued coldly, 'that I am not able to give you particulars on this point—some difficulties stand in the way: be assured, however, that I am a knight, and of at least as ancient a family as yourself.'

'Then you must not refuse our request,' cried Franziska, highly interested in the strange manners of the unknown. 'You must come and visit us.'

'I am no boon-companion, and on that account few have invited me of late,' replied the other with his peculiar smile; 'besides, I generally remain at home during the day; that is my time for rest. I belong, you must know, to that class of persons who turn day into night, and night into day, and who love everything uncommon and peculiar.'

'Really? So do I! And for that very reason, you must visit us,' cried Franziska. 'Now,' she continued smiling, 'I suppose you have just risen, and you are taking your morning airing. Well, since the moon is your sun, pray pay a frequent visit to our castle by the light of its rays. I think we shall agree very well, and that it will be very nice for us to be acquainted.'

'You wish it?—You press the invitation?' asked the stranger earnestly and decidedly.

'To be sure, for otherwise you will not come,' replied the young lady shortly.

'Well, then, come I will!', said the other, again fixing his gaze on her. 'If my company does not please you at any time, you will have yourself to blame for an acquaintance with one who seldom forces himself, but is difficult to shake off.'

When the unknown had concluded these words, he made a slight motion with his hand, as though to take leave of them, and passing under the doorway, disappeared among the ruins. The party soon after mounted their horses, and took the road home.

It was the evening of the following day, and all were again seated in the hall of the castle. Bertha had that day received good news. The knight Woislaw had written from Hungary, that the war with the Turks would be brought to a conclusion during the year, and that although he had intended returning to Silesia,* hearing of the knight of Fahnenberg having gone to take possession of his new estates, he should follow the family there, not doubting that Bertha had accompanied her friend. He hinted, that he stood so high in the opinion of his duke on account of his valuable services, that in future his duties would be even more important and extensive; but before settling down to them, he should come and claim Bertha's promise to become his wife. He had been much enriched by his master, as well as by booty taken from the Turks. Having formerly lost his right hand in the duke's service, he had essayed to fight with his left; but this did not succeed very admirably, and so he had an iron one made by a very clever artist. This hand performed many of the functions of a natural one, but there had been still much wanting; now, however, his master had presented him with one of gold, an extraordinary work of art, produced by a celebrated Italian mechanic. The knight described it as something marvellous, especially as to the superhuman strength with which it enabled him to use the sword and lance. Franziska naturally rejoiced in the happiness of her friend, who had had no news of her betrothed for a long time before. She launched out every now and then, partly to plague Franz, and partly to express her own feelings, in the highest praise and admiration of the bravery and enterprise of the knight, whose adventurous qualities she lauded to the skies. Even the scar on his face, and his want of a right hand, were reckoned as virtues; and Franziska at last saucily declared, that a rather ugly man was infinitely more attractive to her than a handsome one, for as a general rule, handsome men were conceited and effeminate. Thus, she added, no one could term their acquaintance of the night before handsome, but attractive and interesting he certainly was. Franz and Bertha simultaneously denied this. His gloomy appearance, the deadly hue of his complexion, the tone of his voice, were each in turn depreciated by Bertha, while Franz found fault with the contempt and arrogance obvious in his speech. The knight stood between the two parties. He thought there was something in his bearing that spoke of good family, though much could not be said for his politeness; however, the man might have had trials enough in his life to make him misanthropical. Whilst they were conversing in this way, the door suddenly opened, and the subject of their remarks himself walked in.

'Pardon me, Sir Knight,' he said coldly, 'that I come, if not uninvited, at least unannounced; there was no one in the ante-chamber to do me that service.'

The brilliantly lighted chamber gave a full view of the stranger. He was a man about forty, tall, and extremely thin. His features could not be termed uninteresting—there lay in them something bold and daring; but the expression was on the whole anything but benevolent. There was contempt and sarcasm in the cold grey eyes, whose glance, however, was at times so piercing, that no one could endure it long. His complexion was even more peculiar than the features: it could neither be called pale nor yellow; it was a sort of gray, or, so to speak, dirty white, like that of an Indian who has been suffering long from fever; and was rendered still more remarkable by the intense blackness of his beard and short cropped hair. The dress of the unknown was knightly, but old-fashioned and neglected; there were great spots of rust on the collar and breastplate of his armour; and his dagger and the hilt of his finely-worked sword were marked in some places with mildew. As the party were just going to supper, it was only natural to invite the stranger to partake of it; he complied, however, only in so far that he seated himself at the table, for he ate no morsel. The knight, with some surprise, inquired the reason.

'For a long time past, I have accustomed myself never to eat at night,' he replied with a strange smile. 'My digestion is quite unused to solids, and indeed would scarcely confront them. I live entirely on liquids.'

'Oh then, we can empty a bumper of Rhine-wine together,' cried the host.

'Thanks; but I neither drink wine nor any cold beverage,' replied the other; and his tone was full of mockery. It appeared as if there was some amusing association connected with the idea.

'Then I will order you a cup of hippocras'*—a warm drink composed of herbs—'it shall be ready immediately,' said Franziska.

'Many thanks, fair lady; not at present,' replied the other. 'But if I refuse the beverage you offer me now, you may be assured that as soon as I require it—perhaps very soon—I will request that, or some other of you.'

Bertha and Franz thought the man had something inexpressibly repulsive in his whole manner, and they had no inclination to engage him in conversation; but the baron, thinking that perhaps politeness required him to say something, turned towards the guest, and commenced in a friendly tone: 'It is now many weeks since we first became acquainted with you; we then had to thank you for a signal service'—

'And I have not yet told you my name, although you would gladly know it,' interrupted the other drily. 'I am called Azzo;* and as'—this he said again with his ironical smile—'with the permission of the Knight of Fahnenberg, I live at the castle of Klatka, you can in future call me Azzo von Klatka.'

'I only wonder you do not feel lonely and uncomfortable amongst those old walls,' began Bertha. 'I cannot understand'—

'What my business is there? Oh, about that I will willingly give you some information, since you and the young gentleman there take such a kindly interest in my person,' replied the unknown in his tone of sarcasm.

Franz and Bertha both started, for he had revealed their thoughts as though he could read their souls. 'You see, lady,' he continued, 'there are a variety of strange whims in the world. As I have already said, I love what is peculiar and uncommon, at least what would appear so to you. It is wrong in the main to be astonished at anything, for, viewed in one light, all things are alike; even life and death, this side of the grave and the other, have more resemblance than you would imagine. You perhaps consider me rather touched a little in my mind, for taking up my abode with the bat and the owl; but if so, why not consider every hermit and recluse insane? You will tell me that those are holy men. I certainly have no pretension that way; but as they find pleasure in praying and singing psalms, so I amuse myself with hunting. Oh, you can have no idea of the intense pleasure of dashing away in the pale moonlight, on a horse that never tires, over hill and dale, through forest and woodland! I rush among the wolves, which fly at my approach, as you yourself perceived, as though they were puppies fearful of the lash.'

'But still it must be lonely, very lonely for you,' remarked Bertha.

'So it would by day; but I am then asleep,' replied the stranger drily; 'at night I am merry enough.'

'You hunt in an extraordinary way,' remarked Franz hesitatingly.

'Yes; but, nevertheless, I have no communication with robbers, as you seem to imagine,' replied Azzo coldly.

Franz again started—that very thought had just crossed his mind. 'Oh, I beg your pardon; I do not know—' he stammered.

'What to make of me,' interrupted the other. 'You would, therefore, do well to believe just what I tell you, or at least to avoid making conjectures of your own, which will lead to nothing.'

'I understand you: I know how to value your ideas, if no one else does,' cried Franziska eagerly. 'The humdrum, everyday life of the generality of men is repulsive to you; you have tasted the joys and pleasures of life, at least what are so called, and you have found them tame and hollow. How soon one tires of the things one sees all around! Life consists in change. Only in what is new, uncommon, and peculiar, do the flowers of the spirit bloom and give forth scent. Even pain may become a pleasure if it saves one from the shallow monotony of everyday life—a thing I shall hate till the hour of my death.'

'Right, fair lady—quite right! Remain in this mind: this was always my opinion, and the one from which I have derived the highest reward,' cried Azzo; and his fierce eyes sparkled more intensely than ever. 'I am doubly pleased to have found in you a person who shares my ideas. Oh, if you were a man, you would make me a splendid companion; but even a woman may have fine experiences when once these opinions take root in her, and bring forth action!'

As Azzo spoke these words in a cold tone of politeness, he turned from the subject, and for the rest of his visit only gave the knight monosyllabic replies to his inquiries, taking leave before the table was cleared. To an invitation from the knight, backed by a still more pressing one from Franziska to repeat his visit, he replied that he would take advantage of their kindness, and come sometimes.

When the stranger had departed, many were the remarks made on his appearance and general deportment. Franz declared his most decided dislike to him. Whether it was as usual to vex her cousin, or whether Azzo had really made an impression on her, Franziska took his part vehemently. As Franz contradicted her more eagerly than usual, the young lady launched out into still stronger expressions; and there is no knowing what hard words her cousin might have received had not a servant entered the room.

The following morning, Franziska lay longer than usual in bed. When her friend went to her room, fearful lest she should be ill, she found her pale and exhausted. Franziska complained she had passed a very bad night; she thought the dispute with Franz about the stranger must have excited her greatly, for she felt quite feverish and exhausted, and a strange dream, too, had worried her, which was evidently a consequence of the evening's conversation. Bertha, as usual, took the young man's part, and added, that a common dispute about a man whom no one knew, and about whom any one might form his own opinion, could not possibly have thrown her into her present state. 'At least,' she continued, 'you can let me hear this wonderful dream.'

To her surprise; Franziska for a length of time refused to do so.

'Come, tell me,' inquired Bertha, 'what can possibly prevent you from relating a dream—a mere dream? I might almost think it credible, if the idea were not too horrid, that poor Franz is not very far wrong when he says that the thin, corpse-like, dried-up, old-fashioned stranger has made a greater impression on you than you will allow.'

'Did Franz say so?' asked Franziska. 'Then you can tell him he is not mistaken. Yes, the thin, corpse-like, dried-up, whimsical stranger is far more interesting to me than the rosy-cheeked, well-dressed, polite, and prosy cousin.'

'Strange!' cried Bertha. 'I cannot at all comprehend the almost magic influence which this man, to me so repulsive, exercises over you.'

'Perhaps the very reason I take his part, may be that you are all so prejudiced against him,' remarked Franziska pettishly. 'Yes, it must be so; for that his appearance should please my eyes, is what no one in his senses could imagine. But,' she continued, smiling and holding out her hand to Bertha, 'is it not laughable that I should get out of temper even with you about this stranger?—I can more easily understand it with Franz—and that this unknown should spoil my morning, as he has already spoiled my evening and my night's rest?'

'By that dream, you mean?' said Bertha, easily appeased, as she put her arm round her cousin's neck and kissed her. 'Now, do tell it to me. You know how I delight in hearing anything of the kind.'

'Well, I will, as a sort of compensation for my peevishness towards you,' said the other, clasping her friend's hands. 'Now, listen! I had walked up and down my room for a long time; I was excited—out of spirits—I do not know exactly what. It was almost midnight ere I lay down, but I could not sleep. I tossed about, and at length it was only from sheer exhaustion that I dropped off. But what a sleep it was! An inward fear ran through me perpetually. I saw a number of pictures before me, as I used to do in childish sicknesses. I do not know whether I was asleep or half awake. Then I dreamed, but as clearly as if I had been wide awake, that a sort of mist* filled the room, and out of it stepped the knight Azzo. He gazed at me for a time, and then letting himself slowly down on one knee, imprinted a kiss on my throat. Long did his lips rest there; and I felt a slight pain, which always went on increasing, until I could bear it no more. With all my strength I tried to force the vision from me, but succeeded only after a long struggle. No doubt I uttered a scream, for that awoke me from my trance. When I came a little to my senses, I felt a sort of superstitious fear creeping over me—how great you may imagine, when I tell you that, with my eyes open and awake, it appeared to me as if Azzo's figure were still by my bed, and then disappearing gradually into the mist, vanished at the door!'

'You must have dreamed very heavily, my poor friend,' began Bertha, but suddenly paused. She gazed with surprise at Franziska's throat. 'Why, what is that?' she cried. 'Just look: how extraordinary—a red streak on your throat!'

Franziska raised herself, and went to a little glass that stood in the window. She really saw a small red line about an inch long on her neck, which began to smart when she touched it with her finger.

'I must have hurt myself by some means in my sleep,' she said after a pause; 'and that in some measure will account for my dream.'

The friends continued chatting for some time about this singular coincidence—the dream and the stranger; and at length it was all turned into a joke by Bertha.

Several weeks passed. The knight had found the estate and affairs in greater disorder than he at first imagined; and instead of remaining three or four weeks, as was originally intended, their departure was deferred to an indefinite period. This postponement was likewise in some measure occasioned by Franziska's continued indisposition. She who had formerly bloomed like a rose in its young fresh beauty, was becoming daily thinner, more sickly and exhausted, and at the same time so pale, that in the space of a month not a tinge of red was perceptible on the once glowing cheek. The knight's anxiety about her was extreme, and the best advice was procured which the age and country afforded; but all to no purpose. Franziska complained from time to time that the horrible dream with which her illness commenced was repeated, and that always on the day following she felt an increased and indescribable weakness. Bertha naturally set this down to the effects of fever, but the ravages of that fever on the usually clear reason of her friend filled her with alarm.

The knight Azzo repeated his visits every now and then. He always came in the evening, and when the moon shone brightly. His manner was always the same. He spoke in monosyllables, and was coldly polite to the knight; to Franz and Bertha, particularly to the former, contemptuous and haughty; but to Franziska, friendliness itself. Often when, after a short visit, he again left the house, his peculiarities became the subject of conversation. Besides his old way of speaking, in which Bertha said there lay a deep hatred, a cold detestation of all mankind with the exception of Franziska, two other singularities were observable. During none of his visits, which often took place at supper-time, had he been prevailed upon to eat or drink anything, and that without giving any good reason for his abstinence. A remarkable alteration, too, had taken place in his appearance; he seemed an entirely different creature. The skin, before so shrivelled and stretched, seemed smooth and soft, while a slight tinge of red appeared in his cheeks, which began to look round and plump. Bertha, who could not at all conceal her ill-will towards him, said often, that much as she hated his face before, when it was more like a death's-head than a human being's, it was now more than ever repulsive; she always felt a shudder run through her veins whenever his sharp piercing eyes rested on her. Perhaps it was owing to Franziska's partiality, or to the knight Azzo's own contemptuous way of replying to Franz, or to his haughty way of treating him in general, that made the young man dislike him more and more. It was quite observable, that whenever Franz made a remark to his cousin in the presence of Azzo, the latter would immediately throw some ill-natured light on it, or distort it to a totally different meaning. This increased from day to day, and at last Franz declared to Bertha, that he would stand such conduct no longer, and that it was only out of consideration for Franziska that he had not already called him to account.

At this time, the party at the castle was increased by the arrival of Bertha's long-expected guest. He came just as they were sitting down to supper one evening, and all jumped up to greet their old friend. The knight Woislaw was a true model of the soldier, hardened and strengthened by war with men and elements. His face would not have been termed ugly, if a Turkish sabre had not left a mark running from the right eye to the left cheek, and standing out bright red from the sunburned skin. The frame of the Castellan of Glogau might almost be termed colossal. Few would have been able to carry his armour, and still fewer move with his lightness and ease under its weight. He did not think little of this same armour, for it had been a present from the palatine of Hungary* on his leaving the camp. The blue wrought-steel was ornamented all over with patterns in gold; and he had put it on to do honour to his bride-elect, together with the wonderful gold hand, the gift of the duke.

Woislaw was questioned by the knight and Franz on all the concerns of the campaign; and he entered into the most minute particulars relating to the battles, which, with regard to plunder, had been more successful than ever. He spoke much of the strength of the Turks in a hand-to-hand fight, and remarked that he owed the duke many thanks for his splendid gift, for in consequence of its strength, many of the enemy regarded him as something superhuman. The sickliness and deathlike paleness of Franziska was too perceptible not to be immediately noticed by Woislaw; accustomed to see her so fresh and cheerful, he hastened to inquire into the cause of the change. Bertha related all that had happened, and Woislaw listened with the greatest interest. This increased to the utmost at the account of the often-repeated dream, and Franziska had to give him the most minute particulars of it; it appeared as though he had met with a similar case before, or at least had heard of one.* When the young lady added, that it was very remarkable that the wound on her throat which she had at first felt had never healed, and still pained her, the knight Woislaw looked at Bertha as much as to say, that this last fact had greatly strengthened his idea as to the cause of Franziska's illness.

It was only natural that the discourse should next turn to the knight Azzo, about whom every one began to talk eagerly. Woislaw inquired as minutely as he had done with regard to Franziska's illness, about what concerned this stranger, from the first evening of their acquaintance down to his last visit, without, however, giving any opinion on the subject. The party were still in earnest conversation, when the door opened, and Azzo entered. Woislaw's eyes remained fixed on him, as he, without taking any particular notice of the new arrival, walked up to the table, and seating himself, directed most of the conversation to Franziska and her father, and now and then made some sarcastic remark when Franz began to speak. The Turkish war again came on the tapis, and though Azzo only put in an occasional remark, Woislaw had much to say on the subject. Thus they had advanced late into the night, and Franz said smiling to Woislaw: 'I should not wonder if day had surprised us, whilst listening to your entertaining adventures.'

'I admire the young gentleman's taste,' said Azzo, with an ironical curl of the lip. 'Stories of storm and shipwreck are, indeed, best heard on *terra firma*,* and those of battle and death at a hospitable table or in the chimney-corner. One has then the comfortable feeling of keeping a whole skin, and being in no danger, not even of taking cold.' With the last words, he gave a hoarse laugh, and turning his back on Franz, rose, bowed to the rest of the company, and left the room. The knight, who always accompanied Azzo to the door, now expressed himself fatigued, and bade his friends good-night.

'That Azzo's impertinence is unbearable,' cried Bertha when he was gone. 'He becomes daily more rough, unpolite, and presuming. If only on account of Franziska's dream, though of course he cannot help that, I detest him. Now, to-night, not one civil word has he spoken to any one but Franziska, except, perhaps, some casual remark to my uncle.'

'I cannot deny that you are right, Bertha,' said her cousin. 'One may forgive much to a man whom fate has probably made somewhat misanthropical; but he should not overstep the bounds of common politeness. But where on earth is Franz?' added Franziska, as she looked uneasily round.—The young man had quietly left the room whilst Bertha was speaking.

'He cannot have followed the knight Azzo to challenge him?' cried Bertha in alarm.

'It were better he entered a lion's den to pull his mane!' said Woislaw vehemently. 'I must follow him instantly,' he added, as he rushed from the room.

He hastened over the threshold, out of the castle, and through the court, before he came up to them. Here a narrow bridge with a slight balustrade passed over the moat by which the castle was surrounded. It appeared that Franz had only just addressed Azzo in a few hot words, for as Woislaw, unperceived by either, advanced under the shadow of the wall, Azzo said gloomily: 'Leave me, foolish boy—leave me; for by that sun'—and he pointed to the full moon above them—'you will see those rays no more if you linger another moment on my path.'

'And I tell you, wretch, that you either give me satisfaction for your repeated insolence, or you die,' cried Franz, drawing his sword.

Azzo stretched forth his hand, and grasping the sword in the middle, it snapped like a broken reed. 'I warn you for the last time,' he said in a voice of thunder, as he threw the pieces into the moat. 'Now, away—away, boy, from my path, or, by those below us, you are lost!'

'You or I! you or I!' cried Franz madly, as he made a rush at the sword of his antagonist, and strove to draw it from his side. Azzo replied not; only a bitter laugh half escaped from his lips; then seizing Franz by the chest, he lifted him up like an infant, and was in the act of throwing him over the bridge, when Woislaw stepped to his side. With a grasp of his wonderful hand, into the springs of which he threw all his strength, he seized Azzo's arm, pulled it down, and obliged him to drop his victim. Azzo seemed in the highest degree astonished. Without concerning himself further about Franz, he gazed in amazement on Woislaw.

'Who art thou who darest to rob me of my prey?' he asked hesitatingly. 'Is it possible? Can you be'—

'Ask not, thou bloody one! Go, seek thy nourishment! Soon comes thy hour!' replied Woislaw in a calm but firm tone.

'Ha, now I know!' cried Azzo eagerly. 'Welcome, blood-brother! I give up to you this worm, and for your sake will not crush him. Farewell; our paths will soon meet again.'

'Soon, very soon; farewell!' cried Woislaw, drawing Franz towards him. Azzo rushed away, and disappeared.

Franz had remained for some moments in a state of semi-stupefaction, but suddenly started as from a dream. 'I am dishonoured, dishonoured for ever!' he cried, as he pressed his clenched hands to his forehead.

'Calm yourself; you could not have conquered,' said Woislaw.

'But I will conquer, or perish!' cried Franz incensed. 'I will seek this adventurer in his den, and he or I must fall.'

'You could not hurt him,' said Woislaw. 'You would infallibly be the victim.'

'Then shew me a way to bring the wretch to judgment,' cried Franz, seizing Woislaw's hands, while tears of anger sprang to his eyes. 'Disgraced as I am, I cannot live.'

'You shall be revenged, and that within twenty-four hours, I hope; but only on two conditions'—

'I agree to them! I will do anything'—began the young man eagerly.

'The first is, that you do nothing, but leave everything in my hands,' interrupted Woislaw. 'The second, that you will assist me in persuading

Franziska to do what I shall represent to her as absolutely necessary. That young lady's life is in more danger from Azzo than your own.'

'How? What?' cried Franz fiercely. 'Franziska's life in danger! and from that man? Tell me, Woislaw, who is this fiend?'

'Not a word will I tell either the young lady or you, until the danger is passed,' said Woislaw firmly. 'The smallest indiscretion would ruin everything. No one can act here but Franziska herself, and if she refuses to do so, she is irretrievably lost.'

'Speak, and I will help you. I will do all you wish, but I must know'—

'Nothing, absolutely nothing,' replied Woislaw. 'I must have both you and Franziska yield to me unconditionally. Come now, come to her. You are to be mute on what has passed, and use every effort to induce her to accede to my proposal.'

Woislaw spoke firmly, and it was impossible for Franz to make any further objection; in a few moments they both entered the hall, where they found the young girls still anxiously awaiting them.

'Oh, I have been so frightened,' said Franziska, even paler than usual, as she held out her hand to Franz. 'I trust all has ended peaceably.'

'Everything is arranged; a couple of words were sufficient to settle the whole affair,' said Woislaw cheerfully. 'But Master Franz was less concerned in it than yourself, fair lady.'

'I! How do you mean?' said Franziska in surprise.

'I allude to your illness,' replied the other.

'And you spoke of that to Azzo? Does he, then, know a remedy which he could not tell me himself?' she inquired, smiling painfully.

'The knight Azzo must take part in your cure; but speak to you about it he cannot, unless the remedy is to lose all its efficacy,' replied Woislaw quietly.

'So it is some secret elixir, as the learned doctors say, who have so long attended me, and through whose means I only grow worse,' said Franziska mournfully.

'It is certainly a secret, but is as certainly a cure,' replied Woislaw.

'So said all, but none has succeeded,' said the young lady peevishly.

'You might at least try it,' began Bertha.

'Because your friend proposes it,' said the other smiling. 'I have no doubt that you, with nothing ailing you, would take all manner of drugs to please your knight; but with me the inducement is wanting, and therefore also the faith.'

'I did not speak of any medicine,' said Woislaw.

'Oh! a magical remedy! I am to be cured—what was it the quack who was here the other day called it?—"by sympathy." Yes, that was it.'

'I do not object to your calling it so, if you like,' said Woislaw smiling; 'but you must know, dear lady, that the measures I shall propose must be attended to literally, and according to the strictest directions.'

'And you trust this to me?' asked Franziska.

'Certainly,' said Woislaw hesitating; 'but'—

'Well, why do you not proceed? Can you think that I shall fail in courage?' she asked.

'Courage is certainly necessary for the success of my plan,' said Woislaw gravely; 'and it is because I give you credit for a large share of that virtue, I venture to propose it at all, although for the real harmlessness of the remedy I will answer with my life, provided you follow my directions exactly.'

'Well, tell me the plan, and then I can decide,' said the young lady.

'I can only tell you that when we commence our operations,' replied Woislaw.

'Do you think I am a child to be sent here, there, and everywhere, without a reason?' asked Franziska, with something of her old pettishness.

'You did me great injustice, dear lady, if you thought for a moment I would propose anything disagreeable to you, unless demanded by the sternest necessity,' said Woislaw; 'and yet I can only repeat my former words.'

'Then I will not do it,' cried Franziska. 'I have already tried so much, and all ineffectually.'

'I give you my honour as a knight, that your cure is certain, but—you must pledge yourself solemnly and unconditionally to do implicitly* what I shall direct,' said Woislaw earnestly.

'Oh, I implore you to consent, Franziska. Our friend would not propose anything unnecessary,' said Bertha, taking both her cousin's hands.

'And let me join my entreaties to Bertha's,' said Franz.

'How strange you all are!' exclaimed Franziska, shaking her head; 'you make such a secret of that which I must know if I am to accomplish it, and then you declare so positively that I shall recover, when my own feelings tell me it is quite hopeless.'

'I repeat, that I will answer for the result,' said Woislaw, 'on the condition I mentioned before, and that you have courage to carry out what you commence.'

'Ha! now I understand; this, after all, is the only thing which appears doubtful to you,' cried Franziska. 'Well, to shew you that our sex are neither wanting in the will nor in the power to accomplish deeds of daring, I give my consent.'

With the last words, she offered Woislaw her hand.

'Our compact is thus sealed,' she pursued smiling. 'Now say, Sir Knight, how am I to commence this mysterious cure?'

'It commenced when you gave your consent,' said Woislaw gravely. 'Now, I have only to request that you will ask no more questions, but hold yourself in readiness to take a ride with me to-morrow an hour before sunset. I also request that you will not mention to your father a word of what has passed.'

'Strange!' said Franziska.

'You have made the compact; you are not wanting in resolution; and I will answer for everything else,' said Woislaw encouragingly.

'Well, so let it be. I will follow your directions,' said the lady, although she still looked incredulous.

'On our return you shall know everything; before that, it is quite impossible,' said Woislaw in conclusion. 'Now go, dear lady, and take some rest; you will need strength for to-morrow.'

It was on the morning of the following day, the sun had not risen above an hour, and the dew still lay like a veil of pearls on the grass, or dripped from the petals of the flowers, swaying in the early breeze, when the knight Woislaw hastened over the fields towards the forest, and turned into a gloomy path, which by the direction, one could perceive, led towards the towers of Klatka. When he arrived at the old oak-tree we have before had occasion to mention, he sought carefully along the road for traces of human footsteps, but only a deer had passed that way; and seemingly satisfied with his search, he proceeded on his way, though not before he had half drawn his dagger from its sheath, as though to assure himself that it was ready for service in time of need.

Slowly he ascended the path; it was evident he carried something beneath his cloak. Arrived in the court, he left the ruins of the castle to the left, and entered the old chapel. In the chancel, he looked eagerly and earnestly round. A deathlike stillness reigned in the deserted sanctuary, only broken by the whispering of the wind in an old thorn-tree which grew outside. Woislaw had looked long around him ere he perceived the door leading down to the vault; he hurried towards it, and descended. The sun's position enabled its rays to penetrate the crevices, and made the subterranean chamber so light, that one could read easily the inscriptions at the head and feet of the coffins. The knight first laid on the ground the packet he had hitherto carried under his cloak, and then going from coffin to coffin, at last remained stationary before the oldest of them. He read the inscription carefully, drew his dagger thoughtfully from its case, and endeavoured to raise the lid with its point. This was no difficult matter, for the rusty iron nails kept but a slight hold of the rotten wood. On looking in, only a heap of ashes,* some remnants of dress, and a skull were the contents. He quickly closed it again, and went on to the next, passing over those of a woman and two children. Here things had much the same appearance, except that the corpse held together till the lid was raised, and then fell into dust, a few linen rags and bones being alone perceptible. In the third, fourth, and nearly the next half-dozen, the bodies were in better preservation: in some, they looked a sort of yellow brown mummy;* whilst in others, a skinless skull covered with hair grinned from the coverings of velvet, silk, or mildewed embroideries; all, however, were touched with the loathsome marks of decay. Only one more coffin now remained to be inspected; Woislaw approached it, and read the inscription. It was the same that had before attracted the Knight of Fahnenberg: Ezzelin von Klatka, the last possessor of the tower, was described as lying therein. Woislaw found it more difficult to raise the lid here; and it was only by the exertion of much strength he at length succeeded in extracting the nails. He did all, however, as quietly as if afraid of rousing some sleeper within; he then raised the cover, and cast a glance on the corpse. An involuntary 'Ha!' burst from his lips as he stepped back a pace. If he had less expected the sight that met his eyes, he would have been far more overcome. In the coffin lay Azzo as he lived and breathed, and as Woislaw had seen him at the supper-table only the evening before. His appearance, dress, and all were the same; besides, he had more the semblance of sleep than of death—no trace of decay was visible—there was even a rosy tint on his cheeks. Only the circumstance that the breast did not heave, distinguished him from one who slept. For a few moments Woislaw did not move; he could only stare into the coffin. With a hastiness in his movements not usual with him, he suddenly seized the lid, which had fallen from his hands, and laying it on the coffin, knocked the nails into their places. As soon as he had completed this work, he fetched the packet he had left at the entrance, and laying it on the top of the coffin, hastily ascended the steps, and quitted the church and the ruins.

The day passed. Before evening, Franziska requested her father to allow her to take a ride with Woislaw, under pretence of shewing him the country. He, only too happy to think this a sign of amendment in his daughter, readily gave his consent; so, followed by a single servant, they mounted and left the castle. Woislaw was unusually silent and serious. When Franziska began to rally him about his gravity, and the approaching sympathetic care, he replied, that what was before her was no laughing matter; and that although the result would be certainly a cure, still it would leave an impression on her whole future life. In such discourse they reached the wood, and at length the oak, where they left their horses. Woislaw gave Franziska his arm, and they ascended the hill slowly and silently. They had just reached one of the half-dilapidated outworks where they could catch a glimpse of the open country, when Woislaw, speaking more to himself than to his companion, said: 'In a quarter of an hour, the sun will set, and in another hour the moon will have risen; then all must be accomplished. It will soon be time to commence the work.'

'Then, I should think it was time to intrust me with some idea of what it is,' said Franziska, looking at him.

'Well, lady,' he replied, turning towards her, and his voice was very solemn, 'I entreat you, Franziska von Fahnenberg, for your own good, and as you love the father who clings to you with his whole soul, that you will weigh well my words, and that you will not interrupt me with questions which I cannot answer until the work is completed. Your life is in the greatest danger from the illness under which you are labouring; indeed, you are irrecoverably lost if you do not fully carry out what I shall now impart to you. Now, promise me to do implicitly as I shall tell you; I pledge you my knightly word it is nothing against Heaven, or the honour of your house; and, besides, it is the sole means for saving you.' With these words, he held out his right hand to his companion, while he raised the other to heaven in confirmation of his oath.

'I promise you,' said Franziska, visibly moved by Woislaw's solemn tone, as she laid her little white and wasted hand in his.

'Then, come; it is time,' was his reply, as he led her towards the church. The last rays of the sun were just pouring through the broken windows. They entered the chancel, the best preserved part of the whole building; here there were still some old kneeling-stools, placed before the high-altar, although nothing remained of that but the stonework and a few steps; the pictures and decorations had all vanished.

'Say an Ave;* you will have need of it,' said Woislaw, as he himself fell on his knees.

Franziska knelt beside him, and repeated a short prayer. After a few moments, both rose.

'The moment has arrived! The sun sinks, and before the moon rises, all must be over,' said Woislaw quickly.

'What am I to do?' asked Franziska cheerfully.

'You see there that open vault!' replied the knight Woislaw, pointing to the door and flight of steps: 'you must descend. You must go alone; I may not accompany you. When you have reached the vault you will find, close to the entrance, a coffin, on which is placed a small packet. Open this packet, and you will find three long iron nails and a hammer. Then pause for a moment; but when I begin to repeat the Credo* in a loud voice, knock with all your might, first one nail, then a second, and then a third, into the lid of the coffin, right up to their heads.'*

Franziska stood thunderstruck; her whole body trembled, and she could not utter a word. Woislaw perceived it.

'Take courage, dear lady!' said he. 'Think that you are in the hands of Heaven, and that, without the will of your Creator, not a hair can fall from your head. Besides, I repeat, there is no danger.'

'Well, then, I will do it,' cried Franziska, in some measure regaining courage.

'Whatever you may hear, whatever takes place inside the coffin,' continued Woislaw, 'must have no effect upon you. Drive the nails well in, without flinching: your work must be finished before my prayer comes to an end.'

Franziska shuddered, but again recovered herself. 'I will do it; Heaven will send me strength,' she murmured softly.

'There is one thing more,' said Woislaw hesitatingly; 'perhaps it is the hardest of all I have proposed, but without it your cure will not be complete. When you have done as I have told you, a sort of'—he hesitated—'a sort of liquid will flow from the coffin; in this dip your finger, and besmear the scratch on your throat.'*

'Horrible!' cried Franziska. 'This liquid is blood. A human being lies in the coffin.'

'An *unearthly one* lies therein! That blood is your own, but it flows in other veins,' said Woislaw gloomily. 'Ask no more; the sand is running out.'

Franziska summoned up all her powers of mind and body, went towards the steps which led to the vault, and Woislaw sank on his knees before the altar in quiet prayer. When the lady had descended, she found herself before the coffin on which lay the packet before mentioned. A sort of twilight reigned in the vault, and everything around was so still and peaceful, that she felt more calm, and going up to the coffin, opened the packet. She had hardly seen that a hammer and three long nails were its contents, when suddenly Woislaw's voice rang through the church, and broke the stillness of the aisles. Franziska started, but recognised the appointed prayer. She seized one of the nails, and with one stroke of the hammer drove it at least an inch into the cover. All was still; nothing was heard but the echo of the stroke. Taking heart, the maiden grasped the hammer with both hands, and struck the nail twice with all her might, right up to the head into the wood. At this moment commenced a rustling noise; it seemed as though something in the interior began to move and to struggle. Franziska drew back in alarm. She was already on the point of throwing away the hammer, and flying up the steps, when Woislaw raised his voice so powerfully, and it sounded so entreatingly, that in a sort of excitement, such as would induce one to rush into a lion's den, she returned to the coffin, determined to bring things to a conclusion. Hardly knowing what she did, she placed a second nail in the centre of the lid, and after some strokes, this was likewise buried to its head. The struggle now increased fearfully, as if some living creature were striving to burst the coffin. This was so shaken by it, that it cracked and split on all sides. Half distracted, Franziska seized the third nail; she thought no more of her ailments, she only knew herself to be in terrible danger, of what kind she could not guess: in an agony that threatened to rob her of her senses, and in the midst of the turning and cracking of the coffin, in which low groans were now heard, she struck the third nail in equally tight. At this moment, she began to lose consciousness. She wished to hasten away, but staggered; and mechanically grasping at something to save herself by, she seized the corner of the coffin, and sank fainting beside it on the ground.

A quarter of an hour might have elapsed, when she again opened her eyes. She looked around her. Above was the starry sky, and the moon, which shed her cold light on the ruins and on the tops of the old oak-trees. Franziska was lying outside the church walls, Woislaw on his knees beside her, holding her hand in his.

'Heaven be praised that you live!' he cried, with a sigh of relief. 'I was beginning to doubt whether the remedy had not been too severe, and yet it was the only thing to save you.'

Franziska recovered her full consciousness very gradually. The past seemed to her like a dreadful dream. Only a few moments before, that fearful scene; and now this quiet all around her. She hardly dared at first to raise her eyes, and shuddered when she found herself only a few paces removed from the spot where she had undergone such terrible agony. She listened half unconsciously, now to the pacifying words Woislaw addressed to her, now to the whistling of the servant, who stood by the horses, and who, to wile away his time, was imitating the evening-song of a belated cow-herd.

'Let us go,' whispered Franziska, as she strove to raise herself. 'But what is this? My shoulder is wet, my throat, my hand'—

'It is probably the evening dew on the grass,' said Woislaw gently.

'No; it is blood!' she cried, springing up with horror in her tone. 'See, my hand is full of blood!'

'Oh, you are mistaken—surely mistaken,' said Woislaw stammering. 'Or perhaps the wound on your neck may have opened? Pray, feel whether this is the case.' He seized her hand, and directed it to the spot.

'I do not perceive anything; I feel no pain,' she said at length, somewhat angrily.

'Then, perhaps, when you fainted, you may have struck a corner of the coffin, or have torn yourself with the point of one of the nails,' suggested Woislaw.

'Oh, of what do you remind me!' cried Franziska shuddering. 'Let us away—away! I entreat you, come! I will not remain a moment longer near this dreadful, dreadful place.'

They descended the path much quicker than they came. Woislaw placed his companion on her horse, and they were soon on their way home.

When they approached the castle, Franziska began to inundate her protector with questions about the preceding adventure; but he declared that her present state of excitement must make him defer all explanations till the morning, when her curiosity should be satisfied. On their arrival, he conducted her at once to her room, and told the knight his daughter was too much fatigued with her ride to appear at the supper-table. On the following morning, Franziska rose earlier than she had done for a long time. She assured her friend it was the first time since her illness commenced that she had been really refreshed by her sleep, and, what was still more remarkable, she had not been troubled by her old horrible dream. Her improved looks were not only remarked by Bertha, but by Franz and the knight; and with Woislaw's permission, she related the adventures of the previous evening. No sooner had she concluded, than Woislaw was completely stormed with questions about such a strange occurrence.

'Have you,' said the latter, turning towards his host, 'ever heard of Vampires?'

'Often,' replied he; 'but I have never believed in them.'

'Nor did I,' said Woislaw; 'but I have been assured of their existence by experience.'

'Oh, tell us what occurred,' cried Bertha eagerly, as a light seemed to dawn on her.

'It was during my first campaign in Hungary,' began Woislaw, 'when I was rendered helpless for some time by this sword-cut of a janizary* across my face, and another on my shoulder. I had been taken into the house of a respectable family in a small town. It consisted of the father and mother, and a daughter about twenty years of age. They obtained their living by selling the very good wine of the country, and the tap-room was always full of visitors. Although the family were well to do in the world, there seemed to brood over them a continual melancholy, caused by the constant illness of the only daughter, a very pretty and excellent girl. She had always bloomed like a rose, but for some months she had been getting so thin and wasted, and that without any satisfactory reason: they tried every means to restore her, but in vain. As the army had encamped quite in the neighbourhood, of course a number of people of all countries assembled in the tavern. Amongst these there was one man who came every evening, when the moon shone, who struck everybody by the peculiarity of his manners and appearance; he looked dried up and deathlike, and hardly spoke at all;

but what he did say was bitter and sarcastic. Most attention was excited towards him by the circumstance, that although he always ordered a cup of the best wine, and now and then raised it to his lips, the cup was always as full after his departure as at first.'

'This all agrees wonderfully with the appearance of Azzo,' said Bertha, deeply interested.

'The daughter of the house,' continued Woislaw, 'became daily worse, despite the aid not only of Christian doctors, but of many amongst the heathen prisoners, who were consulted in the hope that they might have some magical remedy to propose. It was singular that the girl always complained of a dream, in which the unknown guest worried and plagued her.'

'Just the same as your dream, Franziska,' cried Bertha.

'One evening,' resumed Woislaw, 'an old Sclavonian—who had made many voyages to Turkey and Greece, and had even seen the New World*—and I were sitting over our wine, when the unknown walked silently, as usual, into the room, and sat down at the table. The bottle passed quickly between my friend and me, whilst we talked of all manner of things, of our adventures, and of passages in our lives, both horrible and amusing. We went on chatting thus for about an hour, and drank a tolerable quantity of wine. The unknown had remained perfectly silent the whole time, only smiling contemptuously every now and then. He now paid his money, and was going away. All this had quietly worried me—perhaps the wine had got a little into my head—so I said to the stranger: "Hold, you stony stranger; you have hitherto done nothing but listen, and have not even emptied your cup. Now you shall take your turn in telling us something amusing, and if you do not drink up your wine, it shall produce a quarrel between us." "Yes," said the Sclavonian, "you must remain; you shall chat and drink, too;" and he grasped—for although no longer young, he was big and very strong—the stranger by the shoulder, to pull him down to his seat again: the latter, however, although as thin as a skeleton, with one movement of his hand flung the Sclavonian to the middle of the room, and half stunned him for a moment. I now approached to hold the stranger back. I caught him by the arm; and although the springs of my iron hand were less powerful than those I have at present, I must have griped* him rather hard in my anger, for after looking grimly at me for a moment, he bent towards me and whispered in my ear: "Let me go: from the gripe of your fist, I see you are my brother, therefore do not hinder me from seeking my bloody nourishment. I am hungry!" Surprised by such words, I let him loose, and almost before I was aware, he had left the room. As soon as I had in some degree recovered from my astonishment, I told the Sclavonian what I had heard. He started, evidently alarmed. I asked him to tell me the cause of his fears, and pressed him for an explanation of those extraordinary words. On our way to his lodging, he complied with my request. "The stranger," said he, 'is a Vampire!'"

'How?' cried the knight, Franziska, and Bertha simultaneously, in a voice of horror. 'So this Azzo was'—

'Nothing less. He also was a Vampire!' replied Woislaw. 'But at all events *his* hellish thirst is quenched for ever; he will never return.—But I have not finished. As in my country vampires had never been heard of, I questioned the Sclavonian minutely. He said that in Hungary, Croatia, Dalmatia, and Bosnia, these hellish guests were not uncommon. They were deceased persons, who had either once served as nourishment to vampires, or who had died in deadly sin, or under excommunication;* and that whenever the moon shone, they rose from their graves, and sucked the blood of the living.'

'Horrible!' cried Franziska. 'If you had told me all this beforehand, I should never have accomplished the work.'

'So I thought; and yet it must be executed by the sufferers themselves, while some one else performs the devotions,' replied Woislaw. 'The Sclavonian,' he continued after a short pause, 'added many other facts with regard to these unearthly visitants. He said that whilst their victim wasted, they themselves improved in appearance, and that a vampire possessed enormous strength'—

'Now I can understand the change your false hand produced on Azzo,' interrupted Franz.

'Yes, that was it,' replied Woislaw. 'Azzo, as well as the other vampire, mistook its great power for that of a natural one, and concluded I was one of his own species.—You may now imagine, dear lady,' he continued, turning to Franziska, 'how alarmed I was at your appearance when I arrived: all you and Bertha told me increased my anxiety; and when I saw Azzo, I could doubt no longer that he was a vampire. As I learned from your account that a grave with the name Ezzelin von Klatka lay in the neighbourhood, I had no doubt that you might be saved if I could only induce you to assist me. It did not appear to me advisable to impart the whole facts of the case, for your bodily powers were so impaired, that an idea of the horrors before you might have quite unfitted you for the exertion; for this reason, I arranged everything in the manner in which it has taken place.'

'You did wisely,' replied Franziska shuddering. 'I can never be grateful enough to you. Had I known what was required of me, I never could have undertaken the deed.'

'That was what I feared,' said Woislaw; 'but fortune has favoured us all through.'

'And what became of the unfortunate girl in Hungary?' inquired Bertha.

'I know not,' replied Woislaw. 'That very evening there was an alarm of the Turks, and we were ordered off. I never heard anything more of her.'

The conversation upon these strange occurrences continued for some time longer. The knight determined to have the vault at Klatka walled up for ever. This took place on the following day; the knight alleging as a reason that he did not wish the dead to be disturbed by irreverent hands.

Franziska recovered gradually. Her health had been so severely shaken, that it was long ere her strength was so much restored as to allow of her being considered out of danger. The young lady's character underwent a great change in the interval. Its former strength was, perhaps, in some degree diminished, but in place of that, she had acquired a benevolent softness, which brought out all her best qualities. Franz continued his attentions to his cousin; but, perhaps, owing to a hint from Bertha, he was less assiduous in his exhibition of them. His inclinations did not lead him to the battle, the camp, or the attainment of honours; his great aim was to increase the good condition and happiness of his tenants, and to this he contributed the whole energy of his mind. Franziska could not withstand the unobtrusive signs of the young man's continued attachment; and it was not long ere the credit she was obliged to yield to his noble efforts for the welfare of his fellow-creatures, changed into a liking, which went on increasing, until at length it assumed the character of love. As Woislaw insisted on making Bertha his wife before he returned to Silesia, it was arranged that the marriage should take place at their present abode. How joyful was the surprise of the knight of Fahnenberg, when his daughter and Franz likewise entreated his blessing, and expressed their desire of being united on the same day! That day soon came round, and it saw the bright looks of two happy couples.

FITZ-JAMES O'BRIEN

WHAT WAS IT?

A Mystery

IT is, I confess, with considerable diffidence that I approach the strange narrative which I am about to relate. The events which I purpose detailing are of so extraordinary and unheard-of a character that I am quite prepared to meet with an unusual amount of incredulity and scorn. I accept all such beforehand. I have, I trust, the literary courage to face unbelief. I have, after mature consideration, resolved to narrate, in as simple and straightforward a manner as I can compass, some facts that passed under my observation in the month of July last, and which, in the annals of the mysteries of physical science, are wholly unparalleled.

I live at No.—Twenty-sixth Street, in this city.* The house is in some respects a curious one. It has enjoyed for the last two years the reputation of being haunted. It is a large and stately residence, surrounded by what was once a garden, but which is now only a green inclosure used for bleaching clothes. The dry basin of what has been a fountain, and a few fruit-trees, ragged and unpruned, indicate that this spot, in past days, was a pleasant, shady retreat, filled with fruits and flowers and the sweet murmur of waters.

The house is very spacious. A hall of noble size leads to a large spiral staircase winding through its centre; while the various apartments are of imposing dimensions. It was built some fifteen or twenty years since by Mr. A——, the well-known New York merchant, who five years ago threw the commercial world into convulsions by a stupendous bank fraud. Mr. A——, as everyone knows, escaped to Europe, and died not long after of a broken heart. Almost immediately after the news of his decease reached this country, and was verified, the report spread in Twenty-sixth Street that No.—was haunted. Legal measures had dispossessed the widow of its former owner, and it was inhabited merely by a care-taker and his wife, placed there by the house-agent into whose hands it had passed for purposes of renting or sale. These people declared that they were troubled with unnatural noises. Doors were opened without any visible agency. The remnants of furniture scattered through the various rooms were, during the night, piled one upon the other by unknown hands. Invisible feet passed up and down the stairs in broad daylight, accompanied by the rustle of unseen silk dresses and the gliding of viewless hands along the massive balusters.* The care-taker and his wife declared they would live there no longer. The house-agent laughed, dismissed them, and put others in their place. The noises and supernatural manifestations continued. The neighborhood caught up the story, and the house remained untenanted for three years. Several parties negotiated for it; but somehow, always before the bargain was closed, they heard the unpleasant rumors, and declined to treat any further.

It was in this state of things that my landlady—who at that time kept a boarding-house in Bleecker Street, and who wished to move further up town—conceived the bold idea of renting No.—Twenty-sixth Street. Happening to have in her house rather a plucky and philosophical set of boarders, she laid her scheme before us, stating candidly every thing she had heard respecting the ghostly qualities of the establishment to which she wished to remove us. With the exception of one or two timid persons—a sea-captain and a returned Californian, who immediately gave notice that they would leave—every one of Mrs. Moffat's guests declared that they would accompany her in her chivalric incursion into the abode of spirits.

Our removal was effected in the month of May, and we were all charmed with our new residence. The portion of Twenty-sixth Street where our house is situated—between Seventh and Eighth Avenues—is one of the pleasantest localities in New York. The gardens back of the houses, running down nearly to the Hudson, form, in the summer time, a perfect avenue of verdure. The air is pure and invigorating, sweeping, as it does, straight across the river from the Weehawken heights,* and even the ragged garden which surrounded the house on two sides, although displaying on washing-days rather too much clothes-line, still gave us a piece of green sward to look at, and a cool retreat in the summer evenings, where we smoked our cigars in the dusk, and watched the fire-flies flashing their dark-lanterns in the long grass.

Of course we had no sooner established ourselves at No.—than we began to expect the ghosts. We absolutely awaited their advent with eagerness. Our dinner conversation was supernatural. One of the boarders, who had purchased Mrs. Crowe's 'Night Side of Nature'* for his own private delectation, was regarded as a public enemy by the entire household for not having bought twenty copies. The man led a life of supreme wretchedness while he was perusing this volume. A system of espionage was established, of which he was the victim. If he incautiously laid the book down for an instant and left the room, it was immediately seized and read aloud in secret places to a select few. I found myself a person of immense importance, it having leaked out that I was tolerably well versed in the history of supernaturalism, and had once written a story, entitled 'The Pot of Tulips,' for *Harper's Monthly*,* the foundation of which was a ghost. If a table or a wainscot panel happened to warp when we were assembled in the large drawing-room, there was an instant silence, and everyone was prepared for an immediate clanking of chains and a spectral form.

After a month of psychological excitement, it was with the utmost dissatisfaction that we were forced to acknowledge that nothing in the remotest degree approaching the supernatural had manifested itself. Once the black butler asseverated* that his candle had been blown out by some invisible agency while in the act of undressing himself for the night; but as I had more than once discovered this colored gentleman in a condition when one candle must have appeared to him like two, I thought it possible that, by going a step farther in his potations,* he might have reversed this phenomenon, and seen no candle at all where he ought to have beheld one.

Things were in this state when an incident took place so awful and inexplicable in its character that my reason fairly reels at the bare memory of the occurrence. It was the 10th of July. After dinner was over I repaired, with my friend Dr. Hammond, to the garden to smoke my evening pipe. Independent of certain mental sympathies which existed between the Doctor and myself, we were linked together by a secret vice. We both smoked opium.* We knew each other's secret, and respected it. We enjoyed together that wonderful expansion of thought; that marvelous intensifying of the perceptive faculties; that boundless feeling of existence when we seem to have points of contact with the whole universe; in short, that unimaginable spiritual bliss, which I would not surrender for a throne, and which I hope you, reader, will never—never taste.

Those hours of opium happiness which the Doctor and I spent together in secret were regulated with a scientific accuracy. We did not blindly smoke the drug of Paradise,* and leave our dreams to chance. While smoking we carefully steered our conversation through the brightest and calmest channels of thought. We talked of the East, and endeavored to recall the magical panorama of its glowing scenery. We criticized the most sensuous poets, those who painted life ruddy with health, brimming with passion, happy in the possession of youth, and strength, and beauty. If we talked of Shakespeare's 'Midsummer Night's Dream,' we lingered over Ariel and avoided Caliban.* Like the Gebers,* we turned our faces to the East, and saw only the sunny side of the world.

This skillful coloring of our train of thought produced in our subsequent visions a corresponding tone. The splendors of Arabian fairy-land dyed our dreams. We paced that narrow strip of grass with the tread and port of kings. The song of the *Rana arborea** while he clung to the bark of the ragged plum-tree sounded like the strains of divine orchestras. Houses, walls, and streets melted like rain-clouds, and vistas of unimaginable glory stretched away before us. It was a rapturous companionship. We each of us enjoyed the vast delight more perfectly because, even in our most ecstatic moments, we were ever conscious of each other's presence. Our pleasures, while individual, were still twin, vibrating and moving in musical accord.

On the evening in question, the 10th of July, the Doctor and myself found ourselves in an unusually metaphysical mood. We lit our large meerschaums,* filled with fine Turkish tobacco,* in the core of which burned a little black nut of opium, that, like the nut in the fairy tale,* held within its narrow limits wonders beyond the reach of kings; we paced to and fro, conversing. A strange perversity dominated the currents of our thought. They would *not* flow through the sun-lit channels into which we strove to divert them. For some unaccountable reason they constantly diverged into dark and lonesome beds, where a continual gloom brooded. It was in vain that, after our old fashion, we flung ourselves on the shores of the East, and talked of its gay bazaars, of the splendors of the time of Haroun,* of harems and golden palaces. Black afreets continually arose from the depths of our talk, and expanded, like the one the fisherman released from the copper vessel,* until they blotted everything bright from our vision. Insensibly we yielded to the occult force that swayed us, and indulged in gloomy speculation. We had talked some time upon the proneness of the human mind to mysticism, and the almost universal love of the Terrible, when Hammond suddenly said to me,

'What do you consider to be the greatest element of Terror?'

The question, I own, puzzled me. That many things were terrible, I knew. Stumbling over a corpse in the dark; beholding, as I once did, a woman floating down a deep and rapid river, with wildly lifted arms and awful, upturned face, uttering, as she sank, shrieks that rent one's heart, while we, the spectators, stood frozen at a window which overhung the river at a height of sixty feet, unable to make the slightest effort to save her, but dumbly watching her last supreme agony and her disappearance. A shattered wreck, with no life visible, encountered floating listlessly on the ocean, is a terrible object, for it suggests a huge terror, the proportions of which are vailed.* But it now struck me for the first time that there must be one great and ruling embodiment of fear, a King of Terrors to which all others must succumb. What might it be? To what train of circumstances would it owe its existence?

'I confess, Hammond,' I replied to my friend, 'I never considered the subject before. That there must be one Something more terrible than any other thing, I feel. I can not attempt, however, even the most vague definition.'

'I am somewhat like you, Harry,' he answered. 'I feel my capacity to experience a terror greater than any thing yet conceived by the human mind. Something combining in fearful and unnatural amalgamation hitherto supposed incompatible elements. The calling of the voices in Brockden Brown's novel of "Wieland"* is awful; so is the picture of the Dweller of the Threshold in Bulwer's "Zanoni";* but,' he added, shaking his head gloomily, 'there is something more horrible still than these.'

'Look here, Hammond,' I rejoined, 'let us drop this kind of talk for Heaven's sake. We shall suffer for it, depend on it.

'I don't know what's the matter with me to-night,' he replied, 'but my brain is running upon all sorts of weird and awful thoughts. I feel as if I could write a story like Hoffman,* to-night, if I were only master of a literary style.'

'Well, if we are going to be Hoffmanesque in our talk I'm off to bed. Opium and nightmares should never be brought together. How sultry it is! Good-night, Hammond.'

'Good-night, Harry. Pleasant dreams to you.'

'To you, gloomy wretch, afreets, ghouls, and enchanters.'

We parted, and each sought his respective chamber. I undressed quickly and got into bed, taking with me, according to my usual custom, a book, over which I generally read myself to sleep. I opened the volume as soon as I had laid my head upon the pillow, and instantly flung it to the other side of the room. It was Goudon's 'History of Monsters'*—a curious French work, which I had lately imported from Paris, but which, in the state of mind I was then in, was any thing but an agreeable companion. I resolved to go to sleep at once; so turning down my gas until nothing but a little blue point of light glimmered on the top of the tube, I composed myself to rest once more.

The room was in total darkness. The atom of gas that still remained lighted did not illuminate a distance of three inches round the burner. I desperately drew my arm across my eyes, as if to shut out even the darkness, and tried to think of nothing. It was in vain. The confounded themes touched on by Hammond in the garden kept obtruding themselves on my brain. I battled against them. I erected ramparts of would-be blankness of intellect to keep them out. They still crowded upon me. While I was lying still as a corpse, hoping that by a perfect physical inaction I should hasten mental repose, an awful incident occurred. A Something dropped, as it seemed, from the ceiling, plumb upon my chest, and the next instant I felt two bony hands encircling my throat, endeavoring to choke me.*

I am no coward, and am possessed of considerable physical strength. The suddenness of the attack instead of stunning me strung every nerve to its highest tension. My body acted from instinct, before my brain had time to realize the terrors of my position. In an instant I wound two muscular arms around the creature, and squeezed it, with all the strength of despair, against my chest. In a few seconds the bony hands that had fastened on my throat loosened their hold, and I was free to breathe once more. Then commenced a struggle of awful intensity. Immersed in the most profound darkness, totally ignorant of the nature of the Thing by which I was so suddenly attacked, finding my grasp slipping every moment by reason, it seemed to me, of the entire nakedness of my assailant, bitten with sharp teeth in the shoulder, neck, and chest, having every moment to protect my throat against a pair of sinewy, agile hands, which my utmost efforts could not confine—these were a combination of circumstances to combat which required all the strength and skill and courage that I possessed.

At last, after a silent, deadly, exhausting struggle, I got my assailant under by a series of incredible efforts of strength. Once pinned, with my knee on what I made out to be its chest, I knew that I was victor.

I rested for a moment to breathe. I heard the creature beneath me panting in the darkness, and felt the violent throbbing of a heart. It was apparently as exhausted as I was, that was one comfort. At this moment I remembered that I usually placed under my pillow, before going to bed, a large, yellow silk pocket-handkerchief, for use during the night. I felt for it instantly; it was there. In a few seconds more I had, after a fashion, pinioned the creature's arms.

I now felt tolerably secure. There was nothing more to be done but to turn on the gas, and, having first seen what my midnight assailant was like, arouse the household. I will confess to being actuated* by a certain pride in not giving the alarm before; I wished to make the capture alone and unaided.

Never losing my hold for an instant, I slipped from the bed to the floor, dragging my captive with me. I had but a few steps to make to reach the gas-burner; these I made with the greatest caution, holding the creature in a grip like a vice. At last I got within arm's-length of the tiny speck of blue light, which told me where the gas-burner lay. Quick as lightning I released my grasp with one hand and let on the full flood of light. Then I turned to look at my captive.

I cannot even attempt to give any definition of my sensations the instant after I turned on the gas. I suppose I must have shrieked with terror, for in less than a minute afterward my room was crowded with the inmates of the house. I shudder now as I think of that awful moment. *I saw nothing!* Yes; I had one arm firmly clasped round a breathing, panting, corporeal shape, my other hand gripped with all its strength a throat as warm, and apparently fleshly, as my own; and yet, with this living substance in my grasp, with its body pressed against my own, and all in the bright glare of a large jet of gas, I absolutely beheld nothing! Not even an outline—a vapor!

I do not, even at this hour, realize the situation in which I found myself. I can not recall the astounding incident thoroughly. Imagination in vain tries to compass the awful paradox.

It breathed. I felt its warm breath upon my cheek. It struggled fiercely. It had hands. They clutched me. Its skin was smooth, just like my own. There it lay, pressed close up against me, solid as stone—and yet utterly invisible!*

I wonder that I did not faint or go mad on the instant. Some wonderful instinct must have sustained me; for, absolutely, in place of loosening my hold on the terrible Enigma, I seemed to gain an additional strength in my moment of horror, and tightened my grasp with such wonderful force that I felt the creature shivering with agony.

Just then Hammond entered my room at the head of the household. As soon as he beheld my face—which, I suppose, must have been an awful sight to look at—he hastened forward, crying,

'Great heaven, Harry! what has happened?'

'Hammond! Hammond!' I cried, 'come here. Oh! this is awful! I have been attacked in bed by something or other, which I have hold of; but I can't see it—I can't see it!'

Hammond, doubtless struck by the unfeigned horror expressed in my countenance, made one or two steps forward with an anxious yet puzzled expression. A very audible titter burst from the remainder of my visitors. This suppressed laughter made me furious. To laugh at a human being in my position! It was the worst species of cruelty. *Now*, I can understand why the appearance of a man struggling violently, as it would seem, with an airy nothing,* and calling for assistance against a vision, should have appeared ludicrous. *Then*, so great was my rage against the mocking crowd that had I the power I would have stricken them dead where they stood.

'Hammond! Hammond!' I cried again, despairingly, 'for God's sake come to me. I can hold the—the Thing* but a short while longer. It is overpowering me. Help me. Help me!'

'Harry,' whispered Hammond, approaching me, 'you have been smoking too much opium.'

'I swear to you Hammond that this is no vision,' I answered, in the same low tone. 'Don't you see how it shakes my whole frame with its struggles? If you don't believe me convince yourself. Feel it—touch it.'

Hammond advanced and laid his hand in the spot I indicated. A wild cry of horror burst from him. He had felt it!

In a moment he had discovered somewhere in my room a long piece of cord, and was the next instant winding it, and knotting it about the body of the unseen being that I clasped in my arms.

'Harry,' he said, in a hoarse, agitated voice, for, though he preserved his presence of mind, he was deeply moved, 'Harry, it's all safe now. You may let go, old fellow, if you're tired. The Thing can't move.'

I was utterly exhausted, and I gladly loosed my hold.

Hammond stood holding the ends of the cord that bound the Invisible, twisted round his hand, while before him, self-supporting, as it were, he beheld a rope laced and interlaced, and stretching tightly around a vacant space. I never saw a man look so thoroughly stricken with awe. Nevertheless his face expressed all the courage and determination which I knew him to possess. His lips, although white, were set firmly, and one could perceive at a glance that, although stricken with fear, he was not daunted.

The confusion that ensued among the guests of the house, who were witnesses of this extraordinary scene between Hammond and myself—who beheld the pantomime of binding this struggling Something—who beheld me almost sinking from physical exhaustion when my task of jailer was over—the confusion and terror that took possession of the by-standers, when they saw all this, was beyond description. Many of the weaker ones fled from the apartment. The few who remained behind clustered near the door, and could not be induced to approach Hammond and his Charge. Still incredulity broke out through their terror. They had not the courage to satisfy themselves, and yet they doubted. It was in vain that I begged of some of the men to come near and convince themselves by touch of the existence of a living being in that room which was invisible. They were incredulous, but did not dare to undeceive themselves. How could a solid, living, breathing body be invisible? they asked. My reply was this. I gave a sign to Hammond, and both of us—conquering our fearful repugnance to touch the invisible creature—lifted it from the ground, manacled as it was, and took it to my bed. Its weight was about that of a boy of fourteen.

'Now my friends,' I said, as Hammond and myself held the creature suspended over the bed, 'I can give you self-evident proof that here is a solid, ponderable body which, nevertheless, you can not see. Be good enough to watch the surface of the bed attentively.'

I was astonished at my own courage in treating this strange event so calmly; but I had recovered from my first terror, and felt a sort of scientific pride in the affair which dominated every other feeling.

The eyes of the by-standers were immediately fixed on my bed. At a given signal Hammond and I let the creature fall. There was the dull sound of a heavy body alighting on a soft mass. The timbers of the bed creaked. A deep impression marked itself distinctly on the pillow, and on the bed itself. The crowd who witnessed this gave a sort of low, universal cry, and rushed from the room. Hammond and I were left alone with our Mystery.

We remained silent for some time, listening to the low, irregular breathing of the creature on the bed, and watching the rustle of the bed-clothes as it impotently struggled to free itself from confinement. Then Hammond spoke.

'Harry, this is awful.'

'Ay, awful.'

'But not unaccountable.'

'Not unaccountable! What do you mean? Such a thing has never occurred since the birth of the world. I know not what to think, Hammond. God grant that I am not mad, and that this is not an insane fantasy!'

'Let us reason a little, Harry. Here is a solid body which we touch, but which we can not see. The fact is so unusual that it strikes us with terror. Is there no parallel, though, for such a phenomenon? Take a piece of pure glass. It is tangible and transparent. A certain chemical coarseness is all that prevents its being so entirely transparent as to be totally invisible. It is not *theoretically impossible*, mind you, to fabricate a glass which shall not reflect a single ray of light—a glass so pure and homogeneous in its atoms that the rays from the sun shall pass through it as they do through the air, refracted but not reflected. We do not see the air, and yet we feel it.'

'That's all very well, Hammond, but these are inanimate substances. Glass does not breathe, air does not breathe. *This* thing has a heart that palpitates. A will that moves it. Lungs that play and inspire and respire.'

'You forget the strange phenomena of which we have so often heard of late,' answered the Doctor, gravely. 'At the meetings called "spirit circles,"* invisible hands have been thrust into the hands of those persons round the table—warm, fleshly hands that seemed to pulsate with mortal life.'

'What? Do you think, then, that this thing is—'

'I don't know what it is,' was the solemn reply; 'but please the gods I will, with your assistance, thoroughly investigate it.'

We watched together, smoking many pipes, all night long by the bedside of the unearthly being that tossed and panted until it was apparently wearied out. Then we learned by the low, regular breathing that it slept.

The next morning the house was all astir. The boarders congregated on the landing outside my room, and Hammond and myself were lions.* We had to answer a thousand questions as to the state of our extraordinary prisoner, for as yet not one person in the house except ourselves could be induced to set foot in the apartment.

The creature was awake. This was evidenced by the convulsive manner in which the bed-clothes were moved in its efforts to escape. There was something truly terrible in beholding, as it were, those second-hand indications of the terrible writhings and agonized struggles for liberty, which themselves were invisible.

Hammond and myself had racked our brains during the long night to discover some means by which we might realize the shape and general appearance of the Enigma. As well as we could make out by passing our hands over the creature's form, its outlines and lineaments were human. There was a mouth; a round, smooth head without hair; a nose, which, however, was little elevated above the cheeks; and its hands and feet felt like those of a boy. At first we thought of placing the being on a smooth surface and tracing its outline with chalk, as shoemakers trace the outline of the foot. This plan was given up as being of no value. Such an outline would give not the slightest idea of its conformation.

A happy thought struck me. We would take a cast of it in plaster of Paris.* This would give us the solid figure, and satisfy all our wishes. But how to do it? The movements of the creature would disturb the setting of the plastic* covering, and distort the mould. Another thought. Why not give it chloroform?* It had respiratory organs—that was evident by its breathing. Once reduced to a state of insensibility, we could do with it what we would. Doctor X——was sent for; and after the worthy physician had recovered from the first shock of amazement, he proceeded to administer the chloroform. In three minutes afterward we were enabled to remove the fetters from the creature's body, and a well-known modeler was busily engaged in covering the invisible form with the moist clay. In five minutes more we had a mould, and before evening a rough *fac-simile** of the Mystery. It was shaped like a man. Distorted, uncouth, and horrible, but still a man. It was small, not over four feet and some inches in height, and its limbs betrayed a muscular development that was unparalleled. Its face surpassed in hideousness any thing I had ever seen. Gustave Doré, or Callot, or Tony Johannot never conceived anything so horrible. There is a face in one of the latter's illustrations to '*Un voyage où il vous plaira*,'* which somewhat approaches the countenance of this creature, but does not equal it. It was the physiognomy of what I should have fancied a ghoul to be. It looked as if it was capable of feeding on human flesh.*

Having satisfied our curiosity, and bound every one in the house over to secrecy, it became a question what was to be done with our Enigma? It was impossible that we should keep such a horror in our house; it was equally impossible that such an awful being should be let loose upon the world. I confess that I would have gladly voted for the creature's destruction. But who would shoulder the responsibility? Who would undertake the execution of this horrible semblance of a human being? Day after day this question was deliberated gravely. The boarders all left the house. Mrs. Moffat was in despair, and threatened Hammond and myself with all sorts of legal penalties if we did not remove the Horror. Our answer was, 'We will go if you like, but we decline taking this creature with us. Remove it yourself if you please. It appeared in your house. On you the responsibility rests.' To this there was, of course, no answer. Mrs. Moffat could not obtain for love or money a person who would even approach the Mystery.

The most singular part of the affair was, that we were entirely ignorant of what the creature habitually fed on. Every thing in the way of nutriment that we could think of was placed before it, but was never touched. It was awful to stand by, day after day, and see the clothes toss and hear the hard breathing, and know that it was starving.

Ten, twelve days, a fortnight passed, and it still lived. The pulsations of the heart, however, were daily growing fainter, and had now nearly ceased altogether. It was evident that the creature was dying for want of sustenance. While this terrible life-struggle was going on I felt miserable. I could not sleep of nights. Horrible as the creature was, it was pitiful to think of the pangs it was suffering.

At last it died. Hammond and I found it cold and stiff one morning in the bed. The heart had ceased to beat, the lungs to inspire. We hastened to bury it in the garden. It was a strange funeral, the dropping of that viewless corpse into the damp hole. The cast of its form I gave to Doctor X——, who keeps it in his museum in Tenth Street.

As I am on the eve of a long journey from which I may not return, I have drawn up this narrative of an event the most singular that has ever come to my knowledge.

HARRY ESCOTT.*

[NOTE.—It is rumored that the proprietors of a well known museum in this city have made arrangements with Dr. X——to exhibit to the public the singular cast which Mr. Escott deposited with him. So extraordinary a history can not fail to attract universal attention.]

'WAIF WANDERER' [MARY HELENA FORTUNE]

THE WHITE MANIAC; A DOCTOR'S TALE

IN the year 1858 I had established a flourishing practice in London; a practice which I owed a considerable portion of, not to my ability, I am afraid, but to the fact that I occupied the singular position of a man professional, who was entirely independent of his profession. Doubtless, had I been a poor man, struggling to earn a bare existence for wife and family, I might have been the cleverest physician that ever administered a bolus, yet have remained in my poverty to the end of time. But it was not so, you see. I was the second son of a nobleman, and had Honourable attached to my name; and I practised the profession solely and entirely because I had become enamoured of it, and because I was disgusted at the useless existence of a fashionable and idle young man, and determined that I, at least, would not add another to their ranks.

And so I had a handsome establishment in a fashionable portion of the city, and my door was besieged with carriages, from one end of the week to the other. Many of the occupants were disappointed, however, for I would not demean myself by taking fees from some vapourish Miss or dissipated Dowager. Gout in vain came rolling to my door, even though it excruciated the leg of a Duke; I undertook none but cases that enlisted my sympathy, and after a time the fact became known, and my levees* were not so well attended.

One day I was returning on horseback toward the city. I had been paying a visit to a patient in whom I was deeply interested, and for whom I had ordered the quiet and purer air of a suburban residence. I had reached a spot, in the neighbourhood of Kensington,* where the villas were enclosed in large gardens, and the road was marked for a considerable distance by the brick and stone walls that enclosed several of the gardens belonging to those mansions. On the opposite side of the road stood a small country-looking inn, which I had patronized before, and I pulled up my horse and alighted, for the purpose of having some rest and refreshment after my ride.

As I sat in a front room sipping my wine and water, my thoughts were fully occupied with a variety of personal concerns. I had received a letter from my mother that morning, and the condition of the patient I had recently left was precarious in the extreme.

It was fortunate that I was thought-occupied and not dependent upon outward objects to amuse them, for although the window at which I sat was open, it presented no view whatever, save the bare, blank, high brick wall belonging to a house at the opposite side of the road. That is to say, I presume, it enclosed some residence, for from where I sat not even the top of a chimney was visible.

Presently, however, the sound of wheels attracted my eyes from the pattern of the wall-paper at which I had been unconsciously gazing, and I looked out to see a handsome, but very plain carriage drawn up at a small door that pierced the brick wall I have alluded to; and almost at the same moment the door opened and closed again behind two figures in a most singular attire. They were both of the male sex, and one of them was evidently a gentleman, while the other waited on him as if he was the servant; but it was the dress of these persons that most strangely interested me. They were attired in white from head to heel; coats, vests, trousers, hats, shoes, not to speak of shirts at all, all were white as white could be.

While I stared at this strange spectacle, the gentleman stepped into the vehicle; but although he did so the coachman made no movement toward driving onward, nor did the attendant leave his post at the carriage door. At the expiration, however, of about a quarter of an hour, the servant closed the door and re-entered through the little gate, closing it, likewise, carefully behind him. Then the driver leisurely made a start, only, however, to stop suddenly again, when the door of the vehicle was burst open and a gentleman jumped out and rapped loudly at the gate.

He turned his face hurriedly around as he did so, hiding, it seemed to me, meanwhile, behind the wall so as not to be seen when it opened. Judge of my astonishment when I recognized in this gentleman the one who had but a few minutes before entered the carriage dressed in white, for he was now in garments of the hue of Erebus.* While I wondered at this strange metamorphosis the door in the wall opened, and the gentleman, now attired in black, after giving some hasty instructions to the servant, sprang once more into the carriage and was driven rapidly toward London.

My curiosity was strangely excited; and as I stood at the door before mounting my horse, I asked the landlord who and what were the people who occupied the opposite dwelling.

'Well sir,' he replied, looking curiously at the dead wall over against him, 'They've been there now a matter of six months, I dare say, and you've seen as much of them as I have. I believe the whole crew of them, servants and all, is foreigners, and we, that is the neighbours around, sir, calls them the "white mad people."'

'What! do they always wear that singular dress?'

'Always, sir, saving as soon as ever the old gentleman goes outside the gate he puts black on in the carriage, and as soon as he comes back takes it off again, and leaves it in the carriage.'

'And why in the name of gracious does he not dress himself inside?'

'Oh, that I can't tell you, sir! only it's just as you see, always. The driver or coachman never even goes inside the walls, or the horses or any one thing that isn't white in colour, sir; and if the people aren't mad after that, what else can it be?'

'It seems very like it, indeed; but do you mean to say that everything inside the garden wall is white? Surely you must be exaggerating a little?'

'Not a bit on it, sir! The coachman, who can't speak much English, sir, comes here for a drink now and then. He don't live in the house, you see, and is idle most of his time. Well, he told me himself, one day, that every article in the house was white, from the garret to the drawing-room, and that everything *outside* it is white I can swear, for I saw it myself, and a stranger sight surely no eye ever saw.'

'How did you manage to get into the enchanted castle, then?'

'I didn't get in sir, I only saw it outside, and from a place where you can see for yourself too, if you have a mind. When first the people came to the place over there, you see, sir, old Mat the sexton and bell-ringer of the church there, began to talk of the strange goings on he had seen from the belfry; and so my curiosity took me there one day to look for myself. Blest if I ever heard of such a strange sight! no wonder they call them the white mad folk.'

'Well, you've roused my curiosity,' I said, as I got on my horse, 'and I'll certainly pay old Mat's belfry a visit the very next time I pass this way, if I'm not hurried.'

It appeared unaccountable to even myself that these mysterious people should make such a singular impression on me; I thought of little else during the next two days. I attended to my duties in an absent manner, and my mind was ever recurring to the one subject—viz.* an attempt to account for the strange employment of one hue only in the household of this foreign gentleman. Of whom did the household consist? Had he any family? and could one account for the eccentricity in any other way save by ascribing it to lunacy, as mine host of the inn had already done. As it happened, the study of brain diseases had been my hobby during my noviciate, and I was peculiarly interested in observing a new symptom of madness, if this was really one.

At length I escaped to pay my country patient his usual visit, and on my return alighted at the inn, and desired the landlord to have my horse put in the stable for a bit.

'I'm going to have a peep at your madhouse,' I said, 'do you think I shall find old Mat about?'

'Yes, doctor; I saw him at work in the churchyard not half an hour ago, but at any rate he won't be farther off than his cottage, and it lies just against the yard wall.'

The church was an old, ivy-wreathed structure, with a square Norman belfry,* and a large surrounding of grey and grass-grown old headstones. It was essentially a country church, and a country churchyard; and one wondered to find it so close to the borders of a mighty city, until they remembered that the mighty city had crept into the country, year by year, until it had covered with stone and mortar the lowly site of many a cottage home, and swallowed up many an acre of green meadow and golden corn. Old Mat was sitting in the middle of the graves; one tombstone forming his seat, and he was engaged in scraping the moss from a headstone that seemed inclined to tumble over, the inscription on which was all but obliterated by a growth of green slimy-looking moss.

'Good-day, friend, you are busy,' I said. 'One would fancy that stone so old now, that the living had entirely forgotten their loss. But I suppose they have not, or you would not be cleaning it.'

'It's only a notion of my own, sir; I'm idle, and when I was a lad I had a sort o' likin' for this stone, Lord only knows why. But you see I've clean forgotten what name was on it, and I thought I'd like to see.'

'Well, I want to have a look at these "white mad folk" of yours, Mat, will you let me into the belfry? Mr. Tanning tells me you can see something queer up there.'

'By jove you can, sir!' he replied, rising with alacrity, 'I often spend an hour watching the mad folk; faith if they had my old church and yard they'd whitewash 'em, belfry and all!' and the old man led the way into the tower.

Of course my first look on reaching the summit was in the direction of the strange house, and I must confess to an ejaculation of astonishment as I peeped through one of the crevices. The belfry was elevated considerably above the premises in which I was interested, and not at a very great distance, so that grounds and house lay spread beneath me like a map.

I scarcely know how to commence describing it to you, it was something I had never seen or imagined. The mansion itself was a square and handsome building of two stories, built in the Corinthian style, with pillared portico, and pointed windows.* But the style attracted my attention but little, it was the universal white, white everywhere, that drew from me the ejaculation to which I have alluded.

From the extreme top of the chimneys to the basement, roof, windows, everything was pure white; not a shade lurked even inside a window; the windows themselves were painted white, and the curtains were of white muslin that fell over every one of them. Every yard of the broad space that one might reasonably have expected to see decorated with flowers and grass and shrubberies, was covered with a glaring and sparkling white gravel, the effect of which, even in the hot brilliant sun of a London afternoon, was to dazzle, and blind, and aggravate. And as if this was not enough, the inside of the very brick walls was whitewashed like snow, and at intervals, here and there, were placed a host of white marble statues and urns that only increased the, to me, horrible aspect of the place.

'I don't wonder they are mad!' I exclaimed, 'I should soon become mad in such a place myself.'

'Like enough, sir,' replied old Mat, stolidly, 'but you see it *didn't* make they mad, for they did it theirselves, so they must 'a been mad afore.'

An incontrovertible fact, according to the old man's way of putting it; and as I had no answer for it, I went down the old stone stairs, and having given my guide his donation, left the churchyard as bewildered as I had entered it. Nay, more so, for then I had not seen the extraordinary house that had made so painful an impression upon me.

I was in no humour for a gossip with mine host, but just as I was about to mount my horse, which had been brought round, the same carriage drove round to the mysterious gate, and the same scene was enacted to which I had before been a witness. I drew back until the old gentleman had stepped inside and performed his toilet, and when the carriage drove rapidly toward the city, I rode thoughtfully onward toward home.

I was young, you see, and although steady, and, unlike most young gentlemen of my age and position in society, had a strong vein of romance in my character. That hard study and a sense of its inutility* had kept it under, had not rendered it one whit less ready to be at a moment's call; and, in addition to all this, I had never yet, in the seclusion of my student life, met with an opportunity of falling in love, so that you will see I was in the very best mood for making the most of the adventure which was about to befal me, and which had so tragic a termination.

My thoughts were full of the 'White mad folk,' as I reached my own door; and there, to my utter astonishment, I saw drawn up the very carriage of the white house, which had preceded me. Hastily giving my horse to the groom I passed through the hall and was informed by a servant that a gentleman waited in my private consulting-room.

Very rarely indeed had my well-strung nerves been so troublesome as upon that occasion; I was so anxious to see this gentleman, and yet so fearful of exposing the interest I had already conceived in his affairs, that my hand absolutely trembled as I turned the handle of the door of the room in which he was seated. The first glance, however, at the aristocratic old gentleman who rose on my entrance, restored all my self-possession, and I was myself once more. In the calm, sweet face of the perfectly dressed gentleman before me there was no trace of the lunacy that had created that strange abode near Kensington; the principal expression in his face was that of ingrained melancholy, and his deep mourning attire might have suggested to a stranger the reason of that melancholy. He addressed me in perfect English, the entire absence of idiom alone declaring him to be a foreigner.

'I have the pleasure of addressing Doctor Elveston?'* he said.

I bowed, and placed a chair in which he re-seated himself, while I myself took possession of another.

'And Doctor Elveston is a clever physician and a man of honour?'

'I hope to be worthy of the former title, sir, while my position ought at least to guarantee the latter.'

'Your public character does, sir,' said the old gentleman, emphatically, 'and it is because I believe that you will preserve the secret of an unfortunate family that I have chosen you to assist me with your advice.'

My heart was beating rapidly by this time. There *was* a secret then, and I was about to become the possessor of it. Had it anything to do with the mania for white?

'Anything in my power,' I hastened to reply, 'you may depend on; my advice, I fear, may be of little worth, but such as it is—'

'I beg your pardon, Doctor,' interrupted he, 'it is your medical advice that I allude to, and I require it for a young lady—a relative.'

'My dear sir, that is, of course, an every day affair, my professional advice and services belong to the public, and as the public's they are of course yours.'

'Oh, my dear young friend, but mine is not an every day affair, and because it is not is the reason that I have applied to you in particular. It is a grievous case, sir, and one which fills many hearts with a bitterness they are obliged to smother from a world whose sneers are poison.'

The old gentleman spoke in tones of deep feeling, and I could not help feeling sorry for him at the bottom of my very heart.

'If you will confide in me, my dear sir,' I said, 'believe that I will prove a friend as faithful and discreet as you could wish.'

He pressed my hand, turned away for a moment to collect his agitated feelings and then he spoke again.

'I shall not attempt to hide my name from you, sir, though I have hitherto carefully concealed it. I am the Duke de Rohan,* and circumstances, which it is impossible for me to relate to you, have driven me to England to keep watch and ward over my sister's daughter, the Princess d'Alberville.* It is for this young lady I wish your attendance, her health is rapidly failing within the last week.'

'Nothing can be more simple,' I observed, eagerly, 'I can go with you at once—this very moment.'

'Dear Doctor, it is unfortunately far from being as simple a matter as you think,' he replied, solemnly, 'for my wretched niece is mad.'

'Mad!'

'Alas! yes, frightfully—horribly mad!' and he shuddered as if a cold wind had penetrated his bones.

'Has this unhappy state of mind been of long duration?' I questioned.

'God knows; the first intimation her friends had of it was about two years ago, when it culminated in such a fearful event that horrified them. I cannot explain it to you, however, for the honour of a noble house is deeply concerned; and even the very existence of the unfortunate being I beg of you to keep a secret for ever.'

'You must at any rate tell me what you wish me to do,' I observed, 'and give me as much information as you can to guide me, or I shall be powerless.'

'The sight of one colour has such an effect on the miserable girl that we have found out, by bitter experience, the only way to avoid a repetition of the most fearful tragedies, is to keep every hue or shade away from her vision; for, although it is only one colour that affects her, any of the others seems to suggest that *one* to her mind and produce uncontrollable agitation. In consequence of this she is virtually imprisoned within the grounds of the house I have provided for her, and every object that meets her eye is white, even the ground, and the very roof of the mansion.'

'How very strange!'

'It will be necessary for you, my dear sir,' the Duke continued, 'to attire yourself in a suit of white. I have brought one in the carriage for your use, and if you will now accompany me I shall be grateful.'

Of course I was only too glad to avail myself of the unexpected opportunity of getting into the singular household, and becoming acquainted with the lunatic princess; and in a few moments we were being whirled on our way toward Kensington.

On stopping at the gate of the Duke's residence, I myself became an actor in the scene which had so puzzled me on two previous occasions. My companion produced two suits of white, and proceeded to turn the vehicle into a dressing-room, though not without many apologies for the necessity. I followed his example, and in a few moments we stood inside the gate, and I had an opportunity of more closely surveying the disagreeable enclosure I had seen from the church belfry. And a most disagreeable survey it was; the sun shining brilliantly, rendered the unavoidable contact with the white glare, absolutely painful to the eye; nor was it any escape to stand in the lofty vestibule,* save that there the absence of sunshine made the uniformity more bearable.

My companion led the way up a broad staircase covered with white cloth, and balustraded with carved rails, the effect of which was totally destroyed by their covering of white paint. The very stair-rods were of white enamel, and the corners and landing places served as room for more marble statues, that held enamelled white lamps in their hands, lamps that were shaded by globes of ground glass. At the door of an apartment pertaining, as he informed me, to the Princess d'Alberville, the Duke stopped, and shook my hand, 'I leave you to make your own way,' he said, pointing to the door. 'She has never showed any symptoms of violence while under the calm influence of white; but, nevertheless, we shall be at hand, the least sound will bring you assistance,' and he turned away.

I opened the door without a word, and entered the room, full of curiosity as to what I should see and hear of this mysterious princess. It was a room of vast and magnificent proportions, and, without having beheld such a scene, one can hardly conceive the strange cold look the utter absence of colour gave it. A Turkey carpet that looked like a woven fall of snow; white satin damask* on chair, couch, and ottoman; draped satin and snowy lace around the windows, with rod, rings, and bracelets of white enamel. Tables with pedestals of enamel and tops of snowy marble, and paper on the walls of purest white; altogether it was a weird-looking room, and I shook with cold as I entered it.

The principal object of my curiosity was seated in a deep chair with her side toward me, and I had an opportunity of examining her leisurely, as she neither moved or took the slightest notice of my entrance; most probably she was quite unaware of it. She was the most lovely being I had ever beheld, a fair and perfect piece of statuary one might have thought, so immobile and abstracted, nay, so entirely expressionless were her beautiful features. Her dress was pure white, her hair of a pale golden hue, and her eyes dark as midnight. Her hands rested idly on her lap, her gaze seemed intent on the high white wall that shot up outside the window near her; and in the whole room there was neither book, flower, work, or one single *loose* article of ornament, nothing but the heavy, white-covered furniture, and the draping curtains. I advanced directly before her and bowed deeply, and then I calmly drew forward a chair and seated myself. As I did so she moved her eyes from the window and rested them on me, but, for all the interest they evinced, I might as well have been the white-washed wall outside. She was once more returning her eyes to the blank window, when I took her hand and laid my fingers on her blue-veined wrist. The action seemed to arouse her, for she looked keenly into my face, and then she laughed softly.

'One may guess you are a physician,' she said, in a musical, low voice, and with a slightly foreign accent, that was in my opinion, a great improvement to our harsh language.

'I am,' I replied, with a smile, 'your uncle has sent me to see about your health, which alarms him.'

'Poor man!' she said, with a shade of commiseration clouding her beautiful face, 'poor uncle! But I assure you there is nothing the matter with me; nothing but what must be the natural consequence of the life I am leading.'

'Why do you lead one which you know to be injurious then?' I asked, still keeping my fingers on the pulse, that beat as calmly as a sleeping infant's, and was not increased by a single throb though a stranger sat beside her.

'How can I help it?' she asked, calmly meeting my inquisitorial gaze, 'do you think a sane person would choose to be imprisoned thus, and to be surrounded by the colour of death ever? Had mine not been a strong mind I should have been mad long ago.'

'Mad!' I could not help ejaculating, in a puzzled tone.

'Yes, mad,' she replied, 'could *you* live here, month after month, in a hueless atmosphere and with nothing but *that* to look at,' and she pointed her slender finger toward the white wall, 'could you, I ask, and retain your reason?'

'I do not believe I could!' I answered, with sudden vehemence, 'then, again I repeat why do it?'

'And again I reply, how can I help it?'

I was silent. I was looking in the eyes of the beautiful being before me for a single trace of the madness I had been told of, but I could not find it. It was a lovely girl, pale and delicate from confinement, and with a manner that told of a weariness endured at least patiently. She was about twenty years old, perhaps, and the most perfect creature, I have already said, that I had ever beheld; and so we sat looking into each other's eyes; what mine expressed I cannot say, but her's were purity, and sweetness itself.

'Who are you?' she asked, suddenly, 'tell me something of yourself. It will be at least a change from this white solitude.'

'I am a doctor, as you have guessed; and a rich and fashionable doctor,' I added smilingly.

'To be either is to be also the other,' she remarked, 'you need not have used the repetition.'

'Come,' I thought to myself, 'there is little appearance of lunacy in that observation.'

'But you doubtless have a name, what is it?'

'My name is Elveston—Doctor Elveston.'

'Your christian name?'

'No, my christian name is Charles.'

'Charles,' she repeated dreamily.

'I think it is your turn now,' I remarked, 'it is but fair that you should make me acquainted with your name, since I have told you mine.'

'Oh! my name is d'Alberville—Blanche d'Alberville. Perhaps it was in consequence of my christian name that my poor uncle decided upon burying me in white,' she added, with a look round the cold room, 'poor old man!'

'Why do you pity him so?' I asked, 'he seems to me little to require it. He is strong and rich, and the uncle of Blanche,' I added, with a bow; but the compliment seemed to glide off her as if it had been a liquid, and she were made of glassy marble like one of the statues that stood behind her.

'And you are a physician,' she said, looking wonderingly at me, 'and have been in the Duke's company, without discovering it?'

'Discovering what, my dear young lady?'

'That he is mad.'

'Mad!' How often had I already ejaculated that word since I had become interested in this singular household; but this time it must assuredly have expressed the utmost astonishment, for I was never more confounded in my life; and yet a light seemed to be breaking in upon my bewilderment, as I stared in wondering silence at the calm face of the lovely maiden before me.

'Alas, yes!' she replied, sadly, to my look, 'my poor uncle is a maniac, but a harmless one to all but me; it is I who suffer all.'

'And why you?' I gasped.

'Because it is his mania to believe *me* mad,' she replied, 'and so he treats me.'

'But in the name of justice why should you endure this?' I cried, angrily starting to my feet, 'you are in a free land at least, and doors will open!'

'Calm yourself, my friend,' she said, laying her white hand on my arm, and the contact, I confess, thrilled through every nerve of my system, 'compose yourself, and see things as they are; what could a young, frail girl like me do out in the world alone? and I have not a living relative but my uncle. Besides, would it be charitable to desert him and leave him to his own madness thus! Poor old man!'

'You are an angel!' I ejaculated, 'and I would die for you!'

The reader need not be told that my enthusiastic youth was at last beginning to make its way through the crust of worldly wisdom that had hitherto subdued it.

'It is not necessary that anyone should die for me; I can do that for myself, and no doubt shall ere long, die of the want of colour and air,' she said, with a sad smile.

There is little use following our conversation to the end. I satisfied myself that there was really nothing wrong with her constitution, save the effects of the life she was obliged to lead; and I determined, instead of interfering with her at present, to devote myself to the poor Duke, with a hope that I might be of service to him, and succeed in gaining the liberation of poor Blanche. We parted, I might almost say as lovers, although no words of affection were spoken; but I carried away her image entwined with every fibre of my heart, and in the deep sweetness of her lingering eyes I fancied I read hope and love.

The Duke was waiting impatiently in the corridor as I left the lovely girl, and he led me into another apartment to question me eagerly. What did I think of the princess's state of health? Had she shown any symptoms of uneasiness during my visit? As the old gentleman asked these questions he watched my countenance keenly; while on my part I observed him with deep interest to discover traces of his unfortunate mental derangement.

'My dear sir, I perceive nothing alarming whatever in the state of your niece; she is simply suffering from confinement and monotony of existence, and wants nothing whatever but fresh air and amusement, and exercise; in short, life.'

'Alas! you know that is impossible; have I not told you that her state precludes everything of the sort?'

'You must excuse me, my friend,' I said, firmly, 'I have conversed for a considerable time with the Princess d'Alberville, and I am a medical man accustomed to dealing with, and the observation of, lunacy, and I give you my word of honour there is no weakness whatever in the brain of this fair girl; you are simply killing her, it is my duty to tell you so, killing her under the influence of some, to me, most unaccountable whim.'

The duke wrung his hands in silence, but his excited eye fell under my steady gaze. It was apparently with a strong effort that he composed himself sufficiently to speak, and when he did his words had a solemnity in their tone that ought to have made a deep impression upon me; but it did not, for the sweetness of the imprisoned Blanche's voice was still lingering in my ears.

'You are a young man, Doctor Elveston; it is one of the happy provisions of youth, no doubt, to be convinced of its own infallibility. But you must believe that one of my race does not lie, and I swear to you that my niece is the victim of a most fearful insanity, which but to name makes humanity shudder with horror.'

'I do not doubt that you believe such to be the case, my dear sir,' I said, soothingly, for I fancied I saw the fearful light of insanity in his glaring eye at that moment, 'but to my vision everything seems different.'

'Well, my young friend, do not decide yet too hastily. Visit us again, but God in mercy grant that you may never see the reality as I have seen it!'

And so I did repeat my visits, and repeat them so often and that without changing my opinion, that the Duke, in spite of his mania, began to see that they were no longer necessary. One day on my leaving Blanche he requested a few moments of my time, and drawing me into his study, locked the door. I began to be a little alarmed, and more particularly as he seemed to be in a state of great agitation; but, as it appeared, my alarm of personal violence was entirely without foundation.

He placed a chair for me, and I seated myself with all the calmness I could muster, while I kept my eyes firmly fixed upon his as he addressed me.

'My dear young friend; I hope it is unnecessary for me to say that these are no idle words, for I have truly conceived an ardent appreciation of your character; yet it is absolutely necessary that I should put a stop to your visits to my niece. Good Heavens, what could I say—how could I ever forgive myself if any—any—'

'I beg of you to go no farther, Duke,' I said, interrupting him. 'You have only by a short time anticipated what I was about to communicate myself. If your words allude to an attachment between Blanche and myself, your care is now too late. We love each other, and intend, subject to your approval, to be united immediately.'

Had a sudden clap of thunder reverberated in the quiet room the poor man could not have been more affected. He started to his feet, and *glared* into my eyes with terror.

'Married!' he gasped, 'Married! Blanche d'Alberville wedded! Oh God!' and then he fell back into his chair as powerless as a child.

'And why should this alarm you?' I asked. 'She is youthful and lovely, and as sane, I believe in my soul, as I am myself. I am rich, and of a family which may aspire to mate* with the best. You are her only relative and guardian, and you say that you esteem me; whence then this great distaste to hear even a mention of your fair ward's marriage?'

'She is not my ward!' he cried, hoarsely, and it seemed to me angrily, 'her father and mother are both in existence, and destroyed for all time by the horror she had brought around them! But, my God, what is the use of speaking—I talk to a madman!' and he turned to his desk and began to write rapidly.

There I sat in bewilderment. I had not now the slightest doubt but that my poor friend was the victim of monomania; his one idea was uppermost, and that idea was that his unfortunate niece was mad. I was fully determined now to carry her away and make her my wife at once, so as to relieve the poor girl from an imprisonment, to which there seemed no other prospect of an end. And my hopes went still farther; who could tell but that the sight of Blanche living and enjoying life as did others of her sex, might have a beneficial effect upon the poor duke's brain, and help to eradicate his fixed idea.

As I was thus cogitating, the old gentleman rose from his desk, and handed me a letter addressed, but unsealed. His manner was now almost unearthly calm, as if he had come to some great determination, to which he had only been driven by the most dreadful necessity.

'My words are wasted, Charles,' he said, 'and I cannot tell the truth; but if you ever prized home and name, friends or family, mother or wife, send that letter to its address after you have perused it, and await its reply.'

I took the letter and put it into my pocket, and then I took his hand and pressed it warmly. I was truly sorry for the poor old gentleman, who suffered, no doubt, as much from his fancied trouble as if it were the most terrible of realities.

'I hope you will forgive me for grieving you, my dear sir; believe me it pains me much to see you thus. I will do as you wish about the letter. But oh, how I wish you could see Blanche with my eyes! To me she is the most perfect of women!'

'You have *never* seen her yet!'—he responded, bitterly, 'could you—*dare* you only once witness but a part of her actions under one influence, you would shudder to your very marrow!'

'To what influence do you allude, dear sir!'

'To that of colour—one colour.'

'And that colour? have you any objection to name it?'

'It is red!' and as the duke answered he turned away abruptly, and left me standing bewildered, but still unbelieving.

I hastened home that day, anxious to peruse the letter given me by the duke, and as soon as I had reached my own study drew it from my pocket and spread it before me. It was addressed to the Prince d'Alberville, Chateau Gris, Melun,* France; and the following were its singular contents:—

'DEAR BROTHER.—A terrible necessity for letting another into our fearful secret has arisen. A young gentleman of birth and fortune has, in spite of my assurances that she is insane, determined to wed Blanche. Such a sacrifice cannot be permitted, even were such a thing not morally impossible. You are her parent, it is then your place to inform this unhappy young man of the unspoken curse that rests on our wretched name. I enclose his address. Write to him at once.

'Your afflicted brother,

'DE ROHAN.'

I folded up this strange epistle and despatched it; and then I devoted nearly an hour to pondering over the strange contradictions of human nature, and more particularly diseased human nature. Of course I carried the key to this poor man's strangeness in my firm conviction of his insanity, and my entire belief in the martyrdom of Blanche; yet I could not divest myself of an anxiety to receive a reply to this letter, a reply which I was certain would explain the duke's lunacy, and beg of me to pardon it. That is to say if such a party as the Prince d'Alberville existed at all, and I did not quite lose sight of the fact that Blanche had assured me that, with the exception of her uncle, she had not a living relative.

It seemed a long week to me ere the French reply, that made my hand tremble as I received it, was put into it. I had abstained from visiting my beloved Blanche, under a determination that I would not do so until armed with such a letter as I anticipated receiving; or until I should be able to say, 'ample time for a reply to your communication has elapsed; none has come, give me then my betrothed.' Here then at last was the letter, and I shut myself into my own room and opened it; the words are engraven on my memory and will never become less vivid.

'SIR,—You wish to wed my daughter, the Princess Blanche d'Alberville. Words would vainly try to express the pain with which I expose our disgrace—our horrible secret—to a stranger, but it is to save you* from a fate worse than death. Blanche d'Alberville is an *anthropophagus*,* already has one of her own family fallen a victim to her thirst for human blood. Spare us if you can, and pray for us.

'D'ALBERVILLE.'

I sat like one turned to stone, and stared at the fearful paper! An anthropophagus! a cannibal! Good heavens, the subject was just now engaging the attention of the medical world in a remarkable degree, in consequence of two frightful and well authenticated cases that had lately occurred in France!* All the particulars of these cases, in which I had taken a deep interest, flashed before me, but not for one moment did I credit the frightful story of my beloved. Some detestable plot had been formed against her, for what vile purpose, or what end in view I was ignorant; and I cast the whole subject from my mind with an effort, and went to attend to my daily round of duties. During the two or three hours that followed, and under the influence of the human suffering I had witnessed, a revolution took place in my feelings, God only knows by what means induced; but when I returned home, to prepare for my eventful visit to the 'white house,' a dreadful doubt had stolen into my heart, and filled it with a fearful determination.

Having ordered my carriage and prepared the white suit, which I was now possessor of, I went directly to the conservatory, and looked around among the brilliant array of blossoms for the most suitable to my purpose. I chose the flaring scarlet verbena* to form my bouquet; a tasteless one it is true, but one decidedly distinctive in colour. I collected quite a large nosegay of this flower, without a single spray of green to relieve its bright hue. Then I went to my carriage, and gave directions to be driven to Kensington.

At the gate of the Duke's residence I dressed myself in the white suit mechanically, and followed the usual servant into the house, carefully holding my flowers, which I had enveloped in a newspaper. I was received as usual, also by the Duke, and in a few seconds we stood, face to face in his study. In answer to his look of fearful inquiry I handed him my French epistle, and stood silently by as he read it tremblingly.

'Well, are you satisfied now?' he asked, looking at me pitifully in the face, 'has this dreadful exposure convinced you?'

'No!' I answered, recklessly, 'I am neither satisfied nor convinced of anything save that you are either a lunatic yourself, or in collusion with the writer of that abominable letter!' and as I spoke I uncovered my scarlet bouquet and shook out its blossoms. The sight of it made a terrible impression upon my companion; his knees trembled as if he were about to fall, and his face grew whiter than his garments.

'In the name of heaven what are you going to do?' he gasped.

'I am simply going to present my bride with a bouquet,' I said, and as I said so I laughed an empty, hollow laugh. I cannot describe my strange state of mind at that moment; I felt as if myself under the influence of some fearful mania.

'By all you hold sacred, Charles Elveston, I charge you to desist! who or what are *you* that you should set your youth, and ignorance of this woman against my age and bitter experience?'

'Ha, ha!' was my only response, as I made toward the door.

'By heavens, he is mad!' cried the excited nobleman, 'young man, I tell you that you carry in your hand a colour which had better be shaken in the eyes of a mad bull than be placed in sight of my miserable niece! Fool! I tell you it will arouse in her an unquenchable thirst for blood, and the blood may be yours!'

'Let it!' I cried, and passed on my way to Blanche.

I was conscious of the Duke's cries to the servants as I hurried up the broad staircase, and guessed that they were about to follow me; but to describe my feelings is utterly impossible.

I was beginning now to believe that my betrothed was something terrible, and I faced her desperately, as one who had lost everything worth living for, or placed his last stake upon the cast of a die.

I opened the well-known door of the white room, that seemed to me colder, and more death-like than ever; and I saw the figure of Blanche seated in her old way, and in her old seat, looking out of the window. I did not wait to scan her appearance just then, however, for I caught a glimpse of myself in a large mirror opposite, and was fascinated, as it were by the strange sight.

The mirror reflected, in unbroken stillness, the cold whiteness of the large apartment, but it also reflected my face and form, wearing an expression that half awoke me to a consciousness of physical indisposition. There was a wild look in my pallid countenance, and a reckless air in my figure which the very garments seemed to have imbibed, and which was strangely unlike my usual calm propriety of demeanour. My coat seemed awry; the collar of my shirt was unbuttoned, and I had even neglected to put on my neck-tie; but it was upon the blood-red bouquet that my momentary gaze became riveted.

It was such a contrast; the cold, pure white of all the surroundings, and that circled patch of blood-colour that I held in my hand was so suggestive! 'Of what?' I asked myself 'am I really mad?' and then I laughed loudly and turned toward Blanche.

Possibly the noise of the opening door had attracted her, for when I turned she was standing on her feet, directly confronting me. Her eyes were distended with astonishment at my peculiar examination of myself in the mirror, no doubt, but they flashed into madness at the sight of the flowers as I turned. Her face grew scarlet, her hands clenched, and her regards *devoured* the scarlet bouquet, as I madly held it towards her. At this moment my eye caught a side glimpse of half-a-dozen terrified faces peeping in the doorway, and conspicuous and foremost that of the poor terrified Duke; but my fate must be accomplished, and I still held the bouquet tauntingly toward the transfixed girl. She gave one wild look into my face, and recognized the sarcasm which I *felt* in my eyes, and then she snatched the flowers from my hand, and scattered them in a thousand pieces at her feet.

How well I remember that picture to-day. The white room—the torn and brilliant flowers—and the mad fury of that lovely being. A laugh echoed again upon my lips, an involuntary laugh it was, for I knew not that I had laughed; and then there was a rush, and white teeth were at my throat, tearing flesh, and sinews, and veins; and a horrible sound was in my ears, as if some wild animal was tearing at my body! I dreamt that I was in a jungle of Africa, and that a tiger, with a tawney coat, was devouring my still living flesh, and then I became insensible!

When I opened my eyes faintly, I lay in my own bed, and the form of the Duke was bending over me. One of my medical *confreres** held my wrist between his fingers, and the room was still and dark.

'How is this, Bernard?' I asked, with difficulty, for my voice seemed lost, and the weakness of death hanging around my tongue, 'what has happened?'

'Hush! my dear fellow, you must not speak. You have been nearly worried* to death by a maniac, and you have lost a fearful quantity of blood.'

'Oh!' I recollected it all, and turned to the Duke, 'and Blanche?'

'She is dead, thank God!' he whispered, calmly.

I shuddered through every nerve and was silent.

It was many long weeks ere I was able to listen to the Duke as he told the fearful tale of the dead girl's disease. The first intimation her wretched relatives had of the horrible thing was upon the morning of her eighteenth year. They went to her room to congratulate her, and found her lying upon the dead body of her younger sister, who occupied the same chamber; she had literally torn her throat with her teeth, and was sucking the hot blood as she was discovered. No words could describe the horror of the wretched parents. The end we have seen.

I never asked how Blanche had died, I did not wish to know; but I guessed that force had been obliged to be used in dragging her teeth from my throat, and that the necessary force was sufficient to destroy her. I have never since met with a case of anthropophagy, but I never even read of the rare discovery of the fearful disease, but I fancy I feel Blanche's teeth at my throat.

CHARLES BAUDELAIRE

A CARCASS

RECALL to mind the sight we saw, my soul,
   That soft, sweet summer day:
Upon a bed of flints a carrion foul,
   Just as we turn'd the way,

Its legs erected, wanton-like, in air,
   Burning and sweating pest,
In unconcern'd and cynic sort* laid bare
   To view its noisome breast.

The sun lit up the rottenness with gold,
   To bake it well inclined,
And give great Nature back a hundredfold
   All she together join'd.

The sky regarded as the carcass proud
   Oped flower-like to the day;
So strong the odour, on the grass you vow'd
   You thought to faint away.

The flies the putrid belly buzz'd about,
   Whence black battalions throng
Of maggots, like thick liquid flowing out
   The living rags along.

And as a wave they mounted and went down,
   Or darted sparkling wide;
As if the body, by a wild breath blown,
   Lived as it multiplied.

From all this life a music strange there ran,
   Like wind and running burns;*
Or like the wheat a winnower in his fan
   With rhythmic movement turns.

The forms wore off, and as a dream grew faint,
   An outline dimly shown,
And which the artist finishes to paint
   From memory alone.

Behind the rocks watch'd us with angry eye
  A bitch disturb'd in theft,
Waiting to take, till we had pass'd her by,
  The morsel she had left.

Yet you will be like that corruption too,
  Like that infection prove—
Star of my eyes, sun of my nature, you,
  My angel and my love!

Queen of the graces, you will even be so,
  When, the last ritual said,
Beneath the grass and the fat flowers you go,
  To mould among the dead.

Then, O my beauty, tell the insatiate worm,
  Who wastes you with his kiss,
I have kept the godlike essence and the form
  Of perishable bliss!

JOSEPH SHERIDAN LE FANU

CARMILLA

CHAPTER I

An Early Fright

In Styria,* we, though by no means magnificent people, inhabit a castle, or schloss. A small income, in that part of the world, goes a great way. Eight or nine hundred a year does wonders. Scantily enough ours would have answered among wealthy people at home. My father is English, and I bear an English name, although I never saw England. But here, in this lonely and primitive place, where everything is so marvellously cheap, I really don't see how ever so much more money would at all materially add to our comforts, or even luxuries.

My father was in the Austrian service,* and retired upon a pension and his patrimony, and purchased this feudal residence, and the small estate on which it stands, a bargain.

Nothing can be more picturesque or solitary. It stands on a slight eminence in a forest. The road, very old and narrow, passes in front of its drawbridge, never raised in my time, and its moat, stocked with perch, and sailed over by many swans, and floating on its surface white fleets of water-lilies.

Over all this the schloss shows its many-windowed front; its towers, and its Gothic chapel.*

The forest opens in an irregular and very picturesque glade before its gate, and at the right a steep Gothic bridge carries the road over a stream that winds in deep shadow through the wood.

I have said that this is a very lonely place. Judge whether I say truth. Looking from the hall door towards the road, the forest in which our castle stands extends fifteen miles to the right, and twelve to the left. The nearest inhabited village is about seven of your English miles to the left. The nearest inhabited schloss of any historic associations, is that of old General Spielsdorf,* nearly twenty miles away to the right.

I have said 'the nearest *inhabited* village,' because there is, only three miles westward, that is to say in the direction of General Spielsdorf's schloss, a ruined village, with its quaint little church, now roofless, in the aisle of which are the mouldering tombs of the proud family of Karnstein, now extinct, who once owned the equally desolate chateau which, in the thick of the forest, overlooks the silent ruins of the town.

Respecting the cause of the desertion of this striking and melancholy spot, there is a legend which I shall relate to you another time.

I must tell you now, how very small is the party who constitute the inhabitants of our castle. I don't include servants, or those dependents who occupy rooms in the buildings attached to the schloss. Listen, and wonder! My father, who is the kindest man on earth, but growing old; and I, at the date of my story, only nineteen. Eight years have passed since then. I and my father constituted the family at the schloss. My mother, a Styrian lady, died in my infancy, but I had a good-natured governess, who had been with me from, I might almost say, my infancy. I could not remember the time when her fat, benignant face was not a familiar picture in my memory. This was Madame Perrodon, a native of Berne,* whose care and good nature in part supplied to me the loss of my mother, whom I do not even remember, so early I lost her. She made a third at our little dinner party. There was a fourth, Mademoiselle De Lafontaine, a lady such as you term, I believe, a 'finishing governess.' She spoke French and German, Madame Perrodon French and broken English, to which my father and I added English, which, partly to prevent its becoming a lost language among us, and partly from patriotic motives, we spoke every day. The consequence was a Babel,* at which strangers used to laugh, and which I shall make no attempt to reproduce in this narrative. And there were two or three young lady friends besides, pretty nearly of my own age, who were occasional visitors, for longer or shorter terms; and these visits I sometimes returned.

These were our regular social resources; but of course there were chance visits from 'neighbors' of only five or six leagues* distance. My life was notwithstanding rather a solitary one, I can assure you.

My gouvernantes* had just so much control over me as you might conjecture such sage persons would have in the case of a rather spoiled girl, whose only parent allowed her pretty nearly her own way in everything.

The first occurrence in my existence, which produced a terrible impression upon my mind, which, in fact, never has been effaced, was one of the very earliest incidents of my life which I can recollect.

Some people will think it so trifling that it should not be recorded here. You will see, however, by-and-bye, why I mention it. The nursery, as it was called, though I had it all to myself, was a large room in the upper story of the castle, with a steep oak roof. I can't have been more than six years old, when one night I awoke, and looking round the room from my bed, failed to see the nursery-maid. Neither was my nurse there; and I thought myself alone. I was not frightened, for I was one of those happy children who are studiously kept in ignorance of ghost stories, of fairy tales, and of all such lore as makes us cover up our heads when the door creeks suddenly, or the flicker of an expiring candle makes the shadow of a bed-post dance upon the wall, nearer to our faces. I was vexed and insulted at finding myself, as I conceived, neglected, and I began to whimper, preparatory to a hearty bout of roaring; when to my surprise, I saw a solemn, but very pretty face looking at me from the side of the bed. It was that of a young lady who was kneeling, with her hands under the coverlet. I looked at her with a kind of pleased wonder, and ceased whimpering. She caressed me with her hands, and lay down beside me on the bed, and drew me towards her, smiling; I felt immediately delightfully soothed, and fell asleep again. I was wakened by a sensation as if two needles ran into my breast very deep at the same moment, and I cried loudly. The lady started back, with her eyes fixed on me, and then slipped down upon the floor, and, as I thought, hid herself under the bed.

I was now for the first time frightened, and I yelled with all my might and main.* Nurse, nursery-maid, housekeeper, all came running in, and hearing my story, they made light of it, soothing me all they could meanwhile. But, child as I was, I could perceive that their faces were pale with an unwonted look of anxiety, and I saw them look under the bed, and about the room, and peep under tables and pluck open cupboards; and the housekeeper whispered to the nurse: 'Lay your hand along that hollow in the bed; someone *did* lie there, so sure as you did not; the place is still warm.'

I remember the nursery-maid petting me, and all three examining my chest, where I told them I felt the puncture, and pronouncing that there was no sign visible that any such thing had happened to me.

The housekeeper and the two other servants who were in charge of the nursery, remained sitting up all night; and from that time a servant always sat up in the nursery until I was about fourteen.

I was very nervous for a long time after this. A doctor was called in, he was pallid and elderly. How well I remember his long saturnine face, slightly pitted with smallpox, and his chestnut wig. For a good while, every second day, he came and gave me medicine, which of course I hated.

The morning after I saw this apparition I was in a state of terror, and could not bear to be left alone, daylight though it was, for a moment.

I remember my father coming up and standing at the bedside, and talking cheerfully, and asking the nurse a number of questions, and laughing very heartily at one of the answers; and patting me on the shoulder, and kissing me, and telling me not to be frightened, that it was nothing but a dream and could not hurt me.

But I was not comforted, for I knew the visit of the strange woman was *not* a dream; and I was *awfully* frightened.

I was a little consoled by the nursery-maid's assuring me that it was she who had come and looked at me, and lain down beside me in the bed, and that I must have been half-dreaming not to have known her face. But this, though supported by the nurse, did not quite satisfy me.

I remember, in the course of that day, a venerable old man, in a black cassock, coming into the room with the nurse and housekeeper, and talking a little to them, and very kindly to me; his face was very sweet and gentle, and he told me they were going to pray, and joined my hands together, and desired me to say, softly, while they were praying, 'Lord hear all good prayers for us, for Jesus' sake.' I think these were the very words, for I often repeated them to myself, and my nurse used for years to make me say them in my prayers.

I remember so well the thoughtful sweet face of that white-haired old man, in his black cassock, as he stood in that rude, lofty, brown room, with the clumsy furniture of a fashion three hundred years old, about him, and the scanty light entering its shadowy atmosphere through the small lattice. He kneeled, and the three women with him, and he prayed aloud with an earnest quavering voice for, what appeared to me, a long time.

I forget all my life preceding that event, and for some time after it is all obscure also, but the scenes I have just described stand out vivid as the isolated pictures of the phantasmagoria* surrounded by darkness.

CHAPTER II

A Guest

I Am now going to tell you something so strange that it will require all your faith in my veracity to believe my story. It is not only true, nevertheless, but truth of which I have been an eye-witness.

It was a sweet summer evening, and my father asked me, as he sometimes did, to take a little ramble with him along that beautiful forest vista which I have mentioned as lying in front of the schloss.

'General Spielsdorf cannot come to us so soon as I had hoped,' said my father, as we pursued our walk.

He was to have paid us a visit of some weeks, and we had expected his arrival next day. He was to have brought with him a young lady, his niece and ward, Mademoiselle Rheinfeldt, whom I had never seen, but whom I had heard described as a very charming girl, and in whose society I had promised myself many happy days. I was more disappointed than a young lady living in a town, or a bustling neighbourhood can possibly imagine. This visit, and the new acquaintance it promised, had furnished my day dream for many weeks.

'And how soon does he come?' I asked.

'Not till autumn. Not for two months, I dare say,' he answered. 'And I am very glad now, dear, that you never knew Mademoiselle Rheinfeldt.'

'And why?' I asked, both mortified and curious.

'Because the poor young lady is dead,' he replied. 'I quite forgot I had not told you, but you were not in the room when I received the general's letter this evening.'

I was very much shocked. General Spielsdorf had mentioned in his first letter, six or seven weeks before, that she was not so well as he would wish her, but there was nothing to suggest the remotest suspicion of danger.

'Here is the general's letter,' he said, handing it to me. 'I am afraid he is in great affliction; the letter appears to me to have been written very nearly in distraction.'

We sat down on a rude bench, under a group of magnificent lime-trees. The sun was setting with all its melancholy splendor behind the sylvan horizon, and the stream that flows beside our home, and passes under the steep old bridge I have mentioned, wound through many a group of noble trees, almost at our feet, reflecting in its current the fading crimson of the sky. General Spielsdorf's letter was so extraordinary, so vehement, and in some places so self-contradictory, that I read it twice over—the second time aloud to my father—and was still unable to account for it, except by supposing that grief had unsettled his mind.

It said 'I have lost my darling daughter—for as such I loved her. During the last days of dear Bertha's illness I was not able to write to you. Before then I had no idea of her danger. I have lost her, and now learn *all*, too late. She died in the peace of innocence, and in the glorious hope of a blessed futurity. The fiend who betrayed our infatuated hospitality has done it all. I thought I was receiving into my house innocence, gaiety, a charming companion for my lost Bertha. Heavens! what a fool have I been! I thank God my child died without a suspicion of the cause of her sufferings. She is gone without so much as conjecturing the nature of her illness, and the accursed passion of the agent of all this misery. I devote my remaining days to tracking and extinguishing a monster. I am told I may hope to accomplish my righteous and merciful purpose. At present there is scarcely a gleam of light to guide me. I curse my conceited incredulity, my despicable affectation of superiority, my blindness, my obstinacy—all—too late. I cannot write or talk collectedly now. I am distracted. So soon as I shall have a little recovered, I mean to devote myself for a time to enquiry, which may possibly lead me as far as Vienna. Some time in the autumn, two months hence, or earlier if I live, I will see you—that is, if you permit me; I will then tell you all that I scarce dare put upon paper now. Farewell. Pray for me, dear friend.'

In these terms ended this strange letter. Though I had never seen Bertha Rheinfeldt my eyes filled with tears at the sudden intelligence; I was startled, as well as profoundly disappointed.

The sun had now set, and it was twilight by the time I had returned the general's letter to my father.

It was a soft* clear evening, and we loitered, speculating upon the possible meanings of the violent and incoherent sentences which I had just been reading. We had nearly a mile to walk before reaching the road that passes the schloss in front, and by that time the moon was shining brilliantly. At the drawbridge we met Madame Perrodon and Mademoiselle De Lafontaine, who had come out, without their bonnets, to enjoy the exquisite moonlight.

We heard their voices gabbling in animated dialogue as we approached. We joined them at the drawbridge, and turned about to admire with them the beautiful scene.

The glade through which we had just walked lay before us. At our left the narrow road wound away under clumps of lordly trees, and was lost to sight amid the thickening forest. At the right the same road crosses the steep and picturesque bridge, near which stands a ruined tower which once guarded that pass; and beyond the bridge an abrupt eminence rises, covered with trees, and showing in the shadows some grey ivy-clustered rocks.

Over the sward and low grounds a thin film of mist was stealing, like smoke, marking the distances with a transparent veil; and here and there we could see the river faintly flashing in the moonlight.

No softer, sweeter scene could be imagined. The news I had just heard made it melancholy; but nothing could disturb its character of profound serenity, and the enchanted glory and vagueness of the prospect.

My father, who enjoyed the picturesque, and I, stood looking in silence over the expanse beneath us. The two good governesses, standing a little way behind us, discoursed upon the scene, and were eloquent upon the moon.

Madame Perrodon was fat, middle-aged, and romantic, and talked and sighed poetically. Mademoiselle De Lafontaine—in right of her father who was a German, assumed to be psychological, metaphysical, and something of a mystic—now declared that when the moon shone with a light so intense it was well known that it indicated a special spiritual activity. The effect of the full moon in such a state of brilliancy was manifold. It acted on dreams, it acted on lunacy, it acted on nervous people; it had marvellous physical influences connected with life. Mademoiselle related that her cousin, who was mate of a merchant ship, having taken a nap on deck on such a night, lying on his back, with his face full in the light on the moon, had wakened, after a dream of an old woman clawing him by the cheek, with his features horribly drawn to one side; and his countenance had never quite recovered its equilibrium.

'The moon, this night,' she said, 'is full of odylic* and magnetic influence—and see, when you look behind you at the front of the schloss, how all its windows flash and twinkle with that silvery splendour, as if unseen hands had lighted up the rooms to receive fairy guests.'

There are indolent states of the spirits in which, indisposed to talk ourselves, the talk of others is pleasant to our listless ears; and I gazed on, pleased with the tinkle of the ladies' conversation.

'I have got into one of my moping moods tonight,' said my father, after a silence, and quoting Shakespeare, whom, by way of keeping up our English, he used to read aloud, he said:

> 'In truth I know not why I am so sad:
> It wearies me; you say it wearies you;
> But how I got it—came by it.'*

'I forget the rest. But I feel as if some great misfortune were hanging over us. I suppose the poor general's afflicted letter has had something to do with it.'

At this moment the unwonted sound of carriage wheels and many hoofs upon the road, arrested our attention.

They seemed to be approaching from the high ground overlooking the bridge, and very soon the equipage emerged from that point. Two horsemen first crossed the bridge, then came a carriage drawn by four horses, and two men rode behind.

It seemed to be the travelling carriage of a person of rank; and we were all immediately absorbed in watching that very unusual spectacle. It became in a few moments greatly more interesting, for just as the carriage had passed the summit of the steep bridge, one of the leaders taking fright communicated his panic to the rest, and after a plunge* or two the whole team broke into a wild gallop together, and dashing between the horsemen who rode in front, came thundering along the road towards us with the speed of a hurricane.

The excitement of the scene was made more painful by the clear, long-drawn screams of a female voice from the carriage window.

We all advanced in curiosity and horror; my father in silence, the rest with various ejaculations of terror.

Our suspense did not last long. Just before you reach the castle drawbridge, on the route they were coming, there stands by the roadside a magnificent lime-tree, on the other stands an ancient stone cross, at sight of which the horses, now going at a pace that was perfectly frightful, swerved so as to bring the wheel over the projecting roots of the tree.

I knew what was coming. I covered my eyes, unable to see it out, and turned my head away; at the same moment I heard a cry from my lady-friends, who had gone on a little.

Curiosity opened my eyes, and I saw a scene of utter confusion. Two of the horses were on the ground, the carriage lay upon its side with two wheels in the air; the men were busy removing the traces,* and a lady, with a commanding air and figure, had got out, and stood with clasped hands, raising the handkerchief that was in them every now and then to her eyes. Through the carriage door was now lifted a young lady, who appeared to be lifeless. My dear old father was already beside the elder lady, with his hat in his hand, evidently tendering his aid and the resources of his schloss. The lady did not appear to hear him, or to have eyes for anything but the slender girl who was being placed against the slope of the bank.

I approached; the young lady was apparently stunned, but she was certainly not dead. My father, who piqued himself on being something of a physician, had just had his fingers to her wrist and assured the lady, who declared herself her mother, that her pulse, though faint and irregular, was undoubtedly still distinguishable. The lady clasped her hands and looked upward, as if in a momentary transport of gratitude; but immediately she broke out again in that theatrical way which is, I believe, natural to some people.

She was what is called a fine looking woman for her time of life, and must have been handsome; she was tall, but not thin, and dressed in black velvet, and looked rather pale, but with a proud and commanding countenance, though now agitated strangely.

'Was ever being so born to calamity?' I heard her say, with clasped hands, as I came up. 'Here am I, on a journey of life and death, in prosecuting which to lose an hour is possibly to lose all. My child will not have recovered sufficiently to resume her route for who can say how long. I must leave her; I cannot, dare not, delay. How far on, sir, can you tell, is the nearest village? I must leave her there; and shall not see my darling, or even hear of her, till my return, three months hence.'

I plucked my father by the coat, and whispered earnestly in his ear: 'Oh! papa, pray ask her to let her stay with us—it would be so delightful. Do, pray.'

'If Madame will entrust her child to the care of my daughter, and of her good gouvernante, Madame Perrodon, and permit her to remain as our guest, under my charge, until her return, it will confer a distinction and an obligation upon us, and we shall treat her with all the care and devotion which so sacred a trust deserves.'

'I cannot do that, sir, it would be to task your kindness and chivalry too cruelly,' said the lady, distractedly.

'It would, on the contrary, be to confer on us a very great kindness at the moment when we most need it. My daughter has just been disappointed by a cruel misfortune, in a visit from which she had long anticipated a great deal of happiness. If you confide this young lady to our care it will be her best consolation. The nearest village on your route is distant, and affords no such inn as you could think of placing your daughter at; you cannot allow her to continue her journey for any considerable distance without danger. If, as you say, you cannot suspend your journey, you must part with her to-night, and nowhere could you do so with more honest assurances of care and tenderness than here.'

There was something in this lady's air and appearance so distinguished, and even imposing, and in her manner so engaging, as to impress one, quite apart from the dignity of her equipage, with a conviction that she was a person of consequence.

By this time the carriage was replaced in its upright position, and the horses, quite tractable, in the traces again.

The lady threw on her daughter a glance which I fancied was not quite so affectionate as one might have anticipated from the beginning of the scene; then she beckoned slightly to my father, and withdrew two or three steps with him out of hearing; and talked to him with a fixed and stern countenance, not at all like that with which she had hitherto spoken.

I was filled with wonder that my father did not seem to perceive the change, and also unspeakably curious to learn what it could be that she was speaking, almost in his ear, with so much earnestness and rapidity.

Two or three minutes at most I think she remained thus employed, then she turned, and a few steps brought her to where her daughter lay, supported by Madame Perrodon. She kneeled beside her for a moment and whispered, as Madame supposed, a little benediction in her ear; then hastily kissing her she stepped into her carriage, the door was closed, the footmen in stately liveries* jumped up behind, the outriders spurred on, the postillions cracked their whips, the horses plunged and broke suddenly into a furious canter that threatened soon again to become a gallop, and the carriage whirled away, followed at the same rapid pace by the two horsemen in the rear.

CHAPTER III

We Compare Notes

We followed the cortege* with our eyes until it was swiftly lost to sight in the misty wood; and the very sound of the hoofs and the wheels died away in the silent night air.

Nothing remained to assure us that the adventure had not been an illusion of a moment but the young lady, who just at that moment opened her eyes. I could not see, for her face was turned from me, but she raised her head, evidently looking about her, and I heard a very sweet voice ask complainingly, 'Where is mamma?'

Our good Madame Perrodon answered tenderly, and added some comfortable assurances.

I then heard her ask:

'Where am I? What is this place?' and after that she said, 'I don't see the carriage; and Matska,* where is she?'

Madame answered all her questions in so far as she understood them; and gradually the young lady remembered how the misadventure came about, and was glad to hear that no one in, or in attendance on, the carriage was hurt; and on learning that her mamma had left her here, till her return in about three months, she wept.

I was going to add my consolations to those of Madame Perrodon when Mademoiselle De Lafontaine placed her hand upon my arm, saying:

'Don't approach, one at a time is as much as she can at present converse with; a very little excitement would possibly overpower her now.'

As soon as she is comfortably in bed, I thought, I will run up to her room and see her.

My father in the meantime had sent a servant on horseback for the physician, who lived about two leagues away; and a bedroom was being prepared for the young lady's reception.

The stranger now rose, and leaning on Madame's arm, walked slowly over the drawbridge and into the castle gate.

In the hall servants waited to receive her, and she was conducted forthwith to her room.

The room we usually sat in as our drawing room is long, having four windows, that looked over the moat and drawbridge, upon the forest scene I have just described.

It is furnished in old carved oak, with large carved cabinets, and the chairs are cushioned with crimson Utrecht velvet.* The walls are covered with tapestry, and surrounded with great gold frames, the figures being as large as life, in ancient and very curious costume, and the subjects represented are hunting, hawking, and generally festive. It is not too stately to be extremely comfortable; and here we had our tea, for with his usual patriotic leanings he insisted that the national beverage should make its appearance regularly with our coffee and chocolate.

We sat here this night, and with candles lighted, were talking over the adventure of the evening.

Madame Perrodon and Mademoiselle De Lafontaine were both of our party. The young stranger had hardly lain down in her bed when she sank into a deep sleep; and those ladies had left her in the care of a servant.

'How do you like our guest?' I asked, as soon as Madame entered. 'Tell me all about her?'

'I like her extremely,' answered Madame, 'she is, I almost think, the prettiest creature I ever saw; about your age, and so gentle and nice.'

'She is absolutely beautiful,' threw in Mademoiselle, who had peeped for a moment into the stranger's room.

'And such a sweet voice!' added Madame Perrodon.

'Did you remark a woman in the carriage, after it was set up again, who did not get out,' inquired Mademoiselle, 'but only looked from the window?'

'No, we had not seen her.'

Then she described a hideous black woman,* with a sort of colored turban* on her head, who was gazing all the time from the carriage window, nodding and grinning derisively towards the ladies, with gleaming eyes and large white eyeballs, and her teeth set as if in fury.

'Did you remark what an ill-looking pack of men the servants were?' asked Madame.

'Yes,' said my father, who had just come in, 'Ugly, hang-dog looking fellows as ever I beheld in my life. I hope they mayn't rob the poor lady in the forest. They are clever rogues, however; they got everything to rights in a minute.'

'I dare say they are worn out with too long travelling,' said Madame; 'Besides looking wicked, their faces were so strangely lean, and dark, and sullen. I am very curious, I own; but I dare say the young lady will tell us all about it to-morrow, if she is sufficiently recovered.'

'I don't think she will,' said my father, with a mysterious smile, and a little nod of his head, as if he knew more about it than he cared to tell us.

This made me all the more inquisitive as to what had passed between him and the lady in the black velvet, in the brief but earnest interview that had immediately preceded her departure.

We were scarcely alone, when I entreated him to tell me. He did not need much pressing.

'There is no particular reason why I should not tell you. She expressed a reluctance to trouble us with the care of her daughter, saying she was in delicate health, and nervous, but not subject to any kind of seizure—she volunteered that—nor to any illusion; being, in fact, perfectly sane.'

'How very odd to say all that!' I interpolated. 'It was so unnecessary.'

'At all events it *was* said,' he laughed, 'and as you wish to know all that passed, which was indeed very little, I tell you. She then said, "I am making a long journey of *vital* importance—she emphasized the word—rapid and secret; I shall return for my child in three months; in the meantime, she will be silent as to who we are, whence we come, and whither we are travelling." That is all she said. She spoke very pure French. When she said the word "secret," she paused for a few seconds, looking sternly, her eyes fixed on mine. I fancy she makes a great point of that. You saw how quickly she was gone. I hope I have not done a very foolish thing, in taking charge of the young lady.'

For my part, I was delighted. I was longing to see and talk to her; and only waiting till the doctor should give me leave. You, who live in towns, can have no idea how great an event the introduction of a new friend is, in such a solitude as surrounded us.

The doctor did not arrive till nearly one o'clock; but I could no more have gone to my bed and slept, than I could have overtaken, on foot, the carriage in which the princess in black velvet had driven away.

When the physician came down to the drawing-room, it was to report very favourably upon his patient. She was now sitting up, her pulse quite regular, apparently perfectly well. She had sustained no injury, and the little shock to her nerves had passed away quite harmlessly. There could be no harm certainly in my seeing her, if we both wished it; and, with this permission, I sent, forthwith, to know whether she would allow me to visit her for a few minutes in her room.

The servant returned immediately to say that she desired nothing more.

You may be sure I was not long in availing myself of this permission.

Our visitor lay in one of the handsomest rooms in the schloss. It was, perhaps, a little stately. There was a sombre piece of tapestry opposite the foot of the bed, representing Cleopatra with the asps to her bosom;* and other solemn classic scenes were displayed, a little faded, upon the other walls. But there was gold carving, and rich and varied color enough in the other decorations of the room, to more than redeem the gloom of the old tapestry.

There were candles at the bed side. She was sitting up; her slender pretty figure enveloped in the soft silk dressing gown, embroidered with flowers, and lined with thick quilted silk, which her mother had thrown over her feet as she lay upon the ground.

What was it that, as I reached the bed-side and had just begun my little greeting, struck me dumb in a moment, and made me recoil a step or two from before her? I will tell you.

I saw the very face which had visited me in my childhood at night, which remained so fixed in my memory, and on which I had for so many years so often ruminated with horror, when no one suspected of what I was thinking.

It was pretty, even beautiful; and when I first beheld it, wore the same melancholy expression.

But this almost instantly lighted into a strange fixed smile of recognition.

There was a silence of fully a minute, and then at length *she* spoke; *I* could not.

'How wonderful!' she exclaimed. 'Twelve years ago, I saw your face in a dream, and it has haunted me ever since.'

'Wonderful, indeed!' I repeated, overcoming with an effort the horror that had for a time suspended my utterances. 'Twelve years ago, in vision or reality, *I* certainly saw you. I could not forget your face. It has remained before my eyes ever since.'

Her smile had softened. Whatever I had fancied strange in it, was gone, and it and her dimpling cheeks were now delightfully pretty and intelligent.

I felt reassured, and continued more in the vein which hospitality indicated, to bid her welcome, and to tell her how much pleasure her accidental arrival had given us all, and especially what a happiness it was to me.

I took her hand as I spoke. I was a little shy, as lonely people are, but the situation made me eloquent, and even bold. She pressed my hand, she laid hers upon it, and her eyes glowed, as, looking hastily into mine, she smiled again, and blushed.

She answered my welcome very prettily. I sat down beside her, still wondering; and she said:

'I must tell you my vision about you; it is so very strange that you and I should have had, each of the other so vivid a dream, that each should have seen, I you and you me, looking as we do now, when of course we both were mere children. I was a child, about six years old, and I awoke from a confused and troubled dream, and found myself in a room, unlike my nursery, wainscoted clumsily in some dark wood, and with cupboards and bedsteads, and chairs, and benches placed about it. The beds were, I thought, all empty, and the room itself without anyone but myself in it; and I, after looking about me for some time, and admiring especially an iron candlestick, with two branches, which I should certainly know again, crept under one of the beds to reach the window; but as I got from under the bed, I heard someone crying; and looking up, while I was still upon my knees, I saw *you*—most assuredly you—as I see you now; a beautiful young lady, with golden hair and large blue eyes, and lips—your lips—you, as you are here. Your looks won me; I climbed on the bed and put my arms about you, and I think we both fell asleep. I was roused by a scream; you were sitting up screaming. I was frightened, and slipped down upon the ground, and, it seemed to me, lost consciousness for a moment; and when I came to myself, I was again in my nursery at home. Your face I have never forgotten since. I could not be misled by mere resemblance. You *are* the lady whom I then saw.'

It was now my turn to relate my corresponding vision, which I did, to the undisguised wonder of my new acquaintance.

'I don't know which should be most afraid of the other,' she said, again smiling—'If you were less pretty I think I should be very much afraid of you, but being as you are, and you and I both so young, I feel only that I have made your acquaintance twelve years ago, and have already a right to your intimacy; at all events it does seem as if we were destined, from our earliest childhood, to be friends. I wonder whether you feel as strangely drawn towards me as I do to you; I have never had a friend—shall I find one now?' She sighed, and her fine dark eyes gazed passionately on me.

Now the truth is, I felt rather unaccountably towards the beautiful stranger. I did feel, as she said, 'drawn towards her,' but there was also something of repulsion. In this ambiguous feeling, however, the sense of attraction immensely prevailed. She interested and won me; she was so beautiful and so indescribably engaging.

I perceived now something of languor and exhaustion stealing over her, and hastened to bid her good night.

'The doctor thinks,' I added, 'that you ought to have a maid to sit up with you to-night; one of ours is waiting, and you will find her a very useful and quiet creature.'

'How kind of you, but I could not sleep, I never could with an attendant in the room. I shan't require any assistance—and, shall I confess my weakness, I am haunted with a terror of robbers. Our house was robbed once, and two servants murdered, so I always lock my door. It has become a habit—and you look so kind I know you will forgive me. I see there is a key in the lock.'

She held me close in her pretty arms for a moment and whispered in my ear, 'Good night, darling, it is very hard to part with you, but good night; to-morrow, but not early, I shall see you again.'

She sank back on the pillow with a sigh, and her fine eyes followed me with a fond and melancholy gaze, and she murmured again 'Good night, dear friend.'

Young people like, and even love, on impulse. I was flattered by the evident, though as yet undeserved, fondness she showed me. I liked the confidence with which she at once received me. She was determined that we should be very near friends.

Next day came and we met again. I was delighted with my companion; that is to say, in many respects.

Her looks lost nothing in daylight—she was certainly the most beautiful creature I had ever seen, and the unpleasant remembrance of the face presented in my early dream, had lost the effect of the first unexpected recognition.

She confessed that she had experienced a similar shock on seeing me, and precisely the same faint antipathy that had mingled with my admiration of her. We now laughed together over our momentary horrors.

CHAPTER IV

Her Habits—A Saunter

I TOLD you that I was charmed with her in most particulars.

There were some that did not please me so well.

She was above the middle height of women. I shall begin by describing her. She was slender, and wonderfully graceful. Except that her movements were languid—*very* languid—indeed, there was nothing in her appearance to indicate an invalid. Her complexion was rich and brilliant; her features were small and beautifully formed; her eyes large, dark, and lustrous; her hair was quite wonderful, I never saw hair so magnificently thick and long* when it was down about her shoulders; I have often placed my hands under it, and laughed with wonder at its weight. It was exquisitely fine and soft, and in colour a rich very dark brown, with something of gold. I loved to let it down, tumbling with its own weight, as, in her room, she lay back in her chair talking in her sweet low voice, I used to fold and braid it, and spread it out and play with it. Heavens! If I had but known all!

I said there were particulars which did not please me. I have told you that her confidence won me the first night I saw her; but I found that she exercised with respect to herself, her mother, her history, everything in fact connected with her life, plans, and people, an ever wakeful reserve. I dare say I was unreasonable, perhaps I was wrong; I dare say I ought to have respected the solemn injunction laid upon my father by the stately lady in black velvet. But curiosity is a restless and unscrupulous passion, and no one girl can endure, with patience, that her's should be baffled by another. What harm could it do anyone to tell me what I so ardently desired to know? Had she no trust in my good sense or honour? Why would she not believe me when I assured her, so solemnly, that I would not divulge one syllable of what she told me to any mortal breathing.

There was a coldness, it seemed to me, beyond her years, in her smiling melancholy persistent refusal to afford me the least ray of light.

I cannot say we quarreled upon this point, for she would not quarrel upon any. It was, of course, very unfair of me to press her, very ill-bred, but I really could not help it; and I might just as well have let it alone.

What she did tell me amounted, in my unconscionable estimation to—nothing.

It was all summed up in three very vague disclosures:

First.—Her name was Carmilla.

Second.—Her family was very ancient and noble.

Third.—Her home lay in the direction of the west.

She would not tell me the name of her family, nor their armorial bearings,* nor the name of their estate, nor even that of the country they lived in.

You are not to suppose that I worried her incessantly on these subjects. I watched opportunity, and rather insinuated than urged my inquiries. Once or twice, indeed, I did attack her more directly. But no matter what my tactics, utter failure was invariably the result. Reproaches and caresses were all lost upon her. But I must add this, that her evasion was conducted with so pretty a melancholy and deprecation, with so many, and even passionate declarations of her liking for me, and trust in my honour, and with so many promises that I should at last know all, that I could not find it in my heart long to be offended with her.

She used to place her pretty arms about my neck, draw me to her, and laying her cheek to mine, murmur with her lips near my ear, 'Dearest, your little heart is wounded; think me not cruel because I obey the irresistible law of my strength and weakness; if your dear heart is wounded, my wild heart bleeds with yours. In the rapture of my enormous humiliation I live in your warm life, and you shall die—die, sweetly die—into mine. I cannot help it; as I draw near to you, you, in your turn, will draw near to others, and learn the rapture of that cruelty, which yet is love; so, for a while, seek to know no more of me and mine, but trust me with all your loving spirit.'

And when she had spoken such a rhapsody, she would press me more closely in her trembling embrace, and her lips in soft kisses gently glow upon my cheek.

Her agitations and her language were unintelligible to me.

From these foolish embraces, which were not of very frequent occurrence, I must allow, I used to wish to extricate myself; but my energies seemed to fail me. Her murmured words sounded like a lullaby in my ear, and soothed my resistance into a trance, from which I only seemed to recover myself when she withdrew her arms.

In these mysterious moods I did not like her. I experienced a strange tumultuous excitement that was pleasurable, ever and anon, mingled with a vague sense of fear and disgust. I had no distinct thoughts about her while such scenes lasted, but I was conscious of a love growing into adoration, and also of abhorrence. This I know is paradox, but I can make no other attempt to explain the feeling.

I now write, after an interval of more than ten years, with a trembling hand, with a confused and horrible recollection of certain occurrences and situations, in the ordeal through which I was unconsciously passing; though with a vivid and very sharp remembrance of the main current of my story. But, I suspect, in all lives there are certain emotional scenes, those in which our passions have been most wildly and terribly roused, that are of all others the most vaguely and dimly remembered.

Sometimes after an hour of apathy, my strange and beautiful companion would take my hand and hold it with a fond pressure, renewed again and again; blushing softly, gazing in my face with languid and burning eyes, and breathing so fast that her dress rose and fell with the tumultuous respiration. It was like the ardour of a lover; it embarrassed me; it was hateful and yet over-powering; and with gloating eyes she drew me to her, and her hot lips travelled along my cheek in kisses; and she would whisper, almost in sobs, 'You are mine, you *shall* be mine, you and I are one for ever.' Then she has thrown herself back in her chair, with her small hands over her eyes, leaving me trembling.

'Are we related,' I used to ask; 'what can you mean by all this? I remind you perhaps of someone whom you love; but you must not, I hate it; I don't know you—I don't know myself when you look so and talk so.'

She used to sigh at my vehemence, then turn away and drop my hand.

Respecting these very extraordinary manifestations I strove in vain to form any satisfactory theory—I could not refer them to affectation or trick. It was unmistakably the momentary breaking out of suppressed instinct and emotion. Was she, notwithstanding her mother's volunteered denial, subject to brief visitations of insanity; or was there here a disguise and a romance? I had read in old story books of such things. What if a boyish lover had found his way into the house, and sought to prosecute his suit in masquerade, with the assistance of a clever old adventuress. But there were many things against this hypothesis, highly interesting as it was to my vanity.

I could boast of no little attentions such as masculine gallantry delights to offer. Between these passionate moments there were long intervals of commonplace, of gaiety, of brooding melancholy, during which, except that I detected her eyes so full of melancholy fire, following me, at times I might have been as nothing to her. Except in these brief periods of mysterious excitement her ways were girlish; and there was always a languor about her, quite incompatible with a masculine system in a state of health.

In some respects her habits were odd. Perhaps not so singular in the opinion of a town lady like you, as they appeared to us rustic people. She used to come down very late, generally not till one o'clock, she would then take a cup of chocolate, but eat nothing; we then went out for a walk, which was a mere saunter, and she seemed, almost immediately, exhausted, and either returned to the schloss or sat on one of the benches that were placed, here and there, among the trees. This was a bodily languor in which her mind did not sympathize. She was always an animated talker, and very intelligent.

She sometimes alluded for a moment to her own home, or mentioned an adventure or situation, or an early recollection, which indicated a people of strange manners, and described customs of which we knew nothing. I gathered from these chance hints that her native country was much more remote than I had at first fancied.

As we sat thus one afternoon under the trees a funeral passed us by. It was that of a pretty young girl, whom I had often seen, the daughter of one of the rangers of the forest. The poor man was walking behind the coffin of his darling; she was his only child, and he looked quite heartbroken. Peasants walking two-and-two came behind, they were singing a funeral hymn.

I rose to mark my respect as they passed, and joined in the hymn they were very sweetly singing.

My companion shook me a little roughly, and I turned surprised.

She said, brusquely, 'Don't you perceive how discordant that is?'

'I think it very sweet, on the contrary,' I answered, vexed at the interruption, and very uncomfortable, lest the people who composed the little procession should observe and resent what was passing.

I resumed, therefore, instantly, and was again interrupted. 'You pierce my ears,' said Carmilla, almost angrily, and stopping her ears with her tiny fingers. 'Besides, how can you tell that your religion and mine are the same; your forms wound me, and I hate funerals. What a fuss! Why *you* must die—*everyone* must die; and all are happier when they do. Come home.'

'My father has gone on with the clergyman to the churchyard. I thought you knew she was to be buried today.'

'*She*? I don't trouble my head about peasants. I don't know who she is,' answered Carmilla, with a flash from her fine eyes.

'She is the poor girl who fancied she saw a ghost a fortnight ago, and has been dying ever since, till yesterday, when she expired.'

'Tell me nothing about ghosts. I shan't sleep to-night if you do.'

'I hope there is no plague or fever coming; all this looks very like it,' I continued. 'The swineherd's young wife died only a week ago, and she thought something seized her by the throat as she lay in her bed, and nearly strangled her. Papa says such horrible fancies do accompany some forms of fever. She was quite well the day before. She sank afterwards, and died before a week.'

'Well, *her* funeral is over, I hope, and *her* hymn sung; and our ears shan't be tortured with that discord and jargon.* It has made me nervous. Sit down here, beside me; sit close; hold my hand; press it hard—hard—harder.'

We had moved a little back, and had come to another seat.

She sat down. Her face underwent a change that alarmed and even terrified me for a moment. It darkened, and became horribly livid; her teeth and hands were clenched, and she frowned and compressed her lips, while she stared down upon the ground at her feet, and trembled all over with a continued shudder as irrepressible as ague.* All her energies seemed strained to suppress a fit, with which she was then breathlessly tugging; and at length a low convulsive cry of suffering broke from her, and gradually the hysteria subsided. 'There! That comes of strangling people with hymns!' she said at last. 'Hold me, hold me still. It is passing away.'

And so gradually it did; and perhaps to dissipate the somber impression which the spectacle had left upon me, she became unusually animated and chatty; and so we got home.

This was the first time I had seen her exhibit any definable symptoms of that delicacy of health which her mother had spoken of. It was the first time, also, I had seen her exhibit anything like temper.

Both passed away like a summer cloud; and never but once afterwards did I witness on her part a momentary sign of anger. I will tell you how it happened.

She and I were looking out of one of the long drawing-room windows, when there entered the court-yard, over the drawbridge, a figure of a wanderer whom I knew very well. He used to visit the schloss generally twice a year.

It was the figure of a hunchback, with the sharp lean features that generally accompany deformity. He wore a pointed black beard, and he was smiling from ear to ear, showing his white fangs. He was dressed in buff, black, and scarlet, and crossed with more straps and belts than I could count, from which hung all manner of things. Behind, he carried a magic lantern,* and two boxes, which I well knew, in one of which was a salamander,* and in the other a mandrake.* These monsters used to make my father laugh. They were compounded of parts of monkeys, parrots, squirrels, fish, and hedgehogs, dried and stitched together with great neatness and startling effect. He had a fiddle, a box of conjuring apparatus, a pair of foils and masks* attached to his belt, several other mysterious cases dangling about him, and a black staff with copper ferrules in his hand. His companion was a rough spare dog, that followed at his heels, but stopped short, suspiciously at the drawbridge, and in a little while began to howl dismally.

In the meantime, the mountebank, standing in the midst of the courtyard, raised his grotesque hat, and made us a very ceremonious bow, paying his compliments very volubly in execrable French, and German not much better. Then, disengaging his fiddle, he began to scrape a lively air, to which he sang with a merry discord, dancing with ludicrous airs and activity, that made me laugh, in spite of the dog's howling.

Then he advanced to the window with many smiles and salutations, and his hat in his left hand, his fiddle under his arm, and with a fluency that never took breath, he gabbled a long advertisement of all his accomplishments, and the resources of the various arts which he placed at our service, and the curiosities and entertainments which it was in his power, at our bidding, to display.

'Will your ladyships be pleased to buy an amulet* against the oupire,* which is going like the wolf, I hear, through these woods,' he said, dropping his hat on the pavement. 'They are dying of it right and left, and here is a charm that never fails; only pinned to the pillow, and you may laugh in his face.'

These charms consisted of oblong slips of vellum, with cabalistic* ciphers and diagrams upon them.

Carmilla instantly purchased one, and so did I.

He was looking up, and we were smiling down upon him, amused; at least, I can answer for myself. His piercing black eye, as he looked up in our faces, seemed to detect something that fixed for a moment his curiosity,

In an instant he unrolled a leather case, full of all manner of odd little steel instruments.

'See here, my lady,' he said, displaying it, and addressing me, 'I profess, among other things less useful, the art of dentistry. Plague take the dog!' he interpolated. 'Silence, beast! He howls so that your ladyships can scarcely hear a word. Your noble friend, the young lady at your right, has the sharpest tooth,—long, thin, pointed, like an awl, like a needle; ha, ha! With my sharp and long sight, as I look up, I have seen it distinctly; now if it happens to hurt the young lady, and I think it must, here am I, here are my file, my punch, my nippers; I will make it round and blunt, if her ladyship pleases; no longer the tooth of a fish, but of a beautiful young lady as she is. Hey? Is the young lady displeased? Have I been too bold? Have I offended her?'

The young lady, indeed, looked very angry as she drew back from the window.

'How dares that mountebank insult us so? Where is your father? I shall demand redress from him. My father would have had the wretch tied up to the pump, and flogged with a cart-whip, and burnt to the bones with the castle brand!'*

She retired from the window a step or two, and sat down, and had hardly lost sight of the offender, when her wrath subsided as suddenly as it had risen, and she gradually recovered her usual tone, and seemed to forget the little hunchback and his follies.

My father was out of spirits that evening. On coming in he told us that there had been another case very similar to the two fatal ones which had lately occurred. The sister of a young peasant on his estate, only a mile away, was very ill, had been, as she described it, attacked very nearly in the same way, and was now slowly but steadily sinking.

'All this,' said my father, 'is strictly referable to natural causes. These poor people infect one another with their superstitions, and so repeat in imagination the images of terror that have infested their neighbours.'

'But that very circumstance frightens one horribly,' said Carmilla.

'How so?' inquired my father.

'I am so afraid of fancying I see such things; I think it would be as bad as reality.'

'We are in God's hands; nothing can happen without his permission, and all will end well for those who love him. He is our faithful creator; He has made us all, and will take care of us.'

'Creator! *Nature!*' said the young lady in answer to my gentle father. 'And this disease that invades the country is natural. Nature. All things proceed from Nature—don't they? All things in the heaven, in the earth, and under the earth, act and live as Nature ordains? I think so.'

'The doctor said he would come here to-day,' said my father, after a silence. 'I want to know what he thinks about it, and what he thinks we had better do.'

'Doctors never did me any good,' said Carmilla.

'Then you have been ill?' I asked.

'More ill than ever you were,' she answered.

'Long ago?'

'Yes, a long time. I suffered from this very illness; but I forget all but my pain and weakness, and they were not so bad as are suffered in other diseases.'

'You were very young then?'

'I dare say; let us talk no more of it. You would not wound a friend?' She looked languidly in my eyes, and passed her arm round my waist lovingly, and led me out of the room. My father was busy over some papers near the window.

'Why does your papa like to frighten us?' said the pretty girl, with a sigh and a little shudder.

'He doesn't, dear Carmilla, it is the very furthest thing from his mind.'

'Are you afraid, dearest?'

'I should be very much if I fancied there was any real danger of my being attacked as those poor people were.'

'You are afraid to die?'

'Yes, every one is.'

'But to die as lovers may—to die together, so that they may live together. Girls are caterpillars while they live in the world, to be finally butterflies when the summer comes; but in the meantime there are grubs and larvæ, don't you see—each with their peculiar propensities, necessities, and structure. So says Monsieur Buffon,* in his big book, in the next room.'

Later in the day the doctor came, and was closeted with papa for some time. He was a skilful man, of sixty and upwards, he wore powder, and shaved his pale face as smooth as a pumpkin. He and papa emerged from the room together, and I heard papa laugh, and say as they came out:

'Well, I do wonder at a wise man like you. What do you say to hippogriffs* and dragons?'

The doctor was smiling, and made answer, shaking his head—

'Nevertheless life and death are mysterious states, and we know little of the resources of either.'

And so they walked on, and I heard no more. I did not then know what the doctor had been broaching, but I think I guess it now.

CHAPTER V

A Wonderful Likeness

THIS evening there arrived from Gratz* the grave, dark-faced son of the picture cleaner, with a horse and cart laden with two large packing cases, having many pictures in each. It was a journey of ten leagues,* and whenever a messenger arrived at the schloss from our little capital of Gratz, we used to crowd about him in the hall, to hear the news.

This arrival created in our secluded quarters quite a sensation. The cases remained in the hall, and the messenger was taken charge of by the servants till he had eaten his supper. Then with assistants, and armed with hammer, ripping-chisel, and turnscrew, he met us in the hall, where we had assembled to witness the unpacking of the cases.

Carmilla sat looking listlessly on, while one after the other the old pictures, nearly all portraits, which had undergone the process of renovation, were brought to light. My mother was of an old Hungarian family, and most of these pictures, which were about to be restored to their places, had come to us through her.

My father had a list in his hand, from which he read, as the artist rummaged out the corresponding numbers. I don't know that the pictures were very good, but they were, undoubtedly, very old, and some of them very curious also. They had, for the most part, the merit of being now seen by me, I may say, for the first time; for the smoke and dust of time had all but obliterated them.

'There is a picture that I have not seen yet,' said my father. 'In one corner, at the top of it, is the name, as well as I could read, "Marcia Karnstein," and the date "1698;" and I am curious to see how it has turned out.'

I remembered it; it was a small picture,* about a foot and a half high, and nearly square, without a frame; but it was so blackened by age that I could not make it out.

The artist now produced it, with evident pride. It was quite beautiful; it was startling; it seemed to live. It was the effigy* of Carmilla!

'Carmilla, dear, here is an absolute miracle. Here you are, living, smiling, ready to speak, in this picture. Isn't it beautiful, papa? And see, even the little mole on her throat.'

My father laughed, and said 'Certainly it is a wonderful likeness,' but he looked away, and to my surprise seemed but little struck by it, and went on talking to the picture cleaner, who was also something of an artist, and discoursed with intelligence about the portraits or other works, which his art had just brought into light and colour, while *I* was more and more lost in wonder the more I looked at the picture.

'Will you let me hang this picture in my room, papa?' I asked.

'Certainly, dear,' said he, smiling, 'I'm very glad you think it so like. It must be prettier even than I thought it, if it is.'

The young lady did not acknowledge this pretty speech, did not seem to hear it. She was leaning back in her seat, her fine eyes under their long lashes gazing on me in contemplation, and she smiled in a kind of rapture.

'And now you can read quite plainly the name that is written in the corner. It is not Marcia; it looks as if it was done in gold. The name is Mircalla, Countess Karnstein, and this is a little coronet over it, and underneath A.D. 1698. I am descended from the Karnsteins; that is, mamma was.'

'Ah!' said the lady, languidly, 'so am I, I think, a very long descent, very ancient. Are there any Karnsteins living now?'

'None who bear the name, I believe. The family were ruined, I believe, in some civil wars, long ago, but the ruins of the castle are only about three miles away.'

'How interesting!' she said, languidly. 'But see what beautiful moonlight!' She glanced through the hall-door, which stood a little open. 'Suppose you take a little ramble round the court, and look down at the road and river.'

'It is so like the night you came to us,' I said.

She sighed, smiling.

She rose, and each with her arm about the other's waist, we walked out upon the pavement.

In silence, slowly we walked down to the drawbridge, where the beautiful landscape opened before us.

'And so you were thinking of the night I came here?' she almost whispered. 'Are you glad I came?'

'Delighted, dear Carmilla,' I answered.

'And you asked for the picture you think like me, to hang in your room,' she murmured with a sigh, as she drew her arm closer about my waist, and let her pretty head sink upon my shoulder.

'How romantic* you are, Carmilla,' I said. 'Whenever you tell me your story, it will be made up chiefly of some one great romance.'*

She kissed me silently.

'I am sure, Carmilla, you have been in love; that there is, at this moment, an affair of the heart going on.'

'I have been in love with no one, and never shall,' she whispered, 'Unless it should be with you.'

How beautiful she looked in the moonlight!

Shy and strange was the look with which she quickly hid her face in my neck and hair, with tumultuous sighs, that seemed almost to sob, and pressed in mine a hand that trembled.

Her soft cheek was glowing against mine. 'Darling, darling,' she murmured, 'I live in you; and you would die for me, I love you so.'

I started from her.

She was gazing on me with eyes from which all fire, all meaning had flown, and a face colorless and apathetic.*

'Is there a chill in the air, dear?' she said drowsily. 'I almost shiver; have I been dreaming? Let us come in. Come; come; come in.'

'You look ill, Carmilla; a little faint. You must take some wine,' I said.

'Yes. I will. I'm better now. I shall be quite well in a few minutes. Yes, do give me a little wine,' answered Carmilla, as we approached the door. 'Let us look again for a moment; it is the last time, perhaps, I shall see the moonlight with you.'

'How do you feel now, dear Carmilla? Are you really better?' I asked.

I was beginning to take alarm, lest she should have been stricken with the strange epidemic that they said had invaded the country about us.

'Papa would be grieved beyond measure,' I added, 'if he thought you were ever so little ill, without immediately letting us know. We have a very skilful doctor near us,* the physician who was with papa to-day.'

'I'm sure he is. I know how kind you all are; but, dear child, I am quite well again. There is nothing ever wrong with me, but a little weakness. People say I am languid; I am incapable of exertion; I can scarcely walk as far as a child of three years old: and every now and then the little strength I have falters, and I become as you have just seen me. But after all I am very easily set up again; in a moment I am perfectly myself. See how I have recovered.'

So, indeed, she had; and she and I talked a great deal, and very animated she was; and the remainder of that evening passed without any recurrence of what I called her infatuations. I mean her crazy talk and looks, which embarrassed, and even frightened me.

But there occurred that night an event which gave my thoughts quite a new turn, and seemed to startle even Carmilla's languid nature into momentary energy.

CHAPTER VI

A Very Strange Agony

WHEN we got into the drawing-room, and had sat down to our coffee and chocolate, although Carmilla did not take any, she seemed quite herself again, and Madame, and Mademoiselle De Lafontaine, joined us, and made a little card party, in the course of which papa came in for what he called his 'dish of tea.'*

When the game was over he sat down beside Carmilla on the sofa, and asked her, a little anxiously, whether she had heard from her mother since her arrival.

She answered 'No.'

He then asked whether she knew where a letter would reach her at present.

'I cannot tell,' she answered ambiguously, 'but I have been thinking of leaving you; you have been already too hospitable and too kind to me. I have given you an infinity of trouble, and I should wish to take a carriage to-morrow, and post* in pursuit of her; I know where I shall ultimately find her, although I dare not yet tell you.'

'But you must not dream of any such thing,' exclaimed my father, to my great relief. 'We can't afford to lose you so, and I won't consent to your leaving us, except under the care of your mother, who was so good as to consent to your remaining with us till she should herself return. I should be quite happy if I knew that you heard from her: but this evening the accounts of the progress of the mysterious disease that has invaded our neighborhood, grow even more alarming; and my beautiful guest, I do feel the responsibility, unaided by advice from your mother, very much. But I shall do my best; and one thing is certain, that you must not think of leaving us without her distinct direction to that effect. We should suffer too much in parting from you to consent to it easily.'

'Thank you, sir, a thousand times for your hospitality,' she answered, smiling bashfully. 'You have all been too kind to me; I have seldom been so happy in all my life before, as in your beautiful chateau, under your care, and in the society of your dear daughter.'

So he gallantly, in his old-fashioned way, kissed her hand, smiling and pleased at her little speech.

I accompanied Carmilla as usual to her room, and sat and chatted with her while she was preparing for bed.

'Do you think,' I said at length, 'that you will ever confide fully in me?'

She turned round smiling, but made no answer, only continued to smile on me.

'You won't answer that?' I said. 'You can't answer pleasantly; perhaps I ought not to have asked you.'

'You were quite right to ask me that, or anything. You do not know how dear you are to me, or you could not think any confidence too great to look for. But I am under vows, no nun half so awfully, and I dare not tell my story yet, even to you. The time is very near when you shall know everything. You will think me cruel, very selfish, but love is always selfish; the more ardent the more selfish. How jealous I am you cannot know. You must come with me, loving me, to death; or else hate me and still come with me, and *hating* me through death and after. There is no such word as indifference in my apathetic nature.'

'Now, Carmilla, you are going to talk your wild nonsense again,' I said hastily.

'Not I, silly little fool as I am, and full of whims and fancies; for your sake I'll talk like a sage. Were you ever at a ball?'

'No; how you do run on. What is it like? How charming it must be.'

'I almost forget, it is years ago.'

I laughed.

'You are not so old. Your first ball can hardly be forgotten yet.'

'I remember everything about it—with an effort. I see it all, as divers see what is going on above them, through a medium, dense, rippling, but transparent. There occurred that night what has confused the picture, and made its colours faint. I was all but assassinated in my bed, wounded *here*,' she touched her breast, 'and never was the same since.'

'Were you near dying?'

'Yes, very—a cruel love—strange love, that would have taken my life. Love will have its sacrifices. No sacrifice without blood. Let us go to sleep now; I feel so lazy. How can I get up just now and lock my door?'

She was lying, with her tiny hands buried in her rich wavy hair, under her cheek, her little head upon the pillow, and her glittering eyes followed me wherever I moved, with a kind of shy smile that I could not decipher.

I bid her good-night, and crept from the room with an uncomfortable sensation.

I often wondered whether our pretty guest ever said her prayers. *I* certainly had never seen her upon her knees. In the morning she never came down until long after our family prayers were over, and at night she never left the drawing-room to attend our brief evening prayers in the hall.

If it had not been that it had casually come out in one of our careless talks that she had been baptized, I should have doubted her being a Christian. Religion was a subject on which I had never heard her speak a word. If I had known the world better, this particular neglect or antipathy would not have so much surprised me.

The precautions of nervous people are infectious, and persons of a like temperament are pretty sure, after a time, to imitate them. I had adopted Carmilla's habit of locking her bed-room door, having taken into my head all her whimsical alarms about midnight invaders and prowling assassins. I had also adopted her precaution of making a brief search through her room, to satisfy herself that no lurking assassin or robber was 'ensconced.'

These wise measures taken I got into my bed and fell asleep. A light was burning in my room. This was an old habit, of very early date, and which nothing could have tempted me to dispense with.

Thus fortified I might take my rest in peace. But dreams come through stone walls, light up dark rooms, or darken light ones, and their persons make their exits and their entrances as they please, and laugh at locksmiths.

I had a dream that night that was the beginning of a very strange agony. I cannot call it a nightmare, for I was quite conscious of being asleep. But I was equally conscious of being in my room, and lying in bed, precisely as I actually was. I saw, or fancied I saw, the room and its furniture just as I had seen it last, except that it was very dark, and I saw something moving round the foot of the bed, which at first I could not accurately distinguish. But I soon saw that it was a sooty-black animal that resembled a monstrous cat. It appeared to me about four or five feet long, for it measured fully the length of the hearth-rug as it passed over it; and it continued toing and froing with the lithe sinister restlessness of a beast in a cage. I could not cry out, although as you may suppose, I was terrified. Its pace was growing faster, and the room rapidly darker and darker, and at length so dark that I could no longer see anything of it but its eyes. I felt it spring lightly on the bed. The two broad eyes approached my face, and suddenly I felt a stinging pain as if two large needles darted, an inch or two apart, deep into my breast. I waked with a scream. The room was lighted by the candle that burnt there all through the night, and I saw a female figure standing at the foot of the bed, a little at the right side. It was in a dark loose dress, and its hair was down and covered its shoulders. A block of stone could not have been more still. There was not the slightest stir of respiration. As I stared at it the figure appeared to have changed its place, and was now nearer the door; then, close to it, the door opened, and it passed out.

I was now relieved, and able to breathe and move. My first thought was that Carmilla had been playing me a trick, and that I had forgotten to secure my door. I hastened to it, and found it locked as usual on the inside. I was afraid to open it—I was horrified. I sprang into my bed and covered my head up in the bed-clothes, and lay there more dead than alive till morning.

CHAPTER VII

Descending

It would be vain my attempting to tell you the horror with which, even now, I recall the occurrence of that night. It was no such transitory terror as a dream leaves behind it. It seemed to deepen by time, and communicated itself to the room and the very furniture that had encompassed the apparition.

I could not bear next day to be alone for a moment. I should have told papa, but for two opposite reasons. At one time I thought he would laugh at my story, and I could not bear its being treated as a jest; and at another I thought he might fancy that I had been attacked by the mysterious complaint which had invaded our neighbourhood. I had myself no misgivings of the kind, and as he had been rather an invalid for some time, I was afraid of alarming him.

I was comfortable enough with my good-natured companions, Madame Paradon, and the vivacious Mademoiselle de Lafontaine.* They both perceived that I was out of spirits and nervous, and at length I told them what lay so heavy at my heart.

Mademoiselle laughed, but I fancied that Madame Paradon looked anxious.

'By-the-bye,' said Mademoiselle, laughing, 'the long lime-tree walk, behind Carmilla's bedroom-window, is haunted!'

'Nonsense!' exclaimed Madame, who probably thought the theme rather inopportune, 'and who tells that story, my dear?'

'Martin says that he came up twice, when the old yard-gate was being repaired, before sunrise, and twice saw the same female figure walking down the lime-tree avenue.'

'So he well might, as long as there are cows to milk in the river fields,' said Madame.

'I daresay; but Martin chooses to be frightened, and never did I see fool* *more* frightened.'

'You must not say a word about it to Carmilla, because she can see down that walk from her room window,' I interposed, 'and she is, if possible, a greater coward than I.'

Carmilla came down rather later than usual that day.

'I was so frightened last night,' she said, so soon as we were together, 'and I am sure I should have seen something dreadful if it had not been for that charm I bought from the poor little hunchback whom I called such hard names. I had a dream of something black coming round my bed, and I awoke in a perfect horror, and I really thought, for some seconds, I saw a dark figure near the chimney-piece, but I felt under my pillow for my charm, and the moment my fingers touched it, the figure disappeared, and I felt quite certain, only that I had it by me, that something frightful would have made its appearance, and, perhaps, throttled me, as it did those poor people we heard of.'

'Well, listen to me,' I began, and recounted my adventure, at the recital of which she appeared horrified.

'And had you the charm near you?' she asked, earnestly.

'No, I had dropped it into a china vase in the drawing-room, but I shall certainly take it with me to-night, as you have so much faith in it.'

At this distance of time I cannot tell you, or even understand, how I overcame my horror so effectually as to lie alone in my room that night. I remember distinctly that I pinned the charm to my pillow. I fell asleep almost immediately, and slept even more soundly than usual all night.

Next night I passed as well. My sleep was delightfully deep and dreamless. But I wakened with a sense of lassitude and melancholy, which, however, did not exceed a degree that was almost luxurious.

'Well, I told you so,' said Carmilla, when I described my quiet sleep, 'I had such delightful sleep myself last night; I pinned the charm to the breast of my night-dress. It was too far away the night before. I am quite sure it was all fancy, except the dreams. I used to think that evil spirits made dreams, but our doctor told me it is no such thing. Only a fever passing by, or some other malady, as they often do, he said, knocks at the door, and not being able to get in, passes on, with that alarm.'

'And what do you think the charm is?' said I.

'It has been fumigated or immersed in some drug, and is an antidote against the malaria,' she answered.

'Then it acts only on the body?'

'Certainly; you don't suppose that evil spirits are frightened by bits of ribbon, or the perfumes of a druggist's shop? No, these complaints, wandering in the air, begin by trying the nerves, and so infect the brain, but before they can seize upon you, the antidote repels them. That I am sure is what the charm has done for us. It is nothing magical, it is simply natural.'

I should have been happier if I could have quite agreed with Carmilla, but I did my best, and the impression was a little losing its force.

For some nights I slept profoundly; but still every morning I felt the same lassitude, and a languor weighed upon me all day. I felt myself a changed girl. A strange melancholy was stealing over me, a melancholy that I would not have interrupted. Dim thoughts of death began to open, and an idea that I was slowly sinking took gentle, and, somehow, not unwelcome, possession of me. If it was sad, the tone of mind which this induced was also sweet. Whatever it might be, my soul acquiesced in it.

I would not admit that I was ill, I would not consent to tell my papa, or to have the doctor sent for.

Carmilla became more devoted to me than ever, and her strange paroxysms of languid adoration more frequent. She used to gloat* on me with increasing ardour the more my strength and spirits waned. This always shocked me like a momentary glare of insanity.

Without knowing it, I was now in a pretty advanced stage of the strangest illness under which mortal ever suffered. There was an unaccountable fascination in its earlier symptoms that more than reconciled me to the incapacitating effect of that stage of the malady. This fascination increased for a time, until it reached a certain point, when gradually a sense of the horrible mingled itself with it, deepening, as you shall hear, until it discoloured and perverted the whole state of my life.

The first change I experienced was rather agreeable. It was very near the turning-point from which began the descent of Avernus.*

Certain vague and strange sensations visited me in my sleep. The prevailing one was of that pleasant, peculiar cold thrill which we feel in bathing, when we move against the current of a river. This was soon accompanied by dreams that seemed interminable, and were so vague that I could never recollect their scenery and persons, or any one connected portion of their action. But they left an awful impression, and a sense of exhaustion, as if I had passed through a long period of great mental exertion and danger. After all these dreams there remained on waking a remembrance of having been in a place very nearly dark, and of having spoken to people whom I could not see; and especially of one clear voice, of a female's, very deep, that spoke as if at a distance, slowly, and producing always the same sensation of indescribable solemnity and fear. Sometimes there came a sensation as if a hand was drawn softly along my cheek and neck.

Sometimes it was as if warm lips kissed me, and longer and more lovingly as they reached my throat, but there the caress fixed itself. My heart beat faster, my breathing rose and fell rapidly and full drawn; a sobbing, that rose into a sense of strangulation, supervened,* and turned into a dreadful convulsion, in which my senses left me and I became unconscious.

It was now three weeks since the commencement of this unaccountable state. My sufferings had, during the last week, told upon my appearance. I had grown pale, my eyes were dilated and darkened underneath, and the languor which I had long felt began to display itself in my countenance.*

My father asked me often whether I was ill; but, with an obstinacy which now seems to me unaccountable, I persisted in assuring him that I was quite well.

In a sense this was true. I had no pain, I could complain of no bodily derangement. My complaint seemed to be one of the imagination, or the nerves, and, horrible as my sufferings were, I kept them, with a morbid reserve, very nearly to myself.

It could not be that terrible complaint which the peasants called the oupire, for I had now been suffering for three weeks, and they were seldom ill for much more than three days, when death put an end to their miseries.

Carmilla complained of dreams and feverish sensations, but by no means of so alarming a kind as mine. I say that mine were extremely alarming. Had I been capable of comprehending my condition, I would have invoked aid and advice on my knees. The narcotic of an unsuspected influence was acting upon me, and my perceptions were benumbed.

I am going to tell you now of a dream that led immediately to an odd discovery.

One night, instead of the voice I was accustomed to hear in the dark, I heard one, sweet and tender, and at the same time terrible, which said, 'Your mother warns you to beware of the assassin.' At the same time a light unexpectedly sprang up, and I saw Carmilla, standing, near the foot of my bed, in her white night-dress, bathed, from her chin to her feet, in one great stain of blood.

I wakened with a shriek, possessed with the one idea that Carmilla was being murdered. I remember springing from my bed, and my next recollection is that of standing on the lobby, crying for help.

Madame and Mademoiselle came scurrying out of their rooms in alarm; a lamp burned always on the lobby, and seeing me, they soon learned the cause of my terror.

I insisted on our knocking at Carmilla's door. Our knocking was unanswered. It soon became a pounding and an uproar. We shrieked her name, but all was vain.

We all grew frightened, for the door was locked. We hurried back, in panic, to my room. There we rang the bell long and furiously. If my father's room had been at that side of the house, we would have called him up at once to our aid. But, alas! he was quite out of hearing, and to reach him involved an excursion for which we none of us had courage.

Servants, however, soon came running up the stairs; I had got on my dressing-gown and slippers meanwhile, and my companions were already similarly furnished. Recognising the voices of the servants on the lobby, we sallied out together; and having renewed, as fruitlessly, our summons at Carmilla's door, I ordered the men to force the lock. They did so, and we stood, holding our lights aloft, in the doorway, and so stared into the room.

We called her by name; but there was still no reply. We looked round the room. Everything was undisturbed. It was exactly in the state in which I had left it on bidding her good night. But Carmilla was gone.

CHAPTER VIII

Search

At sight of the room, perfectly undisturbed except for our violent entrance, we began to cool a little, and soon recovered our senses sufficiently to dismiss the men. It had struck Mademoiselle that possibly Carmilla had been wakened by the uproar at her door, and in her first panic had jumped from her bed, and hid herself in a press,* or behind a curtain, from which she could not, of course, emerge until the majordomo and his myrmidons* had withdrawn. We now recommenced our search, and began to call her name again.

It was all to no purpose. Our perplexity and agitation increased. We examined the windows, but they were secured. I implored of Carmilla, if she had concealed herself, to play this cruel trick no longer—to come out, and to end our anxieties. It was all useless.

I was by this time convinced that she was not in the room, nor in the dressing room, the door of which was still locked on this side. She could not have passed it. I was utterly puzzled. Had Carmilla discovered one of those secret passages which the old housekeeper said were known to exist in the schloss, although the tradition of their exact situation had been lost.* A little time would, no doubt, explain all—utterly perplexed as, for the present, we were.

It was past four o'clock, and I preferred passing the remaining hours of darkness in Madame's room. Daylight brought no solution of the difficulty.

The whole household, with my father at its head, was in a state of agitation next morning. Every part of the chateau was searched. The grounds were explored. Not a trace of the missing lady could be discovered. The stream was about to be dragged; my father was in distraction; what a tale to have to tell the poor girl's mother on her return. I, too, was almost beside myself, though my grief was quite of a different kind.

The morning was passed in alarm and excitement. It was now one o'clock, and still no tidings. I ran up to Carmilla's room, and found her standing at her dressing-table. I was astounded. I could not believe my eyes. She beckoned me to her with her pretty finger, in silence. Her face expressed extreme fear.

I ran to her in an ecstasy of joy; I kissed and embraced her again and again. I ran to the bell and rang it vehemently, to bring others to the spot, who might at once relieve my father's anxiety.

'Dear Carmilla, what has become of you all this time? We have been in agonies of anxiety about you,' I exclaimed. 'Where have you been? How did you come back?'

'Last night has been a night of wonders,' she said.

'For mercy's sake, explain all you can.'

'It was past two last night,' she said, 'when I went to sleep as usual in my bed, with my doors locked, that of the dressing-room, and that opening upon the gallery. My sleep was uninterrupted, and, so far as I know, dreamless; but I awoke just now on the sofa in the dressing-room there, and I found the door between the rooms open, and the other door forced. How could all this have happened without my being wakened? It must have been accompanied with a great deal of noise, and I am particularly easily wakened; and how could I have been carried out of my bed without my sleep having been interrupted, I whom the slightest stir startles?'

By this time, Madame, Mademoiselle, my father, and a number of the servants were in the room. Carmilla was, of course, overwhelmed with enquiries, congratulations, and welcomes. She had but one story to tell, and seemed the least able of all the party to suggest any way of accounting for what had happened.

My father took a turn up and down the room, thinking. I saw Carmilla's eye follow him for a moment with a sly, dark glance.

When my father had sent the servants away, Mademoiselle having gone in search of a little bottle of valerian and sal-volatile,* and there being no one now in the room with Carmilla, except my father, Madame, and myself, he came to her thoughtfully, took her hand very kindly, led her to the sofa, and sat down beside her.

'Will you forgive me, my dear, if I risk a conjecture, and ask a question?'

'Who can have a better right?' she said. 'Ask what you please, and I will tell you everything. But my story is simply one of bewilderment and darkness. I know absolutely nothing. Put any question you please. But you know, of course, the limitations mamma has placed me under?'

'Perfectly, my dear child. I need not approach the topics on which she desires our silence. Now, the marvel of last night consists in your having been removed from your bed and your room, without being wakened, and this removal's* having occurred apparently while the windows were still secured, and the two doors locked upon the inside. I will tell you my theory, and first ask you a question.'

Carmilla was leaning on her hand dejectedly; Madame and I were listening breathlessly.

'Now, my question is this. Have you ever been suspected of walking in your sleep?'

'Never, since I was very young indeed.'

'But you did walk in your sleep when you were young?'

'Yes; I know I did. I have been told so often by my old nurse.'

My father smiled and nodded.

'Well, what has happened is this. You got up in your sleep, unlocked the door, not leaving the key, as usual, in the lock, but taking it out and locking it on the outside; you again took the key out, and carried it away with you to some one of the five-and-twenty rooms on this floor, or perhaps up-stairs or down-stairs. There are so many rooms and closets, so much heavy furniture, and such accumulations of lumber, that it would require a week to search this old house thoroughly. Do you see, now, what I mean?'

'I do, but not all,' she answered.

'And how, papa, do you account for her finding herself on the sofa in the dressing-room, which we had searched so carefully?'

'She came there after you had searched it, still in her sleep, and at last awoke spontaneously, and was as much surprised to find herself where she was as any one else. I wish all mysteries were as easily and innocently explained as yours, Carmilla,' he said, laughing. 'And so we may congratulate ourselves on the certainty that the most natural explanation of the occurrence is one that involves no drugging, no tampering with locks, no burglars, or poisoners, or witches—nothing that need alarm Carmilla, or any one else, for our safety.'

Carmilla was looking charmingly. Nothing could be more beautiful than her tints. Her beauty was, I think, enhanced by that graceful languor that was peculiar to her. I think my father was silently contrasting her looks with mine, for he said:

'I wish my poor Laura was looking more like herself;' and he sighed.

So our alarms were happily ended, and Carmilla restored to her friends.

CHAPTER IX

The Doctor

As Carmilla would not hear of an attendant sleeping in her room, my father arranged that a servant should sleep outside her door, so that she could not attempt to make another such excursion without being arrested at her own door.

That night passed quietly; and next morning early, the doctor, whom my father had sent for without telling me a word about it, arrived to see me.

Madame accompanied me to the library; and there the grave little doctor, with white hair and spectacles, whom I mentioned before, was waiting to receive me.

I told him my story, and as I proceeded he grew graver and graver.

We were standing, he and I, in the recess of one of the windows, facing one another. When my statement was over, he leaned with his shoulders against the wall, and with his eyes fixed on me earnestly, with an interest in which was a dash of horror.

After a minute's reflection, he asked Madame if he could see my father.

He was sent for accordingly, and as he entered, smiling, he said, 'I dare say, doctor, you are going to tell me that I am an old fool for having brought you here; I hope I am.'

But his smile faded into shadow as the doctor, with a very grave face, beckoned him to him.

He and the doctor talked for some time in the same recess where I had just conferred with the physician. It seemed an earnest and argumentative conversation. The room is very large, and I and Madame stood together, burning with curiosity, at the further end. Not a word could we hear, however, for they spoke in a very low tone, and the deep recess of the window quite concealed the doctor from view, and very nearly my father, whose foot, arm, and shoulder only could we see; and the voices were, I suppose, all the less audible for the sort of closet which the thick wall and window formed.

After a time my father's face looked into the room; it was pale, thoughtful, and, I fancied, agitated.

'Laura, dear, come here for a moment. Madame, we shan't trouble you, the doctor says, at present.'

Accordingly I approached, for the first time a little alarmed; for, although I felt very weak, I did not feel ill; and strength, one always fancies, is a thing that may be picked up when we please.

My father held out his hand to me, as I drew near, but he was looking at the doctor, and he said:

'It certainly *is* very odd; I don't understand it quite. Laura, come here, dear; now attend to Doctor Spielsberg,* and recollect yourself.'

'You mentioned a sensation like that of two needles piercing the skin, somewhere about your neck, on the night when you experienced your first horrible dream. Is there still any soreness?'

'None at all,' I answered.

'Can you indicate with your finger about the point at which you think this occurred?'

'Very little below my throat—*here*,' I answered.

I wore a morning dress, which covered the place I pointed to.

'Now you can satisfy yourself,' said the doctor. 'You won't mind your papa's lowering your dress a very little. It is necessary, to detect a symptom of the complaint under which you have been suffering.'

I acquiesced. It was only an inch or two below the edge of my collar.

'God bless me!—so it is,' exclaimed my father, growing pale.

'You see it now with your own eyes,' said the doctor, with a gloomy triumph.

'What is it?' I exclaimed, beginning to be frightened.

'Nothing, my dear young lady, but a small blue spot, about the size of the tip of your little finger;* and now,' he continued, turning to papa, 'the question is what is best to be done?'

'Is there any danger?' I urged, in great trepidation.

'I trust not, my dear,' answered the doctor. 'I don't see why you should not recover. I don't see why you should not begin *immediately* to get better. That is the point at which the sense of strangulation begins?'

'Yes,' I answered.

'And—recollect as well as you can—the same point was a kind of centre of that thrill which you described just now, like the current of a cold stream running against you?'

'It may have been; I think it was.'

'Ay, you see?' he added, turning to my father. 'Shall I say a word to Madame?'

'Certainly,' said my father.

He called Madame to him, and said:

'I find my young friend here far from well. It won't be of any great consequence, I hope; but it will be necessary that some steps be taken, which I will explain by-and-bye; but in the meantime, Madame, you will be so good as not to let Miss Laura be alone for one moment. That is the only direction I need give for the present. It is indispensable.'

'We may rely upon your kindness, Madame, I know,' added my father.

Madame satisfied him eagerly.

'And you, dear Laura, I know you will observe the doctor's direction.'

'I shall have to ask your opinion upon another patient, whose symptoms slightly resemble those of my daughter, that have just been detailed to you—very much milder in degree, but I believe quite of the same sort. She is a young lady—our guest; but as you say you will be passing this way again this evening, you can't do better than take your supper here, and you can then see her. She does not come down till the afternoon.'

'I thank you,' said the doctor. 'I shall be with you, then, at about seven this evening.'

And then they repeated their directions to me and to Madame, and with this parting charge my father left us, and walked out with the doctor; and I saw them pacing together up and down between the road and the moat, on the grassy platform in front of the castle, evidently absorbed in earnest conversation.

The doctor did not return. I saw him mount his horse there, take his leave, and ride away eastward through the forest.

Nearly at the same time I saw the man arrive from Dranfeld* with the letters, and dismount and hand the bag to my father.

In the meantime, Madame and I were both busy, lost in conjecture as to the reasons of the singular and earnest direction which the doctor and my father had concurred in imposing. Madame, as she afterwards told me, was afraid the doctor apprehended a sudden seizure, and that, without prompt assistance, I might either lose my life in a fit, or at least be seriously hurt. This interpretation did not strike me; and I fancied, perhaps luckily for my nerves, that the arrangement was prescribed simply to secure a companion, who would prevent my taking too much exercise, or eating unripe fruit, or doing any of the fifty foolish things to which young people are supposed to be prone.

About half-an-hour after my father came in—he had a letter in his hand—and said:

'This letter had been delayed; it is from General Spielsdorf. He might have been here yesterday, he may not come till to-morrow or he may be here to-day.' He put the open letter into my hand; but he did not look pleased, as he used when a guest, especially one so much loved as the General, was coming. On the contrary, he looked as if he wished him at the bottom of the Red Sea. There was plainly something on his mind which he did not choose to divulge.

'Papa, darling, will you tell me this?' said I, suddenly laying my hand on his arm, and looking, I am sure, imploringly in his face.

'Perhaps,' he answered, smoothing my hair caressingly over my eyes.

'Does the doctor think me very ill?'

'No, dear; he thinks, if right steps are taken, you will be quite well again, at least, on the high road to a complete recovery, in a day or two,' he answered, a little drily. 'I wish our good friend, the General, had chosen any other time; that is, I wish you had been perfectly well to receive him.'

'But do tell me, papa,' I insisted, '*what* does he think is the matter with me?'

'Nothing; you must not plague me with questions,' he answered, with more irritation than I ever remember him to have displayed before; and seeing that I looked wounded, I suppose, he kissed me, and added, 'You shall know all about it in a day or two; that is, all that *I* know. In the meantime you are not to trouble your head about it.'

He turned and left the room, but came back before I had done wondering and puzzling over the oddity of all this; it was merely to say that he was going to Karnstein,* and had ordered the carriage to be ready at twelve, and that I and Madame should accompany him; he was going to see the priest who lived near those picturesque grounds, upon business, and as Carmilla had never seen them, she could follow, when she came down, with Mademoiselle, who would bring materials for what you call a pic-nic, which might be laid for us in the ruined castle.

At twelve o'clock, accordingly, I was ready, and not long after, my father, Madame, and I set out upon our projected drive. Passing the drawbridge we turn to the right, and follow the road over the steep gothic bridge, westward, to reach the deserted village and ruined castle of Karnstein. No sylvan drive can be fancied prettier. The ground breaks into gentle hills and hollows, all clothed with beautiful wood, totally destitute of the comparative formality which artificial planting and early culture and pruning impart.

The irregularities of the ground often lead the road out of its course, and cause it to wind beautifully round the sides of broken hollows and the steeper sides of the hills, among varieties of ground almost inexhaustible.

Turning one of these points, we suddenly encountered the old General,* riding towards us, attended by a mounted servant. His portmanteaus* were following in a hired wagon, such as we term a cart.

The General dismounted as we pulled up, and, after the usual greetings, was easily persuaded to accept the vacant seat in the carriage, and send his horse on with his servant to the schloss.

CHAPTER X

Bereaved

It was about ten months since we had last seen him; but that time had sufficed to make an alteration of years in his appearance. He had grown thinner; something of gloom and anxiety had taken the place of that cordial serenity which used to characterize his features. His dark blue eyes, always penetrating, now gleamed with a sterner light from under his shaggy grey eyebrows. It was not such a change as grief alone usually induces, and angrier passions seemed to have had their share in bringing it about.

We had not long resumed our drive, when the General began to talk, with his usual soldierly directness, of the bereavement, as he termed it, which he had sustained in the death of his beloved niece and ward; and he then broke out in a tone of intense bitterness and fury, inveighing against the 'hellish arts' to which she had fallen a victim, and expressing, with more exasperation than piety, his wonder that Heaven should tolerate so monstrous an indulgence of the lusts and malignity of hell.

My father, who saw at once that something very extraordinary had befallen, asked him, if not too painful to him, to detail the circumstances which he thought justified the strong terms in which he expressed himself.

'I should tell you all with pleasure,' said the General, 'but you would not believe me.'

'Why should I not?' he asked.

'Because,' he answered testily, 'you believe in nothing but what consists with your own prejudices and illusions. I remember when I was like you, but I have learned better.'

'Try me,' said my father; 'I am not such a dogmatist as you suppose. Besides which, I very well know that you generally require proof for what you believe, and am, therefore, very strongly pre-disposed to respect your conclusions.'

'You are right in supposing that I have not been led lightly into a belief in the marvellous—for what I have experienced *is* marvellous—and I have been forced by extraordinary evidence to credit that which ran counter, diametrically, to all my theories. I have been made the dupe of a preternatural conspiracy.'

Notwithstanding his professions of confidence in the General's penetration, I saw my father, at this point, glance at the General, with, as I thought, a marked suspicion of his sanity.

The General did not see it, luckily. He was looking gloomily and curiously into the glades and vistas of the woods that were opening before us.

'You are going to the Ruins of Karnstein?' he said. 'Yes, it is a lucky coincidence; do you know I was going to ask you to bring me there to inspect them. I have a special object in exploring. There is a ruined chapel, ain't there, with a great many tombs of that extinct family?'

'So there are—highly interesting,' said my father. 'I hope you are thinking of claiming the title and estates?'

My father said this gaily, but the General did not recollect the laugh, or even the smile, which courtesy exacts for a friend's joke; on the contrary, he looked grave and even fierce, ruminating on a matter that stirred his anger and horror.

'Something very different,' he said, gruffly. 'I mean to unearth some of those fine people. I hope, by God's blessing, to accomplish a pious sacrilege here, which will relieve our earth of certain monsters, and enable honest people to sleep in their beds without being assailed by murderers. I have strange things to tell you, my dear friend, such as I myself would have scouted as incredible a few months since.'

My father looked at him again, but this time not with a glance of suspicion—with an eye, rather, of keen intelligence and alarm.

'The house of Karnstein,' he said, 'has been long extinct: a hundred years at least. My dear wife was maternally descended from the Karnsteins. But the name and title have long ceased to exist. The castle is a ruin; the very village is deserted; it is fifty years since the smoke of a chimney was seen there; not a roof left.'

'Quite true. I have heard a great deal about that since I last saw you; a great deal that will astonish you. But I had better relate everything in the order in which it occurred,' said the General. 'You saw my dear ward—my child, I may call her. No creature could have been more beautiful, and only three months ago none more blooming.'

'Yes, poor thing! when I saw her last she certainly was quite lovely,' said my father. 'I was grieved and shocked more than I can tell you, my dear friend; I knew what a blow it was to you.'

He took the General's hand, and they exchanged a kind pressure. Tears gathered in the old soldier's eyes. He did not seek to conceal them. He said:

'We have been very old friends; I knew you would feel for me, childless as I am. She had become an object of very near interest to me, and repaid my care by an affection that cheered my home and made my life happy. That is all gone. The years that remain to me on earth may not be very long; but by God's mercy I hope to accomplish a service to mankind before I die, and to subserve* the vengeance of Heaven upon the fiends who have murdered my poor child in the spring of her hopes and beauty!'

'You said, just now, that you intended relating everything as it occurred,' said my father. 'Pray do; I assure you that it is not mere curiosity that prompts me.'

By this time we had reached the point at which the Drunstall* road, by which the General had come, diverges from the road which we were travelling to Karnstein.

'How far is it to the ruins?' enquired the General, looking anxiously forward.

'About half a league,' answered my father. 'Pray let us hear the story you were so good as to promise.'

CHAPTER XI

The Story

'WITH all my heart,' said the General, with an effort; and after a short pause in which to arrange his subject, he commenced one of the strangest narratives I had ever heard.

'My dear child was looking forward with great pleasure to the visit you had been so good as to arrange for her to your charming daughter.' Here he made me a gallant but melancholy bow. 'In the meantime we had an invitation to my old friend the Count Carlsfeld, whose schloss is about six leagues to the other side of Karnstein. It was to attend the series of fêtes which, you remember, were given by him in honour of his illustrious visitor, the Grand Duke Charles.'

'Yes; and very splendid, I believe, they were,' said my father.

'Princely! But then his hospitalities are quite regal. He has Aladdin's lamp.* The night from which my sorrow dates was devoted to a magnificent masquerade. The grounds were thrown open, the trees hung with coloured lamps. There was such a display of fireworks as Paris itself has never witnessed. And such music—music, you know, is my weakness—such ravishing music! The finest instrumental band, perhaps, in the world, and the finest singers who could be collected from all the great operas in Europe. As you wandered through these fantastically illuminated grounds, the moon-lighted chateau throwing a rosy light from its long rows of windows, you would suddenly hear these ravishing voices stealing from the silence of some grove, or rising from boats upon the lake. I felt myself, as I looked and listened, carried back into the romance and poetry of my early youth.

'When the fireworks were ended, and the ball beginning, we returned to the noble suite of rooms that were thrown open to the dancers. A masked ball, you know, is a beautiful sight; but so brilliant a spectacle of the kind I never saw before.

'It was a very aristocratic assembly. I was myself almost the only "nobody" present.

'My dear child was looking quite beautiful. She wore no mask. Her excitement and delight added an unspeakable charm to her features, always lovely. I remarked a young lady, dressed magnificently, but wearing a mask, who appeared to me to be observing my ward with extraordinary interest. I had seen her, earlier in the evening, in the great hall, and again, for a few minutes, walking near us, on the terrace under the castle windows, similarly employed. A lady, also masked, richly and gravely dressed, and with a stately air, like a person of rank, accompanied her as a chaperon. Had the young lady not worn a mask, I could, of course, have been much more certain upon the question whether she was really watching my poor darling. I am now well assured that she was.

'We were now in one of the *salons*. My poor dear child had been dancing, and was resting a little in one of the chairs near the door; I was standing near. The two ladies I have mentioned had approached, and the younger took the chair next my ward; while her companion stood beside me, and for a little time addressed herself, in a low tone, to her charge.

'Availing herself of the privilege of her mask, she turned to me, and in the tone of an old friend, and calling me by my name, opened a conversation with me, which piqued my curiosity a good deal. She referred to many scenes where she had met me—at Court, and at distinguished houses. She alluded to little incidents which I had long ceased to think of, but which, I found, had only lain in abeyance in my memory, for they instantly started into life at her touch.

'I became more and more curious to ascertain who she was, every moment. She parried my attempts to discover very adroitly and pleasantly. The knowledge she showed of many passages in my life seemed to me all but unaccountable; and she appeared to take a not unnatural pleasure in foiling my curiosity, and in seeing me flounder, in my eager perplexity, from one conjecture to another.

'In the meantime the young lady, whom her mother called by the odd name of Millarca, when she once or twice addressed her, had, with the same ease and grace, got into conversation with my ward.

'She introduced herself by saying that her mother was a very old acquaintance of mine. She spoke of the agreeable audacity which a mask rendered practicable; she talked like a friend; she admired her dress, and insinuated very prettily her admiration of her beauty. She amused her with laughing criticisms upon the people who crowded the ball-room, and laughed at my poor child's fun. She was very witty and lively when she pleased, and after a time they had grown very good friends, and the young stranger lowered her mask, displaying a remarkably beautiful face. I had never seen it before, neither had my dear child. But though it was new to us, the features were so engaging, as well as lovely, that it was impossible not to feel the attraction powerfully. My poor girl did so. I never saw anyone more taken with another at first sight, unless, indeed, it was the stranger herself, who seemed quite to have lost her heart to her.

'In the meantime, availing myself of the license of a masquerade, I put not a few questions to the elder lady.

'"You have puzzled me utterly," I said, laughing. "Is that not enough? won't you, now, consent to stand on equal terms, and do me the kindness to remove your mask?"

'"Can any request be more unreasonable?" she replied. "Ask a lady to yield an advantage! Beside, how do you know you should recognize me? Years make changes."

'"As you see," I said, with a bow, and, I suppose, a rather melancholy little laugh.

'"As philosophers tell us," she said; "and how do you know that a sight of my face would help you?"

'"I should take chance for that," I answered. "It is vain trying to make yourself out an old woman; your figure betrays you."

'"Years, nevertheless, have passed since I saw you, rather since you saw me, for that is what I am considering. Millarca, there, is my daughter; I cannot then be young, even in the opinion of people whom time has taught to be indulgent, and I may not like to be compared with what you remember me.* You have no mask to remove. You can offer me nothing in exchange."

'"My petition is to your pity, to remove it."

'"And mine to yours, to let it stay where it is," she replied.

'"Well, then, at least you will tell me whether you are French or German; you speak both languages so perfectly."

'"I don't think I shall tell you that, General; you intend a surprise, and are meditating the particular point of attack."

'"At all events, you won't deny this," I said, "that being honoured by your permission to converse, I ought to know how to address you. Shall I say Madame la Comtesse?"

'She laughed, and she would, no doubt, have met me with another evasion—if, indeed, I can treat any occurrence in an interview every circumstance of which was pre-arranged, as I now believe, with the profoundest cunning, as liable to be modified by accident.

'"As to that," she began; but she was interrupted, almost as she opened her lips, by a gentleman, dressed in black, who looked particularly elegant and distinguished, with this drawback, that his face was the most deadly pale I ever saw, except in death. He was in no masquerade—in the plain evening dress of a gentleman; and he said, without a smile, but with a courtly and unusually low bow:—

'"Will Madame the Countess permit me to say a very few words which may interest her?"

'The lady turned quickly to him, and touched her lip in token of silence; she then said to me, "Keep my place for me, General; I shall return when I have said a few words."

'And with this injunction, playfully given, she walked a little aside with the gentleman in black, and talked for some minutes, apparently very earnestly. They then walked away slowly together in the crowd, and I lost them for some minutes.

'I spent the interval in cudgelling my brains for a conjecture as to the identity of the lady who seemed to remember me so kindly, and I was thinking of turning about and joining in the conversation between my pretty ward and the Countess's daughter, and trying whether, by the time she returned, I might not have a surprise in store for her, by having her name, title, chateau, and estates at my fingers' ends. But at this moment she returned, accompanied by the pale man in black, who said:

'"I shall return and inform Madame la Comtesse when her carriage is at the door."

'He withdrew with a bow.'

CHAPTER XII

A Petition

'"THEN we are to lose Madame the Countess, but I hope only for a few hours," I said, with a low bow.

'"It may be that only, or it may be a few weeks. It was very unlucky his speaking to me just now as he did. Do you now know me?"

'I assured her I did not.

'"You shall know me," she said, "but not at present. We are older and better friends than, perhaps, you suspect. I cannot yet declare myself. I shall in three weeks pass your beautiful schloss, about which I have been making enquiries. I shall then look in upon you for an hour or two, and renew a friendship which I never think of without a thousand pleasant recollections. This moment a piece of news has reached me like a thunderbolt. I must set out now, and travel by a devious* route, nearly a hundred miles, with all the dispatch I can possibly make. My perplexities multiply. I am only deterred by the compulsory reserve I practise as to my name from making a very singular request of you. My poor child has not quite recovered her strength. Her horse fell with her, at a hunt which she had ridden out to witness, her nerves have not yet recovered the shock, and our physician says that she must on no account exert herself for some time to come. We came here, in consequence, by very easy stages—hardly six leagues a day. I must now travel day and night, on a mission of life and death—a mission the critical and momentous nature of which I shall be able to explain to you when we meet, as I hope we shall, in a few weeks, without the necessity of any concealment."

'She went on to make her petition, and it was in the tone of a person from whom such a request amounted to conferring, rather than seeking a favour. This was only in manner, and, as it seemed, quite unconsciously. Than the terms in which it was expressed, nothing could be more deprecatory. It was simply that I would consent to take charge of her daughter during her absence.

'This was, all things considered, a strange, not to say, an audacious request. She in some sort disarmed me, by stating and admitting everything that could be urged against it, and throwing herself entirely upon my chivalry. At the same moment, by a fatality that seems to have predetermined all that happened, my poor child came to my side, and, in an undertone, besought me to invite her new friend, Millarca, to pay us a visit. She had just been sounding her, and thought, if her mamma would allow her, she would like it extremely.

'At another time I should have told her to wait a little, until, at least, we knew who they were. But I had not a moment to think in. The two ladies assailed me together, and I must confess the refined and beautiful face of the young lady, about which there was something extremely engaging, as well as the elegance and fire of high birth, determined me; and, quite overpowered, I submitted, and undertook, too easily, the care of the young lady, whom her mother called Millarca.

'The Countess beckoned to her daughter, who listened with grave attention while she told her, in general terms, how suddenly and peremptorily she had been summoned, and also of the arrangement she had made for her under my care, adding that I was one of her earliest and most valued friends.

'I made, of course, such speeches as the case seemed to call for, and found myself, on reflection, in a position which I did not half like.

'The gentleman in black returned, and very ceremoniously conducted the lady from the room.

'The demeanor of this gentleman was such as to impress me with the conviction that the Countess was a lady of very much more importance than her modest title alone might have led me to assume.

'Her last charge to me was that no attempt was to be made to learn more about her than I might have already guessed, until her return. Our distinguished host, whose guest she was, knew her reasons. "But here," she said, "neither I nor my daughter could safely remain for more than a day. I removed my mask imprudently for a moment, about an hour ago, and, too late, I fancied you saw me. So I resolved to seek an opportunity of talking a little to you. Had I found that you *had* seen me, I should have thrown myself on your high sense of honour to keep my secret for some weeks. As it is, I am satisfied that you did not see me; but if you now *suspect*, or, on reflection, *should* suspect, who I am,

I commit myself, in like manner, entirely to your honour. My daughter will observe the same secresy,* and I well know that you will, from time to time, remind her, lest she should thoughtlessly disclose it."

'She whispered a few words to her daughter, kissed her hurriedly twice, and went away, accompanied by the pale gentleman in black, and disappeared in the crowd.

'"In the next room," said Millarca, "there is a window that looks upon the hall-door. I should like to see the last of mamma, and to kiss my hand to her."

'We assented, of course, and accompanied her to the window. We looked out, and saw a handsome old-fashioned carriage, with a troop of couriers* and footmen. We saw the slim figure of the pale gentleman in black, as he held a thick velvet cloak, and placed it about her shoulders and threw the hood over her head. She nodded to him, and just touched his hand with hers. He bowed low repeatedly as the door closed, and the carriage began to move.

'"She is gone," said Millarca, with a sigh.

'"She is gone," I repeated to myself, for the first time—in the hurried moments that had elapsed since my consent—reflecting upon the folly of my act.

'"She did not look up," said the young lady, plaintively.

'"The Countess had taken off her mask, perhaps, and did not care to show her face," I said; "and she could not know that you were in the window."

'She sighed, and looked in my face. She was so beautiful that I relented. I was sorry I had for a moment repented of my hospitality, and I determined to make her amends for the unavowed churlishness of my reception.

'The young lady, replacing her mask, joined my ward in persuading me to return to the grounds, where the concert was soon to be renewed. We did so, and walked up and down the terrace that lies under the castle windows. Millarca became very intimate with us, and amused us with lively descriptions and stories of most of the great people whom we saw upon the terrace. I liked her more and more every minute. Her gossip, without being ill-natured, was extremely diverting to me, who had been so long out of the great world. I thought what life she would give to our sometimes lonely evenings at home.

'This ball was not over until the morning sun had almost reached the horizon. It pleased the Grand Duke to dance till then, so loyal people could not go away, or think of bed.

'We had just got through a crowded saloon, when my ward asked me what had become of Millarca. I thought she had been by her side, and she fancied she was by mine. The fact was, we had lost her.

'All my efforts to find her were vain. I feared that she had mistaken, in the confusion of a momentary separation from us, other people for her new friends, and had, possibly, pursued and lost them in the extensive grounds which were thrown open to us.

'Now, in its full force, I recognized a new folly in my having undertaken the charge of a young lady without so much as knowing her name; and fettered as I was by promises, of the reasons for imposing which I knew nothing, I could not even point my inquiries by saying that the missing young lady was the daughter of the Countess who had taken her departure a few hours before.

'Morning broke. It was clear daylight before I gave up my search. It was not till near two o'clock next day that we heard anything of my missing charge.

'At about that time a servant knocked at my niece's door, to say that he had been earnestly requested by a young lady, who appeared to be in great distress, to make out where she could find the General Baron Spielsdorf and the young lady his daughter, in whose charge she had been left by her mother.

'There could be no doubt, notwithstanding the slight inaccuracy, that our young friend had turned up; and so she had. Would to heaven we had lost her!

'She told my poor child a story to account for her having failed to recover us for so long. Very late, she said, she had got to the housekeeper's bedroom in despair of finding us, and had then fallen into a deep sleep which, long as it was, had hardly sufficed to recruit her strength after the fatigues of the ball.

'That day Millarca came home with us. I was only too happy, after all, to have secured so charming a companion for my dear girl.

CHAPTER XIII

The Wood-Man

'THERE soon, however, appeared some drawbacks. In the first place, Millarca complained of extreme languor—the weakness that remained after her late illness—and she never emerged from her room till the afternoon was pretty far advanced. In the next place, it was accidentally discovered, although she always locked her door on the inside, and never disturbed the key from its place till she admitted the maid to assist at her toilet, that she was undoubtedly sometimes absent from her room in the very early morning, and at various times later in the day, before she wished it to be understood that she was stirring. She was repeatedly seen from the windows of the schloss, in the first faint grey of the morning, walking through the trees, in an easterly direction, and looking like a person in a trance. This convinced me that she walked in her sleep. But this hypothesis did not solve the puzzle. How did she pass out from her room, leaving the door locked on the inside? How did she escape from the house without unbarring door or window?

'In the midst of my perplexities, an anxiety of a far more urgent kind presented itself.

'My dear child began to lose her looks and health, and that in a manner so mysterious, and even horrible, that I became thoroughly frightened.

'She was at first visited by appalling dreams; then, as she fancied, by a spectre, sometimes resembling Millarca, sometimes in the shape of a beast, indistinctly seen, walking round the foot of her bed, from side to side. Lastly came sensations. One, not unpleasant, but very peculiar, she said, resembled the flow of an icy stream against her breast. At a later time, she felt something like a pair of large needles pierce her, a little below the throat, with a very sharp pain. A few nights after, followed a gradual and convulsive sense of strangulation; then came unconsciousness.'*

I could hear distinctly every word the kind old General was saying, because by this time we were driving upon the short grass that spreads on either side of the road as you approach the roofless village which had not shown the smoke of a chimney for more than half a century.

You may guess how strangely I felt as I heard my own symptoms so exactly described in those which had been experienced by the poor girl who, but for the catastrophe which followed, would have been at that moment a visitor at my father's chateau. You may suppose, also, how I felt as I heard him detail habits and mysterious peculiarities which were, in fact, those of our beautiful guest, Carmilla!

A vista opened in the forest; we were on a sudden under the chimneys and gables of the ruined village, and the towers and battlements of the dismantled castle, round which gigantic trees are grouped, overhung us from a slight eminence.

In a frightened dream I got down from the carriage, and in silence, for we had each abundant matter for thinking; we soon mounted the ascent, and were among the spacious chambers, winding stairs, and dark corridors of the castle.

'And this was once the palatial residence of the Karnsteins!' said the old General at length, as from a great window he looked out across the village, and saw the wide, undulating expanse of forest. 'It was a bad family, and here its bloodstained annals were written,' he continued. 'It is hard that they should, after death, continue to plague the human race with their atrocious lusts. That is the chapel of the Karnsteins, down there.'

He pointed down to the grey walls of the gothic building, partly visible through the foliage, a little way down the steep. 'And I hear the axe of a woodman,' he added, 'busy among the trees that surround it; he possibly may give us the information of which I am in search, and point out the grave of Mircalla, Countess of Karnstein. These rustics preserve the local traditions of great families, whose stories die out among the rich and titled so soon as the families themselves become extinct.'

'We have a portrait, at home, of Mircalla, the Countess Karnstein; should you like to see it?' asked my father.

'Time enough, dear friend,' replied the General. 'I believe that I have seen the original; and one motive which has led me to you earlier than I at first intended, was to explore the chapel which we are now approaching.'

'What! see the Countess Mircalla,' exclaimed my father; 'why, she has been dead more than a century!'

'Not so dead as you fancy, I am told,' answered the General.

'I confess, General, you puzzle me utterly,' replied my father, looking at him, I fancied, for a moment with a return of the suspicion I detected before. But although there was anger and detestation, at times, in the old General's manner, there was nothing flighty.

'There remains to me,' he said, as we passed under the heavy arch of the gothic church—for its dimensions would have justified its being so styled—'but one object which can interest me during the few years that remain to me on earth, and that is to wreak on her the vengeance which, I thank God, may still be accomplished by a mortal arm.'

'What vengeance can you mean?' asked my father, in increasing amazement.

'I mean, to decapitate the monster,' he answered, with a fierce flush, and a stamp that echoed mournfully through the hollow ruin, and his clenched hand was at the same moment raised, as if it grasped the handle of an axe, while he shook it ferociously in the air.

'What?' exclaimed my father, more than ever bewildered.

'To strike her head off.'

'Cut her head off!'

'Aye, with a hatchet, with a spade, or with anything that can cleave through her murderous throat. You shall hear,' he answered, trembling with rage. And hurrying forward he said:

'That beam will answer for a seat; your dear child is fatigued; let her be seated, and I will, in a few sentences, close my dreadful story.'

The squared block of wood, which lay on the grass-grown pavement of the chapel, formed a bench on which I was very glad to seat myself, and in the meantime the General called to the woodman, who had been removing some boughs which leaned upon the old walls; and, axe in hand, the hardy old fellow stood before us.

He could not tell us anything of these monuments; but there was an old man, he said, a ranger of this forest, at present sojourning in the house of the priest, about two miles away, who could point out every monument of the old Karnstein family; and, for a trifle, he undertook to bring him back with him, if we would lend him one of our horses, in little more than half an hour.

'Have you been long employed about this forest?' asked my father of the old man.

'I have been a woodman here,' he answered in his *patois*,* 'under the forester, all my days; so has my father before me, and so on, as many generations as I can count up. I could show you the very house, in the village here, in which my ancestors lived.'

'How came the village to be deserted?' asked the General.

'It was troubled by *revenants*,* Sir; several were tracked to their graves, there detected by the usual tests,* and extinguished in the usual way, by decapitation, by the stake, and by burning; but not until many of the villagers were killed.

'But after all these proceedings according to law,' he continued—'so many graves opened, and so many vampires deprived of their horrible animation—the village was not relieved. But a Moravian* nobleman, who happened to be travelling this way, heard how matters were, and being skilled—as many people are in his country—in such affairs, he offered to deliver the village from its tormentor. He did so thus: There being a bright moon that night, he ascended, shortly after sunset, the towers of the chapel here, from whence he could distinctly see the churchyard beneath him; you can see it from that window. From this point he watched until he saw the vampire come out of his grave, and place near it the linen clothes in which he had been folded, and then glide away towards the village to plague its inhabitants.

'The stranger, having seen all this, came down from the steeple, took the linen wrappings of the vampire, and carried them up to the top of the tower, which he again mounted. When the vampire returned from his prowlings and missed his clothes, he cried furiously to the Moravian, whom he saw at the summit of the tower, and who, in reply, beckoned him to ascend and take them. Whereupon the vampire, accepting his invitation, began to climb the steeple, and so soon as he had reached the battlements, the Moravian, with a stroke of his sword, clove his skull in twain, hurling him down to the churchyard, whither, descending by the winding stairs, the stranger followed and cut his head off, and next day delivered it and the body to the villagers, who duly impaled and burnt them.*

'This Moravian nobleman had authority from the then head of the family to remove the tomb of Mircalla, Countess Karnstein, which he did effectually, so that in a little while its site was quite forgotten.'

'Can you point out where it stood?' asked the General, eagerly.

The forester shook his head, and smiled.

'Not a soul living could tell you that now,' he said; 'besides, they say her body was removed; but no one is sure of that either.'

Having thus spoken, as time pressed, he dropped his axe and departed, leaving us to hear the remainder of the General's strange story.

CHAPTER XIV

The Meeting

'My beloved child,' he resumed, 'was now growing rapidly worse. The physician who attended her had failed to produce the slightest impression upon her disease, for such I then supposed it to be. He saw my alarm, and suggested a consultation. I called in an abler physician, from Gratz. Several days elapsed before he arrived. He was a good and pious, as well as a learned man. Having seen my poor ward together, they withdrew to my library to confer and discuss. I, from the adjoining room, where I awaited their summons, heard these two gentlemen's voices raised in something sharper than a strictly philosophical discussion. I knocked at the door and entered. I found the old physician from Gratz maintaining his theory. His rival was combating it with undisguised ridicule, accompanied with bursts of laughter. This unseemly manifestation subsided and the altercation ended on my entrance.

'"Sir," said my first physician, "my learned brother seems to think that you want a conjuror, and not a doctor."

'"Pardon me," said the old physician from Gratz, looking displeased, "I shall state my own view of the case in my own way another time. I grieve, Monsieur le General, that by my skill and science I can be of no use. Before I go I shall do myself the honour to suggest something to you."

'He seemed thoughtful, and sat down at a table and began to write. Profoundly disappointed, I made my bow, and as I turned to go the other doctor pointed over his shoulder to his companion who was writing, and then, with a shrug, significantly touched his forehead.

'This consultation, then, left me precisely where I was. I walked out into the grounds, all but distracted. The doctor from Gratz, in ten or fifteen minutes, overtook me. He apologized for having followed me, but said that he could not conscientiously take his leave without a few words more. He told me that he could not be mistaken; no natural disease exhibited the same symptoms; and that death was already very near. There remained, however, a day, or possibly two, of life. If the fatal seizure were at once arrested, with great care and skill her strength might possibly return. But all hung now upon the confines of the irrevocable. One more assault might extinguish the last spark of vitality which is, every moment, ready to die.

'"And what is the nature of the seizure you speak of?" I entreated.

'"I have stated all fully in this note, which I place in your hands upon the distinct condition that you send for the nearest clergyman, and open my letter in his presence, and on no account read it till he is with you; you would despise it else, and it is a matter of life and death. Should the priest fail you, then, indeed, you may read it."

'He asked me, before taking his leave finally, whether I would wish to see a man curiously learned upon the very subject, which, after I had read his letter, would probably interest me above all others, and he urged me earnestly to invite him to visit him there; and so took his leave.

'The ecclesiastic was absent, and I read the letter by myself. At another time, or in another case, it might have excited my ridicule. But into what quackeries will not people rush for a last chance, where all accustomed means have failed, and the life of a beloved object is at stake?

'Nothing, you will say, could be more absurd than the learned man's letter. It was monstrous enough to have consigned him to a madhouse. He said that the patient was suffering from the visits of a vampire! The punctures which she described as having occurred near the throat, were, he insisted, the insertion of those two long, thin, and sharp teeth which, it is well known, are peculiar to vampires; and there could be no doubt, he added, as to the well-defined presence of the small livid mark which all concurred in describing as that induced by the demon's lips, and every symptom described by the sufferer was in exact conformity with those recorded in every case of a similar visitation.

'Being myself wholly sceptical as to the existence of any such portent as the vampire, the supernatural theory of the good doctor furnished, in my opinion, but another instance of learning and intelligence oddly associated with some one hallucination. I was so miserable, however, that, rather than try nothing, I acted upon the instructions of the letter.

'I concealed myself in the dark dressing-room, that opened upon the poor patient's room, in which a candle was burning, and watched there till she was fast asleep. I stood at the door, peeping through the small crevice, my sword laid on the table beside me, as my directions prescribed, until, a little after one, I saw a large black object, very ill-defined, crawl, as it seemed to me, over the foot of the bed, and swiftly spread itself up to the poor girl's throat, where it swelled, in a moment, into a great, palpitating mass. For a few moments I had stood petrified. I now sprang forward, with my sword in my hand. The black creature suddenly contracted toward the foot of the bed, glided over it, and, standing on the floor about a yard below the foot of the bed, with a glare of skulking ferocity and horror fixed on me, I saw

Millarca. Speculating I know not what, I struck at her instantly with my sword; but I saw her standing near the door, unscathed. Horrified, I pursued, and struck again. She was gone; and my sword flew to shivers against the door.

'I can't describe to you all that passed on that horrible night. The whole house was up and stirring. The spectre Millarca was gone. But her victim was sinking fast, and before the morning dawned, she died.'

The old General was agitated. We did not speak to him. My father walked to some little distance, and began reading the inscriptions on the tombstones; and thus occupied, he strolled into the door of a side-chapel to prosecute his researches. The General leaned against the wall, dried his eyes, and sighed heavily. I was relieved on hearing the voices of Carmilla and Madame, who were at that moment approaching. The voices died away.

In this solitude, having just listened to so strange a story, connected, as it was, with the great and titled dead, whose monuments were moldering among the dust and ivy round us, and every incident of which bore so awfully upon my own mysterious case—in this haunted spot, darkened by the towering foliage that rose on every side, dense and high above its noiseless walls—a horror began to steal over me, and my heart sank as I thought that my friends were, after all, not about to enter and disturb this triste* and ominous scene.

The old General's eyes were fixed on the ground, as he leaned with his hand upon the basement* of a shattered monument.

Under a narrow, arched doorway, surmounted by one of those demoniacal grotesques in which the cynical and ghastly fancy of old Gothic carving delights, I saw very gladly the beautiful face and figure of Carmilla enter the shadowy chapel.

I was just about to rise and speak, and nodded smiling, in answer to her peculiarly engaging smile; when with a cry, the old man by my side caught up the woodman's hatchet, and started forward. On seeing him a brutalized change came over her features. It was an instantaneous and horrible transformation, as she made a crouching step backwards. Before I could utter a scream, he struck at her with all his force, but she dived under his blow, and unscathed, caught him in her tiny grasp* by the wrist. He struggled for a moment to release his arm, but his hand opened, the axe fell to the ground, and the girl was gone.

He staggered against the wall. His grey hair stood upon his head, and a moisture shone over his face, as if he were at the point of death.

The frightful scene had passed in a moment. The first thing I recollect after, is Madame standing before me, and impatiently repeating again and again, the question, 'Where is Mademoiselle Carmilla?'

I answered at length, 'I don't know—I can't tell—she went there,' and I pointed to the door through which Madame had just entered; 'only a minute or two since.'

'But I have been standing there, in the passage, ever since Mademoiselle Carmilla entered; and she did not return.'

She then began to call 'Carmilla,' through every door and passage and from the windows, but no answer came.

'She called herself Carmilla?' asked the General, still agitated.

'Carmilla, yes,' I answered.

'Aye,' he said; 'that is Millarca. That is the same person who long ago was called Mircalla, Countess Karnstein. Depart from this accursed ground, my poor child, as quickly as you can. Drive to the clergyman's house, and stay there till we come. Begone! May you never behold Carmilla more; you will not find her here.'

CHAPTER XV

Ordeal and Execution

As he spoke one of the strangest looking men I ever beheld, entered the chapel at the door through which Carmilla had made her entrance and her exit. He was tall, narrow-chested, stooping, with high shoulders, and dressed in black. His face was brown and dried in with deep furrows; he wore an oddly-shaped hat with a broad leaf.* His hair, long and grizzled, hung on his shoulders. He wore a pair of gold spectacles, and walked slowly, with an odd shambling gait, with his face sometimes turned up to the sky, and sometimes bowed down toward the ground, seemed to wear a perpetual smile; his long thin arms were swinging, and his lank hands, in old black gloves ever so much too wide for them, waving and gesticulating in utter abstraction.

'The very man!' exclaimed the General, advancing with manifest delight. 'My dear Baron, how happy I am to see you, I had no hope of meeting you so soon.' He signed to my father, who had by this time returned, and leading the fantastic old gentleman, whom he called the Baron to meet him. He introduced him formally, and they at once entered into earnest conversation. The stranger took a roll of paper from his pocket, and spread it on the worn surface of a tomb that stood by. He had a pencil-case in his fingers, with which he traced imaginary lines from point to point on the paper, which from their often glancing from it, together, at certain points of the building, I concluded to be a plan of the chapel. He accompanied, what I may term, his lecture, with occasional readings from a dirty little book, whose yellow leaves were closely written over.

They sauntered together down the side aisle, opposite to the spot where I was standing, conversing as they went; then they begun measuring distances by paces, and finally they all stood together, facing a piece of the side-wall, which they began to examine with great minuteness; pulling off the ivy that clung over it, and rapping the plaster with the ends of their sticks, scraping here, and knocking there. At length they ascertained the existence of a broad marble tablet, with letters carved in relief upon it.

With the assistance of the woodman, who soon returned, a monumental inscription, and carved escutcheon,* were disclosed. They proved to be those of the long lost monument of Mircalla, Countess Karnstein.

The old General, though not I fear given to the praying mood, raised his hands and eyes to heaven, in mute thanksgiving for some moments.

'To-morrow,' I heard him say; 'the commissioner will be here, and the Inquisition will be held according to law.'*

Then turning to the old man with the gold spectacles, whom I have described, he shook him warmly by both hands and said:

'Baron, how can I thank you? How can we all thank you? You will have delivered this region from a plague that has scourged its inhabitants for more than a century. The horrible enemy, thank God, is at last tracked.'

My father led the stranger aside, and the General followed. I knew that he had led them out of hearing, that he might relate my case, and I saw them glance often quickly at me, as the discussion proceeded.

My father came to me, kissed me again and again, and leading me from the chapel, said:

'It is time to return, but before we go home, we must add to our party the good priest, who lives but a little way from this; and persuade him to accompany us to the schloss.'

In this quest we were successful: and I was glad, being unspeakably fatigued when we reached home. But my satisfaction was changed to dismay, on discovering that there were no tidings of Carmilla. Of the scene that had occurred in the ruined chapel, no explanation was offered to me, and it was clear that it was a secret which my father for the present determined to keep from me.

The sinister absence of Carmilla made the remembrance of the scene more horrible to me. The arrangements for the night were singular. Two servants, and Madame were to sit up in my room that night; and the ecclesiastic with my father kept watch in the adjoining dressing-room.

The priest had performed certain solemn rites that night, the purport of which I did not understand any more than I comprehended the reason of this extraordinary precaution taken for my safety during sleep.

I saw all clearly a few days later.

The disappearance of Carmilla was followed by the discontinuance of my nightly sufferings.

You have heard, no doubt, of the appalling superstition that prevails in upper and lower Styria, in Moravia, Silesia, in Turkish Servia,* in Poland, even in Russia; the superstition, so we must call it, of the Vampire.

If human testimony, taken with every care and solemnity, judicially, before commissions innumerable, each consisting of many members, all chosen for integrity and intelligence, and constituting reports more voluminous perhaps than exist upon any one other class of cases, is worth anything, it is difficult to deny, or even to doubt the existence of such a phenomenon as the Vampire.*

For my part I have heard no theory by which to explain what I myself have witnessed and experienced, other than that supplied by the ancient and well-attested belief of the country.

The next day the formal proceedings took place in the Chapel of Karnstein. The grave of the Countess Mircalla was opened; and the General and my father recognized each his perfidious and beautiful guest, in the face now disclosed to view. The features, though a hundred and fifty years had passed since her funeral, were tinted with the warmth of life. Her eyes were open; no cadaverous* smell exhaled from the coffin. The two medical men, one officially present, the other on the part of the promoter of the enquiry, attested the marvellous fact, that there was a faint but appreciable respiration, and a corresponding action of the heart. The limbs were perfectly flexible, the flesh elastic; and the leaden coffin floated with blood, in which to a depth of seven inches, the body lay immersed.* Here then, were all the admitted signs and proofs of vampirism. The body, therefore, in accordance with the ancient practice, was raised, and a sharp stake driven through the heart of the vampire, who uttered a piercing shriek at the moment, in all respects such as might escape from a living person in the last agony. Then the head was struck off, and a torrent of blood flowed from the severed neck. The body and head were next placed on a pile of wood, and reduced to ashes, which were thrown upon the river and borne away, and that territory has never since been plagued by the visits of a vampire.

My father has a copy of the report of the Imperial Commission, with the signatures of all who were present at these proceedings, attached in verification of the statement. It is from this official paper that I have summarized my account of this last shocking scene.

CHAPTER XVI

Conclusion

I WRITE all this you suppose with composure. But far from it; I cannot think of it without agitation. Nothing but your earnest desire so repeatedly expressed, could have induced me to sit down to a task that has unstrung my nerves for months to come, and reinduced a shadow of the unspeakable horror which years after my deliverance continued to make my days and nights dreadful, and solitude insupportably terrific.*

Let me add a word or two about that quaint Baron Vordenburg, to whose curious lore we were indebted for the discovery of the Countess Mircalla's grave.

He had taken up his abode in Gratz, where, living upon a mere pittance, which was all that remained to him of the once princely estates of his family, in Upper Styria, he devoted himself to the minute and laborious investigation of the marvellously authenticated tradition of Vampirism. He had at his finger's ends* all the great and little works upon the subject. 'Magia Posthuma,' 'Phlegon de Mirabilibus,' 'Augustinus de curâ pro Mortuis,' 'Philosophicæ et Christianæ

Cogitationes de Vampiris,' by John Christofer Herenberg;* and a thousand others, among which I remember only a few of those which he lent to my father. He had a voluminous digest of all the judicial cases, from which he had extracted a system of principles that appear to govern—some always, and others occasionally only—the condition of the vampire. I may mention, in passing, that the deadly pallor attributed to that sort of *revenants*, is a mere melodramatic fiction. They present, in the grave, and when they show themselves in human society, the appearance of healthy life. When disclosed to light in their coffins, they exhibit all the symptoms that are enumerated as those which proved the vampire-life of the long-dead Countess Karnstein. How they escape from their graves and return to them for certain hours every day, without displacing the clay or leaving any trace of disturbance in the state of the coffin or the cerements, has always been admitted to be utterly inexplicable.* The amphibious existence of the vampire is sustained by daily renewed slumber in the grave. Its horrible lust for living blood supplies the vigour of its waking existence. The vampire is prone to be fascinated with an engrossing vehemence, resembling the passion of love, by particular persons. In pursuit of these it will exercise inexhaustible patience and stratagem, for access to a particular object may be obstructed in a hundred ways. It will never desist until it has satiated its passion, and drained the very life of its coveted victim. But it will, in these cases, husband and protract its murderous enjoyment with the refinement of an epicure, and heighten it by the gradual approaches of an artful courtship. In these cases it seems to yearn for something like sympathy and consent. In ordinary ones it goes direct to its object, overpowers with violence, and strangles and exhausts often at a single feast.

The vampire is, apparently, subject, in certain situations, to special conditions. In the particular instance of which I have given you a relation, Mircalla seemed to be limited to a name which, if not her real one, should at least reproduce, without the omission or addition of a single letter, those, as we say, anagrammatically,* which compose it. *Carmilla* did this; so did *Millarca*.

My father related to the Baron Vordenburg, who remained with us for two or three weeks after the expulsion of Carmilla, the story about the Moravian nobleman and the vampire at Karnstein churchyard, and then he asked the Baron how he had discovered the exact position of the long-concealed tomb of the Countess Mircalla? The Baron's grotesque features puckered up into a mysterious smile; he looked down, still smiling on his worn spectacle-case, and fumbled with it. Then looking up, he said:

'I have many journals, and other papers, written by that remarkable man; the most curious among them is one treating of the visit of which you speak, to Karnstein. The tradition, of course, discolours and distorts a little. He might have been termed a Moravian nobleman, for he had changed his abode to that territory, and was, beside, a noble. But he was, in truth, a native of Upper Styria. It is enough to say that in very early youth he had been a passionate and favored lover of the beautiful Mircalla, Countess Karnstein. Her early death plunged him into inconsolable grief. It is the nature of vampires to increase and multiply, but according to an ascertained* and ghostly law.

'Assume, at starting, a territory perfectly free from that pest. How does it begin, and how does it multiply itself? I will tell you. A person, more or less wicked, puts an end to himself. A suicide, under certain circumstances, becomes a vampire.* That spectre visits living people in their slumbers; *they* die, and almost invariably, in the grave, develope* into vampires. This happened in the case of the beautiful Mircalla, who was haunted by one of those demons. My ancestor, Vordenburg, whose title I still bear, soon discovered this, and in the course of the studies to which he devoted himself, learned a great deal more.

'Among other things, he concluded that suspicion of vampirism would probably fall, sooner or later, upon the dead Countess, who in life had been his idol. He conceived a horror, be she what she might, of her remains being profaned by the outrage of a posthumous execution. He has left a curious paper to prove that the vampire, on its expulsion from its amphibious existence, is projected into a far more horrible life; and he resolved to save his once beloved Mircalla from this. He adopted the stratagem of a journey here, a pretended removal of her remains, and a real obliteration of her monument. When age had stolen upon him, and from the vale of years he looked back on the scenes he was leaving, he considered, in a different spirit, what he had done, and a horror took possession of him. He made the tracings and notes which have guided me to the very spot, and drew up a confession of the deception that he had practised. If he had intended any further action in this matter, death prevented him; and the hand of a remote descendant has, too late for many, directed the pursuit to the lair of the beast.'

We talked a little more, and among other things he said was this:

'One sign of the vampire is the power of the hand. The slender hand of Mircalla closed like a vice of steel on the General's wrist when he raised the hatchet to strike. But its power is not confined to its grasp; it leaves a numbness in the limb it seizes, which is slowly, if ever, recovered from.'

The following spring my father took me a tour* through Italy. We remained away for more than a year. It was long before the terror of recent events subsided; and to this hour the image of Carmilla returns to memory with ambiguous alternations—sometimes the playful, languid, beautiful girl; sometimes the writhing fiend I saw in the ruined church; and often from a reverie I have started, fancying I heard the light step of Carmilla at the drawing-room door.*

JULIAN HAWTHORNE

KEN'S MYSTERY

ONE cool October evening—it was the last day of the month, and unusually cool for the time of year—I made up my mind to go and spend an hour or two with my friend Keningale. Keningale was an artist (as well as a musical amateur and poet), and had a very delightful studio built on to his house, in which he was wont to sit of an evening. The studio had a cavernous fire-place, designed in imitation of the old-fashioned fire-places of Elizabethan manor-houses, and in it, when the temperature out-doors warranted, he would build up a cheerful fire of dry logs. It would suit me particularly well, I thought, to go and have a quiet pipe and chat in front of that fire with my friend.

I had not had such a chat for a very long time—not, in fact, since Keningale (or Ken, as his friends called him) had returned from his visit to Europe the year before. He went abroad, as he affirmed at the time, 'for purposes of study,' whereat we all smiled, for Ken, so far as we knew him, was more likely to do anything else than to study. He was a young fellow of buoyant temperament, lively and social in his habits, of a brilliant and versatile mind, and possessing an income of twelve or fifteen thousand dollars a year; he could sing, play, scribble, and paint very cleverly, and some of his heads and figure-pieces were really well done, considering that he never had any regular training in art; but he was not a worker. Personally he was fine-looking, of good height and figure, active, healthy, and with a remarkably fine brow, and clear, full-gazing eye. Nobody was surprised at his going to Europe, nobody expected him to do anything there except amuse himself, and few anticipated that he would be soon again seen in New York. He was one of the sort that find Europe agree with them. Off he went, therefore; and in the course of a few months the rumor reached us that he was engaged to a handsome and wealthy New York girl whom he had met in London. This was nearly all we did hear of him until, not very long afterward, he turned up again on Fifth Avenue, to every one's astonishment; made no satisfactory answer to those who wanted to know how he happened to tire so soon of the Old World; while as to the reported engagement, he cut short all allusion to that in so peremptory a manner as to show that it was not a permissible topic of conversation with him. It was surmised that the lady had jilted him; but, on the other hand, she herself returned home not a great while after, and, though she had plenty of opportunities, she has never married to this day.

Be the rights of that matter what they may, it was soon remarked that Ken was no longer the careless and merry fellow he used to be; on the contrary, he appeared grave, moody, averse from general society, and habitually taciturn and undemonstrative even in the company of his most intimate friends. Evidently something had happened to him, or he had done something. What? Had he committed a murder? or joined the Nihilists?* or was his unsuccessful love affair at the bottom of it? Some declared that the cloud was only temporary, and would soon pass away. Nevertheless, up to the period of which I am writing it had not passed away, but had rather gathered additional gloom, and threatened to become permanent.

Meanwhile I had met him twice or thrice at the club, at the opera, or in the street, but had as yet had no opportunity of regularly renewing my acquaintance with him. We had been on a footing of more than common intimacy in the old days, and I was not disposed to think that he would refuse to renew the former relations now. But what I had heard and myself seen of his changed condition imparted a stimulating tinge of suspense or curiosity to the pleasure with which I looked forward to the prospects of this evening. His house stood at a distance of two or three miles beyond the general range of habitations in New York at this time, and as I walked briskly along in the clear twilight air I had leisure to go over in my mind all that I had known of Ken and had divined of his character. After all, had there not always been something in his nature—deep down, and held in abeyance by the activity of his animal spirits—but something strange and separate, and capable of developing under suitable conditions into—into what? As I asked myself this question I arrived at his door; and it was with a feeling of relief that I felt the next moment the cordial grasp of his hand, and his voice bidding me welcome in a tone that indicated unaffected gratification at my presence. He drew me at once into the studio, relieved me of my hat and cane, and then put his hand on my shoulder.

'I am glad to see you,' he repeated, with singular earnestness—'glad to see you and to feel you; and to-night of all nights in the year.'

'Why to-night especially?'

'Oh, never mind. It's just as well, too, you didn't let me know beforehand you were coming; the unreadiness is all, to paraphrase the poet.* Now, with you to help me, I can drink a glass of tamarind-water* and take a bit draw* of the pipe. This would have been a grim night for me if I'd been left to myself.'

'In such a lap of luxury as this, too!' said I, looking round at the glowing fire-place, the low, luxurious chairs, and all the rich and sumptuous fittings of the room. 'I should have thought a condemned murderer might make himself comfortable here.'

'Perhaps; but that's not exactly my category at present. But have you forgotten what night this is? This is November-eve,* when, as tradition asserts, the dead arise and walk about, and fairies, goblins, and spiritual beings of all kinds have more freedom and power than on any other day of the year. One can see you've never been in Ireland.'*

'I wasn't aware till now that you had been there, either.'

'Yes, I have been in Ireland. Yes—' He paused, sighed, and fell into a reverie, from which, however, he soon roused himself by an effort, and went to a cabinet in a corner of the room for the liquor and tobacco. While he was thus employed I sauntered about the studio, taking note of the various beauties, grotesquenesses, and curiosities that it contained. Many things were there to repay study and arouse admiration; for Ken was a good collector, having excellent taste as well as means to back it. But, upon the whole, nothing interested me more than some studies of a female head, roughly done in oils, and, judging from the sequestered positions in which I found them, not intended by the artist for exhibition or criticism. There were three or four of these studies, all of the same face, but in different poses and costumes. In one the head was enveloped in a dark hood, overshadowing and partly concealing the features; in another she seemed to be peering duskily through a latticed casement, lit by a faint moonlight; a third showed her splendidly attired in evening costume, with jewels in her hair and ears, and sparkling on her snowy bosom. The expressions were as various as the poses; now it was demure penetration, now a subtle inviting glance, now burning passion, and again a look of elfish and elusive mockery. In whatever phase, the countenance possessed a singular and poignant fascination, not of beauty merely, though that was very striking, but of character and quality likewise.

'Did you find this model abroad?' I inquired at length. 'She has evidently inspired you, and I don't wonder at it.'

Ken, who had been heating the tamarind-water, and had not noticed my movements, now looked up, and said: 'I didn't mean those to be seen. They don't satisfy me, and I am going to destroy them; but I couldn't rest till I'd made some attempts to reproduce—What was it you asked? Abroad? Yes—or no. They were all painted here within the last six weeks.'

'Whether they satisfy you or not, they are by far the best things of yours I have ever seen.'

'Well, let them alone, and tell me what you think of this beverage. To my thinking, it goes to the right spot. It owes its existence to your coming here. I can't drink alone, and those portraits are not company, though, for aught I know, she might have come out of the canvas tonight and sat down in that chair.' Then, seeing my inquiring look, he added, with a hasty laugh, 'It's November-eve, you know, when anything may happen, provided it's strange enough. Well, here's to ourselves.'

We each swallowed a deep draught of the smoking and aromatic liquor, and set down our glasses with approval. The punch was excellent. Ken now opened a box of cigars, and we seated ourselves before the fire-place.

'All we need now,' I remarked, after a short silence, 'is a little music. By-the-bye, Ken, have you still got the banjo I gave you before you went abroad?'

He paused so long before replying that I supposed he had not heard my question. 'I have got it,' he said at length, 'but it will never make any more music.'

'Got broken, eh? Can't it be mended? It was a fine instrument.'

'It's not broken, but it's past mending. You shall see for yourself.'

He arose as he spoke, and going to another part of the studio, opened a black oak coffer, and took out of it a long object wrapped up in a piece of faded yellow silk. He handed it to me, and when I had unwrapped it, there appeared a thing that might once have been a banjo, but had little resemblance to one now. It bore every sign of extreme age. The wood of the handle was honey-combed with the gnawings of worms, and dusty with dry-rot. The parchment head was green with mould, and hung in shrivelled tatters. The hoop, which was of solid silver, was so blackened and tarnished that it looked like dilapidated iron. The strings were gone, and most of the tuning-screws had dropped out of their decayed sockets. Altogether it had the appearance of having been made before the Flood, and been forgotten in the forecastle* of Noah's Ark ever since.

'It is a curious relic certainly,' I said. 'Where did you come across it? I had no idea that the banjo was invented so long ago as this. It certainly can't be less than two hundred years old, and may be much older than that.'

Ken smiled gloomily. 'You are quite right,' he said; 'it is at least two hundred years old, and yet it is the very same banjo that you gave me a year ago.'

'Hardly,' I returned, smiling in my turn, 'since that was made to my order with a view to presenting it to you.'

'I know that; but the two hundred years have passed since then. Yes; it is absurd and impossible, I know, but nothing is truer. That banjo, which was made last year, existed in the sixteenth century, and has been rotting ever since. Stay. Give it to me a moment, and I'll convince you. You recollect that your name and mine, with the date, were engraved on the silver hoop?'

'Yes; and there was a private mark of my own there also.'

'Very well,' said Ken, who had been rubbing a place on the hoop with a corner of the yellow silk wrapper; 'look at that.'

I took the decrepit instrument from him, and examined the spot which he had rubbed. It was incredible, sure enough; but there were the names and the date precisely as I had caused them to be engraved; and there, moreover, was my own private mark, which I had idly made with an old etching point not more than eighteen months before. After convincing myself that there was no mistake, I laid the banjo across my knees, and stared at my friend in bewilderment. He sat smoking with a kind of grim composure, his eyes fixed upon the blazing logs.

'I'm mystified, I confess,' said I. 'Come; what is the joke? What method have you discovered of producing the decay of centuries on this unfortunate banjo in a few months? And why did you do it? I have heard of an elixir to counteract the effects of time, but your recipe seems to work the other way—to make time rush forward at two hundred times his usual rate, in one place, while he jogs on at his usual gait elsewhere. Unfold your mystery, magician. Seriously, Ken, how on earth did the thing happen?'

'I know no more about it than you do,' was his reply. 'Either you and I and all the rest of the living world are insane, or else there has been wrought a miracle as strange as any in tradition. How can I explain it? It is a common saying—a common experience, if you will—that we may, on certain trying or tremendous occasions, live years in one moment. But that's a mental experience, not a physical one, and one that applies, at all events, only to human beings, not to senseless things of wood and metal. You imagine the thing is some trick or jugglery. If it be, I don't know the secret of it. There's no chemical appliance that I ever heard of that will get a piece of solid wood into that condition in a few months, or a few years. And it wasn't done in a few years, or a few months either. A year ago to-day at this very hour that banjo was as sound as when it left the maker's hands, and twenty-four hours afterward—I'm telling you the simple truth—it was as you see it now.'

The gravity and earnestness with which Ken made this astounding statement were evidently not assumed. He believed every word that he uttered. I knew not what to think. Of course my friend might be insane, though he betrayed none of the ordinary symptoms of mania; but, however that might be, there was the banjo, a witness whose silent testimony there was no gainsaying. The more I meditated on the matter the more inconceivable did it appear. Two hundred years—twenty-four hours; those were the terms of the proposed equation. Ken and the banjo both affirmed that the equation had been made; all worldly knowledge and experience affirmed it to be impossible. What was the explanation? What is time? What is life? I felt myself beginning to doubt the reality of all things. And so this was the mystery which my friend had been brooding over since his return from abroad. No wonder it had changed him. More to be wondered at was it that it had not changed him more.

'Can you tell me the whole story?' I demanded at length.

Ken quaffed another draught from his glass of tamarind-water and rubbed his hand through his thick brown beard. 'I have never spoken to any one of it heretofore,' he said, 'and I had never meant to speak of it. But I'll try and give you some idea of what it was. You know me better than any one else; you'll understand the thing as far as it can ever be understood, and perhaps I may be relieved of some of the oppression it has caused me. For it is rather a ghastly memory to grapple with alone, I can tell you.'

Hereupon, without further preface, Ken related the following tale. He was, I may observe in passing, a naturally fine narrator. There were deep, lingering tones in his voice, and he could strikingly enhance the comic or pathetic effect of a sentence by dwelling here and there upon some syllable. His features were equally susceptible of humorous and of solemn expressions, and his eyes were in form and hue wonderfully adapted to showing great varieties of emotion. Their mournful aspect was extremely earnest and affecting; and when Ken was giving utterance to some mysterious passage of the tale they had a doubtful, melancholy, exploring look which appealed irresistibly to the imagination. But the interest of his story was too pressing to allow of noticing these incidental embellishments at the time, though they doubtless had their influence upon me all the same.

'I left New York on an Inman Line steamer,* you remember,' began Ken, 'and landed at Havre.* I went the usual round of sight-seeing on the Continent, and got round to London in July, at the height of the season. I had good introductions, and met any number of agreeable and famous people. Among others was a young lady, a country-woman of my own—you know whom I mean—who interested me very much, and before her family left London she and I were engaged. We parted there for the time, because she had the Continental trip still to make, while I wanted to take the opportunity to visit the north of England and Ireland. I landed at Dublin about the first of October, and, zigzagging about the country, I found myself in County Cork about two weeks later.

'There is in that region some of the most lovely scenery that human eyes ever rested on, and it seems to be less known to tourists than many places of infinitely less picturesque value. A lonely region, too: during my rambles I met not a single stranger like myself, and few enough natives. It seems incredible that so beautiful a country should be so deserted. After walking a dozen Irish miles* you come across a group of two or three one-roomed cottages,* and, like as not, one or more of those will have the roof off and the walls in ruins. The few peasants whom one sees, however, are affable and hospitable, especially when they hear you are from that terrestrial heaven* whither most of their friends and relatives have gone before them. They seem simple and primitive enough at first sight, and yet they are as strange and incomprehensible a race as any in the world. They are as superstitious, as credulous of marvels, fairies, magicians, and omens, as the men whom St. Patrick preached to, and at the same time they are shrewd, skeptical, insensible,* and bottomless liars. Upon the whole, I met with no nation on my travels whose company I enjoyed so much, or who inspired me with so much kindliness, curiosity, and repugnance.

'At length I got to a place on the sea-coast, which I will not further specify than to say that it is not many miles from Ballymacheen,* on the south shore. I have seen Venice and Naples, I have driven along the Cornice Road,* I have spent a month at our own Mount Desert,* and I say that all of them together are not so beautiful as this glowing, deep-hued, soft-gleaming, silvery-lighted, ancient harbor and town, with the tall hills crowding round it and the black cliffs and headlands planting their iron feet in the blue, transparent sea. It is a very old place, and has had a history which it has outlived ages since. It may once have had two or three thousand inhabitants; it has scarce five or six hundred to-day. Half the houses are in ruins or have disappeared; many of the remainder are standing empty. All the people are poor, most of them abjectly so; they saunter about with bare feet and uncovered heads, the women in quaint black or dark blue cloaks, the men in such anomalous attire as only an Irishman knows how to get together, the children half naked. The only comfortable-looking people are the monks and the priests, and the soldiers in the fort. For there is a fort there, constructed on the huge ruins of one which may have done duty in the reign of Edward the Black Prince,* or earlier, in whose mossy embrasures* are mounted a couple of cannon, which occasionally sent a practice-shot or two at the cliff on the other side of the harbor. The garrison consists of a dozen men and three or four officers and non-commissioned officers. I suppose they are relieved occasionally, but those I saw seemed to have become component parts of their surroundings.

'I put up at a wonderful little old inn, the only one in the place, and took my meals in a dining-saloon fifteen feet by nine, with a portrait of George I.* (a print varnished to preserve it) hanging over the mantel-piece. On the second evening after dinner a young gentleman came in—the dining-saloon being public property, of course—and ordered some bread and cheese and a bottle of Dublin stout. We presently fell into talk; he turned out to be an officer from the fort, Lieutenant O'Connor, and a fine young specimen of the Irish soldier* he was. After telling me all he knew about the town, the surrounding country, his friends, and himself, he intimated a readiness to sympathize with whatever tale I might choose to pour into his ear; and I had pleasure in trying to rival his own outspokenness. We became excellent friends; we had up a half-pint of Kinahan's whiskey,* and the lieutenant expressed himself in terms of high praise of my countrymen, my country, and my own particular cigars. When it became time for him to depart I accompanied him—for there was a splendid moon abroad—and bade him farewell at the fort entrance, having promised to come over the next day and make the acquaintance of the other fellows. "And mind your eye,* now, going back, my dear boy," he called out, as I turned my face homeward. "Sure 'tis a spooky place, that grave-yard, and you'll as likely meet the black woman* there as anywhere else!"

'The grave-yard was a forlorn and barren spot on the hill-side, just the hither side of the fort: thirty or forty rough head-stones, few of which retained any semblance of the perpendicular, while many were so shattered and decayed as to seem nothing more than irregular natural projections from the ground. Who the black woman might be I knew not, and did not stay to inquire. I had never been subject to ghostly apprehensions, and as a matter of fact, though the path I had to follow was in places very bad going, not to mention a hap-hazard scramble over a ruined bridge that covered a deep-lying brook, I reached my inn without any adventure whatever.

'The next day I kept my appointment at the fort, and found no reason to regret it; and my friendly sentiments were abundantly reciprocated, thanks more especially, perhaps, to the success of my banjo, which I carried with me, and which was as novel as it was popular with those who listened to it. The chief personages in the social circle besides my friend the lieutenant were Major Molloy, who was in command, a racy and juicy old campaigner, with a face like a sunset, and the surgeon, Dr. Dudeen, a long, dry, humorous genius, with a wealth of anecdotical and traditional lore at his command that I have never seen surpassed. We had a jolly time of it, and it was the precursor of many more like it. The remains of October slipped away rapidly, and I was obliged to remember that I was a traveller in Europe, and not a resident in Ireland. The major, the surgeon, and the lieutenant all protested cordially against my proposed departure, but as there was no help for it, they arranged a farewell dinner to take place in the fort on All-halloween.

'I wish you could have been at that dinner with me! It was the essence of Irish good-fellowship. Dr. Dudeen was in great force; the major was better than the best of Lever's novels;* the lieutenant was overflowing with hearty good-humor, merry chaff, and sentimental rhapsodies anent* this or the other pretty girl of the neighborhood. For my part I made the banjo ring as it had never rung before, and the others joined in the chorus with a mellow strength of lungs such as you don't often hear outside of Ireland. Among the stories that Dr. Dudeen regaled us with was one about the Kern of Querin and his wife, Ethelind Fionguala*—which being interpreted signifies "the white-shouldered." The lady, it appears, was originally betrothed to one O'Connor (here the lieutenant smacked his lips), but was stolen away on the wedding night by a party of vampires, who, it would seem, were at that period a prominent feature among the troubles of Ireland. But as they were bearing her along—she being unconscious—to that supper where she was not to eat but to be eaten, the young Kern of Querin, who happened to be out duck-shooting, met the party, and emptied his gun at it. The vampires fled, and the Kern carried the fair lady, still in a state of insensibility to his house. "And by the same token, Mr. Keningale," observed the doctor, knocking the ashes out of his pipe, "ye're after passing that very house on your way here. The one with the dark archway underneath it, and the big mullioned window at the corner, ye recollect, hanging over the street, as I might say—"

'"Go 'long wid the house, Dr. Dudeen, dear," interrupted the lieutenant; "sure can't you see we're all dyin' to know what happened to sweet Miss Fionguala, God be good to her, when I was after getting her safe up-stairs—"

'"Faith, then, I can tell ye that myself, Mr. O'Connor," exclaimed the major, imparting a rotary motion to the remnants of whiskey in his tumbler. "'Tis a question to be solved on general principles, as Colonel O'Halloran said that time he was asked what he'd do if he'd been the Dook o' Wellington, and the Prussians hadn't come up in the nick o' time at Waterloo. 'Faith,'* says the colonel, 'I'll tell ye—'

'"Arrah,* then, major, why would ye be interruptin' the doctor, and Mr. Keningale there lettin' his glass stay empty till he hears—The Lord save us! the bottle's empty!"

'In the excitement consequent upon this discovery, the thread of the doctor's story was lost; and before it could be recovered the evening had advanced so far that I felt obliged to withdraw. It took some time to make my proposition heard and comprehended; and a still longer time to put it in execution; so that it was fully midnight before I found myself standing in the cool pure air outside the fort, with the farewells of my boon companions ringing in my ears.

'Considering that it had been rather a wet evening in-doors, I was in a remarkably good state of preservation, and I therefore ascribed it rather to the roughness of the road than to the smoothness of the liquor, when, after advancing a few rods,* I stumbled and fell. As I picked myself up I fancied I had heard a laugh, and supposed that the lieutenant, who had accompanied me to the gate, was making merry over my mishap; but on looking round I saw that the gate was closed and no one was visible. The laugh, moreover, had seemed to be close at hand, and even to be pitched in a key that was rather feminine than masculine. Of course I must have been deceived; nobody was near me: my imagination had played me a trick, or else there was more truth than poetry* in the tradition that Halloween is the carnival-time of disembodied spirits. It did not occur to me at the time that a stumble is held by the superstitious Irish to be an evil omen,* and had I remembered it it would only have been to laugh at it. At all events, I was physically none the worse for my tumble, and I resumed my way immediately.

'But the path was singularly difficult to find, or rather the path I was following did not seem to be the right one. I did not recognize it; I could have sworn (except I knew the contrary) that I had never seen it before. The moon had risen, though her light was as yet obscured by clouds, but neither my immediate surroundings nor the general aspect of the region appeared familiar. Dark, silent hill-sides mounted up on either hand, and the road, for the most part, plunged downward, as if to conduct me into the bowels of the earth. The place was alive with strange echoes, so that at times I seemed to be walking through the midst of muttering voices and mysterious whispers, and a wild, faint sound of laughter seemed ever and anon* to reverberate among the passes of the hills. Currents of colder air sighing up through narrow defiles and dark crevices touched my face as with airy fingers. A certain feeling of anxiety and insecurity began to take possession of me, though there was no definable cause for it, unless that I might be belated in getting home. With the perverse instinct of those who are lost I hastened my steps, but was impelled now and then to glance back over my shoulder, with a sensation of being pursued. But no living creature was in sight. The moon, however, had now risen higher, and the clouds that were drifting slowly across the sky flung into the naked valley dusky shadows, which occasionally assumed shapes that looked like the vague semblance of gigantic human forms.

'How long I had been hurrying onward I know not, when, with a kind of suddenness, I found myself approaching a grave-yard. It was situated on the spur of a hill, and there was no fence around it, nor anything to protect it from the incursions of passers-by. There was something in the general appearance of this spot that made me half fancy I had seen it before; and I should have taken it to be the same that I had often noticed on my way to the fort, but that the latter was only a few hundred yards distant therefrom,* whereas I must have traversed several miles at least. As I drew near, moreover, I observed that the head-stones did not appear so ancient and decayed as those of the other. But what chiefly attracted my attention was the figure that was leaning or half sitting upon one of the largest of the upright slabs near the road. It was a female figure draped in black, and a closer inspection—for I was soon within a few yards of her—showed that she wore the calla,* or long hooded cloak, the most common as well as the most ancient garment of Irish women, and doubtless of Spanish origin.

'I was a trifle startled by this apparition, so unexpected as it was, and so strange did it seem that any human creature should be at that hour of the night in so desolate and sinister a place. Involuntarily I paused as I came opposite her, and gazed at her intently. But the moonlight fell behind her, and the deep hood of her cloak so completely shadowed her face that I was unable to discern anything but the sparkle of a pair of eyes, which appeared to be returning my gaze with much vivacity.

'"You seem to be at home here," I said, at length. "Can you tell me where I am?"

'Hereupon the mysterious personage broke into a light laugh, which, though in itself musical and agreeable, was of a timbre and intonation that caused my heart to beat rather faster than my late pedestrian exertions warranted; for it was the identical laugh (or so my imagination persuaded me) that had echoed in my ears as I arose from my tumble an hour or two ago. For the rest, it was the laugh of a young woman, and presumably of a pretty one; and yet it had a wild, airy, mocking quality, that seemed hardly human at all, or not, at any rate, characteristic of a being of affections and limitations like unto ours. But this impression of mine was fostered, no doubt, by the unusual and uncanny circumstances of the occasion.

'"Sure, sir," said she, "you're at the grave of Ethelind Fionguala."

'As she spoke she rose to her feet, and pointed to the inscription on the stone. I bent forward, and was able, without much difficulty, to decipher the name, and a date which indicated that the occupant of the grave must have entered the disembodied state between two and three centuries ago.

'"And who are you?" was my next question.

'"I'm called Elsie,' she replied. "But where would your honor be going November-eve?"

'I mentioned my destination, and asked her whether she could direct me thither.

'"Indeed, then, 'tis there I'm going myself," Elsie replied; "and if your honor'll follow me, and play me a tune on the pretty instrument, 'tisn't long we'll be on the road."

'She pointed to the banjo which I carried wrapped up under my arm. How she knew that it was a musical instrument I could not imagine; possibly, I thought, she may have seen me playing on it as I strolled about the environs of the town. Be that as it may, I offered no opposition to the bargain, and further intimated that I would reward her more substantially on our arrival. At that she laughed again, and made a peculiar gesture with her hand above her head. I uncovered my banjo, swept my fingers across the strings, and struck into a fantastic dance measure, to the music of which we proceeded along the path, Elsie slightly in advance, her feet keeping time to the airy measure. In fact, she trod so lightly, with an elastic, undulating movement, that with a little more it seemed as if she might float onward like a spirit. The extreme whiteness of her feet attracted my eye, and I was surprised to find that instead of being bare, as I had supposed, these were incased in white satin slippers quaintly embroidered with gold thread.

'"Elsie," said I, lengthening my steps so as to come up with her, "where do you live, and what do you do for a living?"

'"Sure, I live by myself," she answered; "and if you'd be after knowing how, you must come and see for yourself."

'"Are you in the habit of walking over the hills at night in shoes like that?"

'"And why would I not?" she asked, in her turn. "And where did your honor get the pretty gold ring on your finger?"

'The ring, which was of no great intrinsic value, had struck my eye in an old curiosity shop in Cork. It was an antique of very old-fashioned design, and might have belonged (as the vender assured me was the case) to one of the early kings or queens of Ireland.

'"Do you like it?" said I.

'"Will your honor be after making a present of it to Elsie?" she returned, with an insinuating tone and turn of the head.

'"Maybe I will, Elsie, on one condition. I am an artist; I make pictures of people. If you will promise to come to my studio and let me paint your portrait, I'll give you the ring, and some money besides."

'"And will you give me the ring now?" said Elsie.

'"Yes, if you'll promise."

'"And will you play the music to me?" she continued.

'"As much as you like."

'"But maybe I'll not be handsome enough for ye," said she, with a glance of her eyes beneath the dark hood.

'"I'll take the risk of that," I answered, laughing, "though, all the same, I don't mind taking a peep beforehand to remember you by." So saying, I put forth a hand to draw back the concealing hood. But Elsie eluded me, I scarce know how, and laughed a third time, with the same airy, mocking cadence.

'"Give me the ring first, and then you shall see me," she said, coaxingly.

'"Stretch out your hand, then," returned I, removing the ring from my finger. "When we are better acquainted, Elsie, you won't be so suspicious."

'She held out a slender, delicate hand, on the forefinger of which I slipped the ring. As I did so, the folds of her cloak fell a little apart, affording me a glimpse of a white shoulder and of a dress that seemed in that deceptive semi-darkness to be wrought of rich and costly material; and I caught, too, or so I fancied, the frosty sparkle of precious stones.

'"Arrah, mind where ye tread!" said Elsie, in a sudden, sharp tone.

'I looked round, and became aware for the first time that we were standing near the middle of a ruined bridge which spanned a rapid stream that flowed at a considerable depth below. The parapet of the bridge on one side was broken down, and I must have been, in fact, in imminent danger of stepping over into empty air. I made my way cautiously across the decaying structure; but when I turned to assist Elsie, she was nowhere to be seen.

'What had become of the girl? I called, but no answer came. I gazed about on every side, but no trace of her was visible. Unless she had plunged into the narrow abyss at my feet, there was no place where she could have concealed herself—none at least that I could discover. She had vanished, nevertheless; and since her disappearance must have been premeditated, I finally came to the conclusion that it was useless to attempt to find her. She would present herself again in her own good time, or not at all. She had given me the slip very cleverly, and I must make the best of it. The adventure was perhaps worth the ring.

'On resuming my way, I was not a little relieved to find that I once more knew where I was. The bridge that I had just crossed was none other than the one I mentioned some time back; I was within a mile of the town, and my way lay clear before me. The moon, moreover, had now quite dispersed the clouds, and shone down with exquisite brilliance. Whatever her other failings, Elsie had been a trustworthy guide; she had brought me out of the depth of elf-land into the material world again. It had been a singular adventure, certainly; and I mused over it with a sense of mysterious pleasure as I sauntered along, humming snatches of airs, and accompanying myself on the strings. Hark! what light step was that behind me? It sounded like Elsie's; but no, Elsie was not there. The same impression or hallucination, however, recurred several times before I reached the outskirts of the town—the tread of an airy foot behind or beside my own. The fancy did not make me nervous; on the contrary, I was pleased with the notion of being thus haunted, and gave myself up to a romantic and genial vein of reverie.

'After passing one or two roofless and moss-grown cottages, I entered the narrow and rambling street which leads through the town. This street a short distance down widens a little, as if to afford the wayfarer space to observe a remarkable old house that stands on the northern side. The house was built of stone, and in a noble style of architecture; it reminded me somewhat of certain palaces of the old Italian nobility that I had seen on the Continent, and it may very probably have been built by one of the Italian or Spanish immigrants of the sixteenth or seventeenth century. The moulding of the projecting windows and arched doorway was richly carved, and upon the front of the building was an escutcheon* wrought in high relief, though I could not make out the purport of the device. The moonlight falling upon this picturesque pile enhanced all its beauties, and at the same time made it seem like a vision that might dissolve away when the light ceased to shine. I must often have seen the house before, and yet I retained no definite recollection of it; I had never until now examined it with my eyes open, so to speak. Leaning against the wall on the opposite side of the street, I contemplated it for a long while at my leisure. The window at the corner was really a very fine and massive affair. It projected over the pavement below, throwing a heavy shadow aslant; the frames of the diamond-paned lattices were heavily mullioned. How often in past ages had that lattice been pushed open by some fair hand, revealing to a lover waiting beneath in the moonlight the charming countenance of his high-born mistress! Those were brave days. They had passed away long since. The great house had stood empty for who could tell how many years; only bats and vermin were its inhabitants. Where now were those who had built it? and who were they? Probably the very name of them was forgotten.

'As I continued to stare upward, however, a conjecture presented itself to my mind which rapidly ripened into a conviction. Was not this the house that Dr. Dudeen had described that very evening as having been formerly the abode of the Kern of Querin and his mysterious bride? There was the projecting window, the arched doorway. Yes, beyond a doubt this was the very house. I emitted a low exclamation of renewed interest and pleasure, and my speculations took a still more imaginative, but also a more definite turn.

'What had been the fate of that lovely lady after the Kern had brought her home insensible in his arms? Did she recover, and were they married and made happy ever after? or had the sequel been a tragic one? I remembered to have read that the victims of vampires generally became vampires themselves. Then my thoughts went back to that grave on the hill-side. Surely that was unconsecrated ground. Why had they buried her there? Ethelind of the white shoulder! Ah! why had not I lived in those days? or why might not some magic cause them to live again for me? Then would I seek this street at midnight, and standing here beneath her window, I would lightly touch the strings of my bandore* until the casement opened cautiously and she looked down. A sweet vision indeed! And what prevented my realizing it? Only a matter of a couple of centuries or so. And was time, then, at which poets and philosophers sneer, so rigid and real a matter that a little faith and imagination might not overcome it? At all events, I had my banjo, the bandore's legitimate and lineal descendant, and the memory of Fionguala should have the love ditty.

'Hereupon, having retuned the instrument, I launched forth into an old Spanish love song, which I had met with in some mouldy library during my travels, and had set to music of my own. I sang low, for the deserted street re-echoed the lightest sound, and what I sang must reach only my lady's ears. The words were warm with the fire of the ancient Spanish chivalry, and I threw into their expression all the passion of the lovers of romance. Surely Fionguala, the white-shouldered, would hear, and awaken from her sleep of centuries, and come to the latticed casement and look down! Hist! see yonder! What light*—what shadow is that that seems to flit from room to room within the abandoned house, and now approaches the mullioned window? Are my eyes dazzled by the play of the moonlight, or does the casement move—does it open? Nay, this is no delusion; there is no error of the senses here. There is simply a woman, young, beautiful, and richly attired, bending forward from the window, and silently beckoning me to approach.

'Too much amazed to be conscious of amazement, I advanced until I stood directly beneath the casement, and the lady's face, as she stooped toward me, was not more than twice a man's height from my own. She smiled and kissed her finger-tips; something white fluttered in her hand, then fell through the air to the ground at my feet. The next moment she had withdrawn, and I heard the lattice close.

'I picked up what she had let fall; it was a delicate lace handkerchief, tied to the handle of an elaborately wrought bronze key. It was evidently the key of the house, and invited me to enter. I loosened it from the handkerchief, which bore a faint, delicious perfume, like the aroma of flowers in an ancient garden, and turned to the arched doorway. I felt no misgiving, and scarcely any sense of strangeness. All was as I had wished it to be, and as it should be; the mediæval age was alive once more, and as for myself, I almost felt the velvet cloak hanging from my shoulder and the long rapier dangling at my belt.

Standing in front of the door I thrust the key into the lock, turned it, and felt the bolt yield. The next instant the door was opened, apparently from within; I stepped across the threshold, the door closed again, and I was alone in the house, and in darkness.

'Not alone, however! As I extended my hand to grope my way it was met by another hand, soft, slender, and cold, which insinuated itself gently into mine and drew me forward. Forward I went, nothing loath; the darkness was impenetrable, but I could hear the light rustle of a dress close to me, and the same delicious perfume that had emanated from the handkerchief enriched the air that I breathed, while the little hand that clasped and was clasped by my own alternately tightened and half relaxed the hold of its soft cold fingers. In this manner, and treading lightly, we traversed what I presumed to be a long, irregular passageway, and ascended a staircase. Then another corridor, until finally we paused, a door opened, emitting a flood of soft light, into which we entered, still hand in hand. The darkness and the doubt were at an end.

'The room was of imposing dimensions, and was furnished and decorated in a style of antique splendor. The walls were draped with mellow hues of tapestry; clusters of candles burned in polished silver sconces, and were reflected and multiplied in tall mirrors placed in the four corners of the room. The heavy beams of the dark oaken ceiling crossed each other in squares, and were laboriously carved; the curtains and the drapery of the chairs were of heavy figured damask. At one end of the room was a broad ottoman, and in front of it a table, on which was set forth, in massive silver dishes, a sumptuous repast, with wines in crystal beakers. At the side was a vast and deep fire-place, with space enough on the broad hearth to burn whole trunks of trees. No fire, however, was there, but only a great heap of dead embers; and the room, for all its magnificence, was cold—cold as a tomb, or as my lady's hand—and it sent a subtle chill creeping to my heart.

'But my lady! how fair she was! I gave but a passing glance at the room; my eyes and my thoughts were all for her. She was dressed in white, like a bride; diamonds sparkled in her dark hair and on her snowy bosom; her lovely face and slender lips were pale, and all the paler for the dusky glow of her eyes. She gazed at me with a strange, elusive smile; and yet there was, in her aspect and bearing, something familiar in the midst of strangeness, like the burden of a song heard long ago and recalled among other conditions and surroundings. It seemed to me that something in me recognized her and knew her, had known her always. She was the woman of whom I had dreamed, whom I had beheld in visions, whose voice and face had haunted me from boyhood up. Whether we had ever met before, as human beings meet, I knew not; perhaps I had been blindly seeking her all over the world, and she had been awaiting me in this splendid room, sitting by those dead embers until all the warmth had gone out of her blood, only to be restored by the heat with which my love might supply her.

'"I thought you had forgotten me," she said, nodding as if in answer to my thought. "The night was so late—our one night of the year! How my heart rejoiced when I heard your dear voice singing the song I know so well! Kiss me—my lips are cold!"

'Cold indeed they were—cold as the lips of death. But the warmth of my own seemed to revive them. They were now tinged with a faint color, and in her cheeks also appeared a delicate shade of pink. She drew fuller breath, as one who recovers from a long lethargy. Was it my life that was feeding her? I was ready to give her all. She drew me to the table and pointed to the viands and the wine.

'"Eat and drink," she said. "You have travelled far, and you need food."

'"Will you eat and drink with me?" said I, pouring out the wine.

'"You are the only nourishment I want," was her answer. "This wine is thin and cold. Give me wine as red as your blood and as warm, and I will drain a goblet to the dregs."

'At these words, I know not why, a slight shiver passed through me. She seemed to gain vitality and strength at every instant, but the chill of the great room struck into me more and more.

'She broke into a fantastic flow of spirits, clapping her hands, and dancing about me like a child. Who was she? And was I myself, or was she mocking me when she implied that we had belonged to each other of old? At length she stood still before me, crossing her hands over her breast. I saw upon the forefinger of her right hand the gleam of an antique ring.

'"Where did you get that ring?" I demanded.

'She shook her head and laughed. "Have you been faithful?" she asked. "It is my ring; it is the ring that unites us; it is the ring you gave me when you loved me first. It is the ring of the Kern—the fairy ring, and I am your Ethelind—Ethelind Fionguala."

'"So be it," I said, casting aside all doubt and fear, and yielding myself wholly to the spell of her inscrutable eyes and wooing lips. "You are mine, and I am yours, and let us be happy while the hours last."

'"You are mine, and I am yours," she repeated, nodding her head with an elfish smile. "Come and sit beside me, and sing that sweet song again that you sang to me so long ago. Ah, now I shall live a hundred years."

'We seated ourselves on the ottoman, and while she nestled luxuriously among the cushions, I took my banjo and sang to her. The song and the music resounded through the lofty room, and came back in throbbing echoes. And before me as I sang I saw the face and form of Ethelind Fionguala, in her jewelled bridal dress, gazing at me with burning eyes. She was pale no longer, but ruddy and warm, and life was like a flame within her. It was I who had become cold and bloodless, yet with the last life that was in me I would have sung to her of love that can never die. But at length my eyes grew dim, the room seemed to darken, the form of Ethelind alternately brightened and waxed indistinct, like the last flickerings of a fire; I swayed toward her, and felt myself lapsing into unconsciousness, with my head resting on her white shoulder.'

Here Keningale paused a few moments in his story, flung a fresh log upon the fire, and then continued:

'I awoke, I know not how long afterward. I was in a vast empty room in a ruined building. Rotten shreds of drapery depended* from the walls, and heavy festoons of spiders' webs gray with dust covered the windows, which were destitute of glass or sash; they had been boarded up with rough planks which had themselves become rotten with age, and admitted through their holes and crevices pallid rays of light and chilly draughts of air. A bat, disturbed by these rays or by my own movement, detached himself from his hold on a remnant of mouldy tapestry near me, and after circling dizzily round my head, wheeled the flickering noiselessness of his flight into a darker corner. As I arose unsteadily from the heap of miscellaneous rubbish on which I had been lying, something which had been resting across my knees fell to the floor with a rattle. I picked it up, and found it to be my banjo—as you see it now.

'Well, that is all I have to tell. My health was seriously impaired; all the blood seemed to have been drawn out of my veins; I was pale and haggard,* and the chill—Ah, that chill,' murmured Keningale, drawing nearer to the fire, and spreading out his hands to catch the warmth—'I shall never get over it; I shall carry it to my grave.'

SABINE BARING-GOULD

MARGERY OF QUETHER

I

THIS is written by my own hand, entirely unassisted. I am George Rosedhu,* of Brinsabatch, in the parish of Lamerton,* and in the county of Devon—whether to write myself Mister or Esquire, I do not know. My father was a yeoman, so was my grandfather, item* my great-grandfather. But I notice that when anyone asks of me a favour, or writes me a begging letter, he addresses me as Esquire, whereas he who has no expectation of getting anything out of me invariably styles me Mister. I have held my acres for five hundred years—that is, my family, the Rosedhus, have, in direct lineal descent, always in the male line, and I intend, in like manner, to hand it on, neither impaired nor enlarged, to my own son, when I get one, which I am sure of, as the Rosedhus always have had male issue. But what with Nihilism, and Communism, and Tenant-right, and Agricultural Holdings legislation,* threatened by this Gladstone-Chamberlain Radical Government,* there is no knowing where a man with ancestral acres stands, and, in the general topsy-turvyism* into which we are plunging—thanks to this Radical Government, God bless me!—I may be driven to have only female issue. There is no knowing to what we landed proprietors are coming.

Before I proceed with my story, I must apologize for anything that smacks of rudeness in my style. I do not mean to say that there is anything intrinsically rude in my literary productions, but that the present taste is so vitiated by slipshod English and effeminacy of writing, that the modern reader of periodicals may not appreciate my composition as it deserves. Roast beef does not taste its best after Indian curry.*

My education has been thorough, not superficial. I was reared in none of your 'Academies for Young Gentlemen,' but brought up on the Eton Latin Grammar and cane at the Tavistock Free Grammar School.* The consequence is that what I pretend to know, I know. I am a practical man with a place in the world, and when I leave it, there will be a hole which will be felt, just as when a molar is removed from the jaw.

There is no exaggeration in saying that my family is as old as the hills, for a part of my estate covers a side of that great hog's-back now called Black Down,* which lies right before my window; and anyone who knows anything about the old British tongue will tell you that Rosedhu is the Cornish for Black Down. Well, that proves that we held land here before ever the Saxons came and drove the British language across the Tamar.* My title-deeds don't go back so far as that, but there are some of them which, though they be in Latin, I cannot decipher. The hills may change their names, but the Rosedhus never. My house is nothing to boast of. We have been yeomen, not squires, and we have never aimed at living like gentry. Perhaps that is why the Rosedhus are here still, and the other yeomen families round have gone scatt [I mean, gone to pieces].* If the sons won't look to the farm and the girls mind the dairy, the family cannot thrive.

Brinsabatch is an ordinary farm-house substantially built of volcanic stone, black, partly with age, and partly because of the burnt nature of the stone. The windows are wide, of wood, and always kept painted white. The roof is of slate, and grows some clumps of stonecrop,* yellow as gold.

Brinsabatch lies in a combe, that is, a hollow lap, in Yaffell—or as the maps call it, Heathfield.* Yaffell is a huge elevated bank of moor to the north-west and west, and what is very singular about it is, that at the very highest point of the moor an extinct volcanic cone protrudes, and rises to the height of about twelve hundred feet. This is called Brentor,* and it is crowned with a church, the very tiniest in the world I should suppose, but tiny as it is, it has chancel, nave, porch, and west tower like any Christian parish church. There is also a graveyard round the church. This occupies a little platform on the top of the mountain, and there is absolutely no room there for anything else. To the west, the rocks are quite precipitous, but the peak can be ascended from the east up a steep grass slope strewn with pumice. The church is dedicated to S. Michael, and the story goes that, whilst it was being built, every night the devil removed as many stones as had been set on the foundations during the day. But the archangel was too much for him. He waited behind Cox Tor,* and one night threw a great rock across and hit the Evil One between the horns, and gave him such a headache that he desisted from interference thenceforth. The rock is there, and the marks of the horns are distinctly traceable on it. I have seen them scores of times myself. I do not say that the story is true; but I do say that the marks of the horns are on the stone. It is said also that there is a depression caused by the thumb of S. Michael. I have looked at it carefully, but I express no opinion thereon—that may have been caused by the weather.

Looking up Brinsabatch Coombe, clothed in oak coppice and with a brawling stream dancing down its furrow, Brentor has a striking effect, soaring above it high into the blue air, with its little church and tower topping the peak.

I am many miles from Lamerton, which is my parish church, and all Heathfield lies between, so, as Divine service is performed every Sunday in the church of S. Michael de Rupe,* I ascend the rocky pinnacle to worship there.

You must understand that there is no road, not even a path to the top; one scrambles up over the turf, in windy weather clinging to the heather bushes. It is a famous place for courting, that is why the lads and lasses are such church-going folk hereabout. The boys help the girls up, and after service hold their hands to help them down. Then, sometimes a maiden lays hold of a gorse bush in mistake for a bunch of heath, and gets her pretty hand full of prickles. When that happens, her young man makes her sit down beside him under a rock away from the wind, that is from the descending congregation, and he picks the prickles out of her rosy palm with a pin. As there are thousands of prickles on a gorse bush, this sometimes takes a long time, and as the pin sometimes hurts, and the maid winces, the lad has to squeeze her hand very tight to hold it steady. I've known thorns drawn out with kisses.

I always do say that parsons make a mistake when they build churches in the midst of the population. Dear, simple, conceited souls, do they really suppose that folks go to church to hear them preach? No such thing—that is the excuse; they go for a romp. Parsons should think of that, and make provision accordingly, and set the sacred edifice on the top of moor or down, or in shady corners where there are long lanes well wooded. Church paths are always lovers' lanes.

When a woman gets too old for sweethearting—if that time ever arrives, in her own opinion—she goes to church for scandalmongery, and, of course, the further she has to go, the more time she has for talk and the outpour of gossip. I know the butcher at Lydford* kills once a week. Sunday is the character-killing day with us, and all our womenkind are the butchers.

Well!—this is all neither here nor there. I was writing about my house, and I have been led into a digression on church-going. However, it is not a digression either; it may seem so to my readers, but I know what I am about, and as my troubles came of church-going, what I have said is not so much out of the way as some superficial and inconsiderate readers may have supposed. I return, for a bit, to the description of my farm-house. As I have said once, and I insist on it again, Brinsabatch makes no pretensions to be other than a substantial yeoman's residence. You can smell the pigs' houses as you come near, and I don't pretend that the scent arises from clematis or weigelia.* The cowyard is at the back, and there is plenty of mud in the lane, and streams of water running down the cart ruts, and skeins of oats and barley straw hanging to the hollies in the hedge. There is no gravel drive up to the front door, but there is a little patch of turf before it walled off from the lane, with crystals of white spar ornamenting the top of the wall. In the wall is a gate, and an ascent by four granite steps to a path sanded with mundic* gravel that leads just twelve feet six inches across the grass plot to the front door. This door is bolted above and below, and chained and double-locked, but the back door that leads from the yard into the kitchen is always open, and I go in and out by that. The front door is for ornament, not use, except on grand occasions.

The rooms of Brinsabatch are low, and I can touch the ceiling easily in each with my hand; I can touch that in the bedrooms with my head. Low rooms are warmer and more homelike than the tall rooms of Queen Anne's and King George's reigns.

On the other side of Heathfield is Quether,* a farm that has belonged to the Palmers pretty nigh as long as Brinsabatch has belonged to the Rosedhus. Farmer John Palmer is a man of some substance, one of the old sort of yeomen, fresh in colour, with light blue eyes and fair hair; he is big-made and stout. He is a man who knows the world and can make money. He has a lime-kiln as well as a farm, but the lime-kiln is not his own, he rents it. His daughter Margaret is a very pretty girl. He has several sons, and a swarm of small children of no particular sex. They are all in petticoats.* So Margaret can't take much with her when she marries. Margaret used to go to chapel,* but her religious views underwent a change since one Sunday afternoon she visited Brentor church. This change in her was not produced by anything in the parson's sermon, but by the fact that I was there, aged three-and-twenty, was good-looking, and the sole owner of Brinsabatch. I accompanied her back to Quether. Since that Sunday she has been very regular in her devotions at S. Michael de Rupe; she has, I understand, returned her missionary box to the minister of the chapel, and no longer collects for the conversion of the heathen to humbug. As for me, I became a much more regular attendant at church after that Sunday afternoon than I had been before. When the day was windy, I helped Margaret up the rock, and held her hand very tightly in mine, for had she missed her footing she might have perished. When the day was rainy, we shared one gig* umbrella. When the day was windy *and* rainy, it was better still; for the gig umbrella could not be unfurled, so I folded my wide waterproof over us both. When the day was foggy, that was best of all, for then we lost our way in the fog, and could not find the church door till service was ended. On sunshiny days we were merry; in rain and fog, sentimental.

One Sunday she and I had gone round to the west end of the church after service. I told her that I wanted to show her Kit Hill,* where the Britons made their last stand against King Athelstan* and the Saxons; the real reason was that there is only a narrow ledge between the tower and the precipice, on which two cannot walk abreast, but on which two can stand very well with their backs to the wall, and no one else can come within eye and ear shot of them. Whilst we stood there, a sudden cloud rolled by beneath our feet, completely obliterating the landscape, but we were left above the vapour, in sunlight, looking down, as it were, on a rushing, eddying sea of white foam. The effect was strange; it was as though we were insulated on a little rock in a vast ocean that had no bounds. Margaret pressed my arm and said, 'We two seem to be alone in a little world to ourselves.'

I answered, looking at the fog, 'And a preciously dull world and dreary outlook.'

I have not much imagination, and I did not at the moment take her words as an appeal for a pretty and lover-like reply. I missed the opportunity and it was gone past recall. She let go of my arm in dudgeon, and when I turned my head Margaret had disappeared. With a step she had left the ledge, and a few paces had taken her to her father. The fog at the same time rose and enveloped the top of the Tor and the church, so that I could no longer see Margaret, and the possibility of overtaking her and apologising was lost.

Next Sunday she did not come to church. This made me very uncomfortable. I like to have the even tenor of neither my agricultural nor my matrimonial pursuits disturbed. I had been keeping company with Margaret Palmer for seven or eight months, and I had begun to hope that in the course of a twelvemonth, if things progressed, I might make a declaration of my sentiments, and that after the lapse of some three or four years more we might begin to think of getting married. This little outburst of temper was distasteful to me; I knew exactly what it meant. It showed an undue precipitancy, an eagerness to drive matters to a conclusion, which repelled me. My sentiments are my own, drawn from my own heart, as my cider is from my own apples. I will not allow anyone to go to the tap of the latter and draw off what he likes; and I will not allow anyone to turn the key of my bosom and draw off the sentiments that are therein. On the third Sunday, I did not go to church, but I sent my hind,* and he reported to me that Margaret Palmer had been there. I knew she would be there, expecting to find me ripe and soft to the pitch of a declaration. By my absence I showed her that I could be offended as well as she. That next week there came a revivalist preacher to the chapel; he was a black man, and went by the name of 'Go-on-all-fours-to-glory Jumbo.'* I heard that Margaret Palmer had been converted by him. The week after there came a quack female dentist to Tavistock, and I went to her and had one of my back teeth out. Margaret Palmer learned a lesson by that. I let her understand that if she chose to be revived by Methodies,* I'd have my teeth drawn by quacks. I'd stand none of her nonsense. My plan answered. Margaret Palmer came round, and was as meek as a sheep, and as mild as buttermilk after that. Next Sunday I went as near a declaration as ever a man did without actually falling over the edge into matrimony. Brinsabatch is a property of 356 acres 2 roods 3 poles,* and it won't allow a proprietor to marry much under fifty; my father did not marry till he was fifty-three, and my grandfather not till he was sixty. Young wives are expensive luxuries, and long families ruin a small property. One son to inherit the estate, and a daughter to keep house for him till he marries, then to be pensioned off on 80*l.* a year, that is the Rosedhu system. Now you can understand why I object to being hurried. Brinsabatch will not allow me to marry for twenty-seven years to come. But women are impatient cattle. They are like Dartmoor sheep;* where you don't want them to go, there they go; and when you set up hurdles to keep them in, they take them at a leap. I've known these Dartmoors climb a pile of rocks on the top of which is nothing to be got, and from which it is impossible to descend, just because the Almighty set up those rocks for the sheep *not* to climb. To my mind, courting is the happiest time of life, for then the maiden is on her best behaviour. She knows that there is many a slip between the cup and the lip, and she regulates her conduct accordingly. I've heard that in Turkey females are real angels; they never nag, they never peck, they never give themselves airs. And the reason is, that a Turkish husband can always turn his wife out of the house and sell her in the slave market. With us it is otherwise; when a woman is a wife she has her husband at her feet in chains to trample on as she pleases. He cannot break away. He cannot send her off. She knows that, and it is more than a woman can bear to be placed in a position of unassailable security. As long as a man is courting, he holds the rod, and the woman is the fish hooked at the end; but when they are married, the positions are reversed.

Well, to return to my story. We made up our quarrel and were like two doves. Then came the event I am about to relate, which disturbed our relations.

It had been the custom on Christmas Eve from time immemorial for the sexton and two others to climb Brentor, and ring a peal on the three bells in the church tower at midnight. On a still Christmas night the sound of these bells is carried to a great distance over the moors. I dare say in ancient times there may have been a service in the church at midnight, but there has been none for time out of mind, and the custom being unmeaning would have fallen into disuse were it not that a benefaction is connected with it—a field is held by feoffees* in trust to pay the rent to the sexton and the ringers, on condition that the bells are rung at midnight on Christmas Eve. Of late years there has been some difficulty in getting men together for the job. Wages are so high that labouring men will not turn out of a winter's night to climb a tor to earn a few shillings. Besides, the sexton has been accused of disseminating a preposterous, idle tale of hobgoblins and bogies to frighten others from assisting him, so that he may pocket the entire sum himself.

Be this as it may, it is certain that on the Christmas Eve that followed the quarrel I have spoken of, no additional ringers were forthcoming. The sexton, who was also clerk, Solomon Davy, worked for me and occupied one of my cottages. I beg, parenthetically, to observe that the cottages that belonged to me would do credit to any owner. My maxim is, look to your men and horses and cows that they be well fed and well housed, and they are worth the money. Solomon Davy was an old man. His work was not worth his wages, but I kept him on because he had been on the farm all his life, and had married late in life. During the afternoon of Christmas Eve, Solomon Davy sent for me. He was taken ill with rheumatism and could not leave his cottage.

'I've ventured on the liberty of asking you to step in, sir,' said he, when I entered his door, 'because I've been took across the back cruel bad, and I can't crawl across the room.'

'Sorry to hear it, Solomon. Who will do the clerking for you to-morrow?'

'I'm not troubled about that, master, as Farmer Palmer do the responses in a big voice. That which vexes me is about the ringing the bells this night.'

'It can't be done,' said I.

'But, sir, meaning no offence, it must be done, or I don't get the money. The feoffees won't pay a farthing unless Christmas be rung in.'

'You must send somebody else to do it.'

Solomon shook his head. 'Then that person pockets the money, and I get naught.' He remained silent awhile, and then added, 'Besides, who'd go?'

'Make it worth a man's while, and he'll do anything,' said I.

Again he shook his head, and this time he said, 'There's Margery of Quether.'

'What do you mean?' I asked, flushing. 'What has Miss Palmer to do with the bells? Oh, I understand; she likes to hear the peal, and you would not disappoint her.'

Solomon looked up at me slyly. 'I didn't mean she.'

'Then who the deuce do you mean?'

'Her as never dies.'

'Solomon, the lumbago* has got into your brains. I'll tell you what I'll do. I will ring the bells for you, and you shall draw the fee for having done it. That, I hope, will content you, my good man.'

'Now that be like you, master, the best and kindest of your good old stock,' exclaimed Solomon. 'I never heard of a master as was of such right good stuff as you. You don't turn off an old man because he is past work, nor grudge him a bit of best garden ground, took out of one of your fields, nor deny him skimmed milk because you want it for the pigs and calves, nor refuse him turnips and pertatees* out of the fields as many as he can eat.' So he went on. I do not hesitate to repeat what he said, because he confined himself strictly within the bounds of truth. I flatter myself I always have been a good master, and just, even generous, to my men. I have been more, I have been considerate and kind. Lights were not made to be put under bushels, and I am not one of those who would distort or suppress the truth, even when it concerns myself. I know my own merits, and as for my faults, if I light on any at any time, I shall not scruple to publish them.

The old sexton jumped at my offer—I mean metaphorically, for his lumbago would not allow him to jump literally. I had made the offer out of consideration for him, but without considering myself, and I repented having made it almost as soon as the words had left my lips. However, I am a man of my word, and when I say a thing I stick to it.

'Where is the key?' I asked.

'Her be hanging up on thicky [that] nail behind the door,' answered the old man.

As I took down the great church key, Solomon said, in a hesitating, timid voice, 'If you should chance to meet wi' Margery o' Quether, you won't mind.'

'I do not in the least expect to see her,' I said, getting red, and hot, and annoyed.

'No meb-be not, but her has been seen afore on Christmas Eve.'

'Margaret on the tor at midnight!' I exclaimed; then, highly incensed at the idea of the old man poking fun at me, and even alluding to my weakness for Margaret Palmer—love is a weakness—I said testily, as I walked out swinging the key on my fore-finger, 'Solomon, I object to Miss Palmer's name being brought in in this flippant and impertinent manner. What with the Gladstone-Chamberlain general-topsy-turvyism of the Government, the working classes are forgetting the respect due to their superiors, and allow themselves liberties of speech which their forefathers would have turned green to think of.'

If I was regular in my devotions every Lord's Day, a labouring man in one's employ earning eleven shillings a week had no right to suppose that I did not ascend Brentor from the purest motives of personal piety. It is a duty of one in his position to think so. His insolence jarred my feelings, and I already regretted the offer I had made. It is a mistake to be good-natured. It is lowering in the eyes of inferiors; it is taken for weakness. The man who is universally respected, and obtains ready attention and exact obedience, is he who cares for nobody but himself, is loud, exacting, and self-asserting. To be good-natured involves a man in endless troubles. I had undertaken to ring the bells at midnight in mid-winter in the windiest, most elevated steeple* in England; I had to ascend a giddy peak on which one false step would precipitate me over the rocks, and dash every bone in my body to pieces. I am not one to shrink from danger, or to shirk a responsibility, freely, if inconsiderately undertaken. I have already said that I would frankly admit my faults when I noticed them; and now the opportunity arises. I admit without scruple that I am too prone to do kind acts. This is a fault. A man ought to consider himself. Charity begins at home. In this instance I did not think of myself, of the discomfort and danger involved in ascending Brentor at midnight.

I took a stiff glass of hot rum and water about half-past ten or a quarter to eleven, and then turned out.

There was no snow on the ground; we are not likely to have seasonable weather so long as this Gladstone-Chamberlain-Radical topsy-turvy Government remain in power. Our sheep get cawed* with the wet, the potatoes get the disease, the bullocks get foot-and-mouth complaint, and the rain won't let us farmers get in our harvest. If only we had Beaconsfield* back! But there, politics have nothing to do with my story.

The evening was not cold, it was raw, and the night was black as pitch. I had a lanthorn with me (I spell the substantive advisedly in the old way, *lanthorn* and not *lantern*, for mine had horn, not glass, sides*). I knew my road perfectly. The lane is stony, wet, and overhung. Stony it must be, for it is worn down to the rock, and the rock breaks up as it likes and stones* itself, just as the coats of the stomach renew themselves. Wet it is, because it serves as main drain to the fields on either side. Overhung it is, because trees grow on either side. If the trees were not there, it would not be overhung. You understand me. I like to be explicit. Some intelligences are not satisfied with a hint, everything must be described and explained to them to the minutest particular.

By the lanthorn light I could see the beautiful ferns and mosses in the hedge, and the water oozing out of the sides, and the dribble that ran down the centre of the lane and then spread all over it, then accumulated on one side, and then took a fancy to run over to the other side. I notice that a stream in going down a hill zigzags just as a horse does in ascending a hill, and as a woman does in aiming at anything. The road rises steeply from my backyard gate to the church porch. When I say road, I mean way. For after one comes out on the moor, there is not even a track.

I knew my direction well enough, so I went straight over the heath to the old volcano, and as I ascended the peak I thought to myself, if any traveller were on Heathfield to-night, what a tale he would make up of the Jack-o'-lanthorn seen dancing in and out among the rocks, and winding its way up the height, till at last it hopped in at the church door of S. Michael on the Rock, and then a faint glimmer was visible issuing from all its windows. Probably he would suspect some witches' frolic was going on there such as Tam o' Shanter saw on All Hallowe'en, when—

Kirk Alloway seem'd in a bleeze,*

though the 'bleeze' could not be bright that issued from my tallow candle in a lanthorn.

The sky was overcast. Not a star was visible; only in the S.W. was a little faint light, and a thread of it ran round the horizon. The simile is not poetical, but it is to the purpose, when I say that the earth seemed under a dish-cover which didn't quite fit.

I reached the church in safety, dark as the night was; the few gravestones lit up with a ghastly smile as the lanthorn and I went by them in the little yard. I set down the clickering* article on the stone seat in the porch, turned the key, resumed my lanthorn and went into the tower.

The church was not in first-rate repair. I believe the Duke of Bedford,* who owns all Heathfield, did intend to do something to the church. He brought an architect there, and the architect said he must pull down the old church that dates from the thirteenth century, and build a sort of Norman Gothic* cathedral in its place. You see the architect thought only of the Duke's pocket from which to draw; he gets five per cent. on the outlay. But when the parson heard that, and I too, being churchwarden, we put our foot down and said, No! We loved the little old church; it was seen by Drake and Raleigh as they sailed into Plymouth Sound,* just the same as we see it to-day, and we would not have a stone changed of the carcase.* They might do what they liked with the vitals inside, that we conceded. Since that day we have heard nothing more of the restoration of Brentor church. Consequently, the sacred edifice has been getting more and more out of repair.

The rain had driven for centuries through the joints of the masonry, even through the stone itself, and had streamed down inside, rotting the joists of the bell-chamber where they rested in the wall. I don't blame the builders, they did their best. The walls are thick, but there is no stone in the country that is impervious to a south-western wind charged with rain. Granite is worst of all. You might as well build of sponge. Brentor church is built of the stone of the hill on which it stands, a sort of pumice, full of holes, and therefore by nature spongy. It holds the wet, and weeps it out at every change of weather. Now the belfry joists had given way, rotted right off, and had brought the planking down with them, and lay a wreck at the bottom of the tower. By day, I have no doubt, anyone looking up would see the three bells, and the holes in the lead roof above them. It was difficult for me to get at the ropes, so encumbered was the floor with fallen beams and boards that smelt of mildew and death. I fancy the floor had given way since last Sunday, and that was why the litter lay there. Some of the sexton's tools had been knocked over by the falling beams. He wants strong tools, for the graves have to be hewn in the rock.

After I had removed some of the rotten timber, I made myself space, and stood in a pool of coffee-coloured water that had leaked from the roof, and drained from the sodden joists, and then I began to ring the bells. As I rang I looked round now and then. It was, of course, possible, though hardly probable, that the blacksmith or Luke Petherick might come up and take a turn at the ropes. I did not *expect* anyone, but I thought one *might* come; and I almost wished I had knocked the blacksmith up on my way, and asked him to join me as a personal favour. He couldn't have refused, for he does all my blacksmithing for me. But it might have seemed as if I were afraid to go alone, and it would have deprived Solomon of half the ringer's fee. Looked at in another light, it would not have done, for one in my position is hardly the person to be seen ringing a church bell, and to be known to have done it out of good-nature.

I soon found that, for one unaccustomed to bell-ringing, the exertion was great; it brought into play muscles not usually exercised, and I began to feel the strain. I paused and wiped my forehead. My hands were getting galled.* I did not moisten them in the customary way,* which is vulgar; but I dipped my palms in the coffee-coloured solution on the pavement at my feet. I had hitherto rung the 'cock,' as Solomon designates one old heavy bell that has a curious Latin inscription on it, which begins, '*Gallus vocor*.'* Now, as I rose from moistening my palms, I looked at the rope of the tenor bell, intending to pull that next. As I did so, I noticed something dark, like a ball of dirty cobwebs, hanging to the cord, rather high up. I elevated my lanthorn to see what it was, but the light afforded by the tallow dip was not sufficient to enable me to distinguish the outline of the object. I supposed it might be a great mass of filthy cobweb, or perhaps a piece of broken flooring which had remained attached to the rope, caught when the rest fell away. I considered that if I pulled the rope, I should probably bring the thing—whatever it was—down on my head. You will understand that my desisting from touching that cord was prompted by the wisest discretion, not by inane fear. So I rang the treble bell, and ever and anon* cast up my eye at the remarkable mass above.

Presently, I desisted from ringing altogether. I thought that the object was descending the rope slowly. I say I *thought* so, I did think so at first, but very soon I was certain of it. So certain was I, that I stepped back, and in so doing fell over a balk.* When I had picked myself up the thing had reached the bottom. I should have liked to leave the church, but to do this I must step past this creature; I must do more; it was in the only clear space between me and the tower arch, so that to get out I must lift it from its place to make a passage for myself, and this I did not feel inclined to do. I never have believed in the supernatural. I do not believe in it now. Ghosts, goblins, and pixies are the creations of fevered imaginations and illiterate ignorance. It puts me out of patience to hear people, who ought to know better, speak of such things. I did not for a moment, therefore, suppose that the object before me was a denizen of another world. As far as I can recollect and analyse my sensations at the time, I should say that blank amazement prevailed, attended by a dominating desire to be outside the church and careering down the flank of the hill in the direction of Brinsabatch. I had no theory as to what the thing was;

indeed the inclination to theorize was far from me. The creature I could now see had a human form. It was of the size of a three months' old baby. I have had no experience in babies myself, and am no judge of ages, so that when I say three months I do not wish to be tied down to that period exactly. In colour the object was brown, as if it had been steeped in peat water for a century, and in texture leathery. It scrambled, much as I have seen a bat* scramble, out of the puddle on the pavement to the heap of broken timber, and worked its way with its little brown hands and long claws up a rafter, and seated itself thereon, holding fast by a hand on each side of what I suppose was the body, and then blinked, much in the same way as a monkey blinks, drawing a skin over the eyes different in colour from the skin of the face.

'I be Margery Palmer of Quether,' it said in strange, far-off, mumbling words. 'I couldn't bide up yonder no longer; the wood be that rotten, it is all giving way, and I be afeard I may fall and break my bones. That 'ud be a gashly state o' things, my dear, to hev to bide up there year after year with a body o' bones all scatted abroad [broken to pieces], and never no chance of the bones healing.'*

'Who are you?' I asked, perhaps not as loudly or with as firm a voice as that in which I usually accost a stranger. The creature did not hear me. It went on, however, in its mumbling voice, and with a querulous intonation, 'I be Margery Palmer of Quether. I reckon there be some one there, but, my dear, I cannot see you, and if you speak I cannot hear you. I be deaf as a post, and I've the eyes white wi' caterick.'*

'Are you a spirit?' I inquired. She did not hear me; so, waxing bolder, I put my hands to my mouth and shouted, as through a speaking trumpet, 'are you a spirit?'

'Spirit—spirit!' she echoed. 'Lauk a mussy!* I wish I was! Spirit! No such luck comed to me yet. If I was I'd be thankful. Ah! Wishes don't fulfil themselves like as prayers do.'

'How came you here?' I called.

'Here!' she repeated. 'I can't hear. I be got too old for that, I reckon I be Margery Palmer o' Quether.'

'Impossible,' I said. Were my senses taking leave of me? 'This is a sheer impossibility.' She did not hear my protest, but went mumbling on. 'I lives up yonder among the bells. I've lived there these hundreds of years. I reckoned it were the safest place I could be in. I'd not ha' come down now, but that I were feard the bells would give way and all fall together, and my bones would ha' broke. It 'ud be a gashly thing to live on for hundreds o' years wi' broked arms and legs, and mebbe also a broked neck, so that the head hung down behind, and with no power to move it, not a bit and crumb.* There ain't no healing power in my old bones now; they be as ancient as they in the graves, and no more power of joining in them, than the dead and mouldering bones hev.'

I held up the lanthorn to inspect this curious creature squatted before me on a beam. It was, as I said, of the size of a baby; but otherwise it was a grown woman very aged and withered. The face was not merely wizen, it was dried up to leather, quite tanned brown, the colour of the oak beams; the hands and arms were shrivelled and like those of a bat. There was actually no flesh on them, they were simply dry, tanned skin about bone. The garments seemed to have been tanned like the hide by the liquor distilling from the oak. The eyes were blear.

'I can't see, and I can't hear,' she went on, 'except just a little scrap o' light which I take to be a link.* I gets blinder and ever blinder, till in time I shall look into the sun and see only blackness and darkness for ever. I gets deafer and deafer, but I can hear the bells still. I can also feel a little with my skin, but not much. I've one tooth remains in my head, and I hang on by that. I drive it into the oak beam, and cling round the beam wi' my arms, and strike my nails in too, and so I hold fast. But I knowed very well that the wood were rotten; I knowed it by a sort of instink, and so I've a-comed down to-day. I reckon my hair be all falled off now; I can't tell by the feel, my hands be that numb wi' clinging, that the feeling be most gone from them. But you can see for yourself.' She put her hand to her head and thrust back a leathery hood that had covered it. The little skull was bald. I opened the door of my lanthorn and took out the candle to inspect her better. The head was as if cut out of a thornstick. Only at the back at the junction with the neck was a little frizzle of ragged white hair. I observed as she moved that her neck creased like old hide that threatened to crack at the creases. The flexibility was gone from it. 'Hold the candle before my eyes,' she said; 'I like the light. I can feel it shining through my dull eyes down into my stomick. What be your name, now? '

'George Rosedhu.' I yelled my name into her ear.

'Ah, George! George!' exclaimed old Margery, 'you put off and off too long. You should have married when the fancy first took you. Now it be too late; we be scrumped up [dried up] like old apples.'

What could this extraordinary creature mean?

'Ah, George! George!' she went on. 'That were a cruel, unkind act of yours, keeping company with me so long, and then giving me the slip after all. Do you mind how we used to meet here of Sundays, and how on the windy days you helped me up the rock, and on windy and rainy days you wrapped your cloak round the both of us, and how, when the days were foggy, we used to lose our way in the mist, and never were able to find the church door till the service were over? And do you recall how one day you took me round to the west end of the church, after service, where we could stand at the edge of the rock, wi' our backs to the tower, and you said you wanted to point out Kit Hill to me—'

I sprang forward and put my hand over her mouth.

'Good heavens!' I exclaimed. 'Will you drive me mad? What do you mean? Who are you?'

She went on, when I withdrew my hand, 'Ah, George, George, you knew there was not much to be got with me. There were my brothers and a swarm of little ones coming on, and so you left me out in the cold, and took up with Mary Cake, of Wringworthy,* who was twenty years older than me. You said I were too young; and now Mary Cake that became Mary Rosedhu be dead and mouldered these hundreds of years, and I—I be alive and old enough even for a Rosedhu.'

Then the old creature began to laugh, but stopped with a short scream. 'I must not do it. I dare not laugh. I be too old, and I shall crack my sides and tear my skin. Then what is cracked bides* cracked, and what is tore bides tore.'

What did the creature mean by her allusion to Mary Cake? That was my great, great—I am afraid to say how many times removed—grandmother. She died about two hundred years ago. She brought an addition to the property of fifty-three acres, which I now possess. I have the marriage settlements in the iron deeds-chest under my bed, the date 1605.*

'Well, well,' the little old woman went on, 'we all make mistakes. Life is but a string of them. Coming into the world is the first; courting, marrying, everything in succession is a mistake. You, George, made a mistake in taking Mary Cake instead of me. Her led you a cruel, sour life, to my thinking. Her had a vixenish* temper as would worry any man out of conceit with life. I, on the other hand, was all lightsomeness and fun. You knew that; but what cared you for a pretty face and a sunny temper alongside of a few acres of moorland? You Rosedhus are a calkelating family, and you reckon up everything wi' a bit o' chalk on the table. I hadn't the land that Mary brought, but I'd youth and energy and a cheerful disposition. But, Rosedhus, you are all afraid of long families, and are a grasping and a keeping set. You always marry late in life, and oldish women, lest a lot of children should eat the property as mice eat cheese. It be a mistake, a gashly error. But there, now, I won't aggravate you. Now tell me this: How come you alive at this time? I thought you'd been dead these two hundred and fifty years. Can't you find your rest no more nor I? Did you also pray that you might never die?'

I could not answer. I have no imagination, and I was unable to follow her, mixing up the past and the present in such an unaccountable manner. As far as I could understand, she confused me with a remote ancestor of the same name who died in 1623. That was the George Rosedhu who married Mary Cake, of Wringworthy, in 1605.

'I made my mistake when I prayed for life,' said the old woman. 'I was so joyous and fond of life and full of giddiness that I used to pray every Sunday when I came to church, and every evening when I said my Matthew, Mark, Luke, and John, that I might never die. I were also mortal afraid of death. The graves here be digged out of the living stone, and be full of water afore the coffins be splashed into them, and the corpses don't moulder; they sop away* and go off the bones just as if they was boiled to rags.* That terrified me, so I always prayed for one only thing, that I might never die, and my prayer hev been heard and answered. I cannot die, but I can grow older and more decrepit and drier, for I never considered to pray that I might always bide young. So you see, even when we pray, we make mistakes. Now I cannot die. I get older and older, and shrump [wither] up more and more, and get drier and blinder and deafer. I can no longer taste, and I cannot smell, and I can hardly feel. I have no pleasure in life at all now, and the only feeling in me is fear—fear lest I should get broke or tore, for I be past mending; if I be broke or tore I must so bide to the end of time. On a very hot day, when the sun shines, I seem to have a sort o' a sense of warmth, and the frost must cake me up in ice before I knows I'm cold. I reckon in another hundred years my tongue will have dried up, and then I sha'n't be able to talk no more; but that is the last organ to go in a woman, as her temper is the first; her mind may go, her teeth may go, her sight may go, her hearing may go—but her tongue dies hard. In another hundred years I shall not be able to feel the streak of midsummer sun that falls on my back, nor the winter icicle that hangs from my nose. I sit bunched up on a beam above the bells, and hold on with a tooth drove fast into the wood right home to the gum, and my nails hev grown till they go round the beam I clutch. The dry rot has got into the wood, and it be turned to powder, so that the crust has given way and I've sunk into the dust and mildew. You must put me away where I can be safe for another two or three hundred years out o' the way of dogs and rats and boys. Dogs would tear my skin, and rats gnaw holes in me, and boys pelt me wi' stones and break my bones. What is broke is broke, and what is tore is tore—I be past all healing. I were put up in the belfry above the bells as the place where I might be safest, but now that the rafters and joists be rotten and falling about me, it b'aint safe no more.'

She ceased, and sat blinking at me. The skin of her eyelids was the only part of her that retained any flexibility, and any likeness to human skin in colour and texture. The eyelashes were white like frost needles. I was touched with compassion. As I have already said, I have no intention of disguising or hiding my faults, and I frankly confess that a too great readiness to be moved by a tale or stirred by a spectacle appealing to human sympathy is one of my worst faults. I fear it is ineradicably ingrained in my constitution; I was born with this just as some unfortunates come into the world with the germs of scrofula in their blood and tubercles in their lungs. I remembered now to have heard, when a boy, of a certain girl who was said to have been so much in love with life that she had prayed she might never die, and who, accordingly, was doomed to live for ever; but I thought that she raced on stormy nights with a white owl hooting before her over the moors in the train of the Black Hunter and the Wisht Hounds.* I know my old nurse had told me some such a tale to draw a moral from it of content with what Providence disposes; but it was news to me that this Undying One had been put away to wither up among the bells of Brentor Church. What a wretched existence this poor creature had dragged on! My ancestor, who had flirted with her and then jilted her, had lived over two hundred years ago, and she would be alive, drier and more wretched two hundred years hence, when Margaret and I are fallen to dust, and our lineal descendant in the male line is reigning at Brinsabatch. My kindly disposition was touched—my heart softened. In a sudden access of pity, I put my arms round the poor old creature—she was as light as a doll—and crooking my finger through the ring of the lanthorn, I said, 'I will carry you home, old Margery! You shall feel a Christmas fire, and taste Christmas beef and plum-pudding.'

She did not understand. I do not think she heard me, but she laid hold of me tenaciously, as she had laid hold of the beam on which she had crouched for two centuries; she drove her single tooth through my coat and waistcoat, even cutting my skin, and her bat-like hands and claws clutched me, the nails going into me like knife-blades. I left the church with her, and carried her home; that is to say, she adhered to me so tenaciously—I might say, voraciously—that I had no occasion to use my arms for her support; she was like a knapsack slung on the wrong way, and quite as securely fastened—faster, for a knapsack will oscillate, but old Margery stuck to me as tight as a tick on a dog.

When I got home I said, 'Now, old Margery, shake yourself off and sit by the brave big fire, and I'll give you something warm to drink that will cheer the cockles of your leathery heart.' But, not a bit would she budge. I shouted into her ear, but she could or would not hear. Her tooth, which was driven into my chest like the proboscis of a mosquito, held her fast, and her hands were no more to be unlocked from my arms than the laces of old ivy from an oak. There was nothing for it but for me to sit down in my armchair, nursing her. The situation was almost grotesque; it was altogether undignified. So I sat on, occasionally expostulating, and always in vain; and I thought I should have next morning to get a man with a knife to slit up my coat and waistcoat behind so as to let the old creature slip off with the garments. But I was saved this annoyance by her tooth gradually being withdrawn, and her fingers relaxing. She fell off, and dropped on my knees, and lay there like a sleeping infant after its meal.

I threw a bunch of gorse on the fire, and it roared up the chimney in a sheet of golden flame, filling the little parlour with light. I was able now to study the face of the little creature on my lap, entirely at my ease. It struck me now that old Margery looked younger than I had taken her to be when I saw her in the belfry. She was a very old woman indeed, still, but there was a human-like moisture on the leathery skin, which also looked less liable to part at the folds, and there was even a rosy tinge on the lips. I suppose that from holding her so long I was somewhat more able to appreciate her weight. It was not that of a doll stuffed with bran, but of a baby with milk and flesh and blood in it adapted to its age. I thought her also rather larger than I had at first supposed, but that may be because she was now asleep on my knees, and there is a gain of an inch or two in repose, owing to muscular relaxation.

I put her down very gently on my sofa, and set a chair against the side, lest she should roll off on the floor; then I went in quest of a clothes basket, which I filled with soft pillows. This I set in the ingle nook, and laid old Margery in the maund.* I covered her over with an eider-down quilt taken from my own bed, and she seemed very cozy in the extemporized cradle. I did more. I got a Florence flask* that had contained sweet oil, and rinsed it well out with a strong solution of soda. When it was quite clean, I filled it with hot strong rum and sugar and water. I wished I could find a flexible india-rubber tube, but I was unprovided with such things. There had been no call for them hitherto, in my house—Hold! there was though! I recollected that one of the cows after calving had died of milk-fever, and the calf had been brought up by hand. I remembered a vulcanized india-rubber contrivance that had been tried but had not answered, as the calf disliked the taste of the sulphur.* I now found this, and with some little ingenuity adapted it to the Florence flask, and then put it into the basket beside Margery. I put my finger into her mouth first to encourage her, but she only played with it, and then I inserted between her almost toothless gums the vulcanized india-rubber contrivance—I forget its proper name. I thought it would keep her quiet, but she dragged so hard at it that the tube came out, and all the rum and water ran among the pillows. So I had to take her out again, and dry the cushions before the fire, and make up the bassinet* with fresh pillows. Poor little thing, she slept through it all, like an angel.

All this took me a long time, and gave me great exertion; it called into requisition faculties of the mind and heart that had not been previously exercised. I was very tired; I sat back in my chair and fell asleep. I did not dare to go to bed lest old Margery should wake and want me. When I opened my eyes, it was Christmas Day. The clerk was ill, I was churchwarden, and must be at S. Michael de Rupe on that sacred festival, to give the good day and the best wishes of the season to all my neighbours—sweet, blooming Margaret Palmer of Quether included. I went upstairs and dressed myself in my Sunday suit, and a blue neckcloth, and I put on my cairngorm pin* with a terrier's head in it, put some pomatum* on my hair—that I always do on

Sunday the last thing before going to church—and before I left I drew down the coverlet and looked at old Margery.

She was sleeping still—bless her!—with her old brown thumb in her mouth. I was uneasy because the nail was so long, I thought it might scratch her palate or irritate the uvula, so I got a pair of scissors and cut it. I felt strangely moved with pity, and with that pity there awoke in me a sort of sense of personal property in old Margery. Also, I presume, because of that, I was aware of some pride in her. I knew that she was wizen and old and hideous, and I knew also, that if any woman had come into my house with her baby in her arms and had asked me to admire it, and then had looked disparagingly at Margery, I should have hated that woman ever after. As it was, that day a child was christened in the church. I looked at its soft pink skin, and went away from the sacred edifice with envy and anger rankling in my heart.

II

I LEFT Brinsabatch that morning with great reluctance, and all the time of divine service I was thinking far more of old Margery than of young Margaret, as I ought—and I do not mind confessing my fault openly. My seat is a little forward of the Quether pew on the other side. Usually, when standing for the psalms and hymns, I stand sideways, that the light may fall on my book, and look over the top at Margaret, who does the same; but as she is on the other side and the window opposite mine, she turns towards me that she may get the light on her print, and so our eyes are always meeting. When the parson is praying to us, I lean forward with my head on the book board, and so my eyes go diagonally backward, Margaret leans her head in an opposite fashion, and so her eyes go diagonally forward, and our eyes are always meeting in the prayers, as in the psalms. During the sermon I am obliged to turn round on my seat, as I am hard of hearing in my right ear, owing to a cricket ball having hit it when I was at the Tavistock Grammar School. Margaret always somehow has her bonnet string over her left ear, so she is forced to sit roundabout on her seat and expose the hearing ear to the preacher, and so it always comes about that during the sermon our eyes are meeting. This Christmas Day it was other with me; I could think of nothing but my poor little old Margery in her bassinet by the fire, and I kept on wondering whether she would wake up in my absence and fret for want of me. Then I had all through the sermon a pricking feeling in my chest—I suppose where her tooth and nails had held so tight—and I was restless and uncomfortable to be back at Brinsabatch.

After service, as I was shaking hands all round, feeling eager to get it over and be off, Farmer Palmer said to me, 'Come home to Quether with us, Rosedhu, and eat your Christmas dinner there. We are old friends and hope to be closer friends in time than we are now. I don't like, nor does Margaret here, to think of you sitting lonely down to your meal on Christmas Day. There is a knife and fork laid ready for you, and I will take no refusal.'

I made a lame sort of excuse. I said I was unwell.

'That is true enough,' said Palmer; 'you don't look yourself at all to-day, and Margaret is uneasy about you. Your face is white, your hand shakes, and you look older by some years than when I last saw you. When was that?'

'Sunday, father,' said Margaret with a sigh.

I assured them that I was too indisposed to accept their kind invitation, and I saw that they believed me. Margaret's brown eyes were fixed anxiously and intently on me. I had been up all night, and much worried, that was why I looked older and unwell, but I only said by way of explanation to Palmer, the one magical word 'liver.' When you say that word every man understands you. It touches his heart at once.

As I walked home every person I passed and spoke to said, 'How oldened you are!' or 'How ill you look!' or 'Why, surely that baint you, Mr. George, looking nigher forty than twenty.'

I wish Mr. Palmer would not try to thrust Margaret on me. Margaret invites me to dinner. Margaret is concerned at my looks. Margaret remembers when last we met. That is all hyperbola and figure and flower of speech, and means in plain English, I want you to take my eldest daughter off my hands, but I am not going to give more than a trifle with her.

I never was more pleased than on this occasion when I got home again. I unlocked my parlour door, and ran in and up to the clothes basket, and cried in a sort of fond foolish rapture, 'Bless it! bless it!'

The little old woman opened her eyes—they were not clouded with cataract; that must have been a fancy of mine before; she saw me and smiled, and made a sort of crowing noise in her throat. I stooped over to kiss her, when—click! in an instant she had fastened herself on me, and driven her tooth into my chest, and grabbed me with her hands, so that I was held as in a vice. To wrench her off would have been impossible. I believe if torn away the hands would have held to me still, and the arms come off at the wrists. I know that when a ferret fastens on a rabbit you may kill the beast before he will let go, unless you nip his hind foot; then he opens his mouth to squeal, and loosens his grip to defend himself. I did not think of this at the time, or I might have called in someone to pinch Margery's foot; but I doubt, even if I had remembered this, whether I should have had recourse to this expedient. I did not care to have my situation discussed; moreover, I was conscious of a soothing sensation all the time Margery was fast. Besides, I knew by this time that when the little old woman had had enough she would drop off, just as a leech does when full. I would not have you suppose that Margery was sucking my blood. Nothing of the sort; that is, not grossly in the manner of a leech. But she really did, in some marvellous manner to me quite inexplicable, extract life and health, the blood from my veins and the marrow from my bones, and assimilate them herself.

Presently she fell off, as I knew she would when satisfied, and lay in my lap, across my knees. She looked up at me with a smile that had something really pleasant in it. She was positively taller, her skin fresher, her eye clearer than before; her eyelashes were gray, not snowy; and there was actually a down of grey hairs covering her poll, like the feathers on a cockatoo. I wrapped a blanket round her, and was about to replace it in the basket, when I found, to my surprise, that it would cramp her limbs; she could not kick out of it. So I got a drawer out of my bureau, fitted it up with pillows, and laid her in that.

I really do think there is something taking about her expression. When you consider her age, she gave wonderfully little trouble. At first it was strange to me to have to do with this sort of little creature—it was my first and only—but I saw that I should soon get used to it. In the afternoon I employed myself in making a pair of rockers, which I adjusted to the drawer, and by this means converted it into a very tolerable cradle. I am handy at carpentering. Indeed there are not many things which I cannot do when put to it. When the emergency arose, as the reader will see, I became really a superior nurse, without any training or experience. Indeed, I feel confident that in the event of this Radical Gladstone-Chamberlain-Bradlaugh* Government altering the land laws and robbing me of Brinsabatch, I could always earn my living as a nurse; I could take a baby from the month, if not earlier, or a person of advanced age lapsed into second childhood. Never before have I taken in hand the tools of literature, and yet, I venture to say that—well! there are idiots in the world who don't know the qualities of a cow, and to whom a sample of wheat is submitted in vain. Such persons are welcome to form what opinion they like of my literary style. Their opinion is of no value whatever to me. There is no veneer in my work, it is sterling. There is no padding, as it is called; my literary execution is substantial and thorough as were the rockers I put on thicky [I mean, that there] cradle. The rockers were not put on many days before they were needed. Old Margery became very restless at night, and she would not let me be long out of the house by day. She was cutting her teeth. The back teeth are terribly trying to babies—they have fits sometimes and big heads and water on the brain, all through the molars. If it be so with an infant of a few months, just consider what it must be with an old woman in her three-hundredth year, or thereabouts! I bore with her very patiently, but broken rest is trying to a man. Besides, about the same time I suffered badly in my jaws, for my teeth, which were formerly perfectly sound, began to decay, break off, and fall out. I may say, approximately, that as Margery cut a tooth I lost one; also that, as her hair grew and darkened, mine came out or turned grey. Moreover, as her eye cleared mine became dim, and as her spirits rose mine became despondent.

In this way, weeks, and even months, passed. It really was a pretty sight to see the havoc of ages repaired in the person of Margery; the sight would have been one of unalloyed delight, had not the recovery been effected at my expense. The colour came back into her cheek as it left my once so florid complexion; she filled out as I shrivelled up, she grew tall as I collapsed; the drawer would now no longer contain her, and a bed was made for her by the fire in the parlour. I noticed a gradual change in the tenour of her talk, as she grew younger. At first she could think and speak of nothing but her ailings, but after, she took to talking scandal, bitter and venomous, of neighbours, that is, of neighbours dead and dropped to dust, whose very tombstones are weathered so as to be illegible. Little by little her talk became less virulent, and softened into harmless prattle, and was all about the things of the farm and house. She was a first-rate worker. I was glad she took such an interest in the farm; she brisked about and saw to everything. I was not able now to get about as much as I might have liked, as I suffered much from rheumatism and bronchitis. Neighbours came to see me, and all were in the same tale, that I was becoming an old man before my time, that the change in me was something unprecedented and unaccountable. I could not walk without a stick. I stooped. My hair was thin and grey, my limbs so shrunken that my clothes hung on me as on a scarecrow. I was advised to see a doctor; that is—everyone had a special doctor who was sure to cure me; one said I must go to Dr. Budd at North Tawton,* and another to Dr. Hingston* at Plymouth, and one to this and one to that; they would have sent me flying over the county consulting doctors, and varying them every week. Some said—and I soon found that was the prevailing opinion—that I was bewitched, and advised me strongly to consult the white witch* either in Exeter or Plymouth. I turned a deaf ear to them all. I wanted no doctors. I needed no white witch. I knew well enough what ailed me. I never now went up Brent Tor to church. Dear life! I could not have climbed such a height if I had wished it! My poor old bones ached at the very thought, and my back was nigh broken when I walked through the shippen* one day to the linneye* [cattle shed]. Besides, I had grown terribly short of wind, and I had such a rattling on my chest. I almost choked of a night. That was the bronchitis, and when I coughed it shook me pretty well to pieces.

So time passed, and I knew that I was sinking slowly and surely into my grave; there was no real complaint on me to kill me. I was breaking up of old age, and yet was no more than three and twenty. Everyone said I looked as if I was over ninety years. If I could see the hundred, it would be something to be proud of before I was four and twenty. One thought troubled me sorely. Whatever would become of Brinsabatch without a Rosedhu in it? I should die without leaving a lineal descendant in the male line. It would go out of the family. I had not a relation in the world. We Rosedhus always marry late in life, and never have large families. I was the single thread on which the possible Rosedhu posterity depended. I believe that an aunt had once married, and had a lot of children, but she was never named in the family. It was tantamount to a loss of character in Rosedhu eyes. I did not even know her married name. She was dead; but her issue no doubt remained, though I knew nothing of them. They, I suppose would inherit. I found as I grew older that this fretted me more and more. I would soon pass beyond the grave into the world of spirits, and I knew, the moment I turned up there, that all the Rosedhus would be down on me for not having left male issue to inherit Brinsabatch, each, with intolerable self-assurance, setting himself up before me as an example I ought to have copied. As if, under my peculiar circumstances, I could help myself. The only one of my ancestors with whom I should be able to exchange words would be the George Rosedhu who had married Mary Cake. I could cast it in his teeth that had he been faithful to his first love, this disastrous contingency would not have occurred.

'Ah!' said I, in a fit of spleen, 'it is all very well of you, Margery, to go about the house singing. What is to become of the Rosedhus? To whom will Brinsabatch fall? You have drawn all the flush and health out of me and made yourself young at my charge,—but I get nothing thereby.'

'I will nurse you in your decrepitude, dearest George,' she answered, and a dimple came in her rosy cheek, the prettiest twinkle in her laughing blue eye. Upon my word she was a bonny buxom* wench, and it would have been a delight to be in the house with her, had I been younger. Now I could only gaze on her charms despairingly from afar off, as Moses looked on the Promised Land from Pisgah.* What a worker she was, moreover! What a manager! What an organizer! What a housekeeper, cook, dairywoman, rolled into one! Never was the house so neat, the linen so cared for, the brass pans so scoured, the butter so sweet, the dairy so clean. She had been brought up in the old-fashioned, hard-working, sensible ways of a farm in the reign of Good Queen Bess. In our days, the women are all infected with your Gladstone-Chamberlain topsy-turveyism,* and farmers' daughters play the piano and murder French, and farmers' wives read Miss Braddon and Ouida* and neglect the cows. Her ways were a surprise to all on the estate. The men and the maids had never seen anything like it. Folks could not make Margery out, who she was, and where I had picked her up. Nobody seemed to belong to her; she had never been seen before, and yet she knew the names of every tor, and hamlet, and coombe, and moor, as if she had been reared there. But though she knew the places, she did not know the people. She spoke of the Tremaines of Cullacombe,* whereas the family had left that house two hundred years ago, and were settled at Sydenham.* She talked of the Doidges of Hurlditch,* a family that had been gone at least a hundred years. Kilworthy, she supposed, was still tenanted by the Glanvilles,* whereas that race is extinct, and the place belongs to the Duke of Bedford, who has turned it into a farm. On the other hand, what was curious was, that Margery hit right now and then on the names of some of the labouring poor; she would salute a man by his right Christian and surname, because he was exactly like an ancestor some two hundred and fifty years ago. Though the great families have migrated or disappeared, the poor have stuck to their native villages, and reproduce from century to century the same faces, the same prejudices, the same characteristics. They are almost as unchangeable as the hills.

As I have said, Margery was a puzzle to everyone, and because a puzzle, the workmen and girls looked on her with suspicion. They resented the close way in which they were kept to their work and the rigid supervision exercised over them. Solomon Davy, the clerk, alone suspected who she was. He called several times to see me, and looked hard at me, with an uneasy manner, and seemed as though he wanted to ask me something, but lacked the courage to do so. Margery is always pleasant to Solomon, she knew the Davys that went before him, but he gives her a wide berth; he never lets her come within arm's reach of him. She feels it, I am sure, by her manner; but she is too good-hearted to remark on it.

I cannot deny that she was goodness and attention itself to me, and that I was fond of her. Just as a mother idolizes her baby that draws all its life and growth from her, so was it with me. I begrudged her none of her youth and beauty; I took a sort of motherly pride in her growth and the development of her charms, and for precisely the same reason—they were all drawn out of me.

One day Margery announced that she intended to marry me, and told me I must be prepared to stir my old stumps and go to church with her. She explained her reason candidly to me. She knew that I had a clear business head, and so she consulted me on the subject, which was flattering, and I should have felt more grateful had I not almost reached a condition past acute feeling. She told me that she would nurse me till I expired in her arms, and then, as my widow, would have Brinsabatch. This would secure her future, for with her renewed youth and with her handsome estate she could always command suitors and secure a second husband, from whom she could extract sufficient life and health to maintain her in the bloom of youth. When he was exhausted and withered up and dead, she could obtain a third, and so on *ad infinitum*. She objected to being again consigned to mummification in the tower of Brent Tor Church, and this was the simplest and most straightforward solution to her peculiar difficulties. The plan suggested was feasible, and, from her point of view, admirable. I was now so shattered mentally and physically that I was in no condition to raise an objection. Indeed, I had no objection to raise. I freely, willingly submitted to her proposal. She exercised no undue compulsion on me; she appealed to my reason, and my reason, as far as it remained, told me that her plan was sensible, and in every way worthy of her. She was a handsome woman, with a fine head of brown hair, and the brightest, wickedest, merriest pair of blue eyes. As for her cheeks—quarantines* were nothing to them. A man in the prime of life would be proud to have such a woman as his wife, and her selection of me was, in its way, complimentary, even though I knew that I was taken for the sake of Brinsabatch.

So I consented, and she herself took the banns* to the clerk. Solomon opened his eyes when she told him her purpose, moved uneasily on his seat, and scratched his head. He hardly knew what to make of it. He came to see me, and looked inquiringly at me, but I had one of my fits of coughing on me. When I was sufficiently recovered to speak, I told Solomon how impatient I was for my wedding-day to arrive, and how kind and excellent a nurse Margery was to me. He went away puzzled, and rubbing his forehead. I made but one stipulation with respect to my wedding, that was, that I should be conveyed to the foot of Brent Tor in a spring-cart, laid on straw, and thence be conveyed up the hill to the altar by four strong men, in a litter, laid upon a feather-bed, and with hot bottles at my feet and sides. I was entirely incapable of walking.

This was at the beginning of November. Consequently ten months had elapsed since that fatal Christmas Eve on which I had made the acquaintance of Margery of Quether. So the banns were read on the first Sunday in the month at the afternoon service, there being no service that day in the morning in the little church. The banns were published between George Rosedhu, of Brinsabatch, bachelor, and Margaret Palmer, of Quether, spinster. If anyone knew any just cause or impediment why these two should not be joined together in holy matrimony, they were now to declare it. That was the first time of asking.

A pretty sensation the reading of these banns caused. Farmer Palmer's face turned as mottled as brawn, and Miss Palmer blushed as red as a rose and buried her face in her hymn-book. My old Margery had overshot her mark, as the sequel proved. She had not reckoned with young Margaret, her great, great, great, great grand-niece.

When public worship was concluded, Mr. Palmer and his daughter, instead of directing their steps homeward towards Quether, where tea was awaiting them, walked in the opposite direction, and descended on Brinsabatch, to know of me what was meant by the banns—sober earnest or a silly joke.

Margery was not at home. She always frequented S. Mary Tavy church,* because she had a dislike to Brent Tor; it was associated in her mind with two centuries of chilling and repellant associations. Margery was a regular church-goer. That was part of her bringing up. In her young days, if anyone missed church, he was fined a shilling,* and if he did not take the sacrament, was whipped at the cart-tail. These penalties are no longer exacted; nevertheless, Margery is punctual in her attendance. Such is the force of a habit early acquired.

Thus it came about that Farmer Palmer and his daughter arrived at Brinsabatch before Margery had returned from church. I am sorry that my hand is not expert at describing things which I neither saw nor heard accurately. I have no imagination, which is a delusive faculty leading to serious error. Palmer and his daughter were attended by Solomon Davy, who I believe endeavoured to explain the situation to them and told them who Margery really was. I had become so dull of hearing, and so cataracted in eye, that I was unable to understand all that went on, and to follow and take part in the somewhat heated and animated conversation. If, like a modern writer of fiction, I were to give the whole of what was said, with description of the attitudes assumed, the inflections of the voices, and the degrees of colour that mantled the several cheeks, I might make my narrative more acceptable, no doubt, to the vulgar many, but it would lose its value to the appreciative few, who ask for a true record of what I *observed*.

I believe that Solomon in time made it clear to the dull intellects of the Palmers that the banns were for my marriage with the great, great, great, great-aunt of Margaret, and not with herself. What he said of poor Margery I don't know. I strained my ears to catch what he said, but heard only a buzzing as of bees. I doubt not that he spiced the truth with plenty of falsehood.

Farmer Palmer has a loud voice. I heard him say to his daughter, 'Wait here a bit, Margaret, along with George Rosedhu, and bide till t'other Margery arrives; I back one woman against another.'

'Oh, father!' exclaimed the pretty creature, 'where are you a-going to?'

'My dear, I shall be back directly. This be Fifth o' November, and bonfire night.* The lads be all collecting faggots for a blaze on the moor. I'll fetch 'em here, and they can have the pleasure o' burning the old witch instead of a man o' straw.'

I held out my hands in terror and deprecation. 'You durstn't do it!'

'Why not?' asked the farmer composedly. 'Her's a witch and no mistake. Her have sucked you dry of life as an urchin [hedgehog] sucks a cow of milk.'

'But,' protested Solomon, 'though that be true enough, what about the laws? I won't say but that it be right and scriptural to burn a witch; for it is written, "Thou shalt not suffer a witch to live,"* but I reckon it be against the laws.'

'Not at all,' said Palmer. 'No man can be had up for burning a person who has no existence.'

'But she has existence,' I remonstrated. 'That is the prime cause of her trouble; she has too much of it; she can't die.'

'There is no evidence of her existence,' argued Palmer. 'You, Solomon, tell me how far back your registers go in Brent Tor Church.'

'Back, I reckon, to about 1680.'

'Very well, then they contain no record of her birth and baptism. Now you cannot be hung for killing a person of whose existence there is absolutely no legal evidence. The law won't touch us if we do burn her.'

'But—but,' I said, crying and snuffling, 'she is your own flesh and blood.'

'That may be, but that is no reason against her cremation.* My own Margaret stands infinitely nearer to me, and her interests closer to my heart, than the person and welfare of a remote ancestress. As the banns have been called, Brinsabatch shall go to my daughter and to no one else. In three weeks' time Margaret shall be Mrs. Rosedhu.' He spoke very firmly.

'Father, dear father, how can you be so cruel to me?' cried Margaret. 'Do y' look what an atomy* Mr. Rosedhu be come to?'

The burly yeoman paid no heed to his daughter's protest, knowing, no doubt, its unreality. He said to me, 'Look y' here, George Rosedhu, you've had my daughter's name coupled wi' yours in the church to-day, and read out before the whole congregation, without axing my leave or hers. I won't have her made game of even by a man o' substance like you, so she shall marry you before December comes, whether you like it or not.'

'Oh, Mr. Palmer, sir,' I pleaded, 'how can you think to force your daughter into nuptials which must be distasteful to her?'

'Don't you trouble your head about that. Margaret knows which side her bread is buttered. She can distinguish between clotted cream and skim milk.'

'Besides,' I argued, 'I am bound by the most solemn engagements to my Margery. I have promised to settle Brinsabatch on her.'

'You cannot,' shouted the farmer of Quether. 'The thing is impossible. You cannot marry a woman who has no existence in the eye of the law. The only Margaret Palmer of Quether of whom the law has cognizance is she who now stands before you. She has been baptized, vaccinated,* and confirmed. What more do you want to establish her existence? Whereas, what documentary proof can the other Margery produce that she exists? There is but one Margaret Palmer of Quether in this nineteenth century; that's flat.'* He slapped the table, and then, with the air of one administering a crushing argument, he added, 'Now, tell me, is it possible for a man to marry a woman from whom he is removed by from two to three centuries? Answer me that.'

'Put in that bald way,' I said, 'it does seem unreasonable; but in these Radical-Gladstone-Chamberlain-Bradlaughian times one does not know where one stands. All the lines of demarcation between the possible and the impossible are wiped out, reason and fact do not jump together.'

'I leave you to digest that question,' answered Palmer triumphantly. He saw I was pushed into a corner. Then he went out, along with Solomon Davy.

I do not think that Margaret objected to be left to meet Margery. I noticed her pluming and bridling like a game-cock before an encounter. She stroked down the folds of her gown, and pursed up her lips, and now and then shot out her tongue from between her lips, as I have seen a wasp test his sting before stabbing me. I was getting uneasy for Margery, and was myself uncomfortable. I said, 'Miss Margaret, will you be so good as to pick me up my handkercher; it is lying there on the floor, and I be so cruel bad took with the lumbagie that I can't bend to take it myself.'

She complied with my request somewhat surlily. Then I said, 'Would you mind, now, just uncorking that bottle there on the shelf, and putting a drop or two on a lump of sugar, and giving it me. My hands be that shaky I cannot put it in my mouth myself, and I've no teeth to hold it by. The drops be ipecacuahana,* and be good for bronchitis.'

'No, I won't do it, you nasty old man.'

'Then, miss, will you rub my spine with hartshorn* and oil: you'll find a bottle of the mixture on the sideboard, and a bit of flannel in the cupboard? '

'I will do nothing of the sort,' she said testily.

'You won't, miss? Then please to take me up in your arms and carry me to bed. Margery does it. She is very kind and considerate; she begrudges me no trouble, and feeds me out of a spoon.'

'I will do nothing of the sort,' she said again, in short, angry tones, and with an air of supreme disgust.

'I am sorry for it,' said I. That was Gospel truth. I knew that when the two women met such a storm of words would rage as would wreck my poor nerves, and I wanted to be in bed and out of it before the hurricane broke loose.

'You'll have to do all this for me,' I said, 'when you become Mrs. Rosedhu. A very old person needs just as much attention as a baby. I know that, for I've gone through it myself; I've done the nursing. Why will you not leave me alone, and allow Margery to marry me? She will take care of me; she kisses and fondles me. Will you?'

'You disgusting old scarecrow, certainly not.'

'And atomy—scarecrow and atomy—what next will you call me? Yet you want to marry me!'

'You fool!' said Margaret shortly. 'I put up with you for the sake of Brinsabatch.'

'It's the same with Margery,' I said; 'but she put it more pleasantly. Her manners are better than yours; but then she belongs to the old school*—the good old school!' I sighed.

What I said made her angry. She did not like to have comparisons drawn between herself and her remote great aunt, to her own disadvantage.

'I suppose I am to have a voice in the matter,' I went on; 'and though I have liked you very much, Margaret, yet I like the other Margery better. One thing in her favour is—she is older than you.'

'You are not going to have her—who has drained life and spirit out of you. Do you think I will allow it? Don't you see I bear her a grudge? She has turned the fresh and hale George who courted me into a shrivelled old man. It would have been a pleasure to have young George, it is a penance to have the old one. I owe her that, and I shall scratch her eyes out when we meet.'

'Whatever you do,' I pleaded, 'do not hurt her. Your father has made a dreadful threat. I hope he will not execute it.'

'There she comes!' exclaimed Margaret Palmer, starting to her feet in a tremor of delight. 'I hear her step on the walk.'

'Throw the hearthrug over me,' I entreated, 'I cannot bear to be agitated. Toss the table-cover above the hearthrug, all helps to deaden the sound.'

Margaret complied with my request. Here again my narrative must present an appearance of incompleteness. I cannot describe what I neither saw nor heard during the interview between Margaret and Margery, because I was buried under a heavy sheepskin rug and a thick-painted damask table-cover on the top of that. I have no imagination, and I only relate what I actually saw and heard. I saw nothing, and what I heard resembled the jangling of pots and pans when a host of maids are going after a swarm of bees. Of words I could distinguish none, till after a while the hearthrug and table-cover slipped off, owing to my coughing a great deal, the dust out of the hearthrug having got into my bronchial tubes. Then I saw a sight which filled me with dismay.

My room was full of men and boys, with their caps and hats on. Their faces were flushed, and eager, savage delight danced in their eyes. One had a pitchfork, several had sticks, one was armed with a flail. Head and shoulders above the rest stood Farmer Palmer, keeping back the mob that crowded in at the door. In the front of all, as if in a cockpit, opposite each other, stood the two Margarets, red in face, blazing in temper, their tongues going, their eyes sparkling, their hands extended. I will say that poor Margery acted solely on the defensive. She held up her arms in self-protection. Margaret had driven her nails into her cheek and a red streak down the side showed that she had drawn blood.

'See, see!' exclaimed the younger Margaret, 'the witch! her power is broken. The blood is running.'

This is a popular belief. If you can draw blood from a witch, her power—at least over you—is at an end.*

My poor Margery gazed with alarm at the crowd of red, threatening faces that looked at her. She shrank from the sticks, the clubs, the pitchfork and flail. She drew behind me, as if I, broken down into premature old age, could defend and assist her. I raised my shrill pipe in entreaty, but my words were without effect. Those horrible faces glowered at Margery with the savagery of dogs surrounding a hare they are about to tear to pieces. The fear of witchcraft blotted all human compassion out of their hearts.

Suddenly a red light blazed in at the window. The evening had fallen fast and it was now dark.

'Look! look there!' shouted Farmer Palmer. 'Look there, you witch, at the bed made for you. There are plenty of faggots to heap over you should you complain of the cold.'

Margery uttered a scream of terror and clutched my chair, whilst she cowered on the floor behind it.

'Oh, George!' she cried in her agony of dread, 'save me! save me! They cannot kill me, but they can fry and burn me! Then I shall live on—on—on, a scorched morsel, not like a human being.'

'My darling,' I answered, 'I can do nothing against all these men.' I, however, made a desperate attempt. 'I am master in this house,' I cried in my shrill old tones; 'no one has any right within the doors without my permission, and I order you all to go away peaceably and to leave me alone.'

The men and boys, led by Palmer, laughed, and did not budge an inch. There came a shout from outside,

'Bring out the witch, and let her burn!'

There is an innate cruelty in human nature which neither Christianity, nor education, nor teetotalism, will eradicate. I always thought the peasantry of the West of England wonderfully gentle, kindly, and free from brutality, and yet—scratch the man and the beast appears; here were my peaceable, tender-hearted country men ravening for the life of a poor woman, really pretty, and as good-dispositioned and without malice as an angel. I knew that they would gloat over her anguish in the fire, that they would poke up the fuel to make her burn more thoroughly—they would do so without compassion; not really because they thought her a witch, but because Farmer Palmer had told them they might burn her without fear of the law.

A fresh heap of fuel had been tossed upon the pyre, and the flame spouted up to heaven. A roar from the boys without. 'Bring her out! Let her burn!'

Poor Margery covered her eyes with her hands to shut out the terrible light.

'Oh, George, George!' she cried, 'save me, and I will give you back some of your youth and strength again.'

'Stand back,' thundered Palmer, as the circle of men contracted about her, and hands were thrust forth to grasp and tear her from my chair. 'Do you hear me? She has offered to recover our friend Rosedhu.'

'You cannot do it, my poor darling,' I said.

'Oh, save me, George, and I will indeed.'

'You hear her,' shouted Palmer. 'Stand back, and let her fulfil what she has undertaken.'

Then Margaret put in her voice. She was afraid that her rival would escape. 'No, father, do not trust her. She can do nothing. She is a witch, and wants to cast spells over you all. Take her away, boys, and pitch her into the fire. Don't listen to a word she says, however hard she prays to be let go.'

'Into the flames with her!' shouted the men, and stepped forward. 'That is the place for such as she.'

'Fair play, my lads,' said Palmer, and with his strong arm he drove the rabble back. 'As for you, Margaret, don't you interfere. Now then, you—Margery—or whatever you call yourself, stand up and come forward. None shall hurt you if you really recover Rosedhu of his age and incapacity. But, mind you, if you fail, I swear that with this cudgel I will break every bone in your body, and then throw you into the fire with my own arms.'

Margery quivered and cried out at the threat.

'Are you going to do it or not?' asked Palmer.

Poor Margery, feeling the necessity for prompt action, if she would save herself from terrible torture, rose from her crouching posture and stole tremblingly forward.

'Stand out o' the road, boys,' shouted Palmer; 'clear away with you,' and with his stick he swept a circle round Margery and me.

'Oh, George,' she said, with tears of mortification in her blue eyes, 'I'm sorry to do it. I wouldn't if I could; I really wouldn't. But I cannot help myself. These cruel men do so scare me. We might have been so comfortable together; I'd have nursed you into your grave quite beautiful and convenient like, and then I'd have had Brinsabatch to myself, and it would have gone so well for all parties. But now, you see, that blessed arrangement you managed so nicely for me won't come to nothing because of the wickedness of evil men, who walks about like unto roaming and roaring lions seeking who they may devour.* I cannot help myself, George. You'll do me the justice to say it were against my will and under compulsion. There, give me your two hands into mine.'

She took my hands and stood opposite me, holding them at arm's length, and looking into my eyes. Poor thing! her lips trembled, and the tears stood on her lids and overflowed and trickled down her soft red cheeks. It was a sore trial and disappointment to her, but she bore it like a Christian,* and never cast a word of bitterness at those who forced her to it. And to think what a sacrifice she was making! Those rude creatures knew nothing of that, and could not appreciate the greatness of her self-sacrifice. I submitted, because I saw in this way only the means of rescuing her.

As she held my hands, I felt as if streams of vital force were flowing from her up my arms into my body. The aching in my bones ceased. My legs became stronger, my head lighter and more erect, I could see better, and hear better. I began to smell the peat burning on the hearth, I felt an inclination to draw Margery on to my knees and kiss her; but when I looked at her, the desire passed, she was waning as I waxed. She grew older, the colour left her cheek, her eyes became dim; then, all at once I sprang to my feet and shook off her hands. 'Enough, Margery, enough,' I said. 'You have restored me sufficient of my strength and health, the rest I freely make over to you. Now for the rest of you.' My voice was full and loud as that of Palmer himself. 'Everyone of you listen to me. This is my house, and an Englishman's house is his castle.* Leave this room, leave my land at once, or I prosecute every man jack of you for burglary and trespass. Good Lord! Do you know where you are? Do you know whom I am? This is Brinsabatch, and I am a Rosedhu. Gladstone and Chamberlain and Bradlaugh haven't brought matters quite so far yet that every dirty Radical may come inside a landed proprietor's doors and snap his fingers under his nose.' I snatched the stick out of Palmer's hand and went at the men with it. Not one ventured to show me his face. I saw a sudden change of posture, and a crush and rush out of my door and down my little passage. 'You bide here, Palmer,' I said; 'and Margaret also. But as for all this rag-tag and bob-tail* that you have brought in, I'll make a clean sweep of them in a jiffy.'

'It is all very well, Rosedhu,' said Palmer, folding his arms, and setting his legs wide apart. 'You have got rid of the rabble, and you are right to do so if you choose. But you do not get rid of me and Margaret so fast. The banns have been called between my daughter and you; I take no account of the other, she has no legal existence.'

I was silent, and looked from Margery to Margaret.

'Besides,' Palmer went on, 'you may not think so much of her now. In appearance she is old enough to be your grandmother.'

Certainly Margery looked aged, a hale woman, but still old—too old to be thought of as a bride at the hymeneal* altar. Margaret was young and pretty; I wish she had not been quite so young and opened such an alarming vista of possibilities. But then I looked at myself in a glass opposite, and saw that I was grey-headed and on the turn down the hill of life. That was an advantage. 'There is one thing,' I said musingly: 'in the matter of amiability there is no comparison. Margery is as good—'

'We will have no comparisons drawn,' interrupted Palmer, as the girl darted a look at me that plainly said, 'You shall suffer for this some day.' 'Hold out your fist like a man and say you will take my daughter for better, for worse, and make her mistress of Brinsabatch within the month. The first time of asking took place to-day.'

'Let us say in another couple or three years,' said I, with the principle of the family at heart.

'No,' answered Palmer curtly. 'Within the month. Unless you consent to that—into the fire the old hag goes.'

'Oh, Palmer! 'I exclaimed, 'you passed your word to her that she should be spared.'

'No, no. I said that unless she restored you I would break every bone of her body and throw her into the flames myself. I will certainly not touch her with my stick, nor commit her myself to the flames, but I will let the men outside deal with her as they like. I see what it is, there is no security for you from the witchcrafts of that old hag till there is another woman in this house. That woman must be my daughter, and when she is here I defy all the witches that dance on Cox Tor,* and all the pretty wenches of Devonshire to get so much as foot inside the door.'

'Father!' protested Margaret.

'My dear, I know you.'

'Well, you need not *say* it.'

'Give me a twelvemonth's grace,' I entreated.

'No, not above twenty days.'

A howl from without—a fresh faggot was cast on the fire. The pyre was not on my ground but on a bit of waste adjoining the lane, and as I am not lord of the manor I have no rights over it. That the rascals knew.

Poor Margery laid hold of my arm. Margaret at once intervened and thrust her aside. 'You do not touch him again.'

'You see,' laughed the father, 'it is as I said. Come, your hand.'

I gave it with a sigh.

I have written these few pages to let people know that Margery of Quether is about somewhere—where I do not know for certain, but I believe she has gone off into the remotest parts of Dartmoor, where, probably she will seek herself a cave among the granite tors, in which to conceal herself, where no boys will be likely to find and throw stones at her. I am uneasy now that there is such a rush of visitors to Dartmoor* to enjoy the wonderful air and scenery, lest they should come across her, and in thoughtlessness or ignorance do her an injury. Now that they know her story, I trust they will give her a wide berth.

I think that what I have gone through has taught me a lesson, but it is not one much recommended, though it is largely followed: Never succour those who solicit succour, or they will suck you dry.

ROBERT LOUIS STEVENSON

OLALLA

'NOW,' said the doctor, 'my part is done, and, I may say, with some vanity, well done. It remains only to get you out of this cold and poisonous city, and to give you two months of a pure air and an easy conscience. The last is your affair. To the first I think I can help you. It falls indeed rather oddly; it was but the other day the Padre* came in from the country; and as he and I are old friends, although of contrary professions, he applied to me in a matter of distress among some of his parishioners. This was a family—but you are ignorant of Spain, and even the names of our grandees are hardly known to you: suffice it, then, that they were once great people, and are now fallen to the brink of destitution. Nothing now belongs to them but the residencia,* and certain leagues of desert mountain, in the greater part of which not even a goat could support life. But the house is a fine old place, and stands at a great height among the hills, and most salubriously; and I had no sooner heard my friend's tale, than I remembered you. I told him I had a wounded officer, wounded in the good cause,* who was now able to make a change; and I proposed that his friends should take you for a lodger. Instantly the Padre's face grew dark, as I had maliciously foreseen it would. It was out of the question, he said. Then let them starve, said I, for I have no sympathy with tatterdemalion* pride. Thereupon we separated, not very content with one another; but yesterday, to my wonder, the Padre returned and made a submission: the difficulty, he said, he had found upon enquiry to be less than he had feared; or, in other words, these proud people had put their pride in their pocket. I closed with the offer; and, subject to your approval, I have taken rooms for you in the residencia. The air of these mountains will renew your blood; and the quiet in which you will there live is worth all the medicines in the world.'

'Doctor,' said I, 'you have been throughout my good angel, and your advice is a command. But tell me, if you please, something of the family with which I am to reside.'

'I am coming to that,' replied my friend; 'and, indeed, there is a difficulty in the way. These beggars are, as I have said, of very high descent and swollen with the most baseless vanity; they have lived for some generations in a growing isolation, drawing away, on either hand, from the rich who had now become too high for them, and from the poor, whom they still regarded as too low; and even to-day, when poverty forces them to unfasten their door to a guest, they cannot do so without a most ungracious stipulation. You are to remain, they say, a stranger; they will give you attendance, but they refuse from the first the idea of the smallest intimacy.'

I will not deny that I was piqued, and perhaps the feeling strengthened my desire to go, for I was confident that I could break down that barrier if I desired. 'There is nothing offensive in such a stipulation,' said I; 'and even I sympathize with the feeling that inspired it.'

'It is true they have never seen you,' returned the doctor politely; 'and if they knew you were the handsomest and the most pleasant man that ever came from England (where I am told that handsome men are common, but pleasant ones not so much so), they would doubtless make you welcome with a better grace. But since you take the thing so well, it matters not. To me, indeed, it seems discourteous. But you will find yourself the gainer. The family will not much tempt you. A mother, a son, and a daughter; an old woman said to be halfwitted, a country lout, and a country girl, who stands very high with her confessor, and is, therefore,' chuckled the physician, 'most likely plain; there is not much in that to attract the fancy of a dashing officer.'

'And yet you say they are high-born,' I objected.

'Well, as to that, I should distinguish,' returned the doctor. 'The mother is; not so the children. The mother was the last representative of a princely stock, degenerate* both in parts and fortune. Her father was not only poor, he was mad; and the girl ran wild about the residencia till his death. Then, much of the fortune having died with him, and the family being quite extinct, the girl ran wilder than ever, until at last she married, heaven knows whom, a muleteer* some say, others a smuggler; while there are some who uphold there was no marriage at all, and that Felipe and Olalla are bastards. The union, such as it was, was tragically dissolved some years ago; but they live in such seclusion, and the country at that time was in so much disorder, that the precise manner of the man's end is known only to the priest—if even to him.'

'I begin to think I shall have strange experiences,' said I.

'I would not romance, if I were you,' replied the doctor; 'you will find, I fear, a very grovelling and commonplace reality. Felipe, for instance, I have seen. And what am I to say? He is very rustic, very cunning, very loutish, and, I should say, an innocent;* the others are probably to match. No, no, señor commandante, you must seek congenial society among the great sights of our mountains; and in these at least, if you are at all a lover of the works of nature, I promise you will not be disappointed.'

The next day, Felipe came for me in a rough country cart, drawn by a mule; and a little before the stroke of noon, after I had said farewell to the doctor, the innkeeper, and different good souls who had befriended me during my sickness, we set forth out of the city by the Eastern gate, and began to ascend into the Sierra.* I had been so long a prisoner, since I was left behind for dying after the loss of the convoy, that the mere smell of the earth set me smiling. The country through which we went was wild and rocky, partially covered with rough woods, now of the cork tree, and now of the great Spanish chestnut, and frequently intersected by the beds of mountain torrents. The sun shone, the wind rustled joyously; and we had advanced some miles, and the city had already shrunk into an inconsiderable knoll upon the plain behind us, before my attention began to be diverted to the companion of my drive. To the eye, he seemed but a diminutive, loutish, well-made country lad, such as the doctor had described, mighty quick and active, but devoid of any culture; and this first impression was with most observers final. What began to strike me was his familiar, chattering talk; so strangely inconsistent with the terms on which I was to be received; and partly from his imperfect enunciation, partly from the sprightly incoherence of the matter, so very difficult to follow clearly without an effort of the mind. It is true I had before talked with persons of a similar mental constitution; persons who seemed to live (as he did) by the senses, taken and possessed by the visual object of the moment and unable to discharge their minds of that impression. His seemed to me (as I sat, distantly giving ear) a kind of conversation proper to drivers, who pass much of their time in a great vacancy of the intellect and threading the sights* of a familiar country. But this was not the case of Felipe; by his own account, he was a home-keeper; 'I wish I was there now,' he said; and then spying a tree by the wayside, he broke off to tell me that he had once seen a crow among its branches.

'A crow?' I repeated, struck by the ineptitude of the remark, and thinking I had heard imperfectly.

But by this time he was already filled with a new idea; hearkening with a rapt intentness, his head on one side, his face puckered; and he struck me rudely, to make me hold my peace. Then he smiled and shook his head.

'What did you hear?' I asked.

'O, it is all right,' he said; and began encouraging his mule with cries that echoed unhumanly up the mountain walls.

I looked at him more closely. He was superlatively well-built, light, and lithe and strong; he was well-featured; his yellow eyes were very large, though, perhaps, not very expressive; take him altogether, he was a pleasant-looking lad, and I had no fault to find with him, beyond that he was of a dusky hue, and inclined to hairyness; two characteristics that I disliked. It was his mind that puzzled, and yet attracted me. The doctor's phrase—an innocent—came back to me; and I was wondering if that were, after all, the true description; when the road began to go down into the narrow and naked chasm of a torrent. The waters thundered tumultuously in the bottom; and the ravine was filled full of the sound, the thin spray, and the claps of wind, that accompanied their descent. The scene was certainly impressive; but the road was in that part very securely walled in; the mule went steadily forward; and I was astonished to perceive the paleness of terror in the face of my companion. The voice of that wild river was inconstant; now sinking lower, as if in weariness; now doubling its hoarse tones; momentary freshets* seemed to swell its volume, sweeping down the gorge, raving and booming against the barrier walls; and I observed it was at each of these accessions to the clamour, that my driver more particularly winced and blanched. Some thoughts of Scottish superstition and the River Kelpie,* passed across my mind; I wondered if perchance the like were prevalent in that part of Spain; and turning to Felipe, sought to draw him out.

'What is the matter?' I asked.

'Oh, I am afraid,' he replied.

'Of what are you afraid?' I returned. 'This seems one of the safest places on this very dangerous road.'

'It makes a noise,' he said, with a simplicity of awe that set my doubts at rest.

The lad was but a child in intellect; his mind was like his body, active and swift, but stunted in development; and I began from that time forth to regard him with a measure of pity, and to listen at first with indulgence, and at last even with pleasure, to his disjointed babble.

By about four in the afternoon, we had crossed the summit of the mountain line, said farewell to the western sunshine, and began to go down upon the other side, skirting the edge of many ravines and moving through the shadow of dusky woods. There rose upon all sides the voice of falling water, not condensed and formidable as in the gorge of the river, but scattered and sounding gaily and musically from glen to glen. Here, too, the spirits of my driver mended, and he began to sing aloud in a falsetto voice, and with a singular bluntness of musical perception, never true either to melody or key, but wandering at will, and yet somehow with an effect that was natural and pleasing, like that of the song of birds. As the dusk increased, I fell more and more under the spell of this artless warbling, listening and waiting for some articulate air, and still disappointed; and when at last I asked him what it was he sang—'O,' cried he, 'I am just singing!' Above all, I was taken with a trick he had of unweariedly repeating the same note at little intervals; it was not so monotonous as you would think, or, at least, not disagreeable; and it seemed to breathe a wonderful contentment with what is, such as we love to fancy in the attitude of trees, or the quiescence of a pool.

Night had fallen dark before we came out upon a plateau, and drew up a little after, before a certain lump of superior blackness which I could only conjecture to be the residencia. Here, my guide, getting down from off the cart, hooted and whistled for a long time in vain; until at last an old peasant man came towards us from somewhere in the surrounding dark, carrying a candle in his hand. By the light of this, I was able to perceive a great arched doorway of a Moorish character: it was closed by iron-studded gates, in one of the leaves of which, Felipe opened a wicket. The peasant carried off the cart to some out-building; but my guide and I passed through the wicket, which was closed again behind us; and by the glimmer of the candle, passed through a court, up a stone stair, along a section of an open gallery, and up more stairs again, until we came at last to the door of a great and somewhat bare apartment. This room, which I understood was to be mine, was pierced by three windows, lined with some lustrous wood disposed in panels, and carpeted with the skins of many savage animals. A bright fire burned in the chimney, and shed abroad a changeful flicker; close up to the blaze there was drawn a table, laid for supper; and in the far end a bed stood ready. I was pleased by these preparations, and said so to Felipe; and he with the same simplicity of disposition that I had had* already remarked in him, warmly re-echoed my praises. 'A fine room,' he said; 'a very fine room. And fire, too; fire is good; it melts out the pleasure in your bones. And the bed,' he continued, carrying over the candle in that direction—'see what fine sheets—how soft, how smooth smooth;'* and he passed his hand again and again over their texture, and then laid down his head and rubbed his cheeks among them with a grossness of content that somehow offended me. I took the candle from his hand (for I feared he would set the bed on fire) and walked back to the supper-table, where, perceiving a measure of wine, I poured out a cup and called to him to come and drink of it. He started to his feet at once and ran to me with a strong expression of hope; but when he saw the wine, he visibly shuddered.

'Oh, no,' he said, 'not that; that is for you. I hate it.'

'Very well, Señor,' said I; 'then I will drink to your good health, and to the prosperity of your house and family. Speaking of which,' I added, after I had drunk, 'shall I not have the pleasure of laying my salutations in person at the feet of the Señora, your mother?'

But at these words all the childishness passed out of his face, and was succeeded by a look of indescribable cunning and secrecy. He backed away from me at the same time, as though I were an animal about to leap or some dangerous fellow with a weapon, and when he had got near the door, glowered at me sullenly with contracted pupils. 'No,' he said, at last, and the next moment was gone noiselessly out of the room; and I heard his footing die away downstairs as light as rainfall, and silence closed over the house.

After I had supped I drew up the table nearer to the bed and began to prepare for rest; but, in the new position of the light, I was struck by a picture on the wall.* It represented a woman, still young. To judge by her costume and the mellow unity which reigned over the canvas, she had long been dead; to judge by the vivacity of the attitude, the eyes and the features, I might have been beholding in a mirror the image of life. Her figure was very slim and strong, and of a just proportion; red tresses lay like a crown over her brow; her eyes, of a very golden brown, held mine with a look; and her face, which was perfectly shaped, was yet marred by a cruel, sullen, and sensual expression. Something in both face and figure, something exquisitely intangible, like the echo of an echo, suggested the features and bearing of my guide; and I stood awhile, unpleasantly attracted and wondering at the oddity of the resemblance. The common, carnal stock of that race, which had been originally designed for such high dames as the one now looking on me from the canvas, had fallen to baser uses, wearing country clothes, sitting on the shaft and holding the reins of a mule cart, to bring home a lodger. Perhaps an actual link subsisted; perhaps some inch* of the delicate flesh that was once clothed upon with the satin and brocade of the dead lady, now winced at the rude contact of Felipe's frieze.*

The first light of the morning shone full upon the portrait, and, as I lay awake, my eyes continued to dwell upon it with growing complacency; her beauty crept about my heart insidiously, silencing my scruples one after another; and while I knew that to love such a woman were to sign and seal one's own sentence of degeneration, I still knew that, if she were alive, I should love her. Day after day the double knowledge of her wickedness and of my weakness grew clearer. She came to be the heroine of many day dreams, in which her eyes led on to, and sufficiently rewarded, crimes. She cast a dark shadow on my fancy; and when I was out in the free air of heaven, taking vigorous exercise and healthily renewing the current of my blood, it was often a glad thought to me that my enchantress was safe in the grave, her wand of beauty broken, her lips closed to silence, her philtre spilt. And yet I had a half-lingering terror that she might not be dead after all, but re-arisen in the body of some descendant.

Felipe served my meals in my own apartment; and his resemblance to the portrait haunted me. At times it was not; at times, upon some change of attitude or flash of expression, it would leap out upon me like a ghost. It was above all in his ill tempers that the likeness triumphed. He certainly liked me; he was proud of my notice, which he sought to engage by many simple and childlike devices; he loved to sit close before my fire, talking his broken talk or singing his odd, endless, wordless songs, and sometimes drawing his hand over my clothes with an affectionate manner of caressing that never failed to cause in me an embarrassment of which I was ashamed. But for all that he was capable of flashes of causeless anger and fits of sturdy sullenness. At a word of reproof, I have seen him upset the dish of which I was about to eat, and this not surreptitiously but with defiance; and similarly at a hint of inquisition. I was not unnaturally curious, being in a strange place and surrounded by strange people; but at the shadow of a question, he shrank back, lowering and dangerous. Then it was, that, for a fraction of a second, this rough lad might have been the brother of the lady in the frame. But these humours were swift to pass; and the resemblance died along with them.

In these first days, I saw nothing of any one but Felipe, unless the portrait is to be counted; and since the lad was plainly of weak mind, and had moments of passion, it may be wondered that I bore his dangerous neighbourhood with equanimity. As a matter of fact, it was for some time irksome; but it happened before long that I obtained over him so complete a mastery, as set my disquietude at rest.

It fell in this way. He was by nature slothful, and much of a vagabond, and yet he kept by the house, and not only waited upon my wants, but laboured every day in the garden* to the south of the residencia. Here he would be joined by the peasant whom I had seen on the night of my arrival, and who dwelt at the far end of the enclosure, about half a mile away, in a rude out-house; but it was plain to me that, of these two, it was Felipe who did most; and though I would sometimes see him throw down his spade and go to sleep among the very plants he had been digging, his constancy and energy were admirable in themselves, and still more so since I was well assured they were foreign to his disposition and the fruit of an ungrateful effort. But while I admired, I wondered what had called forth in a lad so shuttle-witted* this enduring sense of duty. How was it sustained? I asked myself, and to what length did it prevail over his instincts? The priest was possibly his inspirer; but the priest came one day to the residencia. I saw him both come and go after an interval of close upon an hour, from a knoll where I was sketching, and all that time Felipe continued to labour undisturbed in the garden.

At last, in a very unworthy spirit, I determined to debauch the lad from his good resolutions, and waylaying him at the gate, easily persuaded him to join me in a ramble. It was a fine day, and the woods to which I led him were green and pleasant and sweet-smelling and alive with the hum of insects. Here he discovered himself in a fresh character, mounting up to heights of gaiety that abashed me, and displaying an energy and grace of movement that delighted the eye. He leaped, he ran round me in mere glee; he would stop, and look and listen, and seem to drink in the world like a cordial; and then he would suddenly spring into a tree with one bound, and hang and gambol there like one at home. Little as he said to me, and that of not much import, I have rarely enjoyed more stirring company; the sight of his delight was a continual feast; the speed and accuracy of his movements pleased me to the heart; and I might have been so thoughtlessly unkind as to make a habit of these walks, had not chance prepared a very rude conclusion to my pleasure. By some swiftness or dexterity the lad captured a squirrel in a tree top. He was then some way ahead of me, but I saw him drop to the ground and crouch there, crying aloud for pleasure like a child. The sound stirred my sympathies, it was so fresh and innocent; but as I bettered my pace* to draw near, the cry of the squirrel knocked upon my heart. I have heard and seen much of the cruelty of lads, and above all of peasants; but what I now beheld struck me into a passion of anger. I thrust the fellow aside, plucked the poor brute out of his hands and, with swift mercy, killed it. Then I turned upon the torturer; spoke to him long out of the heat of my indignation, calling him names at which he seemed to wither; and at length, pointing toward the residencia, bade him begone and leave me, for I chose to walk with men, not with vermin. He fell upon his knees; and, the words coming to him with more clearness than usual, poured out a stream of the most touching supplications, begging me, in mercy to forgive him, to forget what he had done, to look to the future. 'O, I try so hard,' he said. 'O, commandante, bear with Felipe this once; he will never be a brute again!' Thereupon, much more affected than I cared to show, I suffered myself to be persuaded, and at last shook hands with him and made it up. But the squirrel, by way of penance, I made him bury; speaking of the poor thing's beauty, telling him what pains it had suffered, and how base a thing was the abuse of strength. 'See, Felipe,' said I, 'you are strong indeed; but in my hands you are as helpless as that poor thing off the trees. Give me your hand in mine. You cannot remove it. Now suppose that I were cruel like you, and took a pleasure in pain. I only tighten my hold, and see how you suffer.' He screamed aloud, his face stricken ashy and dotted with needle points of sweat; and when I set him free, he fell to the earth and nursed his hand and moaned over it like a baby. But he took the lesson in good part; and whether from that, or from what I had said to him, or the higher notion he now had of my bodily strength, his original affection was changed into a dog-like, adoring fidelity.

Meanwhile I gained rapidly in health. The residencia stood on the crown of a stony plateau; on every side the mountains hemmed it about; only from the roof, where was a bartizan,* there might be seen between two peaks, a small segment of plain, blue with extreme distance. The air in these altitudes moved freely and largely; great clouds congregated there, and were broken up by the wind and left in tatters on the hilltops; a hoarse, and yet faint rumbling of torrents rose from all round; and one could there study all the ruder and more ancient characters of nature in something of their pristine force. I delighted from the first in the vigorous scenery and changeful weather; nor less in the antique and dilapidated mansion where I dwelt. This was a large oblong, flanked at two opposite corners by bastion-like projections, one of which commanded the door, while both were loopholed for musketry.* The lower storey was, besides, naked of windows, so that the building, if garrisoned, could not be carried without artillery. It enclosed an open court planted with pomegranate trees. From this a broad flight of marble stairs ascended to an open gallery, running all round and resting, towards the court, on slender pillars. Thence again, several enclosed stairs led to the upper storeys of the house, which were thus broken up into distinct divisions. The windows, both within and without, were closely shuttered; some of the stone-work in the upper parts had fallen, the roof, in one place, had been wrecked in one of the flurries of wind which were common in these mountains; and the whole house, in the strong, beating sunlight, and standing out above a grove of stunted cork-trees, thickly laden and discoloured with dust, looked like the sleeping palace of the legend.* The court, in particular, seemed the very home of slumber. A hoarse cooing of doves haunted about the eaves; the winds were excluded, but when they blew outside, the mountain dust fell here as thick as rain, and veiled the red bloom of the pomegranates; shuttered windows and the closed doors of numerous cellars, and the vacant, arches of the gallery, enclosed it; and all day long the sun made broken profiles on the four sides, and paraded the shadow of the pillars on the gallery floor. At the ground level there was, however, a certain pillared recess, which bore the marks of human habitation. Though it was open in front upon the court, it was yet provided with a chimney, where a wood fire would be always prettily blazing; and the tile floor was scattered* with the skins of animals.

It was in this place that I first saw my hostess. She had drawn one of the skins forward and sat in the sun, leaning against a pillar. It was her dress that struck me first of all, for it was rich and brightly coloured, and shone out in that dusty courtyard with something of the same relief as the flowers of the pomegranates. At a second look it was her beauty of person that took hold of me. As she sat back—watching me, I thought, though with invisible eyes—and wearing at the same time an expression of almost imbecile good-humour and contentment, she showed a perfectness of feature and a quiet nobility of attitude that were beyond a statue's. I took off my hat to her in passing, and her face puckered with suspicion as swiftly and lightly as a pool ruffles in the breeze; but she paid no heed to my courtesy. I went forth on my customary walk a trifle daunted, her idol-like impassivity haunting me; and when I returned, although she was still in much the same posture, I was half surprised to see that she had* moved as far as the next pillar, following the sunshine. This time, however, she addressed me with some trivial salutation, civilly enough conceived, and uttered in the same deep-chested, and yet indistinct and lisping tones, that had already baffled the utmost niceness of my hearing from her son. I answered rather at a venture; for not only did I fail to take her meaning with precision, but the sudden disclosure of her eyes disturbed me. They were unusually large, the iris golden like Felipe's, but the pupil at that moment so distended that they seemed almost black;* and what affected me was not so much their size as (what was perhaps its consequence) the singular insignificance* of their regard. A look more blankly stupid I have never met. My eyes dropped before it even as I spoke, and I went on my way upstairs to my own room, at once baffled and embarrassed. Yet, when I came there and saw the face of the portrait, I was again reminded of the miracle of family descent. My hostess was, indeed, both older and fuller in person; her eyes were of a different colour; her face, besides, was not only free from the ill-significance that offended and attracted me in the painting; it was devoid of either good or bad—a moral blank expressing literally naught. And yet there was a likeness, not so much speaking as immanent,* not so much in any particular feature as upon the whole. It should seem, I thought, as if when the master set his signature to that grave canvas, he had not only caught the image of one smiling and false-eyed woman, but stamped the essential quality of a race.

From that day forth, whether I came or went, I was sure to find the Señora seated in the sun against a pillar, or stretched on a rug before the fire; only at times she would shift her station to the top round of the stone staircase, where she lay with the same nonchalance right across my path. In all these days, I never knew her to display the least spark of energy beyond what she expended in brushing and re-brushing her copious copper-coloured hair, or in lisping out, in the rich and broken hoarseness of her voice, her customary idle salutations to myself. These, I think, were her two chief pleasures, beyond that of mere quiescence. She seemed always proud of her remarks, as though they had been witticisms: and, indeed, though they were empty enough, like the conversation of many respectable persons, and turned on a very narrow range of subjects, they were never meaningless or incoherent; nay, they had a certain beauty of their own, breathing, as they did, of her entire contentment. Now she would speak of the warmth, in which (like her son) she greatly delighted; now of the flowers of the pomegranate trees, and now of the white doves and long-winged swallows that fanned the air of the court. The birds excited her. As they raked the eaves in their swift flight, or skimmed sidelong past her with a rush of wind, she would sometimes stir, and sit a little up, and seem to awaken from her doze of satisfaction. But for the rest of her days she lay luxuriously folded on herself and sunk in sloth and pleasure.* Her invincible content at first annoyed me, but I came gradually to find repose in the spectacle, until at last it grew to be my habit to sit down beside her four times in the day, both coming and going, and to talk with her sleepily, I scarce knew of what. I had come to like her dull, almost animal neighbourhood; her beauty and her stupidity soothed and amused me. I began to find a kind of transcendental good sense in her remarks, and her unfathomable good nature moved me to admiration and envy. The liking was returned; she enjoyed my presence half unconsciously, as a man in deep meditation may enjoy the babbling of a brook. I can scarce say she brightened when I came, for satisfaction was written on her face eternally, as on some foolish statue's; but I was made conscious of her pleasure by some more intimate communication than the sight. And one day, as I sat within reach of her on the marble step, she suddenly shot forth one of her hands and patted mine. The thing was done, and she was back in her accustomed attitude, before my mind had received intelligence of the caress; and when I turned to look her in the face I could perceive no answerable sentiment. It was plain she attached no moment to the act, and I blamed myself for my own more uneasy consciousness.

The sight and (if I may so call it) the acquaintance of the mother confirmed the view I had already taken of the son. The family blood had been impoverished, perhaps by long inbreeding, which I knew to be a common error among the proud and the exclusive. No decline, indeed, was to be traced in the body, which had been handed down unimpaired in shapeliness and strength; and the faces of to-day were struck as sharply from the mint, as the face of two centuries ago that smiled upon me from the portrait. But the intelligence (that more precious heirloom) was degenerate; the treasure of ancestral memory ran low; and it had required the potent, plebeian crossing of a muleteer or mountain contrabandista* to raise, what approached hebetude* in the mother, into the active oddity of the son. Yet of the two, it was the mother I preferred. Of Felipe, vengeful and placable, full of starts and shyings, inconstant as a hare, I could even conceive as a creature possibly noxious. Of the mother I had no thoughts but those of kindness. And indeed, as spectators are apt ignorantly to take sides, I grew something of a partizan in the enmity which I perceived to smoulder between them. True, it seemed mostly on the mother's part. She would sometimes draw in her breath as he came near, and the pupils of her vacant eyes would contract as if with horror or fear. Her emotions, such as they were, were much upon the surface and readily shared; and this latent repulsion occupied my mind, and kept me wondering on what grounds it rested, and whether the son was certainly in fault.

I had been about ten days in the residencia, when there sprang up a high and harsh wind, carrying clouds of dust. It came out of malarious* lowlands, and over several snowy sierras. The nerves of those on whom it blew were strung and jangled; their eyes smarted with the dust; their legs ached under the burthen of their body; and the touch of one hand upon another grew to be odious. The wind, besides, came down the gullies of the hills and stormed about the house with a great, hollow buzzing and whistling that was wearisome to the ear and dismally depressing to the mind. It did not so much blow in gusts as with the steady sweep of a waterfall, so that there was no remission of discomfort while it blew. But higher upon the mountain, it was probably of a more variable strength, with accesses of fury; for there came down at times a far-off wailing, infinitely grievous to hear; and at times, on one of the high shelves or terraces, there would start up, and then disperse, a tower of dust, like the smoke of an explosion.

I no sooner awoke in bed than I was conscious of the nervous tension and depression of the weather, and the effect grew stronger as the day proceeded. It was in vain that I resisted; in vain that I set forth upon my customary morning's walk; the irrational, unchanging fury of the storm had soon beat down my strength and wrecked my temper; and I returned to the residencia, glowing with dry heat, and foul and gritty with dust. The court had a forlorn appearance; now and then a glimmer of sun fled over it; now and then the wind swooped down upon the pomegranates, and scattered the blossoms, and set the window shutters clapping on the wall. In the recess the Señora was pacing to and fro with a flushed countenance and bright eyes; I thought, too, she was speaking to herself, like one in anger. But when I addressed her with my customary salutation, she only replied by a sharp gesture and continued her walk. The weather had distempered even this impassive creature; and as I went on upstairs I was the less ashamed of my own discomposure.

All day the wind continued; and I sat in my room and made a feint of reading, or walked up and down, and listened to the riot overhead. Night fell, and I had not so much as a candle. I began to long for some society, and stole down to the court. It was now plunged in the blue of the first darkness; but the recess was redly lighted by the fire. The wood had been piled high, and was crowned by a shock of flames, which the draught of the chimney brandished to and fro. In this strong and shaken brightness the Señora continued pacing from wall to wall with disconnected gestures, clasping her hands, stretching forth her arms, throwing back her head as in appeal to heaven. In these disordered movements the beauty and grace of the woman showed more clearly; but there was a light in her eye that struck on me unpleasantly; and when I had looked on awhile in silence, and seemingly unobserved, I turned tail as I had come, and groped my way back again to my own chamber.

By the time Felipe brought my supper and lights, my nerve was utterly gone; and, had the lad been such as I was used to seeing him,

I should have kept him (even by force had that been necessary) to take off the edge from my distasteful solitude. But on Felipe, also, the wind had exercised its influence. He had been feverish all day; now that the night had come he was fallen into a low and tremulous humour that reacted on my own. The sight of his scared face, his starts and pallors and sudden harkenings, unstrung me; and when he dropped and broke a dish I fairly leaped out of my seat.

'I think we are all mad to-day,' said I, affecting to laugh.

'It is the black wind,'* he replied dolefully. 'You feel as if you must do something, and you don't know what it is.'

I noted the aptness of the description; but, indeed, Felipe had sometimes a strange felicity in rendering into words the sensations of the body. 'And your mother, too,' said I; 'she seems to feel this weather much. Do you not fear she may be unwell?'

He stared at me a little, and then said, 'No,' almost defiantly; and the next moment, carrying his hand to his brow, cried out lamentably on the wind and the noise that made his head go round like a mill-wheel. 'Who can be well?' he cried; and, indeed, I could only echo his question, for I was disturbed enough myself.

I went to bed early, wearied with day-long restlessness; but the poisonous nature of the wind, and its ungodly and unintermittent* uproar, would not suffer me to sleep. I lay there and tossed, my nerves and senses on the stretch. At times I would doze, dream horribly, and wake again; and these snatches of oblivion confused me as to time. But it must have been late on in the night, when I was suddenly startled by an outbreak of pitiable and hateful cries. I leaped from my bed, supposing I had dreamed; but the cries still continued to fill the house, cries of pain, I thought, but certainly of rage also, and so savage and discordant that they shocked the heart. It was no illusion; some living thing, some lunatic, or some wild animal was being foully tortured. The thought of Felipe and the squirrel flashed into my mind, and I ran to the door, but it had been locked from the outside; and I might shake it as I pleased, I was a fast prisoner. Still the cries continued. Now they would dwindle down into a moaning that seemed to be articulate, and at these times I made sure they must be human; and again they would break forth and fill the house with ravings worthy of hell. I stood at the door and gave ear to them, till at last they died away. Long after that, I still lingered and still continued to hear them mingle in fancy with the storming of the wind; and when at last I crept to my bed, it was with a deadly sickness and a blackness of horror on my heart.

It was little wonder if I slept no more. Why had I been locked in? What had passed? Who was the author of these indescribable and shocking cries? A human being? It was inconceivable. A beast? The cries were scarce quite bestial; and what animal, short of a lion or a tiger, could thus shake the solid walls of the residencia? And while I was thus turning over the elements of the mystery, it came into my mind that I had not yet set eyes upon the daughter of the house. What was more probable than that the daughter of the Señora, and the sister of Felipe, should be herself insane? Or, what more likely than that these ignorant and half-witted people should seek to manage an afflicted kinswoman by violence? Here was a solution; and yet when I called to mind the cries (which I never did without a shuddering chill) it seemed altogether insufficient: not even cruelty could wring such cries from madness. But of one thing I was sure: I could not live in a house where such a thing was half conceivable, and not probe the matter home, and, if necessary, interfere.

The next day came, the wind had blown itself out, and there was nothing to remind me of the business of the night. Felipe came to my bedside with obvious cheerfulness; as I passed through the court, the Señora was sunning herself with her accustomed immobility; and when I issued from the gateway, I found the whole face of nature austerely smiling, the heavens of a cold blue, and sown with great cloud islands, and the mountain-sides mapped forth into provinces of light and shadow. A short walk restored me to myself, and renewed within me the resolve to plumb this mystery; and when, from the vantage of my knoll, I had seen Felipe pass forth to his labours in the garden, I returned at once to the residencia to put my design in practice. The Señora appeared plunged in slumber; I stood awhile and marked her, but she did not stir; even if my design were indiscreet, I had little to fear from such a guardian; and turning away, I mounted to the gallery and began my exploration of the house.

All morning I went from one door to another, and entered spacious and faded chambers, some rudely shuttered, some receiving their full charge of daylight, all empty and unhomely. It was a rich house, on which Time had breathed his tarnish and dust had scattered disillusion. The spider swung there; the bloated tarantula* scampered on the cornices; ants had their crowded highways on the floor of halls of audience; the big and foul fly, that lives on carrion and is often the messenger of death, had set up his nest in the rotten woodwork, and buzzed heavily about the rooms. Here and there a stool or two, a couch, a bed, or a great carved chair remained behind, like islets on the bare floors, to testify of man's bygone habitation; and everywhere the walls were set with the portraits of the dead. I could judge, by these decaying effigies, in the house of what a great and what a handsome race I was then wandering. Many of the men wore orders on their breasts and had the port* of noble offices; the women were all richly attired; the canvases most of them by famous hands. But it was not so much these evidences of greatness that took hold upon my mind, even contrasted, as they were, with the present depopulation and decay of that great house. It was rather the parable of family life that I read in this succession of fair faces and shapely bodies. Never before had I so realized the miracle of the continued race, the creation and recreation, the weaving and changing and handing down of fleshly elements. That a child should be born of its mother, that it should grow and clothe itself (we know not how) with humanity, and put on inherited looks, and turn its head with the manner of one ascendant, and offer its hand with the gesture of another, are wonders dulled for us by repetition. But in the singular unity of look, in the common features and common bearing, of all these painted generations on the walls of the residencia, the miracle started out and looked me in the face. And an ancient mirror falling opportunely in my way, I stood and read my own features a long while, tracing out on either hand the filaments of descent and the bonds that knit me with my family.

At last, in the course of these investigations, I opened the door of a chamber that bore the marks of habitation. It was of large proportions and faced to the north, where the mountains were most wildly figured. The embers of a fire smouldered and smoked upon the hearth, to which a chair had been drawn close. And yet the aspect of the chamber was ascetic to the degree of sternness; the chair was uncushioned; the floor and walls were naked; and, beyond the books which lay here and there in some confusion, there was no instrument of either work or pleasure. The sight of books in the house of such a family exceedingly amazed me; and I began with a great hurry, and in momentary fear of interruption, to go from one to another and hastily inspect their character. They were of all sorts, devotional, historical, and scientific, but mostly of a great age and in the Latin tongue. Some I could see to bear the marks of constant study; others had been torn across and tossed aside as if in petulance or disapproval. Lastly, as I cruised about that empty chamber, I espied some papers written upon with pencil on a table near the window. An unthinking curiosity led me to take one up. It bore a copy of verses, very roughly metred in the original Spanish, and which I may render somewhat thus—

Pleasure approached with pain and shame,
Grief with a wreath of lilies came.
Pleasure showed the lovely sun;
Jesu dear, how sweet it shone!
Grief with her worn hand pointed on,
Jesu dear, to thee!*

Shame and confusion at once fell on me; and, laying down the paper, I beat an immediate retreat from the apartment. Neither Felipe nor his mother could have read the books nor written these rough but feeling verses. It was plain I had stumbled with sacrilegious feet into the room of the daughter of the house. God knows, my own heart most sharply punished me for my indiscretion. The thought that I had thus secretly pushed my way into the confidence of a girl so strangely situated, and the fear that she might somehow come to hear of it, oppressed me like guilt. I blamed myself besides for my suspicions of the night before; wondered that I should ever have attributed those shocking cries to one of whom I now conceived as of a saint, spectral of mien,* wasted with maceration,* bound up in the practices of a mechanical devotion, and dwelling in a great isolation of soul with her incongruous relatives; and, as I leaned on the balustrade of the gallery and looked down into the bright close of pomegranates and at the gaily-dressed and somnolent woman, who just then stretched herself and delicately licked her lips as in the very sensuality of sloth, my mind swiftly compared the scene with the cold chamber looking northward on the mountains, where the daughter dwelt.

That same afternoon, as I sat upon my knoll, I saw the Padre enter the gates of the residencia. The revelation of the daughter's character had struck home to my fancy, and almost blotted out the horrors of the night before; but at sight of this worthy man the memory revived. I descended, then, from the knoll, and making a circuit among the woods, posted myself by the wayside to await his passage. As soon as he appeared I stepped forth and introduced myself as the lodger of the residencia. He had a very strong, honest countenance, on which it was easy to read the mingled emotions with which he regarded me, as a foreigner, a heretic, and yet one who had been wounded for the good cause. Of the family at the residencia he spoke with reserve, and yet with respect. I mentioned that I had not yet seen the daughter, whereupon he remarked that that was as it should be, and looked at me a little askance. Lastly, I plucked up courage to refer to the cries that had disturbed me in the night. He heard me out in silence, and then stopped and partly turned about, as though to mark beyond doubt that he was dismissing me.

'Do you take tobacco powder?' said he, offering his snuff-box; and then, when I had refused, 'I am an old man,' he added, 'and I may be allowed to remind you that you are a guest.'

'I have, then, your authority,' I returned, firmly enough although I flushed at the implied reproof, 'to let things take their course, and not to interfere?'

He said 'yes,' and with a somewhat uneasy salute, turned and left me where I was. But he had done two things; he had set my conscience at rest, and he had awakened my delicacy.* I made a great effort, once more dismissed the recollections of the night, and fell once more to brooding on my saintly poetess. At the same time, I could not quite forget that I had been locked in, and that night when Felipe brought me my supper, I attacked him warily on both points of interest.

'I never see your sister,' said I casually.

'Oh, no,' said he; 'she is a good, good girl,' and his mind instantly veered to something else.

'Your sister is pious, I suppose?' I asked in the next pause.

'Oh!' he cried, joining his hands with extreme fervour, 'a saint; it is she that keeps me up.'

'You are very fortunate,' said I, 'for the most of us, I am afraid, and myself among the number, are better at going down.'

'Señor,' said Felipe earnestly, 'I could not say that. You should not tempt your angel. If one goes down, where is he to stop?'

'Why Felipe,' said I, 'I had no guess you were a preacher, and I may say a good one; but I suppose that is your sister's doing?'

He nodded at me with round eyes.

'Well, then,' I continued, 'she has doubtless reproved you for your sin of cruelty?'

'Twelve times!' he cried; for this was the phrase by which the odd creature expressed the sense of frequency. 'And I told her you had done so—I remembered that,' he added proudly—'and she was pleased.'

'Then, Felipe,' said I, 'what were those cries that I heard last night? for surely they were cries of some creature in suffering.'

'The wind,' returned Felipe, looking in the fire.

I took his hand in mine, at which, thinking it to be a caress, he smiled with a brightness of pleasure that came near disarming my resolve. But I trod the weakness down. 'The wind,' I repeated; 'and yet I think it was this hand,'—holding it up—'that had first locked me in.' The lad shook visibly, but answered never a word. 'Well,' said I, 'I am a stranger and a guest. It is not my part either to meddle or to judge in your affairs; in these you shall take your sister's counsel, which I cannot doubt to be excellent. But in so far as concerns my own I will be no man's prisoner, and I demand that key.' Half-an-hour later my door was suddenly thrown open, and the key tossed ringing on the floor.

A day or two after I came in from a walk a little before the point of noon. The Señora was lying lapped in slumber on the threshold of the recess; the pigeons dozed below the eaves like snowdrifts; the house was under a deep spell of noontide quiet; and only a wandering and gentle wind from the mountain stole round the galleries, rustled among the pomegranates, and pleasantly stirred the shadows. Something in the stillness moved me to imitation, and I went very lightly across the court and up the marble staircase. My foot was on the topmost round, when a door opened, and I found myself face to face with Olalla.* Surprise transfixed me; her loveliness struck to my heart; she glowed in the deep shadow of the gallery, a gem of colour; her eyes took hold upon mine and clung there, and bound us together like the joining of hands; and the moments we thus stood face to face, drinking each other in, were sacramental and the wedding of souls. I know not how long it was before I awoke out of a deep trance, and, hastily bowing, passed on into the upper stair. She did not move, but followed me with her great, thirsting eyes; and as I passed out of sight it seemed to me as if she paled and faded.

In my own room, I opened the window and looked out, and could not think what change had come upon that austere field of mountains that it should thus sing and shine under the lofty heaven. I had seen her—Olalla! And the stone crags answered, Olalla! and the dumb, unfathomable azure answered, Olalla! The pale saint of my dreams had vanished for ever; and in her place I beheld this maiden on whom God had lavished the richest colours and the most exuberant energies of life, whom he had made active as a deer, slender as a reed, and in whose great eyes he had lighted the torches of the soul. The thrill of her young life, strung like a wild animal's, had entered into me; the force of soul that had looked out from her eyes and conquered mine, mantled about my heart and sprang to my lips in singing. She passed through my veins; she was one with me.

I will not say that this enthusiasm declined; rather my soul held out in its ecstasy as in a strong castle, and was there besieged by cold and sorrowful considerations. I could not doubt but that I loved her at first sight, and already with a quivering ardour that was strange to my experience. What then was to follow? She was the child of an afflicted house, the Señora's daughter, the sister of Felipe; she bore it even in her beauty. She had the lightness and swiftness of the one, swift as an arrow, light as dew; like the other, she shone on the pale background of the world with the brilliancy of flowers. I could not call by the name of brother that half-witted lad, nor by the name of mother that immovable and lovely thing of flesh, whose silly eyes and perpetual simper now recurred to my mind like something hateful. And if I could not marry, what then? She was helplessly unprotected; her eyes, in that single and long glance which had been all our intercourse, had confessed a weakness equal to my own; but in my heart I knew her for the student of the cold northern chamber and the writer of the sorrowful lines; and this was a knowledge to disarm a brute. To flee was more than I could find courage for; but I registered a vow of unsleeping circumspection.

As I turned from the window, my eyes alighted on the portrait. It had fallen dead, like a candle after sunrise; it followed me with eyes of paint. I knew it to be like, and marvelled at the tenacity of type in that declining race; but the likeness was swallowed up in difference. I remembered how it had seemed to me a thing unapproachable in the life, a creature rather of the painter's craft than of the modesty of nature, and I marvelled at the thought, and exulted in the image of Olalla. Beauty I had seen before, and not been charmed, and I had been often drawn to women, who were not beautiful (except to me); but in Olalla all that I desired and had not dared to imagine was united.

I did not see her the next day, and my heart ached and my eyes longed for her, as men long for morning. But the day after, when I returned, about my usual hour, she was once more on the gallery, and our looks once more met and embraced. I would have spoken, I would have drawn near to her; but strongly as she plucked at my heart, drawing me like a magnet, something yet more imperious withheld me; and I could only bow and pass by; and she, leaving my salutation unanswered, only followed me with her noble eyes.

I had now her image by rote, and as I conned the traits in memory it seemed as if I read her very heart. She was dressed with something of her mother's coquetry, and love of positive colour. Her robe, which I know she must have made with her own hands, clung about her with a cunning grace. After the fashion of that country, besides, her boddice* stood open in the middle, in a long slit, and here, in spite of the poverty of the house, a gold coin, hanging by a ribbon, lay on her brown bosom. These* were proofs, had any been needed, of her inborn delight in life and her own loveliness. On the other hand, in her eyes that hung upon mine, I could read depth beyond depth of passion and sadness, lights of poetry and hope, blacknesses of despair, and thoughts that were above the earth. It was a lovely body, but the inmate, the soul, was more than worthy of that lodging. Should I leave this incomparable flower to wither unseen on these rough mountains? Should I despise the great gift offered me in the eloquent silence of her eyes? Here was a soul immured; should I not burst its prison? All side considerations fell off from me; were she the child of Herod* I swore I should make her mine; and that very evening I set myself, with a mingled sense of treachery and disgrace, to captivate the brother. Perhaps I read him with more favourable eyes, perhaps the thought of his sister always summoned up the better qualities of that imperfect soul; but he had never seemed to me so amiable, and his very likeness to Olalla, while it annoyed, yet softened me.

A third day passed in vain—an empty desert of hours. I would not lose a chance and loitered all afternoon in the court, where (to give myself a countenance) I spoke more than usual with the Señora. God knows it was with a most tender and sincere interest that I now studied her; and even as for Felipe, so now for the mother, I was conscious of a growing warmth of toleration. And yet I wondered. Even while

I spoke with her, she would doze off into a little sleep, and presently awake again without embarrassment; and this composure staggered me. And again, as I marked her make infinitesimal changes in her posture, savouring and lingering on the bodily pleasure of the movement, I was driven to wonder at this depth of passive sensuality. She lived in her body; and her consciousness was all sunk into and disseminated through her members, where it luxuriously dwelt. Lastly, I could not grow accustomed to her eyes. Each time she turned on me these great, beautiful and meaningless orbs, wide open to the day, but closed against human inquiry, each time I had occasion to observe the lively changes of her pupils which expanded and contracted in a breath—I know not what it was came over me, I can find no name for the mingled feeling of disappointment, annoyance, and distaste that jarred along my nerves. I tried her on a variety of subjects, equally in vain; and at last led the talk to her daughter. But even there she proved indifferent; said she was pretty, which (as with children) was her highest word of commendation, but was plainly incapable of any higher thought; and when I remarked that Olalla seemed silent, merely yawned in my face and replied that speech was of no great use when you had nothing to say. 'People speak much, very much,' she added, looking at me with expanded pupils; and then again yawned and again showed me a mouth that was as dainty as a toy. This time I took the hint, and, leaving her to her repose, went up into my own chamber to sit by the open window, looking on the hills and not beholding them, sunk in lustrous and deep dreams, and hearkening in fancy to the note of a voice that I had never heard.

I awoke on the fifth morning with a brightness of anticipation that seemed to challenge fate. I was sure of myself, light of heart and foot, and resolved to put my love incontinently to the touch of knowledge. It should lie no longer under the bonds of silence, a dumb thing, living by the eye only, like the love of beasts; but should now put on the spirit, and enter upon the joys of the complete human intimacy. I thought of it with wild hopes, like a voyager to El Dorado;* into that unknown and lovely country of her soul, I no longer trembled to adventure. Yet when I did indeed encounter her, the same force of passion descended on me and at once submerged my mind; speech seemed to drop away from me like a childish habit; and I but drew near to her as the giddy man draws near to the margin of a gulf. She drew back from me a little as I came; but her eyes did not waver from mine, and these lured me forward. At last, when I was already within reach of her, I stopped. Words were denied me; if I advanced I could but clasp her to my heart in silence; and all that was sane in me, all that was still unconquered, revolted against the thought of such an accost. So we stood for a second, all our life in our eyes, exchanging salvos of attraction and yet each resisting; and then, with a great effort of the will, and conscious at the same time of a sudden bitterness of disappointment, I turned and went away in the same silence.

What power lay upon me that I could not speak? And she, why was she also silent? Why did she draw away before me dumbly, with fascinated eyes? Was this love? or was it a mere brute attraction, mindless and inevitable, like that of the magnet for the steel? We had never spoken, we were wholly strangers: and yet an influence, strong as the grasp of a giant, swept us silently together. On my side, it filled me with impatience; and yet I was sure that she was worthy; I had seen her books, read her verses, and thus, in a sense, divined the soul of my mistress. But on her side, it struck me almost cold. Of me, she knew nothing but my bodily favour; she was drawn to me as stones fall to the earth; the laws that rule the earth conducted her, unconsenting, to my arms; and I drew back at the thought of such a bridal,* and began to be jealous for myself. It was not thus that I desired to be loved. And then I began to fall into a great pity for the girl herself. I thought how sharp must be her mortification, that she, the student, the recluse, Felipe's saintly monitress,* should have thus confessed an overweening weakness for a man with whom she had never exchanged a word. And at the coming of pity, all other thoughts were swallowed up; and I longed only to find and console and reassure her; to tell her how wholly her love was returned on my side, and how her choice, even if blindly made, was not unworthy.

The next day it was glorious weather; depth upon depth of blue over-canopied the mountains; the sun shone wide; and the wind in the trees, and the many falling torrents in the mountains filled the air with delicate and haunting music. Yet I was prostrated with sadness. My heart wept for the sight of Olalla, as a child weeps for its mother. I sat down on a boulder on the verge of the low cliffs that bound the plateau to the north. Thence I looked down into the wooded valley of a stream, where no foot came. In the mood I was in, it was even touching to behold the place untenanted; it lacked Olalla; and I thought of the delight and glory of a life passed wholly with her in that strong air, and among these rugged and lovely surroundings, at first with a whimpering sentiment, and then again with such a fiery joy that I seemed to grow in strength and stature, like a Samson.*

And then suddenly I was aware of Olalla drawing near. She appeared out of a grove of cork trees, and came straight towards me; and I stood up and waited. She seemed in her walking a creature of such life and fire and lightness as amazed me; yet she came quietly and slowly. Her energy was in the slowness; but for inimitable strength, I felt she would have run, she would have flown to me. Still, as she approached, she kept her eyes lowered to the ground; and when she had drawn quite near, it was without one glance that she addressed me. At the first note of her voice I started. It was for this I had been waiting; this was the last test of my love. And lo, her enunciation was precise and clear, not lisping and incomplete like that of her family; and the voice, though deeper than usual with women, was still both youthful and womanly. She spoke in a rich chord; golden contralto strains mingled with hoarseness, as the red threads were mingled with the brown among her tresses. It was not only a voice that spoke to my heart directly; but it spoke to me of her. And yet her words immediately plunged me back upon despair.

'You will go away,' she said, 'to-day.'

Her example broke the bonds of my speech; I felt as lightened of a weight, or as if a spell had been dissolved. I know not in what words I answered; but, standing before her on the cliffs, I poured out the whole ardour of my love, telling her that I lived upon her thought,* slept only to dream of her loveliness, and would gladly forswear my country, my language, and my friends, to live for ever by her side. And then, strongly commanding myself, I changed the note; I reassured, I comforted her; I told her I had divined in her a pious and heroic spirit, with which I was worthy to sympathize, and which I longed to share and lighten. 'Nature,' I told her, 'was the voice of God, which men disobey at peril; and if we were thus dumbly drawn together, ay, even as by a miracle of love, it must imply a divine fitness in our souls; we must be made,' I said, 'made for one another. We should be mad rebels,' I cried out—'mad rebels against God, not to obey this instinct.'

She shook her head. 'You will go to-day,' she repeated, and then with a gesture, and in a sudden, sharp note—'no, not to-day,' she cried, 'to-morrow!'

But at this sign of relenting, power came in upon me in a tide. I stretched out my arms and called upon her name; and she leaped to me and clung to me. The hills rocked about us, the earth quailed; a shock as of a blow went through me and left me blind and dizzy. And the next moment she had thrust me back, broken rudely from my arms and fled with the speed of a deer among the cork trees.

I stood and shouted to the mountains; I turned and went back towards the residencia, walking upon air. She sent me away, and yet I had but to call upon her name and she came to me. These were but the weaknesses of girls, from which even she, the strangest of her sex, was not exempted. Go? Not I, Olalla—O, not I, Olalla, my Olalla! A bird sang near by; and, in that season, birds were rare. It bade me be of good cheer. And once more the whole countenance of nature, from the ponderous and stable mountains down to the lightest leaf and the smallest darting fly in the shadow of the groves, began to stir before me, and to put in the lineaments of life and wear a face of awful joy. The sunshine struck upon the hills, strong as a hammer on the anvil, and the hills shook; the earth, under that vigorous insolation,* yielded up heady scents; the woods smouldered in the blaze. I felt the thrill of travail and delight run through the earth. Something elemental, something rude, violent, and savage, in the love that sang in my heart, was like a key to nature's secrets; and the very stones that rattled under my feet appeared alive and friendly. Olalla! Her touch had quickened, and renewed, and strung me up to the old pitch of concert with the rugged earth, to a swelling of the soul that men learn to forget in their polite assemblies. Love burned in me like rage; tenderness waxed fierce; I hated, I adored, I pitied, I revered her with ecstasy. She seemed the link that bound me in with dead things on the one hand, and with our pure and pitying God upon the other: a thing brutal and divine, and akin at once to the innocence and to the unbridled forces of the earth.

My head thus reeling, I came into the courtyard of the residencia, and the sight of the mother struck me like a revelation. She sat there, all sloth and contentment, blinking under the strong sunshine, branded with a passive enjoyment, a creature set quite apart, before whom my ardour fell away like a thing ashamed. I stopped a moment, and, commanding such shaken tones as I was able, said a word or two. She looked at me with her unfathomable kindness; her voice in reply sounded vaguely out of the realm of peace in which she slumbered, and there fell on my mind, for the first time, a sense of respect for one so uniformly innocent and happy, and I passed on in a kind of wonder at myself, that I should be so much disquieted.

On my table there lay a piece of the same yellow paper I had seen in the north room; it was written on with pencil in the same hand, Olalla's hand, and I picked it up with a sudden sinking of alarm, and read, 'If you have any kindness for Olalla, if you have any chivalry for a creature sorely wrought, go from here to-day; in pity, in honour, for the sake of him who died, I supplicate that you should go.' I looked at this awhile in mere stupidity, then I began to awaken to a weariness and horror of life; the sunshine darkened outside on the bare hills, and I began to shake like a man in terror. The vacancy thus suddenly opened in my life unmanned me like a physical void. It was not my heart, it was not my happiness, it was life itself that was involved. I could not lose her. I said so, and stood repeating it. And then, like one in a dream, I moved to the window, put forth my hand to open the casement, and thrust it through the pane. The blood spurted from my wrist; and with an instantaneous quietude and command of myself, I pressed my thumb on the little leaping fountain, and reflected what to do. In that empty room there was nothing to my purpose; I felt, besides, that I required assistance. There shot into my mind a hope that Olalla herself might be my helper, and I turned and went down stairs, still keeping my thumb upon the wound.

There was no sign of either Olalla or Felipe, and I addressed myself to the recess, whither the Señora had now drawn quite back and sat dozing close before the fire, for no degree of heat appeared too much for her.

'Pardon me,' said I, 'if I disturb you, but I must apply to you for help.'

She looked up sleepily and asked me what it was? and with the very words, I thought she drew in her breath with a widening of the nostrils and seemed to come suddenly and fully alive.

'I have cut myself,' I said, 'and rather badly. See!' And I held out my two hands from which the blood was oozing and dripping.

Her great eyes opened wide, the pupils shrank into points; a veil seemed to fall from her face, and leave it sharply expressive and yet inscrutable. And as I still stood, marvelling a little at her disturbance, she came swiftly up to me, and stooped and caught me by the hand; and the next moment my hand was at her mouth, and she had bitten me to the bone.* The pang of the bite, the sudden spurting of blood, and the monstrous horror of the act, flashed through me all in one, and I beat her back; and she sprang at me again and again, with bestial cries, cries that I recognized, such cries as had awakened me on the night of the high winds. Her strength was like that of madness;* mine was rapidly ebbing with the loss of blood; my mind besides was whirling with the abhorrent strangeness of the onslaught, and I was already forced against the wall, when Olalla ran betwixt us, and Felipe, following at a bound, pinned down his mother on the floor.

A trance-like weakness fell upon me; I saw, heard, and felt, but I was incapable of movement. I heard the struggle roll to and fro upon the floor, the yells of that catamount* ringing up to Heaven as she strove to reach me. I felt Olalla clasp me in her arms, her hair falling on my face, and with the strength of a man, raise and half drag, half carry me upstairs into my own room, where she cast me down upon the bed. Then I saw her hasten to the door and lock it, and stand an instant listening to the savage cries that shook the residencia. And then, swift and light as a thought, she was again beside me, binding up my hand, laying it in her bosom, moaning and mourning over it with dove-like sounds. They were not words that came to her, they were sounds more beautiful than speech, infinitely touching, infinitely tender; and yet as I lay there, a thought stung to my heart, a thought wounded me like a sword, a thought, like a worm in a flower, profaned the holiness of my love. Yes, they were beautiful sounds, and they were inspired by human tenderness; but was their beauty human?

All day I lay there. For a long time the cries of that nameless female thing,* as she struggled with her half-witted whelp, resounded through the house, and pierced me with despairing sorrow and disgust. They were the death-cry of my love; my love was murdered; it was not only dead, but an offence to me; and yet, think as I pleased, feel as I must, it still swelled within me like a storm of sweetness, and my heart melted at her looks and touch. This horror that had sprung out, this doubt upon Olalla, this savage and bestial strain that ran not only through the whole behaviour of her family, but found a place in the very foundations and story of our love—though it appalled, though it shocked and sickened me, was yet not of power to break the knot of my infatuation.

When the cries had ceased, there came a scraping at the door, by which I knew Felipe was without; and Olalla went and spoke to him—I know not what. With that exception, she stayed close beside me, now kneeling by my bed and fervently praying, now sitting with her eyes upon mine. So then, for these six hours, I drank in her beauty, and silently perused the story in her face. I saw the golden coin hover on her breaths; I saw her eyes darken and brighten, and still speak no language but that of an unfathomable kindness; I saw the faultless face, and, through the robe, the lines of the faultless body. Night came at last, and in the growing darkness of the chamber, the sight of her slowly melted; but even then the touch of her smooth hand lingered in mine and talked with me. To lie thus in deadly weakness and drink in the traits of the beloved, is to re-awake to love from whatever shock of disillusion. I reasoned with myself; and I shut my eyes on horrors, and again I was very bold to accept the worst. What mattered it, if that imperious sentiment survived, if her eyes still beckoned and attached me; if now, even as before, any* fibre of my dull body yearned and turned to her? Late on in the night some strength revived in me, and I spoke:

'Olalla,' I said, 'nothing matters; I ask nothing; I am content; I love you.'

She knelt down awhile and prayed, and I devoutly respected her devotions. The moon had begun to shine in upon one side of each of the three windows, and make a misty clearness in the room, by which I saw her indistinctly. When she re-arose she made the sign of the cross.*

'It is for me to speak,' she said, 'and for you to listen. I know you can but guess. I prayed, how I prayed for you to leave this place. I begged it of you, and I know you would have granted me even this; or, if not, O let me think so!'

'I love you,' I said.

'And yet you have lived in the world,' she said; after a pause, 'you are a man and wise; and I am but a child. Forgive me, if I seem to teach, who am as ignorant as the trees of the mountain; but those who learn much do but skim the face of knowledge; they seize the laws, they conceive the dignity of the design—the horror of the living fact fades from their memory. It is we who sit at home with evil who remember, I think, and be warned and pity. Go, rather, go now, and keep me in mind. So I shall have a life in the cherished places of your memory: a life as much my own, as that which I lead in this body.'

'I love you,' I said once more; and reaching out my weak hand, took hers, and carried it to my lips, and kissed it. Nor did she resist, but winced a little; and I could see her look upon me with a frown that was not unkindly, only sad and baffled. And then it seemed she made a call upon her resolution; plucked my hand towards her, herself at the same time leaning somewhat forward, and laid it on the beating of her heart. 'There,' she cried, 'you feel the very footfall of my life. It only moves for you; it is yours. But is it even mine? It is mine indeed to offer you, as I might take the coin from my neck, as I might break a live branch from a tree, and give it you. And yet not mine! I dwell, or I think I dwell (if I exist at all), somewhere apart, an impotent prisoner, and carried about and deafened by a mob that I disown. This capsule, such as throbs against the sides of animals, knows you at a touch for its master; ay, it loves you! But my soul, does my soul? I think not; I know not, fearing to ask. Yet when you spoke to me, your words were of the soul; it is of the soul that you ask—it is only from the soul that you would take me.'

'Olalla,' I said, 'the soul and the body are one, and mostly so in love. What the body chooses, the soul loves; where the body clings, the soul cleaves; body for body, soul to soul, they come together at God's signal; and the lower part (if we can call aught low) is only the footstool and foundation of the highest.'

'Have you,' she said, 'seen the portraits in the house of my fathers? Have you looked at my mother or at Felipe? Have your eyes never rested on that picture that hangs by your bed? She who sat for it died ages ago; and she did evil in her life. But, look again: there is my hand to the least line, there are my eyes and my hair. What is mine, then, and what am I? If not a curve* in this poor body of mine (which you love, and for the sake of which you dotingly dream that you love me) not a gesture that I can frame, not a tone of my voice, not any look from my eyes, no, not even now when I speak to him I love, but has belonged to others? Others, ages dead, have wooed other men with my eyes; other men have heard the pleading of the same voice that now sounds in your ears. The hands of the dead are in my bosom; they move me, they pluck me, they guide me; I am a puppet at their command; and I but reinform features and attributes that have long been laid aside from evil in the quiet of the grave. Is it me you love, friend? or the race that made me? The girl who does not know and cannot answer for the least portion of herself? On the stream of which she is a transitory eddy, the tree of which she is the passing fruit? The race exists; it is old, it is ever young, it carries its eternal destiny in its bosom; upon it, like waves upon the sea, individual succeeds to individual, mocked* with a semblance of self-control, but they are nothing. We speak of the soul, but the soul is in the race.'

'You fret against the common law,' I said. 'You rebel against the voice of God, which he has made so winning to convince, so imperious to command. Hear it, and how it speaks between us! Your hand clings to mine, your heart leaps at my touch, the unknown elements of which we are compounded awake and run together at a look; the clay of the earth remembers its independent life and yearns to join us; we are drawn together as the stars are turned about in space, or as the tides ebb and flow, by things older and greater than we ourselves.'

'Alas!' she said, 'what can I say to you? My fathers, eight hundred years ago, ruled all this province: they were wise, great, cunning and cruel; they were a picked race of the Spanish; their flags led in war; the king called them his cousin; the people, when the rope was slung for them or when they returned and found their hovels smoking, blasphemed their name. Presently a change began. Man has risen; if he has sprung from the brutes, he can descend again to the same level. The breath of weariness blew in their humanity and the cords relaxed; they began to go down; their minds fell on sleep, their passions awoke in gusts, heady and senseless like the wind in the gutters of the mountains; beauty was still handed down, but no longer the guiding wit nor the human heart; the seed passed on, it was wrapped in flesh, the flesh covered the bones, but they were the bones and the flesh of brutes, and their mind was as the mind of flies. I speak to you as I dare; but you have seen for yourself how the wheel has gone backward with my doomed race. I stand, as it were, upon a little rising ground in this desperate descent, and see both before and behind, both what we have lost and to what we are condemned to go, farther downward. And shall I—I that dwell apart in the house of the dead, my body loathing its ways—shall I repeat the spell? Shall I bind another spirit, reluctant as my own, into this bewitched and tempest broken tenement that I now suffer in? Shall I hand down this cursed vessel of humanity, charge it with fresh life as with fresh poison, and dash it, like a fire, in the faces of posterity? But my vow has been given; the race shall cease from off the earth. At this hour my brother is making ready; his foot will soon be on the stair; and you will go with him and pass out of my sight for ever. Think of me sometimes as one to whom the lesson of life was very harshly told, but who heard it with courage; as one who loved you indeed, but who hated herself so deeply that her love was hateful to her; as one who sent you away and yet would have longed to keep you for ever, who had no greater* hope than to forget you, and no greater fear than to be forgotten.'*

She had drawn towards the door as she spoke, her rich voice sounding softer and further away; and with the last word she was gone, and I lay alone in the moonlit chamber. What I might have done had not I lain bound by my extreme weakness, I know not; but as it was there fell upon me a great and blank despair. It was not long before there shone in at the door the ruddy glimmer of a lantern, and Felipe coming, charged me without a word upon his shoulders, and carried me down to the great gate, where the cart was waiting. In the moonlight the hills stood out sharply, as if they were of cardboard; on the glimmering surface of the plateau, and from among the low trees which swung together and sparkled in the wind, the great black cube of the residencia stood out bulkily, its mass only broken by three dimly lighted windows in the northern front above the gate. They were Olalla's windows, and as the cart jolted onward I kept my eyes fixed upon them till, where the road dipped into a valley, they were lost to my view for ever. Felipe walked in silence beside the shafts, but from time to time he would check the mule and seem to look back upon me; and at length drew quite near and laid his hand upon my head. There was such kindness in the touch, and such a simplicity, as of the brutes, that tears broke from me like the bursting of an artery.

'Felipe,' I said, 'take me where they will ask no questions.'

He said never a word, but he turned his mule about, end for end, retraced some part of the way we had gone, and striking into another path, led me to the mountain village, which was, as we say in Scotland, the kirkton* of that thinly-peopled district. Some broken memories dwell in my mind of the day breaking on the plain, of the cart stopping, of arms that helped me down, of a bare room into which I was carried, and of a swoon that fell upon me like sleep.

The next day and the days following the old priest was often at my side with his snuff-box and prayer book, and after a while, when I began to pick up strength he told me that I was now on a fair way to recovery, and must as soon as possible hurry my departure; whereupon, without naming any reason, he took snuff and looked at me sideways. I did not affect ignorance; I knew he must have seen Olalla. 'Sir,' said I, 'you know that I do not ask in wantonness. What of that family?'

He said they were very unfortunate; that it seemed a declining race, and they were very poor and had been much neglected.

'But she has not,' I said. 'Thanks, doubtless, to yourself, she is instructed and wise beyond the use of women.'

'Yes,' he said; 'the Señorita is well-informed. But the family has been neglected.'

'The mother?' I queried.

'Yes, the mother too,' said the Padre, taking snuff. 'But Felipe is a well-intentioned lad.'

'The mother is odd?' I asked.

'Very odd,' replied the priest, taking snuff.*

'I think, sir, we beat about the bush,' said I. 'You must know more of my affairs than you allow. You must know my curiosity to be justified on many grounds. Will you not be frank with me?'

'My son,' said the old gentleman, 'I will be very frank with you on matters within my competence; on those of which I know nothing it does not require much discretion to be silent. I will not fence with you, I take your meaning perfectly; and what can I say, but that we are all in God's hands, and that His ways are not as our ways? I have even advised with my superiors in the church, but they, too, were dumb. It is a great mystery.'

'Is she mad?' I asked.

'I will answer you according to my belief. She is not,' returned the Padre, 'or she was not. When she was young—God help me, I fear I neglected that wild lamb—she was surely sane; and yet, although it did not run to such heights, the same strain was already notable; it had been so before her in her father, ay, and before him, and this inclined me, perhaps, to think too lightly of it. But these things go on growing, not only in the individual but in the race.'

'When she was young,' I began, and my voice failed me for a moment, and it was only with a great effort that I was able to add, 'was she like Olalla?'

'Now God forbid!' exclaimed the Padre. 'God forbid that any man should think so slightingly of my favourite penitent. No, no; the Señorita (but for her beauty, which I wish most honestly she had less of) has not a hair's resemblance to what her mother was at the same age. I could not bear to have you think so; though, Heaven knows, it were, perhaps, better that you should.'

At this, I raised myself in bed, and opened my heart to the old man; telling him of our love and of her decision, owning my own horrors, my own passing fancies, but telling him that these were at an end; and with something more than a purely formal submission, appealing to his judgment.

He heard me very patiently and without surprise; and when I had done, he sat for some time silent. Then he begun the words:* 'The church,' and instantly broke off again to apologize. 'I had forgotten, my child, that you were not a Christian,' said he. 'And indeed, upon a point so highly unusual, even the church can scarce be said to have decided. But would you have my opinion? The Señorita is, in a matter of this kind, the best judge; I would accept her judgment.'

On the back of that he went away, nor was he thenceforward so assiduous in his visits; indeed, even when I began to get about again, he plainly feared and deprecated my society, not as in distaste, but much as a man might be disposed to flee from the riddling sphynx.* The villagers, too, avoided me; they were unwilling to be my guides upon the mountain. I thought they looked at me askance, and I made sure that the more superstitious crossed themselves* on my approach. At first I set this down to my heretical opinions; but it began at length to dawn upon me that if I was thus redoubted it was because I had stayed at the residencia. All men despise the savage notions of such peasantry; and yet I was conscious of a chill shadow that seemed to fall and dwell upon my love. It did not conquer, but I may not deify that it restrained my ardour.* Some miles westward of the village, there was a gap in the sierra, from which the eye plunged direct upon the residencia; and thither it became my daily habit to repair. A wood crowned the summit; and just where the pathway issued from its fringes, it was overhung by a considerable shelf of rock, and that, in its turn, was surmounted by a crucifix of the size of life and more than usually painful in design. This was my perch; thence, day after day, I looked down upon the plateau, and the great old house, and could see Felipe, no bigger than a sparrow,* going to and fro about the garden. Sometimes mists would draw across the view, and be broken up again by mountain winds; sometimes the place slumbered below me in unbroken sunshine; it would sometimes be all blotted out by rain. This distant post, these interrupted sights of the place where my life had been so strangely changed, suited the indecision of my humour. I passed whole days there, debating with myself the various elements of our position; now leaning to the suggestions of love, now giving an ear to prudence and in the end halting irresolute between the two opinions.*

One day, as I was sitting on my rock, there came by that way a somewhat gaunt peasant wrapped in a mantle. He was a stranger, and plainly did not know me even by repute; for, instead of keeping the other side, he drew near and sat down beside me, and we had soon fallen in talk. Among other things he told me he had been a muleteer, and, in former years had much frequented these mountains; later on, he had followed the army with his mules, had realized a competence, and was now living retired with his family.

'Do you know that house?' I inquired, at last, pointing to the residencia, for I readily wearied of any talk that kept me from the thought of Olalla.

He looked at me darkly and crossed himself.

'Too well,' he said, 'it was there that one of my comrades sold himself to Satan; the Virgin shield us from temptations! He has paid the price; he is now burning in the reddest place in Hell!'

A fear came upon me; I could answer nothing; and presently the man resumed, as if to himself: 'Yes,' he said, 'O yes, I know it. I have passed its doors. There was snow upon the pass, the wind was driving it; sure enough there was death that night upon the mountains, but there was worse beside the hearth. I took him by the arm, Señor, and dragged him to the gate; I conjured* him, by all he loved and respected, to go forth with me; I went on my knees before him in the snow; and I could see he was moved by my entreaty. And just then she came out on the gallery, and called him by his name; and he turned, and there was she standing with a lamp in her hand and smiling on him to come back. I cried out aloud to God, and threw my arms about him, but he put me by, and left me alone. He had made his choice; God help us. I would pray for him, but to what end? there are sins that not even the Pope can loose.'*

'And your friend—,' I asked, 'what became of him?'

'Nay, God knows,' said the muleteer. 'If all be true that we hear, his end was like his sin, a thing to raise the hair.'

'Do you mean that he was killed?' I asked.

'Sure enough, he was killed,' returned the man. 'But how? Ay, how? But these are things that it is sin to speak of.'

'The people of that house. ... .' I began.

But he interrupted me with a savage outburst. 'The people?' he cried. 'What people? There are neither men nor women in that house of Satan's! What? have you lived here so long, and never heard?' And here he put his mouth to my ear, and whispered, as if even the fowls of that mountain might have overheard and been stricken with horror.* What he told me was not true, nor was it even original; being indeed, but a new edition, vamped up* again by village ignorance and superstition, of stories nearly as ancient as the race of man. It was rather the application that appalled me. 'In the old days,' he said, 'the church would have burned out that nest of basilisks;* but the arm of the church was now shortened; his friend Miguel had been unpunished by the hands of men, and left to the more awful judgment of an offended God. This was wrong; but it should be so no more. The Padre was sunk in age, he was even bewitched himself; but the eyes of his flock were now awake to their own danger; and some day—aye, and before long—the smoke of that house should go up to heaven.'*

He left me filled with horror and fear. Which way to turn I knew not; whether first to warn the Padre, or to carry my ill-news direct to the threatened inhabitants of the residencia. Fate was to decide for me; for, while I was still hesitating, I beheld the veiled figure of a woman drawing near to me up the pathway. No veil could deceive my penetration by every line and every movement; I recognized Olalla; and keeping hidden behind a corner of the rock, I suffered her to gain the summit. Then I came forward. She knew me and paused, but did not speak; I, too, remained silent; and we continued for some time to gaze upon each other with a passionate sadness.

'I thought you had gone,' she said at length. 'It is all that you can do for me—to go. It is all I ever asked of you. And you still stay. But do you know, that every day heaps up the peril of death, not only on your head, but on ours? A report has gone about the mountain; it is thought you love me, and the people will not suffer it.'

I saw she was already informed of her danger, and I rejoiced at it. 'Olalla,' I said, 'I am ready to go this day, this very hour, but not alone.'

She stepped aside and knelt down before the crucifix to pray, and I stood by and looked now at her, and now at the object of her adoration, now at the living figure of the penitent, and now at the ghastly, daubed countenance, the painted wounds, and the projected ribs of the image. The silence was only broken by the wailing of some large birds that circled sidelong, as if in surprise or alarm, about the summit of the hills. Presently Olalla rose again, turned towards me, raised her veil, and, still leaning with one hand on the shaft of the crucifix, looked upon me with a pale and sorrowful countenance.

'I have laid my hand upon the cross,' she said. 'The Padre says you are no Christian; but look up for a moment with my eyes, and behold the face of the man of sorrows.* We are all such as He was—the inheritors of sin; we must all bear and expiate a past which was not ours; there is in all of us—ay, even in me—a sparkle of the divine. Like Him, we must endure for a little while, until morning returns, bringing peace. Suffer me to pass on upon my way alone; it is thus that I shall be least lonely, counting for my friend, Him who is the friend of all the distressed; it is thus that I shall be the most happy, having taken my farewell of earthly happiness, and willingly accepted sorrow for my portion.'

I looked at the face of the crucifix, and, though I was no friend to images, and despised that imitative and grimacing art of which it was a rude example, some sense of what the thing implied was carried home to my intelligence. The face looked down upon me with a painful and deadly contraction; but the rays of a glory encircled it, and reminded me that the sacrifice was voluntary. It stood there, crowning the rock, as it still stands on so many highway sides, vainly preaching to passers-by, an emblem of sad and noble truths; that pleasure is not an end, but an accident; that pain is the choice of the magnanimous; that it is best to suffer all things and do well. I turned and went down the mountain in silence; and when I looked back for the last time before the wood closed about my path, I saw Olalla still leaning on the crucifix.

GUY DE MAUPASSANT

THE HORLA

May 8th

WHAT a magnificent day! I spent the whole morning stretched on the grass, before my house, under the great plane-tree which entirely covers, shelters, and shades it. I love this country, and I love to live here, because here I have my roots, those deep, fine roots which attach a man to the soil where his forefathers were born and buried, which attach him to what is thought there and to what is eaten, to its customs as to its dishes, to its localisms of speech, to the peculiar intonation of its peasants, to the smell of its earth, of its villages, of its very air.

I love the house where I have grown up. From my windows I see the Seine, flowing by my garden; on the other side of the road, almost on my own property:—the great, wide Seine that goes to Havre from Rouen,* covered with the passing boats.

To the left, down there, Rouen—the great city of blue roofs swarming far and wide below a crowd of pointed Gothic bell-towers. These, ponderous or slender, are innumerable, overtowered by the cathedral's cast-iron spire,* and filled with bells which ring in the blue air on fine mornings. Their sweet and distant iron humming, their brazen chant, reaches out to me, brought by the breeze, and now louder, now lower, as the breeze now wakes, now drowses.

How fine it was this morning!

About eleven o'clock, I remember, a long tow* of ships defiled* past my garden railings. They were pulled by a tug the size of a fly; it groaned and vomited forth a thick, black smoke.

Just behind two English schooners, whose red flag* waved against the sky, came a superb Brazilian three-master, quite white, admirably clean and shining. This ship gave me so much pleasure that I saluted her, I don't know why.

May 12th

For some days I have had a little fever; I feel unwell, or rather, properly speaking, I feel depressed.

Whence come these mysterious influences which change our happiness into discouragement and our confidence into distress? One would almost say that the air, the invisible air, was full of unknowable Powers, to whose mysterious proximity we submit. I awake full of gayety, with desires to sing in my throat. Why? I go down to the waterside, and suddenly, after a short walk, return distressed, as though some misfortune awaited me at home. Why? Is it a shiver of cold which, brushing across my skin, has unsettled my nerves and darkened my soul? Is it the shapes of the clouds, or the colors of the day, or the changeable colors of things which have passed in through my eyes, and have troubled my thoughts? Do we know? Everything about us, everything which we see without observing, everything which we brush against without recognizing, everything which we touch without feeling, everything which we encounter without clearly distinguishing, may have upon us, upon our senses, and, through them, upon our minds and upon our hearts, instant effects which are wonderful and not to be explained.

Ah! but it is deep, this mystery of the Invisible! No, we may not sound it with our wretched senses, with our eyes—which can perceive neither what is too small nor too great, nor too near nor too far, nor the inhabitants of a planet nor the inhabitants of a drop of water. And we may not sound it with our ears—which deceive us, transmitting air-waves in the form of sonorous notes. They are the fairies who perform the miracle of changing movement into sound, and by this metamorphosis they give birth to music and to Nature's dumb agitation the power of singing. No, we may not sound it with our sense of smell—feebler than that of the dog; nor with our taste—which can hardly discern the age of wine!

Ah, if we had only other organs which would perform in our favor other miracles like that miracle of music, what new things we should discover all about our lives!

May 16th

I am certainly ill. Last month I was so well! I have a fever, a dreadful fever, or rather a feeling of feverish enervation which causes my mind to suffer as much as my body. I experience that awful sense of some menacing danger, that apprehension of coming misfortune or approaching death, that curious presentiment which is no doubt really the stroke of a still unrecognized sickness germinating in body and in blood.

May 18th

I have just been to consult my physician, for I was not able to sleep. He found my pulse rapid, my eye dilated, my nerves disturbed, but no alarming symptoms. I must take shower-baths and drink a little bromide of potassium.*

May 25th

No change. My condition is truly curious. With the approach of evening a strange anxiety invades me, as if the night concealed for me some dreadful menace. I dine quickly, then try to read, but I do not comprehend the words. I barely distinguish the letters. Then I pace my drawing-room backward and forward, under the oppression of a confused and resistless fear, the fear of sleep and the fear of my bed.

Towards ten o'clock I go up-stairs to my room. As soon as I get inside the door I double-lock it and I push the bolts; I am afraid ... of what? ... Hitherto I feared nothing ... . I open my closets, I look under my bed; I listen ... I listen for what? ... Is it not strange that a simple indisposition, a difficulty in the circulation perhaps, an irritated nerve, a slight congestion, a little disturbance of the works of my delicate, imperfect human machinery, can out of a merry man make a melancholy one—out of a brave man make a coward? Then I go to bed, and I await sleep as one might await an executioner. I wait with terror for its coming. And my heart beats, and my limbs quiver, and my whole body trembles under the warmth of the bedclothes, until the moment when I fall suddenly into slumber, as a man might fall, to drown himself, into a gulf of stagnant water. I do not feel sleep coming in the way I used to feel it coming—calmly. For this sleep, hidden somewhere near me, is perfidious, and it watches and will soon seize me by the head, and close my eyes, and destroy me.

I sleep long—two or three hours—then a dream—no, a nightmare grips me in its arms. I feel that I am in bed and that I am sleeping ... I feel it and I know it ... and I also feel that some one approaches me, looks at me, touches me, mounts upon my bed, kneels upon my breast, seizes my neck in his hands and presses ... presses ... with all his force, to strangle me.*

I—I writhe, bound fast by that awful powerlessness which paralyzes us in dreams. I desire to shout,—I cannot;—to move,—I cannot;—I try, with fearful efforts, panting, to turn myself, to throw off this being who is crushing and suffocating me;—I cannot.

And suddenly I awake, wild, covered with perspiration. I light a candle. I am alone.

After this crisis, which recurs every night, I sleep at last calmly until dawn.

June 2d

My condition is still worse. What is the matter with me? The bromide has no effect; the shower-baths have no effect. Just now, in order to tire myself out (though Heaven knows I am languid enough already!) I went to walk in the forest of Roumare. I thought at first that the fresh, buoyant, balmy air, full of the perfume of herbs and leaves, was pouring new blood into my veins, new energy into my heart. I took a wide glade. Then I turned towards La Bouille,* along a narrow *allée*, between two armies of great trees which built a thick, green, almost black roof between the sky and myself.

Suddenly a shiver seized me—not a shiver of cold, but a strange shiver of anguish.

I quickened my pace, uneasy at being alone in the wood, terrified without reason, stupidly, by the profound loneliness. All at once it seemed to me that I was being followed, that some one was treading on my heels, on the point—on the point—on the point of touching me.

I turned abruptly. I was alone. I saw behind me only the straight, wide glade—empty, high, fearfully empty; and in front of me also it stretched out of sight just the same—dreadful!

I closed my eyes. Why? And I began to turn round and round on my heel, quickly, like a top. I came near falling. I opened my eyes again; the trees danced; the earth swam; I was obliged to sit down. Then, of course, I no longer knew from which direction I had come! Fantastic thought! Strange! Fantastic thought! I set off to the right, and happened into the same avenue which had led me to the middle of the forest.

June 3d

The night was horrible. I shall go away for a few weeks. A little journey will no doubt set me on my feet again.

July 2d

At home again. I am cured; and, besides that, I have made a charming trip. I have visited Mont Saint Michel,* where I had never been.

What a vision, when one arrives, as I did, at Avranches* towards the end of the day! The city is on a little hill; a guide took me to the public garden at the end of the town. A great bay stretched away before me out of sight, between two lonely shores which lost themselves far off in the mists; and in the midst of this immense yellow bay, beneath a golden and glittering sky, rose, sombre and pointed, a strange mount in the midst of the sands. The sun had just disappeared, and against the still flaming horizon there was designed the profile of that fantastic rock which bears upon its summit a fantastic monument.

By daybreak I was on my way towards it. The tide was low, as yesterday at evening, and I watched that wonder-arousing abbey growing taller and taller before me as I approached. After several hours of walking I reached the enormous block of stones which bears the little town dominated by the great church. Having ascended the narrow and steep street, I entered the most admirable Gothic dwelling which has ever been constructed for God on earth, vast as a city, full of low passages borne down by heavy arches, of high galleries borne up by slender columns. I entered that gigantic granite jewel, light as a bit of lace, covered with towers and with slender belfries linked one to the other by fine-carved arches. They are climbed by twisting stair-ways, and they dart into the blue sky of day and into the black sky of night, their fantastic heads bristling with chimeras,* with Devils, and with strange Beasts.

When I reached the top I said to the monk who accompanied me, 'Father, you must be well off here.'

He answered: 'There's a great deal of wind, Monsieur;' and we fell into conversation while we watched the rising sea spread over the sand and cover it with a steely cuirass.*

And the monk told me stories—all the old stories of the place—legends, always legends.

One of them impressed me very strongly. The country people, those of the mount, pretend that talking is heard on the sands by night, then the bleating of two goats, the one with a voice which is high, the other with a voice which is deep. Unbelievers maintain it is the sea-birds' crying, which resembles now a bleat, and now a human wail; but belated fishermen swear that they have met, wandering on the sands, between two tides, about the little city cast out so far from the rest of the world, an old shepherd whose head, shrouded in a cloak, is always invisible, and who leads behind him a he-goat with the face of a man, and a she-goat with the face of a woman. They have long white hair, and they talk incessantly, quarrelling together in an unknown tongue; then suddenly they cease crying and begin to bleat with all their might.

I said to the monk: 'Do you believe it?'

He murmured: 'I do not know.'

I continued: 'If there really existed on the earth any other beings beside ourselves, how is it possible that we should not have known them long ago? How should you have seen them, you? How should I not have seen them, I?'

He answered: 'Do we see the hundred-thousandth part of what exists? For instance, take the wind, which is the greatest force in nature, which knocks down men, lays low buildings, tears up trees by the roots, heaps the sea into mountains of water, destroys coasts, and hurls great ships upon the breakers,—the Wind which kills, which whistles, which moans, which roars,—have you ever seen it? Can you see it? It exists, nevertheless.'

I was silent before this simple reasoning. This man was a wise man or perhaps a fool. I could not have decided which; but I was silent. What he had just said I had often thought.

July 3d

I have slept badly; there is certainly something feverish in the air here, for my coachman suffers from the same complaint as myself. On my return yesterday I noticed that he was looking curiously pale. I asked him:—

'What is the matter, Jean?'

'It is that I cannot sleep, Monsieur; my nights eat up my days. Since Monsieur went away, it holds me like a charm.'

The other servants, however, are well; but I myself am in great fear of a relapse.

July 4th

Yes, I have had a relapse. My old nightmares have returned. Last night I felt some one squatting on my chest with his mouth to mine, drinking my life out through my lips. Yes, like a leech he drew it out of my throat. Then when he was satiated he arose, and I, I awoke, so nearly murdered, so exhausted, so broken, that I had no longer power to move. If this continues many days more I shall certainly go away again.

July 5th

Have I lost my reason? That which has happened, that which I saw last night, is so strange that my head turns when I think of it!

I had, as I now do every evening, locked my door; then, being thirsty, I drank half a glass of water, and I noticed by mere chance that the water-bottle was full up to the glass stopper.

After that I went to bed and fell into one of my dreadful slumbers, from which, two hours later, I was drawn by a shock more awful yet.

Imagine a man who sleeps, who is being murdered, and who awakes with a knife in his breast, and who groans covered with blood, and who cannot breathe, and who is dying, and who does not understand. It was like that!

Having at last recovered my reason, I again felt thirsty; I lit a candle and I went to the table where the water-bottle stood. I raised it, tipping it over the glass; nothing came out. It was empty! It was completely empty! At first I did not understand; then, all at once, I experienced so terrible an emotion that I had to sit down, or rather that I simply fell, upon a chair! Then, with a start, I jumped to my feet, and looked about me! Then, again, I sat down, dazed with astonishment and with fear, before the transparent glass! I glared at it with staring eyes, trying to understand. My hands trembled! Had some one really drunk that water? Who—I? I, without a doubt. It could only be I. Then I was a somnambulist, I was living, without knowing it, that mysterious double life which makes us wonder whether we are in ourselves two beings, or whether some strange being, unknowable and invisible, may not animate, at moments when our will is weak, our bodies captive and more obedient to this stranger than to us.

Ah! who will understand my abominable anguish? Who will understand the emotion of a man, perfectly sane, well educated, full of reason, and yet contemplating in terror, through the glass of a water-bottle, the disappearance, while he slept, of a little water! And I remained there until morning, not daring to go back to bed.

July 6th

I am going mad. The water was again drunk by some one last night; or, rather, I drank it!

But, is it—is it I? Who should it be? Who? Oh, my God! I am going mad. Who shall save me?

July 10th

I have just established the most wonder-arousing proofs.

Yes, I am mad! And yet?

On the 6th of July, before going to bed, I placed some wine, some milk, some water, some bread, and some strawberries on my table.

Some one drank—I drank—all the water, and a little milk. The wine, the bread, and the strawberries were not touched.

On the 7th of July I made the same experiment, with the same result.

On the 8th of July I suppressed the water and the milk. Nothing was touched at all.

Finally, on the 9th of July, I put only the milk and the water on my table, being careful to wrap up the bottles in cloths of white muslin and to tie down the stoppers. Then I rubbed my lips, my beard, my hands, with black-lead,* and I retired.

The invincible slumber seized me, soon followed by the dreadful awaking. I had not stirred; my very sheets bore no stains. I rushed to the table. The cloths covering the bottles were immaculate. I untied the cords, trembling with fear. Some one had drunk all the water! Some one had drunk all the milk! Oh, my God! ...

I leave to-day for Paris.

July 12th

Paris. I must have lost my head completely these last days. I have been undoubtedly the plaything of a nervous imagination, unless, that is, I am really a somnambulist, or that I have been subjected to one of those influences, admitted but not yet explained, which are called 'suggestions.' In any case my perturbation came near insanity, and twenty-four hours of Paris have sufficed to put me on my feet again.

Yesterday, after taking a drive and making some visits which caused a new, revivifying air to pass into my soul, I finished the evening at the Théâtre Français.* They were playing a piece by Alexandre Dumas *fils*;* and that strong, alert spirit completed my cure. Solitude is certainly dangerous for an active intelligence. We need around us men who think and talk. When we are long alone, we people the void with phantoms.

I returned to the hotel in great good spirits, along the boulevards. Reminded by the jostling of the crowd, I thought, not without irony, of my terrors and imaginings of last week, when I believed, yes, really believed, that an invisible being was dwelling under my roof. How easily we lose our heads, how weakly and quickly we become wild with fear the moment we encounter some little incident which cannot be explained!

Instead of concluding with the words: 'The reason I do not understand is that the cause as yet escapes me,' we immediately proceed to imagine some dreadful mystery, some supernatural power.

July 14th

Fête de la République.* I took a walk in the streets. The flags and the fireworks amused me like a child. Nevertheless, it is simply an absurdity—this being joyous on a fixed date, by Government decree. The people is an imbecile herd, now stupidly patient, now ferociously rebellious. Some one says to it: 'Make merry.' It makes merry. Some one says to it: 'Go and fight with your neighbors.' It goes and fights. Some one says to it: 'Vote for the Emperor.' It votes for the Emperor. Then some one says to it: 'Vote for the Republic.' And it votes for the Republic.

Those who give it these orders are fools, also, but instead of obeying men, they obey principles, things whose stupidity, whose barrenness, whose falsity appears in the very name—Principles! Ideas supposed certain and immutable in this world where one is sure of nothing, where even light, even sound are illusions, merely states in the brain, merely states in the brain!

July 16th

Yesterday I saw something which disturbed me very much.

I was dining with my cousin Mme. Sablé,* whose husband commands the 76th Chasseurs at Limoges.* At dinner there were two young ladies, and the husband of one of them, a Doctor Parent, a nerve-specialist, much interested in the extraordinary developments brought to light by the experiments now making in Hypnotism and Suggestion.*

He gave us a long account of the prodigious results obtained by English scientists and by the physicians of the school at Nancy.*

The facts which he advanced appeared to me so extremely fantastic that I declared myself entirely sceptical.

'We are,' he maintained, 'on the point of discovering one of Nature's most important secrets—I mean to say, one of her most important terrestrial secrets; since, of course, she hides forever others quite as important up there in the stars. Ever since Man has been able to think, ever since he has been able to speak and write his thoughts, he has from time to time felt brushing against him the touch of a mystery which is impenetrable to his gross, imperfect senses; and he has tried to supplement this weakness of his bodily organs by an effort of his mind. While his intelligence remained in the rudimentary state this notion of phenomena, all about him, yet invisible, took on shapes of the most vulgar terror. From it were born popular beliefs in the supernatural, legends of wandering spirits, of fairies, of gnomes, of ghosts—I might even add, the vulgar idea of God; for the ordinary conception of a workman-creator, in whatever religion it springs up, is, of all the inventions of the human brain, the most common, the most stupid, the most unacceptable. Nothing is truer than Voltaire's epigram: "God made man in his own image, and man has returned the compliment."*

'But about a century ago people began to have dim forebodings of something new. Mesmer* and several others started us on an unexpected track, and now, and especially in the last three or four years, we have arrived at wonderful results.'

My cousin, as unbelieving as myself, smiled. Doctor Parent said to her: 'May I try to hypnotize you, madame?'

'Certainly you may.'

She seated herself in an arm-chair, and, trying to fascinate* her gaze, he looked at her fixedly. As for me, I felt suddenly troubled—my heart beating, a choking in my throat. I saw the eyes of Mme. Sablé droop, her mouth work, her breast heave. At the end of ten minutes she slept.

'Put yourself behind her,' said the physician.

And I seated myself behind her. In her hands he placed a visiting-card, saying: 'This is a mirror; what do you see in it?'

She answered: 'I see my cousin.'

'What is he doing?'

'He is twisting his mustache.'

'What now?'

'He is taking a photograph out of his pocket.'

'A photograph of whom?'

'Of himself.'

It was true! And the photograph had been sent home only that evening to my hotel.

'How does he look in the photograph?'

'He is standing up, with his hat in his hand.'

So then she saw in this card, in this white card, as well as she would have seen in a glass!

The young ladies, very much frightened, cried: 'Enough! Enough! Enough!'

But the doctor gave her an order: 'You will rise at eight o'clock tomorrow morning; and you will go to find your cousin at his hotel; and you will beg him to lend you five thousand francs, which your husband has said he needs, and hopes to get from you when he comes up shortly to town.'

Then he awoke her.

While returning to the hotel I meditated on this curious *séance*, and I was assailed by doubts, not of the absolute, the indubitable good faith of my cousin, whom I have known like a sister from childhood up, but of a possible trick on the part of the doctor. Might he not, at the same time with his visiting-card, have held before the sleeping lady a mirror hidden in his hand? Professional prestidigitators perform equally extraordinary feats.

So I went home and to bed.

But this morning, about half after eight, I was awaked by my man, who said:

'It is Mme. Sablé. She asks to speak with you, sir, immediately.'

I dressed in all haste, and I bid him show her in.

Very much embarrassed, she sat down, lowering her eyes, not lifting her veil; and she said:

'My dear cousin, I have to ask you for a great favor.'

'What is it, cousin?'

'I hate to ask you, and yet I must. I need—I need five thousand francs; I need it very much.'

'Oh, come now!—You?'

'Yes, I. Or, rather, my husband. He says I must get the money for him somehow.'

I was so stupefied that I stammered. I asked myself if this were not a joke on me which she was playing with Doctor Parent; if this were not a simple farce rehearsed in advance, and very well acted.

But, when I looked at her carefully, all my doubts vanished. She trembled with anguish, the proceeding was so painful for her; and I saw that her throat was full of sobs.

I knew she was very rich, and I continued:

'What! Your husband has not five thousand francs at his disposal? Come! Think a little. Are you sure he told you to ask me for it?'

For some seconds she hesitated as though making a great effort to remember, then she answered:

'Yes … Yes … I am sure of it.'

'Has he written?'

Again she hesitated, reflecting. I divined how she was tortured by the working of her thoughts. She did not know. She knew simply that she must borrow from me, for her husband, five thousand francs. But she gained the courage to lie.

'Yes, he wrote to me.'

'When, then? You said nothing to me of it yesterday.'

'I got the letter this morning.'

'Can you show it me?'

'No … no … no … it had private matters in it … too personal … I … I burnt it.'

'Oh! I suppose then he's been getting into debt.'

Again she hesitated; then murmured:

'I do not know.'

I announced, abruptly:

'The fact is at the moment I haven't five thousand francs to my hand, cousin.'

She uttered a kind of suffering cry.

'Oh, oh! I beg you, I beg you to get it somehow, somehow.' …

She grew excited, clasped her hands before me as though she were praying! I heard her voice change tone; she wept and stammered; she was tormented, overpowered, dominated by the irresistible order which had been laid upon her.

'Oh, oh! I beg you … if you knew how I suffer … I must have it to-day.'

I took pity on her.

'You shall have it, and very soon, I promise.'

'Oh, thank you! thank you! You are good.'

I continued:—'Do you remember what happened at your house last night?'

'Yes.'

'Do you remember that Doctor Parent put you to sleep?'

'Yes.'

'Well, he ordered you to come to me this morning, and borrow five thousand francs. And at this moment you are obeying his suggestion.'

She reflected for a few seconds, and answered:

'But it's my husband who wants it.'

For an hour I tried in vain to convince her.

As soon as she had gone, I hurried to the Doctor. He was on the point of going out; and he listened to me with a smile. Then he said:—

'Do you believe now?'

'Yes, I must.'

'Let us go to your cousin.'

She was already dozing in a long chair, exhausted with fatigue. The physician felt her pulse, looked at her for a time, his raised hand pointing towards her eyes. Little by little she closed them, submitting to the resistless strength of the magnetic power.

When she slumbered:

'Your husband has no longer any need of five thousand francs. You will therefore forget that you have asked your cousin to lend you them; and if he speaks to you of it, you will not understand him.'

Then he awoke her. I drew out a pocket-book.

'Here, my dear cousin, here is what you asked me for this morning.'

She was so surprised that I did not dare to insist. Nevertheless, I tried to arouse her memory; but she denied everything with vehemence, thought I was making fun of her, and at last came near being angry.

* * * * * * * * * * * * * *

There it is!—I have just returned; and I was so disturbed by this experience that at luncheon I could eat nothing.

July 19th

Several people to whom I have related this adventure have made fun of me. I do not know what to think. The wise man says: 'It may be.'

July 21st

I've been to dine at Bougival;* afterwards I went to the Watermen's Ball.* Decidedly everything depends on circumstance and place. To believe in the supernatural on the island of La Grenouillière* would be the height of folly indeed ... But on the top of Mont St. Michel? ... But in the Far East? We are subject fearsomely to the influence of what surrounds us. Next week I shall go home.

July 30th

I arrived yesterday. All well.

August 2d

Nothing new. Beautiful weather. I pass my days watching the Seine flow.

August 4th

Quarrels among the servants. They say that some one breaks the glass at night in the closets. My man accuses the cook, who accuses the laundress, who accuses the two maids. Which one is guilty? It would take a wise man to say.

August 6th

This time I am not mad. I have seen ... I have seen! ... I have seen! ... I can doubt no more ... I have seen! ... I am still chilled to my very finger-nails ... I am still afraid to the very marrow ... I have seen! ...

I was taking a walk about two o'clock, in broad daylight, in my rose-garden, ... along a row of autumn roses which are already beginning to bloom.

Pausing to look at a Géant des Batailles,* which bore three magnificent buds, I saw, I distinctly saw, quite near me the stem of one of these roses bend as though twisted by an invisible hand, then break, as though that hand had plucked it! Then the flower lifted itself, following the curve which would have been described by an arm carrying it to a mouth; and it remained hanging in the empty air, alone, motionless, a terrifying red stain three paces from my eyes.

Maddened, I threw myself forward to seize it! I found nothing; it had disappeared. Then I was overcome with violent anger against myself, since a man who is serious and reasonable should not allow himself to have such hallucinations as this.

But was it really an hallucination? I turned to look for the stem, and I discovered it almost immediately, on the plant, freshly broken, between the two other roses which remained upon the tree.

So I went back to the house with a troubled soul; for now I am certain that near me there exists an invisible being who lives on milk and on water; who can touch objects; can take them up and change their places; whose nature, therefore, though imperceptible to our sense, is material, and who, like myself, dwells under my roof ...

August 7th

I slept quietly. He drank all the water in my bottle, but did not disturb my sleep.

I ask myself if I am mad. While walking just now along the river, doubts about my reason came to me; not vague doubts such as I have hitherto experienced, but doubts precise and absolute. I have seen lunatics, I have known some who remained intelligent, clear-headed, lucid on every subject save one. They talked clearly, easily, profoundly, then suddenly their intelligence, striking on the rock of their monomania, there ground itself to pieces, was broken up and foundered in that terrible, furious sea, full of heaving waves and mists and squalls, the sea which we call 'Madness.'

I should certainly believe that I was mad, quite mad, if I were not so entirely self-conscious, if I did not recognize my condition so perfectly, if I were not always sounding it by an analysis which is so completely clear. I am, then, only a man who suffers from an hallucination, but who is in full possession of his reason? Some trouble has occurred in my brain, one of those troubles which psychologists nowadays endeavor to note and particularize? And this trouble has induced a profound lapse in my intellect, in the order and logic of my thoughts? A similar phenomenon occurs in dreams, where we are led through the most improbable of phantasmagoria* without feeling a shadow of surprise, simply for the reason that the verifying apparatus, our sense of control, is asleep, while our imaginative faculty wakes and is active. May it not be, therefore, that one of the invisible keys of my cerebral piano is paralyzed? People very often, in consequence of an accident, lose their memory of proper names, or of verbs, or of figures, or simply of dates. That the various little bundles of thought are specially localized is now considered proved. Hence what is there surprising if my power of controlling the unreality of certain hallucinations finds itself at the present moment torpid?

I pondered on all this as I followed the bank of the river. The sun covered the stream with radiance, made the earth delicious, filled my eyes with love for life, for the swallows whose swift motions are a joy to look at, for the grasses by the water's edge whose rustling is a joy to me when I listen.

Little by little, however, I was penetrated by a strange uneasiness. It seemed to me that a force, an occult force, benumbed me, checked me, prevented me from going farther, called me back. I experienced a mournful feeling that I must return, a feeling like that which oppresses us when, having left at home some sick person whom we love, we are suddenly seized by a presentiment that she is worse.

So I turned back, against my will, certain that I should find bad news at home, a letter, or a telegram. There was nothing, and I remained more surprised and uneasy than if I had again seen some fantastic vision.

August 8th

I passed a dreadful evening yesterday. He no longer makes his presence evident, but I feel him near me, spying, watching, penetrating me, dominating me, more terrible while thus concealed than if he manifested by supernatural phenomena his invisible and constant presence.

I slept, however.

August 9th

Nothing. But I am afraid.

August 10th

Nothing. What will happen to-morrow?

August 11th

Still nothing; I cannot stay at home any longer with this fear and these thoughts in my soul; I shall go away.

August 12th: 10 P.M.

All day I have wanted to be off; I could not go. I wished to perform an act of freewill, very easy and very simple:—going out of my door—getting into my carriage—driving to Rouen. I was not able. Why?

August 13th

When one is attacked by certain maladies all the powers of the physical being seem broken, all the energies destroyed, all the muscles relaxed, the bones becoming soft as flesh and the flesh liquid as water. I experience this in my moral state after a strange and appalling fashion. I have no longer any strength, courage, self-control, no power to put in motion my own will. I can no longer will; but some one wills for me, and I obey.

August 14th

I am lost! Some one is in possession of my soul and governs it. Some one orders all my acts, all my movements, all my thoughts. I am no longer anything in myself; I am nothing but an enslaved and terrified spectator of the things which I accomplish. I desire to go out; I cannot—he does not wish it, and I remain, frightened, trembling, in the arm-chair where he holds me seated. I desire simply to rise, to get up, so as to prove that I am still my own master. I cannot! I am riveted to my seat, and my seat adheres to the ground with such force that no power could lift us up.

Then, on a sudden, I must, I must, I must go to the end of the garden and pick some strawberries and eat them. And I go. I pick the berries and I eat them. Oh, my God!—my God! If there be a God, deliver me, save me, help me! Pardon! Pity! Grace! Save me! Oh, what suffering! what torture! what horror!

August 15th

Yes, this is the way in which my poor cousin was possessed and dominated when she came to me to borrow five thousand francs. She submitted to a strange will which had entered into her like a new soul—like a new parasite and dominant soul. Is the world ending?

But this being who governs me—what is he, this invisible? Who is he, this unknowable, this prowler of a supernatural race?

And so the Invisibles exist! How is it, then, that since the beginning of the world they have never manifested themselves as they have to me? I never read of any such things as have happened here in my house. Oh, if I could leave it!—if I could go away—flee and never return—I should be saved! But I cannot.

August 16th

I was able to make my escape to-day for two hours, like a prisoner who finds the door of his dungeon, by chance, open. I suddenly felt that I was free, and that he was far away. I ordered the carriage instantly, and I got as far as Rouen. Oh, what joy to say to a man who obeys you—'Go to Rouen.'

I had myself driven to the library, and I took out Hermann Herestauss's great treatise, *The Unrecognized Inhabitants of the Ancient and Modern World.**

Then, as I was getting back into my brougham* I wanted to say: 'To the station!' but cried—I did not say, I shouted—with a voice so loud that the people in the street turned round—'Home!' and I fell, mad with despair, on the cushions of the carriage. He had found and captured me again.

August 17th

Ah! what a night!—what a night! And yet it occurs to me that I ought to rejoice. I read till one o'clock in the morning. Hermann Herestauss is a doctor of philosophy and of theogony;* he has written a complete history of the manifestations of those beings which wander mostly invisible about mankind, or are imagined by him as so doing; he treats exhaustively of their origin, of their domain, of the power which they exercise; and not one of them resembles the one who haunts me. One would say that ever since man could think he has had dim forebodings and fears of a new being, stronger than himself, his successor in the world; and that, feeling him near at hand, and being unable to foresee the real nature of this new master, he has in terror created all that fantastic crowd of occult beings—vague phantoms born of fear.

But to continue. Having read till one o'clock, I went and seated myself at an open window to refresh brow and brain in the calm air of darkness.

The night was gentle and warm. How I should have loved this kind of a night long ago!

No moon. The stars at the back of the black sky glittered and trembled. Who dwell in those worlds up there? What forms? what living things? what animals? what plants? That which thinks in those distant universes, what knows it more than we? What power has it more than we? What sees it that we know not? And some day or another will not one of those beings, traversing space, appear upon the earth and conquer it, just as the Normans of old crossed the sea to subdue more feeble races?

We are so weak, so defenceless, so ignorant, so little, we here on this revolving speck of mud and water.

Thus dozing in the fresh evening breeze, I drowsed off.

But after I had slept about forty minutes, I opened my eyes, making no other movement, awoke by some confused fantastical emotion. At first I saw nothing; then, on a sudden, it seemed to me that a page of the open book lying on my table had just turned by itself. No breath of air came through the window. I was surprised, and I waited. At the end of about four minutes I saw, I saw, yes, I saw with my eyes another page lift itself and fold over down on the preceding one as though a finger had turned it. My arm-chair was empty, seemed empty; but I understood that he was there, he, seated in my place, and that he was reading. With one furious leap, with the bound of a beast who has rebelled at last, and fallen on his master to tear him open, I crossed the room to seize, to grip him in my hands, to kill him! ... But my chair, before I had reached it, was overturned, as though some one fled before me ... my table tottered, my lamp fell and was extinguished, and my window shut itself as though a detected thief had leaped out into the night by catching both the sashes in his hands.

So, he fled! He was afraid, he was afraid of me!

Then ... then ... to-morrow ... or the day after ... or some day ... I shall be able to get him down under my hands, and to crush him against the earth! Do not dogs sometimes bite and throttle their masters?

August 18th

I have reflected all day. Oh yes, I shall obey him, follow his suggestions, accomplish all his desires, appear humble, submissive, cowardly! He is the strongest. But an hour will come ...

August 19th

I know ... I know ... I know all! I have read as follows in the *Revue du Monde Scientifique*:* 'Information of a curious nature comes to us from Rio de Janeiro. An epidemic of madness, comparable to those contagious crazes which attacked the European peoples during the Middle Ages, is, it seems, at present, raging in the province of San Paulo. The inhabitants are leaving their houses in dismay, deserting their villages, and abandoning their crops, maintaining that they are being pursued, taken possession of, governed like a human herd of cattle, by certain invisible but tangible beings, resembling vampires, who suck upon their life-blood during their sleep, and who, besides that, take water and milk, but no other nourishment.

'Professor Don Pedro Henriquez, accompanied by several other scientists of the medical profession, is on his way to the province of San Paulo, to study on the spot the causes and the manifestations of this curious mania; he will then propose to the Emperor whatever measures he decides best for recalling these unhappy lunatics to their reason.'

Ah! Ah! I remember, I remember the beautiful Brazilian three-master which passed up the Seine under my windows on the 8th of last May! I thought it so beautiful, so white, so gay! The Being was aboard it, coming from that distant country where his race was born! And he saw me! He saw that my dwelling was white, likewise; and he leaped from the ship to the river-banks. Oh, my God!

And now, I know, I divine. The kingdom of man is ended.

He has come. He whom primitive peoples dreaded with a naïve terror, He who was exorcized by anxious priests, He whom sorcerers invoked in vain on sombre nights, He to whom the forebodings of man, the transitory master of the earth, have given the monstrous or gracious forms of gnomes and ghosts, of genii, of fairies, and of familiar spirits. After the vulgar conceptions of primitive fear came the clearer presentations of more highly developed minds. Mesmer first divined Him; and the doctors, as long as ten years ago, discovered the exact nature of His power before He himself had ever used it. They have played with this weapon of the new Lord, this domination of a mysterious will over a human soul made captive. They have called it magnetism, hypnotism, suggestion ... what not? I have seen them, like careless children, amusing themselves with that dreadful power! Woe to us! Woe to Man! He is come, the ... the ... how calls he himself ... the ... it seems to me that he is crying out his name, and that I cannot hear it ... the ... yes ... he is crying it ... I am listening ... I cannot ... I repeat ... the ... Horla* ... I heard ... the Horla ... it is he ... the Horla ... he has come! ...

Ah! the vulture has devoured the dove, and the wolf has devoured the sheep, the lion has devoured the buffalo with the pointed horns; and the man has slain the lion by arrows and by his knife and by powder. But the Horla will make of man what man has made of the horse, and of the ox: his thing, his servant, his food, by the sole power of his will. Woe unto us!

Nevertheless, the animal sometimes revolts and kills his master ... and I, too, I wish ... I shall be able ... but I must first know what he is like, I must touch him, see him! Scientists say that the eyes of animals are different from ours, and do not distinguish things as ours do ... Just so my eyes cannot distinguish this new-comer who oppresses me.

Why? Oh! now I remember the words of the monk of Mont St. Michel: 'Do we see the hundred-thousandth part of what exists? For instance, take the wind, which is the greatest force in nature, which knocks down men, lays low buildings, tears up trees by the roots, heaps the sea into mountains of water, destroys coasts, and hurls great ships upon the breakers,—the Wind which kills, which whistles, which moans, which roars,—have you ever seen it? Can you see it? It exists, nevertheless.'

And I continued to reflect: 'My eye is so feeble, so imperfect, that it does not even distinguish solid bodies, if they are transparent—such as glass! ... And if a mirror without a quicksilver back bars the way, my eye allows me to throw myself up against it like a bird which, straying into a room, dashes its head to pieces against the window-panes. A thousand things beside deceive and confuse it. Then what wonder if it cannot see this new transparent body?'

A new being! Why not? Inevitably he must have arisen! Why should we be the last? We cannot see him as we do other beings created before ourselves? That is simply because his nature is more perfect, because his body is more subtilely* and highly developed than ours, than ours so feeble, than ours conceived so roughly, encumbered with organs like over-complex springs, always fatigued, and always straining. For our body lives like a plant and like a beast, gaining a painful sustenance from air, from grasses, and from flesh. A living machine, the prey to sickness, to deformity, and to decay, it is of dust; a work at once coarse and delicate, irregular, pitifully simple, fantastic, and ill-made ingeniously; the first rough sketch of a being which might sometime be developed into something intelligent and perfect.

There are, after all, from the oyster up to the man, so few of us here on the earth. Why not one more, once the period which separates the appearances of different successive species has been accomplished?

Why not one more? Why not other trees with immense flowers dazzling and suffusing entire regions with their perfume? Why not other elements besides Fire, Air, Earth, and Water? They are four, only four, these nursing fathers of being! What a pity! Why are they not forty, four hundred, four thousand? How poor, how mean, how wretched is everything! Granted, but not freely; conceived, but without genius; executed, but with no lightness of touch! The elephant, forsooth, the hippopotamus, how graceful! The camel, how elegant!

But what say you of the butterfly, that flying flower? I dream of one large as a hundred worlds, with wings whose shape, whose beauty, whose color, and whose manner of motion I cannot even describe. But I see it ... it is going from star to star refreshing and perfuming each with the light and harmonious breathing of its course! … And whole peoples, high up there, watch, in ecstasy and ravishment, its passing! …

* * * * * * * * * * * * * *

What is the matter with me? It is he, he, the Horla, who haunts me and makes me dream such follies! He is within me. He has become my soul; I shall kill him!

August 20th

I shall kill him. I have seen him. I sat down last night at my table, and I pretended to be absorbed in writing. I knew very well that he would come and prowl round me, very near, so near that perhaps I should be able to touch him, to seize him. And then! … then I should have the strength of desperation; I should have hands and knees, breast, and brow, and teeth, to strangle, to crush, to bite, to tear.

And, straining every sense, I watched for him.

I had lit my two lamps and the eight candles on my mantel, exactly as though the light would help me to discover him!

Before me was my bed, an old oak bedstead with columns. On my right the chimney-piece. On my left the door, which I had carefully shut, after leaving it open for a while in order to attract him. Behind me, a tall wardrobe, with a looking-glass which I used every day for shaving and for dressing, and in which, every time I passed it, I had a habit of looking myself over from head to foot.

So I pretended to write in order to deceive him; for he, too, was watching. And suddenly I felt, I was certain, that he was reading over my shoulder, that he was there almost brushing my ear.

I jumped up with out-stretched hands, and turned round so quickly that I almost fell. Well? In my chamber it was as light as day, but I did not see myself in the glass! … It was empty, clear, deep, full of light! My image was not in it … and I stood there right in front of it, I! The great glass was clear from top to bottom. And with wild eyes I stared at this thing; and I did not dare to advance, I did not dare to move, feeling indeed that he was there, but that he would escape me, he, whose invisible body had absorbed the reflection of mine.

What fear I suffered! Then, all of a sudden, I began to perceive myself in a mist at the back of the mirror, in a mist as though through a sheet of water; and it seemed to me that this water glided from left to right, slowly, making my figure clearer, from second to second. It was like the ending of an eclipse. That which concealed me did not appear to possess sharp outlines, but merely a kind of opaque transparence, rarefying itself little by little.

At last I could distinguish my whole figure, just as I do each day when I look.

I had seen him! The terror of it remains still on me, causing me still to shiver.

August 21st

Kill him? How? Since I cannot reach him? Poison? But he would see me mixing it in the water; and, besides, would our poisons have any effect on his supersensual* body? No ... no ... of course not ... What then? ... what then? ...

August 22d

I have had up a locksmith from Rouen, and I have ordered for my room some iron shutters like those which certain private houses in Paris have on the ground-floor as a protection against robbers. He is also to make me an iron door. I am appearing like a great coward, but at that I laugh! ...

* * * * * * * * * * * * * *

Sept. 10th

Rouen. Hôtel Continental. It is accomplished ... it is accomplished ... but is he dead? My soul is overwhelmed by what I have seen.

Yesterday the locksmith, having fitted my shutters and my iron door, I left everything open until midnight, although it began to be very cold.

All of a sudden I felt that he was there, and a joy, a mad joy seized me. I rose gently, and I walked up and down for a long time in order to put him off his guard. Then I carelessly took off my boots and put on my slippers. Then I closed my iron shutters, and, returning tranquilly to the door, I closed that also and double-locked it. Again returning to the window, I secured the shutter with a padlock, and put the key in my pocket.

All of a sudden I understood that he was stirring anxiously round me; that, in his turn now, he was afraid; that he was commanding me to open. I came near yielding; I did not yield, but, setting my back against the door, I opened it on a crack just wide enough for me to pass through backward; and as I am very tall, my head touched the lintel. I was sure that he could not have escaped, and I shut him in all alone—all alone! What happiness! I had him fast! Then I went downstairs, running. In the drawing-room under my bed-chamber I took the two lamps, and I poured oil over the carpet, over the furniture, over everything; then I set fire to it and I escaped from the house after having double-locked on the outside the great hall door.

And I hid myself at the bottom of the garden in a thicket of laurels. How long it was! How long it was! All remained black, silent, immobile; not a breath of air, not a star in the great mountains of clouds which I could not see, but which rested on my soul so heavily, so heavily.

I watched my house and I waited. How long it was! I had begun to think that the fire had gone out of itself, or that he—He had extinguished it. Then one of the windows on the ground-floor cracked under the pressure of the inner conflagration, and a tongue of flame—a great tongue of red and yellow flame—long and soft and caressing, climbed up along the white wall and kissed the very roof. A glow ran over the trees, the branches, the leaves, and a shiver—a shiver of fear also! The birds awoke; a dog began to howl; it seemed to me that the day itself was getting up! Soon two other windows burst open, and I saw that the whole ground-floor of my house was nothing but a dreadful brazier. But a cry—an awful cry—sharp, heart-rending—a woman's shriek—came out into the night, and two windows in the garret opened! I had forgotten my servants! I saw their wild faces, their waving arms! ...

Then, mad with horror, I set off running to the village, shouting 'Help!—help! Fire!—fire!' I met people already hastening to the scene, and I returned with them—to look!

The house was now simply a horrible and magnificent stake—a monstrous stake—illuminating all the country—a stake at which men were burning, and at which he burned also—He, He, my prisoner, the new Being, the new master, the Horla!

Suddenly the entire roof fell in between the walls, and a volcano of flame shot upward to the sky. Through the windows open upon the furnace I saw the fiery vat, and I thought: he is there in that burning oven—dead ...

Dead? Perhaps .... But his body? His body, which the light of day could pass through, is it not perhaps indestructible by such means as destroy our bodies?

What if he be not dead? ... Time alone, perhaps, has power over the Being Invisible, the Being Terrible. Why a transparent body? why an imperceptible body? why the body of a Spirit, if he too must fear misfortunes, wounds, infirmities, premature destruction?

Premature destruction? All human terror springs from the idea of that. After Man, the Horla. After him who can die any day, any hour, any moment, by any accident, has come He who shall die only on his appointed day, at his appointed hour, at his appointed minute, having touched the appointed limit of existence!

No ... no ... there is no doubt, there is no doubt ... I have not killed him ... Then ... then ... I see ... it is plain ... yes, it is plain that I must ... kill ... myself! ... *

AMBROSE BIERCE

THE DEATH OF HALPIN FRAYSER

I

FOR by death is wrought greater change than hath been shown. Whereas in general the spirit that hath removed cometh back upon occasion, and is sometimes seen of those in flesh (though appearing in the form of the body it bore), yet it hath happened that the veritable body without the spirit hath walked. And it is attested of those encountering, who have lived to speak thereon, that a lich* so raised up hath no natural affection, nor remembrance thereof, but only hate. Also, it is known that some spirits which in life were benign become by death evil all together.—*Mannon's 'Thoughts on Immortality.'**

ONE dark night in midsummer a man waking from a dreamless sleep in a forest in the Napa Valley* lifted his head from the earth, and staring a few moments into the blackness said: 'Catharine Larue.' He said nothing more; no reason was known to him why he should have said so much.

The man was Halpin* Frayser. He lived in San Francisco,* but where he lives now is uncertain, for he is dead. One who practices sleeping in the woods with nothing under him but the dry leaves and the damp earth, and nothing over him but the branches from which the leaves have fallen and the sky from which the earth has fallen, cannot hope for great longevity, and Frayser had already attained the age of twenty-seven. There are people in this world, millions of people, and far and away the best people, who regard twenty-seven as a very advanced age. They are the children. To those who view the voyage of life from the haven of departure, the bark* that has accomplished any considerable distance appears already in close approach to the farther shore. However, Halpin Frayser did not come to his death by exposure, as we shall see.

He had been all day in the hills west of the Napa Valley, looking for doves and such small game as was in season. Late in the afternoon it had come on to be cloudy and he had lost his bearings; and although he had only to go always down hill—everywhere the way to safety when one is lost—the absence of trails had so impeded him that he was overtaken by night while still in the forest. Unable in the darkness to penetrate the thickets of manzanita* and other undergrowth, utterly bewildered and overcome with fatigue, he had lain down near the root of a large madroño* and fallen into a dreamless sleep. It was hours later, in the very middle of the night, that one of God's mysterious messengers, gliding ahead of the incalculable host of his companions who swept westward with the dawn line, pronounced the awakening word in the ear of the sleeper, who, as we have noted, sat upright and spoke, he knew not why, a name he knew not whose.

Halpin Frayser was not much of a philosopher, nor a scientist. The circumstance that, waking from a deep sleep at night in the midst of a forest, he had mentioned aloud a name that he had not in memory, and hardly had in mind, did not arouse an enlightened curiosity to investigate the phenomenon. He thought it odd, and with a little perfunctory shiver, as if in deference to a numerical* presumption that the night was chill, he lay down again and went to sleep. But his sleep was no longer dreamless.

He thought he was walking along a dusty road that showed white in the gathering darkness of a summer night. Whence and whither it led, and why he travelled it, he did not know, though all seemed simple and natural, as is the way in dreams; for in the Land beyond the Bed surprises cease from troubling and the judgment is at rest. Soon he came to a parting of the ways: leading from the highway was a road less travelled, having the appearance, indeed, of having been long abandoned, because, he thought, it led to something evil; yet he turned into it without hesitation, impelled by some malign necessity.

As he pressed forward he became conscious that his way was haunted by malevolent existences, invisible, and whom he could not definitely figure to his mind. From among the black bodies of the trees on either side he caught broken and incoherent whispers in a strange tongue which yet he partly understood. They seemed to him fragmentary utterances of a monstrous conspiracy against his body and his soul. It was now long after nightfall, yet the interminable forest through which he journeyed was lit with a wan glimmer, having no point of diffusion, for in its uncanny lumination* nothing cast a shadow. A shallow pool in the guttered depression of an old wheel-rut, as from a recent rain, met his eye with a crimson gleam.

He stooped and plunged his hand into it. It stained his fingers; it was blood. Blood, he then observed, was about him everywhere. The weeds growing rankly by the roadside showed it in blots and splashes on their big, broad leaves. Patches of dry dust between the wheelways were pitted and spattered as with a red rain. Defiling the trunks of the trees were broad maculations* of crimson, and blood dripped like dew from their foliage. All this he observed with a terror, which, however, seemed but the fulfillment of a natural expectation. It seemed to him that it was all in expiation of some crime which, though conscious of his guilt, he could not rightly remember. To the menaces and mysteries of his surroundings the consciousness was an added horror. Vainly he sought, by tracing life backward in memory, to reproduce the moment of his sin; scenes and incidents came crowding tumultuously into his mind, one picture effacing another, or commingling with it in confusion and obscurity, but nowhere could he catch a glimpse of what he sought. The failure augmented his terror; he felt as one who has murdered in the dark, not knowing why nor whom. So frightful was the situation,—the mysterious light burned with so silent and awful a menace; the noxious plants, the trees that by common consent are invested with a melancholy or baleful character so openly in his sight conspired against his peace; from overhead and all about came so audible and startling whispers and the sighs of creatures so obviously not of earth, that he could endure it no longer, and with a great effort to break some malign spell that bound his faculties to silence and inaction, he shouted with the full strength of his lungs! His voice, broken, it seemed, into an infinite multitude of various sounds, went babbling and stammering away into the distant reaches of the forest, died into silence, and all was as before. But he had made a beginning at resistance and was encouraged. He said:

'I will not submit unheard. There may be powers which are not malignant travelling this accursed road. I shall leave them a record and an appeal. I shall relate my wrongs, the persecutions that I endure—I, a helpless mortal, a penitent—an unoffending poet!' Halpin Frayser was a poet only as he was a penitent: in his dream.

Taking from his clothing a small red-leather pocketbook, one-half of which was leaved for memoranda, he discovered that he was without a pencil. He broke a twig from a bush, dipped it in a pool of blood and wrote rapidly. He had hardly touched the paper with the point of his twig when a low, wild laugh seemed to break out at a measureless distance away, and growing ever louder, seemed approaching ever nearer; a soulless, heartless, and unjoyous laugh, like that of the loon,* solitary by the lakeside at midnight; a laugh which culminated in an unearthly shout close at hand, then died away by slow gradations, as if the accursed being that uttered it had withdrawn over the verge of the world whence it had come. But the man felt that this was not so—that it was near by and had not moved. A strange sensation began slowly to take possession of his body and his mind. He could not have said which, if any, of his senses it affected; he felt it rather as a consciousness—a mysterious mental assurance of some overpowering presence—some supernatural malevolence different in kind from the invisible existences that swarmed about him, and superior to them in power. He knew that it had uttered that hideous laugh. And now it seemed to be approaching him; from what direction he did not know—dared not conjecture. All his former fears were forgotten or merged in the gigantic terror that now held him in thrall. Apart from that, he had but one thought—to complete his written appeal to the benign powers who, traversing the haunted wood, might sometime rescue him if he should be denied the blessing of annihilation. He wrote with terrible rapidity, the twig in his fingers rilling* blood without renewal; but in the middle of a sentence his hands denied their service to his will, his arms fell to his sides, the book to the earth; and powerless to move or cry out, he found himself staring into the sharply-drawn face and blank, dead eyes of his own mother, standing white and silent in the garments of the grave!

II

In his youth Halpin Frayser had lived with his parents in Nashville, Tennessee. The Fraysers were well-to-do people, having a good position in such society as had survived the wreck wrought by civil war. Their children had the social and educational opportunities of their time and place, and had responded to good associations and instruction with agreeable manners and cultivated minds. Halpin, being the youngest, and not over-robust, was, perhaps, a trifle 'spoiled.' He had the double disadvantage of a mother's assiduity and a father's neglect. Frayser *père* was what no Southern man of means is not—a politician. His country, or rather his section and State, made demands upon his time and attention so exacting that to those of his family he was compelled to turn an ear partly deafened by the thunder of the political captains and the shouting, his own included.

Young Halpin was of a dreamy, indolent, and rather romantic turn, rather more addicted to literature than law, the profession to which he was bred. Among those of his relations who professed the modern faith of Heredity it was well understood that in him the character of the late Myron Bayne, a maternal great-grandfather, had revisited the glimpses of the moon*—by which orb he had in his lifetime been sufficiently affected to be a poet of no small Colonial distinction. If not specially observed, it was observable that while a Frayser who was not the proud possessor of a sumptuous copy of the ancestral 'poetical works' (printed at the family expense, and long ago withdrawn from an inhospitable market) was a rare Frayser indeed, there was an illogical indisposition to honor the great deceased in the person of his spiritual successor. Halpin was pretty generally deprecated as an intellectual black sheep who was likely at any moment to disgrace the flock by bleating in meter. The Tennessee Fraysers were a practical folk—not practical in the popular sense of devotion to sordid* pursuits, but having a robust contempt for any qualities unfitting a man for the wholesome vocation of politics. In justice to young Halpin it should be said that whilst in him were pretty faithfully reproduced most of the mental and moral characteristics ascribed by history and family tradition to the famous Colonial bard, his succession to the gift and faculty divine was purely inferential. Not only had he never been known to court the muse, but in point of fact he could not have written correctly a line of verse to save himself from the Killer of the Wise.* Still, there was no knowing when the dormant faculty might awake and smite the lyre. In the meantime the young man was rather a loose fish,* anyhow.

Between him and his mother was the most perfect sympathy, for secretly the lady was herself a devout disciple of the late and great Myron Bayne, though with the tact so generally and justly admired in her sex (despite the hardy calumniators who insist that it is essentially the same thing as cunning), she had always taken care to conceal her weakness from all eyes but his who shared it. Their common guilt was a tie that bound them very closely together; and if in Halpin's youth she had 'spoiled' him, he had assuredly done his part toward being spoiled. As he grew to such manhood as is attainable by a Southerner who does not care which way elections go, the attachment between him and his beautiful mother—whom from early childhood he had called Katy—became yearly more strong and tender. In these two romantic natures was manifest in a conspicuous way that neglected phenomenon, the dominance of the sexual element in all the relations of life, strengthening, softening, and beautifying even those of consanguinity. The two were nearly inseparable, and by strangers observing their manner, were not infrequently mistaken for lovers.

Entering his mother's boudoir one day Halpin Frayser kissed her upon the forehead, toyed for a moment with a lock of her dark hair which had escaped from its confining pins, and said, with an obvious effort at calmness:

'Would you greatly mind, Katy, if I were called away to California for a few weeks?'

It was hardly needful for Katy to answer with her lips a question to which her tell-tale cheeks had made instant reply. Evidently she would greatly mind; and the tears, too, sprang into her large, brown eyes as corroborative testimony.

'Ah, my boy,' she said, looking up into his face with infinite tenderness, 'I should have known that this was coming. Did I not lie awake a half of the night weeping because, during the other half, Grandfather Bayne had come to me in a dream, and standing by his portrait—young, too, and handsome as that—pointed to yours on the same wall? And when I looked it seemed that I could not see the features; you had been painted with a face-cloth, such as we put upon the dead. Your father has laughed at me, but you and I, dear, know that such things are not for nothing. And I saw below the edge of the cloth the marks of hands on your throat—forgive me, but we have not been used to keep such things from each other. Perhaps you have another interpretation—perhaps it does not mean that you will go to California. Or maybe you will take me with you?'

It must be confessed that this ingenious interpretation of the dream in the light of newly discovered evidence did not wholly commend itself to the son's more logical mind; he had, for the moment at least, a conviction that it foreshadowed a more simple and immediate, if less tragic, disaster than a visit to the Pacific Coast. It was Halpin Frayser's impression that he was to be garroted on his native heath.

'Are there not medicinal springs in California?' Mrs. Frayser resumed before he had had time to give her the true reading of the dream—'places where one recovers from rheumatism and neuralgia? Look—my fingers feel so stiff, and I am almost sure they have been giving me great pain while I slept.'

She held out her hands for his inspection. What diagnosis of her case he may have thought it best to conceal with a smile the historian is unable to state, but for himself he feels bound to say that fingers looking less stiff, and showing fewer evidences of even insensible pain, have seldom been submitted for medical inspection by even the fairest patient desiring a prescription of unfamiliar scenes.

The outcome of it was that these two odd persons having equally odd notions of duty, the one went to California, as the interest of his client required, and the other remained at home in compliance with a wish that her husband was scarcely conscious of entertaining.

While in San Francisco Halpin Frayser was walking one dark night along the water-front of the city, when, with a suddenness that surprised and disconcerted him, he became a sailor. He was in fact 'shanghaied'* aboard a gallant, gallant* ship, and sailed for a far countree.* Nor did his misfortunes end with the voyage; for the ship was cast ashore on an island of the South Pacific, and it was six years afterward when the survivors were taken off by a venturesome trading schooner and brought back to San Francisco.

Though poor in purse, Frayser was no less proud in spirit than he had been in the years that seemed ages and ages ago. He would accept no assistance from strangers, and it was while living with a fellow survivor near the town of St. Helena,* awaiting news and remittances from home, that he went gunning* and dreaming, as we have seen.

III

The apparition confronting the dreamer in the haunted wood—the thing so like yet so unlike his mother—was horrible! It stirred no love nor longing in his heart; it came unattended with pleasant memories of a golden past—inspired no sentiment of any kind: all the finer emotions were swallowed up in fear. He tried to turn and run from before it, but his legs were as lead: he was unable to lift his feet from the ground. His arms hung helpless at his sides; of his eyes only he retained control, and these he dared not remove from the lusterless orbs of the ghost, which he knew was not a soul without a body, but that most dreadful of all existences infesting that haunted wood, a body without a soul! In its blank stare was neither love, nor pity, nor intelligence—nothing to which to address an appeal for mercy. 'An appeal will not lie,'* he thought, with an absurd attrusion* of professional memories making the situation more horrible, as the fire of a cigar might light up a tomb.

For a time which seemed so long that the world grew gray with age and sin, and the haunted forest, having fulfilled its purpose in this monstrous culmination of its terrors, vanished out of his consciousness with all its sights and sounds, the apparition stood within a pace, regarding him with the mindless malevolence of a wild brute; then thrust its hands forward and sprang upon him with appalling ferocity! The act released his physical energies without unfettering his will; his mind was still spell-bound, but his powerful body and agile limbs, endowed with a blind, insensate life of their own, resisted stoutly and well. For an instant he seemed to see this unnatural contest between a dead intelligence and a breathing mechanism only as a spectator—such fancies are in dreams; then he regained his identity almost as if by a leap forward into his body, and the straining automaton had a directing will as alert and fierce as that of its hideous antagonist. But what mortal can cope with a creature of his dream? The imagination creating the enemy is already vanquished; the combat's result is the combat's cause. Despite his struggles—despite his strength and activity, which seemed wasted in a void, he felt the cold fingers close upon his throat. Borne backward to the earth, he saw above him the dead and drawn face within a hand's breadth of his own, and then all was black. A sound as of the grumble of distant drums—a murmur of swarming voices, a sharp, far cry signing all to silence, and Halpin Frayser dreamed that he was dead.

IV

A warm, clear night had been followed by a morning of drenching fog. At about the middle of the afternoon of the preceding day a little whiff of light vapor—a mere thickening of the atmosphere, the ghost of a cloud—had been observed clinging to the western side of Mount St. Helena,* away up along the barren altitudes near the summit. It was so thin, so diaphanous, so like a fancy made visible, that one would have said: 'Look quickly! in a moment it will be gone.'

In a moment it was visibly larger and denser. While with one edge it clung to the mountain, with the other it reached further and further out into the air above the lower slopes. At the same time it extended itself to north and south, joining small patches of mist that appeared to come out of the mountain-side on exactly the same level with an intelligent design to be absorbed. And so it grew and grew until the summit was shut out of view from the valley, and over the valley itself was an ever-extending canopy, opaque and gray. At Calistoga,* which lies near the head of the valley and the foot of the mountain, there was a starless night and a sunless morning. And the fog, sinking into the valley, had reached southward, swallowing up ranch after ranch, until it had blotted out the town of St. Helena, nine miles away. The dust in the road was laid; trees were adrip with moisture; birds sat silent in their coverts; the morning light was wan and ghastly, with neither color nor fire.

Two men left the town of St. Helena at the first glimmer of dawn, and walked along the road northward up the valley toward Calistoga. They carried guns on their shoulders, yet no one having knowledge of such matters could have mistaken them for hunters of bird or beast. They were a deputy sheriff from Napa and a detective from San Francisco—Holker and Jaralson, respectively. Their business was man-hunting.

'How far is it?' inquired Holker, as they strode along, their feet stirring white the dust beneath the damp surface of the road.

'The White Church? Only a half mile further,' the other answered. 'By the way,' he added, 'it is neither white nor a church; it is an abandoned school-house, gray with age and neglect. Religious services were once held in it—when it was white, and there is a graveyard that would delight a poet. Can you guess why I sent for you, and told you to come heeled?'*

'Oh, I never have bothered you about things of that kind. I've always found you communicative when the time came. But if I may hazard a guess, you want me to help you arrest one of the corpses in the graveyard.'

'You remember Branscom,' said Jaralson, treating his companion's wit with the inattention that it deserved.

'The chap who cut his wife's throat? I ought; I wasted a week's work on him and had my expenses for my trouble. There is a reward of $500, but none of us ever got a sight of him. You don't mean to say—'

'Yes, I do. He has been under the noses of you fellows all the time. He comes by night to the old graveyard at the White Church.'

'The devil! That's where they buried his wife.'

'Well, you fellows might have had sense enough to suspect that he would return to her grave sometime.'

'The very last place that anyone would have expected him to return to.'

'But you had exhausted all the other places. Learning your failure at *them*, I laid for* him *there*.'

'And you found him?'

'Damn it! he found *me*. The rascal got the drop on* me—regularly held me up and made me travel. It's God's mercy that he didn't go through* me. O, he's a good one, and I fancy the half of that reward is enough for me if you're needy.'

Holker laughed good humoredly, and explained that his creditors were never more importunate.

'I wanted merely to show you the ground, and arrange a plan with you. I thought it as well for us to be heeled, even in daylight.'

'The man must be insane,' said the deputy sheriff. 'The reward is for his capture and *conviction*. If he's mad he won't be convicted.'

Mr. Holker was so profoundly affected by that possible failure of justice that he involuntarily stopped in the middle of the road, then resumed his walk with abated zeal.

'Well, he looks it,' assented Jaralson. 'I'm bound to admit that a more unshaven, unshorn, unkempt, and uneverything galoot* I never saw outside the ancient and honorable order of tramps. But I've gone in for him, and can't make up my mind to let go. There's glory in it for us, anyhow. Not another soul knows that he is this side of the Mountains of the Moon.'*

'All right,' Holker said; 'we will go, anyhow, and view the ground,' and he added, in the words of a once favorite inscription for tombstones: '"Where you must shortly lie"*—I mean, if old Branscom ever gets tired of you and your impertinent intrusion. By the way, I heard the other day that "Branscom" was not his real name.'

'What is?'

'I can't recall it. I had lost all interest in the wretch, and it did not fix itself in my memory. Yes, I remember—it is Pardee. The woman whose throat he had the bad taste to cut was a widow when he met her. She had come to California to look up some relatives—there are persons who will do that sometimes. But you know all that.'

'Naturally.'

'But not knowing the right name, by what happy inspiration did you find the right grave? The man who told me that the name was Pardee said it had been cut on the head-board.'

'I don't know the right grave.' Jaralson was apparently a trifle reluctant to admit his ignorance of so important a point of his plan. 'I have been watching about the place generally. A part of our work this morning will be to identify that grave. Here is the White Church.'

For a long distance the road had been bordered by fields on both sides, but now on the left there was a forest of oaks, madroños, and gigantic firs whose lower parts only could be seen, dim and ghostly in the fog. The undergrowth was, in places, thick, but nowhere impenetrable. For some moments Holker saw nothing of the building, but as they turned into the woods it revealed itself in faint gray outline through the fog, looking huge and far away. A few steps more, and it was within an arm's length, distinct, dark with moisture, and insignificant in size. It had the usual country school-house form—belonged to the packing-box order of architecture; had an underpinning of stones, a moss-grown roof, and blank window-spaces, whence both glass and sash had been long removed by Time and his ally, the small boy. It was ruined, but not a ruin—a typical Californian substitute for what are known to guide-bookers abroad as 'monuments of the past.' With scarcely a glance at this uninteresting structure, Jaralson moved on into the dripping undergrowth beyond.

'I will show you where he held me up,' he said. 'This is the graveyard.'

Here and there among the bushes were small inclosures containing graves—sometimes no more than one. They were recognized as graves by the rotting boards at head and foot, leaning at all angles, some prostrate; by the ruined picket-fences surrounding them; or, infrequently, by the mound itself, showing its gravel through the fallen leaves. In many instances nothing marked the spot where lay the vestiges of some poor mortal who, leaving 'a large circle of sorrowing friends,'* had been left by them in turn, except a depression in the earth, more lasting than that in the spirits of the mourners. The paths, if any paths had been, were long obliterated; trees of a considerable size had been permitted to grow up from the graves and thrust aside with root or branch the enclosing fences. Over all was that air of abandonment and decay which seems nowhere so fit and right* as in a village of the dead.

As the two men, Jaralson leading, pushed their way through a growth of young madroños, that enterprising man suddenly stopped and brought up his shotgun to the height of his breast, uttered a low note of warning, and stood motionless, his eyes fixed upon something ahead. As well as he could, obstructed by brush, his companion, though seeing nothing, imitated the posture and so stood, prepared for what might ensue. A moment later Jaralson strode forward, the other following.

Under the branches of an enormous madroño lay the dead body of a man. Standing silent above it they noted such particulars as first strike the attention—the face, the attitude, the clothing; whatever most promptly and plainly answers the unspoken questions of a sympathetic curiosity.

The body lay upon its back, the legs spread wide apart. One arm was thrust upward, the other outward; but the latter was bent acutely, and the hand was near the throat. Both hands were tightly clenched. The whole attitude was that of desperate but ineffectual resistance to—what?

Near by lay a shotgun and a game-bag, through the meshes of which was seen the plumage of shot birds. All about were evidences of a furious struggle: small sprouts of poison-oak were bent and denuded of leaf and bark, dead and rotting leaves had been pushed into heaps and ridges on both sides of the legs by the action of other feet than theirs, alongside the waist were unmistakable impressions of human knees. The nature of the struggle was made clear by a glance at the dead man's throat and face. While breast and hands were white, these were purple—almost black. The shoulders lay upon a low mound, and the head was turned back at an angle otherwise impossible, the expanded eyes staring blankly backward in a direction opposite to that of the feet. From the froth filling the open mouth the tongue protruded, black and swollen. The throat showed horrible contusions; not mere finger-marks, but bruises and lacerations wrought by two strong hands that must have buried themselves in the yielding flesh, maintaining their terrible grip until long after death. Breast, throat, face, were wet; the clothing was saturated; drops of water, condensed from the fog, studded the hair and mustache.

All this the two men observed without speaking; almost at a glance. Then Holker said:

'Poor devil! he had a rough deal.'

Jaralson was making a vigilant circumspection of the forest, his shotgun held in both hands and at full cock, his finger upon the trigger.

'The work of a maniac,' he said, without withdrawing his eyes from the enclosing wood. 'It was done by Branscom—Pardee.'

Something half-hidden by the disturbed leaves on the earth caught Holker's attention. It was a red leather pocket-book. He picked it up and opened it. It contained leaves of white paper for memoranda, and upon the first leaf was the name 'Halpin Frayser.' Written in red on several succeeding leaves—scrawled as if in haste and barely legible—were the following lines, which Holker read aloud, while his companion continued scanning the dim gray confines of their narrow world and hearing matter of suspicion* in the drip of water from every burdened branch:

'Enthralled by some mysterious spell, I stood,
In the lit gloom of an enchanted wood.
   The cypress there and myrtle twined their boughs,
Significant, in baleful brotherhood.

'The brooding willow whispered to the yew;
Beneath, the deadly night shade and the rue,
   With immortelles* self-woven into strange
Funereal shapes, and horrid nettles grew.

'No song of bird nor droning of the bees,
Nor light leaf lifted by the wholesome breeze:
   The air was stagnant all, and Silence was
A living thing that breathed among the trees.

'Conspiring spirits whispered in the gloom,
Half-heard, the stilly secrets of the tomb.
   With blood the trees were all adrip, the leaves
Shone in the witch-light with a ruddy bloom.

'I cried aloud!—the spell, unbroken still,
Rested upon my spirit and my will.
   Unsouled, unhearted, hopeless and forlorn,
I strove with monstrous presages of ill!

'At last the viewless—'*

Holker ceased reading; there was no more to read. The manuscript broke off in the middle of a line.

'That sounds like Bayne,' said Jaralson, who was something of a scholar in his way. He had abated his vigilance and stood looking down at the body.

'Who's Bayne?' Holker asked, rather incuriously.

'Myron Bayne, a chap who flourished in the early years of the nation—more than a century ago. Wrote mighty dismal stuff. I have his collected works, and if that poem is not among them it must have been omitted by mistake. It is—'

There came to them out of the fog—seemingly from a great distance—the sound of a laugh, a low, deliberate, soulless laugh, which had no more of joy than that of a hyena night-prowling in the desert; a laugh that rose by slow gradation, louder and louder, clearer, more distinct and terrible, until it seemed barely outside the narrow circle of their vision; a laugh so unnatural, so unhuman, so devilish, that it filled those hardy man-hunters with a sense of dread unspeakable! They did not move their weapons nor think of them; the menace of that horrible sound was not of the kind to be met with arms. As it had grown out of silence so now it died away; with a culminating shout which seemed almost in their ears, it drew itself away into the distance, until its failing notes, joyless and mechanical to the last, sank to silence at a measureless remove.*

The men looked at one another, consciously pale and visibly shuddering. 'It is cold,' they explained, both at once; and, 'let us leave here,' added Holker; 'we must have up the coroner from Napa.'

Jaralson said nothing, but made a movement in compliance. Passing the end of the slight elevation of earth upon which the dead man's head and shoulders lay, his foot struck some hard substance under the rotting forest leaves, and he took the trouble to kick it into view. It was a fallen headboard, and painted on it were the words, 'Catharine Larue.'

'Larue, Larue!' exclaimed Holker, with sudden animation. 'Why, that is the real name of Branscom—not Pardee. And—bless my soul! how it all comes to me—the murdered woman's name had been Frayser!'

'There is some rascally mystery here,' said Detective Jaralson. 'I hate anything of that kind.'

THE KISS OF
JVDAS

'X. L.' [JULIAN OSGOOD FIELD]

A KISS OF JUDAS

'Woman of outer darkness, fiend of death,
From what inhuman cave, what dire abyss,
Hast thou invisible that spell o'erheard?
What potent hand hath touched thy quickened corse,
What song dissolved thy cerements, who unclosed
Those faded eyes and filled them from the stars?'

LANDOR: *Gebir.**

CHAPTER I

TOWARDS the end of September, about eight years ago, the steamship *Albrecht*, under the command of the popular Captain Pellegrini, had on its voyage down the Danube, as far as Rustchuck,* the honour of counting among its passengers a gentleman to whom not inaptly might have been addressed the somewhat audacious remark made by Charles Buller* to a well-known peer, now deceased,* 'I often think how puzzled your Maker must be to account for your conduct.'* And, indeed, a more curious jumble of lovable and detestable qualities than went to the making-up of the personality labelled for formal purposes Lieutenant-Colonel Richard Ulick Verner Rowan, but familiarly known to Society as 'Hippy' Rowan, it would, we think, have been difficult to find. Selfish almost to cruelty, and yet capable of acts of generous self-sacrifice to which many a better man could not perhaps have risen; famous for his unnecessary harshness in the numerous wars wherein he had distinguished himself, and yet enjoying the well-merited reputation of being the best-natured man in London, Hippy Rowan, thanks to the calm and healthy spirit of philosophy within him, had in the course of his fifty odd years of mundane experiences, never allowed a touch of cynicism to chill his heart. It is not so easy or natural as many may imagine to be content with a great deal; but in the golden days when much had been his—at the meridian of his altogether pleasant life, in which even the afternoon shadows were in no wise indicative of the terrors of advancing night—Dick Rowan was possessed of the same serene spirit of content which distinguished him in the later and more troublous times when he found himself forced to look gout and debt in the face on an income barely double the wages he had formerly given to his *cordon bleu*.*

Although, when we present him for the first time to our readers, Colonel Rowan is past fifty, he has been for the last twenty odd years what he himself termed 'hopelessly and irretrievably ruined,' which meant that he could count on but little over a thousand pounds per annum for his maintenance. In former days he had been far better off and, indeed, for a very short time—a period of about twelve months—was the possessor of a very large sum of money, wealth suddenly inherited, which he had squandered in the most extravagant fashion.*

Disraeli used to say, 'When I meet a man whose name I cannot remember, I give myself two minutes: then, if it be a hopeless task, I always say, "And how is the old complaint?"' Now, if the great Tory leader could be imagined by any miracle forgetting the name of his highly-esteemed friend Hippy Rowan, and meeting him and asking him the above searching and comprehensive question, the reply doubtless would have been, 'I only got back last week,' or 'I'm going next month,' or something after that fashion; for certainly Colonel Rowan would have interpreted 'the old complaint' to signify his passionate love for Paris, the theatre of his splendid follies, the sepulchre of his fortune indeed, but the Mecca whither his faithful feet were ever eager to speed—the shrine at which his knees, even when gouty, were glad to kneel. The sole surviving representative of one of the most patrician families of Ireland, a man of remarkable personal beauty—his good looks, by the way, in his youth would have been best described by the slang adjective 'showy,'—for, ever a man of gigantic stature and herculean build, his bright auburn hair and beard had given him during the earlier part of his career a loud and flaming aspect which rendered him a hopelessly compromising Clavaroche for any Jacqueline* to keep clandestine appointments with—as he was reckless and daring to a degree but rarely attained even by his fellow-countrymen, to whom temerity is often ascribed as a national failing, Dick Rowan had certainly distinguished himself in his martial profession; and the same may be said of that portion of his life passed in the House of Commons, in which august assembly he had for many years helped to represent an Irish county; but to the twelve months of riotous living in Paris already spoken of, Hippy, beyond all doubt, chiefly owed his fame; and his laurels, both as warrior and as legislator, paled before the roses which crowned his winecup filled with Yquem of '37,* and the myrtles sacred to Venus of which he wove garlands for that goddess by Seine side. But his career as one of the acknowledged leaders of *la haute noce** in the capital of pleasure had been brief though brilliant. Persistently playing the 'rubicon' at four louis a point at the Petit Club, while at the same time constantly assuming the onerous responsibilities of an open bank at the Jockey,* possess, when unfailing bad luck attends such gallant endeavours to win the smiles of fickle fortune, at least, the advantage not common to all evils of providing in themselves their own antidote and cure; and so, at the end of twelve brief months devoted to such pastimes, and others no less costly though less avowable, the gallant Colonel had been forced to acknowledge his defeat, and retire with his never-failing grace from the French capital, exchanging indeed with regret *Dugléré* for the Speaker,* and leaving with a sigh the sparkle of the Grand Seize for the comparative respectability of St. Stephen's.*

All this had taken place twenty years and more before the opening of our story, and in the course of this score of years Hippy, by reason of certain prolonged and dangerous rambles undertaken by him for purposes of sport and amusement in all kinds of outlandish countries, had acquired among his friends a not inconsiderable reputation as a traveller; for though, while his money lasted, he had been quite content to limit his wanderings to explorations in the *pays du tendre*,* yet, when forced by unmerciful disaster to fold his pleasure tent and steal away, he had sought to solace his soul for the loss of fortune by 'going to and fro in the earth,'* after the fashion of the prince in whose service indeed that very fortune had been spent—one year suffering himself to be entertained by the Emir of Bokhara,* and in the course of the next twelve months accepting the hospitality of the Imaum of Muscat;* becoming acquainted in his rambles, gun and notebook in hand, with all sorts and conditions of men, from sovereign despots, nay, demi-gods, to slaves ranking far below quadrupeds. Nor did he limit his pastimes to sport pure and simple—for this curious being would leave Pall Mall one day to see if Schliemann* had forgotten anything in the Trojan plain, or endeavour to catch Beke* tripping in Sinai the next; in all these expeditions being, of course, greatly aided by his rare and precious gift of easily and accurately acquiring all languages and dialects, the choice Arabic with which it amused him to surprise the Shereef of Wazan* being no less fluent than the Polish in which he flirted with pretty patriots in the land of Kosciuszco.*

But the expedition on which he was bent when we introduce him to our readers was one calling for the lead of neither pencil nor pellet, but a journey of purely social purport. The all too brief days of Hippy's magnificence in Paris had been, so far as they went, concurrent with the reign of splendid folly which has made the name of Djavil Pacha famous in the annals of apolausticism;* and some of the most happy hours of Rowan's Parisian existence having been passed in the celebrated apartment on the corner of the Rue Taitbout and the Boulevard des Italiens,* inhabited by the Turkish millionaire, between his Excellency and the gallant Colonel a warm feeling of friendship had sprung up—not the mere passing liking, born with the *bisque* and ceasing with the coffee,* but a genuine sympathy which lasted when the banquet was all over and the lights put out, which expressed itself in various graceful and cordial shapes after both had retired from Paris, and which, just before our story opens, had taken the form of an invitation from Djavil to his friend to spend a few days with him at his palace on the Bosphorus,* a summons which Dick Rowan was now steaming down the Danube to obey.

He had chosen this particularly monotonous and uncomfortable way of reaching his friend for reasons which do not concern us; but the thought of the unpleasant railway journey from Rustchuck to Varna which awaited him, and then the encounter with the Black Sea, did not tend to assuage the twinges of gout and irritability which assailed him by fits and starts as, during the two dreary days he watched the shores on either side glide slowly by—seeing on the right Hungary at length give place to Servia,* and then Servia to Turkey, while perpetual Wallachia, sad and desolate, stretched unceasingly and for ever to the left—walking up and down the deck leaning on the arm of his trusty valet, or rather, Ancient* or Lieutenant, Adams by name, a man almost as well known and fully as well informed as his master, a Cockney who, without any control over the aspirates in his native English, spoke eight other different languages, including Arabic, accurately and fluently, and whose knowledge of Oriental countries dated indeed from the days when he had been page-boy to the great Eltchi* in Constantinople. There were but few passengers on board—an abnormally small number, in fact—and to this circumstance, doubtless, was it due that Rowan who, as a rule, paid but little attention to his fellow-travellers, happened to remark a mysterious-looking individual—a man, and apparently not an old one—who sat quite apart from the others and by himself, muffled up to the eyes in a very voluminous, albeit rather dirty, white silk handkerchief, and who was evidently an invalid, judging from the listless way in which he sat, the extreme pallor of the only part of his face which could be seen, and above all, the fever-fed light which glared from between sore and lashless eyelids. He was dressed entirely in black, and although his clothes were somewhat shabby, they betokened carelessness on the part of their wearer rather than poverty; and Adams had noticed and called his master's attention to the fact that on one finger of the man's thin, yellow, dirty hand, which every now and then he would lift to rearrange still higher up about his face the silken muffler, sparkled a diamond, which the omniscient valet recognized to be a stone of value.

'What an extremely disagreeable-looking man, Adams!' pettishly murmured the Colonel in English, as he and his servant in their perambulations up and down the deck for the twentieth time on the first morning of the journey passed by where the mysterious stranger sat. 'And how he stares at us! He has the eyes of a lunatic, and there is evidently something horrible the matter with his face. Perhaps he's a leper. Ask the Captain about him.'

But the ever-amiable Captain Pellegrini had not much information to impart, save indeed that the man was certainly neither a madman nor a leper, nor indeed, so far as he knew, an invalid. He was a Moldavian, Isaac Lebedenko by name, a young man, a medical student or doctor, the Captain thought; but, at all events, a man in very well-to-do circumstances, for he always spent his money freely.

'I have known him off and on for two years, please your Excellency,' said the skipper. 'Though I must confess I have never seen his face properly, for he's always muffled up in that way. He takes his meals by himself, and of course pays extra for doing so, and in fact he always, so far as I know, keeps entirely to himself and never speaks to any one. But the steward's boy, who has waited on him and seen his face, says there is nothing the matter with him except indeed that he's the ugliest man he ever saw.'

'Perhaps he's consumptive,' suggested the Colonel. But the all-wise Adams shook his head. That was quite inadmissible. He had seen the man walk, and had noticed his legs. Phthisis* could not deceive him, he could recognize its presence at a glance. This man was as strong on his legs as a panther; no consumption there.

'Well,' said the Colonel impatiently, 'there's evidently something wrong with him, no matter what, and I'm glad I'm not condemned to remain long in his society; for he certainly has the most unpleasant look in his eyes that I've seen since we left the lepers.' And then he turned the current of the conversation, and the subject dropped.

That night very late, when the Colonel was sitting quite alone on deck, smoking a cigarette, and thinking over his approaching visit to Djavil, wondering what persons his old friend would have invited to his palace to meet him, and a thousand souvenirs of the long-past pleasant Paris days thronging to his mind as he dreamily glanced up at the moon which smiled over slowly-receding Servia, a voice close by his ear, a slow, huskily sibilant high-pitched whisper, broke the stillness, saying in lisping French,—

'May I ask, Monsieur, by what right you dare to question persons about me?' and, turning, he saw standing by his shoulder the horrible man in shabby black, his eyes glaring with exceptional ferocity from between the red bare lids, and the diamond-decorated claw-like hand grasping convulsively the soiled white muffler, presumably to prevent the vehemence of his speech from causing it to slip down.

Hippy rose to his feet at once, and, as he did so, his face passed close to the half-shrouded countenance of the man who had addressed him, and the familiar sickening smell of animal musk full of repulsive significance to the experienced traveller assailed his nostrils.

'What do you mean?' he exclaimed, shrinking back, his disgust quite overpowering for the moment every other sentiment. 'Stand back! Don't come near me!'

The man said nothing, stood quite still, but Rowan saw plainly in the moonlight the red-encircled eyes gleam with renewed ferocity, the yellow, claw-like hand wearing the diamond ring and grasping the dirty muffler agitated by a convulsive spasm, and heard beneath the silken covering the husky breathing caught as in a sob. Hippy recovered himself at once. 'Forgive me, Monsieur,' he said, coldly. 'You startled me. Might I beg you to repeat your question?'

The man said nothing. It was evident that he had perceived the disgust he had inspired, and that his anger, his indignation, mastered him, and that he dared not trust himself to speak.

'You asked me, I think,' continued the Colonel in a more gentle tone—for his conscience smote him as he reflected that he might perhaps involuntarily have caused pain to one who, notwithstanding his unpleasant aspect and arrogant, not to say hostile, attitude, was doubtless merely an invalid and a sufferer—'You asked me, I think, Monsieur, by what right I made inquiries concerning you? Pray pardon me for having done so. I have, indeed, no excuse to offer, but I am really sorry if I have offended you. I merely asked the Captain—'

But the man interrupted him, his voice, which was tremulous with passion, coming as a husky, wheezy hiss, which rendered the strong lisp with which he pronounced the French the more noticeable and grotesque.

'You asked him—you dared ask him, if I were not a leper. He told Hoffmann, the steward's boy, who told me. You can't deny it! Dog of an Englishman!'

Here, gasping for want of breath, and apparently quite overpowered by his anger, the man took a step towards Rowan. This outburst of vituperation came as a great relief to the Colonel. Like most persons of refined feeling, he could stand any wounds better than those inflicted by self-reproach, and the suspicion that perhaps by careless rudeness he had caused pain to one worthy only of pity had been as gall to him. The man's violent hostility and bad language entirely altered and brightened the aspect of affairs.

'I am sorry,' said Hippy, with ironical politeness, 'that my nationality should not meet with the honour of your approval. It is not, hélas! the proud privilege of all to be able to boast that they are natives of Moldavia, you know! *Pour le reste*, all I can do is to repeat my apology for—' But the man interrupted him again.

'Apology!' he echoed, if indeed any word indicative of resonance can be applied to the hoarse, damp, lisping whisper in which he spoke—'Apology! Ah, yes! You English curs are all cowards, and only think of apologies. You dare not fight, canaille,* but you shall! I'll force you to!' And again he took a step forward, but this time in so menacing a fashion that the Colonel, half amused and half disgusted, thought it prudent to step back.

'Take care!' he said, half raising his stick as if to push the man back as an unclean thing: 'keep your distance,'—and then, speaking quickly, for he feared an assault from the infuriated Moldavian, and was desirous of avoiding such an absurd complication, he continued,

'If you can prove to me that I ought to meet you, I shall be happy to do so. You're right, of course, in thinking duels are no longer the fashion in England. But I'm an exception to the rule. I've fought two already, and shall be happy to add to the number by meeting you if it can be arranged. But that's hardly a matter you and I can properly discuss between ourselves, is it? Captain Pellegrini knows me. I'll leave my address with him. I have friends in Turkey, and shall be staying in the neighbourhood of Constantinople for a fortnight, so if you care to send me your seconds,* I will appoint gentlemen to receive them. Allow me to wish you good-night!' and Rowan raised his hat with much formal politeness, and stepped aside as if to depart; but the man sprang forward like a cat and stood in his way.

'Coward!' he exclaimed, extending both arms as if to bar Rowan's passage—'Cur! like all your countrymen! You think to run away from me, but you shall not! You shall go on your knees and beg my pardon, you accursed Englishman—you dog—you—'

But just as the enraged Moldavian reached this point in his fury an awful thing happened. The yellow, claw-like hand having been withdrawn from clutching at the dirty muffler, the vehemence of the man's speech began gradually to disarrange this covering, causing it little by little to sink lower and lower and thus to disclose by degrees to Rowan a sight so strange, so awful, that, impelled by a morbid curiosity, he involuntarily bent his head forward as his horror-stricken eyes eagerly noted every step in the infernal progress of this revelation. And thus, gazing at the slowly slipping silk, he saw first, beardless, hollow cheeks, twitching with emotion, but of a most hideous pallor, of indeed that awful hue inseparably associated with the idea of post-mortem changes, then, in the middle of this livid leanness, lighted only by those fever-fed, red-lidded eyes, the beginning—the broad base springing from the very cheekbones as it were—of a repulsive prominence which apparently went narrowing on to some termination which as yet the scarf hid, but which the horrified Colonel felt every second surer and yet more sure could not resemble the nasal organ of a man, but rather the—ah, yes! the silk fell, and in the moonlight Rowan saw the end he had foreseen, the pointed nose as of a large ferret, and beneath it, far in under it, nervously working, the humid, viscous horror of a small mouth almost round, but lipless, from which came in hurried, husky sibilance the lisping words of hate and menace.

This awful revelation, although partly expected, was so inexpressibly horrible when it came, that, doubtless, the expression of disgust in Rowan's face deepened so suddenly in acuteness and intensity as to arrest the attention of the monster who inspired it, infuriated though he was; for he paused in the lisping tumult of his violence, and, as he paused, became suddenly aware that the muffler had slipped down. Then, rightly interpreting the horror he saw written in the Colonel's countenance, and goaded to a fresh fit of fury, too despairing and violent even for words, he, with an inarticulate moan or whimper, rushed blindly forward with extended arms to attack his enemy. But the Colonel, who had foreseen this onslaught, stepped quickly to one side, and, as he did so, quite overpowered by disgust, he could not resist the temptation of giving the hostile monster a violent push with his heavy walking-stick—a thrust of far greater force than he had indeed intended, for it caused the man to totter and fall forward, just as two or three sailors, who from a distance had witnessed the last incidents of the dispute, ran up and stood between the adversaries.

'That man,' exclaimed the Colonel in German, pointing with his stick to where the Moldavian lay sprawling on his knees, hastily readjusting the muffler around his hideous face, 'tried to assault me, and I defended myself. Look after him, but beware of him. He is a wild beast, not a man!' The men looked at the Colonel, whom they knew to be some important grandee held in great honour by their Captain, and then at the shabby mass of black clothes sprawling on the deck, and then at each other, and marvelled greatly, open-mouthed, not knowing what to say or think or do.

'I shall see the Captain about this to-morrow morning,' continued Rowan. 'But in the meantime, as I say, look after this—this—man, but beware of him!' and so speaking, he turned and strode away in the direction of his cabin.

Just before reaching the stairway he turned and looked back. There in the moonlight stood the man in black, gazing after him, the awful face hidden once more in the dirty muffler which was now stained on one side with the blood which came trickling down from a wound on the brow. As he saw the Colonel turn, the man raised his clenched fist and shook it very slowly, solemnly, and deliberately—the gesture of a warning and of a curse—and the sailors, fearing further violence, closed around him. Then the Colonel turned and went his way to bed. The following morning Rowan of course made his faithful

Adams (who, by the way, was never astonished at anything, having acquired through long residence in the East the stolidity of the Oriental) fully acquainted with the strange events of the preceding night, but charged him to say nothing to anybody.

'I have thought the matter over,' said the Colonel, 'and have decided merely to tell the Captain that I had a few words with the man, and in a heated moment struck him, and then give Pellegrini his Excellency's address where we shall be for the next fortnight, so that if this man wants to communicate with me in any way, he can. Of course any question of a duel with such a brute is absurd,* but I hope he won't attempt to assault me again to-day.'

'I'll keep a sharp look-out he doesn't, sir,' said Adams.

But such precautions were unnecessary. Nothing more was seen of the Moldavian, who presumably was confined to his cabin by his wound, and the following morning at early dawn the Colonel and his servant left the steamer at Rustchuck and took the train to Varna and the Black Sea, *en route* for the splendours of the Bosphorus.

CHAPTER II

FROM one end to the other of the Bosphorus, both on the coast of Europe and on the coast of Asia, are numerous little towns and villages—the *faubourgs*,* as it were, of Constantinople—which in the *belle saison* are inhabited by members of the Turkish aristocracy and strangers of distinction; and in one of these, on the European side, within less than an hour's journey by steamboat from the Stamboul bridge, was situated the palace of Hippy Rowan's friend—the whilom plunger* of the Petit and Jockey Clubs—the famous Djavil Pacha.

Of the building we need say but little. It was white—partly marble and partly wood painted to resemble marble—low, rambling, and commodious, but of no special style of architecture, and certainly not Turkish, or even Oriental, but rather Italian in its outward aspect. The principal beauty and advantage of the residence was the extensive garden which surrounded it, and which, rising in banks of flowers and verdure at the back, in front sloped down to a splendid marble terrace, washed by the waters of the Bosphorus, which led to the Pacha's private landing-place and quay, whereby was moored the private steam-launch of his Excellency.

Djavil was a bachelor, kept no harem, and lived in European style, his head cook and the chief assistants of that artist having been imported direct from Bignon's,* while the palace was throughout furnished by a *tapissier** from Paris; the only concession to Turkish prejudices which a careful observer might have remarked being the absence of statuary and paintings—the Koran, as we know, forbidding the reproduction in painting of animate objects,* and Djavil having, before leaving the French capital, disposed of his splendid canvases and marbles in the Rue Drouot*—whether induced to make this sacrifice by religious motives or for more sordid reasons, who shall say?

In Constantinople—which, by the way, is the most backbiting, tittle-tattling, scandalmongering little village in the world—the ex-Ambassador and old Parisian *viveur* was greatly blamed for living in so thoroughly European a fashion, keeping open house, constantly entertaining the most distinguished members, male and female, of the European colony.* The clever and ambitious Djavil, however, cared nothing for such disapproval, so long as he retained the favour of the Sultan and the Grand Vizier (the gambler and *roué* of the Rue Royale and Rue Scribe* having now developed into a hard-working Under-Secretary of State for Foreign Affairs). He quite determined to live his private life as he pleased since he devoted his public life to the service of his country, and when the day's work was over and he embarked on his steam-launch on his return journey to his palace, he left behind him the Turkish statesman and became again purely and simply the cosmopolitan man of pleasure.

Of other permanent guests beside himself at the palace, Hippy found but three—his old friend, a well-known gambler and breaker and taker of banks, Lord Melrose; an amusing French newspaper man, Emile Bertonneux by name, of the Paris *Œil de Bœuf**—and last, but not least, the universally popular Tony Jeratczesco, whom Hippy had last seen in the Birdcage at Newmarket* some months before, and whose sudden and mysterious disappearance from St. James's Street, which loved him so well, to go to take possession of a property just left him in some outlandish country by a recently-deceased relation, was still the talk of London. Not that London had any reason to be astonished at anything, whether good or evil, that might befall the popular sportsman; for Tony Jeratczesco was altogether a mystery, and nobody knew anything whatever about the man familiarly nicknamed 'Cheery and Cheeky,'* whether he was rich or poor, married or single—patrician by birth or plebeian, nor indeed of what nationality he might boast himself to be, whether Austrian, Hungarian, Bohemian, Pole, Moldavian, Russian, Wallachian, Servian, Bulgarian or Montenegrin—Jew, Christian, Mohammedan, Buddhist—he was good-looking, amiable, refined, and well-dressed, and, moreover, was endowed to a very marked degree with the rare and precious gift of being able to both win and lose money admirably well; in no wise allowing either the smiles or frowns of Fortune to disturb the serene reign of the perfect good taste which presided over all his affairs. When this had been said, and the facts chronicled that he was fond of cards and racing, and always seemed to have plenty of money to justify his interest in both these expensive forms of speculation, and that he enjoyed a close personal friendship with some of the most exalted personages of the realm—the authentic data wherewith to compose a biographical sketch of Count Jeratczesco would be perhaps exhausted, although of course scandal both benevolent and malignant was constantly taking up the wondrous tale of the great success of this mysterious stranger and adventurer in the best of our rude island society—and enriching it with rare and marvellous broideries of fancy.

For once, however, rumour, in dealing with the private affairs of 'Cheery and Cheeky,' would appear to have been correct. A relative had died—an uncle—and left Tony a mysterious castle and many acres in Moldavia, not far from the little town of Sereth, and the Count had come on to stay with Djavil solely because he knew Hippy Rowan, Lord Melrose, and others *ejusdem farinæ*,* would be gathered together under the Pacha's hospitable roof-tree, and he was desirous of making up a house-warming party of friends to accompany him to his new possessions, and enjoy some of the shooting for which the place was famous. This plan met with general approval, and Jeratczesco found no difficulty in forming a pleasant company to return with him to Moldavia; for though Dick Rowan, Lord Melrose, the Count, and the French *chroniqueur* were the only permanent residents beneath the Pacha's roof during this fortnight, the four remaining guest-chambers in the palace were never empty, and there was a constant ebb and flow of all kinds of persons, all more or less invited by the Pacha: people from our Embassy, and people from every other Embassy, people of every rank and position: from a very Broad Church* English divine who was sent on, out of sheer mischief, by our Ambassador, Lord Malling, and who came accompanied by his florid, comely, and substantial spouse, both inclined to be slightly querulous about the Holy Places until they had tasted the water-drinking Djavil's incomparable Yquem;* to a very beautiful and wayward Italian diva, who came accompanied by two of her adorers, likewise blest with the gift of song, and who made every one weep (including the *chef* from Bignon's, who listened outside) when she and her friends after dinner (all three slightly intoxicated) interpreted, as only angels fired with a few goblets of St. Marceaux* can, Verdi's divine Requiem.* So pleasantly did the time pass that it was with regret Colonel Rowan saw the termination of his visit drawing nigh, and heard one morning Jeratczesco, impatient to assume his unwonted *rôle* of host, solemnly announce that in four days' time he should depart to his home in the Karpaks,* taking with him the companions he had selected. Then, to celebrate the approaching departure of the popular Hippy Rowan, Djavil gave a sylvan picnic, which, for many months after, was the subject of much gossip on both sides of the Bosphorus, and from the Black Sea to the Sea of Marmora—an entertainment destined, alas! to be fraught with fatal consequences to the gentleman in whose honour it was given. The rendezvous was for ten o'clock in the morning, at the sweet waters of Asia*—where an insignificant little streamlet loses itself in the Bosphorus; and the guests, about twenty in number, arrived at the place of meeting with surprising punctuality,—some coming with Djavil in his steam-launch, and some from Constantinople.

But for our limited space we would introduce each one of these somewhat notable individualities singly to our readers. Leopold Maryx, the dissipated, irregular and eccentric savant, the renowned specialist for nervous diseases, who had been summoned from Vienna on purpose to see the Sultan; Lord Malling, our delightful but impossible Ambassador;* Lord, and especially Lady, Brentford, the champion political bore in petticoats, the victim to high principles, who had bullied her half-witted husband into believing he had a conscience on the occasion of the Reform Bill of 1867,* and who, since then, had been dedicating her life to impotent though vigorous denunciations of what she termed the 'treachery' of the Tory County Members, and the 'infamy' of the County Caucus; Mr. Leonard P. Beacon, the New York millionaire and sportsman, a rough, boasting, but withal good-hearted giant, who, although vulgar beyond even the power of dynamite to purify, was vastly amusing, owing to the fact of his having only begun his boisterous youth at the age of forty-five;* Frank Silveyra, the famous Hebrew financier and prince of good fellows from Vienna, and his friend, the no-less-delightful young Jew millionaire and artist, Raphael Sciama; the smart and enterprising little Alec Torquati, who had won our Derby at far distant Epsom* the previous year with 'Kyber'; and, finally, three very beautiful and witty, and altogether attractive, ladies of high degree from Paris, who, accompanied by their husbands, had come all the way from the Seine to the Bosphorus on purpose to be admired, and three very magnificent young Cavaliers of the Guard who had come all the way from the Neva* to the Bosphorus on purpose to admire them and to manifest their admiration.

Ten carriages awaited Djavil's guests on the Asian coast, and into nine of these the party clambered; the tenth and last being reserved for a valet-de-chambre provided with all that could be required for the dispensing of light refreshments *en route*. And thus, with servants of the Pacha mounted on faultless little Arab horses racing up and down on either side of the carriages, bringing every now and then from the hindmost vehicle fruit and sandwiches, and bottles of champagne and Bordeaux wherewith the weary travellers might be refreshed, this gay and brilliant party dashed into the interior of Asia at full gallop. It had been arranged that the *déjeuner champétre** should take place in the Forest of Alem-Dagh;* and when, after a drive at steeplechase speed of three hours' duration, this spot was reached, it was indeed made manifest that Djavil had neglected nothing to make this fantastic breakfast a success. Here, to this wild, deserted, picturesque spot in the heart of a forest in Asia, a romantic nook apparently miles away from any trace of European civilization, this very *grand seigneur* had sent the evening before—accompanied by an army of *marmitons**—his *chef*, whose education had been perfected in the famous kitchen on the corner of the Chaussée d'Antin and the Boulevard des Italiens;* and with this great artist and his assistants had come vast and numerous vans drawn by bullocks, and containing all the requisites for cooking, and the food, and wine, and silver, and decorations, and furniture,—in fact, all that could be imagined by a wealthy and experienced voluptuary and man of the world to be necessary to make this *déjeuner sur l'herbe** for twenty persons an entertainment worthy of both host and guests.

The viands provided by Djavil (who, being a Turk, possessed that stubborn and rough Oriental palate which apparently can never be trained to a proper appreciation of the most precious and delicate secrets and traditions of *la grande cuisine*) were of a very substantial character; but the long journey had aroused appetites wholly beyond the power of sandwiches and goblets of St. Marceaux to satisfy, and the Pacha's guests eagerly sought consolation in the introductory *œufs à la Béchamel*, as a hidden orchestra of the best musicians to be found in Constantinople ravished the Asian air with heaven-inspired passages telling of the jealousy of Amneris and of the ill-fated love of Radamès and Aïda.*

'This is the most perfect still champagne I ever drank! Where did you get it, Djavil?' And so speaking, Mr. Leonard P. Beacon put down his glass and felt in his pocket for the note-book wherein he was accustomed to inscribe such precious addresses.

Life at best is short, but he, Mr. Leonard P. Beacon, had, to speak Hibernicé,* only begun when already half through it; and as he always wanted the best of everything and had no time to lose in personal quests after supreme excellence, he was always glad to take advantage of short cuts through the experience of friends. But the good-natured and adipose Pacha shook his head and smiled.

'No, no, *mon cher*. 'Tis a secret. Were I to tell you, you'd buy it all up and take it back with you to America. But, if you like it, I daresay I can spare you a few dozen. Ask Hassan yourself.'

Here a very high-pitched 'Oh! how terrible!' from Lady Brentford disturbed the wit-winged chatter of the three lovely Seine-side dames with their three adoring flowers of Slav chivalry; disturbed the husbands of these dames, who were engaged in an animated discussion among themselves as to the merits of cooking in oil; disturbed the Dowager Duchess, who, while listening to Raphael Sciama's enthusiastic account of the priceless Giulio Clovio* he had unearthed a fortnight before in Venice, had been endeavouring, and not without success, to rekindle by means of a visual current of sympathy with the youthful Alec Torquati the flame of passion in those orbs which had first flashed with that all-devouring fire early in the fifties: disturbed Tony Jeratczesco, who was explaining some Newmarket matters to Baron Silveyra while Lord Brentford and our Ambassador listened; and disturbed, in fact, the original cause of this disturbing cry, the loud-voiced Leopold Maryx, whose remarks to Hippy Rowan had elicited this startling exclamation from Lady Brentford, who sat next to him and had overheard them.

'Dr. Maryx is saying such awful things,' said her ladyship, shaking her head. 'He says he believes in people being possessed of devils.' Then, even as she spoke, her mind reverted to the terrible events of 1867,* those famous 'Resolutions' and the way the Borough members had been treated, and she felt that the great Professor might not perhaps after all be mistaken.

'Ah, no! you misunderstood me, Lady Brentford!' exclaimed Maryx, laughing. 'What I said was, I saw no reason why, if people were ever possessed of evil spirits, as we are told they used to be, we should believe such things to be impossible now. Is the world any better now than it was on the day when the swine ran down that steep place and were choked in the lake?* I didn't say that I believed in such things, for I don't; but, certainly, if I believed they ever existed, I should think they were as likely to exist now as ever.'

'Maryx was telling me about the Children of Judas,'* remarked Hippy Rowan, by way of explanation.

'The Children of Judas!' echoed Emile Bertonneux, the Parisian newspaper man, scenting a possible *article à sensation*—for it is, we suppose, hardly necessary to remind our readers that in so cosmopolitan a gathering the conversation was carried on in French—'Who are they? I had no idea that Judas was a *père de famille*.'

'It's a Moldavian legend,' replied the great specialist. 'They say that Children of Judas, lineal descendants of the arch traitor, are prowling about the world seeking to do harm, and that they kill you with a kiss.'

'Oh! how delightful!' murmured the Dowager Duchess, glancing at Alec Torquati, as if inviting, and indeed expecting, just such homicidal osculatory* tribute from* the lips of the young Derby winner.

'But how do they get at you to kiss you?' gasped Mr. Leonard P. Beacon, his thirst for information leading him to ignore the fact that his mouth was full of *loup sauce homard*.*

'The legend is,' said Maryx, 'that in the first instance they are here in every kind of shape—men and women, young and old, but generally of extraordinary and surpassing ugliness, but *are* here merely to fill their hearts with envy, venom, and hatred, and to mark their prey. In order to really do harm, they have to sacrifice themselves to their hatred, go back to the infernal regions whence they came—but go back by the gate of suicide—report to the Chief of the Three Princes of Evil, get their diabolical commission from him, and then return to this world and do the deed. They can come back in any form they think the best adapted to attain their object, or rather satisfy their hate: sometimes they come as a mad dog who bites you and gives you hydrophobia*—that's one form of the kiss of Judas; sometimes as the breath of pestilence, cholera, or what not—that's another form of the kiss of Judas; sometimes in an attractive shape, and then the kiss is really as one of affection, though as fatal in its effect as the mad dog's bite or the pestilence. When it takes the form of a kiss of affection, however, there is always a mark on the poisoned body of the victim—the wound of the kiss. Last summer, when I was at Sinaia* in attendance on the Queen, I saw the body of a peasant girl whose lover had given her the kiss of Judas, and there certainly was on her neck a mark like this:'* and Maryx took up his fork and scratched on the tablecloth three **X**'s,—thus, **X X X**. 'Can you guess what that's supposed to signify?' inquired the great physician.

'It looks like a hurdle,' remarked Torquati.

'Thirty,' exclaimed Lady Brentford.

'Of course,' replied Maryx, 'thirty—the thirty pieces of silver, of course—the mark of the price of blood.'

'*Vous êtes impayable, mon cher*!'* exclaimed Djavil, grinning. 'Whenever you find it no longer pays you to kill your patients you can always make money at the *foires*.* Set Hippy Rowan to beat the drum at the door and you sit inside the van telling your wonderful *blagues*,* and you'll make a fortune in no time.'

'I hope you don't tell those horrible tales to the Sultan, Maryx,' said Lord Malling, laughing. 'You cure nervous diseases by frightening people to death, I think.'

But the great Professor paid no attention to these flippant remarks; he was, indeed, notwithstanding his marvellous intelligence and extraordinary science and experience and skill, at heart a very charlatan and mountebank in his love of a gaping crowd; and the interest he saw depicted on the faces of his listeners delighted him.

'Did you say that in the first instance these Children of Judas are supposed to be very ugly?' inquired Colonel Rowan, his thoughts reverting to the awful face of that man Isaac Lebedenko who had assaulted him on the boat. The incident had almost wholly passed away from his memory until then, though he had noted it down in his carefully-kept diary; and he had, by the way, long ago told himself that he must have been mistaken in what he thought that horrible muffler had disclosed to him; that such things could not be, and that he must have been deceived either by some trick of shadow, or by some prank played on him by gout astride of his imagination.

'Yes,' replied Maryx, 'so runs the legend. This physical ugliness betokens, of course, the malignant spirit within. At that stage they may be recognized and avoided, or better still, slain; for they only really become dangerous when their hatred has reached such a pitch that they are prompted to seek a voluntary death and re-incarnation in order to completely satisfy their malignancy; for it is by the gate of suicide alone that they can approach the Arch-Fiend to be fully commissioned and equipped to return to earth on their errand of destruction. So if they are killed in their first stage of development, and not allowed to commit suicide, they are extinguished. When they return fully armed with power from Hell, it is too late; they cannot be recognized, and are fatal; for they have at their command all the weapons and artillery of Satan, from the smile of a pretty woman to the breath of pestilence. This voluntary self-sacrifice of hate in order to more fully satisfy itself by a regeneration, this suicide on the *reculer pour mieux sauter** principle, is of course nothing but a parody of the Divine Sacrifice of Love on which the Christian religion is based.'

'I'm both sorry and astonished, my dear Leopold,' said Baron Silveyra, smiling, 'to see that your knowledge of diabolical matters is so faulty. How can you speak of three princes of evil? You must know there are seventy-two!'

'Ah! you believe in the old system,' rejoined Maryx, laughing, and pouring himself out a tumblerful of Mouton Rothschild:* 'six multiplied by twelve, and then the seven million four hundred and five thousand nine hundred and twenty-six demons* of inferior rank. But, *mon cher*, that's altogether out of fashion now; that brings you to six multiplied by one million two hundred and thirty-four thousand three hundred and twenty-one, or the old mysterious "tetrade" of Pythagoras and Plato counting both ways.[1]* We've altogether changed that down in Hades now.' And then the great savant, who delighted

[1] Perhaps the meaning of the Professor will be more apparent if we put the numbers in figures. He speaks of 72 Princes of Darkness (6 multiplied by 12) and 7,405,926 demons of an inferior rank. This last number, so strange apparently, is still the product of 6 multiplied by 1,234,321; and, as our readers can see, 1,234,321 presents to us both from right to left and from left to right the four numbers constituting the mysterious 'tetrade' of Pythagoras and of Plato.

above all things in gravely clothing nonsense in a garb of erudition, launched forth into a fantastic and witty description of the internal economy of the Kingdom of Satan, a satire in which he not only displayed an extraordinary amount of mystical knowledge, but which he enlivened by sly and apposite allusions to the Governments represented by Djavil and Lord Malling respectively; and these gentlemen replying to this banter in the same spirit, and appealing to the other guests, the conversation soon became general.

When the repast was at length over, every one began strolling about the woods, and Hippy Rowan, lighting a cigar, started for a ramble with his old friend Lord Malling. But they had not gone far when their host sent a servant after them to request his lordship to return and speak with him; and so, the Ambassador turning back, Hippy continued his saunter by himself, penetrating by degrees into a somewhat remote and secluded part of the forest, the voices and laughter of the other guests becoming gradually fainter and fainter as he strolled on.

Suddenly, from behind a tree, a man sprang out upon him, and a knife gleamed in the sunlight, swiftly descending upon his heart. Hippy, quick as lightning, leapt to one side, striking up as he did so with his heavy walking-stick at the would-be assassin's arm, and with such force that he sent the knife flying out of the man's hand into the air; and then turning, he dealt the villain a blow on the side of the head which brought him to the ground as one dead. It was the Moldavian, Isaac Lebedenko. Hippy had recognized the eyes gleaming over the dirty-white muffler the moment the man sprang out upon him; and now, as he lay on the ground insensible, there could, of course, be no shadow of doubt about his identity, although he had so fallen, on one side, that the wrapper had not been disarranged from his face. We have said that, although enjoying the well-merited reputation of being the best-natured man in London, Dick Rowan had laid himself open to the reproach of having been most unduly harsh and severe in the numerous wars in which he had been engaged; and this harshness, not to say cruelty, presumably ever latent in his nature, but which seemed only to be called to the surface under certain special conditions closely connected with peril and the excitement engendered thereby, now made itself apparent. The Moldavian had fallen on his side, and the shock of his fall had been so violent that, while one hand lay palm upwards and half open on the trunk of a large fallen tree, the other hand, palm downwards, had been thrown upon its fellow. It was rather a peculiar position for the shock resulting from a fall to have thrown the hands into, and of course indicated that the blow had been so severe that the man had not been able to make any attempt to break his fall, but had sunk to the ground like a doll. Such, at least, was the way Rowan explained the matter as he stood over his prostrate enemy, wondering in his mind how he could possibly contrive to secure the violent would-be assassin until such time as he should be able to obtain assistance and have him handed over to the authorities for punishment; and just as he noticed the position of his hands his eyes caught the gleaming of the knife, which had fallen in the grass a little farther off. Hippy went to where it lay, and picked it up. It was a murderous-looking weapon indeed: broad, double-edged, and very sharp, though rather thick and not long; and fitted with a big round handle of lead, destined, of course, to lend terrible momentum to any blow struck by it. Rowan looked at the knife, and then at the hands of the Moldavian, lying in so diabolically tempting a position; and just then a quivering of the man's legs plainly indicated that he was recovering his senses. If it was to be done at all there was evidently no time to be lost; so Rowan, taking the sharp instrument, and poising it point downwards over the man's hands, which were already beginning to twitch with returning consciousness, and using his huge walking-stick as a hammer, with one powerful blow on the broad heavy handle of the knife, drove it through both the hands of the Moldavian and into the trunk of the tree up to the very hilt. A slight and almost inaudible groan came from behind the white wrapper—that was all; but Rowan could see that under the sting of the sudden pain the man had completely recovered consciousness, for the awful eyes, just visible above the muffler, were now open and fixed upon him.

'You miserable scoundrel!' exclaimed Rowan in German, his voice hoarse with anger. 'You may think yourself lucky I didn't kill you like a dog when you lay there at my mercy. But I'll have you punished—never fear. Lie quiet there until I have you sent to prison.'

The man said nothing: his awful eyes simply looked at Rowan.

'I have been forced, as you see,' continued the Colonel, leisurely taking out a cigar and lighting it, 'to nail you to the tree to prevent your escaping. Vermin is often treated so, you know. But I sha'n't inconvenience you for long. In a very few minutes I shall be sending people to unpin you and bind you properly, and have you taken off to prison. We have not seen the last of each other yet, my good friend—believe me, we have not.'

Then the man spoke—it was almost in a whisper, but the words came with the horrible liquid lisp Rowan remembered with so much disgust. 'No,' he murmured, 'we have not seen the last of each other yet—we have not.'

'There's but little fear, I fancy, of your not being here when I send for you,' resumed Rowan, after a moment's pause, during which he and the Moldavian had been steadfastly gazing at each other. 'So we needn't waste more time now, and especially as you must be rather uncomfortable. So *à bientôt*.'* Then, just as he was turning away, he stopped. 'In case,' said he very quietly, 'you should succeed in wriggling away before I send for you, and prefer mutilating your hands to suffering the very many lashes I shall certainly have administered to you, it's as well you should know, perhaps, that when travelling I invariably carry a revolver. I'm without it to-day—very luckily for you—by the merest accident. But I'm not likely to forget it again. So take care.'

And then Rowan turned and began strolling very leisurely back to where he had left his friends. His last words had not been idly spoken, but were intended to first of all suggest, to the miserable wretch whom he left nailed to the fallen tree, that escape was not altogether impossible, provided he were ready to pay the terrible price of self-mutilation required; and, secondly, to indicate the humiliating nature and severity of the punishment in store for him, that he might decide whether escape at any cost were not preferable to such torture and degradation. For, as a matter of fact, Hippy Rowan, directly the first moment of anger and the accompanying spasm of malignant cruelty had passed away, had decided in his mind to proceed no further in the matter, and by no means to take upon himself the *ennui* and trouble of having the paltry villain more seriously punished than he had already been. Had he had his revolver with him, he would of course have killed the man; but, as it was, he had nailed him as vermin to a tree in a lonely forest in Asia, and there he would leave him to his fate. He might starve to death there, or escape by a terrible mutilation, or possibly with his teeth remove the knife; or somebody might happen to pass by and relieve him—though this last was hardly likely: but at all events he, Hippy Rowan, having warned the villain what to expect in the event of his again molesting him, would have nothing more to do with the matter, and, indeed, not even mention the disagreeable episode to his friends—at least, not at present.

When Rowan got back to the scene of the picnic, he found the preparations for departure just being completed; and in a few minutes all Djavil's guests were once more comfortably ensconced in the carriages and on their way back to the Bosphorus, but this time by another road, which their host had reserved as an agreeable surprise, and which led through scenery of great beauty,—first, after fairy vistas of sylvan solitudes and entanglements, through a squalid though picturesque little village, the inhabitants of which, men and women and children, came running out after the carriages in great excitement, calling out and holding up their hands for alms; then past an encampment of Tziganes,* who were singing and playing and dancing; then across a lonely plain, over which here and there in the far distance, and standing out in bold relief against the horizon now all ablaze with the glory of the setting sun, passed bullock carts full of peasants, grouped together with Oriental and artistic grace, going home after the day's toil; and then at last, as the sun disappeared to their left behind the islands of the Sea of Marmora, to where the splendid panorama of the Bosphorus bathed in twilight lay at their feet. There, by the waterside, the party broke up—all but those persons staying with Djavil going back to Constantinople in a steamboat provided for their convenience by their host, and the others, including of course Hippy Rowan, returning to the Pacha's palace in his Excellency's steam-launch.

The scene returning home was beautiful indeed.* It was evening, and the sea was very quiet, for after sundown no boat leaves the Bosphorus, neither is any vessel allowed to enter therein before the dawn; so that the only sound which broke the stillness when the music had died away in the distance was the noise of the screw, which, working in the phosphorescent waters, rolled out showers and sheets of gold as the little steam-launch plodded, plodded, plodded on its course, cleaving and leaving on either side and behind a way of liquid fire. Above were the heavens sparkling with stars, below and around the sea of molten gold, while on either side on the silent banks of the Bosphorus gleamed and streamed innumerable lights from the different harem-windows, at some one of which every now and then an inquisitive head would appear, peeping out at the passing vessel.

All Djavil's guests were tired; so after dinner, a little music and chatting, and some very harmless gambling, they retired to rest much earlier than usual, Rowan being indeed glad when the time came that, unobserved and alone, he could deliver himself up wholly to his reflections, which happened that night to be of a strangely melancholy complexion. His rooms were on the ground floor, the windows indeed opening out on to the garden which sloped down to the marble terrace bordering the Bosphorus; and since it was to meditate rather than to sleep that Rowan sought retirement,* the Colonel sent the faithful Adams to bed, lit a cigar and went out, descending to the waterside to enjoy the view. Hardly had he reached the terrace, however, when from its farther end, which lay in shadow, emerged, crawling in the moonlight along the white marble pavement, an awful figure, which he knew but too well—that of Isaac Lebedenko the Moldavian, the man whom he had left but a few hours before nailed to a tree in the forest in Asia. As Rowan saw the man, the man saw him; and as Hippy stepped back and hurriedly felt in his pocket for his revolver, remembering, even as he did so, that he had left that useful weapon on his dressing-table, the Moldavian drew himself up and sprang towards his enemy, pulling, as he did so, with one hand the muffler from his face, and disclosing with hideous distinctness in the moonlight the indescribable horror of the countenance of a monster not born of woman, while with the other hand he fumbled in his pocket.

'The only way!' he gasped, in lisping German: 'the only way! But I am ready—glad; for I shall come to you now and you cannot escape me! See!' And so saying, and before Rowan could realize what was taking place, the man stabbed himself to the heart, and with a loud groan fell backwards into the waters of the Bosphorus, which closed over him.

CHAPTER III

'And you say you were not frightened?' exclaimed Bertonneux of the *Œil de Bœuf*.

Hippy Rowan shook his head and smiled. 'No, of course not,' he said. Then he added, lowering his voice lest the others should hear him, 'Do you know, it's a strange thing, *mon cher*, that never in my life have I known what fear is. It's no boast, of course, but a fact; and you can ask anyone who's been with me in danger. There are plenty of them about, for I began with Inkermann and only ended with Candahar,* not to speak of innumerable little private adventures more or less unpleasant between times, like the one I've just been telling you about, in fact. You know me well enough to feel that I'm neither a fool nor a coxcomb, and as a matter of fact this is not exactly courage, I fancy, but rather an absolute inability to entertain such a sentiment as fear. Just as some people are born blind and deaf and dumb.'

The scene was an immense and lofty chamber, luxuriously furnished, half drawing-room, half smoking-room, in Tony Jeratczesco's house in Moldavia, in the Karpak Mountains, and the time about a month after the events recorded in the last chapter had taken place. It had been raining all day as it only can rain in the Danubian principalities, and so the sportsmen had been unable to get out: a particularly deplorable *contretemps*, seeing that, with the exception of the small contingent which had come on from the Bosphorus, and which included Rowan, the French journalist, Lord Melrose, the three very magnificent *Chevaliers Gardes* from the shores of the Neva, and Mr. Leonard P. Beacon, the guests of 'Cheery and Cheeky' were wild, rough and boisterous neighbouring magnates, many of whom had never travelled beyond Bucharest, and none of whom possessed any of those very rare and precious qualities of heart and head, a combination of which in a fellow-captive can alone reconcile us to the common chain. These Boyards* were, indeed, so inconceivably rough and uncouth that Tony Jeratczesco greatly regretted having on the occasion of his taking possession of his property conformed to the almost feudally hospitable custom of the country and invited these loud-voiced Nimrods* and their retainers to take up their residence under his roof-tree for such time as the sport in the neighbourhood might meet with their approval. As it was, however, the mistake had been made: these strange beings had been asked and had come, and the evil was past recall; and although at certain times, and especially after dinner, and when the alcohol began to lift its voice, the society of the wealthy barbarians became almost unendurable, it had, of course, to be put up with and made the best of, all that Tony's more civilized friends could do being, almost in self-defence, as it were, to keep to themselves as much as was possible without risking giving offence to their unpleasant fellow-guests by this reserve. The house party was composed entirely of men, which, of course, did not add to the refinement of the gathering; and when, as at the beginning of this chapter, the tedium of a long and rainy day, thoroughly saturated with alcohol and tobacco, had reached the hour preceding midnight, the atmosphere of Jeratczesco's salon, either from an ethical or from a purely social point of view, would assuredly have compared unfavourably with that of most drawing-rooms in Mayfair.

To the French journalist Rowan had already told the story of his horrible adventure with Isaac Lebedenko and of the man's suicide—all of which events, together with minutes of what Maryx had said about the Children of Judas, were found carefully noted down in the Colonel's diary after his death—from which source of information and the testimony of Adams the present authentic account of these strange occurences is taken; but Mr. Leonard P. Beacon not having heard the story before, Hippy had been prevailed upon to repeat it to him, the question and answer with which this chapter opens being the immediate consequences of the telling of this tale.

Hippy had spoken in a low tone, to avoid attracting attention; but he had not taken into consideration the boisterous nature of his American auditor, who now exclaimed at the top of his voice; 'What! do you mean seriously to tell me, Rowan, that you have never known what fear is? that you simply can't be frightened by anything?'

Annoying as it was under the circumstances to have such a question put in so trumpet-tongued a fashion, Hippy plainly saw that the American would insist upon a reply to his thundered query, and that it would in no wise better matters to delay giving it.

'I do,' said he simply; and then added, in a half-whisper, 'I wish you wouldn't yell so, Beacon.'

But it was too late; the half-tipsy Boyards, bored to death, and eager to seize upon any topic of conversation likely to furnish a pretext for violence of language, had heard the question and the answer, and an uproar ensued which Jeratczesco was powerless to quell, and in the course of which the amiability and good breeding of Dick Rowan were both put to a severe test by the clumsy banter and coarsely expressed incredulity of these uncouth noblemen. One gentleman especially, a certain Prince Valerian Eldourdza, who, owing to the fact of his having been educated at a Lycée in Paris, was looked upon as the Admirable Crichton* of that part of Moldavia, pressed Hippy very hard, plying him with most personal and impertinent questions as to his belief in a future life, future punishment, the devil, and so forth, and at last, indeed, going so far as to solemnly declare that not only did he not believe in Colonel Rowan's inability to experience terror, but that he would himself undertake under a penalty of £4000 to frighten him. This somewhat offensive boast had, in the first instance, fallen from Eldourdza's lips in the heat of excitement, and probably without the speaker himself attaching any very great meaning or importance to his words; but the statement having been received with vociferous approval by the other Boyards, his Highness had been constrained to repeat the bet, and the second time give it a more specific form. 'One hundred thousand francs,' he repeated, bringing his very small and very unclean fist down on the table with much violence, 'that I frighten you, Colonel, before you leave here—that is, of course, always provided you're not leaving at once.'

'My friend is staying with me another month,' interposed Jeratczesco, rather angrily. 'But I can't allow such bets to be made in my house, Eldourdza. I hate practical jokes—we have quite enough of that kind of folly in England.'

'They're afraid already!' sneered a very unpleasant-looking old Moldavian statesman, all lip and nose, chewing at his cigar in the corner of his mouth after the fashion of a dog with a bone.

'You leave this to me, Tony,' said Rowan to his host, speaking quickly, and in English; then, turning to Eldourdza: 'Let's understand each other plainly, Prince. What do you mean by fright? Of course you can startle me by jumping out from a dark corner, or by any trick of that kind. I make no bet about that kind of thing, of course; but I'll bet you an even hundred thousand francs, if you like, or a hundred and fifty thousand francs, that you don't make me experience what is generally and by every one understood by the word fright—a sentiment of fear, or of anything even remotely resembling fear. How shall we define it, for we must be clear on this point?'

'Hair standing on end and teeth chattering,' suggested Mr. Leonard P. Beacon, who was greatly delighted at the turn affairs had taken, foreseeing an adventure and new experience of some kind.

'Exactly,' replied Eldourdza, who had been consulting in a whisper with his friends, and absorbing yet another gobletful of champagne strongly laced with brandy. 'Let those very words be used if you like—I'll bet you an even hundred and fifty thousand francs—two hundred thousand if you like' (Hippy nodded)—'that before you leave this place, four weeks from to-day, you will be so frightened that your hair shall stand on end, your teeth will chatter, and what's more, you'll call for help.'

'Very well,' assented Rowan, laughing, '*C'est entendu*;* but I sha'n't make you go so far as that, my dear Prince. I shall be quite ready to pay up if you do more than merely startle me in the way I spoke of just now—by some sudden noise, or jumping out at me, or some such silly prank. Anything even approaching fear, much less terror, of course, and I pay up at once. And,' he added good-naturedly—for he was fond of winning money, and the certainty of this £8000 was very pleasant to him—'luckily for you, Eldourdza, I happen to have the money to pay with if I lose. I was on every winner the last day at Baden*—couldn't do wrong—and sent it all on to Gunzburg* at once, where it is intact, for I didn't want to be tempted to gamble till I got to St. Petersburg.'

And so this strange bet was made, and duly noted down with the approval of all, even Jeratczesco withdrawing his objection when he saw the very evident satisfaction with which the Colonel regarded what he felt sure to be the only possible result of this absurd wager.

But if Hippy Rowan had foreseen the wholly unexpected way in which this waiting day by day, night after night, and hour by hour for the surprise—of course of an apparently unpleasant nature—which Eldourdza and his friends must be preparing for him—had he, we say, foreseen the peculiar and unprecedented way in which this really absurd suspense was destined gradually, and by almost imperceptible degrees, to affect his nerves in the course of the next month—he would most assuredly have let the Prince's silly wager pass unnoticed. And what made this never-absent feeling of care, of perpetual caution, of unceasing vigilance, the more acutely irksome to Hippy, was that these novel sensations could be ascribed but to one altogether disagreeable and detestable cause—namely, the advance of old age. His experience of life had told him that the constitution of a man who had lived as he had lived was apt to break down suddenly, no matter how apparently robust it might be; the supports, the foundation, which kept the structure in its place and seemingly firm and upright, having been little by little, and very gradually but very surely, removed in the course of years, the nights of which had been worn to morning in the fatigue of pleasure, and the days of which had been scornful of repose. He had seen innumerable friends of his, apparently as strong and vigorous as himself, suddenly give way in this fashion—fall down like a house of cards, as it were, and be swept away into the outer darkness. Could it be owing to the approach of some such sudden and disastrous conclusion to his mundane affairs, that he found, day by day, as the next four weeks wore on, his nerves, hitherto apparently of steel, becoming more and more unstrung by this suspense, the cause of which was in reality so utterly puerile and contemptible? This was very certainly not his first experience of suspense: he had been in danger of his life very often, and on a few occasions this danger had been imminent for a considerable period of time, and yet never could he recall having felt before this uneasiness of mind, this perpetual questioning of his heart, which he now experienced while merely waiting for these boorish savages to play some more or less gruesome, and even perhaps dangerous practical joke on him. It must be old age; it could be nothing else—old age, and the beginning, perhaps, of a general breaking-up of the system; the first intimation, as it were, of the second and final payment about to be required of him for those extravagances by Seine side already alluded to, those myrtles sacred to the sparrow-drawn goddess,* those prolonged and oft-repeated saunters from midnight to dawn arm-in-arm with Bacchus and baccarat,*—such outriders of Death's chariot, Rowan told himself, it must be, that induced him, greatly to his own surprise, to waste so much of his time twisting and turning over in his mind all kinds of possible and impossible speculations as to how these wretched Moldavians were going to try and frighten him. This led him to examine carefully his apartments every night before retiring to rest, and see that his revolver had not been tampered with and was safely under his pillow.* Of course this very abnormal condition of mind, which in no wise even remotely resembled fear, and was one merely of perpetual watchfulness, was of very gradual growth, and Hippy Rowan was throughout the whole course of its development, until just before the end, sufficiently master of himself to conceal his feelings, not only from his friends, but even from his valet, the omniscient Adams; and the very visible change in the Colonel's appearance and manner, which by-and-bye came to be remarked, was ascribed by all—and in a great measure justly ascribed—to a very severe chill which he caught shortly after the night of the wager, and which confined him to the house, and indeed to his room, for many days. Neither Prince Eldourdza nor anyone else had made any allusion whatever, in Rowan's hearing, to the wager since the night on which it had been made and formally noted down; and this fact in itself, this studied silence, became in the course of time, and as Rowan's nervous irritability increased, a source of annoyance to him, and induced him at length, suddenly, one morning, when they were all at breakfast together, to boldly allude to the matter, which was becoming more and more constantly uppermost in his mind.

'Pardon me, Prince,' said he, smiling, and with well-assumed carelessness, 'if I allude to the matter of our wager, which you seem to have forgotten, for you have only ten days left now, and—'

'Plenty of time!' interrupted Eldourdza roughly. 'Forgotten it? Not I—have I?' he continued, turning to his friends. 'You know whether I have forgotten it or not!' Significant and sinister grins and much shaking of heads in negation responded to this appeal,—a pantomime which excited the Colonel's curiosity not a little.

'Well,' said he, 'I'm glad to hear it, for I shouldn't like to take your money without your having had some semblance of a run for it. All I want to tell you was this, and I feel sure you'll agree with what I now say. Of course I've no idea what kind of prank you're going to play on me, to endeavour to frighten me, but no doubt it will be as horrible and awful a thing as you can concoct, for I suppose you've no intention of making me a present of two hundred thousand francs.'

'Certainly not!' laughed Prince Valerian; 'if you get it at all you'll have to pay dear for it, believe me.'

'Very well,' replied Hippy—'anything you like; but that's just what I wanted to speak about. Of course I'm at your disposal to do anything you like with, and to try and frighten in any way and every way you can contrive; but you can easily understand that there must be a limit to my endurance, otherwise you'd make me look like a fool. What I mean is, that you're at perfect liberty, say, to send any ghost or vampire or wild beast or devil, or anything else you can think of, to my room to try and frighten me, and for that purpose I am glad to lend you all the aid in my power. As it is, I leave my door unlocked every night now, as perhaps you know. But there must be some limit to this,—I mean that your endeavour to frighten me must have some limit in time, and can't go on for ever. Suppose we put it at one hour—for one hour let your ghost or devil do its worst: then at the end of that time, if it has failed to frighten me, your goblin will become merely a nuisance, and I think I shall be justified in extinguishing it, don't you?'

'Most assuredly,' replied Eldourdza. 'In less than an hour: we don't ask for an hour—half an hour will do,—after half an hour you are perfectly at liberty to do as you like—provided always,' he added grimly, 'that by that time you are not half dead with fright.'

'Very well, then,' rejoined Hippy: 'so that's understood. After half an hour from the time your test, whatever it may be, begins, I shall be free to use any means I care to adopt to put a stop to this test, provided by that time, of course, I have not felt anything even remotely resembling alarm. As in the event of your test being something really offensive and disagreeable to me I should probably use my revolver, I thought it only fair to have this plainly understood, so that what is really only a silly practical joke may not, by a misunderstanding, end in a tragedy.'

The Prince nodded in acquiescence. 'You are quite right,' he said. 'After half an hour do as you please. But you're mistaken in looking upon this as a practical joke, Colonel Rowan: it will be no joke, and may indeed, even against your will, end in a tragedy.'

As may be readily imagined, these few mysterious words of menace from the man pledged, in some way or other, to cause him within ten days' time to experience the novel, but doubtless unpleasant, sensation of terror, did not tend to bring the Colonel to a more restful state of mind; and his never-ending speculations as to what scheme these savages might perchance be planning wherewith to frighten him began again after this conversation to torment his brain with renewed persistency. Of course Eldourdza would do all he could to win his bet—not for the sake of the money, perhaps, for that could be nothing to him, but for the pleasure and delight of triumph; and, equally of course—at least so Hippy told himself, this desired fright the Prince and his friends would only endeavour to bring about by some pseudo-supernatural agency, for they could hardly imagine that any of the vulgar dangers of life—say an attack of many adversaries, whether men or brutes, peril from water, fire, or what not; in fact, any of the thousand-and-one not uncommon evils which threaten human existence—could possibly affright so hardened and experienced a soldier and traveller as he was, a man whose record of perilous adventures was so well known. The supernatural, therefore, the terrors which owe their horror to the fact of their being inexplicable, the power of them unfathomable; the awful enemies which may be lurking crouched behind the last breath of life ready to spring upon us as the heart stops beating; such, or rather the semblance of such, would doubtless be alone the influences which these wild barbarians would seek to bring to bear upon his nerves to try them. And when this probability having been suggested to his imagination, Colonel Rowan began recalling to mind all the gruesome stories he had ever heard of about ghosts, hobgoblins, and the like, his restlessness and nervous watchfulness (to which he only gave way when in the privacy of his own chamber, of course) so increased as the last ten days sped by, that at length Adams, who slept in the next room, remarking his master's condition, arranged, without, of course, the knowledge of any one, to keep watch and ward over the Colonel during these last few nights by means of an aperture high up in the wall, through which he could obtain a perfect view of his master's sleeping apartment, and see all that took place therein.*

So it came to pass that on the last night but two Hippy never retired to rest until the dawn, having decided, after mature reflection, that no matter what absurd practical joke his friends might be going to play on him, he would cut a less ludicrous figure in his dressing-gown than in bed, and that it might indeed be advisable to be thus prepared to follow the tormenting masqueraders from his chamber to punish them elsewhere, and before the whole household, in the event of their conduct proving too outrageous. And so, after having as usual carefully examined every hole and cranny of his sleeping apartment (as the unobserved Adams from his peephole above saw him do very plainly), and lighted many tapers about the old-fashioned and vast chamber, and put many cheering logs upon the fire, the Colonel lit a cigar and began pacing up and down the room, turning over of course in his mind the perpetual question—'What are these uncouth madmen going to do?' and the query for ever followed by the usual reflection—'They can do as they please, provided they don't, by their folly, make me look a fool.' There would probably be the rattling of chains and bones, and some very cleverly contrived apparition; and even, in fact, some real danger, perhaps, for these men were really perfect savages, who would stop at nothing to attain their end; and Hippy would certainly not have been surprised to have found a box of dynamite concealed beneath his bed.

'Luckily, this is the last night but two,' he said to himself—'and after all this bet has taught me one thing I never plainly realized before, and in a certain sense I have really lost the wager, for there is one thing I am afraid of, and very much afraid of, more and more afraid of every minute, and that is being made a fool of.' Then he stopped in his perambulation and stared at himself in the looking-glass. Yes; he was certainly growing old: the grey hairs he cared nothing about—they were entirely insignificant; and the crows' feet and wrinkles were of no importance—they did not in the least annoy him; but the eyes, ah! the eyes were losing their light—that light that had disported itself over so many beautiful things.* But then even a youthful face would look sad in so mystic a mirror—for it was very old, and evidently Venetian, and had doubtless been in that room in that castle in that remote corner of Moldavia for years and years, and seen perchance strange things,—and was destined (who could tell?) before three nights were over to reflect images of even more fantastic terror than had ever darkened it before. What a pity that this old looking-glass could not recall some of the most pleasant images that had been reflected in it in the long ago to keep him company that night! If he stared at it long enough, would he not, perhaps, at length perceive far, far away, there in the most remote and distant and least lighted corner of the room, reflected the fair sad face of some Moldavian dame who had wept and kissed and loved and lost in the old days of the Hospodars?*

'Les miroirs par les jours abrégés de Décembre
Songent—telles les eaux captives—dans les chambres,
Et leur mélancolie a pour causes lointaines
Tant de visages doux fanés dans ces fontaines
Qui s'y voyaient naguère embellis de sourires.'*

Then, drawing up a comfortable armchair before the blazing logs, he seated himself, and taking up *Le Rouge et le Noir*,* which he happened to find lying on the table by his side, ere long had read himself to sleep over the marvellous narrative of the vicissitudes of Julien Sorel, only awaking, indeed, when the

'fair-faced sun,
Killing the stars and dews and dreams and desolations of the night,'*

was plainly visible through the curtains, and the noises of the awakening household warned him that another day had begun. Then he arose and went to bed, fondly believing that by this little comedy he was deceiving the omniscient Adams, who, as a matter of fact, perched on a step-ladder in the adjoining apartment, had kept an unceasing watch over his master. That day, Rowan's last day on earth, passed without any incident worthy of notice. Jeratczesco announced at breakfast that he had engaged a band of *laoutari**—gypsy minstrels—to enliven his friends, but that, as he only expected them to arrive late that night, his guests would not have the opportunity of enjoying their wild and delightful music until the morning.

'I shall lodge them in your wing of the house, where they'll be quiet,' explained Tony to Colonel Rowan, later on in the day, when they happened to be alone. 'You know how beautiful some of these *tsigane** women are, and how jealously guarded by their men, I don't want a row here, and there's no knowing what mad folly Eldourdza and his friends might be up to when drunk.'

And that the prudent Tony was quite justified in taking all precautionary measures to ensure peace and tranquillity during the sojourn of the gypsies beneath his roof was amply proved that very night when they arrived late, for the Moldavian magnates, who, with Eldourdza at their head, would seem to have intentionally got drunk rather earlier than usual that evening, were only with the greatest difficulty restrained by their host from rushing out into the moonlit courtyard and embracing the women of the minstrel band, as they were seen and heard passing and chattering and singing on their way to their quarters. The arrival of these gypsies, and the prospect of the break which their performances would make in the monotony of the daily life at the château (which, by the way, all save the most enthusiastic sportsmen would have found intolerably tedious), greatly enlivened Hippy Rowan's spirits; and when he retired for the night—the last night but one of this absurd waiting for surprises, as he reminded himself with a smile—he opened his window and looked out across the quadrangle to the lights in the rooms occupied by the wandering musicians, wondering whether indeed this band contained any of those really beautiful women such as he remembered having remarked among the Strelna* gypsy musicians of Moscow,—women unlike any other women to be found in any class or country in the world, and whose peculiar charm is as indescribable as it is indisputable, possessing as it does a power partaking of the supernatural, springing as it were from a fountain of infernal fascination. What a splendid night! And nearly Christmas too, the very season for ghostly masquerading, and—— But hark! a woman's voice singing.

Hippy leaned out and listened. The voice was low and very sweet, though the woman singing was evidently engaged in some other occupation which absorbed her attention, for there would be careless pauses in her song, the words of which in a Roumanian dialect ran somewhat as follows:

'Love shot his arrow o'er the Sea,
And all the waters leaped with joy,
Lifting their foam-wreathed arms in glee,
To bid the sunlight hold the boy;
But the Sun said
"My beams are shed
To cheer with flowers the lonely dead."'

Here the singing ceased for a moment, but presently a man's voice took up the song, singing in the same careless fashion, stopping every now and then.

'Death spread his pinions o'er the Sea,
And all the waves with stormed-thrilled breath
In sobs besought the Moon that she
Might break the tear-plumed wings of Death.
But the Moon cried
"My silver tide
Will only——"'*

But here a merry burst of laughter interrupted the singer, and though for some time after Rowan could hear the voices of the gypsies laughing and talking, he could not distinguish what was being said, and there was no more singing.

'What a strange people!' murmured Rowan to himself, as he closed the window, 'and what suitable neighbours to have on such a night as this, when at any moment now I may expect to see a cavalcade of ghosts come galloping into the room!'

Then the watchful Adams saw his master make his usual careful inspection of the room, seat himself by the fire, take up Stendhal* again, and read himself to sleep.

Suddenly Rowan awoke, roused by a sound that stole into his ears very gradually and very gently, but which, when his drowsy faculties had understood its meaning, stirred them to instant activity—the sound of weeping. He sprang to his feet and looked around the room. He was alone; the apartment was brilliantly illuminated, thanks to two large lamps and several tapers in girandoles,* and he could plainly see into the farthest corner: nobody—no animated creature was visible. He listened, but not a sound broke the stillness of the night. He must have been dreaming. But no—hark! there it was again, the sound of weeping, of some one in great and bitter distress: it came from the corridor, and not far from his chamber door. Should he go and see what it was? Could this be any part of the Moldavians' masquerading? Surely not! Hardly would they begin their attempt to frighten a man by such heartrending expressions of anguish, which could evoke but pity and compassion. Again! Oh, what a wealth of woe!

And a woman too; the long-drawn, gasping, tear-clogged suspiration was pitched in a key of peculiar pathos which that treasury of divine tenderness, a woman's heart, alone can find to woo compassion. Again,—yes, certainly a woman: could it perchance be one of the *laoutari*? The corridor led to the part of the house where they were sleeping, and, so far as he knew, they were the only women in the house except the servants. Surely Eldourdza had nothing to do with this; and even if he had, what then? Had not this drunken Moldavian boor already occupied his mind quite long enough with speculations as to what he might and what he might not be about to do? Let him do as he pleased, and what he liked, and go to the devil!

There was a woman in terrible distress just outside his door, and he, Hippy Rowan, must go to her without delay—that was very clear. So, taking his revolver in his hand in case of need, Rowan advanced, opened the door wide, and looked out into the sombre corridor, Adams, greatly frightened, watching his master the while, and, having heard nothing, was at a loss to understand the Colonel's conduct. Even as he opened the door Rowan saw that he had guessed aright, and that it was a woman who was giving utterance to these most pitiful and heartrending expressions of anguish. There she lay, not very near his door after all, weeping bitterly, her face buried in her hands—as if she had been praying on her knees for mercy, and in a very agony of supplication had fallen forward. Rowan saw at once that those white and shapely hands must belong to a young woman; and so his voice assumed a tone of very special tenderness and compassion, as he said, in the Roumanian dialect in which he had heard the gypsies singing:—

'What is it, lady? Can I help you?'

The mourner, who apparently had not remarked the opening of the door, at the sound of Hippy's voice ceased her lamenting; and after a moment's pause slowly raised her head, withdrawing her hands from her face as she did so, and revealing to Rowan's astonished eyes the most faultlessly lovely countenance he had ever gazed upon in living woman—a countenance different to anything Hippy had ever seen. Was it the moonlight pouring in through the uncurtained windows which gave it that ethereal radiance? Who could she be?* That she was not a gypsy was very evident, for her skin was of the most fine and delicate fairness, and her hair, which fell in caressing curls over her forehead, of a soft and tender brown. Moreover, her dress was entirely unlike that of a *tsigane*, both in colour and in form, being all black, and fashioned, so far as Rowan could see, as that of a member of some religious order, the beautiful face being, as it were, framed round about in a covering not unlike a cowl. Rowan had heard, he thought, of some sisterhood in the neighbourhood: perhaps this fair mourner belonged to such a community;—at all events she was assuredly a very lovely woman, and it behoved him, both as a man of heart and as a man of taste, to console her in her sorrow. But to attain this desired end, of course the first and most necessary step would be to make himself understood, and that, apparently, he had not so far succeeded in doing. The lustrous violet eyes looked at him, indeed, with startled surprise and fawn-like timidity, though there was assuredly nothing redoubtable in the kind aspect of Hippy's handsome face, and he had instinctively hidden the revolver in his pocket the moment he had seen the pathetic prostrate figure in the corridor; but beyond this half-frightened expression there was nothing to be recognized but sorrow in that lovely countenance: not the slightest indication that his words had conveyed to the mourner's mind any idea of sympathy and compassion. Again he addressed her, this time in no dialect, but in the purest Roumanian, and in a still more tender and sympathising tone than before; but the look of timid wonder in the sweet Madonna face remained unchanged. Then, feeling that the situation was becoming rather ludicrous, he said, this time speaking in German and beckoning towards the open door of his apartment,—

'Lady, let me beg of you to tell me what troubles you! Come into my room and rest and warm yourself. Believe me, there is nothing I would not gladly do to be of service to you. You have only to command me; I am an Englishman, a gentleman, and a soldier—so you may trust me. Let me help you, lady: come, I beg of you.' Then, after a pause, as the mourner neither spoke nor moved. Hippy bowed, and, motioning her to follow him, walked slowly into his room, turning every now and then and repeating his gesture of invitation;—she the while remaining upon her knees,—looking after him, indeed, but making no attempt to rise and follow.

Although Adams had at no time lost sight of his master, whose back, as he seemed to be engaged in conversation with some invisible person far down the corridor, had always been within the range of the faithful servant's vision, still it was with a feeling of great relief that he now saw the Colonel come back into the room unharmed, although the expression of tenderness and pity in his master's face rather puzzled the man, as did also the Colonel's conduct in turning when he had reached the fireplace and looking anxiously back towards the door which he had left open behind him, as if expecting and indeed longing for the arrival of some visitor. At length, after the lapse of a few minutes—a delay which, though brief, the servant could plainly see his master bore impatiently, the longed-for visitor slowly emerged from the darkness of the corridor until she stood framed in the doorway, against one side of which, as if to support herself, she lightly placed a small white hand. It was thus Adams saw the slender black-robed figure of a sweet girl mourner appear, and for the first time in his life was astonished, nay, astounded rather, at the marvellous resemblance in depth of tenderness, in purity of sorrow-hallowed loveliness, between this nocturnal lady visitor to his master and a Madonna* from a canvas, say, of Raphael, standing apparently before him clothed in flesh.

Perhaps some such fantastic idea of an incarnation of one of Raphael's Holy Virgins occurred to Rowan as he bowed low and advanced to welcome his fair visitor, for this time he addressed her in Italian, thanking her for the great honour she was doing him, making all kinds of graceful and very Italian protestations of sympathy and respect, and concluding a very pretty speech by begging her not to stay there on the threshold, but to come in and seat herself by the fire; adding that if his presence were in any way distasteful to her he would at once withdraw and leave her in undisturbed possession of the room. But this attempt, clothed in the choicest Tuscan, to inspire confidence, met with no greater measure of success than had attended its Roumanian and German predecessors. The sweetly sorrowful lady stood on the threshold in the same timid attitude, staring at the Colonel with no abatement in the tender melancholy of her face, but apparently in no wise understanding his words, and even, indeed, ignoring his gesture inviting her to enter and be seated.

What was to be done? He could hardly, of course, take this lovely girl-Madonna in his arms and drag her into his room by force; and yet it seemed intolerably absurd, and indeed impossible, to leave her standing there in the doorway. Why had she come even to the threshold of his door, if she had not intended coming farther in the event of her seeing nothing to alarm her? Of course, and beyond all doubt, if he could only make her understand his sympathy and respect, and that she need have no fear of him, she would come in and perhaps tell him the cause of her distress, and let him help her; and on the other hand, knowing so many languages and even dialects and patois as he did, it seemed almost impossible that he should not be able at length to hit upon some form of speech by which he could convey to this most perfect incarnate type of spiritual purity and loveliness the expression of his devoted homage.

So he started off on a wild polyglottic* steeplechase, making protestations of respect and sympathy and offers of aid and friendship in every language and dialect he could remember, from his native English to the patois spoken by the Jews in White Russia. But all to no purpose; and at length he was constrained to pause and acknowledge that he was utterly defeated.*

'You're very beautiful,' said he at last, with a sigh, speaking in his native English, the inability of his fair auditor to understand him possessing at least the meagre and thankless advantage of allowing him to express his admiration in words no matter how impassioned, provided, of course, he took care his face should not betray the significance and ardour of his speech—'the most beautiful woman I think I ever saw; but you're a beautiful riddle, and I don't know how to read you. What language can you speak, I wonder? Only the language of love, perhaps! Were I to kneel down there before you, or take you in my arms and kiss you, in what language would you repulse me, or—?'

Here he paused, greatly surprised: were his eyes deceiving him, or was at length a change stealing over the Madonna face, and the timidity and sadness in it slowly giving place to an expression of some brighter sentiment? That she could not understand the language he was speaking he felt sure, for he had already addressed her in it, and his words had evidently failed utterly to convey any meaning to her mind. But surely there was a difference now, and something he had said, or some gesture he had made, or some expression in his face, had been pleading to her, for the great shadow of melancholy was slowly passing from her. But between the language, the English he had used before and that which he had just spoken, what difference was there? None, of course, save in the sense: then the words had been of respect and sympathy, now of love and tenderness. Could it be that by some marvellous intuition her woman's instinct had at once divined the more tender words? or indeed was it not possible, nay, likely, that in speaking them he had involuntarily let their meaning be reflected in his eyes, and that she had read it there?

But then such tenderness and affection were not displeasing to her, and this Mask of the Madonna, this ideal type of womanly purity, could be lighted by the joy of love.

The thought set Rowan's blood coursing through his veins like fire, and made his heart beat as if he had been but twenty. He must see, and at once: he would speak to her again in words of affection, and let his eyes partly and by degrees interpret what he said, carefully of course, and always guided by what he should see her eyes reply to his, lest he should offend her. And so he began telling this lovely woman in very low, quiet and grave tones, but in words of great tenderness, how fair he found her, and as he spoke his eyes expressed the meaning of his words more and more clearly and ardently as he recognized with ever-growing delight that the Madonna face was being gradually illuminated and transfigured by joy, as word after word of ever-increasing passion, echoed in tender glances from his eyes, fell from his lips.

And as he spoke he did not advance towards her, but only clasped his hands and stood still far from her, looking at her in the doorway; while she, more and more visibly affected by his ever-growing emotion, first withdrew her hand from the side of the door where she had leant it, and pushed back the cowl from her face a little, still further disclosing, by so doing, the wavy wealth of soft brown curls, and then, as the violet eyes became by degrees lighted with great joy and the sweet lips melted to a smile of ineffable rapture, clasped both hands together just beneath her cheek in an attitude of girlish and innocent delight.

So she stood until the fervour of Rowan's words and voice and eyes rose to an ecstasy of passion, and then leaning forward her head, not indeed to hide the sweet blushes which were rising to her cheeks, but as a child eager to rush to a beloved embrace, and her eyes answering the ardour she read in those she gazed into, she half stretched forth her arms as if her longing to twine them in a caress were but restrained by maiden bashfulness. Rowan saw the gesture, stepped forward, opened wide his arms, and the girl Madonna rushed to his embrace, nestling her blushing face upon his neck, as in a rapture of fondness he clasped her to his bosom.

At the same moment a terrible cry rang through the room and through the house, waking the *tsiganes*, who sprang from their beds in mad terror, and startling the stupid Moldavians, who, despairing of really frightening Rowan, had decided on merely making him look a fool, and were at that very moment creeping up the staircase, dressed in absurd costumes and armed with monster squirts* and all kinds of grotesque instruments—the cry of a strong man in an agony of terror. The horrified Adams saw his master hurl the woman from him with great violence, snatch his revolver from his pocket, discharge three chambers of it at her in quick succession, and then reel and fall forward on his face, while she, rising from the floor apparently unhurt, glided from the apartment by the still open door. When Adams reached his master's side he found him quite dead, and the body presenting two most remarkable peculiarities: first a very strong odour of musk—and secondly, on the neck three small wounds shaped like three **X**'s joined together. The medical man, a German, who was immediately called in, ascribed the death of Colonel Rowan to aneurism* of the heart, and declined to attach the least importance to the three small wounds or bites on the neck, the post-mortem examination proving that so far as the cause of death was concerned the physician was right in his conjecture.

As for the strange lady with the Madonna face, Adams was far too shrewd a man of the world to make known the extraordinary circumstance to every one. He told Tony Jeratczesco, and inquiries were made; but no such person had been seen or heard of, and so the matter dropped; and it is only within the last few months that Mr. Adams, now retired from his delicate and difficult profession of valet and living in the neighbourhood of Newmarket, could be prevailed upon to give a detailed account of all the strange facts connected with the death of his master, show Hippy Rowan's diary, and complete his story by producing a photograph which he himself had taken of the dead man's neck, on which is plainly visible the imprint of the Kiss of Judas.

ERIC, COUNT STENBOCK

THE TRUE STORY OF A VAMPIRE

VAMPIRE stories are generally located in Styria;* mine is also. Styria is by no means the romantic kind of place described by those who have certainly never been there. It is a flat, uninteresting country, only celebrated by its turkeys, its capons,* and the stupidity of its inhabitants. Vampires generally arrive at night, in carriages drawn by two black horses.

Our Vampire arrived by the commonplace means of the railway train, and in the afternoon. You must think I am joking, or perhaps that by the word 'Vampire' I mean a financial vampire. No, I am quite serious. The Vampire of whom I am speaking, who laid waste our hearth and home, was a *real* vampire.

Vampires are generally described as dark, sinister-looking, and singularly handsome. Our Vampire was, on the contrary, rather fair, and certainly was not at first sight sinister-looking, and though decidedly attractive in appearance, not what one would call singularly handsome.

Yes, he desolated our home, killed my brother—the one object of my adoration—also my dear father. Yet, at the same time, I must say that I myself came under the spell of his fascination, and, in spite of all, have no ill-will towards him now.

Doubtless you have read in the papers *passim* of 'the Baroness and her beasts.'* It is to tell how I came to spend most of my useless wealth on an asylum for stray animals that I am writing this.

I am old now; what happened then was when I was a little girl of about thirteen. I will begin by describing our household. We were Poles; our name was Wronski:* we lived in Styria, where we had a castle. Our household was very limited. It consisted, with the exclusion of domestics, of only my father, our governess—a worthy Belgian named Mademoiselle Vonnaert—my brother, and myself. Let me begin with my father: he was old, and both my brother and I were children of his old age. Of my mother I remember nothing: she died in giving birth to my brother, who is only one year, or not as much, younger than myself. Our father was studious, continually occupied in reading books, chiefly on recondite subjects and in all kinds of unknown languages. He had a long white beard, and wore habitually a black velvet skull-cap.

How kind he was to us! It was more than I could tell. Still it was not I who was the favourite. His whole heart went out to Gabriel*—Gabryel as we spelt it in Polish. He was always called by the Russian abbreviation Gavril—I mean, of course, my brother, who had a resemblance to the only portrait of my mother, a slight chalk sketch which hung in my father's study. But I was by no means jealous: my brother was and has been the only love of my life. It is for his sake that I am now keeping in Westbourne Park* a home for stray cats and dogs.

I was at that time, as I said before, a little girl; my name was Carmela.* My long tangled hair was always all over the place, and never would be combed straight. I was not pretty—at least, looking at a photograph of me at that time, I do not think I could describe myself as such. Yet at the same time, when I look at the photograph, I think my expression may have been pleasing to some people: irregular features, large mouth, and large wild eyes.

I was by way of being naughty—not so naughty as Gabriel in the opinion of Mlle. Vonnaert. Mlle. Vonnaert, I may intercalate,* was a wholly excellent person, middle-aged, who really *did* speak good French, although she was a Belgian, and could also make herself understood in German, which, as you may or may not know, is the current language of Styria.

I find it difficult to describe my brother Gabriel; there was something about him strange and superhuman, or perhaps I should rather say præter-human,* something between the animal and the divine. Perhaps the Greek idea of the Faun* might illustrate what I mean; but that will not do either. He had large, wild, gazelle-like eyes: his hair, like mine, was in a perpetual tangle—that point he had in common with me, and indeed, as I afterwards heard, our mother having been of gipsy race, it will account for much of the innate wildness there was in our natures. I was wild enough, but Gabriel was much wilder. Nothing would induce him to put on shoes and stockings, except on Sundays—when he also allowed his hair to be combed, but only by me. How shall I describe the grace of that lovely mouth, shaped verily 'en arc d'amour.'* I always think of the text in the Psalm, 'Grace is shed forth on thy lips, therefore has God blessed thee eternally'*—lips that seemed to exhale the very breath of life. Then that beautiful, lithe, living, elastic form!

He could run faster than any deer: spring like a squirrel to the topmost branch of a tree: he might have stood for the sign and symbol of vitality itself. But seldom could he be induced by Mlle. Vonnaert to learn lessons; but when he did so, he learnt with extraordinary quickness. He would play upon every conceivable instrument, holding a violin here, there, and everywhere except the right place: manufacturing instruments for himself out of reeds—even sticks. Mlle. Vonnaert made futile efforts to induce him to learn to play the piano. I suppose he was what was called spoilt, though merely in the superficial sense of the word. Our father allowed him to indulge in every caprice.

One of his peculiarities, when quite a little child, was horror at the sight of meat. Nothing on earth would induce him to taste it. Another thing which was particularly remarkable about him was his extraordinary power over animals. Everything seemed to come tame to his hand. Birds would sit on his shoulder. Then sometimes Mlle. Vonnaert and I would lose him in the woods—he would suddenly dart away. Then we would find him singing softly or whistling to himself, with all manner of woodland creatures around him,—hedgehogs, little foxes, wild rabbits, marmots, squirrels, and such like. He would frequently bring these things home with him and insist on keeping them. This strange menagerie was the terror of poor Mlle. Vonnaert's heart. He chose to live in a little room at the top of a turret; but which, instead of going upstairs, he chose to reach by means of a very tall chestnut-tree, through the window. But in contradiction to all this, it was his custom to serve every Sunday Mass in the parish church, with hair nicely combed and with white surplice and red cassock. He looked as demure and tamed as possible. Then came the element of the divine. What an expression of ecstasy there was in those glorious eyes!

Thus far I have not been speaking about the Vampire. However, let me begin with my narrative at last. One day my father had to go to the neighbouring town—as he frequently had. This time he returned accompanied by a guest. The gentleman, he said, had missed his train, through the late arrival of another at our station, which was a junction, and he would therefore, as trains were not frequent in our parts, have had to wait there all night. He had joined in conversation with my father in the too-late-arriving train from the town: and had consequently accepted my father's invitation to stay the night at our house. But of course, you know, in those out-of-the-way parts we are almost patriarchal in our hospitality.

He was announced under the name of Count Vardalek*—the name being Hungarian. But he spoke German well enough: not with the monotonous accentuation of Hungarians, but rather, if anything, with a slight Slavonic intonation. His voice was peculiarly soft and insinuating. We soon afterwards found out he could talk Polish, and Mlle. Vonnaert vouched for his good French. Indeed he seemed to know all languages. But let me give my first impressions. He was rather tall, with fair wavy hair, rather long, which accentuated a certain effeminacy about his smooth face. His figure had something—I cannot say what—serpentine about it. The features were refined; and he had long, slender, subtle, magnetic-looking hands, a somewhat long sinuous nose, a graceful mouth, and an attractive smile, which belied the intense sadness of the expression of the eyes. When he arrived his eyes were half closed—indeed they were habitually so—so that I could not decide their colour. He looked worn and wearied. I could not possibly guess his age.

Suddenly Gabriel burst into the room: a yellow butterfly was clinging to his hair. He was carrying in his arms a little squirrel. Of course he was bare-legged as usual. The stranger looked up at his approach; then I noticed his eves. They were green: they seemed to dilate and grow larger. Gabriel stood stock-still, with a startled look, like that of a bird fascinated by a serpent. But nevertheless he held out his hand to the newcomer. Vardalek, taking his hand—I don't know why I noticed this trivial thing,—pressed the pulse with his forefinger. Suddenly Gabriel darted from the room and rushed upstairs, going to his turret-room this time by the staircase instead of the tree. I was in terror what the Count might think of him. Great was my relief when he came down in his velvet Sunday suit, and shoes and stockings. I combed his hair, and set him generally right.

When the stranger came down to dinner his appearance had somewhat altered; he looked much younger. There was an elasticity of the skin, combined with a delicate complexion, rarely to be found in a man. Before, he had struck me as being very pale.

Well, at dinner we were all charmed with him, especially my father. He seemed to be thoroughly acquainted with all my father's particular hobbies. Once, when my father was relating some of his military experiences, he said something about a drummer-boy who was wounded in battle. His eyes opened completely again and dilated: this time with a particularly disagreeable expression, dull and dead, yet at the same time animated by some horrible excitement. But this was only momentary.

The chief subject of his conversation with my father was about certain curious mystical books which my father had just lately picked up, and which he could not make out, but Vardalek seemed completely to understand. At dessert-time my father asked him if he were in a great hurry to reach his destination: if not, would he not stay with us a little while: though our place was out of the way, he would find much that would interest him in his library.

He answered, 'I am in no hurry. I have no particular reason for going to that place at all, and if I can be of service to you in deciphering these books, I shall be only too glad.' He added with a smile which was bitter, very very bitter: 'You see I am a cosmopolitan, a wanderer on the face of the earth.'

After dinner my father asked him if he played the piano. He said, 'Yes, I can a little,' and he sat down at the piano. Then he played a Hungarian csardas*—wild, rhapsodic, wonderful.

That is the music which makes men mad. He went on in the same strain.

Gabriel stood stock-still by the piano, his eyes dilated and fixed, his form quivering. At last he said very slowly, at one particular motive*—for want of a better word you may call it the *relâche** of a csardas, by which I mean that point where the original quasi-slow movement begins again—'Yes, I think I could play that.'

Then he quickly fetched his fiddle and self-made xylophone, and did actually, alternating the instruments, render the same very well indeed.

Vardalek looked at him, and said in a very sad voice, 'Poor child! you have the soul of music within you.'

I could not understand why he should seem to commiserate instead of congratulate Gabriel on what certainly showed an extraordinary talent.

* * * * * *

Gabriel was shy even as the wild animals who were tame to him. Never before had he taken to a stranger. Indeed, as a rule, if any stranger came to the house by any chance, he would hide himself, and I had to bring him up his food to the turret chamber. You may imagine what was my surprise when I saw him walking about hand in hand with Vardalek the next morning, in the garden, talking livelily with him, and showing his collection of pet animals, which he had gathered from the woods, and for which we had had to fit up a regular zoological gardens. He seemed utterly under the domination of Vardalek. What surprised us was (for otherwise we liked the stranger, especially for being kind to him) that he seemed, though not noticeably at first—except perhaps to me, who noticed everything with regard to him—to be gradually losing his general health and vitality. He did not become pale as yet; but there was a certain languor about his movements which certainly there was by no means before.

My father got more and more devoted to Count Vardalek. He helped him in his studies: and my father would hardly allow him to go away, which he did sometimes—to Trieste,* he said: he always came back, bringing us presents of strange Oriental jewellery or textures.*

I knew all kinds of people came to Trieste, Orientals included. Still, there was a strangeness and magnificence about these things which I was sure even then could not possibly have come from such a place as Trieste, memorable to me chiefly for its necktie shops.

When Vardalek was away, Gabriel was continually asking for him and talking about him. Then at the same time he seemed to regain his old vitality and spirits. Vardalek always returned looking much older, wan, and weary. Gabriel would rush to meet him, and kiss him on the mouth. Then he gave a slight shiver: and after a little while began to look quite young again.

Things continued like this for some time. My father would not hear of Vardalek's going away permanently. He came to be an inmate of our house. I indeed, and Mlle. Vonnaert also, could not help noticing what a difference there was altogether about Gabriel. But my father seemed totally blind to it.

One night I had gone downstairs to fetch something which I had left in the drawing-room. As I was going up again I passed Vardalek's room. He was playing on a piano, which had been specially put there for him, one of Chopin's nocturnes,* very beautifully: I stopped, leaning on the banisters to listen.

Something white appeared on the dark staircase. We believed in ghosts in our part. I was transfixed with terror, and clung to the banisters. What was my astonishment to see Gabriel walking slowly down the staircase, his eyes fixed as though in a trance! This terrified me even more than a ghost would. Could I believe my senses? Could that be Gabriel?

I simply could not move. Gabriel, clad in his long white night-shirt, came downstairs and opened the door. He left it open. Vardalek still continued playing, but talked as he played.

He said—this time speaking in Polish—*Nie umiem wyrazic jak ciechi kocham,**—'My darling, I fain would spare thee; but thy life is my life, and I must live, I who would rather die. Will God not have *any* mercy on me? Oh! oh! life; oh, the torture of life!' Here he struck one agonized and strange chord, then continued playing softly, 'O Gabriel, my beloved! my life, yes *life*—oh, why life? I am sure this is but a little that I demand of thee. Surely thy superabundance of life can spare a little to one who is already dead. No, stay,' he said now almost harshly, 'what must be, must be!'

Gabriel stood there quite still, with the same fixed vacant expression, in the room. He was evidently walking in his sleep. Vardalek played on: then said, 'Ah!' with a sigh of terrible agony. Then very gently, 'Go now, Gabriel; it is enough.' And Gabriel went out of the room and ascended the staircase at the same slow pace, with the same unconscious stare. Vardalek struck the piano, and although he did not play loudly, it seemed as though the strings would break. You never heard music so strange and so heart-rending!

I only know I was found by Mlle. Vonnaert in the morning, in an unconscious state, at the foot of the stairs. Was it a dream after all? I am sure now that it was not. I thought then it might be, and said nothing to any one about it. Indeed, what could I say?

Well, to let me cut a long story short, Gabriel, who had never known a moment's sickness in his life, grew ill: and we had to send to Gratz* for a doctor, who could give no explanation of Gabriel's strange illness. Gradual wasting away, he said: absolutely no organic complaint. What could this mean?

My father at last became conscious of the fact that Gabriel was ill. His anxiety was fearful. The last trace of grey faded from his hair, and it became quite white. We sent to Vienna for doctors. But all with the same result.

Gabriel was generally unconscious, and when conscious, only seemed to recognize Vardalek, who sat continually by his bedside, nursing him with the utmost tenderness.

One day I was alone in the room: and Vardalek cried suddenly, almost fiercely, 'Send for a priest at once, at once,' he repeated. 'It is now almost too late!'

Gabriel stretched out his arms spasmodically, and put them round Vardalek's neck. This was the only movement he had made for some time. Vardalek bent down and kissed him on the lips. I rushed downstairs: and the priest was sent for. When I came back Vardalek was not there. The priest administered extreme unction.* I think Gabriel was already dead, although we did not think so at the time.

Vardalek had utterly disappeared; and when we looked for him he was nowhere to be found; nor have I seen or heard of him since.

My father died very soon afterwards: suddenly aged, and bent down with grief. And so the whole of the Wronski property came into my sole possession. And here I am, an old woman, generally laughed at for keeping, in memory of Gabriel, an asylum for stray animals—and—people do not, as a rule, believe in Vampires!

R. MURRAY GILCHRIST

THE CRIMSON WEAVER

My Master and I had wandered from our track and lost ourselves on the side of a great 'edge.' It was a two-days' journey from the Valley of the Willow Brakes, and we had roamed aimlessly; eating at hollow-echoing inns where grey-haired hostesses ministered, and sleeping side by side through the dewless midsummer nights on beds of fresh-gathered heather.

Beyond a single-arched wall-less bridge that crossed a brown stream whose waters leaped straight from the upland, we reached the Domain of the Crimson Weaver. No sooner had we reached the key-stone when a beldam, wrinkled as a walnut and bald as an egg, crept from a cabin of turf and osier* and held out her hands in warning.

'Enter not the Domain of the Crimson Weaver!' she shrieked. 'One I loved entered.—I am here to warn men. Behold, I was beautiful once!'

She tore her ragged smock apart and discovered the foulness of her bosom, where the heart pulsed behind a curtain of livid skin. My Master drew money from his wallet and scattered it on the ground.

'She is mad,' he said. 'The evil she hints cannot exist. There is no fiend.'

So we passed on, but the bridge-keeper took no heed of the coins. For awhile we heard her bellowed sighs issuing from the openings of her den.

Strangely enough, the tenour of our talk changed from the moment that we left the bridge. He had been telling me of the Platonists, but when our feet pressed the sun-dried grass I was impelled to question him of love. It was the first time I had thought of the matter.

'How does passion first touch a man's life?' I asked, laying my hand on his arm.

His ruddy colour faded, he smiled wryly.

'You divine what passes in my brain,' he replied. 'I also had begun to meditate ..... But I may not tell you ..... In my boyhood—I was scarce older than you at the time—I loved the true paragon. 'Twere sacrilege to speak of the birth of passion. Let it suffice that ere I tasted of wedlock the woman died, and her death sealed for ever the door of that chamber of my heart ..... Yet, if one might see therein, there is an altar crowned with ever-burning tapers and with wreaths of unwithering asphodels.'*

By this time we had reached the skirt of a yew-forest, traversed in every direction by narrow paths. The air was moist and heavy, but ever and anon a light wind touched the tree-tops and bowed them, so that the pollen sank in golden veils to the ground.

Everywhere we saw half-ruined fountains, satyrs vomiting senilely, nymphs emptying wine upon the lambent flames of dying phœnixes, creatures that were neither satyrs nor nymphs, nor gryphins, but grotesque adminglings of all, slain by one another, with water gushing from wounds in belly and thigh.

At length the path we had chosen terminated beside an oval mere that was surrounded by a colonnade of moss-grown arches. Huge pike quivered on the muddy bed, crayfish moved sluggishly amongst the weeds.

There was an island in the middle, where a leaden Diana, more compassionate than a crocodile, caressed Actæon's horns ere delivering him to his hounds.* The huntress' head and shoulders were white with the excrement of a crowd of culvers* that moved as if entangled in a snare.

Northwards an avenue rose for the space of a mile, to fall abruptly before an azure sky. For many years the yew-mast* on the pathway had been undisturbed by human foot; it was covered with a crust of greenish lichen.

My Master pressed my fingers. 'There is some evil in the air of this place,' he said. 'I am strong, but you—you may not endure. We will return.'

''Tis an enchanted country,' I made answer, feverishly. 'At the end of yonder avenue stands the palace of the sleeping maiden who awaits the kiss. Nay, since we have pierced the country thus far, let us not draw back. You are strong, Master—no evil can touch us.'

So we fared to the place where the avenue sank, and then our eyes fell on the wondrous sight of a palace, lying in a concave pleasaunce,* all treeless, but so bestarred with fainting flowers, that neither blade of grass nor grain of earth was visible.

Then came a rustling of wings above our heads, and looking skywards I saw flying towards the house a flock of culvers like unto those that had drawn themselves over Diana's head. The hindmost bird dropped its neck, and behold it gazed upon us with the face of a mannikin!

'They are charmed birds, made thus by the whim of the Princess,' I said.

As the birds passed through the portals of a columbary* that crowned a western tower, their white wings beat against a silver bell that glistened there, and the whole valley was filled with music.

My Master trembled and crossed himself. 'In the name of our Mother,' he exclaimed, 'let us return. I dare not trust your life here.'

But a great door in front of the palace swung open, and a woman with a swaying walk came out to the terrace. She wore a robe of crimson worn into tatters at skirt-hem and shoulders. She had been forewarned of our presence, for her face turned instantly in our direction. She smiled subtly, and her smile died away into a most tempting sadness.

She caught up such remnants of her skirt as trailed behind, and strutted about with the gait of a peacock. As the sun touched the glossy fabric I saw eyes inwrought in deeper hue.

My Master still trembled, but he did not move, for the gaze of the woman was fixed upon him. His brows twisted and his white hair rose and stood erect, as if he viewed some unspeakable horror.

Stooping, with sidelong motions of the head, she approached; bringing with her the smell of such an incense as when amidst Eastern herbs burns the corse* ..... She was perfect of feature as the Diana, but her skin was deathly white and her lips fretted with pain.

She took no heed of me, but knelt at my Master's feet—a Magdalene before an impregnable priest.

'Prince and Lord, Tower of Chastity, hear!' she murmured. 'For lack of love I perish. See my robe in tatters!'

He strove to avert his face, but his eyes still dwelt upon her. She half rose and shook nut-brown tresses over his knees.

Youth came back in a flood to my Master. His shrivelled skin filled out; the dying sunlight turned to gold the whiteness of his hair. He would have raised her had I not caught his hands. The anguish of foreboding made me cry:

'One forces roughly the door of your heart's chamber. The wreaths wither, the tapers bend and fall.'

He grew old again. The Crimson Weaver turned to me.

'O marplot!'* she said laughingly, 'think not to vanquish me with folly. I am too powerful. Once that a man enter my domain he is mine.'

But I drew my Master away.

''Tis I who am strong,' I whispered. 'We will go hence at once. Surely we may find our way back to the bridge. The journey is easy.'

The woman, seeing that the remembrance of an old love was strong within him, sighed heavily, and returned to the palace. As she reached the doorway the valves opened, and I saw in a distant chamber beyond the hall an ivory loom with a golden stool.

My Master and I walked again on the track we had made in the yew-mast. But twilight was falling, and ere we could reach the pool of Diana all was in utter darkness; so at the foot of a tree, where no anthill rose, we lay down and slept.

Dreams came to me—gorgeous visions from the romances of eld.* Everywhere I sought vainly for a beloved. There was the Castle of the Ebony Dwarf, where a young queen reposed in the innermost casket of the seventh crystal cabinet; there was the Chamber of Gloom, where Lenore danced, and where I groped for ages around columns of living flesh; there was the White Minaret, where twenty-one princesses poised themselves on balls of burnished bronze; there was Melisandra's arbour, where the sacred toads crawled over the enchanted cloak.

Unrest fretted me: I woke in spiritual pain. Dawn was breaking—a bright yellow dawn, and the glades were full of vapours.

I turned to the place where my Master had lain. He was not there. I felt with my hands over his bed: it was key-cold. Terror of my loneliness overcame me, and I sat with covered face.

On the ground near my feet lay a broken riband, whereon was strung a heart of chrysolite. It enclosed a knot of ash-coloured hair—hair of the girl my Master had loved.

The mists gathered together and passed sunwards in one long many-cornered veil. When the last shred had been drawn into the great light, I gazed along the avenue, and saw the topmost bartizan* of the Crimson Weaver's palace.

It was midday ere I dared start on my search. The culvers beat about my head. I walked in pain, as though giant spiders had woven about my body.

On the terrace strange beasts—dogs and pigs with human limbs,—tore ravenously at something that lay beside the balustrade.

At sight of me they paused and lifted their snouts and bayed. Awhile afterwards the culvers rang the silver bell, and the monsters dispersed hurriedly amongst the drooping blossoms of the pleasaunce, and where they had swarmed I saw naught but a steaming sanguine pool.

I approached the house and the door fell open, admitting me to a chamber adorned with embellishments beyond the witchery of art. There I lifted my voice and cried eagerly: 'My Master, my Master, where is my Master?' The alcoves sent out a babble of echoes, blended together like a harp-cord on a dulcimer: 'My Master, my Master, where is my Master? For the love of Christ, where is my Master?' The echo replied only, 'Where is my Master?'

Above, swung a globe of topaz, where a hundred suns gambolled. From its centre a convoluted horn, held by a crimson cord, sank lower and lower. It stayed before my lips and I blew therein, and heard the sweet voices of youth chant with one accord.

'Fall open, oh doors: fall open and show the way to the princess!'

Ere the last of the echoes had died a vista opened, and at the end of an alabaster gallery I saw the Crimson Weaver at her loom. She had doffed her tattered robe for one new and lustrous as freshly drawn blood. And marvellous as her beauty had seemed before, its wonder was now increased a hundredfold.

She came towards me with the same stately walk, but there was now a lightness in her demeanour that suggested the growth of wings.

Within arm's length she curtseyed, and curtseying showed me the firmness of her shoulders, the fulness of her breast. The sight brought no pleasure: my cracking tongue appealed in agony:

'My Master, where is my Master?'

She smiled happily. 'Nay, do not trouble. He is not here. His soul talks with the culvers in the cote.* He has forgotten you. In the night we supped, and I gave him of Nepenthe.'*

'Where is my Master? Yesterday he told me of the shrine in his heart—of ever-fresh flowers—of a love dead yet living.'

Her eyebrows curved mirthfully.

''Tis foolish boys' talk,' she said. 'If you sought till the end of time you would never find him—unless I chose. Yet—if you buy of me—myself to name the price.'

I looked around hopelessly at the unimaginable riches of her home. All that I have is this Manor of the Willow Brakes—a moorish* park, an ancient house where the thatch gapes and the casements swing loose.

'My possessions are pitiable,' I said, 'but they are all yours. I give all to save him.'

'Fool, fool!' she cried. 'I have no need of gear.* If I but raise my hand, all the riches of the world fall to me. 'Tis not what I wish for.'

Into her eyes came such a glitter as the moon makes on the moist skin of a sleeping snake. The firmness of her lips relaxed; they grew child-like in their softness. The atmosphere became almost tangible: I could scarce breathe.

'What is it? All that I can do, if it be no sin.'

'Come with me to my loom,' she said, 'and if you do the thing I desire you shall see him. There is no evil in't—in past times kings have sighed for the same.'

So I followed slowly to the loom, before which she had seated herself, and watched her deftly passing crimson thread over crimson thread.

She was silent for a space, and in that space her beauty fascinated me, so that I was no longer master of myself.

'What you wish for I will give, even if it be life.'

The loom ceased. 'A kiss of the mouth, and you shall see him who passed in the night.'

She clasped her arms about my neck and pressed my lips. For one moment heaven and earth ceased to be; but there was one paradise, where we were sole governours .....

Then she moved back and drew aside the web and showed me the head of my Master, and the bleeding heart whence a crimson cord unravelled into many threads.*

'I wear men's lives,' the woman said. 'Life is necessary to me, or even I—who have existed from the beginning—must die. But yesterday I feared the end, and he came. His soul is not dead—'tis truth that it plays with my culvers.'

I fell back.

'Another kiss,' she said. 'Unless I wish, there is no escape for you. Yet you may return to your home, though my power over you shall never wane. Once more—lip to lip.'

I crouched against the wall like a terrified dog. She grew angry; her eyes darted fire.

'A kiss,' she cried, 'for the penalty!'

My poor Master's head, ugly and cadaverous, glared from the loom. I could not move.

The Crimson Weaver lifted her skirt, uncovering feet shapen as those of a vulture. I fell prostrate. With her claws she fumbled about the flesh of my breast. Moving away she bade me pass from her sight .....

So, half-dead, I lie here at the Manor of the Willow Brakes, watching hour by hour the bloody clew* ever unwinding from my heart and passing over the western hills to the Palace of the Siren.

MARY ELIZABETH BRADDON

GOOD LADY DUCAYNE

I

Bella Rolleston had made up her mind that her only chance of earning her bread and helping her mother to an occasional crust was by going out into the great unknown world as companion to a lady. She was willing to go to any lady rich enough to pay her a salary and so eccentric as to wish for a hired companion. Five shillings told off reluctantly from one of those sovereigns which were so rare with the mother and daughter, and which melted away so quickly, five solid shillings, had been handed to a smartly-dressed lady in an office in Harbeck Street, W.,* in the hope that this very Superior Person would find a situation and a salary for Miss Rolleston.

The Superior Person glanced at the two half-crowns as they lay on the table where Bella's hand had placed them, to make sure they were neither of them florins,* before she wrote a description of Bella's qualifications and requirements in a formidable-looking ledger.

'Age?' she asked, curtly.

'Eighteen, last July.'

'Any accomplishments?'

'No; I am not at all accomplished. If I were I should want to be a governess—a companion seems the lowest stage.'

'We have some highly accomplished ladies on our books as companions, or chaperon companions.'

'Oh, I know!' babbled Bella, loquacious in her youthful candour. 'But that is quite a different thing. Mother hasn't been able to afford a piano since I was twelve years old, so I'm afraid I've forgotten how to play. And I have had to help mother with her needlework, so there hasn't been much time to study.'

'Please don't waste time upon explaining what you can't do, but kindly tell me anything you can do,' said the Superior Person, crushingly, with her pen poised between delicate fingers waiting to write. 'Can you read aloud for two or three hours at a stretch? Are you active and handy, an early riser, a good walker, sweet tempered, and obliging?'

'I can say yes to all those questions except about the sweetness. I think I have a pretty good temper, and I should be anxious to oblige anybody who paid for my services. I should want them to feel that I was really earning my salary.'

'The kind of ladies who come to me would not care for a talkative companion,' said the Person, severely, having finished writing in her book. 'My connection lies chiefly among the aristocracy, and in that class considerable deference is expected.'

'Oh, of course,' said Bella; 'but it's quite different when I'm talking to you. I want to tell you all about myself once and for ever.'

'I am glad it is to be only once!' said the Person, with the edges of her lips.

The Person was of uncertain age, tightly laced in a black silk gown. She had a powdery complexion and a handsome clump of somebody else's hair on the top of her head. It may be that Bella's girlish freshness and vivacity had an irritating effect upon nerves weakened by an eight hours day in that over-heated second floor in Harbeck Street. To Bella the official apartment, with its Brussels carpet,* velvet curtains and velvet chairs, and French clock, ticking loud on the marble chimney-piece, suggested the luxury of a palace, as compared with another second floor in Walworth* where Mrs. Rolleston and her daughter had managed to exist for the last six years.

'Do you think you have anything on your books that would suit me?' faltered Bella, after a pause.

'Oh, dear, no; I have nothing in view at present,' answered the Person, who had swept Bella's half-crowns into a drawer, absent-mindedly, with the tips of her fingers. 'You see, you are so very unformed—so much too young to be companion to a lady of position. It is a pity you have not enough education for a nursery governess; that would be more in your line.'

'And do you think it will be very long before you can get me a situation?' asked Bella, doubtfully.

'I really cannot say. Have you any particular reason for being so impatient—not a love affair, I hope?'

'A love affair!' cried Bella, with flaming cheeks. 'What utter nonsense. I want a situation because mother is poor, and I hate being a burden to her. I want a salary that I can share with her.'

'There won't be much margin for sharing in the salary you are likely to get at your age—and with your—very—unformed manners,' said the Person, who found Bella's peony cheeks, bright eyes, and unbridled vivacity more and more oppressive.

'Perhaps if you'd be kind enough to give me back the fee I could take it to an agency where the connection isn't quite so aristocratic,' said Bella, who—as she told her mother in her recital of the interview—was determined not to be sat upon.

'You will find no agency that can do more for you than mine,' replied the Person, whose harpy* fingers never relinquished coin. 'You will have to wait for your opportunity. Yours is an exceptional case: but I will bear you in mind, and if anything suitable offers I will write to you. I cannot say more than that.'

The half-contemptuous bend of the stately head, weighted with borrowed hair, indicated the end of the interview. Bella went back to Walworth—tramped sturdily every inch of the way in the September afternoon—and 'took off'* the Superior Person for the amusement of her mother and the landlady, who lingered in the shabby little sitting-room after bringing in the tea-tray, to applaud Miss Rolleston's 'taking off.'

'Dear, dear, what a mimic she is!' said the landlady. 'You ought to have let her go on the stage, mum. She might have made her fortune as a hactress.'

II

BELLA waited and hoped, and listened for the postman's knocks which brought such store of letters for the parlours* and the first floor, and so few for that humble second floor, where mother and daughter sat sewing with hand and with wheel and treadle,* for the greater part of the day. Mrs. Rolleston was a lady by birth and education; but it had been her bad fortune to marry a scoundrel; for the last half-dozen years she had been that worst of widows, a wife whose husband had deserted her. Happily, she was courageous, industrious, and a clever needle-woman; and she had been able just to earn a living for herself and her only child, by making mantles and cloaks for a West-end house. It was not a luxurious living. Cheap lodgings in a shabby street off the Walworth Road, scanty dinners, homely* food, well-worn raiment, had been the portion of mother and daughter; but they loved each other so dearly, and Nature had made them both so light-hearted, that they had contrived somehow to be happy.

But now this idea of going out into the world as companion to some fine lady had rooted itself into Bella's mind, and although she idolized her mother, and although the parting of mother and daughter must needs tear two loving hearts into shreds, the girl longed for enterprise* and change and excitement, as the pages of old longed to be knights, and to start for the Holy Land to break a lance with the infidel.

She grew tired of racing downstairs every time the postman knocked, only to be told 'nothing for you, miss,' by the smudgy-faced drudge who picked up the letters from the passage floor. 'Nothing for you, miss,' grinned the lodging-house drudge, till at last Bella took heart of grace* and walked up to Harbeck Street, and asked the Superior Person how it was that no situation had been found for her.

'You are too young,' said the Person, 'and you want a salary.'

'Of course I do,' answered Bella; 'don't other people want salaries?'

'Young ladies of your age generally want a comfortable home.'

'I don't,' snapped Bella; 'I want to help mother.'

'You can call again this day week,' said the Person; 'or, if I hear of anything in the meantime, I will write to you.'

No letter came from the Person, and in exactly a week Bella put on her neatest hat, the one that had been seldomest caught in the rain, and trudged off to Harbeck Street.

It was a dull October afternoon, and there was a greyness in the air which might turn to fog before night. The Walworth Road shops gleamed brightly through that grey atmosphere, and though to a young lady reared in Mayfair or Belgravia such shop-windows would have been unworthy of a glance, they were a snare and temptation for Bella. There were so many things that she longed for, and would never be able to buy.

Harbeck Street is apt to be empty at this dead season of the year, a long, long street, an endless perspective of eminently respectable houses. The Person's office was at the further end, and Bella looked down that long, grey vista almost despairingly, more tired than usual with the trudge from Walworth. As she looked, a carriage passed her, an old-fashioned, yellow chariot, on cee springs,* drawn by a pair of high grey horses, with the stateliest of coachmen driving them, and a tall footman sitting by his side.

'It looks like the fairy god-mother's coach,' thought Bella. 'I shouldn't wonder if it began by being a pumpkin.'

It was a surprise when she reached the Person's door to find the yellow chariot standing before it, and the tall footman waiting near the doorstep. She was almost afraid to go in and meet the owner of that splendid carriage. She had caught only a glimpse of its occupant as the chariot rolled by, a plumed bonnet, a patch of ermine.

The Person's smart page ushered her upstairs and knocked at the official door. 'Miss Rolleston,' he announced, apologetically, while Bella waited outside.

'Show her in,' said the Person, quickly; and then Bella heard her murmuring something in a low voice to her client.

Bella went in fresh, blooming, a living image of youth and hope, and before she looked at the Person her gaze was riveted by the owner of the chariot.

Never had she seen anyone as old as the old lady sitting by the Person's fire: a little old figure, wrapped from chin to feet in an ermine mantle; a withered, old face under a plumed bonnet—a face so wasted by age that it seemed only a pair of eyes and a peaked* chin. The nose was peaked, too, but between the sharply pointed chin and the great, shining eyes, the small, aquiline nose was hardly visible.

'This is Miss Rolleston, Lady Ducayne.'

Claw-like fingers, flashing with jewels, lifted a double eyeglass* to Lady Ducayne's shining black eyes, and through the glasses Bella saw those unnaturally bright eyes magnified to a gigantic size, and glaring at her awfully.

'Miss Torpinter has told me all about you,' said the old voice that belonged to the eyes. 'Have you good health? Are you strong and active, able to eat well, sleep well, walk well, able to enjoy all that there is good in life?'

'I have never known what it is to be ill, or idle,' answered Bella.

'Then I think you will do for me.'

'Of course, in the event of references being perfectly satisfactory,' put in the Person.

'I don't want references. The young woman looks frank and innocent. I'll take her on trust.'

'So like you, dear Lady Ducayne,' murmured Miss Torpinter.

'I want a strong young woman whose health will give me no trouble.'

'You have been so unfortunate in that respect,' cooed the Person, whose voice and manner were subdued to a melting sweetness by the old woman's presence.

'Yes, I've been rather unlucky,' grunted Lady Ducayne.

'But I am sure Miss Rolleston will not disappoint you, though certainly after your unpleasant experience with Miss Tomson, who looked the picture of health—and Miss Blandy, who said she had never seen a doctor since she was vaccinated—'*

'Lies, no doubt,' muttered Lady Ducayne, and then turning to Bella, she asked, curtly, 'You don't mind spending the winter in Italy, I suppose?'

In Italy! The very word was magical. Bella's fair young face flushed crimson.

'It has been the dream of my life to see Italy,' she gasped.

From Walworth to Italy! How far, how impossible such a journey had seemed to that romantic dreamer.

'Well, your dream will be realized. Get yourself ready to leave Charing Cross by the train deluxe this day week at eleven. Be sure you are at the station a quarter before the hour. My people will look after you and your luggage.'

Lady Ducayne rose from her chair, assisted by her crutch-stick,* and Miss Torpinter escorted her to the door.

'And with regard to salary?' questioned the Person on the way.

'Salary, oh, the same as usual—and if the young woman wants a quarter's pay in advance you can write to me for a cheque,' Lady Ducayne answered, carelessly.

Miss Torpinter went all the way downstairs with her client, and waited to see her seated in the yellow chariot. When she came upstairs again she was slightly out of breath, and she had resumed that superior manner which Bella had found so crushing.

'You may think yourself uncommonly lucky, Miss Rolleston,' she said. 'I have dozens of young ladies on my books whom I might have recommended for this situation—but I remembered having told you to call this afternoon—and I thought I would give you a chance. Old Lady Ducayne is one of the best people on my books. She gives her companion a hundred a year, and pays all travelling expenses. You will live in the lap of luxury.'

'A hundred a year! How too lovely! Shall I have to dress very grandly? Does Lady Ducayne keep much company?'

'At her age! No, she lives in seclusion—in her own apartments—her French maid, her footman, her medical attendant, her courier.'

'Why did those other companions leave her?' asked Bella.

'Their health broke down!'

'Poor things, and so they had to leave?'

'Yes, they had to leave. I suppose you would like a quarter's salary in advance?'

'Oh, yes, please. I shall have things to buy.'

'Very well, I will write for Lady Ducayne's cheque, and I will send you the balance—after deducting my commission for the year.'

'To be sure, I had forgotten the commission.'

'You don't suppose I keep this office for pleasure.'

'Of course not,' murmured Bella, remembering the five shillings entrance fee; but nobody could expect a hundred a year and a winter in Italy for five shillings.

III

'From Miss Rolleston, at Cap Ferrino,* to Mrs. Rolleston, in Beresford Street, Walworth.

'How I wish you could see this place, dearest; the blue sky, the olive woods, the orange and lemon orchards between the cliffs and the sea—sheltering in the hollow of the great hills—and with summer waves dancing up to the narrow ridge of pebbles and weeds which is the Italian idea of a beach! Oh, how I wish you could see it all, mother dear, and bask in this sunshine, that makes it so difficult to believe the date at the head of this paper. November! The air is like an English June—the sun is so hot that I can't walk a few yards without an umbrella. And to think of you at Walworth while I am here! I could cry at the thought that perhaps you will never see this lovely coast, this wonderful sea, these summer flowers that bloom in winter. There is a hedge of pink geraniums under my window, mother—a thick, rank hedge, as if the flowers grew wild—and there are Dijon roses* climbing over arches and palisades all along the terrace—a rose garden full of bloom in November! Just picture it all! You could never imagine the luxury of this hotel. It is nearly new, and has been built and decorated regardless of expense. Our rooms are upholstered in pale blue satin, which shows up Lady Ducayne's parchment complexion; but as she sits all day in a corner of the balcony basking in the sun, except when she is in her carriage, and all the evening in her armchair close to the fire, and never sees anyone but her own people, her complexion matters very little.

'She has the handsomest suite of rooms in the hotel. My bedroom is inside hers, the sweetest room—all blue satin and white lace—white enamelled furniture, looking-glasses on every wall, till I know my pert little profile as I never knew it before. The room was really meant for Lady Ducayne's dressing-room, but she ordered one of the blue satin couches to be arranged as a bed for me—the prettiest little bed, which I can wheel near the window on sunny mornings, as it is on castors and easily moved about. I feel as if Lady Ducayne were a funny old grandmother, who had suddenly appeared in my life, very, very rich, and very, very kind.

'She is not at all exacting. I read aloud to her a good deal, and she dozes and nods while I read. Sometimes I hear her moaning in her sleep—as if she had troublesome dreams. When she is tired of my reading she orders Francine, her maid, to read a French novel to her, and I hear her chuckle and groan now and then, as if she were more interested in those books than in Dickens or Scott.* My French is not good enough to follow Francine, who reads very quickly. I have a great deal of liberty, for Lady Ducayne often tells me to run away and amuse myself; I roam about the hills for hours. Everything is so lovely. I lose myself in olive woods, always climbing up and up towards the pine woods above—and above the pines there are the snow mountains that just show their white peaks above the dark hills. Oh, you poor dear, how can I ever make you understand what this place is like—you, whose poor, tired eyes have only the opposite side of Beresford Street? Sometimes I go no farther than the terrace in front of the hotel, which is a favourite lounging-place with everybody. The gardens lie below, and the tennis courts where I sometimes play with a very nice girl, the only person in the hotel with whom I have made friends. She is a year older than I, and has come to Cap Ferrino with her brother, a doctor—or a medical student, who is going to be a doctor. He passed his M.B. exam at Edinburgh* just before they left home, Lotta told me. He came to Italy entirely on his sister's account. She had a troublesome chest attack last summer and was ordered to winter abroad. They are orphans, quite alone in the world, and so fond of each other. It is very nice for me to have such a friend as Lotta. She is so thoroughly respectable. I can't help using that word, for some of the girls in this hotel go on in a way that I know you would shudder at. Lotta was brought up by an aunt, deep down in the country, and knows hardly anything about life. Her brother won't allow her to read a novel, French or English, that he has not read and approved.

'"He treats me like a child," she told me, "but I don't mind, for it's nice to know somebody loves me, and cares about what I do, and even about my thoughts."

'Perhaps this is what makes some girls so eager to marry—the want of someone strong and brave and honest and true to care for them and order them about. I want no one, mother darling, for I have you, and you are all the world to me. No husband could ever come between us two. If I ever were to marry he would have only the second place in my heart. But I don't suppose I ever shall marry, or even know what it is like to have an offer of marriage. No young man can afford to marry a penniless girl nowadays. Life is too expensive.

'Mr. Stafford, Lotta's brother, is very clever, and very kind. He thinks it is rather hard for me to have to live with such an old woman as Lady Ducayne, but then he does not know how poor we are—you and I—and what a wonderful life this seems to me in this lovely place. I feel a selfish wretch for enjoying all my luxuries, while you, who want them so much more than I, have none of them—hardly know what they are like—do you, dearest?—for my scamp of a father began to go to the dogs soon after you were married, and since then life has been all trouble and care and struggle for you.'

This letter was written when Bella had been less than a month at Cap Ferrino, before the novelty had worn off the landscape, and before the pleasure of luxurious surroundings had begun to cloy. She wrote to her mother every week, such long letters as girls who have lived in closest companionship with a mother alone can write; letters that are like a diary of heart and mind. She wrote gaily always; but when the new year began Mrs. Rolleston thought she detected a note of melancholy under all those lively details about the place and the people.

'My poor girl is getting home-sick,' she thought. 'Her heart is in Beresford Street.'

It might be that she missed her new friend and companion, Lotta Stafford, who had gone with her brother for a little tour to Genoa and Spezzia, and as far as Pisa.* They were to return before February; but in the meantime Bella might naturally feel very solitary among all those strangers, whose manners and doings she described so well.

The mother's instinct had been true. Bella was not so happy as she had been in that first flush of wonder and delight which followed the change from Walworth to the Riviera. Somehow, she knew not how, lassitude had crept upon her. She no longer loved to climb the hills, no longer flourished her orange stick in sheer gladness of heart as her light feet skipped over the rough ground and the coarse grass on the mountain side. The odour of rosemary and thyme, the fresh breath of the sea, no longer filled her with rapture. She thought of Beresford Street and her mother's face with a sick longing. They were so far—so far away! And then she thought of Lady Ducayne, sitting by the heaped-up olive logs in the over-heated salon—thought of that wizened-nut-cracker profile, and those gleaming eyes, with an invincible horror.

Visitors at the hotel had told her that the air of Cap Ferrino was relaxing—better suited to age than to youth, to sickness than to health. No doubt it was so. She was not so well as she had been at Walworth; but she told herself that she was suffering only from the pain of separation from the dear companion of her girlhood, the mother who had been nurse, sister, friend, flatterer, all things in this world to her. She had shed many tears over that parting, had spent many a melancholy hour on the marble terrace with yearning eyes looking westward, and with her heart's desire a thousand miles away.

She was sitting in her favourite spot, an angle* at the eastern end of the terrace, a quiet little nook sheltered by orange trees, when she heard a couple of Riviera habitués talking in the garden below. They were sitting on a bench against the terrace wall.

She had no idea of listening to their talk, till the sound of Lady Ducayne's name attracted her, and then she listened without any thought of wrong-doing. They were talking no secrets—just casually discussing an hotel acquaintance.

They were two elderly people whom Bella only knew by sight. An English clergyman who had wintered abroad for half his lifetime; a stout, comfortable, well-to-do spinster, whose chronic bronchitis obliged her to migrate annually.

'I have met her about Italy for the last ten years,' said the lady; 'but have never found out her real age.'

'I put her down at a hundred—not a year less,' replied the parson. 'Her reminiscences all go back to the Regency.* She was evidently then in her zenith; and I have heard her say things that showed she was in Parisian society when the First Empire was at its best—before Josephine was divorced.'*

'She doesn't talk much now.'

'No; there's not much life left in her. She is wise in keeping herself secluded. I only wonder that wicked old quack, her Italian doctor, didn't finish her off years ago.'

'I should think it must be the other way, and that he keeps her alive.'

'My dear Miss Manders, do you think foreign quackery ever kept anybody alive?'

'Well, there she is—and she never goes anywhere without him. He certainly has an unpleasant countenance.'

'Unpleasant,' echoed the parson, 'I don't believe the foul fiend himself can beat him in ugliness. I pity that poor young woman who has to live between old Lady Ducayne and Dr. Parravicini.*'

'But the old lady is very good to her companions.'

'No doubt. She is very free with her cash; the servants call her good Lady Ducayne. She is a withered old female Crœsus,* and knows she'll never be able to get through her money, and doesn't relish the idea of other people enjoying it when she's in her coffin. People who live to be as old as she is become slavishly attached to life. I daresay she's generous to those poor girls—but she can't make them happy. They die in her service.'

'Don't say they, Mr. Carton; I know that one poor girl died at Mentone* last spring.'

'Yes, and another poor girl died in Rome three years ago. I was there at the time. Good Lady Ducayne left her there in an English family. The girl had every comfort. The old woman was very liberal to her—but she died. I tell you, Miss Manders, it is not good for any young woman to live with two such horrors as Lady Ducayne and Parravicini.'

They talked of other things—but Bella hardly heard them. She sat motionless, and a cold wind seemed to come down upon her from the mountains and to creep up to her from the sea, till she shivered as she sat there in the sunshine, in the shelter of the orange trees in the midst of all that beauty and brightness.

Yes, they were uncanny, certainly, the pair of them—she so like an aristocratic witch in her withered old age; he of no particular age, with a face that was more like a waxen mask than any human countenance Bella had ever seen. What did it matter? Old age is venerable, and worthy of all reverence; and Lady Ducayne had been very kind to her.

Dr. Parravicini was a harmless, inoffensive student, who seldom looked up from the book he was reading. He had his private sitting-room, where he made experiments in chemistry and natural science—perhaps in alchemy. What could it matter to Bella? He had always been polite to her, in his far-off way. She could not be more happily placed than she was—in this palatial hotel, with this rich old lady.

No doubt she missed the young English girl who had been so friendly, and it might be that she missed the girl's brother, for Mr. Stafford had talked to her a good deal—had interested himself in the books she was reading, and her manner of amusing herself when she was not on duty.

'You must come to our little salon when you are "off," as the hospital nurses call it, and we can have some music. No doubt you play and sing?' upon which Bella had to own with a blush of shame that she had forgotten how to play the piano ages ago.

'Mother and I used to sing duets sometimes between the lights,* without accompaniment,' she said, and the tears came into her eyes as she thought of the humble room, the half-hour's respite from work, the sewing-machine standing where a piano ought to have been, and her mother's plaintive voice, so sweet, so true, so dear.

Sometimes she found herself wondering whether she would ever see that beloved mother again. Strange forebodings came into her mind. She was angry with herself for giving way to melancholy thoughts.

One day she questioned Lady Ducayne's French maid about those two companions who had died within three years.

'They were poor, feeble creatures,' Francine told her. 'They looked fresh and bright enough when they came to Miladi;* but they ate too much, and they were lazy. They died of luxury and idleness. Miladi was too kind to them. They had nothing to do; and so they took to fancying things; fancying the air didn't suit them, that they couldn't sleep.'

'I sleep well enough, but I have had a strange dream several times since I have been in Italy.'

'Ah, you had better not begin to think about dreams, or you will be like those other girls. They were dreamers—and they dreamt themselves into the cemetery.'

The dream troubled her a little, not because it was a ghastly or frightening dream, but on account of sensations which she had never felt before in sleep—a whirring of wheels that went round in her brain, a great noise like a whirlwind, but rhythmical like the ticking of a gigantic clock: and then in the midst of this uproar as of winds and waves she seemed to sink into a gulf of unconsciousness, out of sleep into far deeper sleep—total extinction. And then, after that blank interval, there had come the sound of voices, and then again the whirr of wheels, louder and louder—and again the blank—and then she knew no more till morning, when she awoke, feeling languid and oppressed.*

She told Dr. Parravicini of her dream one day, on the only occasion when she wanted his professional advice. She had suffered rather severely from the mosquitoes before Christmas—and had been almost frightened at finding a wound upon her arm which she could only attribute to the venomous sting of one of these torturers. Parravicini put on his glasses, and scrutinized the angry mark on the round, white arm, as Bella stood before him and Lady Ducayne with her sleeve rolled up above her elbow.

'Yes, that's rather more than a joke,' he said, 'he has caught you on the top of a vein. What a vampire! But there's no harm done, signorina, nothing that a little dressing of mine won't heal. You must always show me any bite of this nature. It might be dangerous if neglected. These creatures feed on poison and disseminate it.'

'And to think that such tiny creatures can bite like this,' said Bella; 'my arm looks as if it had been cut by a knife.'

'If I were to show you a mosquito's sting under my microscope you wouldn't be surprised at that,' replied Parravicini.

Bella had to put up with the mosquito bites, even when they came on the top of a vein, and produced that ugly wound. The wound recurred now and then at longish intervals, and Bella found Dr. Parravicini's dressing a speedy cure. If he were the quack his enemies called him, he had at least a light hand and a delicate touch in performing this small operation.

'Bella Rolleston to Mrs. Rolleston.—April 14th.

'Ever Dearest,—Behold the cheque for my second quarter's salary—five and twenty pounds. There is no one to pinch off a whole tenner for a year's commission as there was last time, so it is all for you, mother, dear. I have plenty of pocket-money in hand from the cash I brought away with me, when you insisted on my keeping more than I wanted. It isn't possible to spend money here—except on occasional tips to servants, or sous* to beggars and children—unless one had lots to spend, for everything one would like to buy—tortoise-shell, coral, lace—is so ridiculously dear that only a millionaire ought to look at it. Italy is a dream of beauty: but for shopping, give me Newington Causeway.*

'You ask me so earnestly if I am quite well that I fear my letters must have been very dull lately. Yes, dear, I am well—but I am not quite so strong as I was when I used to trudge to the West-end to buy half a pound of tea—just for a constitutional walk—or to Dulwich to look at the pictures. Italy is relaxing; and I feel what the people here call "slack."* But I fancy I can see your dear face looking worried as you read this. Indeed, and indeed,* I am not ill. I am only a little tired of this lovely scene—as I suppose one might get tired of looking at one of Turner's pictures* if it hung on a wall that was always opposite one. I think of you every hour in every day—think of you and our homely little room—our dear little shabby parlour, with the arm-chairs from the wreck of your old home, and Dick singing in his cage over the sewing-machine. Dear, shrill, maddening Dick, who, we flattered ourselves, was so passionately fond of us. Do tell me in your next that he is well.

'My friend Lotta and her brother never came back after all. They went from Pisa to Rome. Happy mortals! And they are to be on the Italian lakes in May; which lake was not decided when Lotta last wrote to me. She has been a charming correspondent, and has confided all her little flirtations to me. We are all to go to Bellaggio* next week—by Genoa and Milan. Isn't that lovely? Lady Ducayne travels by the easiest stages—except when she is bottled up in the train de luxe. We shall stop two days at Genoa and one at Milan. What a bore I shall be to you with my talk about Italy when I come home.

'Love and love—and ever more love from your adoring, BELLA.'

IV

HERBERT STAFFORD and his sister had often talked of the pretty English girl with her fresh complexion, which made such a pleasant touch of rosy colour among all those sallow faces at the Grand Hotel. The young doctor thought of her with a compassionate tenderness—her utter loneliness in that great hotel where there were so many people, her bondage to that old, old woman, where everybody else was free to think of nothing but enjoying life. It was a hard fate; and the poor child was evidently devoted to her mother, and felt the pain of separation—'only two of them, and very poor, and all the world to each other,' he thought.

Lotta told him one morning that they were to meet again at Bellaggio. 'The old thing and her court are to be there before we are,' she said. 'I shall be charmed to have Bella again. She is so bright and gay—in spite of an occasional touch of home-sickness. I never took to a girl on a short acquaintance as I did to her.'

'I like her best when she is home-sick,' said Herbert; 'for then I am sure she has a heart.'

'What have you to do with hearts, except for dissection? Don't forget that Bella is an absolute pauper. She told me in confidence that her mother makes mantles for a West-end shop. You can hardly have a lower depth than that.'

'I shouldn't think any less of her if her mother made match-boxes.'

'Not in the abstract—of course not. Match-boxes are honest labour. But you couldn't marry a girl whose mother makes mantles.'

'We haven't come to the consideration of that question yet,' answered Herbert, who liked to provoke his sister.

In two years' hospital practice he had seen too much of the grim realities of life to retain any prejudices about rank. Cancer, phthisis, gangrene,* leave a man with little respect for the outward differences which vary the husk of humanity. The kernel is always the same—fearfully and wonderfully made—a subject for pity and terror.*

Mr. Stafford and his sister arrived at Bellaggio in a fair May evening. The sun was going down as the steamer approached the pier; and all that glory of purple bloom which curtains every wall at this season of the year flushed and deepened in the glowing light. A group of ladies were standing on the pier watching the arrivals, and among them Herbert saw a pale face that startled him out of his wonted composure.

'There she is,' murmured Lotta, at his elbow, 'but how dreadfully changed. She looks a wreck.'

They were shaking hands with her a few minutes later, and a flush had lighted up her poor pinched face in the pleasure of meeting.

'I thought you might come this evening,' she said. 'We have been here a week.'

She did not add that she had been there every evening to watch the boat in, and a good many times during the day. The Grand Bretagne was close by, and it had been easy for her to creep to the pier when the boat bell rang. She felt a joy in meeting these people again; a sense of being with friends; a confidence which Lady Ducayne's goodness had never inspired in her.

'Oh, you poor darling, how awfully ill you must have been,' exclaimed Lotta, as the two girls embraced.

Bella tried to answer, but her voice was choked with tears.

'What has been the matter, dear? That horrid influenza, I suppose?'

'No, no, I have not been ill—I have only felt a little weaker than I used to be. I don't think the air of Cap Ferrino quite agreed with me.'

'It must have disagreed with you abominably. I never saw such a change in anyone. Do let Herbert doctor* you. He is fully qualified, you know. He prescribed for ever so many influenza patients at the Londres.* They were glad to get advice from an English doctor in a friendly way.'

'I am sure he must be very clever!' faltered Bella, 'but there is really nothing the matter. I am not ill, and if I were ill, Lady Ducayne's physician—'

'That dreadful man with the yellow face? I would as soon one of the Borgias* prescribed for me. I hope you haven't been taking any of his medicines.'

'No, dear, I have taken nothing. I have never complained of being ill.'

This was said while they were all three walking to the hotel. The Staffords' rooms had been secured in advance, pretty ground-floor rooms, opening into the garden. Lady Ducayne's statelier apartments were on the floor above.

'I believe these rooms are just under ours,' said Bella.

'Then it will be all the easier for you to run down to us,' replied Lotta, which was not really the case, as the grand staircase was in the centre of the hotel.

'Oh, I shall find it easy enough,' said Bella. 'I'm afraid you'll have too much of my society. Lady Ducayne sleeps away half the day in this warm weather, so I have a good deal of idle time; and I get awfully moped* thinking of mother and home.'

Her voice broke upon the last word. She could not have thought of that poor lodging which went by the name of home more tenderly had it been the most beautiful that art and wealth ever created. She moped and pined in this lovely garden, with the sunlit lake and the romantic hills spreading out their beauty before her. She was home-sick and she had dreams: or, rather, an occasional recurrence of that one bad dream with all its strange sensations—it was more like a hallucination than dreaming—the whirring of wheels; the sinking into an abyss; the struggling back to consciousness. She had the dream shortly before she left Cap Ferrino, but not since she had come to Bellaggio, and she began to hope the air in this lake district suited her better, and that those strange sensations would never return.

Mr. Stafford wrote a prescription and had it made up at the chemist's near the hotel. It was a powerful tonic, and after two bottles, and a row or two on the lake, and some rambling over the hills and in the meadows where the spring flowers made earth seem paradise, Bella's spirits and looks improved as if by magic.

'It is a wonderful tonic,' she said, but perhaps in her heart of hearts she knew that the doctor's kind voice, and the friendly hand that helped her in and out of the boat, and the watchful care that went with her by land and lake, had something to do with her cure.

'I hope you don't forget that her mother makes mantles,' Lotta said, warningly.

'Or match-boxes: it is just the same thing, so far as I am concerned.'

'You mean that in no circumstances could you think of marrying her?'

'I mean that if ever I love a woman well enough to think of marrying her, riches or rank will count for nothing with me. But I fear—I fear your poor friend may not live to be any man's wife.'

'Do you think her so very ill?'

He sighed, and left the question unanswered.

One day, while they were gathering wild hyacinths in an upland meadow, Bella told Mr. Stafford about her bad dream.

'It is curious only because it is hardly like a dream,' she said. 'I daresay you could find some common-sense reason for it. The position of my head on my pillow, or the atmosphere, or something.'

And then she described her sensations; how in the midst of sleep there came a sudden sense of suffocation;* and then those whirring wheels, so loud, so terrible; and then a blank, and then a coming back to waking consciousness.

'Have you ever had chloroform given you—by a dentist, for instance?'

'Never—Dr. Parravicini asked me that question one day.'

'Lately?'

'No, long ago, when we were in the train de luxe.'

'Has Dr. Parravicini prescribed for you since you began to feel weak and ill?'

'Oh, he has given me a tonic from time to time, but I hate medicine, and took very little of the stuff. And then I am not ill, only weaker than I used to be. I was ridiculously strong and well when I lived at Walworth, and used to take long walks every day. Mother made me take those tramps to Dulwich or Norwood, for fear I should suffer from too much sewing-machine; sometimes—but very seldom—she went with me. She was generally toiling at home while I was enjoying fresh air and exercise. And she was very careful about our food—that, however plain it was, it should be always nourishing and ample. I owe it to her care that I grew up such a great, strong creature.'

'You don't look great or strong now, you poor dear,' said Lotta.

'I'm afraid Italy doesn't agree with me.'

'Perhaps it is not Italy, but being cooped up with Lady Ducayne that has made you ill.'

'But I am never cooped up. Lady Ducayne is absurdly kind, and lets me roam about or sit in the balcony all day if I like. I have read more novels since I have been with her than in all the rest of my life.'

'Then she is very different from the average old lady, who is usually a slave-driver,' said Stafford. 'I wonder why she carries a companion about with her if she has so little need of society.'

'Oh, I am only part of her state. She is inordinately rich—and the salary she gives me doesn't count. Apropos of Dr. Parravicini, I know he is a clever doctor, for he cures my horrid mosquito bites.'

'A little ammonia would do that, in the early stage of the mischief. But there are no mosquitoes to trouble you now.'

'Oh, yes, there are; I had a bite just before we left Cap Ferrino.'

She pushed up her loose lawn sleeve,* and exhibited a scar, which he scrutinized intently, with a surprised and puzzled look.

'This is no mosquito bite,' he said.

'Oh, yes it is—unless there are snakes or adders at Cap Ferrino.'

'It is not a bite at all. You are trifling with me. Miss Rolleston—you have allowed that wretched Italian quack to bleed* you. They killed the greatest man in modern Europe* that way, remember. How very foolish of you.'

'I was never bled in my life, Mr. Stafford.'

'Nonsense! Let me look at your other arm. Are there any more mosquito bites?'

'Yes; Dr. Parravicini says I have a bad skin for healing, and that the poison acts more virulently with me than with most people.'

Stafford examined both her arms in the broad sunlight, scars new and old.

'You have been very badly bitten, Miss Rolleston,' he said, 'and if ever I find the mosquito I shall make him smart. But, now tell me, my dear girl, on your word of honour, tell me as you would tell a friend who is sincerely anxious for your health and happiness—as you would tell your mother if she were here to question you—have you no knowledge of any cause for these scars except mosquito bites—no suspicion even?'

'No, indeed! No, upon my honour! I have never seen a mosquito biting my arm. One never does see the horrid little fiends. But I have heard them trumpeting under the curtains, and I know that I have often had one of the pestilent wretches buzzing about me.'

Later in the day Bella and her friends were sitting at tea in the garden, while Lady Ducayne took her afternoon drive with her doctor.

'How long do you mean to stop with Lady Ducayne, Miss Rolleston?' Herbert Stafford asked, after a thoughtful silence, breaking suddenly upon the trivial talk of the two girls.

'As long as she will go on paying me twenty-five pounds a quarter.'

'Even if you feel your health breaking down in her service?'

'It is not the service that has injured my health. You can see that I have really nothing to do—to read aloud for an hour or so once or twice a week; to write a letter once in a way to a London tradesman. I shall never have such an easy time with anybody else. And nobody else would give me a hundred a year.'

'Then you mean to go on till you break down; to die at your post?'

'Like the other two companions? No! If ever I feel seriously ill—really ill—I shall put myself in a train and go back to Walworth without stopping.'

'What about the other two companions?'

'They both died. It was very unlucky for Lady Ducayne. That's why she engaged me; she chose me because I was ruddy and robust. She must feel rather disgusted at my having grown white and weak. By-the-bye, when I told her about the good your tonic had done me, she said she would like to see you and have a little talk with you about her own case.'

'And I should like to see Lady Ducayne. When did she say this?'

'The day before yesterday.'

'Will you ask her if she will see me this evening?'

'With pleasure! I wonder what you will think of her? She looks rather terrible to a stranger; but Dr. Parravicini says she was once a famous beauty.'

It was nearly ten o'clock when Mr. Stafford was summoned by message from Lady Ducayne, whose courier came to conduct him to her ladyship's salon. Bella was reading aloud when the visitor was admitted; and he noticed the languor in the low, sweet tones, the evident effort.

'Shut up the book,' said the querulous old voice. 'You are beginning to drawl like Miss Blandy.'

Stafford saw a small, bent figure crouching over the piled-up olive logs; a shrunken old figure in a gorgeous garment of black and crimson brocade, a skinny throat emerging from a mass of old Venetian lace, clasped with diamonds that flashed like fire-flies as the trembling old head turned towards him.

The eyes that looked at him out of the face were almost as bright as the diamonds—the only living feature in that narrow parchment mask. He had seen terrible faces in the hospital—faces on which disease had set dreadful marks—but he had never seen a face that impressed him so painfully as this withered countenance, with its indescribable horror of death outlived, a face that should have been hidden under a coffin-lid years and years ago.

The Italian physician was standing on the other side of the fireplace, smoking a cigarette, and looking down at the little old woman brooding over the hearth as if he were proud of her.

'Good evening, Mr. Stafford; you can go to your room, Bella, and write your everlasting letter to your mother at Walworth,' said Lady Ducayne. 'I believe she writes a page about every wild flower she discovers in the woods and meadows. I don't know what else she can find to write about,' she added, as Bella quietly withdrew to the pretty little bedroom opening out of Lady Ducayne's spacious apartment. Here, as at Cap Ferrino, she slept in a room adjoining the old lady's.

'You are a medical man, I understand, Mr. Stafford.'

'I am a qualified practitioner, but I have not begun to practise.'

'You have begun upon my companion, she tells me.'

'I have prescribed for her, certainly, and I am happy to find my prescription has done her good; but I look upon that improvement as temporary. Her case will require more drastic treatment.'

'Never mind her case. There is nothing the matter with the girl—absolutely nothing—except girlish nonsense; too much liberty and not enough work.'

'I understand that two of your ladyship's previous companions died of the same disease,' said Stafford, looking first at Lady Ducayne, who gave her tremulous old head an impatient jerk, and then at Parravicini, whose yellow complexion had paled a little under Stafford's scrutiny.

'Don't bother me about my companions, sir,' said Lady Ducayne. 'I sent for you to consult you about myself—not about a parcel of anæmic girls. You are young, and medicine is a progressive science, the newspapers tell me. Where have you studied?'

'In Edinburgh—and in Paris.'

'Two good schools. And you know all the new-fangled theories, the modern discoveries—that remind one of the mediæval witchcraft, of Albertus Magnus,* and George Ripley;* you have studied hypnotism—electricity?'

'And the transfusion of blood,'* said Stafford, very slowly, looking at Parravicini.

'Have you made any discovery that teaches you to prolong human life—any elixir—any mode of treatment? I want my life prolonged, young man. That man there has been my physician for thirty years. He does all he can to keep me alive—after his lights.* He studies all the new theories of all the scientists—but he is old; he gets older every day—his brain-power is going—he is bigoted—prejudiced—can't receive new ideas—can't grapple with new systems. He will let me die if I am not on my guard against him.'

'You are of an unbelievable ingratitude, Ecclenza,'* said Parravicini.

'Oh, you needn't complain. I have paid you thousands to keep me alive. Every year of my life has swollen your hoards; you know there is nothing to come to you when I am gone. My whole fortune is left to endow a home for indigent women of quality who have reached their ninetieth year. Come, Mr. Stafford, I am a rich woman. Give me a few years more in the sunshine, a few years more above ground, and I will give you the price of a fashionable London practice—I will set you up at the West-end.'

'How old are you, Lady Ducayne?'

'I was born the day Louis XVI. was guillotined.'*

'Then I think you have had your share of the sunshine and the pleasures of the earth, and that you should spend your few remaining days in repenting your sins and trying to make atonement for the young lives that have been sacrificed to your love of life.'

'What do you mean by that, sir?'

'Oh, Lady Ducayne, need I put your wickedness and your physician's still greater wickedness in plain words? The poor girl who is now in your employment has been reduced from robust health to a condition of absolute danger by Dr. Parravicini's experimental surgery; and I have no doubt those other two young women who broke down in your service were treated by him in the same manner. I could take upon myself to demonstrate—by most convincing evidence, to a jury of medical men—that Dr. Parravicini has been bleeding Miss Rolleston, after putting her under chloroform, at intervals, ever since she has been in your service. The deterioration in the girl's health speaks for itself; the lancet marks upon the girl's arms are unmistakable; and her description of a series of sensations, which she calls a dream, points unmistakably to the administration of chloroform while she was sleeping. A practice so nefarious, so murderous, must, if exposed, result in a sentence only less severe than the punishment of murder.'

'I laugh,' said Parravicini, with an airy motion of his skinny fingers; 'I laugh at once at your theories and at your threats. I, Parravicini Leopold, have no fear that the law can question anything I have done.'

'Take the girl away, and let me hear no more of her,' cried Lady Ducayne, in the thin, old voice, which so poorly matched the energy and fire of the wicked old brain that guided its utterances. 'Let her go back to her mother—I want no more girls to die in my service. There are girls enough and to spare in the world, God knows.'

'If you ever engage another companion—or take another English girl into your service, Lady Ducayne, I will make all England ring with the story of your wickedness.'

'I want no more girls. I don't believe in his experiments. They have been full of danger for me as well as for the girl—an air bubble,* and I should be gone. I'll have no more of his dangerous quackery. I'll find some new man—a better man than you, sir, a discoverer like Pasteur, or Virchow,* a genius—to keep me alive. Take your girl away, young man. Marry her if you like. I'll write her a cheque for a thousand pounds, and let her go and live on beef and beer, and get strong and plump again. I'll have no more such experiments. Do you hear, Parravicini?' she screamed, vindictively, the yellow, wrinkled face distorted with fury, the eyes glaring at him.

The Staffords carried Bella Rolleston off to Varese next day, she very loth to leave Lady Ducayne, whose liberal salary afforded such help for the dear mother. Herbert Stafford insisted, however, treating Bella as coolly as if he had been the family physician, and she had been given over wholly to his care.

'Do you suppose your mother would let you stop here to die?' he asked. 'If Mrs. Rolleston knew how ill you are, she would come post haste to fetch you.'

'I shall never be well again till I get back to Walworth,' answered Bella, who was low-spirited and inclined to tears this morning, a reaction after her good spirits of yesterday.

'We'll try a week or two at Varese first,' said Stafford. 'When you can walk half-way up Monte Generoso* without palpitation of the heart, you shall go back to Walworth.'

'Poor mother, how glad she will be to see me, and how sorry that I've lost such a good place.'

This conversation took place on the boat when they were leaving Bellaggio. Lotta had gone to her friend's room at seven o'clock that morning, long before Lady Ducayne's withered eyelids had opened to the daylight, before even Francine, the French maid, was astir, and had helped to pack a Gladstone bag* with essentials, and hustled Bella downstairs and out of doors before she could make any strenuous resistance.

'It's all right.' Lotta assured her. 'Herbert had a good talk with Lady Ducayne last night, and it was settled for you to leave this morning. She doesn't like invalids, you see.'

'No,' sighed Bella, 'she doesn't like invalids. It was very unlucky that I should break down, just like Miss Tomson and Miss Blandy.'

'At any rate, you are not dead, like them,' answered Lotta, 'and my brother says you are not going to die.'

It seemed rather a dreadful thing to be dismissed in that off-hand way, without a word of farewell from her employer.

'I wonder what Miss Torpinter will say when I go to her for another situation,' Bella speculated, ruefully, while she and her friends were breakfasting on board the steamer.

'Perhaps you may never want another situation,' said Stafford.

'You mean that I may never be well enough to be useful to anybody?'

'No, I don't mean anything of the kind.'

It was after dinner at Varese, when Bella had been induced to take a whole glass of Chianti, and quite sparkled after that unaccustomed stimulant, that Mr. Stafford produced a letter from his pocket.

'I forgot to give you Lady Ducayne's letter of adieu!' he said.

'What, did she write to me? I am so glad—I hated to leave her in such a cool way; for after all she was very kind to me, and if I didn't like her it was only because she was too dreadfully old.'

She tore open the envelope. The letter was short and to the point:—

'Good-bye, child. Go and marry your doctor. I enclose a farewell gift for your trousseau.*—ADELINE DUCAYNE.'

'A hundred pounds, a whole year's salary—no—why, it's for a—"A cheque for a thousand!"' cried Bella. 'What a generous old soul! She really is the dearest old thing.'

'She just missed being very dear to you, Bella,' said Stafford.

He had dropped into the use of her Christian name while they were on board the boat. It seemed natural now that she was to be in his charge till they all three went back to England.

'I shall take upon myself the privileges of an elder brother till we land at Dover,' he said; 'after that—well, it must be as you please.'

The question of their future relations must have been satisfactorily settled before they crossed the Channel, for Bella's next letter to her mother communicated three startling facts.

First, that the inclosed cheque for £1,000 was to be invested in debenture stock in Mrs. Rolleston's name, and was to be her very own, income and principal, for the rest of her life.

Next, that Bella was going home to Walworth immediately.

And last, that she was going to be married to Mr. Herbert Stafford in the following autumn.

'And I am sure you will adore him, mother, as much as I do,' wrote Bella. 'It is all good Lady Ducayne's doing. I never could have married if I had not secured that little nest-egg for you. Herbert says we shall be able to add to it as the years go by, and that wherever we live there shall be always a room in our house for you. The word "mother-in-law"* has no terrors for him.'

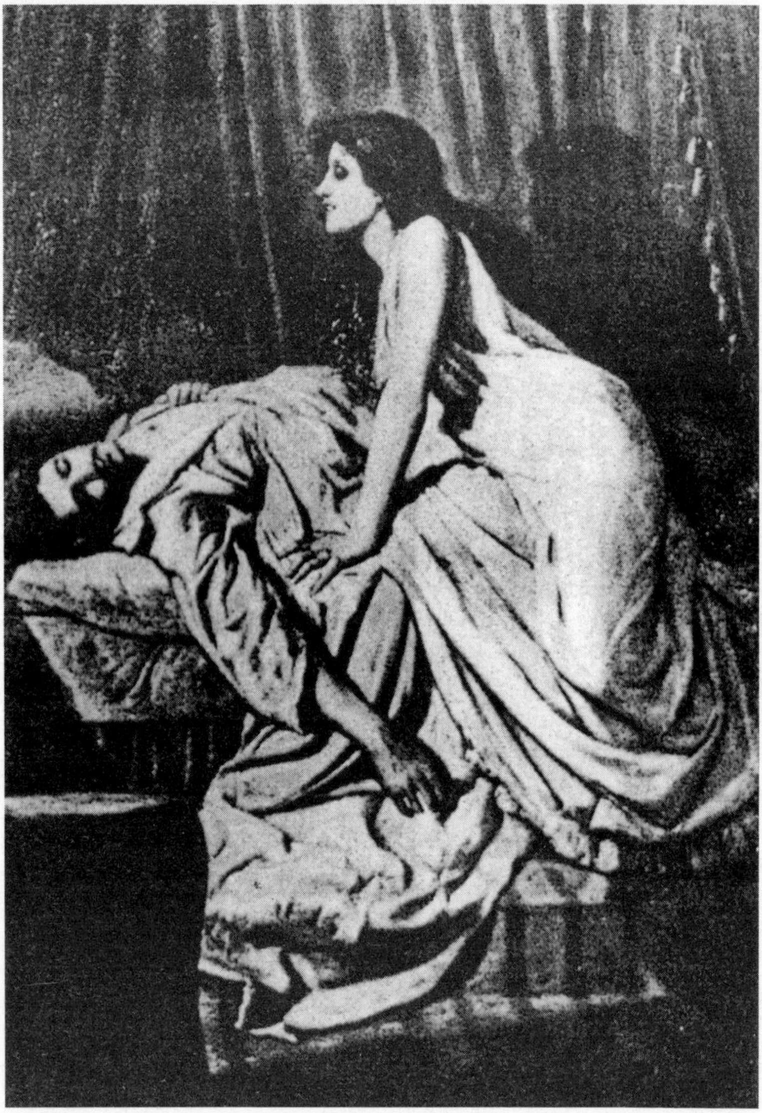

RUDYARD KIPLING

THE VAMPIRE

A FOOL there was and he made his prayer
(Even as you and I!)
To a rag and a bone and a hank of hair
(We called her the woman who did not care)
But the fool he called her his lady fair—
(Even as you and I!)

Oh, the years we waste and the tears we waste
And the work of our head and hand
Belong to the woman who did not know
(And now we know that she never could know)
And did not understand!

A fool there was and his goods he spent
(Even as you and I!)

Honour and faith and a sure intent
(And it wasn't the least what the lady meant)
But a fool must follow his natural bent
(Even as you and I!)
Oh, the toil we lost and the spoil we lost
And the excellent things we planned
Belong to the woman who didn't know why
(And now we know that she never knew why)
And did not understand!

The fool was stripped to his foolish hide
(Even as you and I!)
Which she might have seen when she threw him aside—
(But it isn't on record the lady tried)
So some of him lived but the most of him died—
(Even as you and I!)

'And it isn't the shame and it isn't the blame
*That stings like a white hot brand—**
It's coming to know that she never knew why
(Seeing, at last, she could never know why)
And never could understand!'

EXPLANATORY NOTES

For convenience, all Shakespearean quotations and allusions are identified in the format of *The Oxford Shakespeare: The Complete Works*, gen. eds Stanley Wells and Gary Taylor (Oxford: Clarendon Press, 1988). All biblical citations are from the King James Authorized Version (Oxford and New York: Oxford University Press, 1997). The following abbreviations are used for online editions:

ANB	*American National Biography* (referenced only in individual notes rather than in headnotes)
CE	*Catholic Encyclopaedia*
EB	*Encyclopædia Britannica*
DIB	*The Dictionary of Irish Biography*
DSL	*Dictionary of the Scots Language*
Green	*Green's Dictionary of Slang*
OCAL	*The Oxford Companion to American Literature*
ODNB	*The Oxford Dictionary of National Biography* (individual notes)
OED	*The Oxford English Dictionary* (*OED*)

In addition:

DEF	Jacqueline Simpson and Steve Roud, *A Dictionary of English Folklore* (Oxford: Oxford University Press, 2000)
EDD	Joseph Wright, *The English Dialect Dictionary*, 6 vols (London: Henry Frowde (English Dialect Society), and Oxford: Oxford University Press, 1898–1905)
ODEP	refers to *The Oxford Dictionary of English Proverbs*, 3rd edn (Oxford: Clarendon Press, 1980), compiled by William George Smith, ed. F. P. Wilson

References to other works are given in full in the general and author bibliographies in the Bibliography.

GEORGE GORDON, LORD BYRON, *A FRAGMENT*

Published—much to the author's annoyance—in 1819, appended to the poem *Mazeppa* by the best-selling poet and literary celebrity George Gordon, Lord Byron (1788–1824). The story may have autobiographical elements, and Byron may even have based the fragment and plans for its development on two uncanny anecdotes. In 1810, while Byron was dangerously ill with malaria in Patras (then part of the Ottoman Empire), an old school friend encountered his doppelgänger in St James's Street in London, and another witnessed him visit Buckingham Palace to enquire after the king's health (for a full discussion, see the notes to 'A Fragment' in *Complete Miscellaneous Prose*, 331–2).

Byron wrote 'A Fragment' in an old account book belonging to his estranged wife. It is precisely dated to '*June* 17, 1816', consistent with Polidori's entry in his diary for the same date (*Diary*, 125; see the Explanatory Headnote to Polidori's 'The Vampyre' for the context of the composition of 'A Fragment', pp. 501–3). The manuscript, which is very loosely punctuated with numerous dashes, is now in the Brotherton Library, University of Leeds (BC MS 19c Byron/23), where it is catalogued as 'Fragment of a Novel'. The version given here is from *Mazeppa*, 59–69, compared with the manuscript transcription in *Complete Miscellaneous Prose*, 58–63, where it is retitled by the editor Andrew Nicholson 'Augustus Darvell: A Fragment of a Ghost Story (1816)'. Byron expected his printer to punctuate his texts, so only changes to the wording are noted.

3 *Augustus Darvell*: surprisingly, the name does not appear to be significant.

inquietude: disturbance of mind, uneasiness (*OED*).

concentred: directed towards a single (other) point (*OED*).

4 *hectic*: consumptive—having flushed cheeks and hot, dry skin (*OED*); vampires are associated with inexplicable contagion.

5 *Smyrna*: the Turkish city of İzmir in Anatolia on the Aegean coast; the original ancient Greek name was still current at this time in Britain.

Ephesus and Sardis: Ephesus was a port on the River Kaystros (now Küçük Menderes, Turkey, 50 miles south of Smyrna, which is now İzmir) and is rich in Hellenistic and Roman architectural remains; it was also an important early Christian site and is addressed in the *Revelation of St John the Divine*. Sardis (now Sart, Turkey, 50 miles east of Smyrna) was the capital of Lydia and was described by the Greek historian Herodotus; it too is an important ancient archaeological site and is also one of the seven churches of Asia identified in Revelation. Byron visited Ephesus with John Cam Hobhouse in March 1810 (*Journey through Albania*, 659–65).

a serrugee and a single janizary: *sürücü*: a driver of post-horses (see Nicholson's notes to *Complete Miscellaneous Prose*, 333); janizary: a Turkish soldier (*OED*).

broken columns of Diana: the Temple of Artemis (to the Romans, Diana) was one of the Seven Wonders of the Ancient World; it was destroyed by the Goths in AD 262.

turbaned tombstones: traditional Ottoman Islamic gravestones surmounted by stylized carved turbans.

caravansera: a large quadrangular building with a spacious court in the middle where caravans can be put up (*OED*).

city of the dead: Nicholson notes Byron's 'On the Star of "The Legion of Honour"', stanza 7, ll. 37–8: 'And Freedom hallows with her tread | The silent cities of the dead' (*Complete Miscellaneous Prose*, 333).

he said . . . water: Turkish—*Ver*, give; *bana*, to me; *su*, water (notes to *Complete Miscellaneous Prose*, 333).

I have also been here before: a resonant phrase.

6 *I received*: the MS reads 'he returned'.

a request to make: the MS reads 'to request to make'.

Bay of Eleusis: the annual Eleusinian Mysteries, the most significant of the ancient Greek mystery cults, took place at Eleusis, and it was also the site of the Plutonion Cave—the entrance to the Underworld; the Sacred Way led 14 miles north-west from Athens to Eleusis, and as it reaches Eleusis there are the Rheitoi salt-springs (see Miles, 'The Roman Propylon', 114–51).

temple of Ceres: Ceres derived from the ancient Greek agricultural goddess Demeter; the ruins of the temple of Ceres at Eleusis were a popular subject for artists, and in 1818 Joseph Gandy painted a vision of what the building may have looked like before the fall of the Roman Empire.

ninth day of the month: the MS text emphasizes the date: '9th day of the month'.

a stork, with a snake in her beak: in ancient Rome the stork represented piety and in Christian symbolism it signifies Christ, reflecting the established belief that it hunts snakes—which of course denote original sin in the Old Testament—to feed to its young and thereby nurture the next generation. A stork neither devouring nor passing a snake to its nestlings consequently subverts Christian order. Among the 'Dreadful portents' of medieval Christianity, Friedrich Nietzsche describes 'a stork holding a snake in its beak but *hesitating* to swallow it' and being 'approached by the figures of dead relatives' (*Morgenröthe* (1881), translated as *Daybreak*, 46).

7 *ten might be counted*: the MS emphasizes the number: '*ten* might be counted'.

ataghan: Byron's note to *The Giaour* reads 'a long dagger worn with pistols in the belt, in a metal scabbard, generally of silver; and, among the wealthier, gilt, or of gold' (4n.).

some Mahometan tenant: the MS has 'some preceding Mahometan tenant'.

JOHANN WOLFGANG VON GOETHE, *THE BRIDE OF CORINTH*

'Die Braut von Korinth' was written by Goethe (1749–1832) in 1797—his 'Year of Ballads'—and published in German in 1798. It draws on the Greek myths of Philinnion, described by both Phlegon and Proclus, and of Menippus Lycius and the Lamia—but with a decidedly dark Romantic contemporary twist. The poem was translated by the Irish writer and later jurist John Anster, and published to acclaim in *Blackwood's Magazine* in 1819 as 'The Bride of Corinth', '*From Goethe*'. It was subsequently reprinted in *The Common-Place Book of Ancient and Modern Ballad [sic] and Metrical Legendary Tales* (1824), 215–21, and elsewhere, and in Anster's edition of Goethe's *Faustus* (1835), 325–34 (see *The Quarterly Review*, 68 (June & Sept. 1826), 136). Many other, more faithful translations appeared throughout the century, but Anster's had a reach and an influence that considerably outweighs the others, and also explicitly names the Bride as a vampire. The version given here is from *Blackwood's Edinburgh Magazine*, 4 (Mar. 1819), 688–9, and includes archaic use of the apostrophe; a month later *The New Monthly Magazine* published John William Polidori's 'The Vampyre'.

8 *Corinth*: ancient Greek city on the Isthmus of Corinth, between Athens and Sparta. It lay in ruins after the Greek War of Independence (1821–30), and suffered further damage due to an earthquake in 1858.

plighted: pledged, bound oneself to (*OED*).

9 *scathe*: sorrow (*OED*).

10 *falls*: kills, i.e. of livestock (*OED*).

gravings: incisions, inscriptions, engravings (*OED*).

ringlet: a lock of hair, a corkscrew-shaped curl (*OED*).

11 *strains*: tightly clasps (*OED*).

ween: consider, believe (*OED*).

12 *cock crows*: in British and European folklore, ghosts and other undead entities haunting the earth return to their own abodes at the crowing of the cock; the Ghost of Hamlet's father, for example, 'faded on the crowing of the cock' (*Hamlet, Prince of Denmark*, I. i. 138); the belief is recorded by the fourth-century Roman Christian poet Prudentius (see Brand, *Observations on Popular Antiquities*, 54).

a maid | Thus shameless: i.e. a prostitute.

13 *mummery song*: ridiculous ceremonial hymning (*OED*).

fane: temple (*OED*).

creed: articles of belief or faith (*OED*).

funeral pile: cremation was practised in ancient times but was frowned upon by the Christian church as heathen; it was consequently extremely rare in Britain and Europe. Being sentenced to be burnt at the stake had been a penalty reserved for the gravest crimes as well as for the execution of women, and since at least the Middle Ages was an established way of disposing of the undead; in the eighteenth century it was consequently revived as a highly dependable way to slay vampires. Burning at the stake was abolished in Britain in 1790, and, while not strictly illegal, cremation was only endorsed by Act of Parliament in 1902.

JOHN WILLIAM POLIDORI, ed. ALARIC WATTS, *EXTRACT OF A LETTER FROM GENEVA, WITH ANECDOTES OF LORD BYRON, &C.*

John William Polidori (1795–1821) was Lord Byron's physician and an aspiring writer; he is credited with the inaugural vampire English-language tale 'The Vampyre' (see pp. 22–40), first published prefaced with this letter and an introduction (see pp. 19–21). The gossipy 'Letter from Geneva' is almost wholly derived from Polidori's account of his trip to Switzerland in 1816 accompanying Lord Byron, giving vivid details of Byron, Mary Godwin, and Percy Shelley during their stay at the Villa Diodati, and the circumstances surrounding the composition of both *Frankenstein; or, The Modern Prometheus* (1818) and, it is implied, 'The Vampyre'. Byron was furious that the 'Letter' leaked details of his private life, but concurred that it was a true account, clearly believing that Polidori was primarily responsible (*Byron's Letters and Journals*, vi. 126). However, the text itself was probably devised by Alaric Watts (1797–1864), sub-editor on the *New Monthly*. Watts explicitly denied the 'Letter' was written by Polidori and strongly suggested that he himself was the author—although it could not have been written without Polidori's assistance and direct access to his diary (see Groom, 'Composition, Publication, Deception', 54–5). Despite this, various other candidates have been put forward as the author. Henry Viets proposes Henry Colburn, proprietor of *The New Monthly Magazine* (96), while D. L. Macdonald and Kathleen Scherf attribute the 'Letter' and the accompanying editorial introduction to the jobbing journalist John Mitford (*The Vampire* (1994), 177; reiterated in *The Vampire* (2008), 35–6).

The 'Letter from Geneva' was included in part in the book version of *The Vampyre* (half-titled 'Extract of a Letter to the Editor'—see headnote to 'The Vampyre', pp. 501–3), together with Watts's 'Introduction' to 'The Vampyre' and another supplementary text, the fictitious 'Extract of a Letter, containing an Account of Lord Byron's Residence in the Island of Mitylene [Lesbos]'—a piece of hackwork by Mitford (see Macdonald, *Poor Polidori*, 178, 246n.). By the third edition of this book, William Godwin had objected strongly to the salacious mention of his daughter and stepdaughter, demanding that the specific reference to them be removed; he offered to pay, and the offending lines were expunged from the text of the third issue (Viets, 'London Editions', 97); Byron also made a similar objection in a letter to his publisher John Murray of 15 May 1819 (*Byron's Letters and Journals*, vi. 126).

The 'Letter from Geneva' sets the scene for the ensuing tale of 'The Vampyre' in linking it to Byron's inspired—if notorious—time in Switzerland, his wayward celebrity, the region's cosmopolitan intellectual élite, radical British history, and Polidori's plans for the publication of his novel *Ernestus Berchtold; or, The Modern Œdipus* (1819) and other literary works; it also helped to precipitate the authorship controversy that immediately engulfed 'The Vampyre'. The text is from the first printing in *The New Monthly Magazine*, vol. 11, no. 63 (1 Apr. 1819), 193–5.

14 *Ed.*: the prefatory note was written by Colburn, proprietor of the *New Monthly*, after he had cancelled Watts's original disclaimer that Byron was author of 'The Vampyre' (see headnote to 'The Vampyre', p. 502).

Rousseau . . . under its roof: Jean-Jacques Rousseau, philosopher, was born on 28 June 1712 at 40 Grand-Rue in Geneva Old Town; he is best known for *Julie, ou La Nouvelle Héloïse* (1761), *Émile* and *The Social Contract* (both 1762), and *The Confessions* (1764–6); he died in France in 1778.

Ferney the residence of Voltaire: François-Marie Arouet (1694–1778)—known as Voltaire—was a writer, historian, philosopher, and outspoken critic of the Roman Catholic Church. Voltaire's chateau was built between 1759 and 1766 at Ferney, an estate in France close to the Swiss border; it was there that he entertained Enlightenment luminaries and celebrities.

Bonnet's abode: Charles Bonnet (1720–93), Swiss lawyer, natural scientist, and philosopher who discovered parthenogenesis and later developed the catastrophe theory of evolution. He gave his name both to Rue Charles-Bonnet in Geneva and the medical condition Charles Bonnet Syndrome.

Madame de Stael: Anne-Louise-Germaine Necker, Baroness de Staël-Holstein (1766–1817), French-Swiss writer and public intellectual; she kept a salon at Château de Coppet on Lake Geneva.

Heloise . . . Abeilard: the love affair between Héloïse, a brilliant student, and her tutor Abelard in twelfth-century France was celebrated for developing epistolary literature and affording women a scholarly standing equal to that of men.

M. Schlegel: August Wilhelm Schlegel (1767–1845), philosopher and poet, met Madame de Staël in 1804; he became tutor to her children and influenced her own ideas on Romanticism.

Gibbon, Bonnivard, Bradshaw: the classical historian Edward Gibbon (1737–94) finished the last three volumes of *The History of the Decline and Fall of the Roman Empire* (1788) at Lausanne, overlooking Lake Geneva; and the Genevan patriot François Bonivard (1493–1570), hero of Byron's poem *The Prisoner of Chillon* (1816), was head of the Priory of St Victor, near Geneva. Regarding Bradshaw, Polidori may have mistakenly been thinking of the lawyer and regicide John Bradshaw (1602–59) who presided over the trial of Charles I and was later a friend of John Milton's; several of the regicides escaped to Lausanne, where they remained in exile.

Diodati: Byron rented Villa Belle Rive on 6 June 1816 for six months, naming it Villa Diodati—the owners were related to John Milton's friend Charles Diodati, and it was suggested that Milton himself may have stayed there.

15 *the Third Canto of Childe Harold*: published by John Murray in 1816.

Byron resided many months in this neighbourhood: Byron and Polidori arrived in Geneva on 25 May; Byron dismissed his physician on 16 September after which they both left.

never eat animal food: both Byron and Percy Shelley followed strict dietary regimes.

English boat: Polidori's diary describes several boating expeditions across Lake Geneva (99, 105, 110, 120, 121).

scathed: blasted by lightning (*OED*); see Mary Shelley's *Frankenstein*: 'we witnessed a most violent and terrible thunder-storm . . . on a sudden I beheld a stream of fire issue from an old and beautiful oak, which stood about twenty yards from our house; and so soon as the dazzling light vanished, the oak had disappeared, and nothing remained but a blasted stump' (24).

16 *The sky is changed! . . . themselves to wage*: *Canto the Third* of Byron's *Childe Harold* (London: John Murray, 1816), stanzas 92–4, with 'Rhine' for 'Rhone', 'hastes' for 'hates', 'winter' for 'winters', and minor and insignificant changes in punctuation and spelling from the first edition.

M. Pictet: Marc Auguste Pictet (1752–1825), editor of *Bibliotheque Universelle* (see Giddey, 'Byron and Switzerland', 179); Byron insisted to Murray that it was in fact Polidori who had invited Pictet to dinner (*Byron's Letters and Journals*, vi. 127).

Bonstetten: Charles Victor de Bonstetten (1745–1832), Swiss writer and friend of Thomas Gray, whom he met in 1769 (Polidori, *Diary*, 105–6).

a gentleman who travelled with him: Polidori himself—his *Diary* records that when Pictet visited on 26 and 27 May, Byron instructed Polidori to say that he was 'not at home' (98, 99).

Lady D— H—: Lady Dalrymple Hamilton, Michael Rossetti noting 'a daughter of Viscount Duncan, and wife of Sir Hew D. Hamilton' (Polidori, *Diary*, 140–1); Byron wrote to Murray, 'It is true that I returned without entering Lady Dalrymple Hamilton's—because I saw it full' (*Byron's Letters and Journals*, vi. 127).

upon paying his first visit at Coppet . . . a lady carried out fainting: Byron to Murray: 'It is true—that Mrs. Hervey (She writes novels) fainted at my entrance into Coppet—& then came back again' (*Byron's Letters and Journals*, vi. 127); at the time there were three Herveys who wrote novels.

17 *an outcast*: Polidori lists the Coppet set in his *Diary* (137–9).

Countess of Breuss: Countess Catherine [Yekaterina] Musin-Pushkin-Bruce (d. 1829), only daughter of Count James [Yakov Alexandrovich] Bruce (1732–91), last of the 'Russian Bruces' (known as 'Scottish kings, Russian soldiers': see Fedosov, 'The First Russian Bruces', 64), and Countess Praskovya Bruce (1729–85)—'Brussja', notorious confidante and supposed *'l'eprouveuse'* (love-tester) for Catherine the Great. In 1793 Catherine Bruce had married the Russian aristocrat and patron of the arts Vasily Musin-Pushkin (?1775–1836), who added her name to his—hence in Polidori's *Diary* she is dubbed 'Countess Mouskinpouskin, Breuss' (139). The Countess held salons at her Genthod home, the sumptuous Villa Le Saugy, and according to Polidori, who spent much time in her company, she had 'acted plays at the Hermitage under Catherine [the Great]' and had two husbands 'one in Russia, one at Venice' but was now separated (*Diary*, 141).

17 *agrémens de la Société*: commendations of society (or a social circle)—a phrase used, for example, by Rousseau in his *Confessions* (*Collection complète des oeuvres* (Geneva, 1780–9): www.rousseauonline.ch (2012), xvi, 124).

Αθεος in the Album at Chamouny: on 23 July 1816, Percy Shelley wrote in the visitors' book of the Hôtel de Londres in Chamonix that he was travelling from London 'a l'Enfer'—to Hell—and added 'eimi philanthropos, demokratikos, atheos te'—'I am a lover of mankind, a democrat, and an atheist'; '*Αθεος*' ('atheos') translates as 'atheist' or 'godless' (Crewe 116.23, Wren Library, Trinity College, Cambridge).

daughters of the celebrated Mr Godwin: Byron thought that Polidori openly identifying Mary Shelley and Claire Clairmont was 'a blundering piece of exculpation!' (*Byron's Letters and Journals*, vi. 127); neither was Godwin impressed (see headnote).

Phantasmagoriana: *Fantasmagoriana, ou Recueil d'Histoires d'Apparitions de Spectres, Revenans, Fantômes, etc.; Traduit de l'Allemand, par un Amateur*, trans. Jean Baptiste Benoit Eyriès, 2 vols (F. Schoell: Paris, 1812).

18 *ghost stories . . . out of the room*: Polidori conflates two distinct episodes—the ghost story challenge (17 June) and the effect of Samuel Taylor Coleridge's poem 'Christabel' (18 June) (Polidori, *Diary*, 125–8).

bosom of one of the ladies with eyes: Mary Shelley may well have been breast-feeding her five-month-old baby, William.

ebauches: *ébauches*, first draft (*OED*).

ALARIC WATTS, *INTRODUCTION* TO *THE VAMPYRE*

Watts's 'Introduction' was first printed as a crotcheted preface to 'The Vampyre' and signed 'ED.', subtly different from Colburn signing his contribution '*Ed.*'; it was titled 'Introduction' in the separate book publication of *The Vampyre* (see headnotes to 'Letter from Geneva' and 'The Vampyre'). Macdonald and Scherf point out that the details given of vampires in the editorial introduction are not consistent with Polidori's tale, which seriously undermines Patricia Skarda's claim that Polidori was responsible for all the prefatory material ('Vampirism and Plagiarism', 258–69). Nevertheless, Watts's introduction, which derives from eighteenth-century accounts and the notes to Robert Southey's *Thalaba the Destroyer* (1801) and Byron's *The Giaour* (1813), provides concise historical background material about vampires and was usually reprinted alongside Polidori's text. In an important sense, then, Watts's essay was at least as influential as Polidori's fiction. The text is again from the first printing of 'The Vampyre' in *The New Monthly Magazine*, vol. 11, no. 63 (1 Apr. 1819), 195–6.

19 *the division of the Latin and Greek churches*: the East–West Schism or Great Schism of 1054, which after centuries of theological dispute separated the

Eastern Orthodox Church (Greek) from the Western Catholic Church (Latin); Michael Cerularius, Patriarch of Constantinople, and Pope (later Saint) Leo IX mutually excommunicated one another.

Hungary . . . Lorraine: see Groom, *The Vampire*, 24–8, 86–7.

Arnold Paul: the celebrated case of the vampire *hajduk* (guerrilla soldier) Arnold Paul (an Anglicized version of the name Arnond Paole) was investigated by imperial Habsburg medical officers in 1731, scrupulously documented, and widely disseminated throughout Europe the following year (see Groom, *The Vampire*, 33–9).

20 *corses*: corpses (*OED*).

21 *But first on earth . . . more accursed than they*: the lines are from Byron's *The Giaour* (1813), 23–5; Watts makes a handful of minor changes.

poem of 'Thalaba': Robert Southey, *Thalaba the Destroyer*, 2 vols (London: T. N. Longman and O. Rees, 1801).

pretends: claims, professes (*OED*).

Tournefort . . . Calmet: in *A Voyage into the Levant* (1718), Joseph Pitton de Tournefort, botanist to the French king Louis XIV, described a 'Vroucolacas' on the Greek island of Mykonos, dated to 1 January 1701. Byron cites this in a note to *The Giaour*:

> The Vampire superstition is still general in the Levant. Honest Tournefort tells a long story, which Mr. Southey, in the notes on Thalaba, quotes about these 'Vroucolochas,' as he calls them. The Romaic term is 'Vardoulacha,' which the worthy old traveller has thus transposed. I recollect a whole family being terrified by the scream of a child, which they imagined must proceed from such a visitation. The Greeks never mention the word without horror. (23n.)

Dom Augustin Calmet was a Benedictine abbot whose books ranged from a 26-volume commentary on the Bible to *Dissertations sur les Apparitions des Anges, des Démons & des Esprits. Et sur les Revenans et Vampires. De Hongrie, de Boheme, de Moravie & de Silesie*, published in France in 1746, and in English in 1759 as *Dissertations upon the Apparitions of Angels, Dæmons, and Ghosts, and concerning the Vampires of Hungary, Bohemia, Moravia, and Silesia* (see Groom, *The Vampire*, 27, 101, 228n., and 73–81).

Vroucolocha . . . Broucoloka, &c.: the Greek legend of the *vrocolocas* or *vrykolakas*; the vampiric *vrykolakas* was first recorded in the seventeenth century by Leo Allatius, *De quorumdam Graecorum opinationibus* (1645) and Fr Francois Richard, SJ, *Relation de l'Isle de Sant-Erini* (1657) (see Groom, *The Vampire*, 214n.; see previous note).

JOHN WILLIAM POLIDORI, *THE VAMPYRE*

'The Vampyre' was based on a tale told by Lord Byron and written by John Polidori, before being edited by Alaric Watts (see preceding headnotes). When it came to publication, Watts also wrote a disclaimer to be printed before the prefatory 'Letter from Geneva' (see headnote, p. 497):

> The tale which accompanied the letter we also present to our readers, without pledging ourselves positively for its authenticity, as the production of Lord Byron. We may, however, observe, that it bears strong internal evidence of having been conceived by him; though from the occasional inaccuracies, probably the result of haste, which occur throughout the whole, we should suppose it to have been committed to paper rather from the recital of a third person, than under the immediate direction of its noble author. (Macdonald, *Poor Polidori*, 178.)

However, Henry Colburn, publisher of the *New Monthly*, deleted the passage and added the byline, 'A TALE BY LORD BYRON'. This led Watts to resign in protest, and Polidori to come forward with demands for acknowledgement and compensation (for a full account see Groom, 'Composition, Publication, Deception'; see also Viets, 'London Editions' and Camilletti, 'A Note on the Publication History'). At the same time, *The Vampyre* was published as a book by Sherwood, Neely, and Jones acting for Colburn, together with three supplementary texts: the 'Letter from Geneva' (see pp. 14–18), Watts's 'Introduction' (see pp. 19–21), and the 'Account of Lord Byron's Residence in the Island of Mitylene' (see headnote to 'Letter from Geneva', p. 497).

'The Vampyre' immediately exploded over the Western world's cultural scene: in 1819 there were three Paris English-language editions (ascribed to Byron), a French translation (attributed to Byron), a German translation, and the book crossed the Atlantic to America to be published simultaneously in three editions; by 1830 the tale was also available in Italian, Spanish, and Swedish translations. In 1820 *Le Vampire* appeared on the Paris stage in a celebrated version by Charles Nodier, Pierre-Frédéric-Adolphe Carmouche, and Achille de Jouffroy, followed by at least five other adaptations. *Le Vampire* was subsequently translated into English by James Robinson Planché as *The Vampire, or the Bride of the Isles* (1820) and performed in London, inspiring the invention of the 'vampire trap'—a spring-loaded trapdoor that enabled actors to appear to pass through walls or floors. Both the French and English dramas were performed in America in the same year, and there was also a German stage version. The tale was extended into a two-volume French novel (Cyprian Bérard, *Lord Ruthven ou les Vampires*), and in 1826 into a full opera, *Der Vampyr*, by Wilhelm August Wohlbrück and Heinrich August Marschner. The opera was first performed in Germany, then in England (in Planché's translation, 1829), and subsequently in France, the Netherlands, and Russia; another German opera followed in 1828 (see Viets, 'London Editions', 98–100). However, 'Poor Polidori' did not live to see the success of his 'mere trifle'. He died in 1821; the coroner ruled death by natural causes, possibly resulting from a concussion sustained when he was thrown from his carriage in 1817, although it is more likely that Polidori committed suicide using prussic acid, as his family maintained (see Groom, 'Chatterton and Polidori').

Polidori also wrote about vampires in his poetry. In *Ximenes*, the central character determines to destroy his enemy vampirically: 'I will lay by him, and here | Will live a vampire on his son and him, | Sucking in living drops his very blood' (20, see also 69). Similarly, in his lines on the poet Thomas Chatterton ('Chatterton to his Sister') in the same volume, he writes

> When most the men shall softly smile,
> They fondly hope they may beguile,
> And hope to hurt when most they please,
> As vampire bat excites a breeze
> Soft, cooling, lulling to repose
> The child whose life's blood quickly flows,
> Feeding the filthy beast with all
> A mother's fondest name may call. (138)

Polidori was an aficionado of nightmares and related phenomena as well, having written his medical thesis on somnambulism, or, as he termed it, '*oneirodynia*' (see Macdonald, *Poor Polidori*, 35–41).

The most important editions of 'The Vampyre' are those edited by D. L. MacDonald and Kathleen Scherf in 1994 and reissued in revised form in 2008, and Robert Morrison and Chris Baldick in 1998, reissued in 2008. There is also an unannotated edition by Franklin Charles Bishop (2005), a revised reissue of his 1991 version published by The Gothic Society. Morrison and Baldick correct two tenses, and make minor corrections to the punctuation to clarify the meaning, such as replacing commas with semicolons or full stops (xxiii). In their first version, MacDonald and Scherf present the tale with a full scholarly apparatus, basing their text on a copy in the Houghton Library annotated by Polidori himself and presumably intended for a second, authorized edition which was never published (*EC8.P7598.819va, Sherwood, Neely, and Jones third issue: see *The Vampyre* (1994), 21–6, and, for a detailed list of variants, 145–52). The most striking revision here is in the name of the protagonist: Polidori changed 'Ruthven' to 'Strongmore'. Possibly he had discovered that there was indeed an actual Lord Ruthven, or perhaps he wished to distance his own villain from Lady Caroline Lamb's scandalous character Clarence Ruthven, her portrayal of Byron in the novel *Glenarvon* (1816: see notes to pp. 24, 22).

The present text follows the first printing in *The New Monthly Magazine* (vol. 11, no. 63 (1 Apr. 1819), 196–206). Despite the confusion over the composition and delivery of the tale, and the controversial supplementary material that accompanied publication—but also bearing in mind that the changes Polidori made in planning a second edition were very minor—this version can be treated as reasonably authoritative. It was the moment when the vampire first appeared in fiction in English literature and thus became a cultural sensation.

22 *ton*: fashionable world (*OED*).

dead grey eye: possibly an allusion to Luke 11: 34–5, 'The light of the body is the eye: therefore when thine eye is single, thy whole body also is full of light; but when thine eye is evil, thy body also is full of darkness. Take heed therefore that the light which is in thee be not darkness' (also, Matthew 6: 22–3; see Phillips, 'Tropes of Vision', 169).

ennui: mental weariness through want of occupation (*OED*).

deadly hue of his face: Ruthven is deathly pallid; as the vampires of the previous century were rubicund, this drew criticism from the *Monthly Review*, which carped, 'this in direct opposition to the account of a vampyre's complexion, which is reported, by those who are learnedly cognizant of the fact, to be florid, healthy, and full of blood' (90: see Introduction, p. xi).

Lady Mercer: probably based on Lady Caroline Lamb, with whom Byron had had an affair that she recounted in lurid and fantastical terms in her novel *Glenarvon* (1816) (see note to p. 24; see Macdonald, *Poor Polidori*, 95–8; Skarda, 'Vampirism and Plagiarism', 250; and Twitchell, *The Living Dead*, 108).

mountebank: itinerant entertainer (*OED*); Lamb had dressed as a pageboy to insinuate her way into Byron's bedroom.

23 *Aubrey*: possibly a portrait of Polidori; Skarda argues that the name alludes to the antiquary John Aubrey (1626–97), whose celebrated memoir *Brief Lives* was first published in 1813 as *Lives of Eminent Men* ('Vampirism and Plagiarism', 251)—if so, Polidori may be alluding to his role as a chronicler of Byron's European tour.

the painter's eye: a critique of the picturesque fashion in painting which sentimentalized its subjects; it was popularized by William Gilpin.

in fine: in short, in a word (*OED*).

He thought . . . the realities of life: this is reminiscent of Walton's admission in *Frankenstein* that he had ambitions to be a poet; the conversations at the Villa Diodati doubtless covered art and life (see Shelley, *Frankenstein*, 8).

gay: charming; showy; dissolute and promiscuous; the word was also a euphemism for prostitution (*OED*).

congeries: mass (*OED*).

24 *Lord Ruthven's*: the name of the protagonist is withheld until this stage of the narrative; he is a nobleman, and by inference therefore a rake. The name is clearly taken from *Glenarvon*, Lamb's novel attacking Byron: Lord Glenarvon being Clarence Ruthven. The party at Diodati had a copy of *Glenarvon* with them, which Byron at least read while there (*Byron's Letters and Journals*, v. 86). Moreover, Lord Grey de Ruthyn had leased Newstead Abbey (ancestral seat of the Byrons) in 1803, befriending the young aristocrat, taking him shooting, and possibly seducing him as well—with the result that they were irreparably estranged. Upon discovering that there

really was a Lord Ruthven, Polidori planned to revise the name to Strongmore for the second edition (see headnote, p. 503); the name Ruthven was presumably provided by Watts (see Groom, 'Composition, Publication, Deception', 56). The Scottish clan Ruthven (pronounced '*riven*') were lowlanders.

Lord Ruthven's affairs were embarrassed . . . he was about to travel: as were Byron's affairs when he left England on 25 April 1816, fleeing from bailiffs.

the circling waters: the sea encircling Britain; possibly a reference to Anna Laetitia Barbauld's 'Hymn XXIII: Praise to the Creator', 'The circling waters round her winding shores' (l. 28), first published in 1772 in *Hymns for Public Worship* (29).

25 *faro table*: a card game in which players bet on the order of cards drawn from the top of the deck (*OED*); it was made illegal in Britain in 1739 and remained outlawed into the nineteenth century, yet continued to be played behind closed doors (see 'Chronicle', *Annual Register . . . 1797*, 14). The inveterate gambler and Whig politician Charles Edward Fox ran a faro bank at Brooks's Club, and so many society ladies were running private games at their homes that in 1796 the Lord Chief Justice threatened to pillory them, resulting in several raids and fines (see Russell, 'Faro's Daughters'). James Gillray's drawing of 'The Faro Table' (1792) gives a sense of the heaving and rambunctious atmosphere of a busy game (British Museum, 1867,1012.608). Byron himself had no interest in card games, although he did observe that 'I have a notion that Gamblers are as happy as most people—being always *excited*;—women—wine—fame—the table—even Ambition—*sate* now & then—but every turn of the card—& cast of the dice—keeps the Gambler alive—besides one can Game ten times longer than one can do any thing else' (*Byron's Letters and Journals*, ix. 23). In 1817, the name of one proprietor of a gambling 'hell' or 'shop', Mrs Leach, was described as being 'singularly appropriate' (see Ashton, *History of Gambling*, 114)—gambling was, in other words, recognized as being highly addictive and the dealers who preyed on the gamesters were effectively vampiric.

gilder: guilder, currency coin of the Netherlands, introduced in 1816

Lord Ruthven ... carriage: bearing (*OED*); with consummate conceit, Byron had left England in a carriage modelled on that of Napoleon Bonaparte.

27 *the faithful in Mahoment's paradise . . . those who had no souls . . . the gazelle*: alluding to Byron's poem *The Giaour* (1813):

> Her eye's dark charm 'twere vain to tell,
> But gaze on that of the Gazelle,
> It will assist thy fancy well,
> As large, as languishingly dark,
> But Soul beam'd forth in every spark
> That darted from beneath its lid,
> Bright as the gem of Giamschid.

Yea, *Soul*, and should our prophet say
That form was nought but breathing clay,
By Alla! I would answer nay;
Though on Al-Sirat's arch I stood,
Which totters o'er the fiery flood,
With Paradise within my view,
And all his Houris beckoning through.
Oh! who young Leila's glance could read
And keep that portion of his creed
Which saith, that woman is but dust,
A soulless toy for tyrant's lust? (11–12)

Byron adds the footnote:

> A vulgar error; the Koran allots at least a third of Paradise to well-behaved women; but by far the greater number of Mussulmans interpret the text their own way, and exclude their moieties from heaven. Being enemies to Platonics, they cannot discern 'any fitness of things' in the souls of the other sex, conceiving them to be superseded by the Houris.

Patricia Skalda discusses Polidori's possible inspiration from Byron's poetry, especially *The Giaour* (Skarda, 'Vampirism and Plagiarism', 249–69), and Polidori's novel *Ernestus Berchtold* (1819) has an epigraph from *The Giaour*.

27 *Ianthe*: one of the 'Oceanids', or sea nymphs; the name means 'violet flower' (see note to p. 31). 'Ianthe' was the name given by Byron to Lady Charlotte Mary Harley, daughter of the fifth Earl of Oxford (1801–80); he dedicated the first two cantos of *Childe Harold's Pilgrimage* (1812) to her and had an affair with her mother; whether or not he was sexually attracted to the 11-year-old girl herself is not clear. She too was compared to a gazelle (Canto I, 'To Ianthe', l. 28, p. 5), as well as a Peri, a Persian elf descended from fallen angels (l. 19, p. 4). Furthermore, Percy Bysshe Shelley also had a daughter Eliza Ianthe (1813–76) by Harriet née Westbrook, his first wife who died by her own hand in 1816; Percy Shelley also wrote verses to Ianthe and in his poem *Queen Mab: A Philosophical Poem* (1813) the queen of the fairies takes the character Ianthe above the earth to observe human folly.

Kashmere butterfly: alluding again to Byron's *The Giaour*,

As rising on its purple wing
The insect-queen of eastern spring,
O'er emerald meadows of Kashmeer
Invites the young pursuer near,
And leads him on from flower to flower
A weary chace and wasted hour . . . (8)

Byron's footnote glosses the 'insect-queen' as 'The blue-winged butterfly of Kashmeer, the most rare and beautiful of the species'; he also on 22 November 1813 referred to Lady Charlemont as 'that Kasmeer butterfly of the "Blues"' (*Byron's Letters and Journals*, iii. 171). Polidori, after Byron, may be thinking of the Adonis Blue.

Pausanias: Greek geographer (*fl.* AD 143–76) whose tour of his homeland is described in his *Periegesis Hellados*.

28 *living vampyre*: the Greek legend of the *vrocolocas*: see note to p. 21.

29 *orgies*: occasions of excessive indulgence (*OED*).

blue forked lightning: the tempestuous weather recalls both the Burkean sublime and the 'Year Without A Summer' Polidori spent with Byron and the Shelley ménage at the Villa Diodati, which was characterized by electrical storms; electricity is also key to Mary Shelley's *Frankenstein* (Shelley, *Frankenstein*, pp. xxvi–xxviii).

30 *baffled*: foiled, confounded, cheated; also, throughout the seventeenth century, disgraced (*OED*).

enormous force: the abnormal strength of the vampire, which became a later characteristic (see Groom, *The Vampire*, 103, 244n.).

the marks of teeth having opened the vein: most eighteenth-century accounts of vampires recorded them as strangling their victims and then sucking blood from the corpse.

31 *tideless waves*: the tranquil waters of the Saronic Gulf (Saronikós Gulf), in the Aegean Sea.

modest violet: Ianthe, forlornly playing on her name.

32 *defile*: narrow pass or gorge (*OED*).

order: a written mandate directing a bank to release funds (*OED*).

in two days mortification ensued: the unnervingly rapid putrefaction of Ruthven's body is in contrast to the incorrupt bodies of most other vampires; this has its roots in the Eastern Orthodox belief that the bodies of excommunicants did not decay (see Groom, *The Vampire*, 78).

33 *'Swear!' cried the dying man*: both Polidori's tale and Byron's 'Fragment' centre on an unbreakable oath (see 'A Fragment', p. 6); Macdonald argues that the oath was a key innovation of Byron and Polidori and became a characteristic of later vampire tales; Polidori's membership of the Freemasons may have suggested the ploy (Macdonald, *Poor Polidori*, 190–1, 143).

first cold ray of the moon: Polidori's idea would prove influential—it is how Varney the Vampire was repeatedly revived as a vampire (see Macdonald, *Poor Polidori*, 278–9n.). According to Galenic medical theory, moonlight and astrological influences quickened the decay of the flesh (Macdonald and Scherf, *The Vampyre* (2008), 51n., citing Philippe Ariès, *The Hour of*

Our Death, trans. Helen Weaver (New York: Vintage Books, 1982), 360). In classical medical theory and practice, the moon has traditionally had generative powers and was strongly linked to pregnancy and childbirth, but was also instrumental in dispersing moisture and stimulating change. The supposed humidity of moonbeams was thought to cause both the ripening and then rotting of fruit and vegetables, and associated phenomena such as fermentation, curdling, and putrefaction; its affect on the 'moist' organs of the body could cause cataracts, headaches, and lunacy; and blood flow waxed and waned with the moon's cycles, in turn affecting the ebb and flow of fever. The moon also had long-established associations with witchcraft—particularly the 'Evil Eye'—and could be 'milked' for its potent fluid.

33 *Aubrey astonished*: both the text in the *New Monthly* and the independently printed book of 1819 have this construction; Polidori appears to be drawing attention to the archaic meanings of the word—stupefied, bewildered, shocked out of self-possession—by omitting the linking verb (*OED*).

34 *Smyrna*: see note to p. 5.

Otranto: Italian harbour town at the south-east extremity of the peninsula; possibly a sly allusion to Horace Walpole's Gothic novel *The Castle of Otranto* (1764).

ataghans: see note to p. 7.

infantine: infantile (*OED*, noting two instances in Percy Shelley's poetry); Miss Aubrey is thus compared with the 'infantile' Ianthe (p. 28).

35 *voluptuary*: one addicted to sensuous pleasures (*OED*).

drawing room: a formal reception by a person of rank at which ladies are 'presented' (*OED*).

busy scene: fashionable society; adaptations of Thomas Percy's popular song 'O Nancy' include the lines 'Say, canst thou quite the busy scene, | Where thou art fairest of the fair?' (*Apollo's Lyre*, 60).

36 *besought him . . . to support nature*: another parallel with *Frankenstein*, in which Victor has a comparable breakdown, having spent a restless night outside his apartment 'walking up and down in the greatest agitation' then traverses the streets 'without any clear conception of where I was, or what I was doing, . . . not daring to look about me' (Shelley, *Frankenstein*, 37–8). The subsequent emphasis on the locket containing a fateful miniature also echoes the death of William and the framing of Justine in Shelley's novel.

38 *Earl of Marsden*: the peerage is Polidori's (or Watts's) invention.

39 *serpent's art*: Satan tempted Eve in the form of a guileful and loquacious snake: see Genesis 3: 1–5 and John Milton, *Paradise Lost* (1667), Bk IX.

conjuring: earnestly imploring or beseeching; the word is also used in swearing oaths (*OED*).

40 *Lord Ruthven had disappeared*: Ruthven escapes, and Polidori planned to continue the tale. He informed his sister in November 1819 that, 'I have just written to Longman to see if they would undertake to buy a second part of the *Vampyre* from me—as I must have something to engage my mind & I now find nothing to do' (Macdonald, *Poor Polidori*, 173). There was, however, to be no sequel—at least not by Polidori.

JOHN KEATS, *LA BELLE DAME SANS MERCI*

The textual history of this short ballad by the Romantic poet John Keats (1795–1821) is surprisingly complicated as there are various manuscript and printed versions (see Jones, 'Knight or Wight'; and Murfin and Stampone, 'Romantic Quotation'). The version presented here derives from the earliest manuscript version in Keats's letter to George and Georgina Keats (14 Feb. to 3 May 1819), and is dated 21 April 1819—just twenty days after Polidori's tale appeared. It was subsequently published in a revised version in Leigh Hunt's journal *The Indicator* on 10 May 1820, while Keats was resident in Hunt's house. The earliest version has been selected in its manuscript state to show the possible influence of 'The Bride of Corinth' and 'The Vampyre' (the printed versions are in any case readily available elsewhere). The text is taken from *Letters of John Keats*, ii. 356–7, with the correction 'why' for 'way' in line 45. Keats's deletions are not included, although it is nevertheless worth noting that he twice deleted the word 'death's' in lines 9 and 11; neither have speech marks been added to indicate speakers. This gives the lines the hallucinatory quality of an echo-chamber, which adds a haunting resonance to the linguistic ambiguities, such as 'fairy'/'faery' on which Keats plays.

Title: the title is French (spelt with variations in the different versions), meaning the beautiful lady without mercy, or without pity; it is taken from the title of a fifteenth-century poem by Sir Richard Roos, a translation of an earlier work by Alain Chartier that until the late eighteenth century was often attributed to Chaucer.

41 *sedge*: coarse greenish- or reddish-brown grass growing in wetland, specifically the cyperaceous genera *Carex* and *Cladium*, the Sweet Flag (*Acorus*), and the Wild Iris (*Iris Pseudacorus*); also in heraldry a 'spear reed' or flag carried as a charge, underlining Keats's medievalism (*OED*).

Meads: meadows (*OED*).

a faery's child: La Belle Dame is either a changeling or literally one of the faery folk—the ambiguous word 'faery' is used in its darker sense of supernatural beings 'remarkable for their riches, activity and malevolence' (Percy, *Northern Antiquities*, ii. 48); 'faery' also means an enchantress (*OED*), while the archaic spelling suggests Edmund Spenser's *The Faerie Qveene* (1590–6).

fragrant Zone: encircling girdle of flowers.

41 *manna dew*: miraculous or spiritual sustenance, often associated with the Eucharist (Numbers 11: 9; Psalm 78: 24–5; John 6: 50–1); this overtly Christian reference turns La Belle Dame into a chimera of conflicting and discordant elements. Traditionally, it is extremely perilous to dine with faery folk.

elfin grot: Keats is again invoking more sinister Spenserian meanings beneath apparently sentimental language—'her base Elfin brood there for thee left. | Such men do Chaungelings call' (Spenser, *Faerie Qveene*, Book I, Canto X, stanza 65). Like later vampires, elves were originally associated with contagion, the seductive demons *incubi* and *succubi*, and nightmares, as well as substituting human babies for eldritch changelings. Similarly, 'grot' for grotto or a picturesque cave also suggests grotesque distortion later associated with the Gothic (*OED*).

42 *lulled*: with the accent on the second syllable, lullèd.

thrall: bondage to a power, enslaved; also, misery or distress (*OED*).

gloam: evening twilight, derived from 'gloaming' (*OED*, which quotes this line as the earliest usage); the archaic word also, of course, suggests 'gloom'.

gaped: with the accent on the second syllable, gapèd.

sojourn: tarry, delay; also, unnervingly, describing a lodger in another's dwelling—as if the 'Knight at arms', having accepted La Belle Dame's perverse hospitality, is now bound to her (*OED*).

'URIAH DERICK D'ARCY' [RICHARD VARICK DEY], *THE BLACK VAMPYRE; A LEGEND OF ST. DOMINGO*

The immediate popularity of Polidori's 'The Vampyre' in the United States is evident from its republication in journals such as the *Atheneum* and *Robinson's Magazine* in June 1819, and in the same month the appearance of a 72-page chapbook *The Black Vampyre; A Legend of St Domingo*, attributed to one 'Uriah Derick D'Arcy'. *The Black Vampyre* had sufficient impact to go into a second edition in August of the same year, and inspired literary responses such as a comic poem by 'Goliah F'Arcy' (1819: see Dubay, 'Works like a Charm', 12).

The Black Vampyre is most likely to be the work of Revd Richard Varick Dey (1801–37)—'Uriah Derick D'Arcy' being an anagram of Dey's name (the letter *v* substituted for *u*, consistent with the 'printers alphabet': see Bray, '*The Black Vampyre* and the Hemispheric Gothic', 19–20n.); 'D'Arcy' also published poems in the *New-York Evening Post* in 1819. However, a heavily redacted version of the text was later reprinted in *The Knickerbocker* for January and February 1845 (vol. xxv, pp. 73–7, 171–3), where it is unambiguously attributed to a youthful Robert Charles Sands (1799–1832). Yet Sands—a journalist and author and later editor of *The New York Review and Athenæum Magazine* and *Commercial Advertiser* (*OCAL*)—was a member of the 'Knickerbocker' group of writers, mercilessly parodied and criticized in the text and its paratexts in attacks that seem too savage to be self-deprecating mockery (Bray, '*The Black Vampyre* and the Hemispheric Gothic', 19n.). On the other hand, Andrew Barger points out that Dey delivered the valedictory address at Columbia on the day Sands was awarded his MA degree in Law, and so may indeed be the target (*Best Vampire Stories*, 145–8). Whoever the author, the later version attributed to Sands is in any case severely emasculated: cuts include links made between Haiti and the US, feuding criticisms of the Knickerbocker literary group, and problematic episodes such as the suppression of the slave insurrection and mixed-race marriage and childbirth.

The text is taken from the second edition of 1819, printed for the author in New York; the first edition does not appear to be extant. The second edition is prefaced by an epigraph, an ironic letter of dedication, and an 'Introduction', and is followed by a 'Moral', 'Vampyrism; A Poem' (itself prefaced by a letter addressed to two magazine editors), and finally a note on authorship in a partly versified letter first printed in *The New-York Evening Post* in August 1819. The 'Introduction' and 'Moral' are included in the present text, but not the obvious additions to the second edition that are dated after June 1819; moreover, these paratexts make highly specific satirical references to liberal writers of the period that even with the benefit of explanatory notes would remain opaque to the majority of readers today (see Bray, '*The Black Vampyre* and the Hemispheric Gothic', 7–9). Barger has edited the tale (without the paratexts) for *Best Vampire Stories* (first published 2010), 145–70; the full text has been edited and helpfully annotated by Ed White, Duncan Faherty, and Toni Wall Jaudon in an online edition (Just Teach One; subsequently reprinted with dubious additional material by Leamington Books, 2020). The present version has been re-edited from the earliest extant edition.

43 *Bombast. Furios.*: *Bombastes Furioso, A Tragic Burlesque Opera; in One Act* written by William Barnes Rhodes (1772–1826) and first published in 1810; the lines, based on a mocking response by Artaxomines to similar lines uttered by General Bombastes, are slightly rewritten, being originally, 'So have I heard on Afric's burning shore | Another lion give a grievous roar, | And the last lion thought the first a boar [bore]' (13).

WALL-STREET: *Wall Street: Or, Ten Minutes Before Three; A Farce, in Three Acts* (1819) written by one Mead, and mockingly praised by the Knickerbocker poet Fitz-Greene Halleck: 'And who would now the Athenian dramas read | When he can get "Wall-street," by Mr. Mead' (Wegelin, *Early American Plays*, 57; Halleck, *Fanny*, 19, 25). The play is often wrongly attributed to Patrick Walker (1666?–1745?); Walker was a Scottish Covenanter (a member of the Cameronians, a strict Presbyterian sect opposed to any alliance between Church and State), a prolific historian of the Covenanting movement, and a folklorist.

temple of the Muses: the Nine Muses were ancient Greek divinities who inspired the arts and learning, including Thalia (comedy), Melpomene (tragedy), and Erato (love poetry); the phrase also possibly suggests James Lackington's celebrated bookshop in Finsbury Square, London, which opened in 1794 and traded under this name.

43 *literature of the Auction Room*: a disparaging reference to books being knocked down at cheap prices; there may also be an allusion here to the Panic of 1819, a catastrophic financial crisis that had begun the previous year when land values in some states collapsed, the price of cotton plummeted, and the US was plunged into an economic recession.

tangled skein: an allusion to the 'puzzled skein' and 'entangled skein' of Laurence Sterne's idiosyncratic novel *The Life and Opinions of Tristram Shandy, Gent.* (1759–67); the phrases appear in vol. 2, chapter 19; vol. 4, 'Slawkenbergius's Tale'; and vol. 7, chapter 28.

44 *two afternoons*: interestingly, John Polidori claimed that he had written 'The Vampyre' 'in two idle mornings' (*Diary*, 15–17).

the 'White Vampyre': meaning Polidori's 'The Vampyre' (pp. 22–40).

garbelled: archaic form of *garbled*.

45 *'But first on earth . . . ' Byron*: the text quotes the same lines from Byron's *The Giaour* (1813), 23–5, quoted in Alaric Watts's 'Introduction' to Polidori's 'The Vampyre' (pp. 20–1). Both extracts make the same minor changes to the text, indicating that D'Arcy's source was Watts rather than Byron's original.

ancestors: the tale is set in the early eighteenth century, long before Haitian independence; its alleged source, given at the end of the narrative, being family papers.

St. Domingo: under the Treaty of Rijswijk (1697), Spain ceded the eastern third of the Caribbean island of Hispaniola to France, who named it Saint-Domingue. The territory, which by the 1780s was worked by some half-million slaves, was France's most profitable colony in the Americas, but it was also disastrously over-cultivated, environmentally degraded, and politically incendiary. Escaped slaves (known as *Maroons*, from the French *marron*: fugitive) increasingly harassed the colonial authorities and a number of slave revolts broke out in the 1790s. These culminated in a declaration of independence on 1 January 1804 and the country was renamed Haiti (derived from the Arawak); however, it continued to be known under its French colonial title throughout the nineteenth century—particularly by European and North American commentators.

yaws: *framboesia*, a tropical skin disease presenting as tubercles shaped like raspberries (in French, *framboises*), believed to be a sexually transmitted infection from which Europeans had natural immunity (*OED*); two strains were identified in the nineteenth century—*frambœsia Guineensis*, common on the coast of Guinea, and *frambœsia Americana*, prevalent among the slaves of St Domingo (see *Encyclopædia Perthensis*, xiv, pt II, pp. 368–9).

the moon then shining bright: in Polidori's 'The Vampyre', Lord Ruthven rises under the 'first cold ray of the moon' (see note to p. 33).

Mr. P*ERSONNE*: anyone, anybody; or no-one, nobody (French).

Obi: obeah—in one sense folk medicine and healing techniques or (pejoratively) hostile witchcraft practised by African slaves in the Caribbean; here personified as a demon. However, the identification, depiction, and subsequent regulation of obeah, notably by the British colonial authorities, is complex, and amalgamated multiple beliefs and practices, some of which originated in West Africa, into a single collective term of resistance that, despite being criminalized in 1760 as a capital offence, continued to have significant social, political, cultural, and ritual significance (see Paton, *The Cultural Politics of Obeah Religion*, 16; see also Moseley, *Treatise on Sugar*, 170–80).

46 *Tunc perculit horror . . . tenuit vestigia ripa. LVC.*: 'Then trembling smote the leader's limbs, his hair stood on end, a faintness stopped his motion and fettered his feet on the edge of the river-bank' (Lucan, *De Bello Civili* [*c.* AD 61], Bk I, ll. 192–4: in Lucan, *The Civil War (Pharsalia)*, 17); the first word is transcribed *tunc* rather than the original *tum*, which translates as 'then he was struck with trembling'.

altitude: full height.

small toys . . . called witches and hobgoblins: a gravity device known as the 'posture master', the top of which is elderwood pith, the bottom weighted with lead so that its equilibrium is standing upright (see Vieth, *The Pleasing Preceptor*, i. 233–4; the terms *witch* and *hobgoblin* are unrecorded by *OED* and *Green*).

halloing: shouting, from *halloo*—calling to hounds to urge them on (*OED*).

ignaqueous: a portmanteau word combining *igneous*, meaning fiery, and *aqueous*, meaning watery—hence, living in both fire and water.

Indian Rubber: sap from the plant *Siphonia elastica* used in a variety of ways as gum (*OED*); here referring to a black-lead pencil eraser.

Moloch: Canaanite demon to whom children were sacrificed (1 Kings 11: 7; 2 Kings 23: 10; Jeremiah 32: 35); in John Milton's *Paradise Lost*, Moloch is a devil in league with Satan—'Moloch, horrid King besmeared with blood | Of human sacrifice, and parents' tears' (Bk I, ll. 392–3).

salamander: a mythical lizard or a daemonic spirit reputed to inhabit burning fire.

Hercules: in Greek myth Heracles [*sic*: the name was later Romanized] was a divinity celebrated for his 'Twelve Labours' and many other superhuman feats who died when his wife Deianira mistakenly poisoned him with a shirt soaked in the blood of the centaur Nessus, believing that it would rekindle Heracles' love for her; rather than suffer a lingering death Heracles instead built his own funeral pyre and was immolated by his comrade Philoctetes (*OCD*).

squizzed: drunk (US slang, pre-dating earliest *OED* citation).

46 *'His whole body . . . ' as Virgil or some other poet*: 'totus est pro volnere corpus' (Lucan, *De Bello Civili*, Bk IX, l. 814, in Lucan, *The Civil War (Pharsalia)*, 565), referring to the bite of the mythical *haemorrhois* or 'bleeder', a venomous serpent whose poison violently evacuated the blood from a victim's body and was thereby analogous to a vampire.

47 *Cayenne bath*: a preparation of lemon juice, salt, and cayenne pepper rubbed into the wounds of slaves to prevent infection; perhaps surprisingly, cayenne pepper may also have acted as a pain reliever (see Weaver, *Medical Revolutionaries*, 69).

Euphemia: the name is from the ancient Greek, meaning 'well-spoken'.

skin, hair, and nails: reflecting the consequences of the bite of the *haemorrhois* snake, the carcass being entirely drained of blood.

exsiccation: the complete removal of moisture (*OED*).

Scudder's Museum: a collection of curiosities put on display in New York City's lower Eastside in 1810 and eventually purchased by P. T. Barnum in 1841 to form the basis of his American Museum; among the early exhibits was the desiccated corpse of a Native American female—the 'Fawn Hoof Mummy'—discovered in Kentucky in 1811.

spasmodic affection: agitated and abnormal bodily state (*OED*).

sacre: *sacré* (French), a profane oath (pre-dating inaugural *OED* usages).

holocaust: sacrifice by burning (*OED*).

interesting infant: child concerned (*OED*).

unripe orange: oranges grown in the Caribbean remain green.

marks . . . upon their backs: Article 42 of the *Code noir* (1685), Louis XIV's edict regarding the treatment of slaves in the French American colonies, allowed planters to beat slaves with rods or straps; in Saint-Domingue the *Code* remained in force until 1793.

Time . . . Greek tragedians, Solomon: 'Time, as its age advanceth, teaches all things' (Aeschylus, *Prometheus Chain'd*, in *The Tragedies of Æschylus*, 60); 'To every thing there is a season, and a time to every purpose under the heaven: A time to be born, and a time to die . . . ' (Ecclesiastes 3: 1–8; Solomon is the 'Preacher' of Ecclesiastes).

elasticity: vigour, buoyancy (*OED*).

second mourning: the period following strict mourning when a more relaxed dress code was permitted.

Burton's Anatomy . . . Poems of Dr Farmer: Robert Burton (1577–1640), author of *The Anatomy of Melancholy* (1621), a copious work on the psychology of despair; and Henry Tudor Farmer, MD (1782–1828), whose *Imagination; The Maniac's Dream, and Other Poems* (1819) included several poems on disordered mental states and which cited Burton's *Anatomy* in 'An Essay on Taste' (126).

orangerie: an orchard of orange trees.

48 *Congo Apollo*: the Apollo Belvedere, a Roman copy of a Greek bronze, was discovered in the fifteenth century and considered the epitome of physical perfection—here presented as the archetype of central African masculinity.

Moorish Prince: the Moors were originally of Mauretania (an ancient region of north-west Africa), but the word was used loosely (and pejoratively) to describe Black Africans, Muslims, and Arabic culture generally (*OED*).

tristful: sorrowful (*OED*).

set down: sit down (*OED*, a rare usage).

brought out: a mistake for *bought* (i.e. purchased), in early use the word referred specifically to buying slaves; the Prince is himself a slaver—slavery being widespread in the Muslim world until the nineteenth century.

regal port: stately deportment or bearing (*port*, an inaugural usage).

crescent: a distinguishing emblem of Islam; also a reminder of the moonlight that originally revived the Prince when he was a child (see note to p. 45).

criticized: evaluated and commented upon, as opposed to condemning (*OED*).

ideologist of Lady Morgan: Sydney, Lady Morgan (1783 (baptized)–1859), Irish poet, novelist, and socialite; her novel *Florence Macarthy* (1818) includes various characters who quote, misquote, and discuss Shakespeare, including the bookish Edward De Vere and the pragmatic General Fitzwalter—'The one spoke in epic, the other in epigram'—either may be the character here alluded to (i. 40).

Abbe Reynal: 'Abbé' Guillaume-Thomas-François Raynal (1713–96), revolutionary propagandist and author-editor of *Histoire des deux Indes* ('History of the East and West Indies'), first published in six volumes in 1770 and republished in some thirty expanded editions over the following twenty years; Denis Diderot may have contributed to the work. Raynal was a pacifist and fiercely opposed to European colonialism, displaying a notable sympathy towards non-White races, commenting, for example, on the people of Guinea that, 'On the banks of the Niger, the women are generally handsome . . . Modest, affable, and faithful, an air of innocence appears in their looks . . . The men are of a proper size, their skin is as black as ebony, and their features and countenances pleasing', while

> The Creoles [at the time referring to those of black African descent born in the Caribbean, *OED*] are in general well made ... They are strangers to dissimulation, craft, and suspicion. The pride they take in their frankness, the opinion they have of themselves, together with their extreme vivacity, exclude from their commercial transactions all that mystery and reserve which stifles natural goodness of disposition, extinguishes the social spirit, and diminishes our sensibility. (Raynal, *Philosophical and Political History* (1798), iv. 55–6; see also iii. 403–4; iv. 154).

48 *This was a man!*: 'His life was gentle, and the elements | So mixed in him that Nature might stand up | And say to all the world "This was a man"' (William Shakespeare, *Julius Caesar*, V. v. 72–4); almost the last lines of the play, spoken by Mark Antony.

empyrean: the visible sky (*OED*).

Surgeon's Hall: probably referring to the collections of Surgeons' Hall at the Royal College of Surgeons of Edinburgh, although the first medical school building in America was Surgeons' Hall in Fifth Street, Philadelphia at the University of Pennsylvania, built in the 1790s.

block of Helen: slang term for the head or face of renowned beauty Helen of Troy (*Green*).

Medusa: most notorious of the monstrous Gorgons of Greek mythology—winged females crowned with snakes rather than hair; ironically, Medusa, Queen of the Gorgons, was sometimes depicted by artists with a beautiful face.

Black men . . . ladies' eyes: 'the old saying is, | "Black men are pearls in beauteous ladies' eyes"' (William Shakespeare, *The Two Gentlemen of Verona*, V. ii. 11–12), spoken by Proteus; although presented as proverbial, *ODEP* cites the first recorded usage as Shakespeare's *Titus Andronicus* (V. i. 42).

49 *Bambuck*: Bambuhu (named Bambouk by the French) is a region rich in gold fields on the western coast of Africa, traditionally covering parts of Senegal and western Mali; Raynal describes Bambouk [*sic*] as 'an aristocratic state . . . where each village was governed by a chief called Farim' (Raynal, *Philosophical and Political History* (1798), iv. 53).

perambulate: travel through; the rare and obsolete meaning 'encircle' is also possible here (*OED*).

gump: fool, dolt (possibly Scottish dialect, but this appears to be an inaugural usage: see *OED* and *Green*).

Zara: the Bobo people of Burkina Faso.

golden coast: Gulf of Guinea on the west coast of Africa; Raynal notes that the women scarred their faces (Raynal, *Philosophical and Political History* (1798), iv. 57).

See Reynal, Vol. III. pp. 385 and 387.: 'On the banks of the Niger, the women are generally handsome, if beauty may be said to consist in symmetry of proportion, and not in colour. Modest, affable, and faithful, an air of innocence appears in their looks, and their language is an indication of their bashfulness. The names of Zilia, Calypso, Fanny, Zama, which seem to be names of voluptuousness, are pronounced with an inflection of voice, of the softness and sweetness of which our organs are not susceptible' (Raynal, *Philosophical and Political History* (1804), iv. 48, 50).

Hottentot Venus: Saartjie Baartman (c.1789–1815), a South African Khoisan woman and sufferer from steatopygia who arrived in London in 1810 and was exhibited as an erotic sideshow; on her death she was dissected, an account of the event followed in 1816, and her body parts were publicly displayed (see Shelley, *Frankenstein*, 219n.).

Abyssinia: Kingdom of Ethiopia, now Ethiopia and Eritrea.

Mrs. Dubois: third married name of Euphemia Personne.

fructify: bear fruit.

Zembo: a variant of *zambo* (Spanish) or *sambo* (French, also *Foulah*, meaning uncle, and *Hausa*, meaning second son or spirit), a derogatory term for an individual of mixed race (at this time specifically meaning mixed-race and Black parents). The word was originally neutral but later derogatively applied to slaves and Africans (*Green*); as Zembo has already been described as a 'pale European' its use here seems to be ironic through his association with the Prince.

50 *sweetmeats*: any confectionery, usually candied fruit or sugar lozenges.

dishabille: partially or carelessly dressed (*OED*).

place of sepulture: burial place (*OED*).

tamarind: the tree *Tamarindus indica*, characterized by dark green leaves, yellow and red flowers, and pods harvested for an acidic pulp used in medicine and cooking (*OED*).

Lord Ruthven: the vampire of Polidori's tale (see note to p. 24), explicitly connecting the two texts and audaciously suggesting that Ruthven has a French Caribbean background.

blues: melancholy, the 'blue devils'; *Green* notes that the word is an English coinage from 1741, 'despite assumption that the term was created/ patented by US blacks' (*OED*; *Green*).

genii: a sardonic reference to the supernatural spirits of Arabian stories able to take human form (*OED*).

turned towards the East . . . handfuls of earth . . . over their heads: these actions may loosely allude to Islamic burial rites in facing the Qibla (Mecca) and casting three handfuls of earth into a grave, although this practice is also common at Christian funerals; the verses of the Koran and the Hebrew Bible are not dissimilar on this point—'Out of the ground have we created you; and to the same will we cause you to return, and we will bring you forth from thence another time' (Quran 20: 55 (ii. 143)); 'dust thou *art*, and unto dust shalt thou return' (Genesis 3: 19).

51 *Ed. New Mon. Mag.*: the sub-editor of *The New Monthly Magazine*, Alaric Watts (see headnote to 'Letter from Geneva', p. 497). The child, meanwhile, exhibits the typical characteristics of eighteenth-century European vampires: the body is fresh and uncorrupted, and has a ruddy face—like that of Arnond Paole, as reported in Watts's 'Introduction' (see p. 19; and Groom, *The Vampire* 13, 31, 36, 240n.).

blood . . . mingled with . . . earth: eating earth from the grave of a vampire or bread baked with the blood of a vampire afforded protection against the creatures (see Groom (2020), 23, 42, 79); this concoction may also be an allusion to obeah practices (see note to p. 45).

51 *lymph*: water; i.e. a stream (*OED*).

See Edwards, vol. II. p. 86. '. . . if the truth be not spoken': accurately transcribed with minor changes to punctuation from Edwards, *History*, ii. 278.

gripe: grasp; possibly, from Irish slang, the hand (*Green*).

52 *wrong sow by the ear*: inverting the proverbial 'To have the sow by the right ear' (*ODEP*) to mean having made a poor choice or a mistake; pigs are caught by the ear.

pharmacopeia: reserve of drugs (*OED*).

calomel and jalap, ipecacuanha, rhubarb, and tartar-emetic: mercurous chloride (horn-quicksilver), root of *Exogonium* (*Ipomœa*) *Purga*, root of *Cephaëlis ipecacuanha*, garden rhubarb, and potassio-antimonious tartrate, respectively; all were used medicinally as purgatives or emetics (see *Medical Transactions*).

slaver: saliva, although here perhaps refers to sweat.

tumuli: barrows or ancient burial mounds; here, a poetic archaism (*OED*).

cicatrized: healed by inducing a scar (*OED*).

prospect of immortality before her: early vampire accounts do not dwell on the delights of immortality; this is the first tale to do so.

for a subject to satisfy: corrected from 'for subject to a satisfy'.

got up out of his coffin: the Personnes are perhaps more like zombies than vampires, hinting, as elsewhere in the tale, at ancient African sources for European vampirism (see Bray, 10, 12–13).

53 *divorce*: complete separation (*OED*).

according to the old proverb: 'He is on the ground' (*ODEP*), meaning he is coming to pay his debts.

Salam: a sign of respect, being a low bow of the head and body with the palm of the right hand on the forehead; *salām* (Arabic), meaning 'peace (be upon you)' (*OED*).

gentlemanly satisfaction: a dignified settlement, a phrase of over-politeness common in boxing reports of the time, which this passage imitates (see, for example, McLaren, *The Battle of the Dandies*, 15).

claret: blood; boxing jargon (*Green*).

54 *fibbed*: punched; likewise boxing—or *fibbery*—jargon (*Green*).

sconce: head (*Green*).

a facer under the gills: a blow to the face below the cheeks (*Green*).

the giant of old: Antaeus, son of Poseidon and Earth who wrestled and then killed challengers, and who became stronger each time he was thrown to the ground—the ground being his mother; he was eventually slain by Heracles (*OCD*).

driving stakes . . . sledge hammer: this detail, like that of Arnond Paole, derives from Watts's 'Introduction' rather than from Polidori's tale (see p. 20).

nailed to the counter: commonly means 'exposed as false', but here, prostrate upon the ground.

small or broad sword: the small sword, also known as the court sword, was a light thrusting or fencing weapon; the broad sword was a heavier edged sword often used by cavalrymen.

noddle: the head, especially of a fool (*Green*).

pocketed the affront: accepted or submitted to the insult without resentment (*OED*).

55 *dingy*: derogatory US slang for a Black or mixed-race individual (*Green*).

take French leave: leave unnoticed (*OED*; the phrase more usually means leaving without prior permission: see *Green*).

searments: grave-clothes, i.e. cerements.

bread-basket: stomach; again, common in boxing reports (*Green*).

Counsellor Phillips's harangue, about ' . . . rejected altar': Charles Phillips (1786/7?–1859), Irish Protestant barrister and writer strongly supportive of Catholic emancipation (*DIB*) known as 'Counsellor O'Garnish' for his oratorical extravagance; the quotation is taken from 'A Speech delivered at an Aggregate Meeting of the Roman Catholics of Cork', in *Speeches of Charles Phillips*, 19–36, at 30.

the pale planet of magic adoration: the moon (see notes to pp. 45, 48).

serried files: 'Nor served it to relax their serried files' (Milton, *Paradise Lost*, Bk VI, l. 599); *serried* meaning armed ranks shoulder to shoulder (*OED*)—hence, figuratively, closely packed.

bright armoury: arsenal; a figurative use referring to the supernatural impact of moonbeams.

No cymbal clash'd . . . was dumb: Walter Scott, *The Lady of the Lake* (1810), Canto VI ('The Guard-Room'), stanza xvi (p. 265).

56 *'The ring-leaders . . . ' &c.—Edwards, Vol. III. p 52.*: referring to Vincent Ogé *jeune* (the younger) and Jean-Baptiste Chavanne, free men of colour of Saint-Domingue, who led a slave revolt for which they were executed in 1791—Ogé is considered the first martyr of the Haitian Revolution; quoted, omitting a sub-clause (referring to their 'atrocious project'), from Edwards, *History*, iv. 52; see Garrigus, 'Vincent Ogé *jeune*').

ramifications: branches, in this case of subterranean tunnels (*OED*); an unusual usage.

catachrestically: here, the 'artful concealment' by 'nature' is *catachresis*—the 'necessary misuse' of language (see Quintilian, quoted by Dupriez, *Dictionary of Literary Devices*, 92).

Buccaniers: variant spelling of *Bucaniers*, meaning those who smoke and dry flesh on a *boucan*, the name being given to French hunters of

St Domingo (*OED*); later, the term was adapted to reflect their piratical activities on the Spanish Main as *Buccaneers*.

56 *Professors of the* Obeah *art*: the phrase appears in Stephen Fuller's paper 'Obiah Trials' in The British Board of Trade's *Report . . . of all Matters relating to Trade and Foreign Plantations* (1789): 'In the Year 1760, the Influence of the Professors of the *Obiah Art* was such, as to induce a great many of the Negro Slaves in Jamaica to engage in the Rebellion which happened in that Year, and which gave rise to the Law which was then made against the Practice of *Obiah*' (Part III, sig. D2[v]); it was later quoted by Edwards and, at length, by William Earle in *Obi; or, The History of Three-Fingered Jack* (54–61n.).

midnight orgies: alluding to Polidori's 'The Vampyre' (see p. 29).

spars: the aforementioned 'immense shafts', being rafters or props, often of undressed wood (*OED*).

See Edwards, Vol. II p. 111.: 'The *Obi* is usually composed of a farrago of materials, most of which are enumerated in Jamaica law [note: passed 1760], viz. blood, feathers, parrots beaks, dogs teeth, alligators teeth, broken bottles, grave dirt, rum, and egg shells' (Edwards, *History* (1806–7), ii. 301; see also Moseley, *Treatise on Sugar*, 171, which lists 'grave dirt, hair, teeth of sharks, and other creatures, blood, feathers, egg-shells, images in wax, the hearts of birds, and some potent roots, weeds, and bushes', and which was in turn quoted by Earle (*Obi*, 98n.; see too William Burdett, *Life and Exploits of Mansong, commonly called Three-Finger'd Jack* (1800), which lists 'rags, feathers, bones of cats, and a thousand other articles' (27)).

blackamoors: Black individuals, now of course both derogatory and offensive; however, the context here also alludes to a rare secondary meaning—that of devils (*OED*).

Gouls: variant spelling of *ghoul*; in Islamic demonology, a ghoul (*ghūl*) is a jinn that robs graves and eats human flesh, aligning them with Orthodox Christian vampires (*OED*, which cites J. R. Lowell in 1873, 'It sucks with the vampire, gorges with the ghoule').

her late husband: a confusing reference to the Prince; the text conflates ghouls and afrits with vampires (see note to p. 58).

Merriwang . . . Dundo . . . Goombay: among musical instruments, 'they have the *Banja* or *Merriwang*, the *Dundo*, and *Goombay*; all of African origin. The first is an imperfect kind of violincello; except that it is played on by the finger like the guitar; producing a dismal monotony of four notes. The Dundo is precisely a tabor; and the Goombay is a rustick drum; being formed of the trunk of a hollow tree, one end of which is covered with a sheep's skin. From such instruments nothing like a regular tune can be expected, nor is it attempted' (Edwards, *History* (1793), ii. 84).

57 *lyre of Orpheus*: singer and musician of Greek mythology able to charm wild beasts, trees, and rock with his voice and playing, and famed for

rescuing his wife Eurydice from the Underworld through the power of song (*OCD*).

hosts of Pandemonium: Pandemonium is the city built by devils after they have roused themselves in Hell (Milton, *Paradise Lost*, Bk I, ll. 710–51, 756).

Mr Burke: Edmund Burke (1729/30–1797), statesman and Whig politician, famed for his brilliance in parliamentary debate and his masterly public oratory; over twenty years after his death his reputation remained unmatched.

esculent: vegetable food (*OED*).

Gentlemen of colour: non-White men, the term dating from 1786 (*OED*); Edwards comments that, 'THE Inhabitants . . . were composed of three great classes: 1st, pure whites. 2d, people of colour, and blacks of free condition. 3d, negroes and mulattoes in a state of slavery. The reader is apprised that the class which, by a strange abuse of language, is called *people of colour*, originates from an intermixture of the whites and the blacks' (Edwards, *History* (1801), iii. 25).

Prometheus Vinctus: the ancient Greek tragedy *Prometheus Bound*, probably written by Aeschylus *c.*466–459 BC; in Aeschylus' version of the myth Prometheus steals fire from the gods for the benefit of mankind and is consequently punished by Zeus by being chained to a rock and having his liver torn out by an eagle—and every night his liver regenerates to allow him to be disembowelled again at dawn. Prometheus was a central figure in British Romanticism: Mary Shelley's *Frankenstein* (1818), for example, is subtitled *The Modern Prometheus* (see pp. xxviii–xxxii).

a dog . . . ερπων . . . an insect . . . a bird: alternatives to the eagle sent to eviscerate Prometheus; ερπων also refers to a crawling reptile.

Crows . . . pirate Bat of Madagascar . . . Ivunches . . . Krakens . . . Cape-cod Sea Serpents . . . the Incubi;—and the Succubi: crows are bad luck and omens of death; the Madagascan flying fox (*Pteropus rufus*) was considered carnivorous; Chilean sorcerers, 'who at night transform themselves into nocturnal birds', were attended by familiars or 'man-animals' (*ivunches*: see Abbe Molina, *Geographical, Natural, and Civil History of Chili*, ii. 88); the kraken was a vast sea serpent of the Norwegian Sea; New England sea serpents were witnessed along various parts of the east coast—most notably in 1817–19 at Gloucester, Essex County—and consequently entered US folklore in the nineteenth century; and incubi and succubi were demonic sexual predators known for bringing nightmares and suffocating their victims, and which in the eighteenth century were strongly associated with vampires.

Titan . . . Cyclopes . . . Anthropophagi: the Titans were pre-Olympian gods of ancient Greek mythology, while the Cyclopes were giant and savage humanoids with a single eye—both were the offspring of Gaia (Earth) and Uranus (Sky)—while the Anthropophagi were humanoids who ate humans; all three have cannibalistic tendencies (*OCD*, *OED*).

57 *See Edwards, Vol. II. p. 90, and Reynal, Vol. III. p. 388*:

> THE depression of spirits which these people seem to be under, on their first arrival in the West Indies, gives them an air of softness and submission, which forms a striking contrast to the frank and fearless temper of the Koromantya Negroes. Nevertheless, the Eboes are in fact more truly savage than any nation of the Gold Coast; inasmuch as many tribes among them, especially the Moco tribe, have been, without doubt, accustomed to the shocking practice of feeding on human flesh. This circumstance I have had attested beyond the possibility of dispute, by an intelligent trust-worthy domestick of the Ebo nation, who acknowledged to me, though with evident shame and reluctance, (having lived many years among the Whites) that he had himself, in his youth, frequently regaled on this horrid banquet: and his account received a shocking confirmation from a circumstance which occurred in the year 1770 in Antigua, where two Negroes of the same country were tried for killing and devouring one of their fellow-slaves in that island. (Edwards, *History* (1793), ii. 76)

Raynal attributes to native Brazilians the practices of cannibalism ('anthropophagy') and preserving the decapitated heads of enemies as trophies (Raynal, *Philosophical and Political History* (1798), iii. 279).

58 *bowl of the Coco, the soft bloom of the* ANANA: either coconut milk or the drink cocoa (chocolate), and either pineapple or the Central American fruit *Bromelia pinguin* (penguin, or wild pineapple); Bryan Edwards's poem 'On Seeing a Negro Funeral' contains the lines 'For thee, the dulcet reed shall spring, | Her milky bowl the coco bring, | Th' anana bloom for thee' (*Poems*, 46; later partly republished with revisions in *History* (1793), ii. 87, and elsewhere).

Afrits,—or Vampyres;—Vroucolochas,—Vardoulachos,—or Broucolokas: afrits (*efreeti*) are Qur'anic demons or supernatural spirits of Arabian stories, which in Byron's poem *The Giaour* (1813) are associated with ghouls and in this text are identified with vampires; the remaining terms are alternative names for vampires from Greece, Macedonia, Turkey, and Serbia cited by Byron, Southey, and others (see Groom, *The Vampire*, 14, 27, 87, etc.).

relics and relicts: a variant on the dead and the living—*relics* being bodily remains (often sacred), *relicts* being survivors (*OED*); the original text has a rogue inverted comma at the beginning of this phrase, but this is not a quotation.

at once . . . what must be!: alluding to Phillips, 'A Speech delivered at a Public Dinner given to Mr. Finlay by the Roman Catholics of the Town and County of Sligo'—'the relic of WHAT WAS; the solemn and sublime memento of WHAT MUST BE' (*Speeches of Charles Phillips*, 1–18, at 6).

a fee-tail: an inheritance limited to particular heirs (*OED*).

docked: in law, blocking a settlement or similar, or breaking a succession to inherit (*OED*).

manes: spirits of the dead requiring appeasement (*OED*).

the LEOPHARES *and the* JAKOFFS: Edwards quotes from Richard Hakluyt's *The Principall Navigations, Voiages and Discoveries of the English Nation* (1589): 'The people of Cape Verde . . . are called *Leophares*, and are counted the goodliest men of all others . . . These Leophares have wars against the Jaloffs [*sic*: Hakluyt has 'Jeloffes'], which are borderers [neighbours] by them' (Edwards, *History* (1793), ii. 42).

the SAMBOES *and the* SAWPITS: Samboses and Sapies, again quoted by Edwards from Hakluyt: 'These inhabitants (who were called *Samboes* [*sic*]) hold divers of the Sapies taken in war as their slaves' (Edwards, *History* (1793), ii. 43).

a brig . . . a schooner . . . a seventy-four: a seagoing vessel with two large square-rigged masts; a smaller, swifter coastal vessel with between two and four masts, forerunner of the clipper; a large warship armed with seventy-four cannon, respectively (*OED*).

curculio: *Entimus imperialis*, a brilliantly iridescent species of weevil, also known as the *Curculio imperialis* or Brazilian diamond beetle.

car of the æronaut . . . ligaments are cut: the basket of a hot-air balloonist when its anchor ropes are severed.

59 *discandied*: melted (*OED*).

our chains dissolved . . . by the irresistible genius of UNIVERSAL EMANCIPATION*!!!*: alluding to John Philpot Curran's celebrated (if unsuccessful) defence of Archibald Hamilton Rowan of the Society of United Irishmen—'his body swells beyond the measure of his chains, that burst from around him, and he stands redeemed, regenerated, and disenthralled, by the irresistible genius of UNIVERSAL EMANCIPATION' (O'Regan, *Memoirs*, 62–3; the defence was first published in 1794); Curran (1750–1817) was an Irish Protestant politician and lawyer renowned for his radicalism in supporting Catholics and Irish patriotism.

Corybantes: priests devoted to the ancient Phrygian deity Cybele, goddess of fertility and health (and disease), protector in times of war, and guardian of wild creatures.

Phyrricks: pyrrhic dances, being ancient Greek war dances performed in full armour (*OED*).

chevaux-de-frise: 'CHEVAL *de frise*, in *Fortification*, a large piece of timber, either round or cut into several faces, pierced, and traversed with wooden spikes, armed or pointed with iron, five or six feet long' (Chambers and Rees, *Cyclopædia*, vol. i).

to die game: to meet death resolutely, maintaining spirit to the last (*OED*).

ridicule: a small decorated ladies' handbag, popular from the late eighteenth century (*OED*).

quicksilver: liquid mercury.

59 *curvetting*: in equestrianism, a curvet is a move in which a horse rears and jumps forward on its hind legs—hence, more generally, capering (*OED*).

Mr. Maffey: The Maffey family were French puppeteers, one of whom toured the US in 1817–18 as an 'artist, mechanician, proprietor, inventor', staging a display of mechanical figures in New York in 1818 (*The New-York Evening Post* (23 June 1818), 3: see Huhtamo, 'Mechanical Theatre', 60).

60 *the renowned knight of the Bed-chamber*: probably referring to Don Quixote, the deluded knight errant of Miguel de Cervantes Saavedra's celebrated novel (1604–14); in part 1, chapter 35, Don Quixote, asleep in his room at an inn, dreams that he is fighting a giant and consequently battles several wineskins in his bedchamber, flooding the room.

soused: fell heavily (*OED*).

Johannes Porco Latinus: Pig Latin (*Porco Latinus*: incorrect or mock Latin) is first recorded by *OED* in 1844, so this may be an inaugural use; alternatively, the allusion may be to Johannes Latinus (Juan de Sessa, known as Juan Latino, 1518–1594/7?), the Afro-Hispanic Professor of Latin Grammar at Granada Cathedral; he is mentioned in passing at the beginning of *Don Quixote* and occasionally in contemporary studies of race, but it seems unlikely that readers at the time would have recognized the Latinized name of a sixteenth-century academic.

in principia fundimentalia: literally, 'in fundamental principles', but really referring to the buttocks, alluding to Samuel Johnson's fearsome pun on *fundament* related by James Boswell: 'collecting himself, and looking aweful . . . and as it were searching his mind for a still more ludicrous word, he slowly pronounced, "I said the *woman* was *fundamentally* sensible;" as if he had said, hear this now, and laugh if you dare' (*Boswell's Life of Johnson*, iv. 99).

Gœtulian lion: an African lion of Gaetuli (Libya, in Roman times), referenced proverbially by Horace and other writers to indicate a ferocious beast that may nevertheless easily be subdued through guile.

Enceladus under Ætna: the Gigante (giant) Enceladus, another son of Gaia (Earth) and Uranus (Sky), was slain by either Zeus or Athena and buried or crushed beneath the Sicilian volcano Mount Etna.

compeers: equals, peers, companions (*OED*).

With burning chains . . . by hell's inexorable doors: Homer's *Iliad*, trans. Alexander Pope (1715–20), Book 8, ll. 17–18; part of the description of Tartarus, 'the place of torture for the impious after death' (p. 401).

the caverns of Delphos: the Pythia, housed in the caves of Delphi upon the slopes of Mount Parnassus, was the presiding ancient Greek oracle through whom the god Apollo spoke (*OCD*).

in statu quo: in the same state (*OED*).

Barabbas: in the New Testament, the prisoner whom the crowd called to be released by Pontius Pilate in preference to Jesus; Matthew describes him as a 'notable prisoner' (27: 16), Mark and Luke as a murderer and insurrectionary (15: 7, 23: 19), and John as a 'robber' (18: 40). Barabas [*sic*] is also the Machiavellian villain, murderer, and eponymous character in Christopher Marlowe's play *The Jew of Malta* (*c.*1592), to whom Shakespeare alludes in *The Merchant of Venice* (*c.*1596–7). The name literally means 'son of the father' in Aramaic.

mulatto: specifically at the time 'a name given, in the Indies, to those who are begotten by a Negro man on an Indian woman; or an Indian man on a Negro woman' (Chambers and Rees, *Cyclopædia*, vol. iii); now both derogatory and offensive.

61 *a Forum trope*: probably referring to the New-York Forum, where issues of public interest were presented and debated *c.*1816–19.

must remain buried . . . of futurity: untraced, probably an invented quotation; however, a similar phrase occurs in a review of Mrs B. Hooper, *A Poem occasioned by the Cessation of Public Mourning for H. R. H. the Princess Charlotte; together with Sonnets and Other Productions* (London: Suttaby and Co., 1818) in *The European Magazine, and London Review; containing the Literature, History, Politics, Arts, Manners and Amusements of the Age* (Nov. 1818), 'for who can tell the dark mysteries of fate, or penetrate the bowels of futurity' (vol. lxxiv, p. 435).

namesake at Elizabeth-town: Thomas Gibbons (1757–1826), planter, lawyer, and fractious politician who in 1819 was being sued for infringing a steamboat monopoly between New York and Elizabethtown Point—a case that went to the Supreme Court and which he ultimately won in 1824 (*ANB*); Elizabeth-Town is now the City of Elizabeth in Union County, New Jersey and adjacent to Essex County.

bowels for so diabolical a profession: i.e. vampirism; Gibbons was known for being overweight.

GLUT THE THIRST OF A VAMPYRE!!!: an almost direct quotation of the last words of Polidori's 'The Vampyre', 'glutted the thirst of a VAMPYRE!' (see p. 40); strangely, however, in this text the phrase refers to Anthony Gibbons, who is a direct descendant of the child of Euphemia Personne and the Prince—he is himself part of the vampire bloodline as well as being the custodian of the family papers from which the narrative is supposedly taken.

machinery: use of the supernatural in a literary work (*OED*).

our climate . . . in enchanters: the long list of middle-class professionals (and a few others) as being vampires is typical of earlier eighteenth-century uses of the figure in social critiques.

the counter: the token used as a substitute for money in gambling and games of chance, especially cards (*OED*).

62 *exenterates*: eviscerates; figuratively speaking, takes out the meaning of (*OED*).

62 *Burke, and Curran, and Phillips*: Edmund Burke (see note to p. 57); John Philpot Curran (see note to p. 59); and Charles Phillips (see note to p. 55), who eulogized the late Curran in a popular biographical memoir.

Second-handed: having derivative or plagiarized ideas or arguments (*OED*).

Theologue: a theological student (US colloquialism; *OED*).

Tillotson and Toplady: John Tillotson (1630–94), Archbishop of Canterbury known for the fluency of his published sermons, an invaluable resource for eighteenth-century parsons; Augustus Montague Toplady (1740–78), clergyman and hymn writer best known for 'Rock of Ages', although he was also an influential commentator on Calvinism.

Empiric: an unqualified medical practitioner, either advocating folk cures or simply a quack (*OED*).

Bibliopolist: a bookseller (*OED*).

who guts the fobs: empties the pockets; the phrase appears in Thomas Moore's mock-epic poem to pugilism, *Tom Crib's Memorial to Congress* (1819), where *gutting* is defined as 'Taking out the contents' (p. 1, l. 6).

Lord Byron . . . never saw: such as, perhaps most notoriously, 'The Vampyre' (see headnote, pp. 501–2).

lime and horse-beef: both contain vitamin C and were therefore consumed to prevent scurvy; however, limes were adopted by the British Navy for reasons of cost and were not as effective as lemons, particularly when stored, and although eating horse meat was commonplace in revolutionary France for political reasons and was then favoured by Napoleon's armies (for example, at the siege of Alexandria in 1801), the meat has never been popular in Britain, Ireland, or the US (*OED*).

quantum-meruit: a fair sum paid but not stipulated in a contract (*OED*).

resurrectionist's: bodysnatcher, an illegal exhumer of corpses who profits by selling the cadavers to medical schools or anatomizing them for such things as teeth for dentists and tallow for candle-makers; in 1794 a corpse could realize about 5 guineas, or 5 pounds and 5 shillings (see Groom, *The Vampire*, 114–16).

the anthropophagous Caribs in Robinson Crusoe: the South American cannibals of Daniel Defoe's novel *The Life and Strange Surprizing Adventures of Robinson Crusoe, of York, Mariner* (1719).

pinguidity and unctuousness: fatness and richness (usually of meat; *OED*).

Shylock, impatient to attack the ilia: Shylock, the Jewish moneylender of Shakespeare's *Merchant of Venice*, intends to take payment of a pound of flesh from Antonio by slicing into his breast 'Nearest his heart' (IV. i. 251); however, the ilia were the flanks below the ribs.

Johnson . . . 'have spun this discourse out of my own bowels': not Samuel Johnson, but Horace Walpole in a letter to Lady Ossory, 5 January 1774—'I have no news; and if [I] spin out of my own bowels, what can I find there but the poison I have been swallowing these eight months' (*Horace Walpole's Correspondence*, xxxii. *Horace Walpole's Correspondence with the Countess of Upper Ossory*, 179). Walpole's correspondence and 'Walpoliana' began to be published in 1799, within two years of his death.

ERNST BENJAMIN SALOMO RAUPACH, *WAKE NOT THE DEAD*

First published in German as 'Laßt die Todten Ruhen. Ein Märchen' ('Wake not the dead. A fairy tale') in *Minerva: Taschenbuch für das Jahr 1823* (Leipzig: Gerhard Fleischer, 1823), 35–88; first published in English later in the same year in an anonymous translation, and also subsequently published under the title 'The Bride of the Grave'. The tale is correctly attributed in the *Minerva* volume yet has been persistently but erroneously attributed to Ludwig Tieck (e.g. by Frayling, *Vampyres*, 165; for a comprehensive discussion of the authorship, see Crawford, 'Raupach's Vampire Story'). Crawford outlines Raupach's career: born in 1784, he studied at the University of Halle, ostensibly reading theology but in reality pursuing a wide range of scholarly interests from French to mathematics; he graduated with a doctorate in 1814. Raupach lived in St Petersburg, teaching and writing dramas, before returning to Germany in 1823. He wrote a staggering ninety-eight plays from 1820 to 1842, and died ten years later.

As Crawford points out, there is a strong theme of necrophilia in this tale. There are also echoes of Gottfried August Bürger's vampire poem 'Lenore' (first published in 1774: see Groom, *The Vampire*, 99–100) through the repeated figures of horse and rider. True to its original German subtitle, there are also many fairy-tale elements: 'magic in the form of the sorcerer, the magical root, the cave as a safe hiding place, a crossroads, animal helpers in the form of an eagle and a raven, and the almost excessive use of the numbers 7 and 3'—although these are usually incidental to the plot (Crawford, 'Raupach's Vampire Story', 1199); the return of a dead lover is in any case an enduring motif in ballads and in folklore. Raupach's vampire is characterized by rendering its prey unconscious and causing a gradual collapse of health through repeated bloodsucking, linking earlier identifications of vampirism with wasting diseases and contagion with later medicalizations of the condition. The tale inspired George Blink's comic horror drama *The Vampire Bride: or, The Tenant of the Tomb* (1830), and was also probably a direct influence on Edgar Allan Poe's 'Ligeia' (pp. 88–100) (see Lewis, 'The Intellectual Functions of Gothic Fiction', although here Raupach's tale is attributed to Tieck).

The present text is taken from the first English version published in *Popular Tales and Romances of the Northern Nations* (1823), i. 233–91; there is a dated archness in the vocabulary, and a reliance on colons and semicolons for punctuation; the text also has several different spellings of the word 'ecstasy' and its cognates, which have been regularized to a single archaic form, 'exstasy'.

63 *Wake not the Dead . . . enshrouded deep*: the epigraph appears to be by Raupach himself.

Brunhilda: the names Brunhilda (in Brynhild and other variants, meaning 'armoured in battle') and Swanhilda allude to Germanic and Old Norse myth. Brunhilda, a warrior princess and in some sources a Valkyrie or divine shield-maiden, is a central character who exacts a fatal revenge upon Siegfried (Sigurd) for his duplicity.

64 *gem*: the word is used as a verb, to adorn with gems (*OED*).

Swanhilda: like Brunhilda, a legendary Germanic name meaning 'battle-swan'.

animal life: animal or fleshly nature (*OED*).

67 *sooth*: truth; by this time the word was a conscious literary archaism (*OED*).

weal: of a person, a source of felicity or object of delight; also often opposed to woe (*OED*).

68 *inquiet*: uneasy, anxious (*OED*).

69 *Drink . . . warm stream*: thus, she is raised a vampire.

70 *my eye is yet too weak to ensure the light of day*: aversion to light was characteristic of nineteenth-century and later vampires, deriving from earlier cases of the undead being limited to roaming at certain times; most eighteenth-century vampire assaults, such as those by Arnond Paole, took place at night—their activities being understood as part of the demonic spectrum of incubi, succubi, and nightmares (see Groom, *The Vampire*, 34, 45–8, 52).

aweful: the Burkean sublime: inspiring awe, terror, or dread (*OED*).

sacred music . . . temple: reminiscent of Thomas De Quincey, who in *Confessions of an English Opium Eater* (first published in the *London Magazine* in 1821, and published as a book in 1822) recalled, 'The dream commenced with a music which now I often heard in dreams—a music of preparation and of awakening suspense [which] . . . gave the feeling of a vast march—of infinite cavalcades filing off—and the tread of innumerable armies' (76).

71 *mouldering taint . . . never disappeared*: although vampires were incorruptible, by the end of the nineteenth century the vampires in *Dracula* have the smell of the grave upon them, a characteristic that Bram Stoker picked up from Herbert Mayo, who observed that, 'you feel his face, fresh with the smell of the grave, bent over your throat, while his keen teeth make a fine incision in your jugular, preparatorily to his commencing his plain but nutritive repast' (Mayo, 'Vampyrism', 21)—compare with the child corpse in *The Black Vampyre*: 'the body of her child was perfectly fresh, and the olfactory nerves experienced no unsavoury sensation from its proximity' (p. 51); violets have a complex folklore, combining death and mourning with love and fertility.

moon . . . horn: until the crescent moon waxes into a gibbous and then the full moon.

72 *cross heath*: i.e. across the heath.

ill assorted with: ill matched to (*OED*).

74 *gold . . . silver*: an idiosyncratic inversion, as vampires usually stay away from silver, which traditionally has protective properties, and Dracula of course has heaps of gold in his castle; nevertheless, silver is particularly associated with the moon: the traditional astrological pictogram for the moon and one of the alchemical symbols for silver is ☽.

pearls: ironically, pearls are associated with calming, purity, truth, and integrity, as well as with the moon.

crowing of the cock: see note to p. 12.

malignant withering . . . eye: the evil eye of the vampire, as well as of other dread beings; early theories of contagion proposed that the eye of an infected person could spread disease by look alone—a quality that became associated with vampires and vampirism (see Groom, *The Vampire*, 17, and *passim*).

75 *infantine*: see note to p. 34.

pestilence: vampires were associated with contagion from the early eighteenth century, and Bram Stoker's mother's memories of cholera epidemics in Ireland influenced *Dracula* (see Groom, 'Viral Vampires' and *The Vampire*, 161–8).

simple: medicine containing a single active ingredient, especially a herb (*OED*).

76 *them*: *sic*, i.e. reassuring them both.

77 *her next victims*: vampires usually attack those closest to them first, so this is another inversion of the developing lore surrounding them (see Groom, *The Vampire*, 12–13, 104).

visions of ... magnificence attend their dreams: Brunhilda's tales and dreams—indeed her breath—are opiated, and influenced by De Quincey's Oriental dreams described with terrifying opulence in 'The Pains of Opium':

> Under the connecting feeling of tropical heat and vertical sun-lights, I brought together all creatures, birds, beasts, reptiles, all trees and plants, usages and appearances, that are found in all tropical regions, and assembled them together in China or Indostan. From kindred feelings, I soon brought Egypt and all her gods under the same law. I was stared at, hooted at, grinned at, chattered at, by monkeys, by paroquets, by cockatoos. I ran into pagodas: and was fixed, for centuries, at the summit, or in secret rooms; I was the idol; I was the priest; I was worshipped; I was sacrificed. I fled from the wrath of Brama through all the forests of Asia: Vishnu hated me: Seeva laid wait for me. I came suddenly upon Isis and Osiris. I had done a deed, they said, which the ibis and the crocodile trembled at. I was buried, for a thousand years, in stone coffins, with mummies and sphynxes, in narrow chambers at the

heart of eternal pyramids. I was kissed, with cancerous kisses, by crocodiles; and laid, confounded with all unutterable slimy things, amongst reeds and Nilotic mud. (De Quincey, *Confessions*, 72–3)

77 *broidery*: ornamental needle-work, embroidery (*OED*).

cates: choice viands, dainties (*OED*).

79 *sports of the chase*: hunting game.

pungent: piercing, stabbing, pricking pain (*OED*).

pamper: cram (with an excessively rich or luxurious diet) (*OED*).

80 *make mouths . . . like a puppet*: i.e. gaping speechlessly.

ideot: idiot, an archaic form seldom used after the eighteenth century (*OED*).

terrific: terrifying, terrible (*OED*).

82 *sharpened dagger*: an alternative to the usual stake for dispatching vampires.

swearing: both Polidori's 'The Vampyre' and Byron's 'A Fragment' have oaths at their heart.

Most horrible: see Shakespeare's Ghost of Hamlet's Father—'O horrible, O horrible, most horrible!' (*The Tragedy of Hamlet, Prince of Denmark*, I. v. 80).

I'll do it: see Shakespeare's Hamlet—'And now I'll do't' (*Hamlet*, III. iii. 74).

83 *empoisoned*: polluted, tainted (*OED*).

cave: a suggestive slip in the copy-text prints this as 'grave'.

84 *unnerved*: unsettled, disconcerted (*OED*).

corse: see note to p. 20.

fire-wisp: an *ignis fatuus* that misleads travellers with dancing fires; will-o'-the-wisp or marsh fire (*OED*).

85 *incessant pour*: constant flow (*OED*).

the mark of Cain: the sign of God's protection of Cain so he would not be killed for murdering his brother Abel, it has come to mean the branding of an outcast (Genesis 4: 15).

complicated: tangled, intimately combined (*OED*).

86 *raven*: see Shakespeare's Hamlet—'Come, the croaking raven doth bellow for revenge' (*Hamlet*, III. ii. 241–2).

87 *riot*: a noisy, wanton, and unruly feast or revel (*OED*).

Flames crackled: the snake is dragonish.

EDGAR ALLAN POE, *LIGEIA*

Edgar Allan Poe (1809–49), leading American writer, poet, and critic, was orphaned at 3 and he was educated in London and at the University of Virginia. He published his first poems in 1827, joined the army, and entered the US Military Academy at West Point. After initially thriving there his guardian disowned him and Poe left (having been court martialled), turning in earnest (and of necessity) to freelance writing, occasionally made less precarious by editorships. *Tales of the Grotesque and Arabesque* (1839) and his poem 'The Raven' (1845) cemented his national reputation (if not his financial security) while he inaugurated the detective story and worked as a prominent critic; his drinking, always excessive, developed into the alcoholism that led to the tempestuousness of his later years and eventually to his death.

Poe claimed that this story came to him in a dream. As Paul Lewis argues, Raupach's tale clearly influenced Poe—there are clear parallels in the contrast and antipathy between the two women and the wayward senses of the male protagonist (see headnote to 'Wake Not the Dead', p. 527). Poe also perhaps found inspiration in 'A Madman's Manuscript', part of chapter 11 of Charles Dickens's *Pickwick Papers* (1836–7), which he reviewed in late 1836.

The publication history is complicated. 'Ligeia' was first published in the *American Museum* for September 1838, then in *Tales of the Grotesque and Arabesque* (dated 1840, revised for a projected second edition, *Phantasy-Pieces*, 1842, but not published), and subsequently in revised magazine versions for *New World* (Feb. 1845) and the *Broadway Journal* (Sept. 1845), which Poe later further annotated with revisions. It was then included in Mabbott's 1850 *Collected Works of Edgar Allan Poe* (ii. 310–29). This magisterial edition uses the annotated *Broadway Journal* version as copy-text, but Mabbott also helpfully reproduces all the textual variants (ii. 310–30). The text here is from the first collection of stories by Poe, *Tales of the Grotesque and Arabesque* (dated 1840), i. 171–92; Poe restlessly meddled with the punctuation and language of the tale, but only the significant changes to the proposed second edition (*Phantasy-Pieces*) are noted. Poe claimed that 'Ligeia' 'may be called my *best* tale' (Mabbott (ed.), *Tales and Sketches*, ii. 305).

88 *JOSEPH GLANVILL*: Anglican clergyman, natural philosopher, and controversialist theologian (1636–80) fascinated by the inexplicable, who wrote extensively on the supernatural world of spirits—notably *Saducismus Triumphatus* (1681)—and who was renowned as a believer in witchcraft; ironically, for Poe, he was also an advocate of plain and simple prose. The epigraph, which reverberates through 'Ligeia', does not appear in Glanvill's works and so was probably written by Poe himself.

Ligeia: the Hellenistic name seems to be based on Ligea, a nymph in Virgil's *Georgics* (IV. 336) and Milton's *Comus* (Bridgewater MS, l. 815).

Rhine: the river rises in Switzerland and flows through many cities in Germany and the Netherlands, situating the beginning of the tale in northern Europe.

Ashtophet: probably the pre-Christian goddess Ashtoreth or Astarte, the 'abomination of the Zidonians' (2 Kings 23: 13), mentioned by Milton in *Paradise Lost* as a rebel angel, 'Ashtoreth, whom the Phœnicians called | Astarte, queen of heaven with crescent horns' (Bk I, ll. 438–9); Poe glosses her significance himself.

89 *daughters of Delos*: in ancient Greek myth, the three daughters of Anius, the King of Delos, were Oeno (wine), Spermo (seeds), and Elais (olive oil)—they were collectively known as the Oenotropoe (Winegrowers) and, through the agency of Dionysius, had the magical ability to produce those three staples; Poe thus links the intoxicated states of opium and alcohol with metamorphosis.

Bacon, Lord Verülam: Francis Bacon (1561–1626), statesman, philosopher, and writer; he was made Lord Chancellor in 1618 and later in the same year was created Baron Verulam of Verulam.

without some strangeness in the proportions: see Bacon's essay 'Of Beauty'—'There is no Excellent Beauty, that hath not some Strangenesse in the Proportion' (*Essayes*, no. 43, p. 132); the *Broadway Journal* and subsequent texts have 'proportion'.

hyacinthine: in Homer's *Odyssey*, locks of hair are compared to the hyacinth; the flower and gem are both violet or blue, so this more likely refers to the flowing curls of the flower's petals (see Bk VI, l. 231).

Apollo . . . the Athenian: Apollo was leader of the Muses and god of music, poetry, and prophecy, among other things; the Venus de' Medici is (unusually, and possibly fraudulently) signed Cleomenes, son of Apollodorus and an Athenian sculptor of the first century BC.

90 *of our race*: Ligeia is made increasingly non-human; large and bewitching eyes were characteristic of she-vampires of the period—a quality that Poe characteristically fetishizes and which could also stand for other physical assets (see Groom, *The Vampire*, 125 and *passim*).

Gazelle: 'gazelle-eyed' derives from Arabic love poetry—'A gazelle-eyed beauty is considered as the highest compliment that a lover can pay' (Shaw, *Panorama of Nature*, 238).

Nourjahad: 'All parts of the earth shall be explored for women of the most exquisite beauty'; Nourjahad's seraglio was 'adorned with a number of the most beautiful slaves, of almost every nation, whom he purchased at a vast expence' (Sheridan, *History of Nourjahad*, 28, 39).

Houri: an Islamic nymph of paradise, applied to 'a voluptuously beautiful woman' (*OED*).

jetty lashes: jet-black eyelashes.

more profound: deeper (*OED*).

well of Democritus: Democritus (*c.*460–*c.*370 BC), nicknamed 'Wisdom' and 'The Laughing Philosopher', developed the Atomist theory of matter, which relies on the principles of atoms (substance) as opposed to void (nothingness)—hence his 'well' is the infinite abyss; Democritus was much admired by Aristotle.

twin stars of Leda: Castor and Pollux, the two brightest stars at the head of the constellation of Gemini, the Twins; Castor and Pollux hatched from an egg after their mother, Leda, was raped by Zeus in the form of a swan and on the same night conceived a child by her mortal husband, Tyndareus.

Not for . . . my soul: this sentence deleted in texts after *Phantasy-Pieces*.

91 *a star . . . in Lyra*: the brightest star in the constellation of Lyra is Vega, or Alpha Lyrae, second brightest star in the northern hemisphere; Epsilon Lyrae is the Double-Double star, a system of five stars that using a telescope could, in the period, be resolved into four stars.

but: corrected to 'save' in *Phantasy-Pieces*, consistent with the epigraph.

old: word deleted in *Phantasy-Pieces*.

92 *flee*: revised to 'fly' in *Phantasy-Pieces*.

transcendentalism: American school of thought that allows ideas and imagination to prevail over commonsense realities; the founding and defining work was Ralph Waldo Emerson's *Nature* (1836), in which he argued that nature can sanctify human experience to a sublime level of revelation.

Saturnian lead: the influence of the planet Saturn was to spread melancholy, gloominess, and slowness of spirits; in alchemy (and poetry), the dull and heavy element lead was identified with Saturn—'Here pleas'd behold her mighty wings out-spread | To hatch a new Saturnian age of Lead' (Alexander Pope, *The Dunciad* (1729), Bk I, ll. 27–8); Saturnian also figuratively referred to the followers of the religion of Saturn, that is, the Romans.

Letters . . . lustre of her eyes: clauses inverted in *Phantasy-Pieces* and later versions.

Azrael: the Islamic angel of death.

93 *Methinks . . . feeble will*: in the 1845 version of the tale published in *New World* these sentences were replaced by the following passage and the poem 'The Conquering Worm', which give emphasis to the implicit vampirism of the tale.

> At high noon of the night in which she departed, beckoning me, peremptorily, to her side, she bade me repeat certain verses composed by herself not many days before. I obeyed her.—They were these:
>
> Lo! 'tis a gala night
> Within the lonesome latter years!
> An angel throng, bewinged, bedight
> In veils, and drown'd in tears,
> Sit in a theatre, to see
> A play of hopes and fears,
> While the orchestra breathes fitfully
> The music of the spheres.
>
> Mimes, in the form of God on high,
> Mutter and mumble low,

And hither and thither fly—
  Mere puppets they, who come and go
At bidding of vast formless things
  That shift the scenery to and fro,
Flapping from out their Condor wings
  Invisible Wo!

That motley drama!—oh, be sure
  It shall not be forgot!
With its Phantom chas'd forever more,
  By a crowd that seize it not,
Through a circle that ever returneth in
  To the self-same spot,
And much of Madness and more of Sin
  And Horror the soul of the plot.

But see, amid the mimic rout,
  A crawling shape intrude!
A blood-red thing that writhes from out
  The scenic solitude!
It writhes!—it writhes!—with mortal pangs
  The mimes become its food,
And the seraphs sob at vermin fangs
  In human gore imbued.

Out—out are the lights—out all!
  And, over each quivering form,
The curtain, a funeral pall,
  Comes down with the rush of a storm,
And the angels, all pallid and wan,
  Uprising, unveiling, affirm
That the play is the tragedy, 'Man,'
  And its hero the Conqueror Worm.

'O God!' half shrieked Ligeia, leaping to her feet and extending her arms aloft with a spasmodic movement, as I made an end of these lines—'O God! O Divine Father!—shall these things be undeviatingly so?—shall this Conqueror be not once unconquered [for 'conquered']? Are we not part and parcel in Thee? Who—who knoweth the mysteries of the will with its vigor? Man doth not yield him to the angels, *nor unto death utterly*, save only through the weakness of his feeble will.'

And now, as if exhausted with emotion, she suffered her white arms to fall, and returned solemnly to her bed of death. And as she breathed her last sighs there came mingled with them, a low murmur from her lips. I bent to them my ear and distinguished, again, the concluding words of the passage in Glanvill—'*Man doth not yield him to the angels, nor unto death utterly, save only through the weakness of his feeble will.*'

94 *bedlam*: mad, derived from Bethlehem Hospital—the London lunatic asylum.

Lady Rowena Trevanion, of Tremaine: Rowena, daughter of Hengist and wife to Vortigern, was a legendary queen of the Ancient Britons, and there is also a strong Cornish component to her name—Trevena being the name of Tintagel in Cornwall and site of the reputed ruins of Camelot Castle (proverbially, 'By Tre, Pol, and Pen, you shall know the Cornish men' (*ODEP*)); Poe thus underlines the ancient northern roots of his tale.

pentagonal: the five-sided room suggests that this is a magical chamber—the pentagon is at the centre of the pentacle or five-pointed star, which was a magical device used in summoning demons and for other witcheries.

95 *semi-Gothic, semi-Druidical*: mixing two non-classical architectural styles, medieval Gothic and Ancient British.

Saracenic: in some accounts this was another strand of non-classical Gothic architecture and culture: '*Gothic* SAXON, in which the pure *Saxon* began to receive some tincture of the *Saracen* fashion . . . the massy rotund column became split into a cluster of agglomerated pilasters . . . and the short round-headed window, was lengthened into a narrow oblong form, with a pointed top' (Warton, *Observations on The Fairy Queen of Spenser*, ii. 187).

Luxor: city on the Nile built on the site of the ancient Greek city of Thebes and rich in Egyptian archaeological sites, including the Valley of the Kings and the Valley of the Queens.

volutes: spiral twists (*OED*).

suddenly: among his later revisions, Poe changed this in the *New World* text (1845) to 'gradually'.

Northman: Viking; in the *Broadway Journal* text (1845) this was revised to 'Norman'—another order of Gothic architecture and thus emphatically non-classical.

phantasmagoric: a phantasmagoria was a performance of moving-images cast by moving magic lanterns, and light, smoke, and sound effects, dating from the beginning of the nineteenth century, in which illusions of supernatural beings and events were particularly popular subjects; figuratively, a rapid succession of feverish hallucinations (*OED*).

96 *Ligeia*: deleted in *Phantasy-Pieces*.

the departed Ligeia: revised to 'her' in *Phantasy-Pieces*.

98 *wo*: woe, an archaic spelling.

my brain reel: deleted in *Phantasy-Pieces*.

99 *revivification*: corrected in MS note in 1848 from 'revivication'.

repeated, and: revised in *Phantasy-Pieces* to 'repeated;'.

death?: following phrase added in *Phantasy-Pieces*—'how each agony wore the aspect of a struggle; and how each struggle was succeeded by I know not what of wild change in the personal appearance of the corpse?'

100 *and*: deleted from *Phantasy-Pieces*.

countenance—the limbs relaxed: revised to 'countenance, the limbs relaxed,' in *Phantasy-Pieces*.

and,: deleted from *Phantasy-Pieces*.

trembled: revised to 'spoke' in *Phantasy-Pieces*.

air: external impression or manner (*OED*).

it was: revised to 'was it not' in *Phantasy-Pieces*.

Tremaine: question mark added in *Phantasy-Pieces*.

Lady Ligeia!: 'lady Ligeia!' in *Phantasy-Pieces*.

JAMES MALCOLM RYMER, extract from *VARNEY, THE VAMPYRE; OR, THE FEAST OF BLOOD*

Varney, the Vampyre (the title is variously spelt and punctuated) was published from 1845 as a 'penny blood' in 109 weekly parts, each costing a penny, and then in 1847 as a 232-chapter book (misnumbered as 220 chapters); it was a runaway success. Although sometimes attributed to Thomas Preskett Prest (1810–*c.*1859), it was more probably written by James Malcolm Rymer (1814–84), a dizzyingly prolific writer who published under a series of half a dozen, often anagrammatic, pseudonyms, as well as anonymously. Rymer would work on several stories simultaneously, and alongside *Varney, the Vampyre* may also have been writing *The String of Pearls, or, The Barber of Fleet Street*, the sensationalist tale of Sweeney Todd: barber, murderer, and cannibal.

The text is taken from a version published in the 1850s (London: E. Lloyd, [*c.*1854?]), edited (conceivably by Rymer himself) and cutting several episodes to create a more consistent, less prolix, and hence more readable text than the serial version (British Library, digital store RB.23.a.31447). The design of the page is particularly pleasing, the initial letter of each chapter being a decorative woodcut and with many further woodcut illustrations inventively interspersed throughout.

The edited extract given here comes as the lengthy saga is being concluded and concerns Clara Crofton, a young bride vampirized on the eve of her wedding, and the consequences for her, her family, and her community.

101 *sawdust*: 'THE request of Will Stephens to be allowed to put some sawdust in the vault of the Croftons, was one of those regular things that he always propounded to any one who had a vault opened beneath the old church' (opening of ch. XCVII, p. 408); sawdust was customarily spread over the inside of coffins to absorb bodily fluids.

102 *vapour*: Dracula has the ability to turn to mist, a quality Stoker possibly took from *Varney*.

guinea: twenty-one shillings sterling, or 252 old pennies (£1.05 decimal).

103 *ingress and egress*: entry and exit.

green baize: coarse woollen material used to soundproof doors.

105 *Miss Clara Crofton*: Clara was discovered in a swoon with a tooth bite on her neck, but she recovered sufficiently to describe a nightmare she had experienced: 'Something came; something not quite human, yet having the aspect of a man. Something that flew at me, and fastened its teeth upon my neck' (ch. XCIII, p. 398). Her sister, Emma, simultaneously has a similar dream, but both dreams are ascribed to the girls' overactive imaginations; by the end of the chapter, the 16-year-old Clara is, however, dead. Like Carmilla, Varney has a protruding fang.

body snatchers: anyone, from students to professional dealers, illicitly obtaining a cadaver, usually for the purposes of teaching anatomy and dissection in medical schools; exhuming and removing a corpse was not technically illegal until the 1832 Anatomy Act.

106 *Sir George Crofton*: father of the dead bride, Clara, and therefore sworn enemy of Varney.

resurrectionists: body snatchers (see note to p. 62); the word was first used in 1777 (*OED*).

108 *jetty*: as black as jet.

110 *terrific*: frightful (*OED*).

111 *Chapters C, CI, CII, CIII*: these cover 'The Alarm from the Belfry.—The Beadle in a Quandary'; 'The Clergyman's visit to the Vault.—Rescue of the Sexton'; 'The Young Lover's Midnight Watch'; 'The Horrors of the Grave.—A Frightful Adventure'. The bell arouses the beadle, Mr Anthony Dorey, who visits the church with Mr Wiggins, the bell-ringer, before they both flee in terror to the vicar, Mr Bevan. Bevan then goes to the church and discovers Stephens, who tells his tale—but the coffin appears to be undisturbed and so Bevan concludes Stephens has been dreaming. Bevan goes to Crofton to acquaint him with the night's events and encounters Mr Ringwood (Clara's fiancé), who resolves to keep watch in the church. He goes forth armed with pistols and conceals himself in the pulpit.

irksome: distressing, painful (*OED*).

Graves give up . . . with wild vagary: Rymer's own lines.

Ringwood: the dead Clara's fiancé; he has elected to keep a vigil in the church, as explained to Mr Bevan (ch. CII).

112 *no, no, no!*: Shakespeare's Lear—'No, no, no, no' (*The Tragedy of King Lear*, V. iii. 8).

She comes—she comes!: Sir Walter Scott's modernized 'Part Third' of the traditional ballad 'Thomas the Rhymer' describing the lovelorn Isolde,

> She comes! she comes! like flash of flame
> Can lover's footsteps fly:
> She comes! she comes! she only came
> To see her Tristrem die.

(Scott, *Minstrelsy of the Scottish Border*, ii. 286–94, at 290; the phrase also appears in an epigraph to Scott's *Kenilworth* (1821), ch. 30, and elsewhere.)

114 *distanced*: outstripped (*OED*).

115 *great force*: Rymer emphasizes the physical strength of the vampire; see note to p. 30.

the Grange: the seat of Sir George Crofton, 'a wealthy warm-hearted country gentleman' and father of Clara (ch. LIIIV, p. 380).

117 *a strange sucking sound*: bestial manducation is typical of vampires, and influenced Stoker in his account of the she-vampire approaching Jonathan Harker with a 'churning sound of her tongue as it licked her teeth and lips' (Stoker, *Dracula*, 39; see Groom, *The Vampire*, 241n.41).

119 *Mr Bevan*: a clergyman; a reluctant believer in vampires and the unlikely confessor of Varney.

for the nonce: temporarily, for the time being (*OED*).

Charles and Edwin: sons of Sir George Crofton, brothers to Clara.

Emma: remaining daughter of Sir George Crofton, sister to Clara.

123 *exordium*: introductory discourse (*OED*).

interested in: concerned by, affected by (*OED*).

124 *Chapters CVII, CVIII*: these cover 'The Grand Consultation at the Ale-House.—The Awful Suggestion' and 'The Night Watch.—The Vault'. The villagers gather in the parlour of the alehouse; it is a stormy night and the blacksmith rallies a lynch mob to march on the church against the vampires. Meanwhile, Sir George Crofton and his company venture forth to the vault, where they discover that the marble slab sealing it has been broken into—or out of.

126 *evolved*: released or emitted through chemical reaction (*OED*).

128 *chancel*: eastern part of a church used by those officiating and separated by railings or screens (*OED*).

131 *deprecated*: earnestly wished or prayed against (*OED*).

wild dominion: 'Fantastic thoughts return'd; | And, by their wild dominion led, | My heart within me burn'd' (Walter Scott, *Marmion* (1808), Canto 4, stanza xix).

132 *tarry*: delay, wait (*OED*).

134 *links and matches*: torches of tow and pitch, and small torches (*OED*).

136 *in a cross-road with a stake through its body*: burying and staking a corpse at a crossroads was an accepted way of treating suicides until the 1823 Suicide Act; it persisted in popular memory (see the treatment of Daniel Quilp in Charles Dickens's *The Old Curiosity Shop* (1842), 569).

139 *Varney the vampyre*: the episode ends with Varney's profound remorse. He leaves his memoirs to Mr Bevan and, although throughout his existence

he has been killed several times only to be revived by moonlight, he is by now weary of immortality. He accordingly destroys himself by casting himself into the crater of the Neapolitan volcano Mount Vesuvius.

KARL ADOLF VON WACHSMANN, *THE MYSTERIOUS STRANGER*

First published in German as 'Der Fremde' ('the stranger') in *Erzählungen und Novellen*, 3rd series, vol. vii. pp. 119–230 (Leipzig: Verlag von Carl Fode, 1844); first published in English in an anonymous translation in *Chambers's Repository of Instructive and Amusing Tracts* (William and Robert Chambers: London and Edinburgh, 1854), vol. viii, no. 62, pp. 1–32 [separately paginated], subtitled 'TRANSLATED FROM THE GERMAN'. Von Wachsmann was born in Silesia in 1787 and served for several years with the Prussian army in different European campaigns, before commencing a prolific career as a journalist, short story writer, and novelist. He settled in Dresden, where he died in 1862.

The tale is significant for several reasons. Von Wachsmann describes vampire predation in detail and an idiosyncratic method of vampire slaying, and also draws on his military experience for elements of the story. 'Der Fremde' is also probably the first vampire tale to be set in the Carpathians, which would become the cauldron of European vampirism. As such, it would prove highly influential on later depictions.

140 *Hamlet*: from the celebrated speech in Shakespeare's *Hamlet*, III. i. 66–7; Shakespeare's text repeats the phrase 'to sleep'.

Boreas: god of the north wind (*OED*).

Adriatic: an arm of the Mediterranean Sea between the peninsulas of Italy and the Balkans.

Carpathian Mountains: European mountain range covering parts of the contemporary Czech Republic, Hungary, Poland, Romania, Serbia, the Slovak Republic, and Ukraine.

Knight of Fahnenberg: the name may have been inspired by the peaceable Franz Ferdinand Mayer, Baron von Fahnenberg (1679–1741), known the 'Saviour of Freiburg' for preventing the destruction of the city when it was besieged by French forces in 1713.

141 *mewed up*: confined (*OED*).

effeminate: unmanly; also enervated, self-indulgent (*OED*).

142 *Castellan . . . of Woislaw*: governor of Glogau Castle—Glogau (now Głogów) being a Silesian duchy that became part of the Kingdom of Prussia in 1748; von Wachsmann lived in Kreidelwitz (now Krzydłowice) near Glogau after leaving Prussian military service. He may have been aware of the medieval history associated with the region: Anna of Glogau was the second wife of Louis II, Duke of Bavaria, whom she married in 1260 after Louis had beheaded his first wife for adultery—later accounts depicted the Duke on

a killing spree on his way to mete out justice on his wife and stabbing various unfortunates who were in his path, including his own castellan. Wojsław is a village near the former Silesian Duchy of Grodków, now in Poland, though the word is more likely a variant of 'Vojislav' (Војислав)—a Slavic name derived from the words for 'warrior' and 'glory'.

143 *the Boreas . . . Trieste*: the Bora, a powerful north-north-easterly wind that blows down from the Carpathian Mountains through the Habsburg town of Sežana (now in Slovenia) into the Gulf of Trieste in the Adriatic, with gusts often exceeding 90 mph; inhabitants of the Italian port of Trieste strongly identify their city with the Bora.

castle of Klatka: 'Klatka' is Polish for a small cage for confining animals, and might also suggest a human gibbet cage.

fidget: trouble, worry (*OED*).

reed-wolves: European golden jackals or Caucasian jackals (*Canis aureus moreoticus*), indigenous to south-east Europe and parts of Asia Minor; they were first identified in 1833.

147 *Turkish-Sclavonian*: the Kingdom of Slavonia was a border state created from territories ceded by the Ottoman to the Habsburg Empire in 1699 and lasting until 1868, now comprising parts of Croatia and Serbia; it can accordingly be identified with the Ottoman/Habsburg borderlands in which the first cases of vampirism were investigated (see Groom, *The Vampire*, 44).

cheese fried in butter: there are various fried cheese recipes popular in Eastern European, including syrniki—curd cheese pancakes.

148 *on the tapis*: on the tablecloth, i.e. under discussion (*OED*).

ennuyant: boring, wearisome (unrecorded by *OED*).

149 *freak*: capricious whim (*OED*).

151 *mere*: absolute, veritable (*OED*; now obsolete).

Ezzelin von Klatka: 'Ezzelin' is an Italian name; von Wachsmann may have been inspired by Ezzelino III da Romano (1194–1259), an Italian tyrant known as the 'son of Satan', whose extreme cruelty condemns him to being eternally boiled in Dante's *Inferno* (Canto XII, l. 110, where he is called 'Azzolino'). Another possible source may be Henry Fuseli's painting 'The Italian Count (Ezzelin Bracciaferro, "Iron Arm", Musing over Meduna, Destroyed by him for Disloyalty, during His Absence in the Holy Land)' (*c.*1780) (see also note to p. 155).

Eques: knight (*OED*).

153 *Silesia*: German region seized by Prussia in the eighteenth century to become the Province of Silesia in 1815; now part of Poland.

155 *hippocras*: a restorative drink of wine sweetened, spiced, and flavoured (*OED*; an archaicism after the eighteenth century).

Azzo: an Italian name; Dante alludes to Azzo VIII d'Este, Marquis of Ferrara (d. 1308) in the *Inferno*, where it is implied he assassinated his father, the tyrant Opizzo II d'Esti (Canto XII, ii, ll. 111–12; see also Canto XVIII, ll. 50–7 regarding Venedico Caccianemico); Azzo VIII was also notorious for buying his child bride from her father (see also note to p. 151). The implied anagrammatic connection between the names Ezzelin/Azzolino and Azzo was taken up by Joseph Sheridan Le Fanu in 'Carmilla' (see p. 273).

158 *Then I dreamed . . . that a sort of mist*: like the demonic incubus, vampires can bring forth nightmares (Groom, *The Vampire*, 45–7); like Varney and Dracula, Azzo can transform into mist (see note to p. 102).

161 *palatine of Hungary*: official who takes decisions on behalf of the imperial Habsburg authorities (*OED*).

had heard of one: reports of vampire activity in the Habsburg Empire were often investigated and dealt with by the military (see Groom, *The Vampire*, 29–30).

162 *terra firma*: dry (i.e. firm) land (*OED*).

165 *implicitly*: obediently (*OED*; there is uncertainty in the use of this word—it may be a not uncommon error for 'explicitly').

167 *ashes*: dust of the ground, mortality (*OED*).

mummy: a naturally preserved human body, desiccated through exposure to dry air (*OED*).

169 *Ave*: Ave Maria—the 'Hail Mary', a devotional recitation to the Christian Mother of God (*OED*).

Credo: an utterance of the Christian Creed, or profession of faith, often the Nicene or Apostles' Creed (*OED*).

first one nail . . . to their heads: in the vampire manual *Dissertations . . . concerning the Vampires*, Dom Augustin Calmet describes the Count de Cabreras slaying a vampire by driving a nail into its head (198–9: see note to p. 21); deviant burials throughout history have often involved nailing the dead to their coffins or to the ground.

170 *besmear the scratch on your throat*: one of the inaugural cases of vampirism, that of Arnond Paole, noted the alleged prophylactic effects of smearing oneself with the blood of a vampire (Groom, *The Vampire*, 34).

172 *janizary*: see note to p. 5.

173 *the New World*: the continents of America (*OED*).

griped: clutched, grasped, seized tenaciously; now more commonly 'gripped' (*OED*) (see note to p. 51).

174 *nourishment to vampires . . . under excommunication*: three of the ways in which, according to Eastern European belief, one could become a vampire: by being vampirized, by leading a sinful life, and by excommunication (which, according to the Orthodox Church, prevented a corpse from corrupting); there were also other ways and means, such as a congenital vampirism, or a cat happening to jump over one's corpse before burial.

FITZ-JAMES O'BRIEN, *WHAT WAS IT?: A MYSTERY*

Fitz-James O'Brien (1828–62), 'The Celtic Poe', was born in County Cork, educated at Trinity College Dublin, and claimed to have served with the British army and worked as an editor before emigrating to the US in 1852. He became a prolific journalist, fought for the Union with the Seventh Regiment of the National Guard of New York, was shot at Cumberland, Virginia in February 1862, and died of an infection resulting from his injuries seven weeks later. 'What Was It?' was apparently 'written at odd moments, in the lodging of his friend Aldrich, in Clinton Place [The Bronx]' (O'Brien, *Poems and Stories*, xxiii). It was first published in *Harper's New Monthly Magazine* in 1859; reprinted in *Poems and Stories*, 390–407; and has since been edited most notably by Darryl Jones in *Horror Stories*, 128–39. I am indebted to Jones's edition, although he takes as his copy text the 1881 reprint, and we differ on some explanatory points. The present text is taken from the first printing in *Harper's New Monthly Magazine*, 18/106 (Mar. 1859), 504–9.

176 *this city*: New York City; O'Brien had settled in New York and the tale has some autobiographical elements, as well as being precise about the city's streets and rivers—as here.

177 *balusters*: bannisters of a staircase (*OED*).

Weehawken heights: The Heights is a district of the New Jersey township of Weehawken, west of Greenwich Village over the Hudson River and considered part of the New York metropolitan area; its elevation above New York City made it a neighbourhood favoured by the wealthy for its fresh air.

Mrs Crowe's 'Night Side of Nature': Catherine Crowe (1790–1872), *The Night-Side of Nature; or, Ghosts and Ghost Seers*; first published in 1848, it soon became a bestseller. Crowe was a spiritualist and her book is the first sustained scientific analysis of the paranormal, analysing scores of case studies; in 1854 she appears to have had a breakdown and wandered naked through Edinburgh, believing herself to be invisible.

178 *'The Pot of Tulips,' for Harper's Monthly*: printed in *Harper's* 11/66 (Nov. 1855) as a work by 'Harry Escott' (i.e. Fitz-James O'Brien); the title is not included in later editions.

asseverated: solemnly affirmed (*OED*).

potations: excessive drinking (*OED*).

opium: recreational use of opium spread through America in the nineteenth century.

drug of Paradise: this phrase and the ensuing visions described in the text are indebted to Thomas De Quincey's 'The Pleasures of Opium', which concludes:

> Oh! just, subtle, and mighty opium! ... —thou buildest upon the bosom of darkness, out of the fantastic imagery of the brain, cities and temples, beyond the art of Phidias and Praxiteles—beyond the splendour

of Babylon and Hekatómpylos: and 'from the anarchy of dreaming sleep,' callest into sunny light the faces of long-buried beauties, and the blessed household countenances, cleansed from the 'dishonours of the grave.' Thou only givest these gifts to man; and thou hast the keys of Paradise, oh, just, subtle, and mighty opium! (De Quincey, *Confessions*, 49–50)

179 *Ariel . . . Caliban*: characters in Shakespeare's *The Tempest* rather than *A Midsummer Night's Dream*; corrected in later versions, although the mistake suggests an addled cultural mind, and, in any case, *A Midsummer Night's Dream* is quoted later in the story (see note to p. 183).

the Gebers: a Persian term for the Zoroastrians, followers of Zoroaster (or Zarathustra)—prophet of an ancient pre-Islamic Iranian religion, which influenced the major monotheistic and dualist religions, and which has connections to Pythagoras, astrology, and magic; later revised to 'Guebers'.

Rana arborea: tree frog; *Rana arborea* actually refers to the European tree frog, the American being *Hyla cinerea*.

meerschaums: pipes made with bowls of meerschaum, akin to a pale hardened clay and often carved (*OED*).

Turkish tobacco: a highly aromatic, small-leaf tobacco also known as Oriental tobacco and grown in Turkey, Greece, and neighbouring regions; in the early nineteenth century the Governor of Egypt provided his troops with this variety of tobacco, whereupon they invented the cigarette.

nut in the fairy tale: the folktale 'Allerleirauh' (translated as 'Coat o' Skins', 'All Kinds of Fur', or 'Thousandfurs'), published by the Brothers Grimm in 1819. A widowed king wishes to marry his daughter; she demands a cloak of a thousand different furs and three beautiful dresses, which she conceals in a nutshell before fleeing; however, after working in the palace kitchens she is eventually discovered and wedded to her father.

Haroun: Harun al-Rashid is the principal character in a number of the tales told by Scheherazade in *One Thousand and One Nights*, first published in English as *The Arabian Nights' Entertainments* (1704–17); other characters include Aladdin, Ali Baba, and Sinbad.

Black afreets . . . copper vessel: in 'The Story of the Fisherman' from *The Arabian Nights' Entertainments*, a poor fisherman nets a sealed copper jar which he opens and releases a jinn or afrit whom he has to trick in order to imprison him again back in the jar (see note to p. 58).

180 *vailed*: occasional alternative spelling of 'veil' (*OED*).

calling of the voices . . . 'Wieland': Charles Brockden Brown's *Wieland; or The Transformation* (1798), considered to be the first American Gothic novel, echoes with uncanny, ventriloquized voices.

the Dweller . . . Bulwer's 'Zanoni': 'The Dweller on the Threshold' is the fourth section of Edward Bulwer-Lytton's Rosicrucian novel *Zanoni* (1842) and refers to an occult power or gnosis that initiates strive to overcome in ascending to the mysteries; the concept influenced the later Theosophical movement.

180 *Hoffman*: Ernst Theodor Amadeus Hoffmann [*sic*] (1776–1822), Prussian artist, composer, and writer celebrated for his supernatural tales and subsequent influence on Sigmund Freud's essay 'The "Uncanny"' (1919).

181 *Goudon's 'History of Monsters'*: the work does not exist; as Irene Bulla notes, 'This detail probably paves the way for the manifestation of something completely unprecedented and never before conceived by human mind, suggesting that a new chapter in that History of Monsters is about to be written' (77n.).

A Something . . . choke me: eighteenth-century reports of vampire attacks presented them as strangling their victims before sucking their blood.

182 *actuated*: initiated, prompted (*OED*).

invisible: in Islamic demonology, jinn are corporeal yet invisible and amoral beings with affinities to the daemons of ancient Greece; they are also defined as fire spirits that can only be bound by magic, such as the Seal of Solomon. Comparable entities also haunted Europe in earlier periods: in fourteenth-century Montaillou in France, the invisible-yet-corporeal dead 'were everywhere' to the extent that 'One risked running into them if, while walking, one stuck one's arms or legs out too quickly' (Schmitt, *Ghosts in the Middle Ages*, 141).

183 *airy nothing*: Shakespeare's Theseus—'And as imagination bodies forth | The forms of things unknown, the poet's pen | Turns them to shapes, and gives to airy nothing | A local habitation and a name' (*A Midsummer Night's Dream*, V. i. 14–17).

the Thing: the word reverberates throughout the century's vampire tales: 'The Thing in the coffin writhed' (Stoker, *Dracula*, 201).

185 *spirit circles*: the séance—enthusiasm for spiritualism began on the outskirts of New York in 1848.

lions: persons of note or celebrity, those much sought after (*OED*).

186 *plaster of Paris*: a paste of water and gypsum that hardens into a white solid; primarily used by artists in sculpture and by physicians for making casts for broken bones (*OED*).

plastic: clay or wax medium for modelling (*OED*).

chloroform: a colourless liquid (a triatomic haloid ether) discovered in the 1830s, the vapour producing insensibility (*OED*).

fac-simile: an exact likeness or reproduction (*OED*), so used loosely here.

Gustav Doré . . . Un voyage où il vous plaira: Paul-Gustave Doré (1832–83), influential French artist and printmaker celebrated for his hallucinatory illustrations of Dante's *Inferno* (1861), Milton's *Paradise Lost* (1866), and, with Blanchard Jerrold, *London: A Pilgrimage* (1872); Jacques Callot (1592–1635), innovative French artist and printmaker known for his unflinching *The Miseries and Misfortunes of War* (1633) and for his grotesque caricatures;

Antoine Johannot (1803–52), popular and prolific French artist and printmaker responsible for the illustrations and possibly the concept too of Alfred de Musset and P.-J. Stahl's *Voyage où il vous Plaira* ('travel wherever you like') (1843)—a fantastical picaresque journey into dreams and the literary imagination.

ghoul . . . feeding on human flesh: a ghoul is a jinn of Islamic demonology and Arabic folklore that dwells in cemeteries and eats corpses (see note to p. 58, where they are identified as vampiric).

187 *HARRY ESCOTT*: O'Brien's fictional narrator; although the name appears in other stories such as 'The Pot of Tulips' (1855), Escott does not develop into a consistent figure.

'WAIF WANDERER' [MARY HELENA FORTUNE], *THE WHITE MANIAC: A DOCTOR'S TALE*

Mary Helena Fortune *nèe* Wilson (*c.*1833–*c.*1910) was a highly successful, if now neglected, author. She was born in Belfast, Ireland; was raised and married in Canada; and in 1855 abandoned her husband and with her baby son emigrated to Australia. There, she bigamously remarried, separated (while her second husband himself bigamously remarried), and led a maverick life in the goldfields. Writing as 'W. W.' or 'Waif Wanderer' she epitomized the colonial 'New Woman'. She was the first professional writer in Australia, and is credited with over 500 detective and police procedural stories: she was one of—if not the—first female crime novelists in English, frequently writing as a first-person male narrator. Her extraordinary life is described by Lucy Sussex and Tihana Klepač.

Despite Fortune's colonial travels, this bracing tale is set in one of the most affluent areas of London, showing an easy familiarity with the district. It is taken from *The Australian Journal*, vol. 2, no. 98 (13 July 1867), 725–8.

188 *levees*: receptions, usually in the morning (*OED*).

Kensington: originally, Kensington was a rural part of London with farms, market gardens, and nurseries; between 1850 and 1880, however, it was transformed into a predominantly urban district of premium villas and mansion blocks, squares and gardens, and artists' studios. Queen Victoria was born in Kensington Palace in 1819, and it remains a royal residence.

189 *Erebus*: Ἔρεβος, 'a place of nether darkness, forming a passage from Earth to Hades' (*Greek–English Lexicon*).

190 *viz.*: that is to say—abbreviated from the Latin, *videlicit* (*OED*).

191 *Norman belfry*: Norman architecture was characterized by rounded-arch windows, from which the pointed arch of the Gothic later developed; Norman belfries were often round towers—hence the qualification (see note to p. 95). Chelsea Old Church (All Saints), south of Kensington, has a square tower with Norman Revival features.

192 *Corinthian style . . . pointed windows*: the building is fashionably neoclassical, having a covered colonnade acting as a porch and triangular pediments over the windows, and built in the Corinthian style—the lightest and most ornate of the three orders of ancient Greek architecture; it therefore conforms to the proportions and values described in Vitruvius' *Ten Books on Architecture*.

193 *inutility*: uselessness, unprofitableness (*OED*).

Elveston: possibly a slight allusion to Elvaston Castle, rebuilt in the 1800s by James Wyatt as an early example of the Gothic Revival.

194 *Duke de Rohan*: the last Duke de Rohan, Henri, died in 1638 and his daughter married Henri Chabot to create the House of Rohan-Chabot, for which in 1867 Fernand held the title of duke; Rohan is in north-west Brittany.

Princess d'Alberville: Alberville is a town in south-eastern France (Savoy, Auvergne-Rhône-Alpes) created in the nineteenth century by merging the municipalities of Conflans and L'Hôpital.

195 *vestibule*: an enclosed or partially enclosed space before the main entrance of a classical building (*OED*).

196 *damask*: rich silk fabric usually woven with elaborate designs of different colours, so making the contrast here more stark; originally produced at Damascus (*OED*).

201 *mate*: claim equality with (*OED*).

202 *Chateau Gris, Melun*: Castle Grey; Melun was a town to the south-east of Paris (of which it is now a suburb), near to the Baroque palace Château de Vaux-le-Vicomte, which by this time had fallen into disrepair.

203 *you*: word omitted from printed text, perhaps to indicate mental distress.

anthropophagus: cannibal (see note to p. 57, where they are associated with vampires).

two frightful . . . in France: two notorious cases in nineteenth-century France are suggested here—that of François Bertrand, and that of the village of Hautefaye. Bertrand was a necrophiliac (technically, a necrosadist) who from 1848 to 1849 desecrated a number of graves in Parisian cemeteries for sexual satisfaction; the crimes of the 'Vampire of Montparnasse' were sensationally described by Sabine Baring-Gould in his influential *Book of Werewolves* (1865), although here it is the gender reversal that makes the association particularly disturbing (see Groom, *The Vampire*, 133, 233n.). At Hautefaye in 1870, the young aristocrat Alain de Monéys was savagely beaten with farming tools and burnt alive in broad daylight at the village fair, leading to rumours that he had been roasted and eaten by a village of cannibals (see Corbin, *Village of Cannibals*).

verbena: Red Devil Perennial Verbena (*Verbena Peruviana*), native to Argentina, is a dazzling crimson-flowered groundcover garden plant.

205 *confreres*: fellow-members of a learned profession (*OED*).

206 *worried*: seized by the throat to tear and lacerate the flesh with the teeth (*OED*).

CHARLES BAUDELAIRE, *A CARCASS*

Charles-Pierre Baudelaire (1821–67) was a French poet, art critic, dandy, decadent, and translator of Poe; his enduring achievement was his first book of poetry, *Les Fleurs du mal* ('the flowers of evil'), which had an immediate and profound impact. Baudelaire refers to vampirism several times in his verse—most notoriously in 'Les Métamorphoses du Vampire', published in 1857 in the first printing of *Les Fleurs du mal*. This edition was however seized by the French authorities, Baudelaire was fined, and 'Les Métamorphoses du Vampire' and five other poems were ordered to be removed; the ban remained in France until 1949, although the expunged poems were published in Belgium in 1866; meanwhile, Baudelaire's work gained a reputation as the quintessence of depraved immorality and pornographic obscenity.

Vampires had already appeared in French literature in, for example, Théophile Gautier's novella 'La Morte Amoureuse' ('the dead love', 1836, translated as 'The Dead Leman' and 'Clarimonde') and the later poem 'Les Taches Jaunes' ('the yellow stains', 1882), and indeed Baudelaire made a further allusion to the figure in the title of another poem in *Les Fleurs du Mal*, 'Le Vampire'. However, very little of Baudelaire's work was translated into English in the nineteenth century—just a handful of poems and his critical essay on Edgar Allan Poe. This poem, the scandalous 'Une Charogne' from *Les Fleurs du Mal*, escaped censorship despite its characteristically rancid aesthetic and fetishization of the abject; it was translated by the bibulous editor and bibliographer Richard Herne Shepherd, and appears in his collection *Translations from Charles Baudelaire. With a Few Original Poems* (London: John Camden Hotten, 1869), 11–13, from which this text is drawn.

207 *sort*: character, disposition (*OED*).

burns: brooks, streams (*OED*).

JOSEPH SHERIDAN LE FANU, *CARMILLA*

Joseph Thomas Sheridan Le Fanu (1814–73) was descended from French Huguenots and the renowned Sheridan family (the dynasty of playwright Richard Brinsley Sheridan, 1751–1815), born in Dublin, and raised an Irish Protestant. He studied at Trinity College and the King's Inns, Ireland's oldest law school, but abandoned his legal career in the late 1830s to become a writer. Le Fanu edited the newspaper *The Warder* (which he owned while also having interests in other Dublin papers), wrote many short stories, and published over a dozen novels to become a best-selling author. He fell out of fashion at the end of the nineteenth century, but his reputation was revived by the polymathic scholar and occasional writer of ghost stories M. R. James, who edited a selection of his tales of mystery in 1923.

Carmilla was first published as a four-part serial in the journal *The Dark Blue* in 1871 and 1872 with illustrations by David Henry Friston, before appearing in Le Fanu's collection *In a Glass Darkly* (1872), iii. 49–270; see Le Fanu, *Carmilla*, xiii. The text here is based on the original serialized version in *The Dark Blue*: December 1871 (vol. 2, no. 10, pp. 434–48), January 1872 (vol. 2, no. 11, pp. 592–606), February 1872 (vol. 2, no. 12, pp. 701–14), and March 1872 (vol. 3, no. 13, pp. 59–78). For the later version, see Le Fanu, *In a Glass Darkly*, ed. Tracy, 243–319—an edition to which I am particularly indebted. The changes to the text in *In a Glass Darkly* are negligible and are recorded in detail by Kathleen Costello-Sullivan in her edition; only the most significant are noted below.

When 'Carmilla' was published with four other stories in *In a Glass Darkly*, it was, consistent with the other tales, prefaced by the following prologue ostensibly written by the personal assistant to Dr Martin Hesselius.

Prologue

> *Upon a paper attached to the Narrative which follows, Doctor Hesselius has written a rather elaborate note, which he accompanies with a reference to his Essay on the strange subject which the MS. illuminates.*
>
> *This mysterious subject he treats, in that Essay, with his usual learning and acumen, and with remarkable directness and condensation. It will form but one volume of the series of that extraordinary man's collected papers.*
>
> *As I publish the case, in this volume, simply to interest the 'laity' I shall forestall the intelligent lady, who relates it, in nothing; and after due consideration, I have determined, therefore, to abstain from presenting any précis of the learned Doctor's reasoning, or extract from his statement on a subject which he describes as 'involving, not improbably, some of the profoundest arcana of our dual existence, and its intermediates'.*
>
> *I was anxious on discovering this paper, to reopen the correspondence commenced by Doctor Hesselius, so many years before, with a person so clever and careful as his informant seems to have been. Much to my regret, however, I found that she had died in the interval.*
>
> *She, probably, could have added little to the Narrative which she communicates in the following pages, with, so far as I can pronounce, such conscientious particularity.*

In '*some of the profoundest arcana of our dual existence, and its intermediates*' Tracy argues that Hesselius is a follower of the Swedish philosopher and mystic Emmanuel Swedenborg (1688–1772), noting that for Swedenborg 'the world of spirits' is 'a place intermediate between heaven and hell and . . . also the intermediate state of man after death' (Le Fanu, *In a Glass Darkly*, ed. Tracy, 320, 344); this apparent—but invented—quotation might, however, simply refer to the Roman Catholic realm of Purgatory.

209 *Styria*: at the time, a central duchy of Austro-Hungary, now south-east Austria and north-east Slovenia; the landscape mixes deep forests with alpine peaks. Matthew Gibson argues that Le Fanu chose this province for his setting as he intended the tale as a covert critique on the political history of the region (see *Dracula and the Eastern Question*, 53); Gibson also suggests that Le Fanu appears to have taken descriptive details from Basil Hall's 1836 travelogue *Schloss Hainfeld*, as well as possibly details of Carmilla's charater and behaviour ('Jane Anne Cranstoun, Countess Purgstall').

Austrian service: Habsburg imperial authorities; in the previous century Habsburg officialdom had investigated outbreaks of vampirism at considerable length (see Introduction, pp. x–xii).

Gothic chapel: the story also features a 'Gothic bridge', and 'the cynical and ghastly fancy of old Gothic carving'.

General Spielsdorf: like the imperial authorities, the Habsburg military were mobilized to investigate vampires.

210 *Berne*: Bern (French: Berne) is the federal city of Switzerland, effectively the capital.

Babel: having one language, humankind resolve to build a tower to heaven: 'Therefore is the name of it called Babel; because the LORD did there confound the language of all the earth: and from thence did the LORD scatter them abroad upon the face of all the earth' (Genesis 11: 9).

five or six leagues: between about 15 and 18 miles; in England, a league is about 3 miles, although it was never formally defined.

gouvernantes: governesses and chaperones (*OED*).

211 *might and main*: utmost strength (*OED*).

212 *phantasmagoria*: series of optical illusions and moving images, especially of preternatural phenomena, produced by magic lanterns and other devices; the phantasmagoria was first exhibited in London in 1802 (*OED*; see note to p. 95).

214 *soft*: free from rough winds, or from cold: calm and balmy (*OED*).

215 *odylic*: the od or odyle was a natural force proposed by Baron Karl Ludwig von Reichenbach (1788–1869) emanating from individuals of a sensitive temperament, and a quality of magnets, crystals, heat, light, and chemical action; it was believed to account for mesmerism and animal magnetism (*OED*). The word was later and erroneously revised in the text to 'idyllic'.

216 *In truth . . . came by it*: 'In sooth, I know not why I am so sad. | It wearies me, you say it wearies you, | But how I caught it, found it, or came by it, | What stuff 'tis made of, whereof it is born, | I am to learn'—the opening lines of Shakespeare's *The Merchant of Venice*, I. i. 1–5.

plunge: lurch (*OED*), particularly used of horses shying.

217 *traces*: ropes or leather straps by which the collar of a draught-animal is connected to the swingletree or crossbar of a carriage (*OED*).

218 *liveries*: characteristic uniforms of household retainers or servants (*OED*).

219 *cortege*: a train of attendants, people in procession (*OED*).

Matska: a regional nickname, being Bulgarian for 'cat'.

220 *Utrecht velvet*: a strong plush of worsted, mohair, or cotton for upholstering furniture (*OED*).

black woman: this mysterious figure also appears in an earlier tale by Le Fanu and may be drawn from oral folklore:

> a black woman, with a wonderfully long neck, hung round with many strings of large variously-coloured beads, and on her head was a sort of turban of silk, striped with all the colours of the rainbow, and fixed in it was a golden star.
>
> This black woman had a face as thin almost as a death's-head, with high cheek-bones, and great goggle eyes, the whites of which, as well her wide range of teeth, showed in brilliant contrast with her skin.

She accompanies a fairy princess in a glass-sided carriage who abducts a young, golden-haired boy; as the child is taken she stuffs a silk handkerchief into her mouth to stifle her laughter. The boy briefly returns as an emaciated ghost before disappearing completely ('The Child that Went with the Fairies', *All the Year Round*, 3.62 (5 Feb. 1870), 228–33, at 231).

turban: a wound cotton or silk headdress at the time associated with Muslims, Jews, the East, and also Black women of the West Indies (*OED*).

222 *Cleopatra with the asps to her bosom*: the popular tradition is that Cleopatra VII committed suicide by holding a venomous Egyptian cobra, in antiquity known as an asp, to her breast and then another to her arm (see Shakespeare, *The Tragedy of Antony and Cleopatra*, V. ii); however, the Roman sources suggest that she may have used poison or stabbed herself with a hairpin (see Tronson, 'Cleopatra's Suicide').

225 *hair . . . thick and long*: associated with toxic femininity in, for example, Algernon Charles Swinburne's *Atalanta in Calydon* (1865)—'Not fire nor iron and the wide-mouthed wars | Are deadlier than her lips or braided hair' (24).

226 *armorial bearings*: heraldic devices identifying a family, as depicted on an escutcheon or shield (*OED*).

229 *jargon*: a 'babel' of sounds, originally twittering inarticulate birdsong—an early meaning revived in the nineteenth century; also a contemptuous description of a language one does not understand (*OED*).

ague: a fit of shaking and shivering (*OED*).

230 *magic lantern*: an optical device magnifying and projecting images on slides in a darkened room as used in phantasmagoria (*OED*).

salamander: elemental lizard reputed to inhabit fires.

mandrake: *Mandragora officinum*, an aphrodisiac, soporific, and cure-all, the forked root resembling the human form; mandrakes grew beneath the gallows when hanged felons ejaculated onto the ground at the moment of death and howled when uprooted—as noted by Shakespeare ('shrieks like mandrakes torn out of the earth, | That living mortals hearing them, run mad', *The Most Excellent and Lamentable Tragedy of Romeo and Juliet*, IV. iii. 46–7).

foils and masks: fencing swords and protective headgear.

amulet: a protective charm against disease or witchcraft (*OED*).

oupire: French for 'vampire', of Slavonic origin and comparable words in, for example, Russian and Polish (*upir*, *upyr*; *upior*: *OED*); here, the word is used to thwart the reader's comprehension.

231 *cabalistic*: taken from the Cabbala (the esoteric interpretation of the Old Testament), mystic (*OED*).

castle brand: the brutal practice of branding criminals on the face was replaced in English law in the early eighteenth century by branding on the hand, which survived into the second half of the nineteenth century as tattooing (Ikin, 'Medical Notes', 25).

233 *Monsieur Buffon*: Georges-Louis Leclerc, Comte de Buffon (1707–88), French naturalist and celebrated author of the first thirty-six volumes of *Histoire naturelle, générale et particulière* (1749–88); it was completed after his death in another eight volumes (1788–1802).

hippogriffs: mythical creatures combining the head, wings, and forelegs of an eagle or griffin with the body and hind legs of a horse; proverbially difficult to control (*OED*).

Gratz: capital city of Styria, and for a time the residence of the Habsburgs.

ten leagues: some thirty miles.

234 *a small picture*: see 'The Vampyre' and 'Olalla', pp. 38 and 339–40.

effigy: a sculptured representation (*OED*).

235 *romantic*: Le Fanu was writing just as the word was gaining amorous and sexual meanings (1866 and 1885, respectively), as opposed to displaying idealized or sentimentalized love, or simply being fanciful or overly imaginative (*OED*).

romance: the word was first used to describe a love affair in 1844, alongside the earlier sense of an extravagant or wild fantasy (*OED*): Le Fanu is again playing on the ambiguity of meaning.

apathetic: insensible to suffering or emotion (*OED*).

236 *us*: misprinted as 'this'; corrected in *In a Glass Darkly*.

dish of tea: it was common practice in nineteenth-century England to pour tea from the cup to the saucer in order to cool it—consequently, this is an assertion of displaced national identity; a saucer of tea is taken in *Dracula* (278).

237 *post*: to travel in haste by relays of horses (*OED*).

240 *Madame Paradon . . . Mademoiselle de Lafontaine*: in both *The Dark Blue* serial and *In a Glass Darkly* both names change here—a peculiar error that

in a tale focused on names may be a deliberate way of alerting the reader to spellings and anagrams.

240 *fool*: both the texts of *The Dark Blue* and *In a Glass Darkly* lack the indefinite article.

242 *gloat*: gaze with intense and lustful or malignant satisfaction (*OED*).

Avernus: a deep lake near Roman Naples surrounded by dark woods over which mephitic vapours hung and reputed to lead to the Underworld; hence, the depths of nightmare.

243 *supervened*: changed, interrupted (*OED*).

countenance: in *Satan in Society* (1871), Nicholas Francis Cooke characterized the forensic evidence of the 'crime' of female masturbation as

> A general condition of languor, weakness, and loss of flesh; the absence of freshness and beauty, of color from the complexion, of the vermilion from the lips, and whiteness from the teeth, which are replaced by a pale, lean, puffy, flabby, livid physiognomy; a bluish circle around the eyes, which are sunken, dull, and spiritless; a sad expression, dry cough, oppression and panting on the least exertion, the appearance of incipient consumption. (111)

244 *press*: large, usually shelved cupboard for linen and clothes, often placed in a wall recess (*OED*: Scottish and Irish English).

majordomo and his myrmidons: the head servant and his assistants (literally, bodyguard: *OED*).

245 *Had Carmilla . . . been lost*: neither of the texts of *The Dark Blue* and *In a Glass Darkly* pose this remark as a question.

246 *valerian and sal-volatile*: the root of *Valeriana* plants is used to treat insomnia and anxiety, although it can act as a stimulant and also inspire vivid dreams; sal volatile is ammonium carbonate used as a restorative following fainting fits (*OED*).

removal's: revised to 'removal' in *In a Glass Darkly*.

248 *Doctor Spielsberg*: another professional authority figure, with an oddly similar name to General Spielsdorf.

249 *small blue spot . . . little finger*: characteristic bruising was recorded on the necks of early victims of vampires, one of Arnond Paole's victims displaying a 'bloodshot blue mark, the length of a finger'—such forensic details were crucial to early reports (see Barber, *Vampires, Burial, and Death*, 18).

250 *Dranfeld*: fictitious.

251 *Karnstein*: fictitious; however, a link has been proposed to the 1422 siege of Karlštejn in which rotting corpses and dung were catapulted into the castle to spread infection (Stephanou, *Reading Vampire Gothic Through Blood*, 54).

we suddenly encountered the old General: revised to 'we suddenly encountered our old friend, the old General' in *In a Glass Darkly*.

portmanteaus: cases or bags for transporting possessions when travelling (*OED*).

254 *subserve*: be instrumental in promoting or assisting (*OED*).

Drunstall: fictitious.

Aladdin's lamp: in 'The Story of Aladdin: or, The Wonderful Lamp' from *The Arabian Nights Entertainments* (1704–17), the young boy Aladdin is enlisted to retrieve a magic lamp from a subterranean cave; the lamp contains a jinn that, after various adventures, eventually helps Aladdin to marry the Sultan's daughter.

257 *remember me*: neither of the texts of *The Dark Blue* and *In a Glass Darkly* include a preposition.

258 *devious*: off the main road, circuitous (*OED*).

260 *secresy*: a variant spelling (*OED*).

couriers: servants accompanying a traveller who make all the arrangements necessary for the journey (*OED*).

262 *appalling dreams . . . strangulation; then came unconsciousness*: the incubus, the demon of nightmares that constricted the breathing of those asleep; a symptom of both vampirism and female hysteria (see notes to 'The Mysterious Stranger'; and Groom, *The Vampire*, 45–7, 145, 184–5).

264 *patois*: regional dialect (*OED*).

revenants: those who return from the dead, consequently used as a synonym for 'vampire'—from the French, it appears in the original title of Calmet's *Dissertations sur les Apparitions des Anges, des Démons & des Esprits. Et sur les Revenans et Vampires . . .* (1746) (see 'Introduction', p. 21).

usual tests: exhumation, which would reveal corpses uncorrupted, often smeared with blood about the lips, the eyes staring, the nails and even skin renewed, the coffins often filled with blood (see Groom, *The Vampire*, 34–6; 'Introduction', p. 20).

Moravian: region of central Europe, which in the Middle Ages comprised the Kingdom of Great Moravia, subsequently incorporated into Bohemia and then Silesia, and which now forms part of the Czech Republic.

265 *impaled and burnt them*: this is taken directly from Calmet's *Dissertations . . . concerning the Vampires*, probably in a later translation by Henry Christmas (*The Phantom World*, ii. 209–10); salient details are copied—the vantage point on the church steeple, the confiscation of the linen cerements, the ascent of the vampire to retrieve them, and his ensuing decapitation (see Le Fanu, *In a Glass Darkly*, ed. Tracy, 346).

268 *triste*: dismal, doleful (*OED*).

basement: in architecture, the lowest part of a structure (*OED*).

her tiny grasp: the superhuman strength of the vampire also characterized she-vampires (see notes to pp. 30 and 115).

269 *leaf*: brim of a hat (*OED*, which gives several Irish English examples).

270 *escutcheon*: sculptured shield depicting heraldic coat of arms (*OED*).

according to law: again, a characteristic of Habsburg vampire investigations was to involve the military, physicians, magistrates, the church, and testimonies taken from witnesses (see Calmet, *Dissertations*, 198–9).

271 *Servia*: antiquated English term for Serbia; the modern form was adopted during the Great War, 1914–18.

Vampire: Calmet and other authorities emphasized forensic evidence, testimonials, and official reports of vampires activity (see Groom, *The Vampire*, 24).

cadaverous: corpse-like (*OED*).

272 *the body lay immersed*: the account is derived from Calmet's description of Peter Plogojowitz (*Dissertations . . . concerning the Vampires*, 286–8 (ch. 56): see Groom, *The Vampire*, 29).

terrific: terrifying, terrible (*OED*).

He had at his finger's ends: revised to plural in *In a Glass Darkly*.

'Magia Posthuma' . . . John Christofer Harenberg: classics of early vampirology and deviant burial—Karl Ferdinand Schertz, *Magia Posthuma per Juridicum Illud Pro & Contra Suspenso Non Nullibi Judicio Investigata* (Olmütz, 1704); Phlegon, *Opuscula de Rebus Mirabilibus* (compiled second century AD: see headnote to 'The Bride of Corinth', p. 495); St Augustine of Hippo, *De cura pro Mortuis Gerenda* (composed fourth century AD); and Johann Christoph Harenberg, *Philosophicæ et Christianæ Cogitationes de Vampiriis* (Leipzig, 1733)—this citation may indicate Harenberg's *Vernünftige und Christliche Gedanken über die Vampirs Oder Blutsaugende Todten* (Wolffenbüttel, 1733) (see Groom, *The Vampire*, especially 215n.).

273 *inexplicable*: see Calmet, *Dissertations . . . concerning the Vampires*, 186–7 (ch. 3).

anagrammatically: anagrams have been part of Cabbalistical traditions as well as of mystic linguistics up until the twentieth century.

274 *ascertained*: certain, fixed (*OED*).

How does it begin . . . becomes a vampire: Slavonic lore identified the 'persons who turn vampires' to be 'generally wizards, witches, suicides and those who have come to a violent end or have been cursed by their parents or by the church'; however, vampirism could also be a communicable infection, a congenital condition, or even the consequence of an animal leaping over one's corpse (see Vámbéry, 'Vampire').

develope: a variant spelling not considered archaic at the time (*OED*).

275 *took me a tour*: the construction is in both *The Dark Blue* and *In a Glass Darkly*, but is usually corrected to 'took me on a tour'.

the light step . . . at the drawing-room door: the implication is that General Spielsdorf's niece, Bertha Rheinfeldt, has been vampirized and is now stalking Laura to complete the work of Carmilla; the dead of a past generation no longer constitute a threat—it is the undead of the present, implicated in contemporary class and society, who are to be feared.

JULIAN HAWTHORNE, *KEN'S MYSTERY*

Julian Hawthorne (1846–1934), son of the painter Sophia Peabody (1809–71) and the acclaimed American novelist Nathaniel Hawthorne (1804–64), was born in Boston, travelled widely with his parents, and was educated at Harvard and Dresden before returning America to work in New York where he pursued a career as a civil engineer before publishing his first story in 1870 and turning to literature. He wrote prolifically across a range of genres, from a biography of his parents (*Nathaniel Hawthorne and His Wife*, 1884) to travel journalism to metaphysical and occult novels (dubbed 'Swedenborgian Gothic', *ANB*), and he edited sixty-one volumes of *World's Great Classics* (1899); he also spent time in London where he befriended Bram Stoker. In his later years, Hawthorne's relentless promotion of fraudulent investment schemes brought him considerable profits and ultimately, in 1913, a year in prison.

'Ken's Mystery', inspired in part by the winter Hawthorne spent in Kinsale in County Cork (1881–2), was first published in *Harper's Monthly Magazine* (Nov. 1883), vol. lxvii, no. 402, pp. 925–35, and reprinted five years later in *David Poindexter's Disappearance and Other Tales* (1888), 50–93; he frequently reworked his published work. The text here is taken from its first appearance in print.

277 *Nihilists*: nihilism was an extreme nineteenth-century ideology of utilitarianism and rationalism; politically opposed to absolutism, it was strongly associated with revolutionary Russian dissidents—particularly after being popularized in Ivan Turgenev's novel *Fathers and Sons* (1862) and following the assassination by bombing of Tsar Alexander II in 1881. Turgenev characterized a nihilst as 'a man who doesn't acknowledge any authorities, who doesn't accept a single principle on faith, no matter how much that principle may be surrounded by respect' (23).

278 *the unreadiness is all, to paraphrase the poet*: Shakespeare's Hamlet—'If it be not now, yet it will come. The readiness is all' (*The Tragedy of Hamlet, Prince of Denmark*, V. ii. 167–8).

tamarind-water: infusion of tamarinds (fruit of the tree *Tamarindus indica*), prepared as a cooling drink; also has medicinal qualities (*OED*; see note to p. 50).

bit draw: a small puff (of a pipe); originally Scottish dialect (*DSL*).

November-eve: 31 October, i.e. Hallowe'en—the eve of 1 November, which is All Saints' Day.

Ireland: while Hallowe'en is now, throughout Britain, Ireland, and North America (and beyond), a celebration of ghostly witcheries, those associations are a comparatively recent development and its roots are firmly in the supernatural Irish Celtic associations of the first night of Samhain ('summer's end'), which then spread to the west of Scotland and which Robert Burns drew upon in his poem 'Hallowe'en' (1786).

280 *forecastle*: the fo'c'sle, a short raised deck at the fore end of a nautical vessel (*OED*).

282 *Inman Line steamer*: the Inman Line (formally the Liverpool, New York and Philadelphia Steamship Company) ran from 1850 to 1885 and was popular with emigrants; in January of 1883 (the year in which 'Ken's Mystery' was published), SS *City of Brussels*, an Inman passenger liner, collided with a cargo ship off Mersey Sands, Liverpool, with the loss of ten lives.

Havre: Le Havre, literally 'the harbour', a seaport on the north coast of Normandy, France on the estuary of the River Seine.

Irish miles: longer than imperial miles—2,240 yards as opposed to 1,760 yards, or simply an indeterminate distance (*OED*).

one-roomed cottages: Irish rural labourers were commonly tenants of one-room, mud-and-thatch 'cabins', often in a state of dilapidation; following legislation in the 1880s the labourers began to be rehoused in cottages with allotments.

that terrestrial heaven: the Famine of 1845 led directly to the second wave of Irish immigration to America with whole families relocating; estimates are that there were in total some 4.5 million Irish immigrants between 1820 and 1930, with the home population reduced to just 4.7 million by 1891.

283 *insensible*: imperceptible (*OED*); i.e. inscrutable.

Ballymacheen: fictitious.

Cornice Road: Strada del Cornicione, coastal road to the small Roman city of Ventimiglia in Liguria, near Italy's north-west border with France.

Mount Desert: Italian farmstead.

Edward the Black Prince: son and heir apparent of Edward III, he was born in 1330 and fought at the battles of Crécy (1346) and Poitiers (1356), before becoming Prince of Aquitaine; he died in 1376, his son succeeding to the throne as Richard II a year later. During the reign of Edward III (1327–77), Lionel of Antwerp, Duke of Clarence, served as the king's lieutenant in Ireland.

embrasures: in military architecture, an opening in a fortification or parapet for cannon fire (*OED*).

George I: George Louis of Brunswick-Lüneburg (1660–1727), Elector of Hanover (1698–1727), who became the first Hanoverian king of Great Britain in 1714 by virtue of the Act of Settlement (1701), which secured a Protestant succession; the commemoration of the monarch in the predominantly Roman Catholic country of Ireland indicates that the landlord is a Protestant loyalist.

Irish soldier: the eight Irish regiments of the British Army were romanticized in the nineteenth century as being composed of natural fighters; Irish soldiers were predominantly Anglo-Irish Anglican Protestant loyalists.

284 *Kinahan's whiskey*: celebrated brand of whiskey established in Dublin in 1779 and particularly popular in America.

mind your eye: be careful (*Green*, where the lifetime of the phrase is given as 1834–1915).

the black woman: see note to p. 220.

285 *Lever's novels*: Charles Lever (1806–72), prolific and bestselling Anglo-Irish novelist, chief literary rival to Charles Dickens; his early works were comic sketches of Irish military life.

anent: towards (*OED*).

Kern of Querin and . . . Ethelind Fionguala: the traditional story of the Kern of Querin is 'The Stolen Bride' (see 'Speranza', *Ancient Legends*, i. 49–51); the woman is not named, but 'Ken's Mystery' has been republished in the twenty-first century as 'The Grave of Ethelind Fionguala'.

Faith: 'in faith', an intensifier to emphasize the truth of a statement (*OED*).

Arrah: an Anglo-Irish expletive, expressing excitement or emotion (*OED*).

286 *rods*: units of measurement standardized at 5½ yards (16½ feet: just over 5 metres) (*OED*).

more truth than poetry: an accepted, if not established, saying (see diary entry for 2 April 1812 in Mackintosh, *Memoirs*, ii. 236).

a stumble . . . evil omen: 'If any one stumbles at a grave it is a bad omen; but if he falls and touches the clay, he will assuredly die before the year is out' ('Speranza', *Ancient Legends*, i. 154); there is a rich folklore throughout Britain and Ireland associated with stumbling first recorded in 1180, but previously mentioned by Pliny and St Augustine of Hippo (*DEF*, 346).

ever and anon: ever and again (*OED*, by this time archaic).

287 *therefrom*: from that place (*OED*).

calla: in the Irish–English dictionary *Foclóir Gaeilge-Béarla*, Niall Ó Dónaill defines the word as either a cowl or hood, or as wrappings or finery; however, it does not appear to be a particular style of cloak or cape.

291 *escutcheon*: heraldic coat of arms and its bearing (*OED*).

292 *bandore*: a guitar or lute, with three, four, or six strings, arguably used as a bass to the cittern; its relationship to the banjo is debatable (*OED*, which cites this sentence).

Hist! see yonder! What light: deliberately alluding to Shakespeare's Romeo—'But soft, what light through yonder window breaks?' (*The Most Excellent and Lamentable Tragedy of Romeo and Juliet*, II. i. 44).

295 *depended*: hung down (*OED*).

pale and haggard: strongly reminiscent of the Knight in Keats's 'La Belle Dame Sans Merci', 'Alone and palely loitering . . . | So haggard, and so woe begone' (p. 41).

SABINE BARING-GOULD, *MARGERY OF QUETHER*

Sabine Baring-Gould (1834–1924), 'Squarson' of Lewtrenchard in Devon (he inherited both positions of squire and parson), was a tireless polymath: a writer, folklorist, song collector, archaeologist, and hagiographer. Among his highly varied fiction are the vampire stories 'Glámr' (an episode from the Old Icelandic *Grettis Saga* describing the undead *draugr*, first published in 1863), 'A Dead Finger' (1904), and 'A Professional Secret' (also 1904). Baring-Gould's *Book of Were-Wolves* (1865) was a major source for Stoker's *Dracula*; notwithstanding this, he also wrote the hymn 'Onward, Christian Soldiers'. On publication, *Dracula* was compared with *The Mysteries of Udolpho*, *Frankenstein*, *Wuthering Heights*, 'The Fall of the House of Usher'—and 'Marjery [*sic*] of Quether' (*Daily Mail*, 1 June 1897). More significantly, *Dracula* reworks motives introduced by Baring-Gould, such as property ownership and legal matters—if in a less explicit and exacting way; Stoker also seems to have been influenced by Baring-Gould's trenchant sense of humour.

'Margery of Quether' was first published in the *Cornhill Magazine* in 1884 with illustrations by Harry Furniss, and reprinted in *Margery of Quether: And Other Stories* (1891), 1–61. The text presented here is from the *Cornhill Magazine*, April 1884 (new series vol. 2, pp. 337–60) and May 1884 (vol. 2, pp. 466–85), checked against the 1891 publication. Baring-Gould provides occasional parenthetical glosses to the West Country dialect; these have been retained in square brackets as they form part of the original text. Most of the place names are based on actual locations half a dozen miles south of Baring-Gould's family home, Lewtrenchard Manor, and are on Dartmoor in Devon rather than in Cornwall—although there was much traffic between east Cornwall and west Dartmoor at the time. A special issue of the *Transactions of the Sabine Baring-Gould Appreciation Society* (vol. 10, 2010) devoted to 'Margery of Quether', with essays by Roger Bristow, Jane Marchand, and Troy White, is here referred to as *SBGAS*; Baring-Gould's own *Book of Dartmoor* (1900) contains much background information for this tale and is referenced as *Dartmoor*.

296 *Rosedhu*: Cornish for 'black/dark moor' (*ros dhu*, pronounced 'ros thuu'; Johnston, *Place-Names of Scotland*, 212); it is also recorded as a Cornish name, in reference to a local area.

Brinsabatch . . . Lamerton: Brinsabach is south-east of Brentor hill, and when Baring-Gould wrote the story had been occupied by the same family since 1559; it is actually in the parish of Brentor, not Lamerton—Lamerton village being less than 2 miles south-west of Brentor (*SBGAS*). The name Brinsabatch was revised to 'Foggaton' in later editions.

item: likewise (*OED*).

Nihilism, and Communism . . . Agricultural Holdings legislation: a constellation of political prejudices. Nihilism was a political ideology of utilitarianism and rationalism opposed to absolutism (see note to p. 277);

Communism, popularized by Karl Marx and Friedrich Engels's *Communist Manifesto* (1848), embraced comparable left-wing values in advocating a post-capitalist economy to end the exploitation of workers; a tenant's right to sell their landholding to an incoming tenant and accordingly pay less rent to an (absentee) British landlord was a key aspect of the Irish Land Question that dominated Parliamentary debate in the last third of the nineteenth century; and the Agricultural Holdings Act (1883) allowed farmers to claim compensation for improvements, thereby protecting individual tenant farmers. Rosedhu owns his acreage through generations of prudent inheritance and is therefore not a tenant farmer, but he sees himself, his livelihood, and his land at risk from new tenancy arrangements.

Gladstone-Chamberlain Radical Government: William Ewart Gladstone (1809–98) was leader of the Liberal Party and British Prime Minister 1868–74, 1880–5, 1886, and 1892–4; Joseph Chamberlain (1836–1914) had a reputation as an urban radical, entered Parliament in 1876, and by 1880 was President of the Board of Trade. Both Gladstone and Chamberlain had a particular commitment to Irish affairs, and in 1881 introduced the Irish Land Act against a background of civil unrest in Ireland and Fenian terrorism in Britain (including the immediately ensuing assassination of the Chief Secretary for Ireland, Lord Frederick Cavendish, on the day he was appointed in 1882). By 1886, Chamberlain had split the Liberal Party by forming the Liberal Unionist Party.

topsy-turvyism: inversion of the natural order, leading to utter confusion (*OED*).

Indian curry: curry was being served in London coffee-houses by the 1730s, and Hannah Glasse included recipes for the dish in *The Art of Cookery Made Plain and Easy* (first published in 1747)—although it was still unusual enough for William Makepeace Thackeray's character Becky Sharp to experience it as a novice in *Vanity Fair* (1847–8), 23 (ch. 3).

Tavistock Free Grammar School: Tavistock Grammar School was established in 1552; Baring-Gould uniquely refers to it as Tavistock Free Grammar School.

297 *Black Down*: 'an extensive ridge of moorland traversed by the high road from Okehampton to Tavistock [now the A386]. The highest point is called Gibbet Hill, but tradition is silent as to who hung there' (*Dartmoor*, 136).

Tamar: the river and valley that form an almost complete border between Devon and Cornwall; the river runs about 6 miles west from the edge of Dartmoor.

scatt: not only meaning broken in pieces, but also having gone bankrupt (*OED*); Baring-Gould also uses the word elsewhere—in, for example, *The Gaverocks* (1887), i. 233 (ch. 16), ii. 180 (ch. 33), where it is first glossed 'broken to pieces'.

297 *stone-crop*: *Sedum acre*, a yellow-flowered herb whose favoured habitat is walls and rocks (*OED*).

Yaffell . . . Heathfield: the countryside surrounding Brentor is Heathfield, pronounced locally as 'Yaffell'.

Brentor: a steeply rising hill of volcanic rock on the west edge of Dartmoor, at the summit of which is the thirteenth-century church of St Michael de Rupe, 1,096 feet above sea level (*SBGAS*); 'On Brent Tor summit it is sometimes almost impossible to stand against the wind' (*Dartmoor*, 103). The hill and parish are referred to as both Brentor and Brent Tor.

Cox Tor: a Dartmoor summit south-west of Brentor; the rock, the marks of the devil's horns 'distinctly traceable on it', remains on Brentor.

298 *church of S. Michael de Rupe*: St Michael of the Rock; in 1625 it was described as 'a church, full bleak, and weather beaten, all alone, as it were forsaken, whose church yard doth hardly afford depth of earth to bury the dead' (Risdon, *Chorographical Description . . . of Devon*, 218).

Lydford: village north-east of Brentor, known for its thirteenth-century castle; in the ninth and tenth centuries it was a major Saxon town in the region, later developed by the Normans.

299 *clematis or weigelia*: sweet-scented ornamental flowering and twining shrubs.

mundic: sparkling iron pyrite common in tin-mining regions such as Dartmoor; 'fool's gold' consists of grains of yellow mundic.

Quether: the tiny hamlet of Quither, west of Brentor (*SBGAS*), originally (in the thirteenth century) 'Quedre'; the etymology may be broadly 'Celtic', referring to the Welsh *cwthr*, 'execretory orifice, anus'—which perhaps casts the story in a particular light (see James Johnston, *The Place-Names of England and Wales* (London: John Murray, 1915), 409).

petticoats: skirts worn by children, including young boys who were not yet old enough for trousers or breeches (*OED*).

chapel: Methodist services, not the Holy Communion Service of the established Church of England (*OED*).

300 *gig*: simple; Sairey Gamp carries 'a species of gig umbrella' in Charles Dickens's *Martin Chuzzlewit* (see *OED*), 267 (ch. 19).

Kit Hill: Cornish hill 8 miles south-west of Brentor, and of a comparable height (1,094 ft) (*SBGAS*).

King Athelstan: in 936 Athelstan established the Tamar as the border of the westernmost extremity of the Anglo-Saxon kingdom of Wessex with that of Cornwall (see Payton, *Cornwall*, 82).

301 *hind*: farm servant (*OED*).

Go-on-all-fours-to-glory Jumbo: satirizing hortatory Puritan Christian names of the seventeenth century, such as Praisegod, Fight-the-good-fight-of-faith, and other, possibly apocryphal, examples; Baring-Gould was a connoisseur of the oddities of faith (see Collinson, 'What's in a Name?').

Methodies: colloquial (indeed, disparaging) term for Methodists (*OED*).

acres . . . roods . . . poles: measurements of land—an acre was the area that could be ploughed by a yoke of oxen in a day, later defined in law as 220 yards (40 poles) long by 22 yards (4 poles) broad (a pole or perch being thereby standardized as 1/160th of an acre); a rood was a quarter of an acre (*OED*).

Dartmoor sheep: Whiteface Dartmoors (or Widecombe Whitefaces) were bred from heath sheep of the seventeenth and eighteenth centuries and are hardy and good for milk; Greyface Dartmoors (or Improved Dartmoors) were developed from the nineteenth century—they have longer and thicker fleeces for use in blanket and carpet making and are placid livestock, if equally as hardy as their cousins. Both breeds remain on Dartmoor and are agile and easily capable of scaling dry-stone walls.

302 *feoffees*: board of nominated trustees holding land for charitable or similar public purposes (*OED*); 'A late curate of Tavistock, whose function it was to take the service on Brent Tor, and who found it often desperate work to scramble to the summit in storm and sleet and rain . . . supplied himself with several bottles of whisky, and when he saw a sturdy labourer standing idle in the marketplace he . . . plied him with hot grog, till the man in a moist and smiling condition assented to the proportion that he should give a day to the Brent Tor path' (*Dartmoor*, 103).

303 *lumbago*: rheumatism in the lower back or loins (*OED*).

304 *pertatees*: potatoes—an extreme example of the phonetic spelling of regional dialect.

305 *steeple*: originally the tower of a church, only later meaning specifically the spire (*OED*); St Michael de Rupe has a rectangular tower, probably first raised in the fifteenth century.

cawed: gasping for breath (*OED*, which notes that this is usually northern dialect; Baring-Gould's first church appointment was in Yorkshire).

Beaconsfield: Benjamin Disraeli, Earl of Beaconsfield (1804–81), novelist and leader of the Conservative Party and Prime Minister in 1868 and 1874–80.

horn . . . sides: translucent leaves of animal horn.

stones: to pave with stones (*OED*); Baring-Gould also uses the word elsewhere—in, for example, *Cheap Jack Zita* (1893), ii. 72 (ch. 17; 'a highway had been new stoned').

306 *Tam o' Shanter . . . in a bleeze*: the Hallowe'en poem 'Tam o' Shanter: A Tale' (1791) was written by the Scottish poet Robert Burns (1759–96) for the maverick antiquary Francis Grose (1731–91); the drunken Tam rides his grey mare to the ruins of Auld Kirk Alloway (Alloway Old Church), which are all lit up ('in a bleeze') and witnesses 'Warlocks and witches in a dance' (Grose, *Antiquities of Scotland*, ii. 199–201, at 200).

clickering: possibly a figurative use of the Devonian dialect word *clicker* or *clicquer* meaning tongue (i.e. tongue of flame), or, more generally, chattering (*EDD*).

306 *Duke of Bedford*: Francis Russell, ninth Duke of Bedford (1819–91), owned Kilworthy at the time Baring-Gould was writing, and had rebuilt it 1851–3; he was a keen agriculturalist, owning some 90,000 acres in Bedfordshire, Buckinghamshire, Cambridgeshire, Devonshire, Dorset, Huntingdonshire, Northamptonshire, and Cornwall (*ODNB*).

Norman Gothic: see note to p. 191.

307 *Drake and Raleigh . . . Plymouth Sound*: Sir Francis Drake (1540–96), mariner and explorer, lived in Plymouth, embarked on his expeditions from the coastal city, and ended his three-year circumnavigation of the world there in 1580; it was supposedly while playing bowls on Plymouth Hoe that Drake received news that the Spanish Armada had been sighted en route to Plymouth, whereupon he delayed engaging the attacking force until he had completed his game. Sir Walter Raleigh (or 'Ralegh', 1554–1618), explorer and writer, also used Plymouth as the base for his expeditions; he is credited (if wrongly) with introducing both potatoes and tobacco into Britain and Ireland. Both Drake and Raleigh were born in Devon. The Sound is an inlet into which several rivers flow—hence it was an important trading hub and heavily defended with fortifications. It was reputed that the light from the tower of Brentor could be seen in The Sound and had enabled various vessels to navigate to safety.

carcase: the framework of a building; also a ruin (*OED*).

308 *galled*: sore through chafing (*OED*).

customary way: i.e. by spitting on the palms of his hands.

cock . . . Gallus vocor: there are currently five bells in the tower, all recast in 1909; two bear a medieval inscription, which is in full 'Gallus vocor ego, solus per omne sono'—'I am called the cock [chief or dominant (*OED*)], and I alone sound above all'.

ever and anon: ever and again (*OED*, archaic).

balk: wooden tie-beam or cross-beam (*OED*).

309 *leathery . . . bat*: the creature is a mix of natural wonder (a preserved bog body) and natural history—the 'quadrupedal gait' of the bat being first described in 1869 ('vampires can walk rather than grovel like other bats': see Ditmars and Greenhall, 'The Vampire Bat', 301).

That 'ud . . . bones healing: West Devon dialect; the word 'gashly' (ghastly, frightful (*OED*)) appears in the traditional song 'Widdecombe Fair', possibly added by Baring-Gould himself (see *Songs and Ballads of the West*, 35).

caterick: variant spelling of *cataract*, a clouding of the lens of the eye (a figurative use of the earlier meaning of a portcullis, *OED*).

Lauk a mussy: Lord have mercy (*OED*); one of several instances where Margery makes a Christian appeal.

310 *a bit and crumb*: altogether (*EDD*), i.e. at all.

link: see note to p. 134.

311 *Wringworthy*: Mary Tavy, a village south-east of Brentor (*SBGAS*).

bides: remains (*OED*, *EDD*).

1605: the year of the Gunpowder Plot, thus a possible portent of what may be to come.

vixenish: ill-tempered and snappish (*OED*).

312 *sop away*: be carried away by soaking (*OED*, where only an instance in Dickens's *Bleak House* (1853) is recorded, 18 (ch. 2)).

The graves here . . . boiled to rags: Baring-Gould had surveyed Brentor and found it to be riddled with springs: 'According to popular belief the graves, which are cut in the volcanic tufa, fill with water, and the dead dissolve in a sort of soup. But this is not true; the rock is dry and porous. It discharges its drainage by a little spring on the north-east that in process of ages has worked itself from stage to stage lower down the hill' (*Dartmoor*, 104).

313 *white owl . . . Black Hunter and the Wisht Hounds*: a conflation of two Dartmoor legends. The white bird of Oxenham, more usually a smaller and white-breasted bird, foretells the death of a member of the Oxenham family of South Tawton in west Devon (see Charles Kingsley, *Westward Ho!* (1855), vol. i, ch. 1: 'How Mr. Oxenham saw the White Bird'); the Wisht Hounds comprise a supernatural hunt that preys on travellers on Dartmoor—in some accounts they are led by Old Crockern, the spirit of Dartmoor, in others by Richard Cabell, the vampire of Buckfastleigh Church and an influence on Arthur Conan Doyle's *The Hound of the Baskervilles* (1902). 'Whisht' is West Country dialect meaning in Somerset miserable or bewitched by the evil eye, and in Cornwall dismal or rough (see Elworthy, *Somerset Word Book*, 835; and Jago, *Ancient Language and the Dialect of Cornwall*, 313).

315 *maund*: wickerwork basket with handles (*OED*).

Florence flask: bulbous glass bottle with a long narrow neck covered in wickerwork or similar material, in which wine and olive oil were exported from Italy (*OED*).

sulphur: natural ('india') rubber is stabilized and hardened by being mixed with sulphur; old vulcanized rubber may consequently taste sulphurous.

bassinet: wickerwork basket with a hood at one end, used as a cradle for babies (*OED*).

cairngorm pin: souvenir tiepin or brooch; Victorian examples were often Celtic in design.

pomatum: hair oil (*OED*).

318 *Bradlaugh*: Charles 'Iconoclast' Bradlaugh (1833–91), was a lawyer, free-thinker, and Liberal MP who led the Reform League, formed the Secular Society, and assisted the Fenians in drafting their manifesto—his commitment to radical politics and personal freedoms making him 'a symbol of people against parliament' (*ODNB*). Baring-Gould was writing at the height of Bradlaugh's celebrity: he won the parliamentary seat for

Northampton in 1880, but being an atheist refused to take the Oath of Allegiance—thereby precipitating a parliamentary crisis. He successfully recontested the seat in 1881, 1882, 1884, and 1885, eventually being allowed to swear the Oath despite being an unbeliever, took his seat in 1886, and changed the law in 1888. During this time he was satirized in *Punch* in a portrait depicting him as 'The Northampton Cherub': a vampire bat (10 Sept. 1881).

320 *North Tawton*: market town in West Devon, over 20 miles north-east of Brentor.

Hingston: a West Country name, deriving specifically from the South Hams in Devon; there is a Hingston Down in east Cornwall (visible from Brentor), a Hingston Down and Hingston Hill on Dartmoor (the latter crowned with an impressive stone circle and row, as well as other neolithic remains), as well as the hamlet of Hingston in south Devon.

white witch: there were many white witches in Devon in the nineteenth century, healing patients who had been 'overlooked' by black witches by a variety of means, including divining rods and astrology; Baring-Gould knew of one named 'Old Snow' who practised in Tiverton, 60 miles from Lewtrenchard (*Book of the West* (London: Methuen & Co., 1900), i. 109).

shippen: cattle shed (*OED*), here mistaken for a sheep shed.

linneye: a variant of *linny*, *linney*, and *linhay* meaning an open farm building, often a cattle shed (*EDD*, *OED*; chiefly SW dialect); Baring-Gould also uses the word 'linney' elsewhere—in, for example, *In the Roar of the Sea* (1891), 89, 93, 182 (chs 11, 21).

321 *buxom*: plump and comely (*OED*).

Moses . . . Pisgah: 'AND Moses went up from the plains of Moab unto the mountain of Nebo, to the top of Pisgah, that is over against Jericho. And the LORD shewed him all the land . . . And the LORD said unto him, This is the land which I sware unto Abraham, unto Isaac, and unto Jacob, saying, I will give it unto thy seed: I have caused thee to see it with thine eyes, but thou shalt not go over thither' (Deuteronomy 34: 1–4).

topsy-turveyism: *sic*.

Miss Braddon and Ouida: Mary Elizabeth Braddon (1835–1915), a prolific author who, after writing for the 'Penny Dreadfuls', soon became a leading writer of 'sensation fiction' through novels such as *Lady Audley's Secret* (1861) and *Aurora Floyd* (1862) that featured strong, independent, and often amoral women (see pp. 466–89); Marie Louise de la Ramée (1839–1908) wrote melodramatic novels under the pseudonym 'Ouida', the best-seller *Under Two Flags* (1867) making her a fortune and leading her into a life of luxury, scandal, and eccentricity (*ODNB*).

Cullacombe: Collacombe, south-west of Brentor and roughly equidistant from it and Kit Hill.

Sydenham: seventeenth-century manor house in Marystow, about 2½ miles west of Brentor.

Hurlditch: an area just west of the village of Lamerton.

Kilworthy . . . Glanvilles: from 1559 the Glanville family had occupied Kilworthy Farm, less than 2 miles south of Brentor (*SBGAS*).

323 *quarantines*: i.e. isolation did not affect her complexion.

banns: public notice proclaimed in church of an intended marriage, a legal requirement in England (*OED*).

324 *S. Mary Tavy church*: 'picturesquely situated, not on the Tavy, but on a little confluent, was barbarously renovated some years ago, but of late much loving care has been bestowed upon the structure, and something has been done to efface the mischief wrought by the architect who had dealt with it previously' (*Dartmoor*, 137); despite her vampirism, Margery is a devout church-goer.

fined a shilling: by the 1559 Act of Uniformity recusants (those who refused to attend church) were fined a shilling a week.

325 *Fifth o' November . . . bonfire night*: the anniversary of the failure of the 1605 Gunpowder Plot to blow up Parliament was celebrated in incendiary fashion as a lawless and riotous Protestant festival at which locally and nationally reviled figures were often burnt in effigy; it became a national holiday in 1859.

Thou shalt not suffer a witch to live: Exodus 22: 18.

cremation: in England, those convicted of witchcraft were hanged—Baring-Gould himself wrote an account of the Bideford witches, who were executed in 1682; cremation was legalized as a way of disposing corpses in Britain in 1885 (see note to p. 13).

atomy: emaciated and withered living body, a walking skeleton (*OED*).

326 *vaccinated*: deliberately injected with cowpox as inoculation against smallpox; the Vaccination Act (1853) required babies to be vaccinated against smallpox within three months of birth.

that's flat: (defiantly) that is the undeniable truth (*OED*).

327 *ipecacuahana*: root of *Cephaëlis ipecacuanha*, a South American shrub, which acts as an emetic, diaphoretic, and purgative, and was therefore used as a household drug (*OED*; see note to p. 52).

hartshorn: aqueous solution of ammonia, obtained from rasping the horn of the hart (*OED*).

the old school: according to traditional, if old-fashioned, methods, principles, and values (*OED*).

328 *blood from a witch . . . at an end*: a belief that goes back at least to the Middle Ages, as described by Shakespeare—'Devil or devil's dam, I'll conjure thee. | Blood will I draw on thee—thou art a witch— | And straightway give thy soul to him thou serv'st' (*The First Part of Henry the Sixth*, I. vii. 5–7).

331 *roaming and roaring . . . they may devour*: 'Be sober, be vigilant; because your adversary the devil, as a roaring lion, walketh about, seeking whom he may devour' (1 Peter 5: 8).

Christian: another ironic comment regarding the morality and mortal condition of Margery.

an Englishman's . . . castle: proverbial since at least 1581 (*ODEP*).

rag-tag and bob-tail: disreputable rabble of people, riff-raff (*OED*).

332 *hymeneal*: concerning weddings, matrimonial (*OED*).

witches . . . Cox Tor: Dartmoor witches are attached to locations such as Vixen Tor and Bowerman's Nose; Cox Tor has no specific legends of witchcraft, but it is haunted by the ghost of a suicide supposedly buried nearby at 'Stephen's Grave'.

333 *visitors to Dartmoor*: Dartmoor became an increasingly popular tourist attraction from the mid-nineteenth century onwards.

ROBERT LOUIS STEVENSON, *OLALLA*

Robert Louis Stevenson (1850–94) was born in Edinburgh to a strict Church of Scotland family, and although he later rejected Calvinist Christianity while an undergraduate his Presbyterian upbringing left a deep impression. Stevenson's father planned a legal career for his son, who accordingly read law at Edinburgh University; however, despite completing his studies and being called to the Scottish bar, Stevenson quickly established himself as a prolific reviewer, short-story writer, and novelist—most famously for *Treasure Island* (1881–2) and *Strange Case of Dr Jekyll and Mr Hyde* (1886). Despite persistent bouts of ill health, Stevenson travelled widely—including trips to America and voyages around the South Seas; he died in Samoa, where he lived for the last four years of his life.

'Olalla' is set in Spain but was probably based on Stevenson's time in the South of France, 1882–4, when he was dangerously ill with congestion of the lungs and haemorrhages—possibly reflected in the story, which begins by contrasting the 'cold and poisonous city' with the 'pure air' of the countryside. The tale was, he later admitted, based on a dream:

> the court, the mother, the mother's niche, Olalla, Olalla's chamber, the meetings on the stair, the broken window, the ugly scene of the bite, were all given me in bulk and detail as I have tried to write them; to this I added only the external scenery (for in my dream I never was beyond the court), the portrait, the characters of Felipe and the priest, the moral, such as it is, and the last pages, such as, alas! they are. And I may even say that in this case the moral itself was given me; for it arose immediately on a comparison of the mother and the daughter, and from the hideous trick of atavism in the first. (Stevenson, 'A Chapter on Dreams', in *Strange Case*, ed. Luckhurst, 160; first published in *Scribner's Magazine*, (1888) 122–7)

It was also inspired by contemporary theories of degeneration (see note to p. 335), Théophile Gautier's short story 'La Morte Amoureuse', and the novels *Inès de la Sierras* by Charles Nodier (1837) and *The Marble Faun* by Nathaniel Hawthorne (1860) (see Stevenson, *Strange Case*, ed. Luckhurst, 196n.; and Beattie, 'Dreaming, Doubling and Gender'). These themes would be much more fully developed the following year in *Dr Jekyll and Mr Hyde*, a novella that is clearly indebted to 'Olalla' in, for example, the character of Felipe—a prototype for Edward Hyde—and which may be one reason why Stevenson apparently came to loathe the tale.

'Olalla' was written for *The Christmas Number of the Court and Society Review* (7 Dec. 1885), 3–15, before being reprinted in Stevenson's collection *The Merry Men* (1887), 161–223. Roger Luckhurst has edited the later version for *Strange Case of Dr Jekyll and Mr Hyde and Other Tales*, 101–38. I am indebted to Luckhurst's edition and introduction, although we inevitably differ on some explanatory points. The 1887 text has many minor revisions (mainly to punctuation, such as adding an apostrophe to 'friend's' in the first paragraph), but only significant changes are noted and obvious corrections to mend punctuation and typographic errors have been silently adopted. Despite Stevenson condemning 'Olalla' as 'not very defensible' ('A Chapter on Dreams', 160) it is a hallucinatory and highly wrought—perhaps overwrought—tale and, with arresting subtlety, only implicitly rather than explicitly concerns vampires and vampirism.

334 *Padre*: the tale contrasts Roman Catholic Spain not with British Protestantism, as might be expected from earlier Gothic fiction, but with English atheism. The secular humanist journal *The Freethinker* was first published in May 1881, describing itself as 'an anti-Christian organ and [which] must therefore be chiefly aggressive. It will wage relentless war against superstition in general, and against Christian superstition in particular' (quoted by Brake and Demoor (eds), *Dictionary of Nineteenth-Century Journalism*, 232); it proved very popular.

residencia: home (Spanish).

the good cause: the traditionalist Carlist uprisings that endeavoured to revert the Bourbon monarchy in Spain to the line of Don Carlos, brother of Ferdinand VII, from the line of Ferdinand's daughter Isabella II, which had controversially been legitimated through revising the Salic law of succession in 1830; there were Carlist wars from 1833 to 1876. Queen Isabella, known as *La de los Tristes Destinos* ('she of the sad fates'), was deposed in 1868; her son Alfonso XII became king in 1874.

tatterdemalion: beggarly (*OED*).

335 *degenerate*: in addition to the general sense of a deterioration in character or qualities (*OED*), Stevenson is alluding to a nineteenth-century theory of reversion to primal types—as becomes clear later in the tale. This quasi-scientific idea of 'degeneration' was first theorized in 1857 by Benedict Morel, who argued that conditions such as madness resulting

from physiological damage or immoral behaviour could become inherited disorders transmitted to later generations. The criminal anthropologist Cesare Lombroso then combined these ideas with Darwinian models of evolution to argue that criminals were regressive throwbacks—a primitive, subhuman racial type with an 'irresistible craving for evil for its own sake, the desire not only to extinguish life in the victim, but to mutilate the corpse, tear its flesh, and drink its blood' (Lombroso, *Criminal Man*, xv). *L'Uomo Delinquente* was first published in 1876, with revised editions following in 1878, 1884, 1889, and 1896–7; Stevenson's *Strange Case of Dr Jekyll and Mr Hyde* (1886) is similarly predicated on the theory.

335 *muleteer*: a mule-driver or muleskinner (*OED*).

336 *innocent*: an unusual usage—while there is a dialect sense of a half-witted imbecile, in most senses the word has meanings of artlessness and a lack of cunning (*OED*).

Sierra: Sierra Nevada, a mountain range in Andalucia; also used generally of the rising peaks reminiscent of the teeth of a saw (*OED*).

threading the sights: presumably wandering through familiar landmarks, although possibly an unrecorded Scottish dialect phrase.

337 *freshets*: small currents of fresh water (*OED*).

River Kelpie: the kelpie is a legendary water demon appearing in the form of a horse that haunts the lakes and rivers of Lowland Scotland, delighting in drowning travellers (*OED*).

339 *had had*: *sic*.

smooth smooth: *sic*.

a picture on the wall: portraits are central to the Gothic literature of the period, particularly vampire tales (see in the present volume 'The Vampyre' and 'Carmilla', pp. 38 and 234)—the device is strikingly developed in 'Olalla'.

340 *inch*: revised to 'scruple' in 1887's *The Merry Men*.

frieze: a type of coarse woollen cloth with a nap (*OED*).

341 *garden*: 'or small farm' added to 1887 text.

shuttle-witted: of unsteady or shaky understanding, from the dialect word 'shittle' (*OED*); Stevenson also uses the word in *The Black Arrow* (1888), 31, 40 (chs 1, 2).

342 *pace*: corrected from 'place', a not-inconceivable reading.

343 *bartizan*: an overhanging battlemented turret extending at an angle from the top of a tower (*OED*).

loopholed for musketry: cut with narrow vertical slits to allow for defensive gunfire (*OED*); Stevenson uses the exact same phrase in *Treasure Island* (1888), 88 (ch. 16).

the sleeping palace of the legend: the fairy tale known today as 'Sleeping Beauty' was originally a sexually violent medieval romance published in

Italy in the seventeenth century, rewritten by Charles Perrault (1697; translated as 'The Sleeping Beauty in the Wood', 1729), and published by the Brothers Grimm in 1812 ('Briar-Rose'). The Grimms' version tells of a princess cursed by a Wise Woman to sleep for a hundred years if she pricks her finger; she does so, casting the whole of her castle into a slumber from which they awake when, after a century, a prince errant arrives and kisses the princess.

344 *scattered*: revised to 'littered' in the 1887 text.

had: word missing in original.

unusually large . . . almost black: a fine example of the nineteenth-century fascination with vampiric female eyes (see Groom, *The Vampire*, 125 and *passim*).

insignificance: meaninglessness (*OED*).

not so much speaking as immanent: not so much manifested or expressed as inherent (*OED*); 'imminent' in the original later corrected to 'immanent', a not uncommon error, in the 1887 text.

345 *sloth and pleasure*: the Señora is depicted as the epitome of the sin of sloth; the *Catechism of the Catholic Church* warns that 'acedia or spiritual sloth goes so far as to refuse the joy that comes from God and to be repelled by divine goodness' (§ 2094), which underscores her family's transgression. John Calvin, meanwhile, wrote that with regard to the achievements of the ancient Greeks and Romans and other non-Christians, 'if the Lord has been pleased to assist us by the work and ministry of the ungodly in physics, dialectics, mathematics, and other similar sciences, let us avail ourselves of it, lest, by neglecting the gifts of God spontaneously offered to us, we be justly punished for our sloth' (Calvin, *Institutes of the Christian Religion*, i. 319)—Stevenson may therefore be reflecting on the relationship between moral philosophy and contemporary psychology.

346 *contrabandista*: a trafficker in contraband, a smuggler (*OED*).

hebetude: dullness, obtuseness (*OED*).

malarious: infested with malarial mosquitos (*OED*); malaria was endemic in Spain until the twentieth century and was eventually eradicated in 1964.

348 *black wind*: the Llevantades, or intense stormy gales on the east coast of Spain blowing from between north-north-east and east-north-east (see Oliver (ed.), *Encyclopedia of World Climatology*, 471).

unintermittent: not in fits and starts, i.e. continuous (*OED*).

349 *tarantula*: *Lycosa tarantula*, a large wolf-spider of Southern Europe, famed for its poisonous bite that was believed to cause tarantism, or hysterical dancing (*OED*).

350 *port*: deportment, bearing (*OED*).

351 *Pleasure approached . . . to thee!*: Stevenson's lines; 'the' corrected to 'thee' in the final line, as in the 1887 text.

351 *mien*: bearing, look (*OED*).

maceration: wasting away through fasting (*OED*); Stevenson also used the word in his essay 'Æs Triplex', published in *Virginibus Puerisque* (1881), 164–83, 167.

352 *delicacy*: keenness, acuteness, or subtlety of observation, perceptiveness; Stevenson also used the word several times in *New Arabian Nights* (1882) in an archaic sense, meaning a source of delight or enjoyment (*OED*): see 'The Suicide Club', 3–35, 22.

353 *Olalla*: Spanish version of the name Eulalia, meaning a sweet-spoken girl; St Eulalia of Barcelona (probably the same saint as St Eulalia of Mérida) was a 13-year-old martyred in the fourth century by flagellation and then being tied to a saltire cross and having her flesh torn—as depicted in the fourteenth-century reliefs on her sarcophagus in the crypt of Barcelona Cathedral.

355 *boddice*: variant of *bodice* endorsed by Johnson (*OED*).

These: corrected in the 1887 text from 'There', a not-inconceivable reading.

the child of Herod: in a frenzied attempt to eradicate the infant Jesus Christ, Herod the Great, King of Judea, decreed the 'Massacre of the Innocents'—the slaughter of all male children up to the age of two years in the region of Bethlehem (Matthew 2: 16). The Roman philosopher Macrobius Ambrosius Theodosius claimed that when the Emperor Augustus learnt that Herod's savage dogma had led him to execute his own, he commented, 'It is better to be Herod's hog [*ous*], than his son [*houios*]'—referring to the Jewish prohibition against killing and eating pigs (*Saturnalia*, Bk II, pp. xiii, 348: see *CE*).

356 *El Dorado*: a legendary country or city brimming with gold, reputed to lie on the Amazon River (*OED*).

357 *bridal*: a wedding or a union, both meanings becoming archaic and obsolete at the time (OED).

monitress: female monitor, a student with authority over her peers (*OED*).

358 *Samson*: the story of Samson is told in Judges 13–16; he first killed a young lion with his bare hands, later slew a thousand Philistines with the jawbone of an ass, and finally, having been captured and blinded, brought down the Temple of Dagon upon his head to slay thousands more Philistines.

her thought: revised to 'the thought of her' in the 1887 text.

359 *insolation*: exposure to sunlight, both a medical treatment but also liable to cause madness or fever (*OED*).

361 *bitten me to the bone*: part of the dream that inspired the tale (see headnote).

Her strength . . . of madness: like their fathomless eyes, the exceptional strength of the Señora and of Olalla is a tell-tale sign; see note to p. 268.

catamount: originally a panther, then a North American name for a puma or cougar (*Felis concolor*; *OED*)—an incongruous reference, though doubtless inspired by Stevenson's experiences in the United States; Luckhurst suggests that the word subsequently developed to 'refer to the "wild men" of mountainous regions' (*Strange Case*, 197n.).

nameless female thing: see note to p. 183.

362 *any*: revised to 'every' in the 1887 text.

the sign of the cross: as with 'Margery of Quether', there is a Christian contradiction—or indeed, potential salvation—running through this tale.

363 *curve*: corrected in the 1887 text from 'curse', another not-inconceivable reading.

364 *mocked*: corrected in 1887 from 'worked', again a possible reading.

365 *greater*: revised in 1887 to 'dearer', which removes the effective repetition.

My fathers . . . be forgotten: Olalla's fear is her children would carry the degeneracy of her family to future generations in a horrifying form of backwards evolution, ultimately returning to an inhuman primordial state—'the hideous trick of atavism' Stevenson refers to in 'A Chapter on Dreams' (160: see headnote); her thinking is consistent with theories of the time (see note to p. 335).

kirkton: hamlet or village by a church (*OED*, which cites this usage).

366 *taking snuff*: this dose of snuff was deleted in the 1887 text.

367 *begun the words*: revised in 1887 simply to 'began'; the colon is added from 1887.

riddling sphynx: referring to Greek mythology, in which the sphinx (a monster with a woman's head and a winged lion's body) terrorized Thebes until a riddle it posed could be solved; Oedipus did so and either subsequently slew the sphinx or, in some versions of the myth, allowed it to commit suicide (*OCD*).

the more superstitious crossed themselves: the villagers and the muleteer are implicitly criticized for their 'Christian superstition' (see note to p. 334).

ardour: the end of the paragraph in the 1887 text.

sparrow: revised to 'fly' in the 1887 text.

368 *opinions*: deleted in the 1887 text.

conjured: beseeched, implored often—often by appealing to the divine (*OED*).

loose: discharge; figuratively, absolve.

369 *horror*: the end of the paragraph in the 1887 text.

vamped up: patched up; a figurative use that knits together the features of the tale with a calculated pun on the word 'vampire'.

basilisks: supernatural reptiles hatched by a serpent from a cock's egg and possessing lethal breath and a fatal gaze, here used figuratively (*OED*).

369 *In the old days . . . go up to heaven*: inverted commas removed in the 1887 text, shifting the unstable direct speech to indirect speech.

370 *the man of sorrows*: 'He is despised and rejected of men; a man of sorrows, and acquainted with grief: and we hid as it were *our* faces from him; he was despised, and we esteemed him not' (Isaiah 53: 3).

GUY DE MAUPASSANT, *THE HORLA*

Henry-René-Albert-Guy de Maupassant (1850–93), French author celebrated for his short stories. Maupassant served in the Franco-German war (1870–1) before working as a civil servant, becoming a close disciple of Gustave Flaubert, and establishing himself as a best-selling writer of over three hundred short stories and six novels. Maupassant had a particular fascination for French sexual mores in the early years of the Belle Époque and a keen eye for incriminating detail; he travelled widely and while valuing solitude had a compulsive series of affairs. He contracted syphilis in his early twenties and died in his early forties in the advanced stages of the disease, having attempted suicide and been confined to an asylum.

The psychological classic 'The Horla' was first published as 'Lettre d'un fou' ('the diary of a madman') in 1885 before being thoroughly revised as 'Le Horla' in 1886, and again in 1887; Maupassant may have been influenced by Fitz-James O'Brien's tale 'What Was It?' (see pp. 176–87 in the present volume). The first English translation appeared in 1890, and was later published in *Weird Tales* (Aug. 1926). The version here is the original translation by Jonathan Sturges, edited with considerable care by George William Curtis in *Modern Ghosts* (1890), 1–55. Aside from correcting a handful of American English spellings and minor changes to punctuation, the text is reproduced exactly, and while some editorial decisions may appear at first sight to be wayward, it seems that elements such as ellipses indicate faultlines in the narrator's mind. 'Le Horla' has since been translated by David Coward in Maupassant, *A Day in the Country and Other Stories*, 275–302; and Charlotte Mandell has translated all three versions for a single-volume edition.

371 *to Havre from Rouen*: Rouen is 42 miles (72 km) inland from the port of Le Havre in Normandy; the River Seine loops along the route for 78 miles (125 km) before it continues to Paris and the Seine Basin.

the cathedral's cast-iron spire: the spire of Rouen Cathedral, built in 1876 of cast-iron, is an audacious example of French Gothic Revival architecture and succeeded in making the cathedral the tallest building in the world for the next four years; the main bell tower of the building is the fifteenth-century Tour de Beurre, built in the Flamboyant Gothic style.

tow: line of vessels being towed (*OED*).

defiled: literally, marching in line (*OED*, military usage).

red flag: the Red Ensign or 'red duster'—a red flag with the Union Jack in the quadrant, flown by vessels of the Merchant Navy of the United Kingdom.

373 *bromide of potassium*: KBr, also known simply as bromide—a sedative used as an anti-seizure medication and in the treatment of epilepsy; the compound was first isolated from the Mediterranean Sea in 1826.

kneels upon my breast... to strangle me: the incubus, the demon that would bear down on the chest of a sleeping victim, bringing nightmares and often suffocation or strangulation; considered a symptom of vampirism and repeated in the tale (see notes to pp. 158, 262; and Groom, *The Vampire*, 45–7, 145, 184–5).

374 *La Bouille*: Normandy village on the Seine, some dozen miles (20 km) south-west of Rouen.

Mont Saint Michel: Benedictine abbey built in the Gothic style from the eleventh to sixteenth centuries, and spectacularly situated on a rock outcrop off the coast of Normandy and Brittany. The 'Wonder of the West' was a major Christian site, but the abbey was dissolved in 1789 by the revolutionary government and the building became a state prison until 1863; it was classified as a national monument in 1874, restoration began, and a causeway was built in 1879.

375 *Avranches*: Maupassant also describes this 'ancient and pretty Norman city' in his novel *Notre Cœur* (1903), 62.

chimeras: in painting and architecture the term is used figuratively for a grotesque monster, or one composed of parts of miscellaneous animals; here referring to the prominent gargoyles of Mont Saint-Michel (*OED*).

cuirass: armour protecting the body, a breastplate (*OED*).

378 *black-lead*: the graphite core of a pencil; also the black polish used on stoves and grates (*OED*).

Théâtre Français: national theatre of France, established in 1680 and located at Salle Richelieu, 2 Rue de Richelieu, Paris.

Alexandre Dumas fils: prolific French author and playwright (1824–95), celebrated for his treatments of contemporary moral dilemmas and the 'play of ideas'; he and Maupassant were on cordial terms.

379 *Fête de la République*: 14 July was made an annual national holiday in France on 6 July 1880 to commemorate the Fête de la Fédération (14 July 1790), although it is generally associated with the storming of the Bastille (14 July 1789).

Mme. Sablé: the name may allude to Madeleine de Souvré, Marquise de Sablé (1598–1678), a theological philosopher and patron of the moralist François de La Rochefoucauld (1613–80).

Limoges: city in central France, its prosperity in the nineteenth century was due to porcelain manufacture.

Hypnotism and Suggestion: like many of his contemporaries (including, of course, Bram Stoker), Maupassant was fascinated by mental suggestion and psychological states.

379 *school at Nancy*: in the second half of the nineteenth century research into hypnosis was led by the Nancy School and the Salpêtrière School; the Nancy School, directed by Ambroise-Auguste Liébeault and Hippolyte Bernheim, presented hypnosis as a therapeutic treatment functioning through mental suggestibility.

380 *Voltaire . . . returned the compliment*: 'Si Dieu nous a faits à son image, nous le lui avons bien rendu', from Voltaire's *Le Sottisier*, XXXII, *Faits Détachés* (*Œuvres Complètes*, xxxii. 562); 'Voltaire' was the pen-name of François-Marie Arouet (1694–1778), a leading figure of the Enlightenment.

Mesmer: Franz Anton Mesmer (1734–1815), controversial German physician who proposed a theory of 'animal magnetism' from which he developed the therapeutic practice of 'mesmerism', a precursor of hypnotism.

fascinate: entrance or render unable to move by the power of one's stare (*OED*).

383 *Bougival*: originally a village on the banks of the Seine near Paris, but by the mid-nineteenth century a chic suburb of the capital.

Watermen's Ball: balls and cabarets opportunistically named after the Parisian boatmen (*nautes*) were popular on the banks of the Seine; originally, the Boatmen's guild had been a powerful institution that controlled trade on the Seine and whose coat of arms was adopted by the city.

island of La Grenouillière: La Grenouillère ('the frog pond'), a fashionable Parisian water resort on the Seine—the haunt of tawdry prostitutes, sleazy dandies, and underworld lowlife, and popular as a subject for Impressionist painters; Maupassant also refers to it in his short story 'Femme Fatale' (1881) (see *A Parisian Affair* (2004), 75–92).

384 *Géant des Batailles*: 'giant of battles', a rose hybrid of a vivid crimson colour introduced in the mid-nineteenth century and very popular at the time.

385 *phantasmagoria*: see notes to pp. 95 and 212.

387 *Hermann Herestauss's . . . Ancient and Modern World*: fictitious.

brougham: closed carriage drawn by a single horse, with two or four wheels and so carrying two or four passengers; the word was first used in 1851 (*OED*).

388 *theogony*: discipline studying the birth and genealogy of pagan deities (*OED*).

389 *Revue du Monde Scientifique*: a fictitious journal.

390 *Horla*: presumably derived from the French words *hors* (outside) and *là* (there), suggesting something uncanny, outlandish, and alien.

391 *subtilely*: ingeniously, precisely (*OED*).

393 *supersensual*: beyond what is perceptible by the (human) senses, transcendent (*OED*).

395 *I must . . . kill . . . myself! . . .* : the journal is ultimately revealed to be the last testament of a multiple killer and a suicide note.

AMBROSE BIERCE, *THE DEATH OF HALPIN FRAYSER*

Ambrose Gwinnett Bierce (1842–1914?) was an American writer known as 'Bitter Bierce' due to his acerbic and unforgiving wit. He served in the American Civil War (1861–5), fighting for the Union in the 9th Indiana Regiment and was commended for his bravery on the battlefield, leaving the army as a lieutenant and eventually becoming a leading polemical journalist in San Francisco and Washington, as well as living in England in 1872–5. Bierce is celebrated for his short stories, which often bear the scars of his experiences of warfare, and he also published novels and several volumes of poetry; he is, however, perhaps best known for *The Devil's Dictionary* (originally titled *The Cynic's Word Book*, 1906). The circumstances of Bierce's death are unknown: he disappeared in Mexico during the protracted violence that followed the Mexican Revolution of 1910.

'The Death of Halpin Frayser' was first published in the Christmas 1891 issue of *The Wave*, and later appeared in the collection *Can Such Things Be?* (1893), 1–26, with many minor revisions, the more significant of which are noted below. The text here is taken from *The Wave* (19 Dec. 1891), pp. 2–5.

396 *lich*: corpse (*OED*).

Mannon's 'Thoughts on Immortality': fictitious—the epigraph is by Bierce; in the version given in the 1893 text (*Can Such Things Be?*) the attribution is revised to 'Hali'.

Napa Valley: Californian region with a Mediterranean climate, consequently planted with vines and by the end of the nineteenth century the heart of American viticulture with over 140 wineries in business.

Halpin: Anglicized form of the Irish surname Ó hAilpín, originating in Co. Monaghan.

San Francisco: St Helena in the 1893 text.

bark: literally a sail boat, but here (as often) used figuratively (*OED*); perhaps alluding to Percy Bysshe Shelley's final stanza of *Adonais* (1821): 'my spirit's bark is driven, | Far from the shore', 25.

397 *manzanita*: bearberry shrubs (*Arctostaphylos*; *OED*).

madroño: large evergreen trees with red berries native to North America (*Arbutus*; *OED*, which cites *American Humour* (May 1888): 'Here and there a madrona tree grows, with its bark peeling off in its own peculiar way, leaving the tree bright red and as smooth as satin').

numerical: presumably a hamfisted reference to temperature; the barely better 1893 text reads 'seasonal'.

lumination: emission of light (*OED*, which notes that the word is rare and gives no citations beyond 1855).

398 *maculations*: stains (*OED*).

399 *loon*: Great Northern Diver (*Gavia immer*), a bird noted for its strange cry, variously described as 'whistling', 'laughing', and 'weird' (*OED*).

rilling: flowing in a stream (*OED*).

400 *moon*: perhaps alluding to Shakespeare's *A Midsummer Night's Dream*, V. i. 12–17:

The poet's eye, in a fine frenzy rolling,
Doth glance from heaven to earth, from earth to heaven,
And as imagination bodies forth
The forms of things unknown, the poet's pen
Turns them to shapes, and gives to airy nothing
A local habitation and a name.

sordid: menial (*OED*, which records the word as obsolete, its last citation being 1751).

the Killer of the Wise: a pseudo-idiomatic phrase coined by Bierce, presumably meaning pride.

loose fish: an individual with no settled way of life (*Green*, who also notes meanings of a promiscuous woman and a prostitute).

402 *shanghaied*: knocked out, kidnapped, and compelled serve aboard a ship (*OED*).

gallant: noble—when used of a ship (*OED*), ironically so in this case.

countree: in many traditional Anglo-Scottish ballads, popular in nineteenth-century America, the stress of 'country' falls on the second syllable to create a winsome pronunciation of the word; with the repetition of 'gallant' earlier in the sentence the effect is of ironic euphony.

St Helena: at the time a small town established by settlers in Napa Valley (see note to p. 396).

gunning: shooting, hunting with a gun (*OED*).

403 *An appeal will not lie*: legal phraseology—an appeal will not be set.

attrusion: possibly an error for 'detrusion'—thrusting away (*OED*); the phrase was rewritten in 1893 to read, 'reversion to professional slang'.

Mount St. Helena: part of the Sonoma Volcanics, its highest point (at 4,343 ft) is in Napa County; Robert Louis Stevenson spent his honeymoon in the area in 1880 and described his experiences there in *The Silverado Squatters* (1883).

404 *Calistoga*: named for its hot springs—the 'Saratoga of California'.

heeled: armed (*Green*)—US slang recorded from 1852, later popular in 'Wild West' stories.

405 *laid for*: lay in wait for (*OED*); the whole phrase is given in quotation marks in *Can Such Things Be?*

got the drop on: became aware of—or possibly, was tipped off about (*Green*).

go through: rob; also beat up (*OED*; *Green*).

galoot: an awkward or uncouth fellow, sometimes a term of affection (*OED*; *Green*).

Mountains of the Moon: believed since ancient times to be a vast snow-capped mountain range in southern Africa and the source of the Nile; the phrase is used here figuratively to describe something both iconic and unknown.

'Where you must shortly lie': the line is from Isaac Watts's hymn lxiii, 'A Funeral Thought', also known as 'Hark! from the Tombs a doleful sound!' (*Hymns and Spiritual Songs* (1709), 187).

406 *'a large circle of sorrowing friends'*: a conventional phrase of mourning, as shown by its inclusion in the mock obituary for English cricket that appeared in the *Sporting Times* on 2 September 1882, thus inaugurating the biennial Ashes series of Test Matches played between England and Australia.

407 *right*: revised to 'significant' in 1893 text.

408 *suspicion*: revised to 'apprehension' in 1893 text.

Enthralled by some mysterious spell . . . the viewless: Bierce's composition.

immortelles: generic name for papery flowers that retain their colour being dried, such as species of *Helichrysum* and *Xeranthemum*; also known as 'everlasting flowers' (*OED*).

409 *There came to them . . . a measureless remove*: the text printed in 1893 (*Can Such Things Be?*) places this paragraph at the very end and cuts the sentence 'The men looked at one another, consciously pale and visibly shuddering'.

'X. L.' [JULIAN OSGOOD FIELD], *A KISS OF JUDAS*

Julian Osgood Field (1852–1925) was an American, educated in England, a European cosmopolitan, and an unrepentant gossip. He wrote sensational horror stories under the pseudonyms 'X. L.' and 'Sigma' and several volumes of 'uncensored' and consequently scandalous memoirs; at the same time he was tried for defrauding his high-society acquaintances through forgeries and confidence scams, for which he received a prison sentence.

'A Kiss of Judas' was first printed in 1893 in the *Pall Mall Magazine* with illustrations including a notable frontispiece by Aubrey Beardsley (1872–98), leading artist of 1890s Aestheticism renowned for his erotic and grotesque black-and-white images, and then reprinted in Field's collection *Aut Diabolus Aut Nihil* ('the Devil or nothing'), in which Field made preposterous claims for the title story's authenticity. Notwithstanding this tissue of misinfomation, the maverick scholar Montague Summers conflates 'A Kiss of Judas' with genuine Eastern European folklore:

> Red was the colour of the hair of Judas Iscariot, and of Cain . . . I have not met with the following tradition save orally, but it is believed in Serbia, Bulgaria, and Rumania, that there are certain red-polled vampires who are called 'Children of Judas,' and that these, the foulest of the foul, kill their victim with one bite or kiss which drains the blood as it were at a single draught. The poisoned flesh of the victim is

wounded with the Devil's stigmata, three hideous scars shaped thus, XXX, signifying the thirty pieces of silver, the price of blood. (Summers, *The Vampire* (1928), 183)

This claim has since been absorbed into popular vampire lore.

The version given here is from the *Pall Mall Magazine* for July 1893, pp. 338–66. The handful of punctuation idiosyncrasies, such as double em-rule, are retained; only significant textual changes made in the version published the following year in *Aut Diabolus Aut Nihil and Other Tales* (1894), 145–226, are noted.

411 *Gebir*: quoted (with minor changes) from Walter Savage Landor, *Gebir* (1798), ll. 53–8, p. 45.

Rustchuck: Ruse, Bulgaria, on the high bank of the Danube; the town was extensively developed during the period.

Charles Buller: Buller (1806–48) was a radical politician and wit, known as 'the Cornish Voltaire' (*ODNB*).

peer, now deceased: Richard Monckton Milnes (1809–85), first Baron Houghton (elevated to the peerage 1863), Liberal politician and man of letters best known for his two-volume *Life, Letters and Literary Remains of John Keats* (1848); in his own estimation he was 'a man of no common imaginative perceptions, who never gave his full conviction to anything but the closest reasoning; of acute sensibilities, who always distrusted the affections; of ideal aspirations and sensual habits; of the most cheerful manners and of the gloomiest philosophy' (*ODNB*).

I often think . . . your conduct: Buller's words are quoted by Monckton Milnes's son, Robert Offley Ashburton Crewe-Milnes, Marquess of Crewe (see Granville-Barker (ed.), 'Lord Houghton and his Circle', 9).

412 *cordon bleu*: originally a blue ribbon identifying the Knights-Grand-Cross of the chivalric French Order of the Holy Ghost, the insignia came to represent first-rate accomplishment and hence figuratively, at the time, an excellent cook (*OED*).

fashion: later editions add the following clause to the sentence, 'but his excesses thoroughly enjoying the while, as a refined, healthy, handsome, and hot-blooded beggar mounted on a two-year-old thoroughbred, and bound for that uncomfortable capital described by St Theresa as a place where there is a bad smell and no love, might reasonably be expected to do'.

Clavaroche . . . Jacqueline: in Alfred de Musset's dark comedy *Le Chandelier* ('the candlestick', 1835), Captain Clavaroche is the lover of Jacqueline, young wife of an elderly notary; this three-act play was first staged in 1848, before being banned upon publication in 1850.

413 *Yquem of '37*: Château d'Yquem in Bordeaux is the most celebrated producer of Sauternes, or dessert, wine; Bordeaux enjoyed an abundant harvest in 1837, but the wines were ordinary—according to Tastet & Lawton (Courtiers Assermentés, Bordeaux wine brokers established in 1740), 1834 was a far better year.

la haute noce: literally, 'the high wedding'; here referring to a volume by the French journalist and art critic Albert Wolff, who wrote several volumes of *Mémoires d'un Parisien* describing society life; *La Haute-Noce*, concerning marriage customs, was published in 1885.

'rubicon' . . . four louis . . . Petit Club . . . the Jockey: references to gambling culture. The rubicon in card games is a target score (100 in piquet, 1,000 in bezique) which increases the penalty paid by a losing player who fails to attain it (*OED*). The louis was a silver coin equivalent to the English crown (five shillings), and in the nineteenth century a five-franc piece. The Petit Club and Jockey Club were high-class gaming houses; the exclusive and aristocratic Jockey Club in particular was targetted by the mob during the Prussian Siege of Paris in 1870–1 (see Whitehurst, *My Private Diary*, i. 27, 270).

Dugléré for the Speaker: referring to Adolphe Dugléré (1804–85), from 1866 head chef at the premier Parisian restaurant the Café Anglais, and John Evelyn Denison (1800–73), Speaker of the House of Commons—a man not known for his finesse in the kitchen.

Grand Seize . . . St Stephen's: Le Grand Seize was the most sumptuous of the private rooms in the Café Anglais and the venue for 'Le Dîner des Trois Empereurs' (1867), here contrasted with St Stephen's Hall in the Palace of Westminster—originally the debating chamber of the House of Commons.

pays du tendre: the realm of love, sometimes depicted in fanciful maps.

going to and fro in the earth: in Job 1: 7, Satan answers the Lord's question 'Whence comest thou?' with the reply, 'From going to and fro in the earth, and from walking up and down in it'.

Emir of Bokhara: Nasrulla, the ruler of Bukhara, now in southern Uzbekistan, referred to in newspaper reports on the Eastern Question; he was described by Captain Arthur Conolly (1807–42?), the British envoy he imprisoned and murdered, as a 'demon' and a 'fiend' (Kaye, *Lives Of Indian Officers*, ii. 166).

Imaum of Muscat: ruler of the capital city of Oman; the Governor-General of British India arbitrated in the Oman succession in 1856, and in 1862 signed the Zanzibar Guarantee Treaty confirming the independence of both countries.

Schliemann: Heinrich Schliemann (1822–90), archaeologist famed for discovering Troy—including, he believed, the tombs of Agamemnon and Clytemnestra.

Beke: Charles Tilstone Beke (1800–74), a prolific and controversial biblical geographer and African explorer of Abyssinia and the source of the Nile (*ODNB*).

414 *Shereef of Wazan*: the principal Islamic leader of North Morocco wielding more power than the Sultan; he also enjoyed the patronage of France.

414 *Kosciuszco*: Tadeusz Kościuszko (1746–1817), Polish officer in both the American and Polish armies, engineer, and revolutionary republican; he fought for American independence before returning to Poland and, with French Jacobin support, led the Kościuszko Uprising of 1794 in Kraków against Russian and Prussian imperial control.

apolausticism: devotion to enjoyment (*OED*, first recorded in 1883; 'A Kiss of Judas' provides the only other citation, although the word was current in Oxford in the first decades of the twentieth century).

Rue Taitbout and the Boulevard des Italiens: the fashionable and chic Café Tortoni, famous for its ices and frozen desserts, stood at this corner. It is mentioned by both Alexandre Dumas *père* in *Le Comte de Monte-Cristo* (1844–6), trans. Coward, 877, and Émile Zola in *La Carée* (1872), trans. Nelson, 192, and was also frequented by Léo Delibes (1836–91), Edgar Degas (1834–1917), the Goncourt brothers (Edmond, 1822–96; Champrosay, 1830–70), Édouard Manet (1832–83), and Jacques Offenbach (1819–80; see Crisci-Richardson, *Mapping Degas*, 203).

bisque . . . coffee: the duration of a meal, from fish soup to post-prandial coffee.

Bosphorus: the Bosporus, a 19-mile-long strait through Turkey that joins the Black Sea with the Sea of Marmara; Istanbul lies on its western and eastern banks.

Servia: see note to p. 271.

Ancient: ensign; originally a 'standard-bearer' (*OED*).

great Eltchi: Stratford Canning (1786–1880), Viscount Stratford de Redcliffe (elevated to the peerage 1852), diplomat—known as the 'Great Elchi' (*elchi* being a Turkic word for 'ambassador') from his position in Constantinople, where he had first been appointed ambassador in 1825 and where he served almost continuously from 1841; he was again sent in 1853 to deal with the developing crisis in the East, a crisis that rapidly developed into the Crimean War (1853–6).

416 *Phthisis*: tuberculosis (also known as consumption), a wasting disease of the lungs (*OED*).

417 *canaille*: rabble (*OED*); in French, a scoundrel.

418 *seconds*: those representing the principal opponents in a duel and who make the challenge, arrange the time and place, and load the weapons (*OED*).

420 *absurd*: later editions add the following sentences:

> I'd as soon accept a challenge from a stoat or a ferret. But after all, the initial fault was mine. This wretched creature is not responsible either for his face or for his manners, and I feel I owe him some reparation for my impertinent curiosity. So I'll just say a word to Pellegrini and give him our address at Djavil Pacha's, to give to this man if he requires it.

faubourgs: suburbs outside a city's gates (*OED*).

whilom plunger: former reckless gambler (*OED*); the phrase was used of Ernest Benzon (d. 1911), the 'Jubilee Plunger', in American and Australasian newspaper reviews of his book, *How I Lost £250,000 in Two Years* (1889).

421 *Bignon's*: Louis Bignon (1816–1906) was proprietor of both the Café de Foy and the Café Riche, ultra-fashionable restaurants on the Boulevard des Italiens with a similar clientele to the Café Tortoni; it is mentioned by Guy de Maupassant in 'Le Protecteur' (1884) (translated as 'The Patron', *A Day in the Country*, trans. Coward, 154) (see note to p. 414).

tapissier: upholsterer (French).

the Koran . . . painting of animate objects: no verse in the Qur'an prohibits paintings and sculptures of living creatures; the *Hadith* (traditions or sayings of the Prophet) do, however, generally oppose such depictions.

Rue Drouot: known for the major Parisian auction house Hôtel Drouot, as well as art dealers and philately.

colony: later editions add the following clause to the sentence, 'and, in fact, conducting his life by the Bosphorus very much on the same lines as any man of wealth and refinement might conduct his by the Seine, the Danube, the Neva, or the Thames'.

Rue Scribe: at the time the location of the Jockey Club (see note to p. 413).

Œil de Bœuf: a small round window through which one can assess visitors—specifically the title of an antechamber in the Palace of Versailles where guests gathered (*OED*); hence, here the title of a fictitious newspaper.

the Birdcage at Newmarket: the saddling paddock at Newmarket Racecourse, an élite enclosure in which to view the horses—for which privilege admission was charged; the crowded scene, celebrating Paradox's victory at the 2,000 Guineas Stakes in 1885, was painted by Lowes Cato Dickinson (1819–1908) and includes Paradox and third-placed The Child of the Mist as well as many racing celebrities.

422 *'Cheery and Cheeky'*: an indication of how the name Jeratczesco is pronounced.

ejusdem farinæ: of the same sort (sometimes used derogatively, especially of scholastics).

Broad Church: liberal and tolerant Anglican; the term was first popularized in 1848 (*OED*).

423 *Yquem*: later editions add the following clause to the sentence:

> she, indeed, almost brought at length to forget the Turkish woman's burning wrongs in the delightful dulchatz served in dainty silver saucers; but he, more robust in faith, finding it helpful to let his soul occasionally carol bracing and encouraging snatches from 'Hymns Ancient and Modern,' as healthy Anglican protests against the errors of the Crescent, even though his lips, engaged in negotiation with the Moslem's woodcock, of a necessity remained silent.

St Marceaux: a sparkling wine of the Champagne region.

423 *Requiem*: later editions add the following clause to the sentence:

> persons of both sexes, and of every nationality and religion, who would arrive in time for dinner one evening, stay the night, and perhaps the following day and night, and then disappear without thinking of subjecting their host to a formal leave-taking, being well aware that his Excellency's time was very precious, since he was up and about by six o'clock every morning, and very often steaming down in the direction of Stamboul to look after the foreign affairs of the empire before many of his guests had awakened from their slumbers.

the Karpaks: the vast Carpathian mountain range, running for almost a thousand miles through Central to South-East Europe, across modern Poland, the Czechia, Slovakia, Ukraine, Moldova, Hungary, Serbia, and Romania.

sweet waters of Asia: European name for two streams, the Göksu and the Küçüksu, that flowed into the Bosphorus at its narrowest point near the Anatolian Fortress (Anadolu Hisarı); the meadow between the two streams was a fashionable resort for the modish élite of Ottoman and European society.

Ambassador: later editions add the following clause to the sentence:

> accompanied by such representatives of the power and supremacy of Great Britain as the wicked and sempiternally-beautiful Dowager Duchess of Brompton, who, since the close of the Crimean War, had been giving her undivided attention to an exhaustive study of the Eastern Question, her head reclining on the shoulders of two successive generations of susceptible attachés.

1867: later editions add the following clause to the sentence, 'and expressing his delighted surprise at the discovery of his novel possession in a fashion so offensive to his party as to have merited and brought about his final extinction at the hands of "the impetuous earl, the Rupert of debate"'.

424 *forty-five*: later editions add the following clause to the sentence, '(he had been a collier till then), and who thus at fifty experienced the delightful surprises of a lad of eighteen, and confided them to you with a frankness which would even have brought blushes to the cheeks of Jean Jacques'.

Derby . . . Epsom: the Derby Stakes, one of England's classic flat horse races; it is run at Epsom Downs Racecourse.

Neva: river in north-west Russia, Leningrad province, flowing into the Baltic Sea at St Petersburg—some 1,500 miles north of the Bosphorus.

déjeuner champétre: lunch in the country (French); possibly alluding to the painting *Les Charmes de la Vie Champêtre* (c.1740) by the celebrated Rococo artist François Boucher (1703–70).

Alem-Dagh: mountain range north-west of Anatolia from the Bosphorus.

marmitons: assistant chefs, or scullions (*OED*).

kitchen on the corner of... Boulevard des Italiens: Restaurant Paillard, established 1880—a small restaurant, but supposedly one of the best in Paris and later frequented by Arnold Bennett.

déjeuner sur l'herbe: lunch on the grass (French); almost certainly alluding to the famed erotic painting of the same title by Édouard Manet (1832–83; 1863).

425 *Amneris... Radamès and Aïda*: characters in the 1871 opera *Aida*, composed by Giuseppe Verdi (1813–1901). Radamès, commander of the Egyptian army, loves Aida, the Ethiopian slave of Princess Amneris—who in turn loves Radamès and is jealous of Aida; Radamès unwittingly betrays his country to the Ethiopians, is sentenced to death, and dies in a vault with Aida while Amneris prays for his salvation.

Hibernicé: Irish (Latin; usually, Hibernicè).

Giulio Clovio: Juraj (Giorgio) Glovicic (1498–1578), born in Croatia before moving to Italy to train as a miniature painter, at which he excelled—his masterpiece being the *Farnese Hours* (1546).

426 *events of 1867*: the Second Great Reform Bill, which extended the vote to men over the age of 21 who were either householders, lodgers who paid rent of £10 a year or more, agricultural landowners, or tenants with small holdings of land; this doubled voters from one to two million and was greeted with shock by the existing electorate.

when the swine . . . choked in the lake?: the Gadarene swine, described in Mark 5: 1–20. Among tombs in the country of the Gadarenes, Jesus encounters an unclean man who is possessed by many devils ('My name is Legion: for we are many'); Jesus casts the devils into a nearby herd of pigs who then 'ran violently down a steep place into the sea . . . and were choked'.

Children of Judas: in Acts 1: 20 it is suggested that the children of Judas are described in Psalm 109, the 'Judas Psalm'; in particular, verse 8 prophesies Judas's fate—'Let his days be few; and let another take his office'. From the Middle Ages the Jewish people were also reviled by the Roman Catholic clergy as the 'children of Judas' (see Michael, *History of Catholic Antisemitism*, 167).

osculatory: kissing-related (*OED*).

tribute from: revised to 'cruelty at' in later editions.

loup sauce homard: sea bass (*loup de mer*) with lobster sauce.

427 *hydrophobia*: rabies, a symptom of which is dread of water (*OED*).

Sinaia: town in Prahova (județ, meaning county) in east-central Romania, north of Bucharest.

a mark like this: correctly punctuated, the sentence continuing after the colon in the act of scratching rather than in words.

Vous êtes impayable, mon cher: you are priceless, my dear fellow.

foires: fairs, i.e. as a sideshow.

427 *blagues*: pretentious falsehoods (*OED*; a French word first used in English in 1839).

428 *reculer pour mieux sauter*: deploying a setback to advance further (*OED*).

Mouton Rothschild: Baron Nathaniel Rothschild (1840–1915) bought Château Brane-Mouton, in the Médoc region, in 1853.

seven million . . . demons: there is occult authority for this figure, calculated from 1,111 legions each of 6,666 souls, and various sixteenth-century demonologists proposed similar figures. Nicolas Fromenteau (*fl.* 1581?) in *Le Cabinet du Roy de France* ('the cabinet of the King of France', 1581) proposed 7,405,926 or 7,409,127 demons (see Givray, *Witchcraft Magic & Alchemy*, 127; and Seignolle, *Les Évangiles du Diable* ('the Devil's gospels'), 115, respectively). Johann Weyer (also Wier, Wierus) (1515–88), Dutch Protestant, physician, demonologist, and pupil of Cornelius Agrippa, identified a further 7,451,926 demons in his treatise *De Praestigiis Daemonum* (1568), revising the figure to 44,435,622 ($6{,}666^2 + 66$) in *Pseudomonarchia Daemonum* ('the false monarchy of demons', 1583, an appendix to *De Praestigiis Daemonum*, 1577), and later still to 1,758,640,176: a rabbit hole down which it is fruitless to plunge. The Talmudic tradition also advances a figure of 7,405,926 (see Bane, *Encyclopedia of Demons*, 118, 238)—although inevitably numbers differ.

'tetrade' . . . counting both ways: typical occult numerology—such mathematics are fascinating for acolytes, but devoid of any higher meaning; the *tetraktys*, 'the four', refers to the first four numbers, which added together equal ten—the perfect number in fifth-century Pythagoreanism, if not part of Platonic philosophy.

431 *à bientôt*: see you soon (a less final farewell than '*au revoir*').

432 *Tziganes*: Gypsys or members of the Romani people, often specifically referring to musicians (*OED*; the identity 'Roma' is endorsed by the European Network Against Racism).

indeed: later editions add the following clauses to the sentence:

> but so familiar to Colonel Rowan that the loveliness of what he saw could hardly have been the sole and only cause of the deep feeling of melancholy which stole over him as he walked the deck and heard the music of the orchestra, which the others were taking back with them to Constantinople, growing fainter and fainter in the distance.

433 *retirement*: following this, 'and as it was early and the night divine' added to subsequent editions.

434 *Inkermann . . . Candahar*: Battle of Inkermann (1854), the 'Soldier's Battle', a notable allied victory of the Crimean War fought in fog outside Sevastopol; Battle of Kandahar (1880), last engagement of the Second Afghan War in which Major-General Sir Frederick Roberts's forces heroically relieved besieged British Raj troops and controversially brought Afghanistan under British control.

Boyards: members of a privileged and politically influential class in Wallachia and Moldavia, and later Romania (*OED*).

Nimrods: the 'mighty hunter' of Genesis 10: 9; thus, a generic term for great hunters, often—as here—used ironically (*OED*).

435 *Admirable Crichton*: James Crichton (1560–82), a Scottish rhetorician who matriculated at St Andrew's aged just 10 years; he gained his BA in 1573 and MA in 1575, acquired military experience in France, and was acclaimed as an orator in Italy—whereupon he was promoted (probably by himself) as a prodigy 'fluent in ten languages (including Hebrew and Chaldean); learned in philosophy, theology, mathematics, astrology, and statecraft; dazzling in disputation, equipped with an almost miraculous memory; eloquent, handsome, courtly, witty in conversation; and soldierly and athletic, as much a master of horsemanship and jousting as of the dance' (*ODNB*).

437 *C'est entendu*: that is understood.

Baden: leading German racecourse at Iffezheim near Baden-Baden and a favourite summer resort for the wealthy; the first thoroughbred event was held in 1858.

Gunzburg: banking firm founded in 1853 by the Russian philanthropist Joseph, Baron Günzburg in St Petersburg.

438 *sparrow-drawn goddess*: Aphrodite, the ancient Greek goddess of love, beauty, and fertility; myrtles and sparrows were sacred to her (*OCD*).

Bacchus and baccarat: the ancient Greek god of wine (also known as Dionysus) and the casino chance card game baccarat, popular in the second half of the nineteenth century; in 1866 the *Daily Telegraph* opined on 'Baccarat, bad luck, and bankruptcy' (quoted by *OED*).

pillow: later editions add the following clause to the sentence, 'and finally, indeed, and just before the end, brought about so chronic a condition of nervous restlessness as to render his seeking that pillow for purposes of prolonged repose, a mockery'.

441 *therein*: later editions add the following paragraph:

> And as this restlessness of the Colonel,—whose general health, by the way, had been greatly impaired by the chill he had caught, and especially by the strong remedies he had taken to counteract its effects—although having nothing whatever in common with a sentiment of alarm, being merely indeed the natural result of the perpetual and fatiguing reiteration of the question in his mind, 'In what absurd fashion are those uncouth boors going to try to frighten me? What is their idea of a very terrible thing, I wonder?'—although, as we say, his uneasiness partook in nowise of the nature of alarm, and he felt perfectly ready to entertain, at a moment's notice and with a smile, a whole army of ghosts and goblins, still, as this disquietude sprang from uncertainty and suspense, it naturally increased in acuteness as the time drew near when it must perforce cease altogether—give

place to knowledge and experience, and, of course, amusement, triumph, and tranquillity.

442 *things*: later editions add the following clause to the sentence: 'and for so many years, was now being withdrawn,—going perhaps to join the fair and dear and dead, or indeed worse than dead, women who had inspired its most brilliant and most ardent scintillations'.

Hospodars: literally 'lord' (Slavonic), a title for governors of Wallachia and Moldavia appointed by the Ottoman authorities.

Les miroirs . . . embellis de sourires: from Part V of 'Du Silence' by leading Belgian symbolist poet and novelist Georges-Raymond-Constantin Rodenbach (1855–98); published in *Le Règne du Silence* (1891), 191, with minor changes. According to Lynne Pudles, 'In the fifth section of his ode to solitude and silence, Rodenbach's poet-hero leans over to kiss the mirror, in which reside the dead faces from his past; the "captive waters" in his glass are identified with Bruges' ('Fernand Khnopff, Georges Rodenbach, and Bruges', 647).

Le Rouge et le Noir: 'the red and the black', 1830 novel by 'Stendhal' (Marie-Henri Beyle, 1783–1842) recounting the fortunes of Julien Sorel during the Bourbon Restoration in France (1814–30).

fair-faced sun . . . desolations of the night: Algernon Charles Swinburne, *Atalanta in Calydon* (1865), 1–2; lineation slightly revised.

443 *laoutari*: as stated, *lăutari* (Romanian) are professional Gypsy musicians who perform *muzica lăutărească*; they consider themselves an élite caste.

tsigane: see note to p. 432.

Strelna: a traditional restaurant noted for its 'Gypsy choir'; the Russian aristocracy of the nineteenth century were enthralled by Gypsy culture and the fabled beauty of Gypsy women.

444 *Love shot his arrow . . . Will only*: Field's composition.

Stendhal: see note to p. 442.

445 *girandoles*: branched candlesticks (*OED*).

446 *a countenance different . . . Who could she be?*: these lines replaced by the following sentence in later editions:

> It was a youthful copy of the most perfect type of the Mater Dolorosa, and never, Rowan told himself, had he known, until he saw those tearful and uplifted eyes, the sweet and wondrous power that violets could lend to grief to stir compassion with; nor, till he noted the delicate oval of that face, all the poetic value and pathetic eloquence of form; nor, till he marked the quivering of those parted, perfect lips, with what resistless tenderness sorrow could light upon the very throne of kisses.

447 *a Madonna*: in later editions these words are preceded with the clause, 'the most inspired efforts of genius to depict the countenance of the Virgin Mother of God, so struck and so amazed the travelled and cultured

valet, that he could hardly perhaps have been more filled with wonder had he actually seen'.

448 *polyglottic*: uttered in several different languages (*OED*).

defeated: later editions add the following clauses to the sentence:

> and quite at the end of his tether, for although in the course of his chatter his hands even had not been idle (for the horrible possibility of this beautiful woman being a deaf mute had occurred to him), nothing that his tongue or fingers could find to tell had been able to bring the faintest gleam of recognition or even of curiosity to that perfect face.

450 *squirts*: tubular devices for squirting water (*OED*).

aneurism: a ruptured artery (*OED*).

ERIC, COUNT STENBOCK, *THE TRUE STORY OF A VAMPIRE*

Eric Magnus Andreas Harry (1860–95), later Count Stanislaus Eric Stenbock, was, in the words of W. B. Yeats, a 'scholar, connoisseur, drunkard, poet, pervert, most charming of men' (*Oxford Book of Modern Verse*, x). He inherited the title Count Stenbock and with it vast estates in Estonia, and took the name Stanislaus from the Roman Catholic saint Stanislaus Kostka after his conversion. Following an education by turns sporadic and desultory, he published slim volumes of homoerotic poetry and lived a life of decadence not unlike that of Duc Jean Des Esseintes in Joris-Karl Huysmans's novel of excess, *À Rebours* (1884).

'The True Story of a Vampire' (also published as 'The Sad Story of a Vampire') is Stenbock's best-known work, first appearing in his last book, *Studies of Death: Romantic Tales* (1894), 120–47, from which the text here is taken. It is, perhaps inevitably, a cocktail of autobiography and self-mythologization—not least in its inclusion of male homosexuality and exotic creatures (among Stenbock's various outré pets was a snake). Although Bram Stoker was probably not aware of the tale, there are nevertheless some suggestive overlaps with *Dracula*, such as the train journey and the trance state of Gabriel.

451 *Styria*: see note to p. 209.

its turkeys, its capons: *The Metropolitan Magazine* described Upper Styria as 'no less famous for its handsome women, than its vicinity is for excellent turkeys and poultry' (vol. 35 (1842), 171).

'the Baroness and her beasts': a generic news story.

Wronski: the portrait of Carmela's father may be indebted to Józef Maria Hoene-Wroński (1778–1853), an eccentric and controversial Polish philosopher of mathematics whose belief that he had discovered the 'Absolute'—the underlying principle of the universe—led to his work being both studied by occultists and dismissed as mad.

452 *Gabriel*: in the Christian tradition, St Gabriel the Archangel is one of the three archangels named in the Bible; he is an agent of mercy and

intercession, and so is the angel of Consolation and Incarnation—it is Gabriel who tells Mary that she will bear Christ, and is accordingly depicted in many paintings of the Annunciation. In Jewish literature the names of angels were considered to have mystic powers (*CE*).

452 *Westbourne Park*: affluent London suburb, characterized at the time by spacious villas and rural land, through which ran the Great Western Railway line terminating at Paddington station; the area was known variously as Westbournia and 'the Bond Street of the west'.

Carmela: like Gabriel, originally a Hebrew name that became popular in Italy and Spain; it also evokes Joseph Sheridan Le Fanu's tale 'Carmilla' (see the present volume, pp. 209–75).

intercalate: interpolate (*OED*).

præter-human: preterhuman, beyond the bounds of what is human (*OED*).

Faun: a forest spirit or *numen* associated with the mysterious sounds of the trees; Faun has affinities both to Pan and the incubus of nightmare, and, like Pan, is usually depicted as a horned human with the hindquarters of a goat (*OCD*).

en arc d'amour: the arch of Love (French)—see, for example, Pétrus Borel's 1838 novel *Madame Putiphar* (Book IV, ch. 1: ii, p. 1); Borel (1809–59) was a writer of the French 'Frenetique' school of horror, styling himself on the title-page of his novel '*le Lycanthrope*' (the wolf-man).

Grace is shed . . . thee eternally: 'Thou art fairer than the children of men: Grace is poured into thy lips: therefore hath God blessed thee for ever' (Psalm 45: 2).

454 *Vardalek*: the Count's name probably derives from the Serbian *vukodlak*, the Bulgarian *varkolak*, and the Greek *vourkólakes*—words meaning both vampire and werewolf (Perkowski, *The Darkling*, 332: cited in Groom, *The Vampire*, xviii).

455 *csardas*: the national dance of Hungary (*OED*; also *csárdás* or *czardas*, derived from the word for an inn); the distinctive two-part form in contrasting tempos dates from about 1830 as a romanticization of peasant dancing, and was, for example, used by Johannes Brahms (1833–97) in his suite of *Hungarian Dances* (1869, 1880).

motive: in music, a short and often recurrent melody or rhythm (*OED*).

relâche: interval (*OED*).

456 *Trieste*: see note to p. 143.

textures: woven fabrics (*OED*, by this time an archaic term).

Chopin's nocturnes: Frédéric Chopin (1810–49) wrote twenty-one 'Nocturnes' ('songs of the night') during his career; they are considered masterly examples of nineteenth-century Romantic solo piano compositions.

457 *Nie umiem . . . ciechi kocham*: 'I cannot find words to express how much I love you' (Polish).

Gratz: see note to p. 233—another allusion to Le Fanu's tale.

458 *extreme unction*: in the Roman Catholic Church, a sacrament for the sick who are in peril of dying; it consists of a priest anointing the subject with oil and repeating appropriate words for the remission of sins (*CE*).

R. MURRAY GILCHRIST, *THE CRIMSON WEAVER*

Robert Murray Gilchrist (1867–1917), author and humanitarian, is an unjustly neglected author of novels, English topographical writing, and decadent Gothic stories. Born in Sheffield, his working life began as a cutler's apprentice before he turned to writing, and although he may then have visited Paris and London, he afterwards spent the rest of his life in the wilds of the Peak District in Derbyshire, England. From this rural retreat he wrote novels of homicide and homosexuality, and many acclaimed short stories—the first of which were collected in *The Stone Dragon and Other Tragic Romances* (1894). He became a much-loved local character and eccentric, and was a champion of Belgian refugees during the Great War.

'The Crimson Weaver' was first published in the bible of decadence, the *Yellow Book*—from which this text is taken (vol. 6, July 1895, pp. 269–77); the idiosyncratic style of ellipses in the *Yellow Book* has been preserved; two minor typographical errors have been corrected.

459 *turf and osier*: grass swards and pliant willow branches (*OED*); associated with the indigenous peoples of California—'their houses were built only of turf and osier, yet so wrought together that they served very well to keep out the cold' (Boucard, *Travels of a Naturalist*, 56).

460 *asphodels*: genus of liliaceous plants notable for its flowers; in poetry an immortal blossom carpeting the Elysian fields (*OED*).

Diana . . . Actæon's . . . hounds: Diana was Roman goddess of wild beasts and the hunt, as well as of women; in Ovid's account in *Metamorphoses*, the hunter Actæon accidentally sees her bathing naked, whereupon she turns him into a stag and he is pursued and brought down by his own pack of hounds (*OCD*).

culvers: doves (*OED*).

yew-mast: fallen fruit (arils) of the yew tree—edible red berries encasing poisonous seeds; yew trees symbolize both death and immortality (*DEF*).

pleasaunce: an enclosed or secluded garden (*OED*).

461 *columbary*: dove-cote (*OED*).

corse: see note to p. 20.

462 *marplot*: one who frustrates a plot or thwarts an undertaking (*OED*).

eld: old, a poetic archaism (*OED*).

bartizan: see note to p. 343.

463 *cote*: dove-cote.

463 *Nepenthe*: Nepenthes, a concoction or drug bringing forgetfulness or driving away sorrow, alluding to Homer's *Odyssey*, Bk IV, ll. 220–1 (*OED*).

moorish: boggy, marshy (*OED*).

464 *gear*: goods and movable property; in northern dialect, also possessions and wealth (*OED*).

the head . . . many threads: the grisly loom alludes to that of the Norns in Norse myth, as described by Thomas Gray: 'See the grisly texture grow, | ('Tis of human entrails made,) | And the weights that play below, | Each a gasping warrior's head' ('The Fatal Sisters, An Ode', in *Poems*, ll. 25–8, pp. 210–20, at 217).

465 *clew*: thread of life, as spun by the Fates (*OED*); in Greek mythology, more literally, Theseus navigates the Cretan Labyrinth by means of a ball of thread.

MARY ELIZABETH BRADDON, *GOOD LADY DUCAYNE*

Mary Elizabeth Braddon (1835–1915) was an actor, poet, and prolific author who graduated from writing 'penny dreadful' shockers to novels—most notably the bestselling bigamy narratives *Lady Audley's Secret* (serialized from 1861 and never out of print in her lifetime) and *Aurora Floyd* (1862), both of which epitomized the new genre of sensation novels. Her unconventional private life became the subject of prurient criticism—not least from fellow authors—yet she continued to write at an astonishing rate, delivering another eighty novels, as well as editing the *Belgravia Magazine*, her plots gradually turning from the sensational to social radicalism. She resumed her place as part of the London literary scene, and numbered Bram Stoker among her friends and he visited her frequently.

This story was first published in 1896 in *The Strand Magazine* vol. 9, illustrated with a headpiece depicting Lady Ducayne shadowed by a vast bat with outstretched wings. The text is taken from that printing, pp. 185–99.

466 *W.*: area in west London including Oxford Street, Soho, Harley Street, Mayfair, and Fitzrovia; Harbeck Street is fictitious.

florins: English silver coins worth two shillings, first minted in 1849 (*OED*).

467 *Brussels carpet*: variety of carpet with a wool upper surface and a back of linen thread (*OED*).

Walworth: a Victorian development of London, south of the River Thames between Camberwell and Elephant and Castle, and described by Charles Dickens in *Great Expectations* (1860–1) as 'a collection of back lanes, ditches, and little gardens' (vol. II, ch. 6, p. 188); by 1896 it had rail links to central London and was rapidly commercializing.

468 *harpy*: a rapacious or grasping individual, after the predatory classical monster—a bird with a woman's face (*OED*).

took off: mimicked, mocked, caricatured (*OED*).

parlours: presumably guest rooms or apartments, although this precise usage is not given by *OED*.

wheel and treadle: a sewing machine, the wheel rotated by a lever worked by foot.

homely: plain, simple (*OED*).

469 *enterprise*: endeavour or productive activities (*OED*).

took heart of grace: plucked up courage (*OED*).

cee springs: c-shaped springs supporting the body of a carriage; the design was still fashionable in 1884 (*OED*).

470 *peaked*: pinched, from illness or malnutrition (*OED*).

double eyeglass: a pair of spectacles.

471 *vaccinated*: inoculated against smallpox; by 1853 vaccination was compulsory in the UK, and within twenty-five years the disease had been all but eradicated in Britain—'small-pox has died out or diminished in severity, in exact proportion as efficient vaccination has been generalised' (Bristowe, *A Treatise on the Theory and Practice of Medicine*, 178). The mention of the practice of vaccination introduces the central medical theme of the tale (see note to p. 326).

crutch-stick: stick with a horizontal handle like the head of a crutch (*OED*).

472 *Cap Ferrino*: Forino, a town in Campania, southern Italy; the surrounding landscape is celebrated as 'Green Irpinia' and is renowned for vineyards that have been producing distinctive wines since the early Roman period.

Dijon roses: Gloire de Dijon, a large and fragrant honey-coloured tea rose first cultivated in 1853.

473 *Dickens or Scott*: the hugely popular and prolific novelists Charles Dickens (1812–70) and Sir Walter Scott (1771–1832).

M.B. exam at Edinburgh: Bachelor of Medicine at the Edinburgh Medical School, one of the most respected qualifications in the world in the nineteenth century.

474 *Pisa*: over 350 miles north of Forino.

475 *angle*: a corner or recess (*OED*).

the Regency: the nine years at the end of George III's reign (1811–20); the king being deemed unfit to reign due to fits of insanity, his son George was appointed Prince Regent to rule in his place until he himself ascended ingloriously to the throne.

the First Empire . . . Josephine was divorced: Napoleon Bonaparte (1769–1821) married Joséphine (Marie-Josèphe-Rose Tascher de La Pageri, known as Joséphine de Beauharnais, 1763–1814) in a civil ceremony in 1796, proclaimed himself Emperor Napoleon I of France in 1804, and on the eve of his coronation they married again in a religious ceremony; Napoleon had this marriage annulled on a technicality in 1810.

476 *Parravicini*: the name suggests a parasite in the vicinity.

476 *Crœsus*: King of Lydia *c.*560–*c.*546 BC, of proverbial wealth.

Mentone: Italian name for the coastal town of Menton, on the French Riviera at the border with Italy; it was particularly popular in the nineteenth century as a winter resort for the British nobility (Queen Victoria visited in 1882), and also had a reputation for curing tuberculosis.

477 *lights*: candles or gas-jets for illumination (*OED*).

Miladi: my Lady, French title for an English noblewoman (*OED*).

478 *oppressed*: of sleep, affected with feelings of pressure or distress (*OED*).

479 *sous*: French coins, worth five centimes (*OED*).

Newington Causeway: London thoroughfare between Elephant and Castle and Borough High Street, boasting several department stores such as Rabbit's Shoes, leading the area to become known as the Piccadilly of the South.

slack: unmotivated or lazy (*Green*).

Indeed, and indeed: really and truly (*OED*, a colloquial phrase).

Turner's pictures: Joseph Mallord William Turner (1775–1851), celebrated English Romantic artist of landscapes and historical scenes who toured Europe extensively; he was known as the 'painter of light' for his shimmering use of colour (*ODNB*).

Bellaggio: Bellagio, a luxury Italian resort on Lake Como in Lombardy; by 1888, the town's three leading hotels—the Genazzini, Grande Bretagne, and Grande Hotel Bellagio—were all wired for electricity; in comparison, Queen Victoria's Osborne House was similarly fitted only in 1893.

480 *phthisis, gangrene*: tuberculosis (see note to p. 416); necrosis, or death of body tissue in the body, accompanied by infection and putrefaction (*OED*).

pity and terror: in chapter 6 of his *Poetics* (*c.*360s–*c.*320s BC), Aristotle defines tragedy as arousing pity and terror to purge the mind of such passions (*catharsis*: see *Poetics*, 46–55); here, these emotions indicate a shared humanity.

481 *doctor*: administer medical treatment to (*OED*, as a verb).

Londres: the Hôtel des Londres, built in 1861 in the Italian city of San Remo, Liguria, on the Mediterranean coast near the north-west border with France; San Remo was a popular resort for English travellers.

Borgias: Italian dynasty of the fourteenth and fifteenth centuries central to political and ecclesiastical affairs and notorious for their intrigue, corruption, depravity, and assassinations.

moped: listless, dejected (*OED*).

482 *suffocation*: an allusion to the incubus, the demon of nightmares and a symptom of both vampirism and female hysteria (see notes to pp. 158, 262, 373; and Groom, *The Vampire*, 45–7, 145, 184–5).

483 *lawn sleeve*: fine linen sleeve, technically part of a Bishop's episcopal dress (*OED*).

bleed: draw blood for medicinal reasons (*OED*), the practice gradually became less common through the nineteenth century.

the greatest man in modern Europe: George Gordon, Lord Byron (1788–1824) died at Missolonghi in Greece, possibly from a combination of epilepsy and malaria; these conditions were profoundly exacerbated by the excessive bloodletting of his physicians, who in the last three days of his life drew over 4½lbs of blood and applied a dozen leeches throughout his last night (see Mills, 'The Last Illness of Lord Byron').

486 *Albertus Magnus*: St Albert of Cologne (b. 1193 or 1206, d. 1280), a Dominican friar known as 'Doctor Universalis' for his comprehensive commentary on Aristotelian philosophy; he was reputed to have constructed a brass head able to answer questions (see Shelley, *Frankenstein*, 23).

George Ripley: fifteenth-century Augustinian canon and alchemist (d. *c.*1490); he was reputed to have discovered the philosophers' stone and accordingly created £100,000 of gold a year to support the Knights Hospitaller against the Turks.

transfusion of blood: blood transfusion became a legitimate medical practice in the nineteenth century and between 1885 and 1892 in Edinburgh the surgeon Dr John Duncan (1839–99) led the largest series of transfusions to date (see Groom, *The Vampire*, 149). There are several such transfusions in Bram Stoker's *Dracula*, and Braddon may also be alluding to the Hungarian Countess Elizabeth (Erzsébet) Báthory (or Báthori, d. 1614), who was reputed to bathe in the blood of young girls to retain her own youth. Báthory allegedly believed maiden's blood was 'the *elixir vitæ*, the source of never failing youth and beauty' and hence 'three hundred maidens were sacrificed at the shrine of vanity and superstition' before she was exposed and imprisoned (Paget, *Hungary and Transylvania*, i. 68, 69); there is also a version of her story in Baring-Gould's *The Book of Were-Wolves* (139–41). Paget's account was quoted in its entirety in notes to the long narrative ballad 'The Princess' Bath: or The Three Maids. A Song of Hungary' in which one victim, Gabrielle, morbidly sings that the autumn leaves 'wear the vampire's hectic hue' (Foxton, *Prémices*, 103).

lights: knowledge, intellectual capacities (*OED*).

Ecclenza: *Eccellenza*, your Excellency (Italian).

487 *the day Louis XVI. was guillotined*: 21 January 1793.

an air bubble: air embolism, the potentially fatal effects of an air bubble blocking an artery or vein causing heart attack, stroke, or respiratory failure.

Pasteur, or Virchow: Louis Pasteur (1822–95), French founder of microbiology among whose discoveries were fermentation, pasteurization, and vaccines for anthrax and rabies; Rudolf Virchow (1821–1902), pioneering German cellular pathologist, anthropologist, politician, and social reformer.

488 *Monte Generoso*: mountain on the Italian–Swiss border near the southern end of Lake Lugano, some 5,580 feet high and about 10 miles from the city of Varese.

Gladstone bag: a light travelling bag (*OED*, which gives the inaugural use in Braddon's 1882 three-decker novel *Mount Royal*).

489 *trousseau*: bridal linen consisting of clothes, bedding, and so forth (*OED*).

mother-in-law: *OED* records the first mention of a 'mother-in-law joke' in 1885, by which stage it was clearly common currency; *Green* concurs, recording 'Mother-in-Law' as slang for ordering the drink 'old and bitter' (old ale and bitter beer) since at least 1869, while 'mother-in-law's bit', meaning an ungenerous portion, dates to the eighteenth century.

RUDYARD KIPLING, *THE VAMPIRE*

Rudyard Kipling and Johann von Goethe bookend this anthology as internationally renowned writers who among their many and varied publications described vampires. Kipling (1865–1936) was born in Bombay to a well-connected family and educated at the United Services College of Westward Ho!, before becoming a journalist in India and being acknowledged as the tireless and pre-eminent laureate of Anglo-Indian culture. He returned to England in 1889 and cemented his career as a man of letters with a best-selling succession of novels, volumes of short stories and poetry, and books of genre-defying prose.

'The Vampire' was written in 1897 to accompany a painting, also titled *The Vampire*, by Kipling's cousin Philip Burne-Jones (1861–1926) when it was exhibited in the New Gallery's summer show held in Regent Street, London (see Dijkstra, *Idols of Perversity*, 350–1). The painting was Burne-Jones's revenge on the actor Mrs Patrick Campbell, who had snubbed his attentions; his response was to depict her as a vampire hanging over a bed occupied by a prostrate male form, a suggestion of blood on his chest. Despite its brevity, the poem caused a storm—particularly when the painting was shown in New York, provoking responses and parodies, inspiring a play and a novel, Emerson Porter Browne's *A Fool There Was* (1909). Browne's book was in turn made into a film in 1915 and starred the kohl-eyed *femme fatale* Theda Bara, who posed seductively with a human skeleton for publicity shots; a remake followed in 1922 starring the similarly seductive Estelle Taylor. The poem and its rich afterlife was therefore instrumental in creating the 'vamp', a term popularized by the films (see Morey and Nelson, 'Phallus and Void', 45–52). Although the word was already in use, Brander Matthews claimed in 1919 that

> Kipling cannot escape the ultimate responsibility for another abbreviated word, which has taken its place in the technical vocabulary of the so-called 'silent drama.' His biting lyric on the 'Vampire,' with its corroding characterization of its heroine villainess as 'a rag and a bone and a hank of hair,' has brought about a belief that a vampire is always the female of the species; and as a logical result of this unfounded

> opinion any fascinating adventuress trying to cajole an innocent hero is now entitled a *vamp*. What is even more picturesque is that this abbreviated noun has also become a verb: 'She *vamps* him.' ('The Latest Novelties in Language', *Harper's*, 841 (June 1920), 83–4)

'The Vampire' was originally printed in the 1897 catalogue *The New Gallery, Regent Street: Tenth Summer Exhibition*, and swiftly reprinted in newspapers on both sides of the Atlantic, as well as in many privately printed and unauthorized editions. In one unauthorized printing (1898), there is a further stanza that begins with one of the poem's lines and is perhaps a continuation:

> "So some of him lived but the most of him died"—
> He has never forgot—for he has not tried
> The years will come and the years will go—
> Happiness also, but oh so slow.
> May 'you and I'—before we die,
> Again be contented, we must both try.

As an afterthought, Kipling added a title, 'Daydreaming—' (Lawrence, 'Rudyard Kipling, *The Vampire*, and the Actress', 306). The piece first appeared as part of Kipling's authorized collected verse in 1919, from which this text is taken (251–2; see Livingston, *Bibliography*, 177–81).

491 *white hot brand*: one would expect the compound adjective to be hyphenated, but the mark is absent from the copy-text, perhaps to make the phrase more ambiguous.

The Oxford World's Classics Website

- Browse the full range of Oxford World's Classics online
- Sign up for our monthly e-alert to receive information on new titles
- Read extracts from the Introductions
- Listen to our editors and translators talk about the world's greatest literature with our Oxford World's Classics audio guides
- Teachers and lecturers can order inspection copies quickly and simply via our website

www.oup.com/uk/worldsclassics

MORE ABOUT **OXFORD WORLD'S CLASSICS**

American Literature

British and Irish Literature

Children's Literature

Classics and Ancient Literature

Colonial Literature

Eastern Literature

European Literature

Gothic Literature

History

Medieval Literature

Oxford English Drama

Philosophy

Poetry

Politics

Religion

The Oxford Shakespeare

A SELECTION OF **OXFORD WORLD'S CLASSICS**

Charles Dickens	Nicholas Nickleby A Christmas Carol and Other Christmas Books Dombey and Son The Old Curiosity Shop Our Mutual Friend The Pickwick Papers Tale of Two Cities
George du Maurier	Trilby
Maria Edgeworth	Castle Rackrent
George Eliot	Adam Bede Daniel Deronda The Lifted Veil and Brother Jacob Middlemarch The Mill on the Floss Silas Marner
Edward FitzGerald	The Rubáiyát of Omar Khayyám
Elizabeth Gaskell	Cranford The Life of Charlotte Brontë Mary Barton North and South Wives and Daughters
George Gissing	New Grub Street The Nether World The Odd Women
Edmund Gosse	Father and Son
Thomas Hardy	Far from the Madding Crowd Jude the Obscure The Mayor of Casterbridge The Return of the Native Tess of the d'Urbervilles The Woodlanders
James Hogg	The Private Memoirs and Confessions of a Justified Sinner

A SELECTION OF **OXFORD WORLD'S CLASSICS**

JOHN KEATS	**The Major Works** **Selected Letters**
CHARLES MATURIN	**Melmoth the Wanderer**
HENRY MAYHEW	**London Labour and the London Poor**
WILLIAM MORRIS	**News from Nowhere**
JOHN RUSKIN	**Praeterita** **Selected Writings**
WALTER SCOTT	**Ivanhoe** **Rob Roy** **Waverley**
MARY SHELLEY	**Frankenstein** **The Last Man**
ROBERT LOUIS STEVENSON	**Kidnapped** **South Sea Tales** **Strange Case of Dr Jekyll and Mr Hyde and Other Tales** **Treasure Island**
BRAM STOKER	**Dracula**
W. M. THACKERAY	**Vanity Fair**
FRANCES TROLLOPE	**Domestic Manners of the Americans**
OSCAR WILDE	**The Importance of Being Earnest and Other Plays** **The Major Works** **The Picture of Dorian Gray**
ELLEN WOOD	**East Lynne**
DOROTHY WORDSWORTH	**The Grasmere and Alfoxden Journals**
WILLIAM WORDSWORTH	**The Major Works**
WORDSWORTH and COLERIDGE	**Lyrical Ballads**

A SELECTION OF **OXFORD WORLD'S CLASSICS**

ANTHONY TROLLOPE

The American Senator
An Autobiography
Barchester Towers
Can You Forgive Her?
Cousin Henry
Doctor Thorne
The Duke's Children
The Eustace Diamonds
Framley Parsonage
He Knew He Was Right
Lady Anna
The Last Chronicle of Barset
Orley Farm
Phineas Finn
Phineas Redux
The Prime Minister
Rachel Ray
The Small House at Allington
The Warden
The Way We Live Now

A SELECTION OF **OXFORD WORLD'S CLASSICS**

Louisa May Alcott	**Little Women**
Hans Christian Andersen	**Fairy Tales**
J. M. Barrie	**Peter Pan in Kensington Gardens and Peter and Wendy** **Peter Pan and Other Plays**
L. Frank Baum	**The Wonderful Wizard of Oz**
Lewis Carroll	**Alice Through the Looking Glass**
Frances Hodgson Burnett	**The Secret Garden**
Lewis Carroll	**Alice's Adventures in Wonderland and Through the Looking-Glass**
Carlo Collodi	**The Adventures of Pinocchio**
Kenneth Grahame	**The Wind in the Willows**
Anthony Hope	**The Prisoner of Zenda**
Thomas Hughes	**Tom Brown's Schooldays**
Charles Perrault	**The Complete Fairy Tales**
Charles Kingsley	**The Water-Babies**
Anna Sewell	**Black Beauty**
Robert Louis Stevenson	**Kidnapped** **Treasure Island**

A SELECTION OF **OXFORD WORLD'S CLASSICS**

Honoré de Balzac	**Cousin Bette** **Eugénie Grandet** **Père Goriot**
Charles Baudelaire	**The Flowers of Evil**
Denis Diderot	**Jacques the Fatalist** **The Nun**
Alexandre Dumas (père)	**The Count of Monte Cristo** **The Three Musketeers**
Gustave Flaubert	**Madame Bovary**
Victor Hugo	**Notre-Dame de Paris**
J.-K. Huysmans	**Against Nature**
Pierre Choderlos de Laclos	**Les Liaisons dangereuses**
Guy de Maupassant	**Bel-Ami**
Molière	**Don Juan and Other Plays** **The Misanthrope, Tartuffe, and Other Plays**
Abbé Prévost	**Manon Lescaut**
Arthur Rimbaud	**Collected Poems**
Jean-Jacques Rousseau	**Confessions**
Marquis de Sade	**The Crimes of Love**
Stendhal	**The Red and the Black** **The Charterhouse of Parma**
Paul Verlaine	**Selected Poems**
Voltaire	**Candide and Other Stories**
Émile Zola	**L'Assommoir** **Germinal**